Y0-DBZ-892

ANALECTA ORIENTALIA 43

A POLITICAL HISTORY OF POST-KASSITE BABYLONIA

1158-722 B. C.

J. A. BRINKMAN

1968
PONTIFICIUM INSTITUTUM BIBLICUM
I-00187 ROMA PIAZZA PILOTTA 35

ANALECTA ORIENTALIA
COMMENTATIONES SCIENTIFICAE DE REBUS ORIENTIS ANTIQUI
43

A POLITICAL HISTORY OF POST-KASSITE BABYLONIA

1158-722 B. C.

1968
PONTIFICIUM INSTITUTUM BIBLICUM
I-00187 ROMA PIAZZA PILOTTA 35

A POLITICAL HISTORY OF POST-KASSITE BABYLONIA

1158-722 B. C.

J. A. BRINKMAN

1 9 6 8

PONTIFICIUM INSTITUTUM BIBLICUM

I-00187 ROMA PIAZZA PILOTTA 35

TIPOGRAFIA S. PIO X — VIA DEGLI ETRUSCHI N. 7-9 — ROMA — IX - 1968

TO MY PARENTS

JOHN AND ALICE BRINKMAN

PREFACE

The original draft of this book was written between November 1961 and February 1962 in partial fulfillment of the requirements for the degree of Doctor of Philosophy in Assyriology at the University of Chicago. The topic was first suggested by Prof. I. J. Gelb, who served as chairman of the dissertation committee and provided notes towards an initial bibliography of the pertinent royal inscriptions published up to 1960. Profs. H. G. Güterbock, Thorkild Jacobsen, A. L. Oppenheim, and M. B. Rowton also served on the dissertation committee and offered helpful criticism of the manuscript.

A preliminary catalogue of the written sources used in this history appeared in the *Journal of Cuneiform Studies* XVI (1962) 83-109. Since that time many scholars have been kind in calling to my attention various unpublished inscriptions or additional bibliography on previously published texts. I wish especially to thank P. Amandry, R. Biggs, R. Borger, P. Calmeyer, M. Gibson, A. K. Grayson, O. R. Gurney, D. A. Kennedy, W. G. Lambert, A. R. Millard, A. L. Oppenheim, E. Reiner, Clyde C. Smith, E. Sollberger, E. Weidner, and D. J. Wiseman. I am also grateful for text collations from Dr. E. Sollberger (British Museum), for the impression of a weight inscription from Dr. Vaughn Crawford (Metropolitan Museum of Art), and for photographs of unpublished texts from Miss Dorothy Hill (Walters Art Gallery) and from Prof. Dr. G. R. Meyer (Vorderasiatisches Museum, Berlin).

Between the writing of the original manuscript and completion of the final revision (June 1967), I have benefitted from collaboration and discussion with Prof. A. K. Grayson, who has generously placed at my disposal various drafts of his forthcoming edition of the Assyrian and Babylonian chronicles. References to Grayson's readings and collations, however, are not based on the final version of his work, which is not yet completed; and readers are advised to check statements given here (especially relating to unpublished chronicles) against Grayson's ultimate publication.

The decision to expand my original manuscript beyond the mere addition of new texts and minor alterations of opinion was made in 1966, when it seemed better to add separate chapters on foreign population groups (principally the Kassites, Chaldeans, and Arameans) and on the government and military. These new chapters plus several expanded notes in Chapter III (chiefly on geographical matters) are the principal changes made from the 1962 edition, which stands substantially unaltered here. Copies of the 1962 edition have been available to Prof. Grayson and my Chicago colleagues, and I have profited from their comments. The pertinent portions of Chapters II-III (Second Isin through Elamite Dynasties) with various addenda were sent to Prof. D. J. Wiseman at his request in early 1964 to assist in his preparation of Chapter XXXI of the revised second volume of the *Cambridge Ancient History*.

I wish to thank the American Council of Learned Societies for a grant enabling me to study the role of the Arameans in Babylonia during the late second and early first millennia; the principal results of that study appear in Chapters III-IV and in Appendix C. I am likewise grateful to the Oriental Institute of the University of Chicago and to its director, Prof. R. M. Adams, for underwriting the expenses of a journey to collate texts in the British Museum. It is also a pleasant duty to acknowledge the financial contribution of the Division of Humanities, University of Chicago, towards typing expenses for the final manuscript of this volume.

During the period of rewriting and expanding this manuscript (1966-1967), I have profited much from discussions with my teacher and colleague Prof. Oppenheim, who has kindly read and criticized most of the revised draft that appears here. I also thank Prof. Gelb, who read and commented on the new portions of Chapters IV-V. The book likewise owes much to the faithful assistants who patiently helped in the preparation of the revised manuscript: Maria de J. Ellis, Harriet P. Osborn, and especially James D. Steakley, who also aided with the proofreading.

Finally, I wish to express my gratitude to the editors of *Analecta Orientalia*, especially Profs. K. Deller, J. Swetnam, and R. Caplice, for accepting this book for publication in the series and for their expeditious and careful handling of the manuscript.

J. A. Brinkman

Oriental Institute
Chicago
July 4, 1967

LIST OF ABBREVIATIONS

A. = (siglum for tablets, etc. in the collection of the Louvre)
A. = Asiatic (siglum for tablets, etc. in the collection of the Oriental Institute, Chicago)
AAA = *Annals of Archaeology and Anthropology*
AASOR = *The Annual of the American Schools of Oriental Research*
ABL = R. F. Harper, *Assyrian and Babylonian Letters*
ACT = O. Neugebauer, *Astronomical Cuneiform Texts*
ADD = C. H. W. Johns, *Assyrian Deeds and Documents*
AfK = *Archiv für Keilschriftforschung*
AfO = *Archiv für Orientforschung*
A.H. = (siglum for tablets in the collection of the British Museum)
AHw = W. von Soden, *Akkadisches Handwörterbuch*
AJ = *The Antiquaries Journal*
AJA = *American Journal of Archaeology*
AJSL = *The American Journal of Semitic Languages and Literatures*
AKA = E. A. W. Budge and L. W. King, *Annals of the Kings of Assyria*
Akitu = S. A. Pallis, *The Babylonian Akîtu Festival*
Alphabetisches Verzeichniss = J. N. Strassmaier, *Alphabetisches Verzeichniss der assyrischen und akkadischen Wörter der Cuneiform Inscriptions of Western Asia*, Vol. II
ANEP = J. B. Pritchard, *The Ancient Near East in Pictures Relating to the Old Testament*
ANET = J. B. Pritchard, *Ancient Near Eastern Texts Relating to the Old Testament*
Annales de Tn. II = V. Scheil, *Annales de Tukulti Ninip II, roi d'Assyrie 889-884*
AnOr = *Analecta Orientalia*
AnSt = *Anatolian Studies*
AO = (siglum for tablets in the collection of the Louvre)
AOB = *Altorientalische Bibliothek*
AOF = *Altorientalische Forschungen*
APN = K. L. Tallqvist, *Assyrian Personal Names*
ARAB = D. D. Luckenbill, *Ancient Records of Assyria and Babylonia*
ARM = *Archives royales de Mari*
ArOr = *Archiv Orientální*
AS = *Assyriological Studies*
Asarhaddon = R. Borger, *Die Inschriften Asarhaddons Königs von Assyrien*
Asb. = M. Streck, *Assurbanipal und die letzten assyrischen Könige bis zum Untergang Nineveh's*
Assur = (prefix for field numbers of tablets, etc. excavated at Assur)
Assyrische Kriegführung = M. Pancritius, *Assyrische Kriegführung von Tiglat-pileser I. bis auf Šamši–adad III.*
BA = *Beiträge zur Assyriologie und semitischen Sprachwissenschaft*
Bab. = (siglum for excavation numbers at the Deutsche Orient-Gesellschaft excavations in Babylon)
Babylon = E. Unger, *Babylon, die heilige Stadt, nach der Beschreibung der Babylonier*

Bagh. Mitt. = *Baghdader Mitteilungen*
BASOR = *Bulletin of the American Schools of Oriental Research*
BBSt = L. W. King, *Babylonian Boundary-Stones and Memorial-Tablets in the British Museum*
BE = *The Babylonian Expedition of the University of Pennsylvania*, Series A: *Cuneiform Texts*
Berens Collection = T. G. Pinches, *The Babylonian Tablets of the Berens Collection*
BHT = S. Smith, *Babylonian Historical Texts Relating to the Capture and Downfall of Babylon*
BIN = *Babylonian Inscriptions in the Collection of James B. Nies*
BiOr = *Bibliotheca Orientalis*
Bischof = B. Landsberger, *Brief des Bischofs von Esagila an König Asarhaddon*
BJV = *Berliner Jahrbuch für Vor- und Frühgeschichte*
BM = British Museum (siglum for tablets, etc. in the collection of the British Museum)
BMQ = *The British Museum Quarterly*
Boundary Stone = W. J. Hinke, *A New Boundary Stone of Nebuchadrezzar I from Nippur*
BOR = *The Babylonian and Oriental Record*
BRM = *Babylonian Records in the Library of J. Pierpont Morgan*
Bronze Reliefs = L. W. King, *Bronze Reliefs from the Gates of Shalmaneser, King of Assyria B.C. 860-825*
Bu. = Budge (siglum for tablets, etc. in the British Museum)
BWL = W. G. Lambert, *Babylonian Wisdom Literature*
CAD = *The Assyrian Dictionary of the Oriental Institute of the University of Chicago*
CAH = *The Cambridge Ancient History*
Camb. = J. N. Strassmaier, *Inschriften von Cambyses*
Catalogue = C. Bezold, *Catalogue of the Cuneiform Tablets in the Kouyunjik Collection of the British Museum*
CBM = (siglum for tablets, etc. in the collection of the Babylonian Section of the University Museum, Philadelphia; now replaced by CBS)
CBS = (siglum for tablets, etc., in the collection of the Babylonian Section of the University Museum, Philadelphia)
CCEBK = L. W. King, *Chronicles Concerning Early Babylonian Kings*
CCT = *Cuneiform Texts from Cappadocian Tablets in the British Museum*
CH = Codex Hammurapi
Chronicles = D. J. Wiseman, *Chronicles of Chaldaean Kings*
CIS = *Corpus Inscriptionum Semiticarum*
Coll. de Clercq = H. F. X. de Clercq, *Collection de Clercq. Catalogue méthodique et raisonné: Antiquités assyriennes*
CPN = A. T. Clay, *Personal Names from Cuneiform Inscriptions of the Cassite Period*
CT = *Cuneiform Texts from Babylonian Tablets, etc. in the British Museum*
CVC = consonant – vowel – consonant (cuneiform sign)
Dar. = J. N. Strassmaier, *Inschriften von Darius*
DN = divine name
D.T. = Daily Telegraph (siglum for tablets, etc. in the collections of the British Museum)
dupl. = duplicate
EA = J. A. Knudtzon, *Die El-Amarna-Tafeln*

EAK = R. Borger, *Einleitung in die assyrischen Königsinschriften*
EBPN = H. Ranke, *Early Babylonian Personal Names*
Épithètes royales = M.-J. Seux, *Épithètes royales akkadiennes et sumériennes*
EHA = S. Smith, *Early History of Assyria*
Esarhaddon = R. C. Thompson, *The Prisms of Esarhaddon and Ashurbanipal...*
Ev.-M. = B. T. A. Evetts, *Inscriptions of the Reigns of Evil-Merodach, Neriglissar and Laborosoarchod*
f. e. = from end
FGrH = F. Jacoby, *Die Fragmente der griechischen Historiker*
Final Vowels = J. P. Hyatt, *The Treatment of Final Vowels in Early Neo-Babylonian*
GAG = W. von Soden, *Grundriss der akkadischen Grammatik*
gen. = genitive
GN = geographical name
Gron. = Groningen (siglum for tablets now in the Böhl collection, Leiden)
Haupt Anniversary Volume = *Oriental Studies Published in Commemoration of the Fortieth Anniversary (1883-1923) of Paul Haupt as Director of the Oriental Seminary of the Johns Hopkins University*
Ḫḫ = ḪAR-ra = *ḫubullu* (lexical series)
Hinke Kudurru = W. J. Hinke, *Selected Babylonian Kudurru Inscriptions*, no. 5, pp. 21-27
H.S. = (siglum for tablets, etc. in the Frau Professor Hilprecht Collection of Babylonian Antiquities, Jena)
HSS = *Harvard Semitic Series*
HUCA = *Hebrew Union College Annual*
ICC = A. H. Layard, *Inscriptions in the Cuneiform Character...*
IEJ = *Israel Exploration Journal*
ILN = *The Illustrated London News*
IM = Iraq Museum (siglum for objects in the collection of the Iraq Museum, Baghdad)
ITT = *Inventaire des tablettes de Tello*
JAOS = *Journal of the American Oriental Society*
JCS = *Journal of Cuneiform Studies*
JEA = *The Journal of Egyptian Archaeology*
JENu = Joint expedition (with the Iraq Museum) at Nuzi (siglum of unpublished tablets)
JEOL = *Jaarbericht van het Vooraziatisch-Egyptisch Genootschap "Ex Oriente Lux"*
JESHO = *Journal of the Economic and Social History of the Orient*
JHS = *The Journal of Hellenic Studies*
JNES = *Journal of Near Eastern Studies*
JRAS = *The Journal of the Royal Asiatic Society*
JSOR = *Journal of the Society of Oriental Research*
JSS = *Journal of Semitic Studies*
K. = Kouyunjik (siglum for tablets in the Kouyunjik collection of the British Museum)
KAH = *Keilschrifttexte aus Assur historischen Inhalts*
KAJ = *Keilschrifttexte aus Assur juristischen Inhalts*
KAR = *Keilschrifttexte aus Assur religiösen Inhalts*
KAV = *Keilschrifttexte aus Assur verschiedenen Inhalts*
KBo = *Keilschrifttexte aus Boghazköi*

Ki. = King (siglum for tablets, etc. in the collections of the British Museum)
"Königsdolche" = W. Nagel, "Die Königsdolche der Zweiten Dynastie von Isin," *AfO* XIX (1959-60) 95-104
Konst. = Konstantinopel (siglum for tablets, etc. in the collections of the Archaeological Museum of Istanbul)
KUB = *Keilschrifturkunden aus Boghazköi*
Kudurru = F. X. Steinmetzer, *Die babylonischen Kudurru (Grenzsteine) als Urkundenform*
Landfahrzeuge = A. Salonen, *Die Landfahrzeuge des alten Mesopotamien*
LBAT = T. G. Pinches and J. N. Strassmaier, *Late Babylonian Astronomical and Related Texts* (A. J. Sachs, ed.)
Lie, *Sargon* = A. G. Lie, *The Inscriptions of Sargon II, King of Assyria.* Part I: *The Annals.*
LIH = L. W. King, *The Letters and Inscriptions of Hammurabi*
LTBA = *Die lexikalischen Tafelserien der Babylonier und Assyrer in den Berliner Museen*
Lyon, *Sargon* = D. G. Lyon, *Keilschrifttexte Sargon's, Königs von Assyrien*
MA = Middle Assyrian
MAD = *Materials for the Assyrian Dictionary*
MAOG = *Mitteilungen der Altorientalischen Gesellschaft*
MB = Middle Babylonian
MDOG = *Mitteilungen der Deutschen Orient-Gesellschaft*
MDP = *Mémoires de la Délégation en Perse*
MIO = *Mitteilungen des Instituts für Orientforschung*
MLC = (siglum for tablets in the J. Pierpont Morgan Library Collection)
MMA = (siglum for objects in the collection of the Metropolitan Museum of Art, New York)
MN = month name
MSL = *Materialien zum sumerischen Lexikon*
MVAG = *Mitteilungen der Vorderasiatisch-aegyptischen Gesellschaft*
N = Nippur (siglum for field numbers of objects excavated at Nippur by the Oriental Institute and other institutions)
NA = Neo-Assyrian
Namengebung = J. J. Stamm, *Die akkadische Namengebung*
NB = Neo-Babylonian
NBC = Nies Babylonian Collection (siglum for tablets in the Babylonian Collection, Yale University)
Nbk. = J. N. Strassmaier, *Inschriften von Nabuchodonosor*
NBN = K. L. Tallqvist, *Neubabylonisches Namenbuch*
Nbn. = J. N. Strassmaier, *Inschriften von Nabonidus*
ND = (siglum for field numbers of tablets, etc. excavated at Nimrud)
Ni. = (siglum for tablets, etc. from Nippur in the Archaeological Museum of Istanbul)
nom. = nominative
Nomades = J.-R. Kupper, *Les nomades en Mésopotamie au temps des rois de Mari*
NPN = I. J. Gelb *et al.*, *Nuzi Personal Names*
NSG = A. Falkenstein, *Die neusumerischen Gerichtsurkunden*
N-T = Nippur text (siglum for field numbers of tablets, etc. excavated at Nippur by the Oriental Institute and other institutions)
Nuzi = R. F. S. Starr, *Nuzi: Report on the Excavations at Yorgan Tepa near Kirkuk, Iraq*
OA = Old Assyrian

OAkk = Old Akkadian
OB = Old Babylonian
obv. = obverse
OECT = *Oxford Editions of Cuneiform Texts*
OIP = *Oriental Institute Publications*
OLZ = *Orientalistische Literaturzeitung*
Orientalia N.S. = *Orientalia, Nova Series*
Pauly-Wissowa = *Paulys Real-Encyclopädie der classischen Altertumswissenschaft,* herausgegeben von G. Wissowa, etc.
PBS = *Publications of the Babylonian Section* (University Museum, University of Pennsylvania)
PN = personal name
PNC = F. J. Stephens, *Personal Names from Cuneiform Inscriptions of Cappadocia*
Provinzeinteilung = E. Forrer, *Die Provinzeinteilung des assyrischen Reiches*
PRT = E. G. Klauber, *Politisch-Religiöse Texte aus der Sargonidenzeit*
PSBA = *Proceedings of the Society of Biblical Archaeology*
PT = Persepolis texts (siglum for tablets, etc. excavated at Persepolis by the Oriental Institute)
R = H. C. Rawlinson, *The Cuneiform Inscriptions of Western Asia*
RA = *Revue d'assyriologie et d'archéologie orientale*
RB = *Revue biblique*
RCAE = L. Waterman, *Royal Correspondence of the Assyrian Empire*
rev. = reverse
RHA = *Revue hittite et asianique*
RHR = *Revue de l'histoire des religions*
RLA = *Reallexikon der Assyriologie*
RLV = *Reallexikon der Vorgeschichte*
Rm. = Rassam (siglum for tablets in the collections of the British Museum)
RMA = R. C. Thompson, *The Reports of the Magicians and Astrologers of Nineveh and Babylon in the British Museum*
RN = royal name
RSO = *Rivista degli studi orientali*
RT = *Recueil de travaux relatifs à la philologie et à l'archéologie égyptiennes et assyriennes*
Une saison = V. Scheil, *Une saison de fouilles à Sippar*
SAKI = F. Thureau-Dangin, *Die sumerischen und akkadischen Königsinschriften*
Sammlung = H. Winckler, *Sammlung von Keilschrifttexten*
Sargon = [see Lie, *Sargon* and Lyon, *Sargon*]
The Sculptures of TP III = R. D. Barnett and M. Falkner, *The Sculptures of Aššur–naṣir–apli II (883-859 B.C.), Tiglath-Pileser III (745-727 B.C.), Esarhaddon (681-669 B.C.) from the Central and South-West Palaces at Nimrud*
SDAS = Seventh Day Adventist Seminary
Sin = C. Virolleaud, *L'Astrologie chaldéenne: Texte cunéiforme, Sin*
ŠL = A. Deimel, *Šumerisches Lexikon*
Sp. = Spartoli (siglum for tablets in the collection of the British Museum)
SPA = A. Pope, *A Survey of Persian Art from Prehistoric Times to the Present*
SSB = F. X. Kugler, *Sternkunde und Sterndienst in Babel*

Stelenreihen = W. Andrae, *Die Stelenreihen in Assur*
STT = O. R. Gurney, J. J. Finkelstein, and P. Hulin, *The Sultantepe Tablets*
Studies Oppenheim = *Studies Presented to A. Leo Oppenheim*
Šurpu = E. Reiner, *Šurpu: A Collection of Sumerian and Akkadian Incantations*
Symbolae van Oven = M. David *et al.* (eds.), *Symbolae ad jus et historiam antiquitatis pertinentes Julio Christiano van Oven dedicatae*
TAPS = *Transactions of the American Philosophical Society*
TCL = *Textes cunéiformes du Louvre*
Tell Umar = L. Waterman, *Preliminary Report(s) upon the Excavations at Tell Umar, Iraq*
Tn. I. = E. Weidner, *Die Inschriften Tukulti-Ninurtas I. und seiner Nachfolger*
TP III = P. Rost, *Die Keilschrifttexte Tiglat-Pilesers III.*
Travels = R. Ker Porter, *Travels in Georgia, Persia, Armenia, Ancient Babylonia, etc.*
TSBA = *Transactions of the Society of Biblical Archaeology*
Tu = (siglum for tablets excavated at Nuzi)
TuM = *Texte und Materialien der Frau Professor Hilprecht Collection of Babylonian Antiquities im Eigentum der Universität Jena*
U. = (siglum for field numbers of objects excavated at Ur by the joint expedition of the British Museum and the University of Pennsylvania)
UDT = J. Nies, *Ur Dynasty Tablets*
UE = *Ur Excavations*
UET = *Ur Excavations, Texts*
UIOM = (siglum for objects in the collection of the University of Illinois Museum, Urbana)
Une saison = V. Scheil, *Une saison de fouilles à Sippar*
Untersuchungen = H. Winckler, *Untersuchungen zur altorientalischen Geschichte*
UVB = *Vorläufiger Bericht über die ... Ausgrabungen in Uruk–Warka*
VA = (siglum for objects in the collections of the Staatliche Museen, Berlin)
VAB = *Vorderasiatische Bibliothek*
var. = variant
VAS = *Vorderasiatische Schriftdenkmäler der Königlich Museen zu Berlin*
VAT = (siglum for tablets in the collections of the Staatliche Museen, Berlin)
W. = (siglum for tablets in the Herbert Weld Collection of the Ashmolean Museum)
W. = (siglum for excavation numbers of the Deutsche Orient-Gesellschaft at Uruk–Warka)
W.-B. = (siglum for tablets in the H. Weld-Blundell Collection of the Ashmolean Museum)
WO = *Die Welt des Orients*
WVDOG = *Wissenschaftliche Veröffentlichung der Deutschen Orient-Gesellschaft*
WZJ = *Wissenschaftliche Zeitschrift der Friedrich-Schiller-Universität Jena*
WZKM = *Wiener Zeitschrift für die Kunde des Morgenlandes*
YBC = Yale Babylonian Collection (siglum for tablets in the Babylonian Collection, Yale University)
YOS = *Yale Oriental Series, Babylonian Texts*
ZA = *Zeitschrift für Assyriologie*
ZDMG = *Zeitschrift der Deutschen Morgenländischen Gesellschaft*
ZDPV = *Zeitschrift des Deutschen Palästina–Vereins*
Zwei Hauptprobleme = C. F. Lehmann, *Zwei Hauptprobleme der altorientalischen Chronologie und ihre Lösung*

TABLE OF CONTENTS

Introduction

The purpose of the present study is to investigate the political history of Babylonia during an obscure segment of her existence as a nation: from the rise of the Second Dynasty of Isin (c. 1158 B.C.) to the death of Shalmaneser V (722 B.C.). Our discussion will be limited almost entirely to political history, that is, the inquiry into the internal and external activities of the body politic, as exemplified in the workings of the government both within and without the country and especially in the focus of political life in ancient Babylonia, the king. The geographical area with which we shall be concerned is relatively small, extending roughly from Dur-Kurigalzu and the Lower Zab in the north (1) to Ur and Eridu in the south and from the Euphrates in the west to the plains, foothills, and marshes flanking the Tigris to the east. We shall touch upon lands outside this region only in so far as their history affects or is affected by the history of Babylonia.

Our procedure for this investigation will be as follows. In the first chapter, we shall consider the written and non-written sources to be utilized, the information conveyed by them, and the relative reliability of this information. In the second chapter, we shall establish a chronological framework for the period, arranging the known kings and dynasties in their proper sequence. Then, in the third chapter, we shall present a detailed narrative of political events in chronological order, ranging the facts and conclusions around the individual kings and dynasties as focal points. In the fourth chapter, we shall give a unified treatment of the role of the large foreign population groups within Babylonia—Kassites, Chaldeans, Arameans, Sutians—who profoundly affected the growth of Babylonia at this period. In the fifth chapter, we shall discuss the apparatus of political and military life, i.e., the government and army. The book will conclude with several appendices, including a bibliography of the written source materials.

Having outlined our purpose as well as the projected means for attaining that purpose, we may now remark about hopes for achieving our goal. Any author dealing with the history of the ancient Near East realizes all too well the ephemeral

(1) The northern border of Babylonia at the time of the Second Dynasty of Isin was generally the Lower Zab east of the Tigris and around Dur-Kurigalzu west of that river. But it fluctuated with the waxing and waning of Babylonian political might.

quality of his work. The sources he uses are noted for their paucity and obscurity. Any attempt to achieve a synthesis of such material is consequently subject to two major weaknesses: (1) the history portrayed is liable at any time to be significantly altered as more material becomes available through excavations and other research; and (2) the historical account may come to represent one individual's creative interpretation of the polyvalent data, having a minimal foundation in fact and a maximal in hypothesis. We propose partially to circumvent these difficulties in the following manner. First, we wish to gather all the sources presently available from our area, thus presenting for future historians an up-to-date corpus of material—to which they may readily add new discoveries, reinterpreting where necessary. Secondly, we hope to indicate precisely what are the bases for each of our interpretations and to distinguish explicitly between what is fact and what is speculation on our part, thus enabling the reader to choose the view which he himself may consider more plausible in each case. When interpretation is still open because of obscurity or conflict of sources, we hope to make this clear; and, wherever an opinion is advanced in such cases, let it be patent that it is an opinion, no more.

On the basis of the sources currently accessible, we cannot expect to reach decisive or incontestable results in this study. It is sufficient if the present work serves to break ground in an undeveloped area of history and succeeds in exposing the present state of our knowledge. Facts and theories may be pointed out and discussed, potential trends may be sketched; but this is only a first attempt to bring light into a period which is still quite obscure. Our best-supported hypotheses, because of the slimness of the evidence, will be resting on relatively thin support; and we shall not be surprised when future finds, research, and interpretation discard them as irrelevant. Our main object here is to provide a map in relatively uncharted territory, as a prelude to future efforts.

CHAPTER I

THE SOURCES

The purpose of this chapter is to provide a brief survey of the sources currently available for a political history of Babylonia during the years immediately following the downfall of the Kassite Dynasty. This will be done in two steps: (1) inspection of the sources according to type, and (2) evaluation of the sources as regards the historical information conveyed and the relative reliability of that information.

In the first section of the chapter, the different types of sources will be examined. (2) Emphasis here will be on the number and the distribution of sources available from each type so that the reader may gain some notion of the extent of the usable material. In most instances, the individual documents under each type will not be enumerated; nor will detailed bibliographical references for them be given within the chapter. Rather, a complete catalogue of sources, listing each text together with pertinent bibliographical data, will be given in Appendix A.

In the second section of the chapter, the sources will be evaluated. Here we shall investigate briefly what information our texts purport to confer and to what extent this information is credible. Once again, the sources will be discussed principally according to type; and the rules put forth for interpretation will be generic only. Specific questions involving factual conflict between data provided in two or more documents will be settled individually as each case arises in the course of subsequent chapters.

TYPES OF SOURCES

The Written Sources

At present, we have about two hundred ancient documents which in one way or another bear upon the history of Babylonia during this epoch. For our present purposes, we divide them as follows: (1) primary documentation, i.e., contemporary

(2) Since this is not a historiographical study nor a study in sources as such, we will use the traditional assignations of documents to certain classes, this being sufficient for our purposes. For example, Chronicle P will be treated as a chronicle despite the fact that it exhibits several features not characteristic of that form of writing.

recording of events; (2) secondary documentation, i.e., later recording of events; and (3) tertiary documentation, i.e., remote tradition concerning events. The first type is comprised of original documents written down at the same time as or soon after the events they describe in the guise of reliable witnesses. The second type includes documents which originate at some distance in time from the events related but which rely usually on other, earlier documents (or traditions) for their historical information. These differ from texts of the third type in that they have access to primary oral or written documentation and make an attempt to interpret it. The documents of the third type, as a general rule, originate much later than those of the second, usually show little utilization of even poor secondary documents, and are generally conspicuous for being outside the direct transmission of historical tradition. We have in mind here chiefly Hellenistic texts like those of Berossos and Josephus, who had lost direct literary contact with earlier ages in Babylonia and presented the history of these ages largely in garbled and almost unrecognizable form.

PRIMARY DOCUMENTATION: CONTEMPORARY RECORDING OF HISTORICAL EVENTS

Babylonian Royal Inscriptions. (3) There are eighteen different royal inscriptions from Babylonia during this period which are known to the present writer. (4) A table listing royal building and votive inscriptions (5), presented opposite on page 5, shows their distribution in time, (6) the language in which each was written, the length of each document, the material on which it was inscribed, the ancient site at which each was originally located, and the general contents of the text. As can be seen from the table, building inscriptions outnumber votive texts 11 to 2, (7) with one text—that of Simbar–Shipak—combining votive and building elements. The sixteen texts average slightly over nineteen lines in length. Noteworthy is the predominance of Sumerian over Akkadian during the early years of the Second

(3) Excluding royal inscriptions on Luristan bronzes (which are treated in a separate section below), brief colophons referring to contemporary kings, and the Assyrian inscriptions of Tiglath–Pileser III and Shalmaneser V. Kudurrus are classified as Babylonian private texts.

(4) This excludes duplicates in the same language, but includes as separate items Sumerian and Akkadian versions of the same inscription (*UET* I 166 and 167) and two unpublished inscriptions (2 N-T 483, a brick of Nebuchadnezzar I, and a brick of Marduk–balassu–iqbi).

(5) The royal inscriptions on weights are treated separately below.

(6) The dates given in the tables in this chapter are those which are established in detail in the second chapter.

(7) The texts of Itti–Marduk–balatu and Marduk–balassu–iqbi are broken, so it cannot be ascertained to which type they belonged. They were probably building inscriptions.

Babylonian Royal Inscriptions of the Post-Kassite Period

DATE	KING	LANGUAGE	LENGTH (IN LINES)	MATERIAL	ORIG. SITE	GENERAL CONTENTS
1140*-1133*	Itti–Marduk–balatu [8]	Akk.	15+	limestone	?	?
1126*-1105*	Nebuchadnezzar I	Sum.-Akk.	47+	limestone	Babylon	temple repair
	Nebuchadnezzar I	Sum.	9	brick	Nippur	temple repair
1100*-1083*	Marduk–nadin–ahhe	Sum.	15	limestone(?)	Ur	temple repair
	Marduk–nadin–ahhe	Sum.	62	copper cylinder	Ur	temple repair
1082*-1070*	Marduk–shapik–zeri	Sum.	17+colophon	clay tablet (COPY)	Borsippa	temple repair
	Marduk–shapik–zeri	Akk.	39+	clay cylinder	Babylon	repair on city wall and gate
1069*-1048*	Adad–apla–iddina	(Akk.?) [9]	4	brick	Babylon	repair of city wall
	Adad–apla–iddina	Sum.-Akk.	22+colophon	clay tablet (COPY)	Borsippa	votive
	Adad–apla–iddina	Sum.	9	stamped brick	Kish	temple repair
	Adad–apla–iddina	Akk.	10	clay cylinder	Nippur	repair of city wall
	Adad–apla–iddina	Sum.	10	brick	Ur	temple repair
	Adad–apla–iddina	Akk.	11	brick	Ur	temple repair
1026*-1009*	Simbar–Shipak	Akk.	27+colophon	clay tablet (COPY)	Nippur	temple repair and votive
c. 850	Marduk–zakir–shumi I	Akk.	8	lapis lazuli seal	Babylon	votive
c. 815	Marduk–balassu–iqbi	(Akk.?) [10]	2+	brick	Tell Umar	? [11]

(8) The rules followed in this book for transcribing personal names are discussed at the beginning of the General Index, p. 397 below.

(9) This brick contains only proper names, hence the language in which it was written cannot be stated with certainty. But, since the Babylonian names in it are spelled out syllabically, the text was possibly written in Akkadian.

(10) Since the latter part of the king's name is written syllabically here as *iq–bi*, the brick may have been written in Akkadian.

(11) Bibliography of these inscriptions is given below in Appendix A under nos. 2.2.1, 4.2.1, 4.2.3, 6.2.1, 6.2.5, 7.2.1, 7.2.2, 8.2.1, 8.2.2, 8.2.3, 8.2.4, 8.2.5, 8.2.6, 12.2.1, 25.2.1, 26.2.1. (Unless statement is made to the contrary, all references to Appendix A in this book will be to the basic catalogue, Section II of that appendix).

Dynasty of Isin, [12] but the use of Sumerian dies out after the reign of Adad–apla–iddina. [13] Six texts are written in Sumerian, six in Akkadian, two are interlinear bilinguals; [14] and their style ranges from terse stereotyped formulae to elaborate learned poetry. Of the surviving original documents, six are written on bricks, [15] four on stone, [16] two on clay cylinders, and one on a copper cylinder; the later copies are all written on clay tablets. Of the building texts, six deal with temple repairs, five with repairs on city walls. The two strictly votive texts record gifts of a girdle and of a seal to statues of the principal Babylonian deities, Marduk and Nabu; and the mixed votive-building inscription tells of the reconstruction of a throne at Nippur for Enlil. Four of the texts come originally from Babylon, four from Ur, three from Nippur, [17] two from Borsippa, [18] one from Kish, one from Tell Umar, and one is of unknown provenience.

Two weights bearing Babylonian royal inscriptions from this time have also survived. The following table shows their time distribution, etc.:

DATE	KING	LANGUAGE	LENGTH (IN LINES)	SHAPE	SIZE	FOUND AT
1034*-1027*	Nabu–shumu–libur	(Akk.)	2	duck	30 mina	Nimrud
c. 770	Eriba–Marduk	Akk.	3	duck	30 mina	Nimrud [19]

These two weights were found in the ruins of the Northwest Palace at Nimrud.

Babylonian Private Legal, Administrative, and Votive Texts. Various texts written by or in the interests of private individuals have survived from the period under consideration. For the sake of clarity, we present the chronological and typological division of the material in the following table. [20]

[12] Its use may have revived in the time of Nebuchadnezzar I, though the present paucity of texts prohibits any fixed conclusions on the matter.

[13] It resumes after this period in the reign of Merodach–Baladan II.

[14] For the two remaining texts see notes 9-10 above.

[15] All on stamped bricks, as far as I can ascertain at present.

[16] Three on limestone and one on a seal of lapis lazuli.

[17] Though one was found at Khorsabad (V. Place, *Ninive et l'Assyrie*, II, 308) and the copy of another was apparently written at Uruk (*JCS* XIX [1965] 123-124).

[18] Both are seventh-century copies, one made in the reign of Esarhaddon (*Studia Orientalia* I [1925] 28-33) and the other in the reign of Kandalanu (*LIH* I 70).

[19] Bibliography for the inscriptions listed in this table is given below in Appendix A under nos. 11.2.1 and 31.2.1.

[20] In this table, the texts published in *MDOG* VII (1901) 25-29 and *BBSt* no. 25 are counted as separate documents, as are columns ii and iv of *YOS* I 37. BM 78156 and BM 40717, unpublished duplicate legal texts from the reign of Tiglath–Pileser III, are counted as one, as are the three duplicates of a single inscription: NBC 2502 (published as *BIN* II 31), YBC 2170 (published as *YOS* IX 74), and BM 113205 (unpublished). Luristan bronzes bearing the inscriptions of private individuals are treated in the next section.

Babylonian Private Texts of the Post-Kassite Period

		ORIGINAL DOCUMENTS (21)							COPY
		WRITTEN ON STONE				WRITTEN ON CLAY			CLAY TABLET
		Steles	Tablets	Weights	Seal	Building Texts (Cyl.)	Legal (Tab.)	Administrative (Tab.)	Legal
1140*-1133*	Itti–Marduk–balatu		1					5	
1126*-1105*	Nebuchadnezzar I	2	1					2	
1104*-1101*	Enlil–nadin–apli	1*	1						
1100*-1083*	Marduk–nadin–ahhe	4+2*	1					1	
1082*-1070*	Marduk–shapik–zeri	2		1				1	
1069*-1048*	Adad–apla–iddina	1*	2					1	
1047*	Marduk–ahhe–eriba	1*							
1026*-1009*	Simbar–Shipak		1						
979*-944*	Nabu–mukin–apli	1						1?	
c. 860	Nabu–apla–iddina	1	3 (4?)						
c. 850	Marduk–zakir–shumi I	2							
c. 815	Marduk–balassu–iqbi								1
	Marduk–bel–zeri							1	
c. 770	Eriba–Marduk						1		
c. 750	Nabu–shuma–ishkun	1				1		2	
747-734	Nabonassar					1	1	18	
731-729+	Nabu–mukin–zeri							1	
728-727	Tiglath–Pileser III						1	3	
	uncertain	1		1	1			6	

(21) Bibliography for the texts cited in this table may be found below in Appendix A under nos. 2.2.2, 2.2.3, 4.2.7, 4.2.8, 4.2.9, 4.2.10, 5.2.2, 5.2.3, 6.2.6, 6.2.7, 6.2.8, 6.2.9, 6.2.10, 6.2.11, 6.2.12, 6.2.13, 7.2.4, 7.2.5, 7.2.6, 7.2.7, 8.2.8, 8.2.9, 8.2.10, 8.2.11, 9.2.1, 12.2.2, 19.2.2, 19.2.3, 24.2.1, 24.2.2, 24.2.3, 24.2.4 (I have not yet found out whether this document was written on a stele or a tablet, hence the question mark in the table), 25.2.2, 25.2.3, 26.2.2, 29.2.1, 31.2.2, 32.2.1, 32.2.2, 32.2.3, 33.2.1, 33.2.2, 33.2.3, 36.2.1, 37.2.1, 37.2.2, and supplement (s) (t) (v) (w). In the table, asterisks indicate probable datings. All texts are written in Akkadian except one of the weights (7.2.7), which is written in Sumerian.

One text not included in the table is a kudurru once in the possession of A. Sayce (*Expository Times* XIX [1907-1908] 498), the script of which—according to Sayce—indicated a date towards the end of the Second Isin Dynasty. The text was never published, and I do not know its present whereabouts.

From the Second Dynasty of Isin (kings 1-11), the most common text types surviving are the stone documents (steles and tablets) dealing with legal matters concerning land (sales, grants, gifts, tax exemptions connected with property, and settling of title disputes). In fact all stone documents from this time, with the exception of the duck weight inscribed with the name of the high priest (*nišakku*) of Nippur, concern land transactions of one sort or another. (22) The clay tablets are dated administrative memoranda from various private or temple estates.

It is noteworthy that there are as yet no legal texts known from the end of the Kassite Dynasty down to the early eighth century other than those written on stone. (23) In the earliest example from the period, a stone tablet from the reign of Itti–Marduk–balatu, the old legal phraseology in Sumerian is partially preserved; (24) but this feature is absent in later texts. Only one example of a stone tablet for such private use is known from the Kassite period, (25) and it is possible that the usage became popular only under the Second Isin Dynasty. These early stone tablets never contain divine symbols; and the reigning monarch is always mentioned in the body of the text, frequently as the prime agent in the legal case. After the Second Dynasty of Isin, the practice changes. Stone tablets as well as steles regularly bear symbols, deal frequently with strictly private affairs (to the exclusion of the king), often include matters not concerned with land, (26) and always contain lists of witnesses. (27)

Documentation in general after the Second Dynasty of Isin is rather sparse. Save for a small cluster of six kudurrus in the mid–ninth century, few private texts are known until the reigns of Nabu–shuma–ishkun and Nabonassar; and then most of the texts are administrative memoranda from estates. Of especial interest are two mid–eighth century inscriptions (28) written on clay cylinders which record temple repairs made by local officials in areas (Uruk, Borsippa) where kings had failed to exercise their royal prerogative of restoring sacral precincts.

(22) This weight also contains the only private text written in Sumerian. All the other private documents are in Akkadian.

(23) I.e., original texts. But a legal document drawn up in the last quarter of the ninth century survives only in a later clay copy (4 N-T 3). The original of this document was probably done on stone, since the phrase *kunuk šarri* [*ša š*]*iprē*[*ti*] (lines 40′-41′) is attested to date only on stone texts. (See J. A. Brinkman, *RA* LXI [1967] 72 for references).

(24) *BBSt* no. 30:14.

(25) *MDP* II pl. 20. F. X. Steinmetzer's contention (*Die babylonischen Kudurru* (*Grenzsteine*) *als Urkundenform*, p. 73) that the text published in *MDP* IV pls. 16-17 was on a stone tablet rather than a stele is subject to dispute; the stone in question is far too broken to opt for either alternative on the basis of external appearance alone.

(26) As time goes on, many matters extraneous to land concerns are mentioned until the last stele in this period (*VAS* I 36) does not mention land at all, only a "divine" grant of temple income.

(27) Lists of witnesses were often missing in kudurrus written under the Kassite and Second Isin Dynasties.

(28) One of which survives in three copies.

The provenience of few of these texts is known. Some of the stone tablets and steles were drawn up at Babylon, yet intended for display at other places. Major cities from which these texts come include: Babylon (4 texts), [29] Borsippa (2), Dilbat (1), Nippur (4), [30] Sippar (1), [31] Ur (1), Uruk (1); [31] minor sites whose names can be read include Ate, Bit–Iddin–Shamash(?), Dur–Sumulael, Kar–bel–matati, Kar–kur–gar–ra(?), Sahritu, Sha–mamitu, Udani, and the mound of Za'aleh. [31]

Luristan Bronzes. Under this heading we are concerned with inscribed bronze objects, chiefly in the shape of weapons (daggers, arrowheads, hatchets) or household vessels (situlae, bowls), which are reputed to have been found in Luristan in western Iran and which bear the names of Babylonian kings or of private individuals who lived between the twelfth and eighth centuries B.C. There is abundant recent literature speculating on how these bronzes inscribed with the name of Babylonians came to Luristan; [32] and the chief theories now propounded suggest (a) that the weapons inscribed with royal names were rewards given to Iranian mercenaries for faithful military service under Babylonian kings, [33] or (b) that they were votive or ceremonial pieces originally kept in Babylonia but later carried off by invaders from the Iranian highlands. [34] There is also some dispute as to whether the weapons were merely display objects or whether they were intended to be functional.

Most of these questions cannot be solved by the evidence presently available. It is probable that the various Luristan bronzes may have served different functions. For instance, the only pertinent inscriptions on contemporary bronzes (a royal hatchet and two private daggers) reveal that these were originally votive objects dedicated to gods. [35] On the other hand, there are contemporary and later reliefs which depict identical daggers being worn by Babylonian and Assyrian kings. [36] Furthermore, it is conceivable that these or similar weapons, originally the perquisite of royalty, could subsequently have been bestowed as a mark of favor for royal service. [37] Those bronzes which were the property of gods or kings pre-

(29) Plus four texts originally written there, but displayed elsewhere.

(30) Plus one text, written for an area near the city.

(31) The texts from Sippar, Uruk, and Za'aleh were written at Babylon but destined for these cities, where they were actually found (see note 29 above).

(32) E.g., L. vanden Berghe, *Archéologie de l'Irān ancien*, pp. 91-97; R. Ghirshman, "À propos des bronzes du Luristan de la Collection Foroughi," *Iranica Antiqua* II (1962) 165-179; Ghirshman and E. Porada in *Dark Ages and Nomads c. 1000 B.C.*, pp. 3-12; Porada, *The Art of Ancient Iran*, pp. 75-89.

(33) E.g., Porada in *Dark Ages and Nomads c. 1000 B.C.*, pp. 11-12 and n. 12.

(34) E.g., Ghirshman in *Iranica Antiqua* II (1962) 174.

(35) The Nebuchadnezzar I hatchet, published by G. Dossin in *Iranica Antiqua* II (1962) 158 no. 14, and the Eriba–Nusku dagger, published by W. Nagel in *AfO* XIX (1959-60) 96, were dedicated to Marduk. The Marduk–nasir dagger (*Iranica Antiqua* II [1962] 153 no. 7), was dedicated to the god Erija.

(36) Some illustrations have been collected by Nagel in *AfO* XIX (1959-60) 101-103.

(37) Presumably to people of lower rank or to people whose service was less noteworthy than those who received formal land grants or tax exemptions from the king, e.g., *BBSt* nos. 8 and 6.

sumably came as booty or as later barter to Iran. Bronzes which were the property of private individuals (albeit occasionally bearing the name of a royal patron) could have come to Iran in a similar fashion or could have belonged to Babylonian subjects, allies, or mercenaries settled in or near Luristan. Bolstering the latter alternative is the fact that most of these inscribed weapons come from the period between 1135 and 940, when there were close ties between the rulers of Babylonia and lands some distance east of the Tigris. ([38]) Though there is as yet no direct evidence for Babylonian political involvement in the Luristan region (or vice versa) at this time, such contact would fit in well with what is known of contemporary Babylonian political and military activity.

There is a total of 38 Luristan bronzes which can be dated exactly because they are inscribed with the names of Babylonian kings who ruled between the twelfth and tenth centuries. They bear a total of 14 different inscriptions belonging to 10 different rulers.

Their distribution in time is as follows:

1132*-1127*	Ninurta–nadin–shumi: 2 daggers
1126*-1105*	Nebuchadnezzar I: 4 daggers, 1 hatchet
1104*-1101*	Enlil–nadin–apli: 1 dagger
1100*-1083*	Marduk–nadin–ahhe: 4 daggers
1082*-1070*	Marduk–shapik–zeri: 1 dagger
1069*-1048*	Adad–apla–iddina: 1 dagger
1005*-989*	Eulmash–shakin–shumi: 14 arrowheads
988*-986*	Ninurta–kudurri–usur I: 2 arrowheads
985*-980*	Mar–biti–apla–usur: 4 arrowheads
979*-944*	Nabu–mukin–apli: 4 arrowheads ([39])

In addition to these 38 bronzes bearing the names of kings, two situlae bearing the names of sons of Nabu–mukin–apli (Ninurta–kudurri–usur, who later succeeded to the throne, and Rimut–ili) are to be dated during his reign. ([40]) Furthermore, there are three daggers with inscriptions preserving part of the royal titulary, but where

([38]) Semi-independent eastern chieftains aided Babylonia in campaigns against Elam and Assyria under the Second Dynasty of Isin (*BBSt* nos. 6 and 8) and, in the early tenth century, the Bazi and Elamite dynasties presumably originated in eastern Babylonia.

([39]) Bibliography of inscriptions below in Appendix A under nos. 3.2.1, 4.2.2, 4.2.4, 4.2.5, 5.2.1, 6.2.2, 6.2.3, 6.2.4, 7.2.3, 8.2.7, 15.2.1, 16.2.1, 18.2.1, 19.2.1. (The arrowheads should perhaps more properly be termed spear points).

([40]) The situla of Ninurta–kudurri–usur has been published by P. Amandry, *Antike Kunst* IX (1966) 59 no. 3 (fig. 3). The situla of Rimut–ili is published in A. U. Pope, *SPA* I 284 no. XIII.

the royal name is no longer visible; (41) G. Dossin has suggested that they be assigned to the reign of Nebuchadnezzar I, (42) and it is probable that they come from approximately that time. (43) From the above table, one cannot but notice the predominance of daggers under the kings of the Second Dynasty of Isin, followed by a predominance of arrowheads under the Bazi and later dynasties. There are no known situlae bearing the name of a reigning monarch.

Besides the two inscribed situlae of the tenth-century princes mentioned in the preceding paragraph, there are about fourteen bronzes inscribed with the names of persons other than kings which may date from Babylonia during this period.

daggers: (1) Ẹriba–Nusku, a scribe (*AfO* XIX [1959-60] 96)
(2) Marduk–nasir (*Iranica Antiqua* II [1962] 153 no. 7)
(3) Shamash–killanni, *ša rēš šarri* (Pope, *SPA* I 284 no. XI)
(4) (*na–pu*[?]; Herzfeld, *Iran in the Ancient East,* pl. XXVIII)
(5-6) personal names not yet readable (*Iranica Antiqua* II [1962] 154 nos. 8-9)

arrowheads: (7) Mar–biti–shuma–ibni (*Iranica Antiqua* II [1962] 161 no. 20)
(8) x–x–x–(x)–Marduk, *bēl pīḫati* (reading of title not altogether certain, *Iranica Antiqua* II [1962] 162 no. 25)
(9) Ninurta–ushallim (*Iranica Antiqua* II [1962] 161 no. 24)
(10-11) personal names not yet readable (*Iranica Antiqua* II [1962] 161 nos. 22-23)

situla: (12) Ẹriba–Marduk (*Iranica Antiqua* II [1962] 164 no. 33)

bowl: (13) Abdi–il (Pope, *SPA* I 285 no. XIV)

macehead(?): (14) personal name not yet readable, *ša rēš šarri* (*Iranica Antiqua* II [1962] 162 no. 26)

None of these can be dated with certainty. Because similar daggers bearing royal names have been dated to the time of the Second Isin Dynasty, one could assume that these private daggers come from approximately the same time. Similarly with the arrowheads, of which the dated royal examples come from the reigns of kings who ruled between 1005* and 944*, and with the situla, which is similar to those which bear tenth-century inscriptions. The bowl, because of the mention of Adinu

(41) Dossin, *Iranica Antiqua* II (1962) 152.
(42) *Ibid.*, 152.
(43) The remaining portion of the titulary is paralleled by daggers of Ninurta–nadin–shumi (*ibid.*, 151 no. 3), Nebuchadnezzar I (*ibid.*, 152 no. 4), Enlil–nadin–apli (*ibid.*, 153 no. 6), and Marduk–nadin–ahhe (*SPA* I 283 nos. VIII-IX). Later dagger inscriptions have an abbreviated titulary.

of the Dakkuru tribe, should probably be dated about the middle of the ninth century. (44) A Marduk–nasir who lived about the time of the reign of Marduk–nadin-ahhe (1100*–1083*) (45) could conceivably be identified with the Marduk–nasir of the dagger; but the name may have been relatively common and no positive identification can be made. A much more likely prospect for identification is the Mar-biti–shuma–ibni of the arrowhead, who may be the same as a Mar–biti–shuma–ibni who is known from the tenth–century kudurru, *BBSt* no. 9 (46) and who flourished during the time when the royal arrowheads are dated. Some of these objects, especially nos. 2, 4, 5, 6, 8, 10, 11, need not have come from Babylonia during this time.

Babylonian Letters. Two fragments, which exist only in Neo-Assyrian copies and may originally have belonged to the same letter or to separate letters, have definitely been dated to this period in Babylonia. They were written by a Babylonian king early in the Second Dynasty of Isin to his royal contemporary in Assyria. The name of neither monarch has been preserved; but one of the fragments alludes to an episode which took place between Ninurta–tukulti–Ashur, an earlier Assyrian monarch, and the father of the current Babylonian king. Because of the relative flexibility of the chronology of the early part of the Second Isin Dynasty, we are still unable to identify either the sender or the receiver of the letter(s) with sufficient precision for unqualified incorporation into this study. We shall, however, touch briefly on possibilities for interpretation of these fragments in the third chapter.

Babylonian Treaties. There is only one document at present which fits into this category. The text, found by H. Rassam at Kuyunjik in the last century, is fragmentary; but enough remains to ascertain that it is a draft of a treaty drawn up between Marduk–zakir–shumi I of Babylon and Shamshi–Adad V of Assyria early in the reign of the latter (in or shortly after 824 B.C.).

Babylonian Miscellany. From the Second Dynasty of Isin has survived a copy of a text describing a process for making artificial gems. It is dated by its colophon, which reads: "Original exemplar from Babylon. Palace of Nebuchadnezzar (I), king of Babylon." (47)

Disputed Documents. Many private votive inscriptions, economic texts, and letters exist which can be classified generically as Neo-Babylonian but whose date cannot now be determined more precisely. Because of the scarcity of docu-

(44) See S. Langdon's remarks in *SPA* I 285 and n. 1.

(45) *BBSt* no. 7 i 11, etc. It is interesting that this Marduk–nasir is called *ša rēš šarri*, a title borne also by other individuals whose names appear on Luristan bronzes about this time (nos. 3 and 14 in the above list).

(46) *BBSt* no. 9 i 19, 25, 35, iii 10, iva 6, 7, 16, 20. This is the only (other) individual known by this name, and his dating from about the same time is at least a great coincidence.

(47) *RA* LX (1966) 31, colophon. See note 642 below.

ments which can be dated with reasonable accuracy within the period under consideration, there is little chance as yet of establishing typological or prosopographical connections which would help in dating these texts. Since reconstruction of the political history of the early Neo-Babylonian period depends heavily on precise dating for elucidation of the scheme of development, it would be of little benefit to make a list of Neo-Babylonian documents of uncertain date which must be excluded from the present study.

Besides documents of uncertain date, there are two other texts which fall within the "disputed" category because it is uncertain whether they should be classified as primary or secondary documentation. Purportedly composed in the name of individual Babylonian kings, these texts give highly poetic accounts of the deliverance of Babylonia from the Elamites, an event which took place early in the Second Isin Dynasty. (48) Neither paleography nor style helps to date these documents, for they survive only in late copies, chiefly from the library of Ashurbanipal; and documents in similar poetic style occur among both primary and secondary documentation relating to this time. (49) We can only inspect the contents of each briefly in order to determine in which of the two classifications, i.e., primary or secondary, they are more likely to belong.

The first text, K. 2660 (50), is a poetic description of the upheavals in Babylonia at the end of the Kassite Dynasty and the later attempts of an unnamed king to recoup Babylonia's losses against Elam. It is quite clear that the text is written in the name of one monarch, but the question is whether the king authorized the composition of the text or whether it was written down at a later date to embellish a kernel of historical truth. The latter alternative seems more likely in the light of our knowledge of ancient historiography. In the inscription the king devotes some space to describing his fears and his flight before the Elamite king; and ancient rulers were not known for subsidizing official records of their own timidity in battle in such humiliating terms. But, despite the fact that this document is probably to be relegated to the realm of secondary documentation, it seems to have been based on good contemporary tradition. Its command of detail surrounding the downfall of the Kassites is precise and accurate and unlikely to have been fabricated out of thin air. (51)

The second text, which survives in several fragmentary copies, (52) is more of an enigma; and it is difficult to reach even a tentative decision on its classification.

(48) Under Nebuchadnezzar I (*BBSt* nos. 6 and 24, *CT* XIII 48, etc.).

(49) Poetic primary: *Bibliotheca Orientalis* VII (1950) 42-46 and *Studia Orientalia* I (1925) 32-33. Poetic secondary: *CT* XIII 48.

(50) Published principally as III *R* 38 no. 2. For further bibliography, see Appendix A under 4.3.9.

(51) The names of the Babylonian and Elamite kings, the removal of Marduk from Babylon, and the names of battle sites are noted exactly and compare favorably, where possible, with other sources relating to these same events.

(52) Full bibliography below in Appendix A under 4.3.10.

The document has been termed a hymn composed on the occasion of Marduk's return to Babylon from Elamite captivity. While it is true that the text centers around that event, it hardly seems a hymn: its contents are too descriptive, specific, and humanly oriented for that. (53) The way in which the principal tablet begins—launching into the midst of a description of corpses strewn around a battlefield—arouses our suspicion that it may have been the second or later tablet in a series. (54) This would hardly be true of a genuine royal inscription. But, on the other hand, if we examine the general mode of composition, the interlinear Sumerian-Akkadian style, we find that the only parallels in this period are legitimate royal inscriptions. (55) Unfortunately, with the beginning of the text missing, we cannot absolutely rule out the possibility of its being a royal inscription, though there are no traces of votive sections in its preserved portions. Under the present circumstances, the classification of the text must be left undecided; but the evidence in favor of its being secondary—rather than primary—documentation seems stronger.

Assyrian Royal Inscriptions. Besides the Babylonian contemporary inscriptions, there are also first-hand witnesses from other lands which mention political activities in and around Babylonia. The Assyrian royal inscriptions will be the first documents of this type to be considered. Many more texts of Assyrian kings have survived from this time than texts of their Babylonian royal contemporaries; but these do not often touch upon events pertinent to Babylonia. In this period, nine kings, beginning with Tiglath–Pileser I and ending with Tiglath–Pileser III, left records—principally of hostility—with Babylonia. Their distribution in time is as follows:

Tiglath–Pileser I	1115-1077
Ashur–bel–kala	1074-1057
Adad–nirari II	911-891
Tukulti–Ninurta II	890-884
Ashurnasirpal II	883-859
Shalmaneser III	858-824
Shamshi–Adad V	823-811
Adad–nirari III	810-783
Tiglath–Pileser III	744-727 (56)

(53) The extant sections describe the activities of the devotee with little direct interest in the god.

(54) Perhaps part of an epic cycle surrounding the feats of Nebuchadnezzar I. See W. G. Lambert in *The Seed of Wisdom*, pp. 9-10.

(55) *Bibliotheca Orientalis* VII (1950) 42-46 and *Studia Orientalia* I (1925) 32-33 of Nebuchadnezzar I and Adad–apla–iddina respectively.

(56) Bibliography below in Appendix A under nos. 6.2.14, 8.2.12, 22.2.1, 24.2.5, 25.2.5, 26.2.4, 26.2.5 (*Gottesbrief*), 27.2.2, 36.2.2, supplement (o) and (r).

As can readily be seen, most of these Assyrian annals which mention contact with Babylonian rulers were written in the ninth century. This may be mere coincidence, since the concentration of Assyrian royal texts known from that century is greater than for any other comparable interval between the end of the Kassite Dynasty and 722.

Assyrian Letters. The only known contemporary Assyrian letters which bear on Babylonian affairs are some of the Nimrud Letters, excavated by British archeologists on the site of ancient Calah in 1952. These tablets stem from eighth-century royal archives, partly from the time of Tiglath-Pileser III. Of the published texts at least thirteen apparently deal with political events in Babylonia and the Sealand in the time of the Chaldean chieftain Mukin-zeri, predecessor of Tiglath-Pileser on the Babylonian throne. (57) Unfortunately, most of these tablets are badly broken; and their contents, even in preserved passages, often remain matter for conjecture. They are written in the contemporary Assyrian dialect and reflect usages known from the slightly later Harper Letters.

Elamite Royal Inscriptions. Contemporary documents in this category do not mention any Babylonian monarch by name. One lone inscription bears information pertinent to the history of Babylonia in this period: the long account by Shilhak-Inshushinak of his incursions into Babylonian territory during the early years of the Second Isin Dynasty. (58) Several other Elamite royal texts inscribed on booty taken from Babylonia date around the end of the Kassite period and will be used to reconstruct the background for the beginning of the Isin Dynasty.

SECONDARY DOCUMENTATION: LATER RECORDING OF HISTORICAL EVENTS

Kinglists. Lists of Babylonian kings of this period may be divided into two chief classes: simple kinglists and synchronistic kinglists. The first type, the simple kinglist, contains names of Babylonian rulers in chronological order and the number of years ruled by each. Other features are sometimes added: summaries giving the total number of kings and years for each dynasty and information concerning the

(57) Partial bibliography below in Appendix A under 36.2.3.

(58) F. W. König, *Die elamischen Königsinschriften*, no. 54 (=*MDP* XI no. 92). The text must date from this time because Shilhak-Inshushinak ruled between Kudur-Nahhunte (king of Elam at the time of Enlil-nadin-ahi, the last Kassite king) and Hulteludish-Inshushinak (king of Elam at the time of Nebuchadnezzar I).

ancestry of the individual monarchs. [59] Two such kinglists have survived which deal with rulers of the period under consideration: (1) Kinglist A, a broken and badly worn tablet which originally included all the Babylonian kings from the First Dynasty of Babylon down to the Chaldean Dynasty; [60] no definite date can be assigned to it in its present form, but the sixth or early fifth century B.C. would be a reasonable assumption; and (2) Kinglist C, a small school tablet dating from the time of the Second Dynasty of Isin, which contains the names of the first seven kings of that dynasty; it presumably dates from the reign of Adad–apla–iddina, since the list is complete only as far as the last year of that king's predecessor. [61] Both these kinglists originated in Babylonia. [62]

The second type of kinglist containing names of Babylonian kings of the period is the synchronistic kinglist. This characteristically Assyrian form ranges the names of Babylonian and Assyrian kings side by side in parallel columns, purportedly indicating which kings ruled at the same time in the two lands. Four such texts are known, all found in the German excavations at Assur. [63] The only texts sufficiently preserved to be dated come from late Assyrian times, i.e., the reigns of Ashurbanipal and Ashur–etil–ilani. [64] Because of the fragmentary state of the surviving synchronistic kinglists, it is often difficult to determine the time range of their original contents. One list, however, states at its conclusion that it included all the Babylonian kings from Sumulael to Kandalanu and all the Assyrian sovereigns from Erishum I to Ashurbanipal. [65]

Though this category strictly speaking includes only kinglists mentioning Babylonian kings, we should briefly advert to the fact that Assyrian kinglists, eponym lists, and eponym chronicles which deal with contemporary Assyria will also be of use in reconstructing the history of Babylonia in this period.

Chronicles. Here again one may distinguish two principal groups of texts, the Babylonian chronicles and the Assyrian chronicles. The Babylonian group embraces six texts which enter at least partially into our study: Chronicle P, the

(59) Statements of this type are restricted chiefly to terse comments like "his son" (i.e., son of the preceding king) or "dynasty of GN" (i.e., the dynastic affiliation of the ruler).

(60) The last monarch occurring in the preserved section is Kandalanu's successor, whose name in the text (iv 23) clearly begins with Sin ([d]30); based on personal collation. But there would have been sufficient space at the end of the list to contain all the kings down through Nabonidus and perhaps even further.

(61) Poebel in *AS* XV 25-26 has presented arguments for dating Kinglist C to the final year of the reign of Marduk–shapik–zeri. This is unquestionably the earliest possible date for the composition of the list; the latest probable date for its composition would be late in the reign of Adad–apla–iddina.

(62) Bibliography for the Babylonian kinglists is contained below in Appendix A, Section I.

(63) Bibliography for the synchronistic kinglists is contained below in Appendix A, Section I.

(64) E.g., Assur 14616c and *KAV* 182.

(65) Assur 14616c iv 17-20. It should also be noted that this text is the only one of the synchronistic kinglists to place the Assyrian kings to the left of their Babylonian contemporaries.

New Babylonian Chronicle, the Religious Chronicle, the Dynastic Chronicle, the Babylonian Chronicle, and the Shamash–shuma–ukin Chronicle; (66) a seventh chronicle (BM 48498), to be published by Grayson in his forthcoming edition of the Assyrian and Babylonian chronicles, may also bear on this period. These present a wide variety of styles and contents, ranging from portrayal of Babylonian military encounters with Assyria and Elam to the perfunctory recording of religious portents or of years in which the New Year festival was not celebrated.

The time range covered by these texts varies considerably. (67) The first identifiable episode in Chronicle P occurred about the middle of the fourteenth century and the latest mentioned event probably sometime in the middle of the twelfth century. (68) The preserved portion of the New Babylonian Chronicle begins just before a section dealing with Marduk–shapik–zeri (early eleventh century) and continues till about the time of Shalmaneser V. (69) The first and last monarchs mentioned in the Religious Chronicle are Nabu–shumu–libur (second half of the eleventh century) (70) and Nabu–mukin–apli (mid–tenth century); from a catchline at the end of the tablet, one may infer that there were other tablets in the series which carried the story beyond this point in time. The Dynastic Chronicle began originally with an age long before the Old Babylonian period and extended down till at least the early eighth century. (71) The Babylonian Chronicle is the first in a series of comprehensive chronicles which began with the reign of Nabonassar; the tablet pertinent to our present purposes was copied in the twenty-second year of Darius I (500 B.C.). The Shamash–shuma–ukin Chronicle is mostly concerned with the reign of that king, but two brief excerpts towards the end of the tablet mention Shirikti–Shuqamuna (early tenth century) and Nabu–shuma–ishkun (mid-eighth century). The fragmentary chronicle BM 48498, to be published by Grayson in his *Assyrian and Babylonian Chronicles*, mentions a Kurigalzu, a Merodach–Baladan, a Nebuchadnezzar, and possibly even Hammurapi; but the document is too badly broken for us to determine the original time range of its contents.

(66) Bibliography for the Babylonian chronicles appears below in Appendix A, Section I.

(67) By "time range" in this context is meant the historical period described by the extant portions of each text.

(68) This is true if the conventional identification of Tukulti–Ashur (Chronicle P iv 12) with Ninurta–tukulti–Ashur, Assyrian king number 84, is accepted; on this point, see note 557 below. If this identification is not accepted, then the latest certainly identifiable occurrence is the restoration of Adad–shuma–usur to the Babylonian throne about 1219.

(69) There is apparently a trace of the name of Tiglath–Pileser III in rev. 18; and a successor of Tiglath–Pileser should therefore be mentioned in rev. 19. (In citing this text, I follow the line numbering of L. W. King, *CCEBK*, II, 57-69, 147-155.)

(70) There are fifteen lines preserved in the text before the mention of Nabu–shumu–libur, and the chronicle may have begun with some other monarch.

(71) *ADD* 888 is a fragment of the reverse of this tablet (probably column vi). See Appendix A, Section I, C 4 for particulars.

It is difficult to date the composition of these Babylonian chronicles on the basis of either external or internal evidence. It is sufficient here to realize that most of them were written down by at least the late Neo-Babylonian or early Persian period, when primary sources were still available and intelligible.

Assyrian chronicles pertaining to this period are three in number: (1) the Synchronistic History, (2) the Ashur–resha–ishi I Chronicle, and (3) the Tiglath–Pileser I Chronicle. ([72]) The Synchronistic History covers events from the late fifteenth to the early eighth century. Some of its later sections, with which we shall be concerned here, bear a remarkable similarity with passages in the Assyrian royal annals; ([73]) and it may plausibly be supposed either that the chronicler borrowed from the annals or that both the chronicler and the annalist derived their material from some common source. The composition of the Synchronistic History may be dated to the first half of the eighth century. ([74])

The other two Assyrian chronicles are of a type somewhat different than the better known Synchronistic History. In so far as they are preserved, their accounts are each confined to the deeds of one Assyrian monarch; and, in this, they are similar to the official royal inscriptions of Assyrian kings. But the narrative is set forth in the third person, entirely in the manner of a chronicle. ([75]) These documents, because of their more detailed treatment of events—as contrasted with the Synchronistic History's cursory sweep over the centuries—might be viewed as fuller sources from which the later, more summary chronicles drew and which would then occupy an intermediate place between the formal field accounts of the royal inscriptions and the large eclectic chronicles. Both chronicles to be used here probably date not long after the late-twelfth- and early-eleventh-century events which they describe. ([76]) They are not classified with the primary documentation because they were not official accounts of royal activities composed in the name of the king and may have been written down after the reigns of the kings involved.

Poetic Narratives. The documents in this classification are poems which touch on historical themes. They are texts of some literary value which portray events of political history from a more universal point of view than that of the strict-

([72]) Bibliography for these texts is given in Appendix A, Section I, D.

([73]) Compare Synchronistic History ii 15′ with *AfO* XVIII (1957-58) 351:50; ii 18′-21′ with *AfO* XVIII (1957-58) 351:45-47; iii 28-35 with *ICC* pl. 91:74-75, 80-81 and *TSBA* VII (1882) 98 iv 1 ff.; iv 1 with *AfO* IX (1933-34) 100:15. Especially noteworthy is the use of the relatively rare word *malmališ* in corresponding passages of the chronicle and the annals of Shalmaneser III.

([74]) The time of the Babylonian border disputes of the Assyrian kings from Adad–nirari III to Ashur–dan III. See p. 219 below.

([75]) Occasional passages in Assyrian royal inscriptions are also in the third person; but these narratives do not refer to the king as "RN, king of Assyria," as do these chronicles.

([76]) In the case of the Tiglath–Pileser I Chronicle, there is some evidence for such a date (see note 151 below).

ly political or military historian. The interest of these compositions is largely theological; and, for the most part, they are preoccupied with justifying or explaining the vicissitudes of Babylonian history in terms of the will of the gods. The texts to be discussed here fall into three groups: (1) the so-called "Kedor–laomer" texts, (2) the poems relating to Nebuchadnezzar I, and (3) the Era Epic. [77]

The "Kedor–laomer" texts are poetic fragments, three in number, which perpetuate the infamy of several foreign arch-malefactors, who acted against Babylonia and its gods. A confusion of Kudur–Nahhunte II, an Elamite king who figures in these texts, with the Kedor–laomer of Genesis xiv led scholars in the last century to give the documents their present name. One of these texts treats briefly of the situation at the close of the Kassite Dynasty, when Kudur–Nahhunte entered Babylon and removed its chief god, Marduk, to Elam; and the meager historical data given is of value for reconstructing the background of the fall of the Kassites and the rise of the Second Isin Dynasty. [78]

The second group of poetic narratives deals with the exploits of Nebuchadnezzar I. We have discussed above under the title "disputed documents" [79] two texts which may belong to this category. A third text, extant only in a copy from the library of Ashurbanipal, mentions Nebuchadnezzar by name [80] and narrates his royal anger at Marduk's continued exile in Elam, his prayer asking the god to return to his land, and part of the god's response to his pleadings before the tablet breaks off. The date of the poem's composition is uncertain. [81]

The Era Epic also paints a picture of part of the Post–Kassite period in theological terms. This rather lengthy poem describes the turmoil created in Babylonia beginning in the middle of the eleventh century by the Sutians, whose raids are viewed as occurring with the permission and even at the instigation of the gods. W. G. Lambert, in a penetrating discussion of the historical background of the epic, has suggested that its composition be dated to the time of the ninth-century ruler Nabu–apla–iddina, who, according to his own inscriptions, seems to have regarded himself as the divinely appointed avenger of Akkad against the Sutians. [82]

(77) Bibliography for these texts is given below in Appendix A: for group no. 1 in supplement (b), for group no. 2 in 4.3.8-4.3.10, for group no. 3 in supplement (l).

(78) The "Kedor–laomer" texts were probably composed sometime during the early Neo-Babylonian period, when the memory of the conflict with the Elamites lived on in hazy fashion—enough to be romanticized but without much detail.

(79) Above, pp. 13-14.

(80) This text is almost perfectly preserved at the beginning, while the other two "disputed" texts are broken (or missing) in this crucial section.

(81) Other poetic fragments have sometimes been placed in this category, e.g., *BA* V (1906) 386-387 (=*AOF* I [1893-97] 540-542), *JRAS* 1932 33ff.; but there is no evidence for connecting these texts with Nebuchadnezzar I. In fact, the latter text refers to an Assyrian goddess (*JRAS* 1932 36:22) and, if Babylonian at all, probably belongs to a later ruler of Assyrian extraction.

(82) *AfO* XVIII (1957-58) 395-401.

Incidental References. Under this heading we group isolated passages alluding to events of this period which occur in various documents from later times. ([83]) These passages are usually brief, parenthetical remarks in contexts primarily concerned with the later period. We have unearthed several such "flashbacks" to date, from both Babylonia and Assyria.

The Babylonian references occur chiefly in royal votive-historical texts. For instance, Merodach–Baladan II mentions Eriba–Marduk as an illustrious ancestor, ([84]) and Nabonidus refers to Nebuchadnezzar I and Eriba–Marduk in connection with earlier religious practices and building. ([85]) There are also a Neo-Babylonian temple inventory text from Ur, which mentions gold votive objects which had originally been presented by two kings of the Second Dynasty of Isin, and a list of temple food-offerings established at Uruk by a ninth-century king. ([86]) Finally, recent German excavations at Uruk found a list of Babylonian sages written in Seleucid times which included the names of two kings of the Second Isin Dynasty and their contemporary *ummânu* official. ([87])

Two of the Assyrian references likewise occur in historical documents. Sennacherib tells of Marduk–nadin–ahhe's removal of the gods of Ekallate over four centuries previously, and Esarhaddon notes Eriba–Marduk's earlier repairs of a temple in Uruk. ([88]) Astrologers and interpreters of portents refer back to earlier times, alluding to an omen series entitled "How Nebuchadnezzar (I) Destroyed Elam," ([89]) mentioning an omen interpretation report submitted to Marduk–nadin–ahhe, ([90]) or making a comparison between Esarhaddon and Marduk–shapik–zeri. ([91]) Colophons of texts in the Kuyunjik collection mention earlier Babylonian kings. ([92]) A seventh-century letter, the "Assur Ostracon," which was written in Aramaic by an Assyrian official, refers to events in Babylonia during the eighth century. ([93])

([83]) This excludes documents written in the period itself which refer to earlier kings: monarchs recounting their pedigree, histories of lawsuits which include records of earlier cases, royal votive-historical texts which give the historical background preceding the present king's benefactions, and contemporary colophons. There are at least two pertinent references in Assyrian historical texts written in this period to earlier Babylonian kings: Ashur–bel–kala to Marduk–nadin–ahhe (*AKA* 129 i 17; see note 729 below) and Ashurnasirpal to Sibir (*AKA* 325:84).

([84]) Bibliography below in Appendix A under 31.3.1-31.3.4.

([85]) *YOS* I 45 i 29; *VAB* IV 274 iii 17.

([86]) *UET* IV 143; *OECT* I pls. 20-21.

([87]) *UVB* XVIII 44-52.

([88]) *OIP* II 83:48-50; *YOS* I 40:13.

([89]) *RMA* 200 rev. 4-5.

([90]) *ABL* 1391 rev. 7 (=*CT* XXXIV 10-11).

([91]) *ABL* 1237 rev. 24.

([92]) Bibliography in Appendix A under 8.3.3 and 24.3.3.

([93]) H. Donner – W. Röllig, *Kanaanäische und aramäische Inschriften*, no. 233.

TERTIARY DOCUMENTATION: REMOTE TRADITION CONCERNING HISTORICAL EVENTS

This category embraces documents outside the main stream of cuneiform historical tradition which are neither contemporary witnesses of the events they depict nor derived directly from the testimony of contemporary witnesses. Composed in a variety of ways, these texts rely principally on earlier compilers of historical data and have no access to more direct sources. For matters relating to kings of Babylonia in the Post–Kassite period, there are four principal tertiary sources known thus far.

The Old Testament. The Bible mentions no native Babylonian king of the period under consideration but only the two Assyrian rulers who were also monarchs of Babylonia shortly before 722 B.C. We are interested in biblical references to them only in so far as they touch upon the years during which these kings were holding the dual monarchy.

For this reason, all biblical passages referring to Tiglath - Pileser or Pul may be ruled out. These sections in II Kings and in I Chronicles describe Tiglath–Pileser's activities in Syria and Palestine before he assumed the crown in Babylonia.

Shalmaneser V, however, ruled both Assyria and Babylonia throughout the whole of his five-year reign; so all biblical references to him necessarily fall during his reign in Babylonia, even though he is invariably referred to merely as king of Assyria. We shall use in our study those passages in II Kings which deal with the siege of Samaria and the subsequent deportation of the people of Israel to Mesopotamia. ([94])

Berossos. The fragments of Berossos preserve for us a third-century (B.C.) tradition concerning two kings who date from the late Post–Kassite period. Berossos explains that any detailed history of Babylonia written in his day was forced to commence with the reign of Nabonassar because that king had destroyed the records of his royal predecessors. Berossos also describes Phul(os), king of the Chaldeans, as the brother of Sennacherib and as a monarch who undertook an expedition against Judea. His convoluted chronological scheme of the dynasties from the time of the flood to the accession of Phul(os) defies unravelling even in the manuscript tradition. ([95])

([94]) II Kings 17:3-6, 18:9-12.
([95]) Bibliography below in Appendix A under 33.3.1 and 37.3.2.

Josephus. In his *Antiquities of the Jews*, written in the late first century A.D., Flavius Josephus treats of the military activities of Shalmaneser V in Syria-Palestine, especially the sieges of Samaria and Tyre. His account borrows heavily from the Old Testament as well as from Menander of Ephesus. (96)

Claudius Ptolemaeus. Any scheme of chronology for post-Nabonassar Babylonia must reckon with the κανὼν τῶν βασιλέων usually attributed to Ptolemy (floruit 127-141 A.D.). (97) This work lists in chronological order kings and their regnal years from Nabonassar down to Antoninus (138-161 A.D.). The first five lines of the text deal with the rulers at the end of the period under consideration here.

As O. Neugebauer has pointed out, it is technically a misnomer to call this list the "Ptolemaic Canon" because, although there was undoubtedly a βασιλέων χρονογραφία originally included in Ptolemy's "Handy Tables," there is no extant version of a royal canon of this sort earlier than the tables of Emperor Heraclius (610-641 A.D.). (98) One may hope that later versions are substantially identical with the now lost canon of Ptolemy, but there is no real certainty that the list had not undergone some alteration over the years. Despite its ineptness, we retain the traditional designation "Ptolemaic Canon," with the title in quotation marks, since an acceptable substitute has yet to be suggested.

We exclude from consideration here later tables such as those of Elias of Nisibis in Syriac or of al–Biruni in Arabic. These chronologies are generally late reflections of the tradition of the "Ptolemaic Canon"; and in them the Babylonian names have often become so garbled as to be of little service to us.

The Non-Written Sources

The time is not yet ripe for utilizing uninscribed archeological materials in a history of this type. Close dating of individual objects and building levels is required before these finds can be incorporated meaningfully into a detailed chronological sketch of Babylonian political history. We are frequently handicapped by the lack of distinctive archeological remains from the Post–Kassite period, i.e., remains that can readily be distinguished from those of the preceding Kassite or the following Neo-Babylonian periods. For instance, R. M. Adams in his surface survey of mounds in the Diyala region was hampered in his attempt to describe the occupation of the

(96) Bibliography below in Appendix A under 38.3.4.
(97) Bibliography below in Appendix A, Section I, E.
(98) O. Neugebauer, "'Years' in Royal Canons" in *A Locust's Leg*, pp. 209-210.

area in Post–Kassite ("Middle Babylonian") (99) times because of the dearth of ceramic features typical of that period. (100) But he gradually succeeded in isolating a few characteristic ceramic features, most of them occupying an intermediate typological position between Kassite and Neo-Babylonian forms. (101) Still these preliminary attempts have aimed only at obtaining broad, approximate dates for uninscribed materials.

Stratification at sites like Babylon, Kish, Nippur, and Ur indicates that these cities were occupied between the Kassite heyday in the fourteenth and thirteenth centuries and the rise of the Chaldean Dynasty under Nabopolassar about 625. (102) But nowhere are we able to reconstruct the detailed scheme of development neces-

(99) Scholars writing on Mesopotamian archeology sometimes use the terms "Middle Babylonian" or "Assyrian" to designate part or all of the period between the Kassite and Chaldean dynasties in Babylonia. These two terms can be somewhat misleading for philologists because: (a) they designate a time beginning just after what many Assyriologists consider the end of the Middle Babylonian period (i.e., the end of the Kassite Dynasty); (b) there is no evidence for actual Assyrian control over Babylonia until nearly the end of the ninth century B.C.

(100) *Land behind Baghdad*, pp. 55-57.

(101) *Ibid.*, pp. 56 and 129, no. 8.

(102) Babylon: O. Reuther, *WVDOG* XLVII 21-25, 60-64, pls. 3-5 and 15; many Kassite houses continued to be used, but they were gradually replaced—if at all—by poorer buildings. Merkes, the principal area of the city in which Post-Kassite remains were found, seems to have declined in popularity or at least in fashionability as a residential site. The houses built after the Kassite period had no strong foundations and were often composed of simple earthen walls, which eroded quickly after abandonment; many Kassite house sites were apparently used as gardens during this time. Reuther (*ibid.*, pp. 22-23) noted several characteristic pottery styles and some distinctive small four-legged clay chests (*ibid.*, fig. 20) and remarked on possible Assyrian influences shown in pottery types, enamel work, and burial customs. The introduction of the fibula is perhaps to be dated to the eighth century (*ibid.*, p. 24). The poverty of the inhabitations of this quarter, not likely to survive if long exposed on the surface, and the subsequent destruction of the city by Sennacherib have undoubtedly contributed to the paucity of our knowledge concerning the site at this time. E. Strommenger has discussed the types of graves found at Babylon dating from the tenth through eighth centuries in *Bagh. Mitt.* III (1964) 166-67.

Kish: Langdon, *Excavations at Kish*, I, 16-17 and 65 (dated principally by inscriptions of Adad–apla–iddina).

Nippur: D. McCown and R. C. Haines, *OIP* LXXVIII 13-14, 17-18, 69, 76, 82, 91-92, and *passim*. In area TA of the Scribal Quarter, after the last Kassite level (VI), there is evidence for a lapse of time before the building of the houses in the next level (V). It should be noted that the two earliest levels classified as "Assyrian" (V-IV) yielded no dated tablets and contained elements reminiscent of the Post–Kassite period at Babylon (e.g., the horse-and-rider figurine in IV); since principally Kassite seal types also occurred in these levels (*ibid.*, p. 82), it is worth wondering whether the date of these levels might not extend earlier than the Assyrian domination of Babylonia under Tiglath–Pileser III. The earliest dated tablet in the subsequent level (III) comes from the first year of Sargon as king of Babylon (=709 B.C.), and it would be surprising if levels V-IV were to represent only the preceding twenty years.

Ur: L. Woolley, *UE* VIII 36, possibly 46-47, 69, etc.; *UE* V 93-95.

At Uruk, there are no traces that can definitely be dated between the time of the Kassite Dynasty and that of Merodach–Baladan II (see the convenient summary of evidence presented by R. North in *Orientalia N.S.* XXVI [1957], especially pp. 250-251). Inscriptions are known which were originally written at Uruk during this time, e.g., *BIN* II 31 and duplicates; but none have turned up in controlled excavations.

At other sites in Mesopotamia, e.g., Sippar, inscriptions have generally furnished the chief clues for dating remains of this period.

sary to pinpoint any particular stratum of remains and assign it to a specific place within the pertinent chronological framework *unless* the vital clue about that complex of remains is furnished by writing. In the present state of our knowledge, only where identification by inscriptions is possible can individual archeological data be assigned to a particular time or monarch. Consequently, we shall not discuss archeological remains separately as such but shall confine ourselves to treating pertinent buildings and smaller objects in conjunction with the inscriptions by which each is dated.

EVALUATION OF THE SOURCES

The sources enumerated above contain much information that cannot be used in a primarily political history. It will be our purpose in this final section of the chapter to outline briefly which information in these sources is pertinent and to propose a few general criteria for the critical evaluation of this material. To that end, we shall review the main source categories listed above, though not in such detail as before, and comment on their informational and critical value.

We begin with the primary documentation from Babylonia. Here contemporary texts mentioning a ruler's name serve to confirm the fact of that individual's reign; and, wherever precise year dates are given, they aid in determining the minimal length of the sovereign's rule. (103) Royal inscriptions reveal what the kings considered significant titulary, in some cases more an indication of ambition than accomplished fact. Royal activities on the battlefield, royal votive and building enterprises, royal land grants and tax exemptions appear in the royal inscriptions and in some of the kudurrus; (104) and one can gain at least a skeletal knowledge of Babylonian officialdom from the names and titles of officials occurring in kudurrus and other private documents. The geographical area over which the king held sway can be gauged from names of places mentioned in contemporary documents (105) as well as from sites where texts were found. (106) A fair-sized corpus of personal names (107) appears in the kudurrus and in other private texts, indicating to some

(103) They serve as a check to information given in the kinglists and, where such information is not available, provide one of the principal means for estimating the duration of a reign.

(104) We take kudurru here in its widest conventional sense, as determined by Steinmetzer, *Die babylonischen Kudurru* (*Grenzsteine*) *als Urkundenform*, pp. 95-100.

(105) At least from the names of those places where the king's dating system or the king's local administration is accepted.

(106) It is obvious, however, that inscribed bronze objects found in Luristan, booty from northern Babylonia found in Elam, and the Babylonian duck weights found at Nimrud are hardly to be construed as indications of Babylonian royal power extending to those sites.

(107) About 500 completely or partially preserved names have survived from this period.

extent the ethnic makeup of the land. (108) The language of the inscriptions helps to determine the current dialect spoken by the people. (109)

The primary documents from Babylonia require little or no historical criticism in themselves. They may, by and large, be accepted at face value. Disregarding occasional poetic flights in kudurrus or royal texts, we find that the contents are otherwise principally utilitarian and that no purpose would be served by prevarication. (110) For these reasons and, in other cases, because of the meagerness of the material available, we have adopted the following general rule regarding primary and secondary documentation from Babylonia: where no sound evidence exists to the contrary, an isolated document, according to its capacity, (111) is to be accepted as historically accurate until proven otherwise. Without this principle, there would be no hope of writing political history for ancient Babylonia.

With the Assyrian primary documentation, we are standing on entirely different ground. The Assyrian royal inscriptions and chronicles like the Synchronistic History have been subjected to repeated critical scrutiny, and rules have been determined for their interpretation. (112) In military matters involving other countries—in this case, military contacts between Assyria and Babylonia—the historian must be wary of accepting Assyrian accounts at face value. Assyrian official documents were notorious for turning any encounter with an enemy into a victory; and the magnitude of the triumph increased as the event receded in time from the redaction on hand. As a consequence, one may often question Assyrian claims of kudos both in fact and in magnitude. However, one may and generally should accept the fact that an encounter took place where and when and with whom it is reported, even though the outcome of the skirmish must be left in doubt in many cases. Only a close scrutiny of prior and subsequent events can place an Assyrian claim of "victory" in sufficient context to determine its veracity. (113)

On the other hand, Assyrian letters, even when written to the king, are usually of a non-public nature and are designed to apprise the recipient of the true state of affairs. (114) For example, the Nimrud correspondence, the only epistolary ar-

(108) On the general method for evaluating such evidence, see I. J. Gelb, "Ethnic Reconstruction and Onomastic Evidence," *Names* X (1962) 45-52. The foreign population groups in Babylonia will be discussed below in the fourth chapter.

(109) I.e., the gradual shift from the Middle-Babylonian to the Neo-Babylonian dialect.

(110) Babylonian contemporary documents tend to be quite vague and dispassionate on military matters in contrast to the Assyrian royal inscriptions, which are quite detailed and sometimes obviously propagandistic.

(111) E.g., one must not attempt to interpret poetic passages by the same rigid canons used for historical prose.

(112) Especially in A. T. Olmstead's *Assyrian Historiography*.

(113) E.g., if the Assyrian king fights his next battle in an area closer to home, then it is likely that the victory existed only in the official documents.

(114) Save in those instances where the writer is obviously pleading his own case or that of another interested party.

chive known thus far from the period under consideration, portrays Assyrian attempts at diplomacy during the Mukin–zeri troubles in southern Babylonia and not always in a light favorable to the Assyrians. Assyrian emissaries are described in their unsuccessful efforts to negotiate a surrender of Babylon—an incident hardly likely to find its way into the official records of the Assyrian march of conquest. These letters undoubtedly present a faithful picture of contemporary affairs.

The chief contribution of the Elamite royal sources to the present study is the list of places in normally Babylonian territory which Shilhak–Inshushinak claims to have bested in the early years of the Second Isin Dynasty. Knowing the power of the Elamites in that era not only from Babylonian tradition but also from the important Babylonian monuments which they stole and transported to their capital at Susa, we may be reasonably sure that Shilhak–Inshushinak is simply stating the facts. We cannot tell whether the Elamites occupied any of these regions for long; but, in line with general Elamite policy, it seems unlikely.

Secondary documentation, of course, provides a much more fertile field for historical criticism. Here, because of the very different types of individual sources within numerically small categories, we must often take each document and evaluate it separately. The disproportionate amount of space spent on the criticism of these texts will, we feel, be justified because of the overwhelming importance of secondary documentation in presenting a history of this type. Without secondary materials, we would often be left only with isolated and unrelated facts presented by individual primary sources, which would in themselves offer little hope of erecting an all-important chronological framework. A prime example of the chaos that can arise in historical reconstruction when it is attempted independently of reliable secondary materials may be seen in the generally accepted reconstructions of the sequence of the first kings of the Second Isin Dynasty prior to the publication of Kinglist C in 1955; the edifice painstakingly erected from tiny clues crumbled almost completely when confronted with the clear-cut evidence of the small kinglist. Any attempt to present a unified history of this period necessarily relies on secondary materials for chronological and other perspectives.

We begin our consideration of the secondary documentation with the kinglists. Kinglist C, though only a schoolboy's exercise tablet (with one obvious uncorrected scribal error), (115) is undoubtedly the best secondary document available for the period which it treats, being almost a contemporary source. (116) Kinglist A, on the other hand, though more removed in time from the kings with which it deals, is the only Babylonian document thus far unearthed that originally listed all the Baby-

(115) See note 187 below.
(116) See note 61 above.

lonian monarchs of this time and the length of their reigns. Since part of the tablet is missing and since its surface has substantially deteriorated through repeated refiring, one must be wary of making categorical statements about its untrustworthiness: errors attributed to the source may sometimes prove to be due to its present physical condition. (117) Furthermore, in estimating the accuracy of the document, one must distinguish between statements regarding regnal years, royal names, and royal ancestry. The numbers given for regnal years, as far as can be judged at present, seem to be reliable, with only one proven exception. (118) The names of the kings are often given in abbreviated form, but are otherwise accurate. Remarks about the ancestry of the kings are less reliable: some of the statements are true, (119) others obviously false. (120)

The synchronistic kinglists may be taken as a group for critical purposes. These lists are written in double columns. Each double column is subdivided by a line down the center, to the left of which are the names of Babylonian kings inscribed in chronological order and to the right the contemporary Assyrian monarchs. (121) (The synchronistic kinglists do not record the number of years reigned by individual kings, but occasionally list *ummânu* officials, "royal secretaries," who are mentioned after their royal masters, Assyrian and Babylonian.) (122) Horizontal division lines are also regularly employed in each double column, according to the following rules.

(117) This is true of the numbers in lines 17′ and 18′ of column two, where the digit rows are blurred. Though the most likely apparent readings are those given on Gadd's copy in *CT* XXXVI 24 (*17* and *6*), one could conceivably defend readings based on the parallel section of Kinglist C (*18* and *8*). These alternatives have also been discussed by Poebel, *AS* XV 24-25.

(118) The number *6* given for the reign of Kudur-Enlil (ii 5′) is almost certainly wrong. Two published economic texts, *BE* XIV 123 and 124, are both dated in the eighth year of Kudur-Enlil. W. von Soden *apud* K. Jaritz, *MIO* VI (1958) 200, mentions a tablet in the Hilprecht Sammlung, Jena, dated in the king's ninth year. M. B. Rowton, on the basis of the unpublished text Ni. 7004, has conjectured that the ninth year of Kudur-Enlil was the same as the accession year of Shagarakti-Shuriash and, therefore, Kudur-Enlil's last year (*JCS* XIII [1959] 5 n. 25; *JNES* XXV [1966] 255).

There is also some apparent disagreement about the total number of years which Shagarakti-Shuriash reigned. Kinglist A reads 13 (ii 6′); but von Soden *apud* Jaritz, *MIO* VI (1958) 200, mentions unpublished texts dated in the eighteenth and perhaps even twenty-first years of the king. However, the unpublished text Ni. 7113, cited by Rowton in *JCS* XIII (1959) 5 n. 25 and *JNES* XXV (1966) 255, apparently equivalates the thirteenth year of Shagarakti-Shuriash with the accession year of his successor, thereby substantiating the figure as transmitted by Kinglist A. It is, therefore, too early to pronounce on the validity of the Kinglist A tradition in this instance; but the balance of evidence seems to favor its reliability at present.

(119) E.g., that Merodach-Baladan I was the son of Meli-Shipak (ii 13′) or that Nabu-nadin-zeri was the son of Nabonassar (iv 4).

(120) E.g., Mukin-zeri's being described as the son of Nabu-nadin-zeri (iv 5) and the two different designations for Merodach-Baladan II (iv 10, 14, see *Studies Oppenheim*, pp. 35-37).

(121) With the sole exception of Assur 14616c (see note 65 above).

(122) E.g., Assur 14616c iv 13. The exact function of the *ummânu* is unknown, but he may have served as a chief official scribe.

If an Assyrian and a Babylonian king are considered to be relatively coextensive in time, then a line is drawn before and after the pair: (123)

m*Aššur–rēša–iši* MIN	md*Mār–bīti–[apla–uṣur* MIN]

However, if a king had two or more contemporaries in the other land, then the king with the longer reign has his name repeated on subsequent lines (124) paralleling his second and later contemporaries; and a horizontal divider line is drawn only after all the contemporaries of one king have been noted: (125)

[md*Marduk–nādin–aḫ]ḫē*	m*Tukulti–apil–E[šarra]*
[m]	md*Ninurta–apil–E[kur]*

The method of expressing overlapping reigns is imperfectly developed, as may be seen from the following example:

[md*Nabû]–kudurrī–uṣur*	md*Ninurta–tukul[ti–Aššur]*
[m]	m*Mutakkil–[*d*Nusku]*
[m]	m*Aššur–rēša–[iši]*
[md*Enlil–nādin]–apli*	m
[md*Marduk–nādin–aḫ]ḫē*	m*Tukulti–apil–E[šarra]* (126)

Here the blank space opposite Enlil–nadin–apli is probably to be interpreted as an extension of the reign of Ashur–resha–ishi I.

(123) Assur 14616c iii 8. MIN here refers to the respective titles "king of Assyria/Babylonia," to be considered as repeated from the first line of the column.

(124) Usually by means of a simple masculine determinative or a ditto sign. The name is seldom written out in full a second time.

(125) *KAV* 12:5-6. The final dividing line is not preserved in the text.

(126) *KAV* 12:1-5. Weidner's interpretation of this list in terms of the relative accession dates for the Assyrian and Babylonian kings (*MVAG* XXVI/2 [1921] 10) was superseded by his later article in *AfO* IV (1927) 213-217, where it was shown that Ashur–resha–ishi I and Ninurta–nadin–shumi were contemporaries.

Royal reigns patently do not coincide with such great regularity, and it is obvious that the highly stylized synchronistic kinglists are not to be interpreted literally. This conclusion is reinforced by other considerations. First, the fiction that the first three dynasties of Babylon were consecutive is preserved in the list Assur 14616c, save for the unique "contemporaneity" of Ea-gamil and Gandush (expressed by writing their names on a single line) with Erishum III of Assyria; this, of course, necessitates some hasty interpolation, accomplished by placing eight Kassite kings opposite Shamshi-Adad II, who ruled for only six years! In addition, a literal interpretation of some data in the synchronistic kinglists is incompatible with the acceptance of otherwise well-attested synchronisms such as that between Ashur-resha-ishi I and Ninurta-nadin-shumi (127) or that between Tiglath-Pileser I and Marduk-shapik-zeri. (128) Thus, though only a few of the synchronisms listed in these kinglists can be directly demonstrated to be wrong, (129) it is clear that these synchronistic kinglists cannot be used as proof for any synchronism without supporting evidence. (130)

The synchronistic kinglists, however, have some use as chronological sources. They preserve the names and the order of kings of Babylonia in otherwise poorly attested eras; and this information, where it can be compared with other sources, has proven uniformly accurate. (131) The names of Babylonian and Assyrian *ummânu* officials, which are also occasionally given, appear to be reliably transmitted. (132)

(127) Provided by the text VAT 10281, published by Weidner in *AfO* IV (1927) 213-217. Compare the synchronistic kinglist *KAV* 12:1-3, in which Ashur-resha-ishi and his two immediate predecessors are listed as contemporaries of Nebuchadnezzar I, the successor of Ninurta-nadin-shumi.

(128) As known from the text VAT 10453+10465, published by Weidner in *AfO* XVII (1954-56) 384. Compare the synchronistic kinglist *KAV* 12:5-6, in which Tiglath-Pileser I's reign ends before the accession of Marduk-shapik-zeri.

(129) Such as the Mutakkil-Nusku—Nebuchadnezzar I synchronism (*KAV* 12:2) or the Ninurta-apil-Ekur—Marduk-nadin-ahhe synchronism (*KAV* 12:6). D. Schötz in *JSOR* IX (1925) 103-104 and Poebel in *JNES* II (1943) 60-61 commented on other untrustworthy synchronisms, but chiefly in the faultily edited column ii of Assur 14616c. Apparent contradictions between the various synchronistic kinglists were discussed already by Weidner in *MDOG* LVIII (1917) 5-6.

(130) Thus, the synchronism between Kashshu-nadin-ahhe (sic) and Ashurnasirpal I proposed by A. Moortgat in *Ägypten und Vorderasien im Altertum*, p. 500, must be rejected, as must the evidence for eleventh- and tenth-century synchronisms proposed by D. J. Wiseman, *CAH* II² xxxi 27, 33, etc.

(131) It should be noted, however, that one of the principal synchronistic kinglists, Assur 14616c, has proven unusable for another reason. Copies of that text by O. Schroeder (*KAV* 216) and by Weidner (*MVAG* XXVI/2 [1921] pls. 1-4 and *AfO* III [1926] 70-71) were made from photographs; and the names of kings, especially in columns i-ii, were heavily restored. Since no emended version of the text is available (both because the tablet itself has deteriorated in the meantime and because the photographs of it taken in 1925 have become yellow with age: *AfO* XVII [1954-56] 383-384 n. 1, XIX [1959-60] 138), the obverse of the text is better disregarded or—at best—accepted with extreme caution. Poebel in *AS* XV 14 has attempted to show how the badly damaged column ii should probably be restored. The reverse of the same text (columns iii-iv), with which we shall also be concerned, was apparently in much better condition when copied and compares favorably with other sources concerning the same period.

(132) E.g., in the case of ᵐMU-PAB, the *ummânu* of Marduk-zakir-shumi I, known both from the synchronistic kinglist *KAV* 10 ii 10′ and from the contemporary kudurru *RA* XVI (1919) 126 iv 23.

The Assyrian simple kinglists, eponym lists, and eponym chronicles provide the only firm foundation for the absolute chronology of ancient Western Asia in the early first millennium. Though Professor Landsberger has criticized the earlier portions of the Assyrian kinglists for apparent omissions, ([133]) there is no sound basis for derogatory judgments about later sections of the lists. The only real conflict in the sources which in any way affects the chronology of the period is the minor discrepancy regarding the length of the reign of Tiglath–Pileser II, recorded as 33 years in the nearly contemporary Nassouhi list, ([134]) but as 32 years in the later Khorsabad list. ([135]) Since the testimony of the Nassouhi list is also supported by the total given in a list of contemporary eponym officials, ([136]) that tradition is here accepted as correct. ([137]) In general, the Assyrian kinglists and eponym texts will be employed in this study chiefly to check possible synchronisms between Babylonia and Assyria, to note incidental references to contemporary Babylonia such as the deportation of Ninurta–tukulti–Ashur thither by Mutakkil–Nusku, and for information concerning the southern campaigns of Assyrian rulers in the ninth and eighth centuries.

The Babylonian chronicles pose peculiar problems of their own because of their variegated scope, contents, and style. The time range of the information given by each has been discussed earlier in this chapter, ([138]) so we confine ourselves here to a few general criticisms of each document.

Chronicle P is concerned chiefly with Babylonian–Assyrian and Babylonian-Elamite military relations. The style of the document varies from poetic sections dealing with Elam ([139]) to dry narrative in portions dealing with Assyria. The text definitely conflicts with other sources, e.g., with the Synchronistic History concerning the Karaindash–Karahardash episode. Only one passage in Chronicle P, however, is potentially involved with the period with which we are directly concerned, and that is the mention of the restoration of the Marduk statue to Babylon in the time of Tukulti–Ashur. This statement does not conflict directly with any other

([133]) "Assyrische Königsliste und 'Dunkles Zeitalter,'" *JCS* VIII (1954) 31 ff., etc. The most significant omission is probably due to differing dynastic traditions rather than to defective transmission of sources.

([134]) *AfO* IV (1927) 5 rev. ii 28; the figure is preserved in the text as [*30*+]⌜*3*⌝.

([135]) *JNES* XIII (1954) 220 iv 13.

([136]) VAT 11256 ii 9′ (=*KAV* 22 v).

([137]) Though we cannot be completely certain that there was no difference between the total number of regnal years for Tiglath–Pileser II and the number of years in his eponym period, it is unlikely in any case that his reign would have been copied as a higher number in later kinglists. See further Rowton's remarks in *Iraq* VIII (1946) 101-104.

([138]) Page 17.

([139]) Elam throughout the many years of its contacts with Babylonia was frequently the subject of poetic narrative and lamentation, from such famous pieces as the Lamentation over the Destruction of Ur down through the Kedor–laomer and Nebuchadnezzar I texts.

source, though it raises chronological problems that will be discussed below in the third chapter. ([140])

The New Babylonian Chronicle, as presently preserved, seems interested primarily in recording the incursions of Aramean nomads into Babylonia, peaceful relations between Babylonia and Assyria, and sundry cultic repairs and restorations made by Babylonian monarchs. The abbreviated style of the document sometimes leads to ambiguity (e.g., the statement *ina* BÁR MU 5 *É–ul–maš*–GAR–MU LUGAL, ([141]) which could be translated either "in Nisan of the fifth year of King Eulmash–shakin–shumi" or "on the dais (in) the fifth year of King Eulmash–shakin–shumi") or obscurity (e.g., an entry mentioning simply "year 14," ([142]) with neither king nor event directly specified). The significance of such allusions is yet to be determined. ([143]) The contents of this text fit in well with information from primary sources, where these touch on the same events; ([144]) and it seems to be a generally reliable source.

The Religious Chronicle is a text primarily occupied with recording portents, e.g., the straying of wild animals into public places or unusual natural phenomena such as exceptionally high floods. Because the document is largely concerned with individual oddities, most of its contents have no place in a political history save in so far as the close observation and recording may reflect disturbed political conditions and a desire to see what omens accompanied them. The various portents are not always set down in strict chronological order, thereby rendering the task of interpretation more difficult. Our principal use of the document will be to note the nature of the historical events, e.g., Aramean invasions, which were attended by the omens recorded.

Two small sections of the Dynastic Chronicle that deal with the period under consideration have survived. The first section treats of the three small dynasties which followed the Second Isin Dynasty. It notes the origin of the individual monarchs, the length of their reigns, and their place of burial. The order of the kings is the same as that given by other sources, though the information regarding royal origins and interments cannot be checked with any other source as yet. The numbers given for the regnal years of some of the kings are suspect: they disagree with the figures in Kinglist A and, moreover, are incorrectly totaled for two of the dynasties. ([145]) The second section deals with kings of the early eighth century. Here only the beginnings of about ten lines are preserved, but enough survives that one may

([140]) Note 465; see also p. 361, supplement (a).
([141]) *CCEBK* II 149:14.
([142]) *Ibid.*, 15.
([143]) But see note 978 below.
([144]) E.g., famine in the reign of Marduk–shapik–zeri and the cultic restorations of Simbar–Shipak.
([145]) E.g., 17 years + 3 months + 3 years = 23 years; 15 years + 2 years + 3 months = 20 years, 3 months.

see that the text divided these kings into dynasties different from the grouping in Kinglist A. [146] Because of internal inconsistencies, this text seems less reliable than Kinglist A, at least on the subject of regnal years.

The Babylonian Chronicle, commencing its account about the year 747 B.C., relates the major military and political events in the lands of Babylonia, Assyria, and Elam, providing exact dates for the royal reigns in each of these lands. The dating is done in terms of the current regnal year of the Babylonian monarch; and major international wars and internal uprisings are duly noted. The tone of the document is impartial, retailing the vicissitudes of all three lands, including Babylonia. This source, in the light of present evidence, seems to be eminently reliable. [147]

The Shamash–shuma–ukin Chronicle, published by Millard in *Iraq* XXVI (1964) 14-35, has two sections dealing with kings of this period. With the exception of one obvious scribal error (writing the name of the brother of Shirikti–Shuqamuna *Nabû–kudurrī–uṣur* rather than *Ninurta–kudurrī–uṣur*), the text seems otherwise reliable. The fragmentary chronicle BM 48498, to be published by Grayson in his edition of the Assyrian and Babylonian chronicles, is too poorly preserved to be properly evaluated. [148]

Assyrian chronicles must also be judged individually. The Synchronistic History, the longest and best preserved of the Assyrian chronicles, is obviously partial in its battle accounts: only Assyrian victories are recounted, and Babylonian victories are either attributed to the Assyrians or omitted entirely from the narrative. [149] Furthermore, the principal version of the Synchronistic History that has come down to us is a carelessly written text. [150] The Tiglath–Pileser I Chronicle is not sufficiently preserved to be the subject of much analysis; but, if the present interpretation of it is correct, it gives a reasonably accurate contemporary description of the Assyrian decline. [151] It is not blind to the losses of the Assyrians and narrates the

(146) The Dynastic Chronicle divides Marduk–apla–usur and his two successors into three separate dynasties; Kinglist A viewed at least the last two rulers as part of a larger single dynasty.

(147) See also A. K. Grayson in *AS* XVI 342 and in his forthcoming edition of the Assyrian and Babylonian Chronicles.

(148) But see note 485 below for difficulties arising in the interpretation of the text.

(149) See Poebel, *JNES* II (1943) 58 and Grayson, *AS* XVI 337-342. Weidner in *AfO* XVII (1954-56) 385 comments on a type of source from which the Synchronistic History may derive its information.

(150) It exhibits scribal errors in names like Tukulti–apil–*Ekur* for Tukulti–apil–*Esharra* (ii 14′), Marduk–shapik–zer–mati for Marduk–shapik–zeri (ii 26′), incorporates a royal historical source without changing the verb from the first to the third person (iv 12), and lists incidents outside proper chronological order (i 5′-7′).

(151) The interpretation followed here is substantially that proposed by H. Tadmor in *JNES* XVII (1958) 133-134. That the text is a contemporary or nearly contemporary witness of the events it describes seems likely from the fact that it was found in the northwest court of the Ashur temple at Assur (and apparently connected with the state archives of Tiglath–Pileser I) and from its late MA script (Weidner, *AfO* XVII [1954-56] 384).

successes of the Arameans and the flight of Tiglath–Pileser I with candor. (152) The Ashur–resha–ishi I Chronicle is so poorly preserved that one can hardly pass judgment on its reliability; but, remembering the propagandistic nature of other Assyrian documents, (153) we shall be duly cautious in assessing its account of the excursion of Ashur–resha–ishi to Arbail.

In the case of poetic sources, where literary creativity and theological interpretation play an important role, one should not expect literal accuracy and exact historical detail. The Kedor–laomer texts, for instance, contain practically no historically usable data beyond the name of the central figure, Kudur–Nahhunte, and his devastation of Babylonia and its shrines. The Nebuchadnezzar I texts and the Era Epic exhibit the same general features—a central core of fact (i.e., Nebuchadnezzar's vanquishing of Elam and returning Marduk to Babylon; the long-term Sutian incursions into Babylonia) imbedded in poetic narrative. It is questionable procedure to accept literally statements in these texts concerning contemporary political conditions; and attempts to identify incidental characters such as the slaughterous king in the fourth tablet of the Era Epic are of dubious value. Although it is conceivable that the historical layer in these texts may penetrate further than we presently suspect, one must keep in mind that the vehicle is primarily literary. Attempts to see historical significance in minor details represent speculation rather than legitimate historical inference. Such speculation, if properly controlled, is not out of place in a study of this type, but it should and will be explicitly labelled as such.

Incidental references in later cuneiform documents must be judged individually. Nabonidus' references to the finding of the earlier stele of Nebuchadnezzar I at Ur are quite credible; and one might infer that Nebuchadnezzar had established his own daughter as *entu*–priestess there. Nabonidus' allusion to the time of Eriba–Marduk as the date for cultic changes at Uruk may be believed, since it is also known from an inscription of Esarhaddon that Eriba–Marduk built in that city. Merodach–Baladan II's tracing his descent from Eriba–Marduk is plausible, since both kings are known to have been powerful tribal chieftains in the southern part of Babylonia. Finally, the inventory text from Ur which mentions several kings of the period as donors of gold votive objects is a strictly utilitarian document and obviously admissible as evidence.

With regard to incidental references in later Assyrian documents, one need not be as cautious as with Assyrian royal inscriptions and chronicles. Assyrian monarchs were not reluctant to describe their country's past losses or their pre-

(152) *AfO* XVII (1954-56) 384:3′-7′, 11′-13′.

(153) We should note, however, that these "improved" accounts were probably for divine rather than human consumption.

decessors' deficiencies. Sennacherib did not hesitate to mention Marduk-nadin-ahhe's plundering of the gods from Ekallate, a tale hardly complimentary to earlier Assyria; and even the dating of this event to a time 418 years before may prove to be substantially accurate. ([154]) Esarhaddon's reference to Eriba-Marduk's building at Uruk is credible, as are the allusions to an omen series concerning Nebuchadnezzar I and to a tablet copied in the time of Adad-apla-iddina; these are too trivial to merit forgery.

Tertiary documentation provides a number of interesting passages concerning the last kings of the period, from Nabonassar through Shalmaneser V. These texts, however, because they are isolated from the direct historical tradition, are in general less acceptable as evidence. We shall refer to them whenever they bear on matters under discussion in subsequent chapters; but their reliability as historical evidence is generally weak.

The biblical texts concerning Shalmaneser V apparently rely on earlier Hebrew chronicles for their information. The compiler of II Kings, however, did not prune his material and presents us with two almost identical accounts of the siege of Samaria in successive chapters. But we gain approximate synchronisms of the chronology of Israel with that of Assyria and Babylonia and learn of the deportation of some Israelites to Mesopotamia. These matters will be discussed further at the end of the third chapter. ([155])

In using Berossos, we are ever aware of the tortuous textual tradition of the surviving fragments of this author. As A. T. Olmstead once wrote:

> Today we must consult a modern Latin translation of an Armenian translation of the lost Greek original of the Chronicle of Eusebius, who borrowed in part from Alexander Polyhistor who borrowed from Berossus direct, in part from Abydenus who apparently borrowed from Juba who borrowed from Alexander Polyhistor and so from Berossus. To make a worse confusion, Eusebius has in some cases not recognized the fact that Abydenus is only a feeble echo of Polyhistor, and has quoted the accounts of each side by side! And this is not the worst. Although his Polyhistor account is in general to be preferred, Eusebius seems to have used a poor manuscript of that author. ([156])

Today we have the benefit of a German translation of the Armenian and additional late Greek citations in Jacoby's critical edition, ([157]) but otherwise the situation

([154]) See p. 84.

([155]) Since the biblical account of the siege of Samaria cannot be compared with anything in the cuneiform sources, save the brief allusion in the Babylonian Chronicle (*CT* XXXIV 47 i 28), we can hardly evaluate the accuracy of this account on the basis of external criteria.

([156]) *Assyrian Historiography*, p. 63. See also "Beros(s)os," *Pauly-Wissowa* V (1897) 314-315.

([157]) *Die Fragmente der griechischen Historiker*, III C/1 (Leiden, 1958), no. 680.

remains much the same. Most of what we cite as Berossos comes directly from the manuscripts of Georgios Synkellos and (pseudo-)Moses of Chorene, both of whom wrote in the early ninth century A.D. and had to rely on third- and fourth-hand sources. The weakness of this tradition is apparent, and we need hardly explain why Berossos is not to be considered as one of our better sources. (158) Information from him, however, will be mentioned in the appropriate places towards the end of the third chapter.

Josephus, in his better passages, echoes the earlier biblical account of the siege of Samaria. Hence his narrative on that subject is liable to the same general criticism as the passage in II Kings. In his discussion of the siege of Tyre, Josephus claims to base his history on Menander of Ephesus and that writer's translation of the official Tyrian archives into Greek. These events, as expressed in Josephus' narrative, probably suffered some distortion after centuries of transmission, as may be seen in the altered personal names and chronology as compared with the biblical account.

The final tertiary source, the "Ptolemaic Canon," is of known and praiseworthy accuracy. (159) Careful scrutiny of its dates beginning with Nabonassar shows that these compare favorably with the best cuneiform sources. For the period under consideration here, the "Ptolemaic Canon" is in almost total agreement with the Babylonian Chronicle, an eminently reliable document. The only differences are: (a) where the Babylonian Chronicle assigns three years to Mukin–zeri and two to Tiglath–Pileser III, the "Ptolemaic Canon" considers the two reigns together and assigns five years as their total; (b) the "Ptolemaic Canon" omits reigns which did not last long enough to be counted as a full (regnal) year; (160) (c) the names of individual kings are slightly changed in their Greek rendering. Though the origin of the list is uncertain, it has generally proved quite trustworthy. (161)

This concludes the consideration of the sources available for the present historical study. We have seen what types of materials can be brought to bear on the

(158) The situation is further complicated by Jacoby's distinction between Berossos of Babylon, author of the Βαβυλωνιακά, and Pseudo-Berossos of Cos, author of the Χαλδαικά.

(159) The appraisal of C. Wachsmuth in *Einleitung in Studium der alten Geschichte* (Leipzig, 1895), pp. 305-312, is still valid.

(160) Fractional reigns of this sort were reckoned as zero in computing eras, see pp. 63-67 below.

(161) Through the time of Nabonidus the "Ptolemaic Canon" shows only minor discrepancies from the regular Babylonian chronological tradition, but none affecting the overall chronological total. For instance, the reigns of Sennacherib in 704-703 and 688-681 are called "kingless" rather than attributed to Sennacherib by name. Also, in the total number of regnal years given for Esarhaddon and Kandalanu, the "Ptolemaic Canon" gives 13 and 22 (rather than 12 or 21) since the last years of these kings' reigns were not identical with the accession years of their successors; so the intervening time, one year in each case, was added to the reign of the recently deceased king. Reigns which did not last for an official regnal year continued to be omitted throughout the list.

subject, what information these sources contain, and—in a general way—how this information can be utilized to reconstruct a critical picture of the political development of Babylonia during the Post–Kassite period. Many matters omitted in this chapter will be discussed in subsequent chapters as we deal with specific questions of source conflict or with ambiguities in the texts; such problems can better be handled in the immediate context of the difficulty where more pertinent factors may be brought into play. For the present, however, we are sufficiently acquainted with the materials on hand to proceed, in the next chapter, to the erection of the basic chronological framework of the period.

Chapter II

CHRONOLOGY

The purpose of this chapter is to set forth a chronological outline for the Post-Kassite period, which can be used as a background for the historical discussion in the succeeding chapters. Two major steps will be followed in constructing this outline. The first will be to determine the relative chronology of the period, that is, the sequence of Babylonian rulers and the number of years which each reigned. The second will be to fix this sequence in terms of years of the pre-Christian era, thus facilitating comparison between the Babylonian history of this period and the history of neighboring lands. Hence the two principal divisions of the chapter will be: (1) relative chronology, (2) absolute chronology.

Relative Chronology

Kinglist A is the only native Babylonian source now available that originally contained a list of all the kings of this period. As such, it forms the backbone of our reconstruction. Where lacunae occur because of its damaged condition, these can be filled in for the most part from other kinglists and chronicles. ([162])

Kinglist A divides the Post–Kassite period as follows: ([163])

([162]) This does not imply that the testimony of Kinglist A is in every case to be preferred to that of other sources. It merely provides the skeleton which will form the outline for our discussion.

([163]) Kinglist A divides the kings into so-called "dynasties" (BALA). The criterion which the Babylonians used for setting up these groups was not blood relationship of the individual rulers but rather their reputed geographical origin. The dynasties are called BALA GN, i.e., "dynasty of such-and-such a place/people"; and this tradition of distinguishing ruling groups by ancestral city or country goes back at least as far as the Sumerian Kinglist (cf. also the Egyptian dynasties of Manetho, usually distinguished by place of origin). Even though modern usage of the term dynasty—implying blood relationship between monarchs—renders the term technically inaccurate in our context, we nonetheless retain the word because of its traditional use in the fields of Mesopotamian and Egyptian history.

The division of Babylonian kings into dynasties was commonly accepted in the sense that different sources dividing sequences of kings regularly divided them into the same groups; so some sort of common tradition is evident. This tradition, however, did not become fixed regarding some of the later periods in

(1) BALA PA.ŠE: the Second Dynasty of Isin
11 kings, 132 years [164] 6 months

(2) BALA KUR *Tam–tim*: the Second Sealand Dynasty
3 kings, 21 years 5 months

(3) BALA *Ba–*⌜*zum*(?)⌝: [165] the Bazi Dynasty
3 kings, 20 years 3 months

(4) [BALA NIM.MA.KI]: the Elamite Dynasty [166]
1 king, 6 years

(5) lacuna
at least 3 kings (number of years unknown)

(6) BALA E: the E Dynasty
at least 5 kings (number of years not given)

(7) three additional rulers with individual dynastic designations [167]
3 kings, 10 years.

From this we obtain the rough outline of the chronology of the period: at least 29 rulers over a span of more than 400 years. [168] Kinglist A preserves the names of twenty kings either wholly or in part; and, on the basis of the information in Kinglist A, the period can be broken up into sections of (a) 179 years for the first four dynasties, [169] (b) an unknown number of years for the lacuna and the E Dynasty, (c) the final ten years of the period.

Babylonia, e.g., the early eighth century, where the end of the E Dynasty in the Kinglist A tradition was split into several dynasties in the tradition of the Dynastic Chronicle (=*ADD* 888). See also note 167 below.

For the original meaning of Sumerian b a l a, see W. W. Hallo, *JCS* XIV (1960) 89, with citation of earlier literature. Other recent comment on the meaning of "dynasty" in Mesopotamian tradition may be found by F. R. Kraus in *ZA* L (1952) 30 n. 2 and by J. J. Finkelstein in *JCS* XX (1966) 105-106.

(164) The number of years here could also be read as 133, though this is a somewhat less likely reading (based on personal collation of the text in spring 1965). This possibility was also noted by Lehmann, *Zwei Hauptprobleme*, p. 15 and pl. 2.

(165) The reading ⌜*zum*⌝ is unsure, since there is little of the sign left and the traces are uncertain (save for a clear long horizontal stroke on top). Readings *zi* or *su* are impossible from the traces.

(166) The name of this dynasty is restored from the Dynastic Chronicle v 13′, 15′.

(167) It is doubtful that the final group of rulers listed in Kinglist A (iv 7-23) was considered as a single dynasty, since many of the names in that section are followed by individual dynastic designations, e.g., BALA *Ḫa–bi–gal*.

(168) The four hundred years are not apparent from Kinglist A alone, but must be calculated from synchronisms with Assyrian history, which has a more fixed chronological framework. The period with which we are concerned in this study parallels the years between Ashur–dan I and Shalmaneser V (inclusive) in Assyria.

(169) The months are to be disregarded in such calculations: see pp. 63-67 below.

The gaps in the overall picture may now be filled with information garnered from the other pertinent kinglists and chronicles, as listed in the concordance on plate I opposite. (170)

The information contained in the concordance may be schematized as follows:

No.	Name of King	Length of Reign	
1.	Marduk–kabit–ahheshu	18 years	
2.	Itti–Marduk–balatu	8 years	
3.	Ninurta–nadin–shumi	6 years	
4.	Nebuchadnezzar I	22 years	
5.	Enlil–nadin–apli	4 years	
6.	Marduk–nadin–ahhe	18 years	
7.	Marduk–shapik–zeri	13 years	
8.	Adad–apla–iddina	22 years	
9.	Marduk–ah[he–eriba] (171)	1 year	6 months
10.	Marduk–zer?–[...]	12 years	
11.	Nabu–shumu–libur	8 years	
12.	Simbar–Shipak	18 years	
13.	Ea–mukin–zeri		5 months
14.	Kashshu–nadin–ahi	3 years	
15.	Eulmash–shakin–shumi	17 years	
16.	Ninurta–kudurri–usur I	3 years	
17.	Shirikti–Shuqamuna		3 months
18.	Mar–biti–apla–usur	6 years	
19.	Nabu–mukin–apli	36 years	
20.	Ninurta–kudurri–usur II		8 months 12 days
21.	Mar–biti–ahhe–iddina	unknown	
22.	Shamash–mudammiq	unknown	
23.	Nabu–shuma–ukin I	unknown	
24.	Nabu–apla–iddina	unknown	

(170) Column ii of Assur 14616c is omitted from this concordance for reasons discussed in note 131 above. Also Millard's Shamash–shuma–ukin Chronicle (*Iraq* XXVI [1964] 14-35) is too random in its chronological selections from this period to be of use here. Grayson's BM 48498 is badly broken, and the allusions in what might have been pertinent entries are uncertain (see note 485 below).

(171) Name partially restored from *BE* I/2 149 i 14.

25. Marduk–zakir–shumi I	unknown	
26. Marduk–balassu–iqbi	unknown	
27. Baba–aha–iddina	unknown	
(unknown number of years in which there was no king)		
28. Ninurta–apl?–[...]	unknown	
29. Marduk–bel–[zeri] ([172])	unknown	
30. Marduk–apla–usur	unknown	
31. Eriba–Marduk	unknown	
32. Nabu–shuma–ishkun	unknown	
33. Nabonassar	14 years	
34. Nabu–nadin–zeri	2 years	
35. Nabu–shuma–ukin II		1 month 13 days
36. [Nabu]–mukin–zeri ([173])	3 years	
37. Tiglath–Pileser (III)/Pulu	2 years	
38. Shalmaneser (V)/Ululaju	5 years	

The following paragraphs are devoted to a brief discussion of some individual kings of the sequence, especially those instances in which there is conflict between the sources.

1. Marduk-kabit-ahheshu. The name and regnal years have been ascertained from Kinglist C, an older but better preserved source than Kinglist A. In 1908, long before the discovery of Kinglist C, Schnabel thought that the correct reading of the figure in Kinglist A was 18, ([174]) though no earlier or subsequent editor of the kinglist has agreed. In 1965 I collated the text of Kinglist A and, although the traces of the number are now somewhat blurred because of repeated refiring of the tablet, the more likely reading is 17. ([175]) Traces of the royal name in Kinglist A are uncertain, though several of the nineteenth-century editors and collators of the tablet thought the name began with [md]*Marduk*(ŠÚ). ([176])

([172]) Name partially restored from *JAOS* XLI (1921) 313:10.

([173]) Name partially restored from *BRM* I 22:13.

([174]) *MVAG* XIII/1 (1908) 51. Schnabel's observations depended on a collation of the tablet made by Lehmann, which, even according to Schnabel, did not correspond to the testimony of other early collators.

([175]) Wiseman (*CAH* II² xxxi 7) believes that Kinglist A may omit the accession year of Marduk–kabit–ahheshu; but this is unlikely, since Babylonian kinglists before the Persian period never counted the accession year as a regnal year. Furthermore, since Kinglists A and C disagree as to the length of reign for both of the first two kings of the Second Dynasty of Isin, defective tradition should be suspected rather than a difference in reckoning systems.

([176]) Fr. Delitzsch, *Berichte über die Verhandlungen der Königlich Sächsischen Gesellschaft der Wissenschaften zu Leipzig, philologisch-historische Classe,* XLV (1893) 186 (with bibliography).

KINGLIST A

1. Marduk–kabit–ahheshu	*17* ᵐᵈŠ[Ú?–]
2. Itti–Marduk–balatu	*6* ᵐ⌈x⌉[ ]
3. Ninurta–nadin–shumi	
4. Nebuchadnezzar I	
5. Enlil–nadin–apli	
6. Marduk–nadin–ahhe	
7. Marduk–shapik–zeri	
8. Adad–apla–iddina	*22* ⌈ᵐᵈ⌉[ ]
9. Marduk–ahhe(?)–[eriba]	MU *1 6* ITI ᵐᵈŠÚ–ŠEŠ?–[x]
10. Marduk–zer(?)–[x]	⌈*12*⌉ ᵐᵈŠÚ–NUMUN?–[x]
11. Nabu–shumu–libur	⌈*8*⌉ ᵐᵈAG–MU–[x]
12. Simbar–Shipak	*18* ᵐ*Sim–bar–ši*
13. Ea–mukin–zeri	ITI *5* ᵐᵈBE–*mu–kin*
14. Kashshu–nadin–ahi	*3* ᵐ*Kaš–šú–u*–MU–ŠEŠ
15. Eulmash–shakin–shumi	*17* ᵐ*É–ul–maš*–⌈GAR–MU⌉
16. Ninurta–kudurri–usur I	*3* ᵐᵈMAŠ–⌈NÍG.DU⌉
17. Shirikti–Shuqamuna	ITI *3* ᵐᵈ*Ši*–⌈*x*-(*x*)-*šu-qa*⌉-*mu*
18. Mar–biti–apla–usur	⌈*6*⌉ ᵐDUMU.⌈É⌉–[ ]
19. Nabu–mukin–apli	⌈*36*⌉ [ ]
20. Ninurta–kudurri–usur II	ITI *8 12* [UD]
21. Mar–biti–ahhe–iddina	⌈*x*⌉ [ ]
22. Shamash–mudammiq	
23. Nabu–shuma–ukin I	
24. Nabu–apla–iddina	
25. Marduk–zakir–shumi I	
26. Marduk–balassu–iqbi	
27. Baba–aha–iddina	
28. Ninurta–apl(?)–[x]	
29. Marduk–bel–zeri	
30. Marduk–apla–usur	
31. Eriba–Marduk	[ ] x–(x) [ ]
32. Nabu–shuma–ishkun	[ ] ᵐᵈAG–MU–GAR–*u*[*n*?]
33. Nabonassar	[ ] ᵐᵈAG–⌈PAB?⌉
34. Nabu–nadin–zeri	⌈*2*⌉ ᵐ[ᵈA]G–MU–NUMUN A–*šú*
35. Nabu–shuma–ukin II	ITI *1 13* UD ᵐ[ᵈA]G–MU–DU A–*šú*
36. (Nabu)–mukin–zeri	*3* ᵐDU–NUMUN BALA *Šá–pi–i*
37. Tiglath–Pileser III/Pulu	*2* ᵐ*Pu–lu*
38. Shalmaneser V/Ululaju	*5* ᵐ*Ú–lu–la–a+a* BALA BAL.TIL

CONCORDANCE OF CHRONOLOGIC

KINGLIST C

18 ^{md}AMAR.UTU–IDIM–ŠEŠ.MEŠ–*šú*
8 ^{m}KI–^{d}AMAR.UTU–DIN
6 ^{md}MAŠ–*na-din*–MU
22 ^{md}AG–NÍG.DU–ŠEŠ
4 ^{md}EN.LÍL–*na-din*–IBILA A–*šú*
18 ^{md}AMAR.UTU–*na-din*–MU
13 ^{md}AMAR.UTU–DUB–NUMUN

ASSUR 14616c iii

^{m}[ ]
^{md}⌈x⌉[ ]
^{md}*Kaš–šu*–[ ]
^{md}*Ul–maš*–[ ]
^{md}MAŠ–*ku*–[ ]
^{m}*Ši-rík-tú*–^{d}[ ]
^{md}DUMU.É–[ ]
[ ]⌈x⌉[ ]–A
[ ]–PAB
[ ]–PAB–AŠ
^{md}UTU–SIG$_5$
^{md}PA–MU–⌈x⌉[x]
^{md}PA–A–SUM–[*na*]
⌈^{md}x⌉[ ]

KAV 182

⌈^{m}⌉[ ]
⌈^{m}x⌉[ ]
^{md}[ ]
^{m}*Š*[*i*–]
^{m}[ ]–⌈A⌉–PAB
^{m}[ ]–DU–A
^{md}MAŠ–[NÍG.D]U–PAB
^{md}A.É–⌈PAB–SUM⌉–*na*
^{md}UTU–SIG$_5$
^{md}PA–MU–*ú-kin*
^{md}PA–A–AŠ
^{md}PA–*za-kir*–MU
^{md}ŠID–TI–*su*–DUG$_4$
⌈^{md}*Ba*⌉–[ ]

"PTOLEMAIC CANON"

Ναβονασσάρου	*14*
Ναδίου	*2*
Χινζῆρος καὶ Πώρου	*5*
Ἰλουλαίου	*5*

ASHUR-RESHA-ISHI I CHRONICLE

m[d]⌈NIN.IB⌉–SUM–MU.MEŠ

TIGLATH-PILESER I CHRONICLE

mdAMAR.UTU–[–Š]EŠ.MEŠ

mdAMAR.UTU–D[UB]–*ik*–NUMUN

RELIGIOUS CHRONICLE

[A]G?–MU–*li*–*bur*

dAG–DU–A/IBILA

SYNCHRONISTIC HISTORY

mdPA–*ku*–*dúr*–PAB

mdAMAR.UTU–SUM–PAB.MEŠ

mdAMAR.UTU–*šá*–*pi*–*ik*–NUMUN–(≪KUR≫)

mdIM–A–SUM–*na*

mdUTU–*mu*–SIG_5

mdPA–MU–GAR–*un*

[ ]–IBILA–SUM–*na*

mdŠID/AMAR.UTU–MU–MU

[*s*]*u*–*iq*–*bi*

md*Ba*–ba_6–PAB–AŠ

14

2

TI 2 UD

3

2

5

AL SOURCES LISTING KINGS OF THE POST-KASSITE PERIOD

KAV 12

[ ]–NÍG.DU–PAB
[ ]–A
[ ].MEŠ

KAV 10

^{m}*Š*[*i*–]
^{md}DU[MU?.É]
^{md}PA–D[U]
^{md}MAŠ–NÍG.DU–PAB
^{md}DUMU.É–PAB–AŠ
^{md}UTU–S[IG$_5$]
^{md}PA–MU–[ ]
^{md}PA–A–[ ]
^{md}ŠID–M[U–]
[ ]⌈^{d}x⌉[ ]

KAV 13

[^{m}]⌈^{d}MAŠ–A?⌉–[ ]
^{md}ŠID–⌈EN⌉–[ ]
^{md}ŠID–A–[ ]
^{m}SU–*Mar*–[ ]
^{md}PA–MU–[ ]

NEW BABYLONIAN CHRONICLE

^{md}AMAR.UTU–DUB–NUMUN
^{md}IM– –MU

^{m}*Sim–bar–ši–i–pak*

É–ul–maš–GAR–MU

^{d}A.É– –ŠEŠ
^{d}AG–DU–[ ]

[ ].ME–MU

^{md}AG–MU–*ú–kin*
[DUMU].UŠ–MU
^{md}AMAR.UTU–*za–kir*–MU
^{md}AMAR.UTU–DIN–*su*–[ ]

⌈*x*⌉ MU.ME MAN *ina* KUR NU GÁL

^{m}*Eri–ba–*^{d}ŠÚ/AMAR.UTU

[*n*]*a–ṣir*

[ ].⌈RA⌉

DYNASTIC CHRONICLE v

^{m}*Sim–bar–ši–pak*	*17*
^{md}*É–a–mu–kin*–NUMUN	*3* ITI
^{md}*Kaš–šú–ú*–SUM–ŠEŠ	*3*
[ ]–*ul–maš*–GAR–MU	*15*
[ ].DU–ŠEŠ	*2*
[ ]–^{d}*Šu–qa–mu–na*	*3* ITI
[–Š]EŠ	*6*

DYNASTIC CHRONICLE vi

^{d}AMAR.UTU–A–ŠE[Š]
^{m}*Eri–ba*–[ ]

BABYLONIAN CHRONICLE

^{d}AG–PAB
$^{(m)}$*Na–din/di–nu*
^{m}MU–DU/GI.NA I
$^{(m)}$DU–NUMUN
$^{(m)}$TUKUL–*ti*–A/IBILA–(≪*ina*≫)–É.ŠAR.RA
^{m}*Šul–man–a–šá–red*

PLATE I

2. Itti-Marduk-balatu. The name and regnal years of this king have been adopted as transmitted in Kinglist C, because it is a more nearly contemporary and better preserved source than either Kinglist A or the synchronistic kinglist Assur 14616c. The reading of the number of regnal years in Kinglist A is not absolutely certain, but *6* is the smallest number possible. (177) In Assur 14616c ii 13′, where one would expect to find the name of Itti–Marduk–balatu, the traces are so obscure that no conclusions can be drawn as to the original contents of the text at this point. (178)

Unfortunately, however, the matter is further complicated because Weidner in a copy of Assur 14616c made from a photograph represented faint traces of the name Itti–Marduk–balatu in ii 18′, just after Marduk–nadin–ahhe. (179) Since Weidner has in the meantime expressed the wish that his copy of this section of the text be disregarded, (180) we do better to follow the clear and almost contemporary testimony of Kinglist C at this point. (181)

3. Ninurta-nadin-shumi. A variant of the name, [Ninurta]–nadin–shumati, appears in an Assyrian text; (182) but this reading is unsubstantiated from any other source. Kinglist C and the other Babylonian documents, both contemporary and later, are unanimous in writing the last element of the name in the singular. (183)

4. Nebuchadnezzar I. The common English form of the name, (184) which is employed throughout the study, is based on a later Hebrew corruption of the

(177) The place where a third row of wedges might be expected is worn smooth now, and the possibility that the text originally read *8* cannot categorically be denied (result of my collation of the tablet in 1965). J. A. Knudtzon's copy of the text in his *Assyrische Gebete an den Sonnengott*, I, 60 clearly raised the possibility of this reading, which was also supported by Poebel, *AS* XV 25.

(178) See Weidner's copy in *AfO* III (1926) 70. But, according to the usual style of the synchronistic kinglists, one would expect a horizontal dividing line to be drawn between ii 12′ and 13′.

(179) *AfO* III (1926) 70. These traces were expected in line with the reconstruction of the Second Isin Dynasty then held (principally because an Itti–Marduk–balatu was said to be the father of Adad–apla–iddina according to the New Babylonian Chronicle obv. 8′).

(180) *AfO* XVII (1954-56) 383-384 n. 1. See also *AfO* XIX (1959-60) 138 and note 131 above. One may gain an impression of the uncertainty of the traces by comparing Weidner's copy in *MVAG* XXVI/2 (1921) pl. II with that in *AfO* III (1926) 70. Wiseman's statement (*CAH* II² xxxi 27) that the "Synchronous Chronicle" (a name applied by him here to Assur 14616c) lists Ashared–apil–Ekur as a contemporary of Itti–Marduk–balatu is obviated by the above evidence.

(181) Supporting evidence for the sequence of kings as listed in Kinglist C may be adduced from Itti–Marduk–balatu's mention of Marduk–kabit–ahheshu as his father in *VAS* I 112:4. Wiseman's "Chronicle C" (*CAH* II² xxxi 8) is to be read "Kinglist C."

(182) *AfO* IV (1927) 215 rev. ii 11: ᵐ[ᵈ]⌈NIN.I⌉B–SUM–MU.MEŠ.

(183) The references are collected below in n. 529.

(184) *Webster's Third New International Dictionary of the English Language Unabridged* (Springfield, Mass.: G. and C. Merriam Company, 1961), p. 1510.

name given to Nebuchadnezzar II in the Bible. (185) The more common Hebrew spelling of the name of that king, as well as the writing of his name in a contemporary Aramaic tablet, (186) speak against the historical correctness of the medial *n*.

6. Marduk-nadin-ahhe. Here our usually impeccable source, Kinglist C, lists the name as Marduk–nadin–shumi. This is a simple case of scribal error, (187) since the Babylonian primary sources and the other secondary sources in our concordance unanimously refer to him as Marduk–nadin–ahhe (188) and no Marduk–nadin–shumi is attested elsewhere as monarch in Babylonia.

One further difficulty is the sequence of rulers at this point. The often-discussed kudurru published by A. T. Clay as *YOS* I 37 poses a question in interpretation, (189) seeming to invert the order of Marduk–nadin–ahhe and Marduk–shapik–zeri, kings number 6 and 7 respectively. The second column of the observe of this kudurru records payments made in the twelfth year of Marduk–shapik–zeri, (190) while the second column of the reverse in a position where one would normally expect to find the date for the whole text mentions the eighth year of Marduk–nadin–ahhe. (191) Since the text as a whole can hardly be dated twenty-two years before a transaction which it cites, we are confronted with a dilemma, which could be resolved in one of two basic ways:

(1) the two dates mentioned do not appear in chronological order either (a) because what Clay regarded as the obverse and reverse of the text are in reality the reverse and obverse, (192) or (b) because two completely un-

(185) נבוכדראצר and its variant forms are slightly less common than נבוכדנאצר and its variants. The more common form, however, is restricted to Jeremiah and Ezechiel.

(186) J. Starcky, "Une tablette araméenne de l'an 34 de Nabuchodonosor," *Syria* XXXVII (1960) 100 B line 5.

(187) Kinglist C was obviously written by an apprentice scribe (cf. the physical description of the tablet by Poebel, *AS* XV 1-2). The young scribe confused MU and ŠEŠ also in line 3 (where the final MU is written over an erased ŠEŠ). His error of MU for ŠEŠ in line 6, however, went uncorrected.

(188) Babylonian primary sources: *UET* I 306:2; *UET* VIII 101:12, 52-53; *SPA* I 283-284 nos. VIII-X:1; *PSBA* XIX (1897) 71 ii 4, 19; *YOS* I 37 iv 32; *BBSt* no. 8 i 4, 28; *BBSt* no. 25:3, 38; *Iranica Antiqua* II (1962) 152 no. 5:1-2. In the campaign records of Tiglath–Pileser I, the final element of this king's name is sometimes written in the singular (references in note 679 below). Cf. a similar confusion in the name of Mar–biti–ahhe/aha–iddina (note 1078 below).

(189) Discussed in detail by A. Ungnad, "Zur Geschichte und Chronologie des zweiten Reiches von Isin," *Orientalia N.S.* XIII (1944) 86-95 and Poebel, *AS* XV 16-20.

(190) *YOS* I 37 ii 4, 6. (Poebel in *AS* XV 19 raised the possibility that there might have been an additional column, now lost, on both sides of the stone, which would necessitate renumbering of the columns.)

(191) *YOS* I 37 iv 31-32.

(192) Poebel (*AS* XV 18-19) strongly favored this hypothesis. But A. Goetze, who at Poebel's request re-examined the stone, backed Clay's original designations of the sides as "observe" and "reverse" (*AS* XV 19).

related transactions were being recorded, or (c) because the contents of the second column of the reverse were added as a sort of postscript; or

(2) another Marduk–nadin–ahhe came to the throne sometime after the reign of Marduk–shapik–zeri. (This possibility cannot be altogether excluded because king number 10 of the Second Isin Dynasty has a name beginning with Marduk and the reading of the remainder of the name is uncertain; this king also ruled for more than eight years.) (193)

At any rate, the dilemma cannot be resolved simply by reversing the order of Marduk–nadin–ahhe and Marduk–shapik–zeri, since that alternative is specifically precluded by the statement of the Tiglath–Pileser I Chronicle. (194) A satisfactory solution to this problem is yet to be presented.

7. Marduk-shapik-zeri. (195) This reading of the king's name is definitely established by two recently published texts, Kinglist C and the Tiglath–Pileser I Chronicle. The older reading Marduk–shapik–zer–mati has been discussed at length by Poebel (196) and seems to be due to a scribal error which originally mistook the MAN(=*šar*) of the king's title for part of his name. As Poebel has remarked, it is unlikely that the Synchronistic History would preserve a fuller form of the royal name than the monarch's own formal inscriptions.

8. Adad-apla-iddina. (197) The sequence of the first seven kings of the Second Isin Dynasty is assured through the testimony of Kinglist C. We know that Adad–apla–iddina directly followed Marduk–shapik–zeri on the throne because of the following evidence. The Synchronistic History states:

> In the time of Ashur–bel–kala, king of [Assyria], Marduk–shapik–zer–« mati », [king] of Karduniash, died. He (198) placed Adad–apla–iddina, son of Esagil–shaduni, son of a nobody, as king over them. (199)

(193) The ninth king of the Second Isin Dynasty is excluded because he ruled for only one year (not the minimum of eight years required by *YOS* I 37 iv 31-32). For the uncertainty regarding the reading of the name of the tenth king of the dynasty, see p. 45 below.

(194) *AfO* XVII (1954-56) 384:8′-9′.

(195) For the apparent insertion of another king between Marduk–nadin–ahhe and Marduk–shapik–zeri in Assur 14616c, see p. 41 above.

(196) *AS* XV 20.

(197) Poebel's statement in *AS* XV 21 that "Adad–apla–iddina ... is known to have been the immediate successor of Marduk–nâdin–aḫḫē" is certainly a *lapsus calami*, as the rest of his book shows.

(198) The subject of the verb apparently refers to the Assyrian king, Ashur–bel–kala, as the only single antecedent still on the scene.

(199) *CT* XXXIV 39 ii 29′-32′. In line 30′ it is uncertain whether to read « KUR » or MAN! after the NUMUN sign.

The New Babylonian Chronicle places Adad–apla–iddina between kings nos. 7 and 12 of the Second Isin Dynasty, and all other rulers within that sequence (i.e., nos. 9-11) are known to have royal names beginning with *Marduk–* or *Nabu–*. Furthermore, the synchronistic kinglist Assur 14616c indicates that the name of the eighth king of the dynasty might begin with *Adad–*. (200) The length of the king's reign, twenty-two years, is known only from Kinglist A, where the royal name is almost totally broken away. (201)

9. Marduk-ah[he?-eriba]. (202) The name of this ruler is not yet definitely established. For kings 9 and 10 of this dynasty, we have only the traces of two names in Kinglist A which read ^{md}ŠÚ–x–[x], one of which may have stood for Marduk–ahhe–eriba. (203) Poebel has examined this topic in detail, (204) and we need not be detained here with what he has already discussed. It is fairly obvious that the sign form (given as the second element in the name of king number 10) can only with difficulty be transformed into a (the normal form for the sign ŠEŠ in Kinglist A); (205) such a transformation would not only require the addition of four small wedges over the principal horizontal stroke but also the deletion of the wedge beneath the stroke and of one of the three wedges at its right end. The second element of the name of the ninth king, however, appears as , which, while it is identical with the normal form for NUMUN in Kinglist A, (206) could quite simply be transformed into ŠEŠ by the addition of wedges over the main horizontal stroke; this would require no removal of traces presently there.

This evidence is not altogether satisfactory or convincing for establishing the name of the ninth king of the Second Dynasty of Isin. If there were not the kudurru of a king Marduk–ahhe–eriba which should be dated to approximately this time on paleographical grounds, we could just as well read the name of this king in Kinglist A as *Marduk–zēru/a–[x]* and place Marduk–ahhe–eriba as a missing king after Baba–aha–iddina, king number 27.

(200) Assur 14616c ii 21′. Because of the physical condition of the kinglist (see note 131 above), this reading cannot be regarded as certain or as sufficient evidence by itself.

(201) Kinglist A iii 1′. The traces of the RN here are now quite illegible, though Delitzsch (*Berichte über die Verhandlungen der Königlich Sächsischen Gesellschaft der Wissenschaften zu Leipzig, philologisch-historische Classe*, XLV [1893] 187) thought that the traces favored a reading ^{md}*Adad*.

(202) For the restoration, see note 171 above.

(203) A ruler whose name occurs in a kudurru (*BE* I/2 149 i 14) which is dated to the time of the Second Dynasty of Isin by means of paleography (W. J. Hinke, *Boundary Stone*, pp. 188-189). The only other available place for a king of this name would be after king number 27.

(204) *AS* XV 22.

(205) Cf. Kinglist A i 8′, 15′.

(206) E.g., iv 4.

10. Marduk-zer?-[x]. We have already discussed the traces of the name of this king in the preceding paragraphs. We regard Poebel's reading, which is followed here, as somewhat uncertain. The traces [cuneiform] in Kinglist A are perhaps closer to some forms of MU which appear elsewhere in the same text, e.g., [cuneiform]. (207) But a reading Marduk–shumu/a/i–[x] is no more certain than the usually accepted alternative. (208)

11. Nabu-shumu-libur. The name is readily restored from the Religious Chronicle, where there is a [*Na*]*bû–šumu–lībur* (209) as king before Nabu–mukin–apli. Since the only Babylonian kings before the time of Nabu–mukin–apli who had names beginning with Nabu were Nebuchadnezzar I and the eleventh ruler of the Second Isin Dynasty, the Nabu–shum(u)–[x] of Kinglist A and the [Na]bu–shumu–libur of the Religious Chronicle should clearly be identified. (210)

12. Simbar-Shipak. The reading of both elements of this name is not as yet established beyond the shadow of a doubt. We read the first element as *Simbar* rather than *Simmash* because there are Kassite proper names written *Sib–bar–*DN. (211) This phenomenon can be explained by interpreting the middle consonants of the first element as *mb* (dissimilated from *bb*). (212) It is unlikely that *mm* could develop from an earlier *bb* or *bm*. As to the second element of the royal name, we concur for the time being with Eilers' remarks in his review of Balkan's *Kassitenstudien* and read *Shipak*. (213)

Kinglist A gives a shortened form of this king's name: Simbar–shi, while the chronicles give the full name. The origin of the abbreviations of royal names in Kinglist A is uncertain. It might be argued that the source from which this kinglist drew had several lines broken at their ends. But then the fact that several of the shortened forms have additional information after them in the same line, e.g., "Kashtil⟨iashu⟩, his son," could be explained only by assuming a plurality of sour-

(207) ii 10′.

(208) Especially since in Kinglist A the MU in the royal name immediately following (i.e., that of king number 11) is written differently than the second element in the name of the tenth king.

(209) For the traces of the PA sign still visible in the chronicle, see L. W. King, *CCEBK* II 72 n. 1.

(210) This identification was early supported by H. Winckler, *Auszug aus der vorderasiatischen Geschichte* (1905), p. 17, and by King, *PSBA* XXIX (1907) 221. It was rejected by F. Weissbach in *ZDMG* LXI (1907) 395 and by C. H. W. Johns in *ADD* II p. 264. See most recently Poebel, *AS* XV 23.

(211) K. Balkan, *Kassitenstudien*, I, 76.

(212) For examples of such dissimilation in the Kassite period, see J. Aro, *Studien zur mittelbabylonischen Grammatik*, pp. 36-37.

(213) *AfO* XVIII (1957-58) 137 and n. 12. For a more comprehensive bibliography of recent discussions, see n. 901. The reading of the last element of the name as *ḫu* or *pak* must be regarded as unsettled.

ces. This, in turn, would give rise to the question why none of the sources for Kinglist A would preserve the full form of the names, since the longer forms were obviously accessible to compilers of the late chronicles. Therefore, it seems better to interpret the shortened forms as abbreviations by the scribe rather than to place the blame on the state of preservation of his sources. (214)

A conflict arises in the number of regnal years assigned to Simbar–Shipak: Kinglist A reads 18, the Dynastic Chronicle 17. For the present, Kinglist A is probably to be preferred in this matter, since the Dynastic Chronicle is not consistent in its handling of the years of the Second Sealand and Bazi Dynasties. (215)

13. Ea-mukin-zeri. (216) For the abbreviated form of this name which occurs in Kinglist A and for our preference for the length of reign as listed in Kinglist A ("5 months"), as contrasted with that given in the Dynastic Chronicle ("3 months"), compare the remarks on Simbar–Shipak in the preceding paragraphs.

15. Eulmash-shakin-shumi. The unique writing [md]*Ul–maš* in Assur 14616c could be explained in one of two ways. First, the shorter form of the temple name Ulmash for Eulmash occurs several times in personal names of the Kassite period. (217) This shorter form is apparently older, since it is attested even in Old Akkadian; (218) and it could be prefixed with the divine determinative. (219) Though Ulmash forms are not otherwise attested after the Kassite period (and certainly not with a divine determinative), this writing does have earlier parallels and is not entirely isolated in the cuneiform tradition.

(214) Rowton in *JNES* XXV (1966) 242 argues that the source from which the scribe compiling Kinglist A copied the Kassite Dynasty was heavily damaged at its right edge, hence the abbreviated form of the royal names. Rowton states that this original source gave, from left to right, the figure for the king's reign, the king's name, and the genealogical relationship to the king's predecessor. It seems unlikely, however, in this case that the original text would be damaged just at the end of the king's name and yet preserve the genealogical relationship perfectly (e.g., *CT* XXXVI 24 ii 6'-7', where the text reads [m]*Šá–ga-rak–*⌜*ti*⌝ [DU]MU–*šú*/[m]*Kaš–til* DUMU–*šú*). Despite the averred plurality of sources from which Kinglist A was compiled, the shortened forms of royal names occur in all sections of the Kinglist (e.g., i 4'-7', 9'-14', ii 6'-7', iii 6'-7', 11'-12', iv 20-22). It seems more likely that abbreviations were deliberately used, especially since a Neo-Babylonian scribe would hardly be ignorant of the full forms of the names of such well-known and almost contemporary figures as Esarhaddon, Shamash–shuma–ukin, and Kandalanu.

(215) See above, pp. 31-32.

(216) Before the publication of the Dynastic Chronicle, the name was restored Ea–mukin–shumi. A history of the old reading is given by Weissbach in *RLA* II 259.

(217) Note Eulmash–bitum (*PBS* II/2 137:5, *BE* XIV 100:7, etc.) and Ulmash–bitum (*BE* XV 169:4, 114:4a, etc.), Ulmash–sharrat (*BE* XV 100:16; a shortened form of Ina–Eulmash–sharrat, CBS 13253 [cited in Clay, *CPN*, p. 88], cf. *BE* XV 155:9). Compare the adjectival PN *Ulmašītu* in *AfO* X (1935-36) 43 no. 100:42 (MA econ.).

(218) Nabi–Ulmash (*MAD* III 195), Ukin–Ulmash (*MAD* III 140).

(219) C. Jean, *Šumer et Akkad* (Paris, 1923), no. XXVI rev. 1 (reference called to my attention by I. J. Gelb).

A second explanation could be based on scribal error. In Assur 14616c, the two lines preceding the one in question and the line following it each begin $^{\text{md-}}$. A slip of the stylus that would make these four consecutive lines begin in the same way is not surprising.

The listing of Eulmash–shakin–shumi's regnal years as 17 in Kinglist A is to be preferred to the 14 (15?) (220) of the Dynastic Chronicle for the reasons mentioned above in our comments on Simbar–Shipak.

16. Ninurta-kudurri-usur I. The name occurs in an abbreviated form in Kinglist A; and the "3 years" of Kinglist A are to be preferred to the "2 years" of the Dynastic Chronicle for the reasons given above.

17. Shirikti-Shuqamuna. The fullest writing of this royal name is preserved in the Shamash–shuma–ukin Chronicle: Shirikti–Shuqam[u]nu. (221) Other variants render the first part of the name as Shiriktu or the second part as Shuqamuna. (222) The form accepted here is based on the classical Babylonian construct of *širiktu* and the more usual form of the Kassite divine name. (223)

18. Mar-biti-apla-usur. The name appears in full only in the New Babylonian Chronicle, but all the other sources agree except the synchronistic kinglist *KAV* 10. Here the first sign after the initial determinatives seems to read , but there is sufficient space above the traces to restore the sign into or some other form of DUMU. The would–be PA sign in this line is much smaller than the corresponding PA in the next line; but, on the other hand, the traces do not fit well with the fully preserved DUMU which occurs three lines lower, unless the first two horizontal wedges were omitted by mistake in the drawing of the earlier sign. This questionable sign, however, cannot be considered as offering decisive evidence against the present reading of the king's name.

The length of the reign of this king is given as 6 years in the Dynastic Chronicle v 13′. The pertinent number cannot be read with certainty in Kinglist A. (224)

(220) Grayson informs me that the number in the Dynastic Chronicle should be read as 14 rather than as 15, the figure given in King's copy. The digit four written as ZA rather than GAR would be relatively rare in late chronological lists; and, unfortunately, no fours occur elsewhere in the Dynastic Chronicle for comparison. But, whether read as 14 or 15, the number nonetheless disagrees with the figure given in Kinglist A.

(221) *Iraq* XXVI (1964) pl. VII 20.

(222) The spellings are listed in detail in note 996 below.

(223) *GAG* §64h; Balkan, *Kassitenstudien*, I, 118-122.

(224) Though there is sufficient space for a 6 in Kinglist A at this point, only one digit can now be seen clearly and another with a fair degree of probability in the badly pitted surface (personal collation). Early

19. Nabu-mukin-apli. In the secondary sources the name of this king is preserved complete only in the Religious Chronicle. His occurrence at this place in the sequence is assured by the evidence of the synchronistic kinglists:

KAV 10: ^{md}PA–D[U–X]
KAV 182: [ ]–DU–A
Assur 14616c: [ ]–A

These combined readings, all occurring at the same place in the sequence, leave no doubt as to the identity of the king.

Nabu–mukin–apli probably reigned for at least 36 years, though the number in Kinglist A is now somewhat blurred and cannot be regarded as certain. As presented in Gadd's copy, (225) the wedges in the bottom row might be four (because of the spacing). But my own recent collation of the text (226) and the general custom in Kinglist A of writing 8 in three horizontal rows (227) rather than in two speak against this alternative.

20. Ninurta-kudurri-usur II. The name is preserved almost complete in *KAV* 10; and any doubt about the final P[AB] in the name is removed by the mention of the same individual as a royal prince in a kudurru drawn up during his father's reign. (228) With the exception of Pinches, (229) copyists of Kinglist A have generally agreed in reading "8 months, 12 [days]" as the length of this king's reign. For the restoration of UD in Kinglist A, (230) one may compare the better preserved ITI *1 13* UD later in the document. (231)

---

copyists of the kinglist generally favored the reading 6: Pinches (*PSBA* VI [1884] pl. between pp. 198-199), Abel (Winckler, *Untersuchungen*, p. 147), and Rost (*MVAG* II [1897] 242) rendered the 6 without shading, while Knudtzon (*Assyrische Gebete an den Sonnengott*, I, 60) and Lehmann (*Zwei Hauptprobleme*, pl. 2) partially shaded the upper row of digits. Gadd, however, in *CT* XXXVI 25 shaded both rows of digits. There are no serious grounds for challenging the chronological information given by the Dynastic Chronicle at this point.

(225) *CT* XXXVI 25 iii 15′. See also Delitzsch, *Berichte über die Verhandlungen der Königlich Sächischen Gesellschaft der Wissenschaften zu Leipzig, philologisch-historische Classe*, XLV (1893) 187.

(226) The three vertical wedges visible in the bottom row of the number seem too close together to permit a fourth to intervene.

(227) i 11′, 15′, 19′, ii 3′, iii 4′, 6′, iv 19.

(228) *BBSt* no. 9 iva 30: ^{md}NIN.IB–NÍG.DU–PAB DUMU LUGAL.

(229) *PSBA* VI (1884) pl. between pp. 198-199. He read "6 months, 12 [days]." Weidner in *MVAG* XX/4 (1915) 93 read the passage as "9 months x days." According to my own collation of the text, Pinches' reading is impossible because the number after ITI has three clear horizontal rows of wedges. The possibility of Weidner's reading cannot be entirely ruled out, but it is less likely than *8* (especially since 9 months is written elsewhere in the text as [sign], ii 16′).

(230) Knudtzon in his copy of the kinglist (*Assyrische Gebete an den Sonnengott*, I, 60), published in 1893, showed clear traces of two wedges at the beginning of an UD at the edge of the tablet here.

(231) Kinglist A iv 5.

21. Mar-biti-ahhe-iddina. We prefer the reading of the Babylonian primary and secondary sources here. (232) The Assyrian sources write the name as Mar–biti–aha–iddina. (233) The majority of the early copyists of Kinglist A—Pinches, (234) Abel (for Winckler), (235) Rost (236)—show no traces whatsoever for a line after Ninurta–kudurri–usur II, while Knudtzon (237) and Lehmann (238) show shaded traces of a figure *12* here. Kinglist A in its present refired state seems to show only the head of a single wedge, which could be interpreted either as ten or as one. (239)

The break in the text of Kinglist A is complete at this point; and, for information on kings 21-27, we are largely dependent upon the synchronistic kinglists. Furthermore, with the cessation of Kinglist A, we are no longer able to ascertain the number of regnal years to be assigned to the individual kings. (240) Consequently, the first real gap in the relative chronology of this period commences with the reign of this king.

22. Shamash-mudammiq. The reading of the element SIG$_5$ is established by the phonetic indicator *mu–* prefixed in the contemporary Assyrian annals of Adad–nirari II (241) and in the Synchronistic History. (242) The regnal years of the king are unknown.

23. Nabu-shuma-ukin I. The Synchronistic History records the name of this king as Nabu–shuma–ishkun (^{md}PA–MU–GAR–*un*), (243) while both the New Babylonian Chronicle and the synchronistic kinglist *KAV* 182 preserve the name as Nabu-shuma–ukin (^{md}PA/AG–MU–*ú–kin*). (244) Since the Synchronistic History is

(232) Babylonian primary: *BBSt* no. 9 iva 32. Babylonian secondary: New Babylonian Chronicle, edge.

(233) Assur 14616c iii 11, *KAV* 182 iii 8′, *KAV* 10 ii 5′.

(234) *PSBA* VI (1884) pl. between pp. 198-199.

(235) *Untersuchungen zur altorientalischen Geschichte*, p. 147.

(236) *MVAG* II (1897) 242. Weidner (*MVAG* XX/4 [1915] 93) followed this reading of *12*.

(237) *Assyrische Gebete an den Sonnengott*, I, 60.

(238) *Zwei Hauptprobleme*, pl. 2. A photograph of Kinglist A taken over seventy years ago and published by Lehmann, *ibid.*, pl. 1, shows that not much more of the line was visible even in those days.

(239) Based on personal collation. Gadd's copy in *CT* XXXVI shows this wedge, but fails to show the poor condition of the beginning of the line.

(240) Where we have information regarding the regnal years of these kings, it comes from sources other than chronological lists, e.g., economic texts, which may list an occasional regnal year and thus provide a minimal figure for the length of reign.

(241) *KAH* II 84:27.

(242) *CT* XXXIV 40 iii 2, 4, 8.

(243) It is possible that the compiler of the Synchronistic History confused the name of this king with that of king number 32, who was named Nabu–shuma–ishkun. We know that the Synchronistic History was probably composed in the first half of the eighth century, perhaps close to the time when the latter ruler came to the throne.

(244) *KAV* 182 iii 10′; New Babylonian Chronicle, rev. 2-3 (reconstructed from the two lines).

guilty elsewhere of such misnomers as Marduk–shapik–zer–mati (for Marduk–shapik–zeri) ([245]) and Tukulti–apil–Ekur (for Tukulti–apil–Esharra), ([246]) the testimony of the other sources is to be preferred. ([247])

24. Nabu-apla-iddina. The sources unanimously agree on the name of this monarch. Fortunately, we have three kudurrus dated from his reign, in the twentieth, ([248]) thirty-first, ([249]) and thirty-third ([250]) years; so we know that he ruled at least thirty-three years.

25. Marduk-zakir-shumi I. Some writers on chronology have inserted an additional king into the sequence of rulers at this point, namely Marduk–bel–usati, ([251]) the rebellious brother of Marduk–zakir–shumi. Some like Moortgat ([252]) have inserted him before Marduk–zakir–shumi, while others like van der Meer ([253]) have placed him after or in the middle of the king's reign. ([254]) The evidence for such an insertion comes solely from Assyrian sources, which dignify the rebel with the title LUGAL IM.GI (=*šar ḫammā'i*: "usurper"). ([255]) In other documents, this appellative has been used to designate kings of Babylonia who were actually included in the canon of rulers. ([256]) But the Synchronistic History nowhere refers to a legitimate king of either Babylonia or Assyria in this fashion; and, more important, no kinglist includes him in its list of rulers. ([257])

([245]) *CT* XXXIV 39 ii 26′.

([246]) *Ibid.*, ii 14′.

([247]) Before the publication of the synchronistic kinglists, it was generally assumed that kings named Nabu–shuma–ukin and Nabu–shuma–ishkun ruled consecutively about this time (e.g., Winckler in *OLZ* X [1907] 591 and Schnabel in *MVAG* XIII/1 [1908] 87). Weidner proposed the solution to these difficulties in *MVAG* XX/4 (1915) 94.

([248]) *BBSt* no. 28 rev. 25-26.

([249]) *BBSt* no. 36 vi 27-29.

([250]) Douglas Kennedy has kindly informed me of an unnumbered kudurru in the Louvre which he intends to publish and which starts *ina* MU *33* KAM dAG–[DUMU.UŠ–S]UM.NA.

([251]) For the reading of this name, see note 1184 below.

([252]) In *Aegypten und Vorderasien im Altertum*, p. 500. Also earlier by Weidner, *MVAG* XX/4 (1915) 97 n. 4.

([253]) P. van der Meer, *The Chronology of Ancient Western Asia and Egypt* (2nd rev. ed., 1955), tab. 4.

([254]) I.e., their charts place the name of Marduk–bel–usati after that of Marduk–zakir–shumi, presuming that the former held power only during the latter's term of office.

([255]) *CT* XXXIV 40 iii 33 (Synchronistic History), *WO* IV/1 (1967) 30 iv 4 (Balawat Gate inscription of Shalmaneser III).

([256]) The same terminology is used in the New Babylonian Chronicle, obv. 8′, of Adad–apla–iddina, king number 8, and in the Dynastic Chronicle v 5′, of Ea–mukin–zeri, king number 13. These references differ in that: (1) the sources are of Babylonian origin, (2) the kings in question were successful in their usurping bids for the throne.

([257]) *KAV* 182, the only complete kinglist for the period, omits Marduk–bel–usati entirely. *KAV* 10 ii 10′ preserves traces that could fit either Marduk–z[akir–shumi] or Marduk–b[el–usati]; and the succeeding line, which apparently reads *1* MU [ ], has been interpreted to mean "one year" and to refer to

On these grounds, we are justified in rejecting Marduk–bel–usati from the canon of rulers. (258)

Although none of the strictly chronological sources gives us the regnal years of Marduk–zakir–shumi, we have kudurrus dated in the second (259) and eleventh (260) years of his reign. Although these prove only that he ruled at least eleven years, we shall see in the following section on absolute chronology that a much longer reign must be postulated for this king on the basis of synchronisms.

The writing mdPA[*-za-kir-*]MU in *KAV* 182 is simply a scribal error, possibly induced by the mdPA– at the beginning of the two preceding lines. All other primary and secondary sources give the first element of the royal name as Marduk.

26. Marduk-balassu-iqbi. The complete name of the king and his place in the sequence are assured principally by the synchronistic kinglist *KAV* 182. (261) We have no way at present of determining how many years he ruled.

27. Baba-aha-iddina. The chronological materials listed in the concordance tell us little beyond the fact that Baba–aha–iddina was king of Babylonia sometime soon after the reign of Marduk–balassu–iqbi. (262) The only proof we have that he was the latter's immediate successor comes from the Assyrian eponym chronicles and the royal inscriptions of Shamshi–Adad V. In the Assyrian king's annals, we learn that he fought successive campaigns (his fifth and sixth) against Marduk-balassu–iqbi (263) and Baba–aha–iddina (264) respectively. These campaigns are to be dated in successive years around 813 and 812, as has been shown by studies of the eponym lists. (265) Thus Baba–aha–iddina is almost certain to have been Marduk-balassu–iqbi's immediate successor on the Babylonian throne.

---

the reign of Marduk–b[el–usati], who was then to be restored in the preceding line (Weidner, *MVAG* XX/4 [1915] 4 and 97 n. 4; *MVAG* XXVI/2 [1921] 10-11). As we have already shown in *JCS* XVI (1962) 96 n. 20, Weidner's former interpretation of these lines cannot be held: (a) because synchronistic kinglists never list the lengths of reigns, (b) because the only information recorded on such lists other than the names of kings, brief royal titles, and the concluding summaries is the names of the *ummânus* of the individual monarchs, (c) and, therefore, *1* MU [x] is to be interpreted as mMU–[PAB/ŠEŠ], the well-known scribe and *ummânu* of Marduk–zakir–shumi I (*KAV* 182 iii 12′, cf. *RA* XVI [1919] 126 iv 23).

(258) A slightly abbreviated form of the rebel's name occurs in the New Babylonian Chronicle, rev. 5. Though the context is destroyed, it is the only Babylonian source at present that may refer to the revolt.

(259) *RA* XVI (1919) 126 iv 25ff.

(260) *VAS* I 35:53.

(261) The traces in *KAV* 10 ii 11′ seem to indicate a sign beginning with a vertical wedge after the personal and divine determinatives, possibly but not certainly ŠÚ.

(262) The Synchronistic History, in its present fragmentary state, presents them as subjects of successive narratives (Marduk–balassu–iqbi: *CT* XXXIV 43 Sm. 2106 rev. 6′-9′; Baba–aha–iddina: *CT* XXXIV 41 iv 1-14) with a lacuna of unknown length in between.

(263) *AfO* IX (1933-34) 93 iii 24.

(264) *AfO* IX (1933-34) 95 iv 16.

(265) *RLA* II 428 and Weidner in *AfO* IX (1933-34) 101. Cf. n. 1291 below.

Dynastic Tradition of Kinglist A: Unknown Kings? There is an apparent lacuna in the extant kinglist and chronicle tradition at this point. No kings between Baba–aha–iddina and Ninurta–apl?–[x] are attested in the available chronological sources, and the question to be answered here is how many—if any—kings ruled between them. Our only present hope for estimating the number of monarchs between these two rulers lies in an analysis of Kinglist A, which originally contained a list of all the Babylonian kings of this period. (266) Because Kinglist A is damaged and the reading of even its preserved portions is often difficult, the interpretations offered here are necessarily hypothetical; but, if we wish to attempt any sort of unified and coherent history of this age, we will have to suggest opinions which are more than usually liable to be superseded by new discoveries bearing more directly on the topic. With this apology, we turn to the calculation of the dynastic tradition of Kinglist A, which calculation will revolve principally around two problems: (a) the reading and interpretation of the line (iv 6) which summarizes dynastic data concerning the rulers immediately preceding Mukin–zeri, (b) the estimated number of lines (and kings) missing in the gap between [Mar–biti–ahhe–iddina] (iii 17′) and [Eriba–Marduk] (iv 1).

Let us begin with an attempt to read the enigmatic summary line (iv 6) in Kinglist A. Most summary lines which give dynastic totals in Kinglist A read: "*x* (years), *x* king(s), dynasty of GN." (267) This line, however, reads simply "*x*, dynasty of GN"; and it is unspecified whether the *x* is to be interpreted as the number of years or the number of kings. This question may be given a probable solution when we note that: (a) the number in question is written in the right half of the column, where the total number of kings is usually recorded, (268) and (b) the number, even with as high a reading as possible (i.e., 32), (269) would still be too low to summarize the number of years reigned by even the five preceding kings. (270) Therefore, it seems

(266) Assur 14616c and *KAV* 182 also at one time contained lists of all the Babylonian kings of this period; but these synchronistic kinglists are of little help here since their spacing of monarchs is irregular (i.e., some kings occupy more than one line, etc.) and one can hardly estimate with any degree of accuracy the number of monarchs to be supplied in the missing space. Nor is the total of "98 kings of Akkad from Sumulael to Kandalanu" given in Assur 14616c iv 19-20 any more revealing, since 75 of these kings would have ruled before Nabu–mukin–apli and at least 11 kings after the E Dynasty. This does not leave room for even the known kings from Nabu–mukin–apli to Nabu–shuma–ukin II, unless one resorts to arbitrary exclusion of certain monarchs from the total.

(267) E.g., i 3′, 15′. Frequently the length of a dynasty's rule is expressed in years and months (e.g., iii 5′, 9′, 13′).

(268) The total number of years for a dynasty is regularly cited in the left half of each summary line. The left half of iv 6, however, is left blank; and the number starts practically at the beginning of the second half of the line. Gadd in *JRAS* 1922 396 suggested that the summary number might mean "twenty-two dynasties"; this would not only be stylistically irregular, but highly unlikely.

(269) To the best of my knowledge, this is the highest reading proposed for this number. It was proposed by Forrer, *MVAG* XX/3 (1915) 19, and also accepted by W. Del Negro, *Klio* XVIII (1923) 18.

(270) These five kings must be classified as part of the E Dynasty because there is no evidence of a summary line in column iv before line 6. They ruled for at least 38 years (Eriba–Marduk for at least 9

quite probable that the number should be interpreted as referring to the total number of kings in the preceding dynasty. (271)

How is the number in Kinglist A iv 6 to be read? There has been some debate on this question over the years. Of the five marks in this line which might be interpreted as numbers only three have generally been read in the same way by editors and collators of the text. Since there has been such discrepancy in interpretation in the years since the text was first published (1884-1967), we present on page 54 a chart of the readings proposed by men who have either collated the text personally or have had it collated specifically for them. (272)

As may be seen from the chart, men who have examined the text have unanimously agreed on interpreting the first mark as a defect in the tablet rather than as a sign, (273) on reading the third mark as 10, and on reading the fifth mark as 1. Almost all viewers of the tablet have interpreted the second mark as 10, with the exception of Delitzsch (1890) and Grayson (1965, etc.); and it must be admitted that the second mark is shallower than the third mark and that it begins slightly to the left of the guideline at the start of the royal-name column in the kinglist. (274) It is this second mark that is the *crux interpretum*, because the fourth mark has been unanimously interpreted as 1 rather than 10 since Knudtzon's edition (despite Delitzsch's "ausser Zweifel" reading); and, depending on whether one interprets this second mark as a 10 or as a defect in the surface of the tablet, one may read the number as 22 or as 12. In all fairness, then, we note both 22 and 12 as possible readings of the line as it presently stands. To determine which of these two readings is more likely to be correct we must examine the context of the line more closely.

---

years, Nabu-shuma-ishkun for at least 13 years, Nabonassar for 14 years, Nabu-nadin-zeri for 2 years, and Nabu-shuma-ukin II for less than two months).

(271) Even though one would expect some such expression as "kings" (LUGAL.MEŠ) after the number, as in the other summary lines. Why it is omitted here is unknown.

(272) Bibliography for opinions expressed in the chart: Pinches, *PSBA* VI (1884) pl. between pp. 198-199; Winckler and Abel in *Untersuchungen zur altorientalischen Geschichte*, p. 147; Delitzsch in *Berichte über die Verhandlungen der Königlich Sächsischen Gesellschaft der Wissenschaften zu Leipzig, philologisch-historische Classe*, XLV (1893) 188; Knudtzon, *Assyrische Gebete an den Sonnengott*, I, 60; Rost, *MVAG* II (1897) 242; Lehmann, *Zwei Hauptprobleme*, pp. 15-16 and pl. 2; Gadd, *CT* XXXVI 25. My collations were made in the spring of 1965. Grayson has kindly communicated his collations to me by private letter; he is preparing an article for publication which will contain his conclusions.

(273) Though Forrer and Del Negro interpreted this mark as a 10 (see note 269), they had not examined the text but were relying on traces in the copies of others.

(274) Delitzsch was the first to note that the second mark began to the left of the guide-line. This seemingly minor stylistic feature should not be minimized since it is strictly adhered to throughout the text. Numbers in the summary lines referring to totals of kings never elsewhere begin to the left of this guide-line, even where there is room to do so (e.g., i 3′, 15′). The only exceptions to the rule of beginning the total of kings on the guide-line occur when the number given for the total reign of the dynasty (i.e., years and months) is too large to be contained within the left half of the line and extends past the guide-line (e.g., ii 16′, iii 5′); then the total of kings necessarily begins somewhat farther to the right than usual.

Proposed Readings of Kinglist A iv 6

EDITOR, COLLATOR	CHARACTER NUMBER					TOTAL READING
	1	2	3	4	5	
Pinches (1884)		10	10	10	1	31
Winckler (1889)		10	10	10	1	31
Delitzsch (1890)		nur scheinbar	10	10	1	ausser Zweifel 21
Knudtzon (1893)	die vorgehenden Spuren sind wahrscheinlich keine Schriftzüge	10	10	1	1	wahrscheinlich 22
Rost (1897)		⌜10⌝	⌜10⌝	1	1	22
Lehmann (1898)	(trace)	10	10	1	1	fraglos 22
Gadd (1921)		10	10	1	1	22
Brinkman (1965)	(pit)	10(?)	10	1	1	probably 22
Grayson (1965, etc.)		uncertain 10	10	1	1	"far from certain" 22 quite possible 12

The line, as stated above, is a summary line giving a dynastic total. This total embraces at least the kings in iv 1-5 and at most the kings from iii 15′-iv 5. Since we have established above that the number in question (22 or 12) cannot refer to the total number of years and probably refers to the total number of kings, it is important for us to ascertain how much of column three is missing after line 17′ to gain some impression of how many kings can be restored there and whether 22 or 12 would be a more apt summary for the missing rulers.

In calculating the size of any of the missing portions of Kinglist A, we must first take a look at the tablet as a whole. The lines in the individual columns of the tablet are spaced at fairly regular intervals so that, with the exception of the slightly larger summary lines (which include horizontal lines drawn across the tablet both above and below the entry), the line correspondence between columns is approximately one to one. (275) This close correspondence helps us in estimating how many lines have been lost in the breaks at the top and the bottom of each column in the kinglist.

There was a total of 36 kings in the Kassite Dynasty (ii 16′). The names of 15 of these kings are preserved (or partially preserved) (276) in the second column, and the names of 7 more of these kings may be seen in the first column. Thus a total of 14 kings is missing in the broken sections at the bottom of column one and the top of column two. From this one may infer that the kinglist must have commenced with the First Dynasty of Babylon, since only 9 kings are required to complete that dynasty at the beginning of column one and a maximum of 10 lines available (277) will not allow room for another dynasty at the beginning of the list. The restoration of these 9 lines (278) at the head of column one gives us a clue as to the size of the gap at the beginning of column two, which is about 4 lines larger than the gap in column one (this can be observed from Gadd's copy). Thus one may see that there are approximately 13 lines missing at the head of column two; and, consequently, only 1 line can be missing in the break at the end of column one. This, in turn, provides us with the figure of 1 line missing at the bottom of column two, which is equilinear to the end of column one at this point.

(275) This is not to say that each line in column one is exactly opposite a line in column two, etc. What is meant is that the lines are approximately the same size and—with due allowance for the slightly larger summary lines—the number of lines preserved in equal space in adjoining columns of the obverse and reverse is approximately the same (i.e., unlikely to vary by more than one or—at most—two lines).

(276) In the mathematical calculations here, for the sake of simplicity, all partially preserved lines are considered as whole lines since vertical rather than horizontal restoration is desired.

(277) The maximum of 10 lines is calculated as follows. The beginning of column one has four more lines preserved than the beginning of equilinear column two. Since the missing portion at the beginning of column two cannot exceed 14 lines (the total number of missing Kassite kings in columns one and two), the beginning of column one is unlikely to be much in excess of 14–4 (or 10) lines.

(278) Once the possibility of a preceding dynasty has been excluded, the restoration at the beginning of column one should be exactly nine lines because the total "11 kings" is preserved in i 3′.

Turning to the reverse of the tablet, we know then (from the total number of kings of the Isin Dynasty, 11, from which must be subtracted the restored total at the end of column two [3 kings] as well as the number of kings still visible on the extant portion of column three [4 kings]) that some 4 kings occurred in the gap at the beginning of column three. This, in turn, assures us that probably no lines at all are missing from the beginning of the equilinear column four ([279]) and that the top of column four is broken at the edge above its first line. The gap at the end of column four is approximately equal to that at the beginning of column one, since they occur back to back on the tablet and break off at almost exactly the same place. Thus the missing bottom of column four would be about 9 lines long. ([280]) The missing bottom of the third column may be seen to be either equal to or about one line longer than the gap at the end of column four: ([281]) therefore about 9 or 10 lines long. ([282])

How then are we to assess the different readings of 22 and 12 in the summary line (iv 6) in the light of the reconstructed contents of Kinglist A? First, we may say that the number 22 (kings) is extremely difficult to reconcile with the reconstruction proposed above. Besides the 5 kings in iv 1-5 and the 3 kings in iii 15′-17′, we would need to restore 14 additional lines in the gap at the end of column three to make a total of 22. This would necessitate fitting 14 lines into a space which would normally have only 9 or 10 lines and would be very unlikely, considering the general style of Kinglist A. ([283])

([279]) Column four has plainly 4 more lines at its beginning than the extant portion of the beginning of column three. Though I became aware of it only after my own calculations had been made, Delitzsch's collation of the tablet in 1890 and his subsequent calculation of the number of lines missing at the bottom of columns i-ii and the top of column iv agree with the conclusions reached here (cf. *Berichte über die Verhandlungen der Königlich Sächsischen Gesellschaft der Wissenschaften zu Leipzig, philologisch-historische Classe* XLV [1893] 184).

([280]) I.e., there is space for 9 more lines on the column. Whether or not this space was filled may be doubted.

([281]) This must be judged from the text itself or from a photograph (where iv 22 may be seen to be on a level between iii 16′ and 17′ and iv 21 between iii 15′ and 16′). Gadd's copy in *CT* XXXVI 25 is not accurate here in its representation of the relative position of the final lines of columns three and four.

([282]) Forrer (*MVAG* XX/3 [1915] 19) reached the same conclusion concerning the size of the gap at the end of column three. He calculated the length of this gap plus the three preceding lines as being "12 1/2 lines and no more."

([283]) Schnabel (*MVAG* XIII/1 [1908] 79) attempted to justify the interpretation of "22 kings" by the assumption that the scribe who drew up Kinglist A wrote much smaller in the missing section of column three. This seems unlikely in view of the uniform size of the lines in the preserved portions of columns three and four: why would the scribe have employed a reduced script just towards the bottom of the second-last column?

The interpretation of the number 22 as referring to kings was also accepted by Weidner (*MVAG* XX/4 [1915] 88, with earlier bibliography in n. 1) and by the present author in the 1962 draft of this manuscript (when the size of the gaps in Kinglist A had to be computed from Gadd's copy rather than from personal observation or photographs), in his bibliography of sources published in *JCS* XVI (1962) 83-109, and in his chronology published in Oppenheim, *Ancient Mesopotamia*, pp. 335-347. Gadd's copy leaves much to be desired in the matter of line-to-line correspondences between the various columns of the text.

Is the number of 12 (kings) compatible with a restoration of 9 or 10 lines at the end of column three? This question may be answered with a qualified affirmative. If we restore 9-10 lines in column three, the last 7 of these lines would contain the names of the first 7 kings whom Kinglist A considered part of the E Dynasty. This would leave 2 or 3 restored lines to conclude the preceding dynasty; and, since one of these lines would have to be a total or summary line, this would mean only one or two rulers could be added to the kings in iii 15′-17′ to fill out the dynasty which succeeded the Elamite Dynasty. In this case, nine or ten kings all told would be inserted between Mar–biti–ahhe–iddina and Eriba–Marduk; and, since we already know the names of nine Babylonian kings between these two monarchs, (284) the estimated restoration in Kinglist A would fit well with what is known from other sources. (285) But, if the nine known monarchs exactly fill the lacuna in Kinglist A, we are confronted with a further difficulty: in accordance with the total of "12" rulers assigned to the E Dynasty, the break between the E Dynasty and the preceding dynasty should come between Nabu–shuma–ukin I (no. 23) and Nabu–apla–iddina (no. 24); a dynastic change at this point seems unlikely because the New Babylonian Chronicle (rev. 3) says that these two kings were father and son. Even if we allow the names of ten or more kings to be restored between Mar–biti–ahhe–iddina and Eriba–Marduk and postulate one or more unknown kings following Baba–aha–iddina, we would have to hypothesize at least three new kings (unlikely for spatial reasons in Kinglist A) before we could find a suitable place for a dynastic break. (286) Thus, while the number 12 is technically possible as a designation for the total number of kings in the E Dynasty, it creates still other problems concerning the division of dynasties. For this reason, it can hardly provide a firm basis for reconstructing the chronology of the early first millennium in Babylonia.

(284) The names of nine kings from Shamash–mudammiq (no. 22) to Marduk–apla–usur (no. 30) are known principally from Assur 14616c iii 13-18, *KAV* 182 iii 9′-14′, *KAV* 10 ii 6′-11′, *KAV* 13:1′-3′, *ADD* 888:3′ (Dynastic Chronicle).

(285) The reconstruction of the missing lines of Kinglist A would then stand as follows:

Column	[Beginning]		Preserved		[End]		Total
i	9	+	22	+	1	=	32
ii	13	+	18	+	1	=	32
iii	4	+	17	+	10	=	31
iv	0	+	23	+	9	=	32

The slightly smaller total of lines in column iii is not unexpected, since this column contains a greater number of the slightly larger summary lines (5′, 9′, 13′, 14′) than any other column.

(286) Because kings nos. 23-26 are successive generations of the same family.

By way of summary and conclusion, then, we make the following statements about the chronological tradition of Kinglist A at this point:

(a) the number preserved in the summary line in iv 6 cannot refer to the total number of years reigned by the E Dynasty, but it can and should refer to the number of kings in that dynasty;

(b) this number in iv 6 has been and can be read either as 22 or as 12;

(c) but there was not enough room in Kinglist A to contain 22 kings between the Elamite Dynasty and the end of the E Dynasty;

(d) there was enough space, however, to contain 12 kings in the E Dynasty; but then the break between the E Dynasty and the preceding dynasty would have to be put in an unlikely place (between rulers who are known to have been father and son).

Since our analysis of Kinglist A leads us to no certain conclusions about either the reading or interpretation of the summary line iv 6 and since the Dynastic Chronicle apparently adds to the confusion by presenting a different dynastic tradition at this point, ([287]) we are better advised at present to restrict ourselves to the following conservative chronological position:

(a) there is no clear evidence that any kings have to be inserted between Baba–aha–iddina (no. 27) and Ninurta–apl?–[x] (no. 28); ([288])

(b) the dynastic affiliation of kings 19-30 is unknown; ([289])

(c) the E Dynasty included at least kings 31-36 (Eriba–Marduk through Nabu–shuma–ukin II) and perhaps earlier kings as well. ([290])

([287]) It begins a new dynasty with the successor of Eriba–Marduk (*ADD* 888:7′-9′).

([288]) Nor, on the other hand, is there any definitive evidence that Ninurta–apl?–[x] was the first Babylonian monarch after Baba–aha–iddina. There is, however, an indication in the New Babylonian Chronicle rev. 7 that several kingless years may have occurred between these two rulers.

([289]) The only evidence for beginning the E Dynasty with Nabu–mukin–apli (no. 19) was the supposed number 22 in Kinglist A. None of the rulers among kings 19-30 is known to have belonged to the E Dynasty.

In discussing this period in *MVAG* XXVI/2 (1921) 20-22, Weidner tried to solve the problem of the conflicting dynastic traditions by distinguishing a Babylonian tradition (represented by Kinglist A and the synchronistic kinglists *KAV* 10+13 and *KAV* 182) and an Assyrian tradition (represented by Assur 14616c and the New Babylonian Chronicle, BM 27859). According to Weidner, the Assyrian tradition considered the E Dynasty as composed of thirteen kings plus an interregnum, while the Babylonian tradition counted 22 kings (no interregnum). Though Weidner was undoubtedly justified in claiming that there were varying traditions about the Babylonian royal succession in this period (see note 163 above and note 287 below), his specific conclusions about a Babylonian and an Assyrian tradition were unwarranted. There are Assyrian and Babylonian documents within each of these "traditions" (and either one of the "traditions" could equally well be called Assyrian or Babylonian); and most of the texts are too incomplete at the pertinent section (early eighth century) for their contents to be restored with any degree of probability.

The uncertain dynastic divisions at this period will be discussed in further detail on pp. 166-168 below.

([290]) According to the tradition of Kinglist A (but in opposition to the tradition of the Dynastic Chronicle, *ADD* 888).

I frankly suspect that something of the same confusion may also have confronted the compiler of Kinglist A, when in the summary line for the E Dynasty he left the space blank for the total number of years and then failed to qualify the number which he did record with any designation such as "kings". (291) Did he too find the number hard to square with the data available to him?

28. Ninurta-apl?-[x]. The only evidence for this king is preserved in *KAV* 13, where the second element of the name cannot be read with certainty. A combination like Ninurta-apla-[usur] or something similar may be envisaged at present, but we must await further documentation before proposing a definite solution. The length of this king's reign is unknown. (292)

29. Marduk-bel-[**zeri**]. The first two elements of the royal name are preserved in *KAV* 13; the last element is restored from an economic text which is dated in the reign of a king of this name (293) and comes from approximately this period. (294) We do not know how long he ruled.

30. Marduk-apla-usur. The name is preserved almost complete in the Dynastic Chronicle (*ADD* 888), (295) where the king appears as the immediate predecessor of Eriba-[Marduk]. The same sequence is confirmed by *KAV* 13, where, even though the ends of the royal names are damaged, the beginning elements are sufficiently distinctive so that they fit only here. This king is not as yet attested in any primary documentation, and the length of his reign is unknown.

31. Eriba-Marduk. The name of this ruler is fully preserved only in the New Babylonian Chronicle among the secondary source materials. His place in the sequence, however, is assured by traces in *KAV* 13 (mSU-*Mar*-[*x*]) and *ADD* 888 (m*Eri-ba*-[ ]) because the name of no other Babylonian king of the time began with *Erība*-. Though he was a famous ruler in his era, the only indication we have of the length of his reign is an unpublished economic text dated in his ninth year. (296)

(291) This double omission—especially the deliberate leaving of the first half of the summary line blank—argues much more for ancient uncertainty than for ancient carelessness.

(292) We have no chronological source that shows Ninurta-apl?-[x] as the first monarch after Baba-aha-iddina (either immediately or after a kingless interval). This position is based on the analysis of Kinglist A just given.

(293) *JAOS* XLI (1921) 313:10. This was recognized by Ungnad in *AfK* II (1924-25) 26.

(294) It is always remotely possible that Marduk-bel-zeri might have been an "unknown king" between Baba-aha-iddina and Ninurta-apl?-[x], but this is much less likely.

(295) Ungnad's collation of the text in 1912 assured the reading *Marduk-apla-uṣur*: *AfK* II (1924-25) 25-26.

(296) BM 40548, called to my attention by Prof. D. J. Wiseman.

32. Nabu-shuma-ishkun. His complete name and his place in the sequence are best attested in Kinglist A and strengthened by *KAV* 13. (297) His highest known regnal year to date is the thirteenth, which occurs in the economic text *BRM* I 3. (298)

33. Nabonassar. Beginning with this king, the succession of rulers over the next several centuries is well established. The name of this monarch is given in full by Kinglist A and the Babylonian Chronicle and rendered in Greek characters in the "Ptolemaic Canon." (299) In this study, we use the classical anglicized form based on the Greek transcription. The length of the king's reign is set at fourteen years by both the Babylonian Chronicle and the "Ptolemaic Canon." (300)

34. Nabu-nadin-zeri. The name is given in full only in Kinglist A. Both the Babylonian Chronicle and the "Ptolemaic Canon" give an abbreviated form—*Nādin(u)*. (301) All three sources list the length of his reign as two years.

35. Nabu-shuma-ukin II. The full form of this royal name appears only in Kinglist A; the Babylonian Chronicle gives the abbreviated form *Šuma–ukīn*. (302) The "Ptolemaic Canon," in accordance with its usual custom, (303) omits this ruler because he had no official regnal year. The length of his reign was somewhere between one and two months. (304)

(297) There is, of course, always the remote possibility that the ^{md}PA–MU–[x] of *KAV* 13 and the ^{md}AG–MU–GAR–*u*[*n*?] of Kinglist A were different individuals; and, in that case, the sequence would have to be adjusted at this point. But it seems highly probable at present that these names, with their first two elements in common, should be regarded as the same.

(298) Line 14.

(299) The rendering of Nab*u* by Nab*o* is easily understood in the light of what we know of the pronunciation of Neo-Babylonian. The transcription of *naṣir* as *nassar* may be explained by the doubled medial consonant rendering the heightened sound of the ṣ and by the obscure quality of the final unaccented vowel.

(300) The "Ptolemaic Canon" may have derived its chronology at least mediately from the Babylonian Chronicle, but they are treated here as separate sources.

(301) Synkellos presents an interesting variant to the name in his excerpt from the Canon: Νάβιος, where the beta, even though late, could reflect an earlier abbreviation based on the first rather than the second element of the royal name. It should likewise be noted here that Synkellos regularly puts the names of the kings in the nominative case, while the Canon proper puts them in the genitive (possessive) preceding ἔτη: "years of RN." See Wachsmuth, *Einleitung in das Studium der alten Geschichte*, p. 305.

(302) The name was undoubtedly pronounced *Šum/w–ukīn* by this time (J. P. Hyatt, *Final Vowels*, pp. 21-23).

(303) As it does later with Marduk–zakir–shumi II and the second reign of Merodach–Baladan II.

(304) Kinglist A gives ITI *1 13* UD; the Babylonian Chronicle gives ITI *2* U[D]. The last reference is ambiguous, since "one month" is usually written ITI *1*; but, if we take the figure *2* with ITI, then the UD cannot be fitted meaningfully into the line, because the royal name must be restored in the gap which follows immediately. Thus the Babylonian Chronicle here seems best interpreted as reading "⟨one⟩ month, two day(s)."

36. (Nabu)-mukin-zeri. The full form of the name is attested only in the economic document *BRM* I 22:13, where it appears as [md]AG–DU–NUMUN. ([305]) Abbreviated forms occur in all three secondary sources: Kinglist A and the Babylonian Chronicle both give [m]DU–NUMUN ([306]) and the "Ptolemaic Canon" gives Χινζῆρος. ([307]) The Greek form indicates that the Babylonian abbreviation may have been pronounced Kin–zer rather than Mukin–zeri ([308]) or Ukin–zer(a); ([309]) but the Greek text is late, and its applicability to earlier times is thus subject to dispute. The king will be referred to as Mukin–zeri or Nabu–mukin–zeri throughout this study.

The king's regnal years are listed as three in both the Babylonian Chronicle and Kinglist A; but the economic text mentioned above is dated in his fourth year ([310]) and the "Ptolemaic Canon" assigns a combined reign of five years to him and his successor, Pulu. ([311]) The most probable explanation is that he ruled over all of Babylonia for three years before his defeat at the hands of Assyria, but that even then his power was not totally broken in the south so that documents were still being dated there in his fourth year (which would coincide with Tiglath–Pileser's first year elsewhere in Babylonia). ([312])

37. Tiğlath-Pileser III/Pulu. That these two names were used to designate a single ruler is no longer seriously called in question. ([313]) It cannot however be assumed, as has often been done, that "Pulu" was this king's official name in Ba-

([305]) For the dating of this text, see Ungnad, *AfK* II (1924-25) 27 and note 1530 below. One cannot entirely rule out the possibility that Nabu–mukin–zeri was an "unknown king" after Baba–aha–iddina and that the name of king no. 36 should be restored in some other way; but the Aramaic docket on *BRM* I 22 makes such an earlier date much less likely.

([306]) It is improbable that such a name could have existed without a divine element; so a fuller original form is postulated.

([307]) Contrary to F. Schmidtke, *Der Aufbau der babylonischen Chronologie*, p. 98, Χινζῆρος is the *genitive* case of this name. This was noted long ago by Wachsmuth, *Einleitung in das Studium der alten Geschichte*, p. 305, n. on line 4.

([308]) If we had only Babylonian sources, Mukin–zeri would be the most logical reading of the abbreviation (employing the simple expedient of dropping the first element).

([309]) An impossible form even though generally in use. Finite verb forms do not regularly occur as the middle element of an Akkadian personal name (with a following object), and the theophoric element is to be supplied at the beginning of this name.

([310]) *BRM* I 22:12-13.

([311]) A similar combined reign (of one year) is assigned to Sin–shumu–lishir and Sin–shar(ra)–ishkun in the kinglist recently found at Uruk (*UVB* XVIII 53:4-5).

([312]) This interpretation would be reinforced by the Aramaic writing on the tablet, since there were many Aramean tribes in southeastern Babylonia by this time.

Another interpretation would be that, although Mukin–zeri was defeated in the south, Tiglath–Pileser had not effectively extended his reign there early in his first regnal year so that citizens, perhaps hoping for a comeback of the old king, continued to use his name for dating; cf. the date in *BRM* I 23:11-12, "the fourth year in which there was no king in the land."

([313]) The identification is made certain on the Assyrian side by the *limmu* lists, which state that Tiglath–Pileser performed the physical ceremony making him king of Babylonia and on the Babylonian side by the Babylonian Chronicle, Kinglist A, and the "Ptolemaic Canon."

bylonia and "Tiglath-Pileser" his name in Assyria, since the source distribution does not bear this out. Contemporary and nearly contemporary documents in both Babylonia and Assyria—the king's own royal inscriptions, the Assyrian kinglists and eponym lists, economic texts coming from Babylon during his reign, and the Babylonian Chronicle—uniformly refer to him as "Tiglath-Pileser". ([314]) Only later sources—Kinglist A in the cuneiform tradition and the Bible, Berossos, Josephus, and the "Ptolemaic Canon" in foreign languages—call the king "Pulu" or Πῶρος. ([315]) There is no evidence that "Pulu" was ever used as a contemporary name for the king in Babylonia or anywhere else. ([316]) How the name later gained currency as an authentic variant for "Tiglath-Pileser" is unknown. ([317]) From the fact that both forms of the name occur in the Bible and in Josephus, it is conceivable that their original designation of a single individual was eventually forgotten.

It is clear that Tiglath-Pileser reigned for two years in Babylonia, though the "Ptolemaic Canon", as already mentioned, combines these two years with the preceding three years of Mukin-zeri and gives a total of five years for the two rulers.

38. Shalmaneser V/Ululaju. As in the case of the preceding king, this monarch bore two different names in the historical tradition; and, here too, the two names do not represent different throne names in Assyria and Babylonia. "Ululaju", ([318]) however, had much less vogue than "Pulu". The form "Shalmaneser" is retained not only in the king's own inscriptions, the Assyrian kinglist and eponym lists, and the Babylonian Chronicle, but also in the Bible and Josephus; ([319]) "Ululaju" occurs in Kinglist A, the "Ptolemaic Canon", and the Assur Ostracon; its use in the Assur Ostracon indicates that this form of the name was current by the middle of the seventh century. ([320])

([314]) Full references for the occurrences of "Pulu" and "Tiglath-Pileser" are listed in note 1544 below.

([315]) The Codex Laurentianus has a variant Πόρου (genitive). The variation of *r* for *l* in the Canon is interesting, but as yet unexplained.

([316]) Furthermore, Pulu is an Assyrian not a Babylonian name (*ADD* 281 rev. 8, 642 rev. 17, etc.).

([317]) One could propose several hypotheses, e.g., that Pulu was his name in Assyria before he came to the throne or that it was employed as a quasi-hypocoristic for the second element of the name Tiglath-Pileser.

([318]) The reading of the end of the Babylonian form in -A.A(-*a*+*a*) is not altogether certain. We read it here as nominative because Babylonian personal names of this type earlier in the Post-Kassite period could be written alternatively as -A.A or as -*a-a-ú* (e.g., *PSBA* XIX [1897] 71 ii 11; *BBSt* no. 25:28; *BBSt* no. 8 ii 1). See also Poebel's remarks on the declension of case endings for gentilics and hypocoristics of this type in *JNES* I (1942) 471-474.

([319]) Full references for these occurrences may be found in note 1560 below.

([320]) For possible occurrences of Ululaju in the Nimrud Letters (when Shalmaneser was crown prince), see note 1564 below. Since Ululaju could serve as an informal name or nickname, it could very well have been an alternate contemporary name for Shalmaneser V but—because of its informality—not used in official documents.

The Babylonian Chronicle, Kinglist A, and the "Ptolemaic Canon" concur in assigning a five-year reign to this king.

We have now reviewed in some detail the reconstruction of the sequence of kings in Babylonia during the Post–Kassite period. The results may be summarized briefly as follows:

Kings 1-27: order of monarchs certain; names for two kings (9, 10) known either incompletely or with probability only; length of reigns known only for the first twenty rulers in succession, though several minimal figures for the reigns of the remaining seven may be postulated;

Kings 28-32: order and names known with certainty; the names for kings 28 and 29 are only partially known thus far (the latter plausibly restored); the restoration of the name of king 32 and the conclusion that ruler 33 immediately follows 32 are highly probable, but not absolutely certain; (321) regnal years unknown, save for a minimal figure for kings 31 and 32;

Kings 33-38: order, names, regnal years all well attested and certain.

With this scheme in mind, we may now turn to the reconstruction of a relative chronology.

Before proceeding to assign definite years to the individual kings, we must consider one more problem. In five instances in the list of monarchs for the Post–Kassite period, (322) we encounter reigns listed in terms of fractions of a year, i.e., in months or days. We are aware of the Babylonian custom for dating which began in the Kassite era—reckoning dates in terms of the number of official regnal years of the king, of which the first would commence when he "took the hand" of Bel in the New Year's festival for the first time. When the old king died before the end of a year, the time between the new king's coming to power and the beginning of his first official regnal year was designated as his accession year. The accession year was never counted in chronological computations, since it was just another name for the last year of the old king. Thus, when Nabonassar died in his fourteenth year, he was credited with fourteen years in the kinglists and chronicles; and the accession year of his son and successor, Nabu–nadin–zeri, was absorbed—for computational purposes—into his father's reign. This simple method of reckoning obviated any cumbersome counting of reigns in terms of years, months, and days for which the king was actually on the throne. Hence, at first glance, it is surprising to find in Kinglist A no fewer than five occurrences of reigns listed in fractions of years

(321) See note 297 above.

(322) Marduk–ahhe–eriba (no. 9): MU *1 6* ITI; Ea–mukin–zeri (no. 13): ITI *5*; Shirikti–Shuqamuna (no. 17): ITI *3*; Ninurta–kudurri–usur II (no. 20): ITI *8 12* [UD]; Nabu–shuma–ukin II (no. 35): ITI *1 13* UD.

since, if these are added in the usual way to the other totals, (323) it would mean that the beginning of the official Babylonian regnal year shifted several times during the course of our period.

There is, however, no evidence that such a change of the beginning of the regnal year ever took place and no indication that the New Year's festival in Babylon was celebrated at various times of the year during this part of the historical period.

But, if we consider the examples of reigns recorded in fractions of years in Kinglist A and compare this information with what is known about the same reigns from other sources, we reach some interesting conclusions. The examples of fractional reigns according to Kinglist A are:

MU *1* ITI *6*	Enlil–nadin–shumi
MU *1* ITI *6*	Kadashman–Harbe II
MU *1* ITI *6*	Marduk–ah[he-eriba]
ITI *5*	Ea–mukin–(zeri)
ITI *3*	Shirikti–Shuqamu(na)
ITI *8* [*12* UD]	[Ninurta–kudurri–usur II]
ITI *1* *13* UD	Nabu–shuma–ukin II
ITI *1*	Marduk–zakir–shumi II
ITI *9*	Merodach–Baladan II (324)

For some of these nine examples, there is extraneous evidence to determine how the reigns were figured in Babylonian chronology. The reign of Nabu-shuma-ukin II was simply disregarded in reckoning years; the "Ptolemaic Canon" omits this king entirely. And, if we reckon his official reign at 0 years, all the synchronisms of the surrounding period balance out perfectly. Similarly, with the reigns of Marduk–zakir–shumi II and Merodach–Baladan II: though these two brief reigns occurred in succession, the "Ptolemaic Canon" omits them both (325)—and the approximately contemporary synchronisms are again undisturbed.

Even more striking evidence is furnished by the reign of Nergal-ushezib in the first decade of the seventh century. This king is listed as ruling 1 year, according to Kinglist A. (326) At the same time, the Babylonian Chronicle states quite plainly

(323) The compiler of Kinglist A actually did add up the totals for individual dynasties in this strictly literal way. But, as we shall see below, this totaling was a late and erroneous interpretation of the earlier data and fortunately did not vitiate the figures for the individual reigns.

(324) I.e., his second reign as king of Babylonia. His first reign lasted for twelve years.

(325) Between the first reign of Sennacherib over Babylon (technically designated as ἀβασίλευτα [*scil.* ἔτη]) and the three-year reign of Bel-ibni, the "Ptolemaic Canon" makes no provision for reckoning these ten months as a year.

(326) *1* mdU+GUR–KAR (iv 17).

that the king was captured in his very first year on the throne (i.e., his first official regnal year) and that he ceased to rule after being on the throne for MU *1 6* ITI. ([327]) Since the king was removed to Assyria in Teshritu (the seventh month) of his first regnal year, it is clear that what is meant here is not "1 year and 6 months", but rather "1 year, that is, 6 months". In other words, the king had one official regnal year; the six months were added to the total to clarify how much of the official regnal year he was actually on the throne. ([328])

The only instance in which there is difficulty in applying this solution is in the case of the consecutive reigns of Enlil–nadin–shumi and Kadashman–Harbe II, Kassite kings shortly after Tukulti–Ninurta I's conquest of Babylon, who are said to have ruled MU *1* ITI *6* each. ([329]) The question of Tukulti–Ninurta's suzerainty over Babylon is problematic. Chronicle P tells that "[Tukulti–Ninurta] set up his governors over Karduniash; Tukulti–Ninurta gave orders to Karduniash for seven years". ([330]) Tukulti–Ninurta, however, was never included in the canon of Babylonian rulers; and it has sometimes been assumed that his "governors over Karduniash" were the following kings in Kinglist A:

MU *1*	ITI *6*	Enlil–nadin–shumi
MU *1*	ITI *6*	Kadashman–Harbe (II)
6		Adad–shuma–iddina ([331])

These seven years—if six months is taken as the actual length of the reigns—would then be equivalent to the seven-year vassalage of Babylon to Tukulti–Ninurta. ([332])

([327]) *CT* XXXIV 48 iii 5.

([328]) It cannot be argued that Nergal–ushezib may have ruled for a full eighteen months (i.e., that he came to the throne almost immediately after the New Year's festival in his predecessor's last year). Since his predecessor was not removed from office until the end of Teshritu, Nergal–ushezib could have ruled at most for only a little over eleven months. The actual time of his reign, then, is not recorded in the Babylonian Chronicle, but only that part of his official regnal year during which he was actually exercising authority. (For a chronological scheme of events in the years 694-693, see my remarks in *Orientalia N. S.* XXXIV [1965] 244-245).

([329]) Kinglist A ii 8′-9′.

([330]) Chronicle P iv 6-8.

([331]) Kinglist A ii 8′-10′.

([332]) This equation is bolstered by the fact that Adad–shuma–usur's reign begins immediately after the seven-year interregnum in Chronicle P (iv 9) and immediately after the reign of Adad–shuma–iddina in Kinglist A (ii 11′). This is a strong argument in favor of identifying the two periods.

Tadmor's attempt to find divergences between the Kinglist A tradition and the Chronicle P tradition in the sequence of kings here (*JNES* XVII [1958] 136) may be disregarded, even though followed by Wiseman (*CAH* II² xxxi 1). It should be noted that Chronicle P unifies its episodes around single royal personages and hence tells the whole Tukulti–Ninurta story at once (iv 1-13), including its conclusion in the accession of Adad–shuma–usur. Then it returns to pick up the chronological thread of the narrative by telling about Enlil–nadin–shumi, etc. (iv 14ff.). Note also that the whole fate of the Marduk statue is trea-

Some objections may be raised to this attempted solution:

(a) the stylistic interpretation of fractional years accepted here would give a total of eight years (1+1+6), not seven; (333)

(b) scholars such as Tadmor (334) and Rowton (335) total the three reigns literally as nine years;

(c) dates in the Middle Babylonian economic texts found at Ur would seem to indicate that Kadashman–Harbe ruled at least fourteen months, not six. (336)

Nor do the difficulties end there. According to the Ur economic texts (note 336), Kadashman–Harbe's reign extended into at least two Nisans; and, accordingly, the kinglist should have given him a minimum of two official regnal years. It is possible that the Kinglist A tradition at this point was defective or that the rapid removal of Enlil–nadin–shumi by the Elamites (337) caused some confusion in the calculations or even, conceivably, that Enlil–nadin–shumi and Kadashman–Harbe were simultaneous contenders for the throne. (338) It is better at present, because of the conflict in the traditions preserved by Kinglist A, Chronicle P, and the economic texts, to suspend judgment and to await further evidence before attempting an interpretation of this instance of fractional years in Kinglist A.

From our previous observations, one clear stylistic rule emerges for the Post–Kassite data in chronological lists: lengths of reign cited in terms of months or days are to be disregarded in chronological computation; only whole years are to be admitted. Thus, when we read of a reign of one month or three months or ten months,

---

ted also in iv 12-13, though it was not returned till many years later. For further commentary on the passage, see Rowton, *JNES* XIX (1960) 19-20.

Tadmor's contention that "*šaknūti* cannot refer to kings, nor would such Babylonian governors be regarded as legitimate rulers in Babylon to be entered in the canonical King List" (*JNES* XVII [1958] 137) seems too strong. Regardless of whether or not *šaknūti* is used elsewhere to refer to kings, Assyrian appointees such as Kandalanu were not omitted from the canonical Babylonian kinglists. (*Šaknu* is used of Mesopotamian kings chiefly in the phrase *šakin* DN; see Seux, *Épithètes royales*, p. 280).

(333) Unless one assumes some sort of copyist's error which deviated from an original text reading ITI *6*... / MU *1* ITI *6*.

(334) *JNES* XVII (1958) 140.

(335) Tables to be appended to *CAH* I² vi; see also *JNES* XIX (1960) 19, where Rowton posits 7 years for Tukulti–Ninurta I, 3 years for Enlil–nadin–shumi and Kadashman–Harbe, 6 years for Adad–shuma–iddina, plus an unknown number of years for an Elamite interregnum under Kidin–Hutrutash.

(336) There are two economic texts from Ur dated in the reign of Kadashman–Harbe (II rather than I because otherwise these two texts would be over a century earlier than the other MB economic texts from Ur: *Orientalia N. S.* XXXIV [1965] 242 n. 2). One (*UET* VII 22) is dated in Tebetu (28th day) of the king's accession year, one (*UET* VII 33) in Abu of a year whose number is broken away, but which ends in KAM— therefore at least his first year. Furthermore, another text (*UET* VII 1) is dated on the thirteenth day of Nisan in the accession year of his successor Adad–shuma–iddina, implying that Kadashman–Harbe died in the first twelve days of that year. Therefore, he ruled a minimum of fourteen months.

(337) Chronicle P iv 16.

(338) Enlil–nadin–shumi as the Assyrian-sponsored candidate, Kadashman–Harbe as the Kassite. This proposal is purely speculative.

that reign is to be reckoned at zero for chronological purposes. When we read of a reign in the cryptic style MU *1* ITI *6*, we know that one year is to be counted for the reign and the six months disregarded save only as an explanation of the actual conditions under which the regnal year was fulfilled. (339) When reigns last more than one regnal year, they are automatically counted as two, three, four, or more years without further explanation. Only when the reign is less than one year is explanation sometimes felt necessary; and the annotations of *x* months and so forth occur only in reference to reigns that last less than a calendar year. If the short reign fails to reach the New Year and thus the king cannot be credited with an official regnal year, (340) then the months (and sometimes the days as well) are listed as the time of reign because the Babylonians, who did not wish to omit all mention of a short-lived king and yet had no way of expressing zero numerically at this time, did not wish to leave the space for the number blank (thus paving the way for later speculation as to whether or not they knew the actual length of reign). If the reign reached the New Year or began with the New Year and did not last for the whole year, then the reign could be recorded as MU *1* (341) or as *1* (342) or as MU *1* ITI *x*. (343) Thus the chronology worked strictly in terms of integral years, and all fractions are to be reckoned as zero.

These observations made, we may now proceed to set up a relative chronology for the period. Disregarding all indications of reigns in terms of months and days, we arrive at the following figures:

Kings	**Years**	
1-11	1-132	Second Isin Dynasty
12-14	133-153	Second Sealand Dynasty
15-17	154-173	Bazi Dynasty
18	174-179	Elamite Dynasty
19-20	180-215	(dynasty unknown)
21-30	—	(dynasty unknown)
31-32	—	E Dynasty
33-38	1′-26′	E Dynasty (last three kings)
		Mukin–zeri through Shalmaneser V

(339) With the possible exception of the presently inexplicable reigns of Enlil–nadin–shumi and Kadashman–Harbe II, as noted above.

(340) The Assyrian kinglists may have expressed roughly the same notion by their use of *ṭuppišu* (especially when kings had no *limmu* period).

(341) Kinglist A ii 14′.

(342) Kinglist A iv 17.

(343) Kinglist A ii 8′, 9′, iii 2′. To date, (MU *1*) ITI *6* is the only number of months recorded; and its recurrence may indicate that it was a round number or stereotyped phrase for one official regnal year which did not last a full calendar year.

Thus we reach a relative chronology firmly established for the first two centuries and for the last quarter century with an uncertain period between them. ([344]) In the remaining portion of this chapter we will attempt to establish absolute dates corresponding to the relative year numbers given here for kings 1-20 and 33-38 and to see whether any absolute dates may be ascertained for the interval between.

Absolute Chronology

For this period we cannot determine any absolutely fixed date from Babylonian chronology alone. ([345]) As with the contemporary chronologies of most other Western Asiatic countries, absolute dating for Babylonia is entirely dependent on synchronisms with the Assyrian chronology of the time. Assyrian chronology, thanks to lengthy eponym lists which exist in numerous, corroborating copies, is the best-attested chronology in Western Asia for the first half of the first millennium B.C. It, in turn, is fixed chiefly by one event recorded towards the middle of the two hundred and sixty-odd consecutive years of eponyms: "In the month of Simanu, there took place a solar eclipse". ([346]) This eclipse, which occurred in the eponymy of Bur–sagale, has been dated to June 15, 763 B.C. (Julian); ([347]) and it serves as a reference point for determining absolute dates for most of the Neo-Assyrian eponymies, the reigns of the Assyrian kings of the first millennium, and—by means of synchronisms—the absolute chronology of Post–Kassite Babylonia.

Before proceeding to a discussion of the Babylonian-Assyrian synchronisms of the Post–Kassite period, we should note that, for the purposes of this study, we are accepting the dates proposed by Rowton ([348]) for the later Assyrian kings, i.e.,

([344]) Another potential element of uncertainty may be introduced if it is someday discovered that any of the early dynasties of this period either overlap or do not succeed one another immediately. As yet, however, there is no evidence for this. The only place where the present calculations would be slightly thrown off by this eventuality is in the small dynasties following the Second Dynasty of Isin and in kings 19-20. The Isin Dynasty itself is reasonably well anchored by synchronisms, as we shall presently see.

([345]) A possible reference to an eclipse of the sun in the Religious Chronicle (ii 14) has been discussed by Rowton in *Iraq* VIII (1946) 106-107. But this passage: (a) does not unmistakably refer to an eclipse (the day can be darkened by other causes, and the Babylonians had an unambiguous expression for recording an eclipse), (b) does not mention any king by name, though it mentions the seventh year and the twenty-sixth day of Simanu. (These difficulties were raised already by Winckler in *OLZ* X [1907] 593). Though Rowton's further calculations point out Simbar–Shipak as the most likely candidate for the unnamed king, his calculations are based on the twentieth rather than the twenty-sixth day. The interpretation of this passage is far too tenuous to provide a reference point for erecting an absolute chronology.

([346]) *I–na* ITI.SIG$_4$ ^{d}UTU AN.GE$_6$ GAR–*an* (*RLA* II 430 rev. 7).

([347]) The dating of the eclipse is discussed by Ungnad together with full bibliographical material in *RLA* II 414. See also F. X. Kugler, *SSB* II 333.

([348]) As adopted for the revised edition of *CAH* and briefly explained in *CAH* I^2 vi 32-35. Until the final bound edition of *CAH* is issued, a complete listing of the Assyrian dates according to this system may be found in Oppenheim, *Ancient Mesopotamia*, pp. 346-347.

from Ashur–uballit I (number 73: 1365-1330) (349) through Shalmaneser V (number 109: 726-722). (350)

Our first step in establishing an absolute chronology for Post–Kassite Babylonia will be to collect and analyze all the direct synchronisms between Assyrian and Babylonian rulers of the period. (351) These synchronisms are furnished by a variety of sources: (1) letters or treaties between the kings of the two countries, (2) annals of Assyrian kings which mention contemporary Babylonian rulers, (352) and (3) later chronicles, both Babylonian and Assyrian, describing events in Mesopotamia as taking place during the reigns of two identified, contemporary kings. (353) Synchronistic kinglists, for reasons of style discussed in the first chapter, are not sufficiently accurate to be used in exact calculations of this type.

The following is a list of attested Babylonian-Assyrian synchronisms of the Post–Kassite period together with the pertinent source references: (354)

1. Ninurta–nadin–shumi – Ashur–resha–ishi I
   Chronicle: *AfO* IV (1927) 215 rev. ii 7-19
2. Nebuchadnezzar I – Ashur–resha–ishi I
   Chronicle: *CT* XXXIV 39 ii 1′-13′ (=Syn. Hist.)
3. Marduk–nadin–ahhe – Tiglath–Pileser I
   Contemporary Annals: *AfO* XVIII (1957-58) 351:44-51
   Later Annals: *OIP* II 83:49-51 (Sennacherib)
   Chronicle: *CT* XXXIV 39 ii 14′-24′ (=Syn. Hist.)
4. Marduk–shapik–zeri – Ashur–bel–kala (355)
   Chronicles: *CT* XXXIV 39 ii 25′-30′ (=Syn. Hist.)
   CCEBK II 147:4-7 (=NB Chron.)
5. Adad–apla–iddina – Ashur–bel–kala
   Chronicles: *CT* XXXIV 39 ii 31′-37′ (=Syn. Hist.)
   CCEBK II 147 and 149:8-11 (=NB Chron.)

(349) *CAH* I² vi 34 mistakenly lists Ashur–uballit as ruling between 1365 and 1320. The latter figure is a misprint for 1330.

(350) The kings are numbered according to the system listed by Poebel in *JNES* II (1943) 87-88.

(351) By direct synchronism we mean an explicit statement in a cuneiform text which says that a specific Assyrian king and a specific Babylonian king were reigning at the same time.

(352) To which may be added the annalistic reference of a later Assyrian king to an event which occurred between one of his predecessors and a specified Babylonian monarch.

(353) When either one of the kings' names is in question, the synchronism will not be used.

(354) Additional abbreviations in the references: Bab. Chron. (Babylonian Chronicle), NB Chron. (New Babylonian Chronicle), Syn. Hist. (Synchronistic History).

(355) An implicit synchronism between Marduk–shapik–zeri and Tiglath–Pileser will be discussed below.

6. Shamash–mudammiq – Adad–nirari II ([356])
   Annals: *KAH* II 84:26-28
   Chronicle: *CT* XXXIV 40 iii 1-8 (=Syn. Hist.)

7. Nabu–shuma–ukin I – Adad–nirari II
   Chronicle: *CT* XXXIV 40 iii 9-21 (=Syn. Hist.)

8. Nabu–shuma–ukin I – Tukulti–Ninurta II
   Chronicle: *CCEBK* II 153:2 (= NB Chron.)

9. Nabu–apla–iddina – Ashurnasirpal II
   Annals: *AKA* 350 ff.: iii 15-20

10. Nabu–apla–iddina – Shalmaneser III
    Chronicle: *CT* XXXIV 40 iii 22-26 (=Syn. Hist.)
    Colophon: *JCS* XI (1957) 5 n. 21, etc.

11. Marduk–zakir–shumi I – Shalmaneser III
    Annals: *ICC* pl. 91:73-84, etc. ([357])
    Chronicle: *CT* XXXIV 40 iii 27-36 (=Syn. Hist.)

12. Marduk–zakir–shumi I – Shamshi–Adad V
    Treaty: *AfO* VIII (1932-33) 28:8, 10

13. Marduk–balassu–iqbi – Shamshi–Adad V
    Annals: *AfO* IX (1933-34) 93 and 95 iii 17 - iv 10
    I *R* 31 iii 70 - iv 45
    Chronicle: *CT* XXXIV 43 Sm. 2106 rev. 6′-8′ (=Syn. Hist.)

14. Baba–aha–iddina – Shamshi–Adad V
    Annals: *AfO* IX (1933-34) 95 iv 11-29

15. Nabonassar – Tiglath–Pileser III ([358])
    Chronicle: *CT* XXXIV 46 i 1-12 (=Bab. Chron.)

16. Nabu–nadin–zeri – Tiglath–Pileser III ([359])
    Chronicle: *CT* XXXIV 46 i 13-15 (=Bab. Chron.)

17. Nabu–shuma–ukin II – Tiglath–Pileser III
    Chronicle: *CT* XXXIV 46 i 16-17 (=Bab. Chron.)

([356]) Between synchronisms 5 and 6, Moortgat in *Ägypten und Vorderasien im Altertum*, p. 500, lists another synchronism between Kashshu–nadin–ahhe (*sic*) and Ashurnasirpal I. This is based solely on a synchronistic kinglist (Assur 14616c iii 4) and must be regarded as unproven.

([357]) Full references in note 1179 below.

([358]) Moortgat, *op. cit.*, p. 502, lists a synchronism between Eriba–Marduk and Shalmaneser IV. This is not attested in any Assyrian or Babylonian source known to me.

([359]) Synchronisms such as this in the better preserved portions of the Babylonian Chronicle are not stated in so many words but are so clear that they may safely be classified with explicit statements.

18. (Nabu)–mukin–zeri – Tiglath–Pileser III
Annals: II *R* 67:23-25
D.T. 3:16-19 (Rost, *TP III*, pl. XXXIV)
Chronicle: *CT* XXXIV 46-47 i 18-22 (=Bab. Chron.)

19. Tiglath–Pileser III – Tiglath–Pileser III
Chronicle: *CT* XXXIV 47 i 23-26 (=Bab. Chron.) ([360])

20. Shalmaneser V – Shalmaneser V
Chronicle: *CT* XXXIV 47 i 27-30 (=Bab. Chron.)

These twenty well-attested, direct synchronisms of the Post–Kassite period fall easily into three chronological groups as follows: ([361])

3. Ninurta–nadin–shumi	86. Ashur–resha–ishi I	C
4. Nebuchadnezzar I	86. Ashur–resha–ishi I	C
6. Marduk–nadin–ahhe	87. Tiglath–Pileser I	CA
7. Marduk–shapik–zeri	89. Ashur–bel–kala	C
8. Adad–apla–iddina	89. Ashur–bel–kala	C
22. Shamash–mudammiq	99. Adad–nirari II	CA
23. Nabu–shuma–ukin I	99. Adad–nirari II	C
23. Nabu–shuma–ukin I	100. Tukulti–Ninurta II	C
24. Nabu–apla–iddina	101. Ashurnasirpal II	A
24. Nabu–apla–iddina	102. Shalmaneser III	C
25. Marduk–zakir–shumi I	102. Shalmaneser III	CA
25. Marduk–zakir–shumi I	103. Shamshi–Adad V	T
26. Marduk–balassu–iqbi	103. Shamshi–Adad V	CA
27. Baba–aha–iddina	103. Shamshi–Adad V	A
33. Nabonassar	108. Tiglath–Pileser III	C
34. Nabu–nadin–zeri	108. Tiglath–Pileser III	C
35. Nabu–shuma–ukin II	108. Tiglath–Pileser III	C
36. (Nabu)–mukin–zeri	108. Tiglath–Pileser III	CA
37. Tiglath–Pileser III	108. Tiglath–Pileser III	CA
38. Shalmaneser V	109. Shalmaneser V	C

([360]) This synchronism, though attested only in the Babylonian Chronicle, is supported by information given in the eponym lists (*šarru qātē Bēl iṣṣabat, RLA* II 431:45) and in the titulary of some of the later annal editions of his reign (e.g., II *R* 67:1; Rost, *TP III*, pl. XXXIV 1).

([361]) Explanation of the table: in the left column are the Babylonian rulers, in the middle column the Assyrian kings. The number preceding the Babylonian monarchs is that already established in the first half of the chapter for their sequence in the Post–Kassite period; the number preceding the Assyrian kings is their standard Poebel number. The right column lists the type(s) of source(s) by which the synchronism is attested: *C* for chronicle(s), *A* for annals, *T* for treaty.

The first group lies roughly between the years 1133 and 1057; (362) its sources are almost exclusively chronicles. Despite the fact that two contacts between Marduk–nadin–ahhe and Tiglath–Pileser I are dated by eponymies, the incompleteness of the eponym canon at this point does not allow us to fix an absolute date for these events. Thus, despite all the direct synchronisms in the first group, we cannot obtain a single fixed date. Any absolute chronology in this period must be based on other calculations. (363)

The second group of synchronisms stretches approximately from the beginning to the end of the ninth century. Here chronicles and Assyrian royal annals furnish most of the information, but a treaty also enters as evidence here. Of the nine synchronisms in this group, four may be dated absolutely:

(1) 878: Nabu–apla–iddina – Ashurnasirpal II; the Assyrian campaign is dated in the eponymy of Dagan–bela–usur, (364) which is fixed by the eponym canon at 878; (365)

(2) 851-850: Marduk–zakir–shumi I – Shalmaneser III; Shalmaneser's annals record that his campaigns to help the Babylonian king against rebels were waged in the eighth and ninth years of his reign; (366)

(3) 814-813: Marduk–balassu–iqbi – Shamshi–Adad V; the two campaigns against the Babylonian king are dated by the eponym chronicle C^{b}1 to 814 and 813; (367)

(4) 812: Baba–aha–iddina – Shamshi–Adad V; this campaign is likewise dated by the eponym chronicle C^{b}1. (368)

The five other synchronisms do not mention any exact dates on either the Assyrian or the Babylonian side. Even those synchronisms which do admit of absolute dating give little information about Babylonian chronology save that certain Babylonian kings were reigning during the years in question. Only in the cases of Marduk–balassu–iqbi and Baba–aha–iddina is anything learned about the beginning or end of a reign: Marduk–balassu–iqbi was captured and taken away to Assyria most

(362) These dates represent the first official year of the reign of Ashur–resha–ishi I and the last year of the reign of Ashur–bel–kala.

(363) See pp. 74-76 below.

(364) *AKA* 346 iii 1. [The name of the eponym is possibly to be read *Dagan–bēla–uṣur*; see addenda].

(365) *RLA* II 418 (C^{a}2:15). As is the custom in most works dealing with this period, we designate each Assyro-Babylonian year with only one number, e.g., 878, rather than the technically more accurate double designation, e.g., 878/877. See Poebel's remarks in *JNES* I (1942) 289 n. 115.

(366) See pp. 194-196 below.

(367) *RLA* II 428 (C^{b}1:3-4). For a possible deviation of one year in these dates between 814 and 812, see note 1291 below.

(368) *RLA* II 428 (C^{b}1:5).

probably in the year 813, and hence Baba–aha–iddina's first official regnal year is quite likely to have been 812. (369) Thus, while the absolute chronology of the ninth century is slightly clarified by the synchronisms presently known, much more must be ascertained before we can date the individual reigns of the Babylonian kings with precision.

The third group of synchronisms, stemming mostly from the third quarter of the eighth century and based almost exclusively on the meticulously accurate Babylonian Chronicle, enables us to reach our only really satisfactory results in the realm of absolute chronology for the Post–Kassite period. In the following chart, we list to the left the information given by the Babylonian Chronicle as it now stands. In the right column, we place the restorations as calculated on the basis of other texts. (370)

Nabonassar: year [x] = acc. year of TP	year 3 = acc. year of TP
total reign = 14 years	year 14 = year 11 of TP
Nabu–nadin–zeri: total reign = 2 years	= years 12-13 of TP
Nabu–shuma–ukin: total reign = 2 months	= year 13 of TP
(Nabu)–mukin–zeri: total reign = 3 years	= years 14-16 of TP
Tiglath–Pileser: reign: 2 years (in Bab.)	= years 17-18 of TP
reign: [x] years (in Ass.)	= 18 years (371)

Then, since it is known from the eponym lists that Tiglath–Pileser's accession year in Assyria was 745 B.C., (372) the following absolute dates for kings number 33-38 are obtained:

33. Nabonassar	747-734
34. Nabu–nadin–zeri	733-732
35. Nabu–shuma–ukin II	732
36. (Nabu)–mukin–zeri	731-729
37. Tiglath–Pileser III	728-727
38. Shalmaneser V	726-722.

(369) In addition, it is not improbable that the revolt against Marduk–zakir–shumi I in Babylonia took place upon his accession, which would then make his first official regnal year either 851 or 850. Unfortunately, there is no explicit mention of his recent assumption of the throne in the texts referring to the revolt.

(370) Abbreviations in the chart: *acc.* for accession; *Ass.*: Assyria; *Bab.*: Babylonia; *TP*: Tiglath–Pileser III. The chart should be read (for the basis of argument) down the left-hand column and then up the right-hand column.

(371) In the Babylonian Chronicle, the space is left blank where the length of Tiglath–Pileser's reign was to be listed (*CT* XXXIV 47 i 25). The regnal years are restored on the basis of the SDAS Kinglist in *JNES* XIII (1954) 223 iv 25.

(372) *RLA* II 430 rev. 26-27.

We have now seen what information may be readily obtained about the absolute chronology of Babylonia in the Post–Kassite period from the study of direct synchronisms. For the ninth century we are able to calculate four absolute dates, of which only one concerns the end of one reign and the beginning of another. The latter half of the eighth century yields more satisfactory results, and we are able to date the official regnal years of the last six kings of the period with precision. The twelfth and eleventh centuries provide five synchronisms but not one certain fixed date. In the succeeding paragraphs, we shall attempt to remedy this last deficiency to some degree.

Let us look again at our chronological results for the early part of the Post–Kassite period. In Babylonia, we have a long sequence of 215 years and 20 kings, but no definite anchor for fixing the sequence at any point. In Assyria, however, reasonably accurate fixed dates have been calculated for the reigns of the kings from the late fifteenth century till the time of Ashurbanipal in the late seventh century. ([373]) Therefore, because of the five established synchronisms between Babylonian and Assyrian rulers in the early Post–Kassite period, there is at least a basis for calculating the relative mobility of that long block of twenty Babylonian reigns. The block can only be moved so early in time without upsetting at least one of the synchronisms with Assyrian rulers and only so late in time without achieving a similar result. We shall now determine what are the chronological limits for the Babylonian kings in question if all the synchronisms are to be fulfilled. ([374])

First, before proceeding to our calculations, we should advert to one additional piece of information, touched upon briefly earlier in the chapter. Besides the five explicit synchronisms pertaining to the early part of the Post–Kassite period, there is another synchronism which, though only implicit, is nonetheless valid and of considerable help for our calculations. This is the mention of Tiglath–Pileser I in a chronicle, a type of document which normally records events in strictly chronological order, ([375]) in an entry immediately following one which deals with the death

([373]) See pp. 68-69 above.

([374]) Most previous methods used for determining absolute dates for the initial rulers of the Post–Kassite period have been invalidated in recent years. Relying on an assumption that kings Adad–shuma–usur of Babylonia and Enlil–kudurri–usur of Assyria were killed in the same battle, past chronologers had computed dates in the early part of the Post–Kassite period by dead reckoning from dates towards the close of the preceding Kassite period. When Tadmor in *JNES* XVII (1958) 131-132 proved that the theory of the almost simultaneous deaths of Adad–shuma–usur and Enlil–kudurri–usur was based on an erroneous translation of a passage in the Synchronistic History, the foundations for previous chronological arguments—including Poebel's in *AS* XV—were effectively destroyed. The whole question of Post–Kassite chronology must be thought out on a new basis.

([375]) There are minor exceptions to this rule. In the first column of the Synchronistic History (i 1′-7′, the eighth-century Assyrian compiler reversed the actual chronological order of the first two events preserved, presumably because he confused Burnaburiash (I/II), successor of Agum (II), with Burnaburiash (II/III), successor of Kadashman–Enlil I. In the Religious Chronicle, events within a single king's reign

of Marduk–nadin–ahhe and the accession of Marduk–shapik–zeri. This arrangement implies that Tiglath-Pileser's reign extended into that of Marduk–shapik–zeri and that, therefore, the two kings were contemporaries for at least a short time.

We have six synchronisms, then, to work into our chronological calculations and must now determine the chronological limits within which each of the six can be true. In the left-hand columns of the following chart, we have placed the Assyrian kings involved in each of the synchronisms and their dates according to Rowton; in the right-hand columns, we have placed the maximal and minimal dates possible for the reigns of the Babylonian kings when all six synchronisms are satisfied. The dates given in the chart are *not* just official regnal years but include the accession year of each king as well, since some of the synchronisms could plausibly have taken place at any time during the reign.

Assyria		**Babylonia**	**Maximum**	**Minimum**
Ashur–resha–ishi I	1134-1116	Ninurta–nadin–shumi	1138-1132	1128-1122
		Nebuchadnezzar I	1132-1110	1122-1100
Tiglath–Pileser I	1116-1077	Marduk–nadin–ahhe	1106-1088	1096-1078
		Marduk–shapik–zeri	1088-1075	1078-1065
Ashur–bel–kala	1075-1057	Adad–apla–iddina	1075-1053	1065-1043

If the maximum figures for the Babylonian kings are shifted one year earlier, then the synchronism between Ashur–bel–kala and Marduk–shapik–zeri is ruled out; if the minimum figures for the Babylonian kings are shifted one year later, then the synchronism between Tiglath–Pileser I and Marduk–shapik–zeri cannot be properly maintained. ([376]) Thus we are able to fix the absolute chronology of these kings and, as a consequence, the absolute chronology of the whole 215-year block of the first 20 kings of the Post–Kassite period within a range of ten years; ([377])

	Maximum Date of Reign	**Minimum Date of Reign**
1. Marduk–kabit–ahheshu	1163-1146	1153-1136
20. Ninurta–kudurri–usur II	949	939

---

are not always listed in strictly chronological order (e.g., iii 10′-11′). The apparent exception in Chronicle P, when Adad–shuma–usur (iv 9) is mentioned before Enlil–nadin–shumi (iv 14, 16) and Adad–shuma–iddina (iv 17), is explained in note 332 above.

([376]) According to the scheme of the chronicle (*AfO* XVII [1954-56] 384), Tiglath–Pileser could not have died before Marduk–shapik–zeri's first official regnal year.

([377]) With the reservations expressed in note 344 above, we resume the practice of listing reigns by official regnal years here.

Thus, while we do not arrive at absolutely fixed dates accurate down to the year, we do reach a serviceable chronology for the period with a rather slight margin of error. (378) Since it would prove unwieldy to refer to a date in every instance by its maximum and minimum figures, we shall abbreviate our references to dates in the first two hundred and fifteen years of the Post–Kassite period in the following manner: Nabu–shumu–libur, 1034*-1027* (the asterisked dates being understood as medial, i.e., subject to a possible fluctuation of five years up or down on the absolute scale). (379)

We are now ready to construct a chronological table for the Post–Kassite period (see plate II opposite). (380)

M. B. Rowton in *CAH* I² vi 34-35 uses a different method of reckoning absolute dates for the Second Isin Dynasty and reaches slightly different results: each reign is dated two years later, with a margin of error of five years either way. Rowton reasons from the implicit synchronism between Ashared–apil–Ekur of Assyria (1076-1075) and Marduk–shapik–zeri, which may be deduced from the explicit synchronisms between Marduk–shapik–zeri and the predecessor and successor of Ashared–apil–Ekur. He asserts, therefore, that Ashared–apil–Ekur's reign was entirely within the time span of that of Marduk–shapik–zeri. Furthermore, it is known from the Assyrian chronicle published in *AfO* XVII (1954-56) 384 that Ashared–apil–Ekur's first official year was equivalent to Marduk–shapik–zeri's second official year—at the earliest. (381) Rowton then reasons:

> And though not certain, it is at least probable that the first four years of the next Assyrian king, Ashur–bel–kala, come before the death of Marduk–shapik–zeri. For we have the annals of the first four years of an Assyrian king who is very probably Ashur–bel–kala, and enough of the damaged text is preserved to show that the intervention of Ashur–bel–kala in Babylonia at the death of Marduk–shapik–zeri was probably not mentioned in any of the four years covered by this text. (382)

Rowton then concludes that the two-year reign of Ashared–apil–Ekur "very probably" comes within the interval between the second and ninth year of Marduk–shapik–zeri. He then equates the years 1076 and 1075 with the fifth and sixth years

(378) Presuming, of course, that our sources in their present state are accurate and our interpretations of them here have been correct.

(379) The king in question could have ruled as early as 1039-1032 or as late as 1029-1022.

(380) It should be noted that the dates in this table for Babylonian kings 1-21 (1158*-943*) are two years higher than those accepted in the revised edition of the *Cambridge Ancient History* and those listed by me in Oppenheim, *Ancient Mesopotamia*, p. 339 (i.e., 1156-941). The latter dates could have been used here, but only with the qualification that they could be raised as much as seven years or lowered as much as three years according to the present calculations. It therefore seemed simpler to specify median dates with a five-year margin of possible change either way. The dates for the contemporary Assyrian kings are the same in both systems.

(381) Because Tiglath–Pileser I outlived Marduk–nadin–ahhe by at least one year.

(382) *CAH* I² vi 34.

R THE POST-KASSITE PERIOD

Babylonia

1.	Marduk–kabit–ahheshu	1158*-1141*	18 yrs.
2.	Itti–Marduk–balatu	1140*-1133*	8 yrs.
3.	Ninurta–nadin–shumi	1132*-1127*	6 yrs.
4.	Nebuchadnezzar I	1126*-1105*	22 yrs.
5.	Enlil–nadin–apli	1104*-1101*	4 yrs.
6.	Marduk–nadin–ahhe	1100*-1083*	18 yrs.
7.	Marduk–shapik–zeri	1082*-1070*	13 yrs.
8.	Adad–apla–iddina	1069*-1048*	22 yrs.
9.	Marduk–ah[he–eriba]	1047*	1 yr.
10.	Marduk–zer?–x	1046*-1035*	12 yrs.
11.	Nabu–shumu–libur	1034*-1027*	8 yrs.
12.	Simbar–Shipak	1026*-1009*	18 yrs.
13.	Ea–mukin–zeri	1009*	5 mos.
14.	Kashshu–nadin–ahi	1008*-1006*	3 yrs.
15.	Eulmash–shakin–shumi	1005*-989*	17 yrs.
16.	Ninurta–kudurri–usur I	988*-986*	3 yrs.
17.	Shirikti–Shuqamuna	986*	3 mos.
18.	Mar–biti–apla–usur	985*-980*	6 yrs.
19.	Nabu–mukin–apli	979*-944*	36 yrs.
20.	Ninurta–kudurri–usur II	944*	8 mos. 12 da.
21.	Mar–biti–ahhe–iddina	943*-	
22.	Shamash–mudammiq (383)	-900(±9)	
23.	Nabu–shuma–ukin I (384)	899(±9) -888(+3-4)	13 (+12-13) yrs.
24.	Nabu–apla–iddina (385)	887(+3-4)-855(+3-4)	37 (+3-4) yrs.
25.	Marduk–zakir–shumi I (386)	854(+3-4)-819(±5)	31 (+3-4) yrs.
26.	Marduk–balassu–iqbi (387)	818(+5-6)-813(-1)	6 (±5) yrs.
27.	Baba–aha–iddina (388)	812(-1)	
	(interregnum; unknown kings?)		
28.	Ninurta–apl?–[x]		
29.	Marduk–bel–zeri		
30.	Marduk–apla–usur	-770(+)	
31.	Eriba–Marduk (389)	769(+)-761(+)	9(+) yrs.
32.	Nabu–shuma–ishkun (390)	760(+)-748	13(+) yrs.
33.	Nabonassar	747-734	14 yrs.
34.	Nabu–nadin–zeri	733-732	2 yrs.
35.	Nabu–shuma–ukin II	732	1 mo. 13 da.
36.	Nabu–mukin–zeri (391)	731-729	3 yrs.
37.	Tiglath–Pileser III/Pulu (392)	728-727	2 yrs.
38.	Shalmaneser V/Ululaju (393)	726-722	5 yrs.

---

(389) The latest possible date for his first regnal year is 769, because the economic text BM 40548 is dated in his ninth year; see also note 390 below.

(390) His last regnal year is known with certainty. Because the economic text *BRM* I 3 is dated in his thirteenth year, the latest date for his first official year is 760. Of course, a number of years could be added to that date, should it be proved that he had reigned longer.

(391) We have discussed the text dated in this king's fourth year (*BRM* I 22:12-13) above p. 61.

(392) Equal to the last two years of his reign in Assyria.

(393) Co-extensive with his reign in Assyria.

Assyria

83.	Ashur–dan I	1179-1134	46 yrs.
84.	Ninurta–tukulti–Ashur	1134	0 yrs.
85.	Mutakkil–Nusku	1134	0 yrs.
86.	Ashur–resha–ishi I	1133-1116	18 yrs.
87.	Tiglath–Pileser I	1115-1077	39 yrs.
88.	Ashared–apil–Ekur	1076-1075	2 yrs.
89.	Ashur–bel–kala	1074-1057	18 yrs.
90.	Eriba–Adad II	1056-1055	2 yrs.
91.	Shamshi–Adad IV	1054-1051	4 yrs.
92.	Ashurnasirpal I	1050-1032	19 yrs.
93.	Shalmaneser II	1031-1020	12 yrs.
94.	Ashur–nirari IV	1019-1014	6 yrs.
95.	Ashur–rabi II	1013-973	41 yrs.
96.	Ashur–resha–ishi II	972-968	5 yrs.
97.	Tiglath–Pileser II	967-935	33 yrs.
98.	Ashur–dan II	934-912	23 yrs.
99.	Adad–nirari II	911-891	21 yrs.
100.	Tukulti–Ninurta II	890-884	7 yrs.
101.	Ashurnasirpal II	883-859	25 yrs.
102.	Shalmaneser III	858-824	35 yrs.
103.	Shamshi–Adad V	823-811	13 yrs.
104.	Adad–nirari III	810-783	28 yrs.
105.	Shalmaneser IV	782-773	10 yrs.
106.	Ashur–dan III	772-755	18 yrs.
107.	Ashur–nirari V	754-745	10 yrs.
108.	Tiglath–Pileser III	744-727	18 yrs.
109.	Shalmaneser V	726-722	5 yrs.

---

(383) The margin of error possible for each king's regnal years is indicated in parentheses after the year date. Thus, 900 (±9) means that Shamash–mudammiq's last official regnal year could have been as early as 909 or as late as 891 without contradicting the evidence available. Because of his synchronism with Adad–nirari II in one of that king's early campaigns after 910 (*KAH* II 84:26-28), we know that he must have been on the throne for one of the years from 909 to 902.

(384) Nabu–shuma–ukin I was a contemporary of both Adad–nirari II and Tukulti–Ninurta II, so he must have been ruling in the year 891. He could not have come to the throne earlier than 909 (accession year) because of his predecessor's synchronism with Adad–nirari II. He could not have ruled longer than 884 (last official year) because his successor's reign of 33 years must have terminated at the latest in 851.

(385) The termini of his reign are determined by his father's synchronism with Tukulti–Ninurta II and his son's synchronism with Shalmaneser III in 851; he reigned at least 33 years (note 250).

(386) Because of Nabu–apla–iddina's 33(+)-year reign, Marduk–zakir–shumi's first official year could not have been before 857. He must have ruled till at least the accession year of Shamshi–Adad V (824) and possibly longer.

(387) The earliest date for his accession year could be 824 because of his father's synchronism with Shamshi–Adad V; the latest date for his accession year would be either 814 or 813 because Shamshi–Adad campaigned against him in Babylonia in one of those years. For the one-year uncertainty in dates between 814 and 812, see note 1291 below.

(388) His first regnal year was probably also his last, since he was captured by the Assyrian Shamshi–Adad V in his campaign of 812(–1).

of Marduk–shapik–zeri, "which is in all probability subject to a margin of error of only three years either way." (394) Adding a year or two for possible error in the date of Ashared–apil–Ekur, he arrives at a date of 1080-1068 for the reign of Marduk–shapik–zeri, with a margin of error of five years either way.

The only major difficulty with this reconstruction lies in its interpretation of the annals which are usually attributed to Ashur–bel–kala. (395) First, the text is very badly damaged—so much so that we cannot tell either against what region the second campaign was conducted or where the first action of the third campaign was fought. (396) If there was any mention of intervention in Babylonia in these years, we would not know it from the text as it is presently preserved. Second, on the basis of parallels with other Assyrian annals, there is no indication that such intervention—if it did take place (397)—would have been mentioned at all, especially if it did not require a campaign to instate the Babylonian king. Tukulti–Ninurta I took over Babylonia completely, but his annals are entirely silent as to whether he himself personally assumed control or whether he appointed puppet kings. (398) Tiglath–Pileser III in 745 marched through northern Babylonia with his army, but mentioned nothing about his relationship with the nominally reigning Babylonian monarch Nabonassar. (399) Later in 728, when Tiglath–Pileser III ascended the throne in Babylon itself, he did not recount his accession, but simply assumed the title "king of Babylonia" in his inscriptions. (400) Assyrian kings before Sargon II were quite reticent about their political meddling with the Babylonian monarchy—either when they assumed the throne themselves or when they raised their supporters to the kingship. (401)

(394) *CAH* I² vi 35.

(395) Published by Weidner in *AfO* VI (1930-31) 75-94.

(396) *AfO* VI (1930-31) 86.

(397) Intervention is postulated on the basis of the subjectless singular *iškun* (Synchronistic History ii 32′), which is usually interpreted as referring back over an intervening sentence (of which Marduk–shapik–zeri is the subject) to Ashur–bel–kala (ii 29′), whose name occurs in the genitive case in the phrase "in the time of Ashur–bel–kala, king of Assyria." The New Babylonian Chronicle calls the Babylonian king installed at this time a usurper (*šar ḫammā'i*, obv. 8′).

(398) Chronicle P would seem to favor the installation of puppet kings, since Adad–shuma–usur is listed as Tukulti–Ninurta's successor (iv 9). This would imply that the three intervening monarchs between Kashtiliash IV and Adad–shuma–usur (iv 14ff.) were regarded as kings during the Assyrian period of suzerainty. Note that inscriptions written after Tukulti–Ninurta's victory over Babylonia (Weidner, *Tn. I*, nos. 5 and 16) do not mention Tukulti–Ninurta's provisions for governing the land.

(399) See p. 231 below.

(400) E.g., Rost, *TP III*, pl. XXIX 2 (Second Nimrud Slab).

(401) Shalmaneser III is the only Assyrian king during these times who makes a definite statement about his interference with the Babylonian monarchy. In the inscription carved on the throne base recently found at Nimrud, he says *Marduk–zākir–šumi ina kussī abišu ukīn* (*Iraq* XXV [1963] 56:46). Considering that a rebellion against Marduk–zakir–shumi had been mentioned in the preceding portion of the text, one should probably translate: "I confirmed Marduk–zakir–shumi('s position) on his father's throne."

Related Problems

Before proceeding to the treatment of the political history of the Post–Kassite period in the next chapter, however, we will touch briefly upon two minor problems connected with the chronology of the period: (1) the Elamite interregnum which some scholars would interpose between the Kassite Dynasty and the Second Dynasty of Isin, and (2) the *Distanzangaben* specifically connected with this period.

With regard to the Elamite interregnum we should first remark that by interregnum here we mean a period of time amounting to at least one official year in which no king recognized by the canonical kinglists occupied the throne. (402) A period of less than one official year would not be reckoned in Babylonian chronology, as we have seen; so it may be disregarded here. To establish an interregnum in Babylonian chronology, we would have to satisfy the following conditions: (1) between two rulers generally regarded as consecutive (403) there must be a clear chronological gap, and (2) this gap must amount to at least one official year.

Because of the style employed in documents like Kinglist A, interregna cannot be established from them alone. (404) On the contrary, there are several examples where rulers proposed as consecutive in kinglists actually overlap in time. (405) It is obvious then that dynasties and rulers listed as consecutive in a Babylonian kinglist need not necessarily be so. But overlaps or interregna must be demonstrated clearly from outside sources either by showing synchronisms between supposedly consecutive monarchs or by demonstrating a gap between two supposedly consecutive rulers. The latter may be done in at least two ways: (a) by showing that the monarchs actually ruled too far apart in terms of absolute or relative dating to satisfy the conditions imposed by the kinglist, or (b) by proving that a ruler unmentioned in the kinglist occupied the throne for at least one year *between* them.

The last serious argument for an Elamite interregnum between the Kassite Dynasty and the Second Dynasty of Isin before the publication of the new material in Kinglist C was made by Ungnad in 1944. (406) Basing his conclusions on (1) the

(402) The kinglists could conceivably either omit the period entirely from their calculation or, like the "Ptolemaic Canon", refer to such a period as x years ἀβασίλευτα.

(403) I.e., placed one after the other in the kinglist tradition, whether belonging to the same dynasty or not.

(404) The Babylonian cuneiform kinglists never mention an interregnum.

(405) Besides the numerous examples in the Sumerian Kinglist, the first three Babylonian dynasties—listed as consecutive by Kinglist A—are known from other sources to have been partially concurrent.

(406) Ungnad, "Zur Geschichte und Chronologie des zweiten Reiches von Isin," *Orientalia N.S.* XIII (1944) 73-101.

end of the Kassite Dynasty in 1160, (407) (2) the regnal years of the first two kings of the Post–Kassite period as attested in Kinglist A, (408) (3) the pre-Kinglist-C reconstruction of the sequence of the first seven kings of the Second Dynasty of Isin, and strengthening his mathematical deductions by (4) III *R* 38 no. 2, (409) which may have alluded to an Elamite interregnum, Ungnad postulated a seven-year rule by the Elamite Kudur–Nahhunte in Babylon to satisfy the otherwise attested Assyro-Babylonian synchronisms of the period. (410)

Poebel, when publishing Kinglist C in 1955, saw no need to postulate an interregnum between the Kassite and Second Isin Dynasties and listed them as strictly consecutive. (411) Weidner, when reviewing Poebel's study in the following year, chided him for neglecting Ungnad's article and especially for not mentioning his "wohlbegrundete Annahme, dass zwischen der Kassiten-Dynastie und der Zweiten Dynastie von Isin eine elamische Fremdherrschaft einzuschieben ist, die in der Königsliste A mit Stillschweigen übergangen wird." (412) This stricture was not entirely deserved since, although Poebel had failed to notice Ungnad's article on other points, one of Ungnad's major arguments had already collapsed when the real sequence of the early kings of the Second Isin Dynasty was ascertained and Itti–Marduk–balatu shown to be the second king. Eight full years had then been added to the chronology of the dynasty before the beginning of the reign of Nebuchadnezzar I, and the need for postulating a seven-year Elamite interregnum had utterly vanished.

In 1958, Tadmor effectively demolished any shred of accuracy remaining in Ungnad's mathematical calculations, when he showed that there was no philological basis for the supposed simultaneous deaths of Enlil–kudurri–usur and Adad–shuma–usur. (413) In the same article, however, he revived the idea of the Elamite interregnum: "Another interregnum in Babylon after the end of the Kassite dynasty has to be inferred from the self-report in the *narû*-style K. 2660 (III, *R* 38, no. 2)...." (414) Tadmor made no estimate of how long such an interregnum might have lasted, but contented himself with the observation: "The assumption of an interregnum between the last Kassite king and the first king of the second Isin Dynasty, as short

(407) Established on the basis of the supposed deaths of Enlil–kudurri–usur and Adad–shuma–usur in one and the same battle in 1192.

(408) I.e., 17 (years) and 6 (years) rather than the 18 and 8 given by Kinglist C.

(409) The poetic text presumably written in the name of Nebuchadnezzar I which describes the downfall of the last Kassite rulers.

(410) I.e., the synchronisms already discussed at length above, save for the Tiglath–Pileser I—Marduk–shapik–zeri synchronism (known only since 1956).

(411) *AS* XV 28.

(412) *AfO* XVII (1954-56) 384.

(413) Tadmor, "Historical Implications of the Correct Rendering of Akkadian *dâku*," *JNES* XVII (1958) 129-141.

(414) *Ibid.*, 137.

as it may have been, is unavoidable; even if the direct allusion to a governor (not king) in line 14 [i.e., of K. 2660] should not be confirmed." ([415])

This opinion may be modified somewhat. Line 14′ of the pertinent text reads: "[ ] ⌜*la*⌝ *nab–nit Ba–bi–*⌜*li ge–ri–e*⌝ [x x x]." ([416]) The isolated reference to an individual who is "not a native of Babylon, (but) an enemy [ ]" can refer to anyone, even to Kudur–Nahhunte himself. There are no positive grounds for saying that this line must refer to a non-Babylonian governor installed in Babylon by the Elamite king. Such a reconstruction is not ruled out by the context: the document is too badly broken to preclude such a possibility. But a serious gap in the chronology of Babylonia cannot be proposed on such slim and ambiguous evidence. Therefore, I wish to bring forth other evidence which may bear on the question of an Elamite interregnum at this time. ([417])

Another text, hitherto undiscussed in this connection, may now be brought into the picture. In the third of the so-called Kedor–laomer texts, there is a poetic passage which might touch on the same events which took place upon the demise of the Kassite Dynasty in Babylonia. The passage is worth citing in full, since it apparently refers to the judgment of the gods regarding Babylon at the time of Kudur–Nahhunte's victory over the Kassites.

(6) *ina mil–ki–šú–nu ki–nim ana* ^{m}KU.KU.KU.KU.GÁ LUGAL KUR *E–la–*[*mat*]

(7) *ú–kan–nu–ú rid–di ga–na šá* UGU–*šú–nu ṭa–a–bi* ⌜x⌝ [x] ([418])

(8) *ina* E.KI URU *Kár–*^{d}*dun–iá–àš* LUGAL–*tam ip–pu–uš* [ ]

(9) *ina* DIN.TIR.KI URU LUGAL DINGIR.MEŠ ^{d}AMAR.UTU *id–du–ú* GIŠ.[GU.ZA–*šú?*]

(10) *su–kul–lum u* UR.BAR.RA *ḫab–ba–a–tú i–ma–ag–ga–*[*ru* x]

(11) *kun–šil–lu!*(text:–*ku*) *ki–i–nu a–ri–bi mut–tap–ri–šu i–ra–m*[*u*]

(12) *i–*ma_5*–gàr a–ri–bi* MUŠ *mut!*(text: *ḫu*)*–tab–bi–ik mar–tum* [ ]

(13) UR.KU *ka–si–is* ⌜GÌR⌝.PAD.DA *i–ma–ag–ga–ár* ^{d}NI[N.KILIM]

(14) ⌜*i*⌝*–*ma_5*–gàr* MUŠ.ḪUŠ LÚ *ḫab–ba–a–tum ta–bi–ik d*[*a–mi*]

(15) [*a*]*–a–ú* LUGAL KUR *E–la–mat šá iz–nun–nu* É.SAG.GÍL *ú–*⌜*x*⌝–[*x*]

(16) [*ki–d*]*in?* LÚ.DUMU.MEŠ E.KI *iš–ku–nu–ma šip–ru–šu–nu i–*[*x x*]

([415]) *Ibid.*, 139.

([416]) Transliteration made on the basis of personal collation of the tablet.

([417]) I do not disagree with Tadmor's general conclusion concerning the temporary rule of Elam over Babylon at the close of the Kassite Dynasty. But I am not convinced that this reign would constitute an interregnum in the strict sense defined above.

([418]) The number of signs missing at the end of the line cannot be determined from the state of the tablet. From the fact that most of the lines make complete sense with very little or no restoration, one may surmise that the text is almost totally preserved.

(6) With their true counsel, (the gods) determined the course of Kudur-Nahhunte, the king of Elam:
(7) "Now, one who is pleasing to them (i.e., the gods)...
(8) shall reign in Babylon, the city of Karduniash....
(9) (For) in Babylon, the city of Marduk, king of the gods, (the gods) have set up [his throne].
(10) Can cattle and rapacious wolf come to terms with one another?
(11) Can the stationary plant(?) [419] and the flitting crow love one another?
(12) Can the crow come to terms with the poisonous serpent?
(13) Can the bone-gnawing dog come to terms with the mon[goose]?
(14) Can the dragon come to terms with the brigand who sheds [blood]?
(15) What king of Elam is there who has endowed Esagil...?
(16) [or has cared for] the Babylonians, or [ ] their works? [420]

The burden of the passage is the judgment of the gods that no Elamite can reign over Babylon. [421] Kudur-Nahhunte can never be considered as king because of the inherent contradiction between the notions of a true Babylonian ruler and of an Elamite prince (stressed in the vivid metaphors of lines 10-14). No Elamite king will endow Babylonian temples nor care for the welfare of Babylonian citizens (lines 15-16). Only one who is pleasing to the gods can rule in the city where Marduk, king of the gods, holds sway (lines 7-9). This forceful exclusion of even the possibility of an Elamite ruling as king in the capital city cannot help but raise the question in our minds as to what caused the verbal outburst. The most probable explanation is that the passage is to be interpreted as a *vaticinium ex eventu*—an indication that the Elamite, Kudur-Nahhunte, actually did exercise power over the city in her darkest hour. The later Babylonian tradition repudiated any notion of his having been a real king of Babylonia on grounds of theological incompatibility; but that he at one time controlled the city seems clear. [422]

My purpose in calling this passage to the attention of the reader is to forestall any difficulties which might arise from some future interpretation of it as a con-

[419] The *kunšillu*, an instrument used for carding (*AHw* 507b), may like the English teasel also refer to a plant, if this passage is any indication.

[420] The text is taken from the obverse of Sp. II 987, published in *MVAG* XXI (1916) 92-95 as the third of the Kedor-laomer texts. The corrections are made after personal collation of the text in the British Museum. I am grateful to Professor Landsberger for his help in translating and restoring lines 10-16 of this passage; the interpretation presented for the section is my responsibility.

[421] G. Cameron, *History of Early Iran*, pp. 110-111, interpreted the passage in exactly the opposite sense.

[422] Cf. III *R* 38 no. 2, where Kudur-Nahhunte appears to be entrusted with power over Akkad (lines 2′ ff.).

vincing proof for an Elamite interregnum at this point. I am not denying the Elamite control over the city of Babylon at the end of the Kassite period. This fact is fairly well substantiated by the two texts, III *R* 38 no. 2 and the Kedor-laomer document just cited; and it is further borne out by the removal of the Marduk statue from Esagila by the Elamites at this time. But such Elamite control does not constitute an interregnum in the sense defined above.

First of all, the text gives no indication as to how long such a reign might have lasted: a few months (and therefore not long enough to occupy an official year) or a few years? Secondly, since we can date neither the end of the Kassite Dynasty nor the beginning of the Isin Dynasty with certainty, we cannot say that sufficient time elapsed between the two dates to constitute an interregnum. On the contrary, we have no assurance that the opposite was not the case: that the first ruler of the Isin Dynasty might not have counted his reign from the time at which he first exercised independence (423)—possibly at some point within the last four years of official Kassite rule. In that case, even though an Elamite may have governed the city of Babylon for a time after the deposition of Enlil-nadin-ahi, (424) no interregnum need enter into our chronological calculations since the dynastic totals themselves would have to be telescoped in order to obtain a true chronology.

What is needed most at this juncture is a few well-attested synchronisms between the various Babylonian regimes at this time. If we could establish that some Elamite ruler exercised power in Babylon for a definite number of years after the removal of the last Kassite and then establish that the first official regnal year of Marduk-kabit-ahheshu began after the removal of the Elamite, we would have an interregnum in the strict sense. If, however, there are only poetic references to the fact that the Elamites were in control of Babylon for a totally unknown period of time after the last Kassite and if there is no way yet of ascertaining whether the first regnal year of Marduk-kabit-ahheshu was reckoned from his first assertion of independence under the dying Kassite rule or from the end of the last official Kassite regnal year or from the close of a supposed Elamite reign in the land, then we can hardly assume that an Elamite interregnum—much less one of seven years duration—*must* be inserted into the chronology at this point. The question of the chronological relationship between the end of the Kassite Dynasty and the beginning of the Second Dynasty of Isin must be left open at present. Neither overlap nor consecution nor interregnum has been demonstrated; nor have any of these alternatives been ruled out. But, since the absolute chronology given here has been

(423) Like Ishbi-Erra of Isin and Naplanum of Larsa while Ibbi-Sin of the Third Dynasty of Ur was still on the throne.

(424) Compare the temporary control of the Elamites over Ur at the end of Ur III.

calculated entirely independently of the end of the Kassite Dynasty, it remains untouched by these considerations. (425)

The last topic for discussion in this chapter is the *Distanzangaben* relating to this period and how they fit into the chronological picture. We have, to date, two such *Distanzangaben*: (1) a statement in the kudurru *BE* I/1 83 that the time which elapsed from Gulkishar, a king of the First Dynasty of the Sealand, to Nebuchadnezzar I was 696 years; (426) (2) a statement by Sennacherib in the Bavian inscription that the gods of Ekallate were in Babylon for 418 years from the time when they were stolen by Marduk–nadin–ahhe (in the time of Tiglath–Pileser I) till the time of their recovery by Sennacherib. (427) A third *Distanzangabe* may have originally been intended in Kinglist C, lines 8-9; (428) but the text is in such poor condition that all one can read is "500 years from... before Marduk–shapik–zeri." (429)

The first of these instances, as noted long ago by Thureau-Dangin (430) and recently repeated by Poebel, (431) probably represents an artificial calculation by a scribe on the basis of the canonical kinglists, in which it is assumed that the First Sealand and Kassite Dynasties were consecutive. The scribe would have had the following figures available:

120 yrs. for the last five kings of the First Sealand Dynasty,
576 yrs. for the entire Kassite Dynasty, and
54 yrs. for the first four kings of the Second Isin Dynasty.

(425) Save that we cannot be reproached for ignoring the end of the Kassite Dynasty as a possible basis for computing the start of the Second Dynasty of Isin. In the present state of our knowledge, such a point of reference cannot be utilized safely.

(426) *BE* I/1 83:6-8.

(427) *OIP* II 83:50.

(428) See already Poebel, *AS* XV 29-41.

(429) Suggestions have been made for reading this difficult passage. Von Soden (*WZKM* LV [1959] 156) proposed that the lacuna in the line be restored in some such way as "the return of the Marduk statue." Although the reading of this section of the tablet is complicated both because of decay of grain particles in its surface and because—due to the curvature of the tablet—the runover from rev. 1 runs directly into the runover from obv. 5 (a conflict not shown in Poebel's copy in *AS* XV 3), the extant traces do not favor a restoration of ⌈dAMAR.UTU⌉ or ⌈dEN⌉ in the pertinent line (personal collation).

D. O. Edzard in *ZA* LIII (1959) 309 and n. 4 suggested very tentatively that the lines might be interpreted as giving a total for the dynasty: "75(!) years, Isin before (Marduk–shapik–zeri)." In answer to the specific inquiries raised by Edzard, our recent collation of the tablet has shown: (a) the PAB sign at the beginning of rev. 1 is not composed of DIŠ+U (i.e., 70), but of a clear horizontal wedge with a very light oblique stroke crossing it; (b) the initial Winkelhaken of the UL is separated from the final wedges of the MEŠ by a short space and is considerably larger than them in size; (c) the two final Winkelhaken at the end of UL and the two at the beginning of TU are separated in such a way that the spacing does not make the reading ŠE likely; (d) the final traces of TU in rev. 1 and the sign KI in obv. 2 do not represent the same sign. Edzard is quite right in reiterating Poebel's doubt whether the traces after *ul–tu* actually represent writing by the scribe; it is quite possible that the phrase was never completed on the original.

(430) *RA* XXIV (1927) 186.

(431) *AS* XV 30 n. 94.

The scribe, however, forgot to add on the figure for the first kings of the Isin Dynasty and thus announced his total for the first two numbers alone. (432) This date, in any case, is hardly usable for our purposes. (433)

The second dating, that contained in the Bavian inscription, was calculated by one of Sennacherib's scribes and could presumably have been based on one of the extant copies of the Assyrian kinglist or on one of the eponym lists. The Bavian text states that 418 years elapsed between Marduk–nadin–ahhe's theft of the statues of Adad and Shala and the return of the same statues to Ekallate by Sennacherib. Our interpretation of this date naturally hinges on the determination of the point in Sennacherib's reign from which the 418 years are to be reckoned. (434) From the context of the Bavian inscription, it seems that the removal of Adad and Shala took place after the fall of Babylon, which is to be dated on the first day of the ninth month (Kislimu) in 689. (435) If the divine statues were removed within the first four months after the capture of the city, then 689 should be taken as the primary reference point; and this would place the theft by Marduk–nadin–ahhe in 1107, one year before the earliest possible date for his accession. (436) If, however, the return of the statues took place slightly later, in 688 or 687, the original theft would have occurred in 1106 or 1105, very early in the reign of Marduk–nadin–ahhe. (437) Thus one can see that the accuracy of the Bavian *Distanzangabe* lies within the realm of present possibility, albeit close to the upper limits of that possibility. (438)

(432) It is, of course, possible that the striking concurrence of the numbers could be ascribed to mere coincidence. See further the remarks of Landsberger in *JCS* VIII (1954) 70 n. 181 and A. Falkenstein in *OLZ* LI (1956) 419 n. 1.

(433) Even if the *Distanzangabe* in this instance were correct, it would not be useful for establishing absolute chronology, since Gulkishar himself has not yet been definitely dated (amidst the current disputes over high, middle, and low chronologies for the first half of the second millennium).

(434) Solutions based on gratuitous textual emendations such as Lehmann's changing 418 to 318 (on the basis of the chronology of Berossos; *Klio* IV [1904] 111) are unreliable.

(435) *CT* XXXIV 49 iii 22, Babylonian Chronicle. The fall of Babylon is not recounted in the Oriental Institute Prism, which is dated in the fourth month of 689 (*OIP* II 131:84). The Bavian text is the only edition of Sennacherib's inscriptions which mentions the fall of Babylon and is probably to be dated in 688 or later (though the final months of 689 cannot be categorically excluded).

(436) See pl. II above. Marduk–nadin–ahhe could not have ascended the throne as early as 1107 because this date cannot be squared with the well-attested synchronism between Marduk–shapik–zeri and Ashur–bel–kala known from both the Assyrian and Babylonian chronicle traditions (*CT* XXXIV 39 ii 25′-30′, Synchronistic History; New Babylonian Chronicle, obv. 6′).

One should realize, of course, that it is somewhat unlikely that the gods were restored and that the Bavian text was redacted (and the chronological calculations made) within four months after the fall of Babylon. If the scribe were drawing up the document sometime in 688 or 687, he may have reckoned from his time of writing rather than strictly from the time of the return of the statues some months earlier.

(437) S. Smith (*EHA*, p. 355) suggested that Sennacherib might have returned the gods in 687; but Smith regarded the Bavian date as substantially inaccurate.

(438) Therefore, if the Bavian date is accurate, it would favor higher rather than lower dates for the Second Isin Dynasty, e.g., 1163-1146 for Marduk–kabit–ahheshu, etc. Another factor that might someday

In conclusion, then, we might sum up the results of the chronological studies in this chapter as follows. We have, through a thorough examination of the various chronological sources at our disposal, arrived at a relatively stable sequence of thirty-eight kings for the Post–Kassite period. (439) If our chronological sources are correct in the main (440) and our calculations reasonably accurate, (441) then we have obtained the following picture of the chronology of the period: two centuries and twenty kings with approximate absolute dates from 1158* to 943*, followed by a span of almost two centuries and probably eleven kings for which we have about half a dozen absolute dates, and concluding with another period from 760 to 722 where we have certain dates and seven known rulers. Except for the chronology of the final brief period, which is completely stable, (442) much work is still to be done on the preceding four centuries; but the publication of further texts is necessary to achieve better results here. In the meantime, the question of the so-called Elamite interregnum before the Second Isin Dynasty must be left undecided pending the discovery of additional evidence; and the table on plate II above should be considered as the most up-to-date attempt at a working chronology.

---

have to be taken into consideration would be the Assyrian use of the lunar calendar (see note 441 below), which could place the theft later in the reign of Marduk–nadin–ahhe.

Before the publication of the Khorsabad Kinglist by Poebel in *JNES* I-II (1942-43), most attempts to compute the chronology of Marduk–nadin–ahhe's theft of the gods of Ekallate in terms of the regnal years of Tiglath–Pileser I were based on dead reckoning from the time of Sennacherib and relied on incorrect dates for the reigns of many twelfth- and eleventh-century monarchs. These attempts, e.g., Olmstead's elaborate argument set forth in the *American Journal of Theology* XX (1916) 280-281, may now be totally disregarded.

Among more recent opinions, R. Borger (*EAK* I 120) has rejected the Bavian date, principally because he feels that Marduk–nadin–ahhe's removal of Adad and Shala must have taken place after Tiglath–Pileser's raid on Babylon; we will discuss the sequence of these events on pp. 124-129 below. Wiseman (*CAH* II² xxxi 25), on the other hand, has proposed that the problem would be solved if Marduk–nadin–ahhe had been a co-regent during the reign of Nebuchadnezzar or Enlil–nadin–ahhe (*sic*; presumably an error for Enlil–nadin–apli). Such a co-regency, however, would not only be unparalleled at this period, but events occurring during it would hardly be ascribed to the lesser co-regent.

(439) The sequence is unlikely to change for kings 1-27 and 28-33. The insertion of a king or kings between nos. 27 and 28 would not change the picture substantially, since the chronology is sufficiently anchored on either side of these rulers.

(440) This seems to be borne out by the way in which most of the sources, especially in the concordance, fit readily into a unified and coherent scheme.

(441) Their potential accuracy cannot transcend that of the source material (and especially the accuracy of its publication). The only real change in our synchronistic calculations may be necessitated if one day we find that the Assyrians used a lunar calendar much later than presently suspected. (See Appendix B below and Rowton, *CAH* I² vi 58-59).

(442) Barring some such unforeseen circumstance as the recalculation of the 763 eclipse or the repudiation of the generally accepted eponym list tradition. These eventualities do not seem within the realm of probability at the present writing.

Chapter III

POST–KASSITE POLITICAL HISTORY

The Rise of Elam: The Downfall of the Kassite Dynasty

On the stage of Mesopotamian history, the dominant power during the years which witnessed the change-over from the Kassite Dynasty to the Second Dynasty of Isin was Elam. As on at least one occasion in the past in Babylonia, (443) the catalytic agent in the death and birth of hegemonic powers came from the plains of Susa. Babylonian history at this point can be understood only in conjunction with its counterpart in Western Iran.

About the year 1230 the dynamic Tukulti–Ninurta I of Assyria defeated the Kassite Kashtiliash IV and gained control of Babylonia for seven years. During this time, three vassal kings administered the country for him. (444) The first of these, Enlil–nadin–shumi, ruled for just a short time before Kidin–Hutrutash, (445) king of Elam, invaded the land and wrought considerable devastation. He destroyed Der, including Edimgalkalamma, its principal temple. He captured Nippur and deported some of its citizens. Then he climaxed his destruction by deposing Enlil–nadin–shumi. (446)

During the reign of Adad–shuma–iddina, (447) the last of the three Babylonian vassals of Tukulti–Ninurta, Kidin–Hutrutash returned for a second time to Ba-

(443) The Third Dynasty of Ur, weakened by Amorite incursions from the west, was finally overthrown by invaders from Elam. (It is noteworthy that both the First and Second Isin Dynasties gained their hegemony in Babylonia after Elamite raids on the former capital).

(444) It is only fair to note that this interpretation of the three Babylonian kings (Enlil–nadin–shumi, Kadashman–Harbe II, Adad–shuma–iddina) as Assyrian vassals is open to question (see page 77 and note 398 above). Until fresh evidence is available, it is unlikely that the problems involved can be settled. For the most recent pertinent observations on these matters, including the possibilities of damage to the relevant section of Kinglist A, of an Elamite interregnum, and of a partial overlap between the seven-year Babylonian suzerainty of Tukulti–Ninurta I and the reigns of the aforementioned three Babylonian kings, see Rowton in *JNES* XXV (1966) 253-254.

(445) The name is written [m]*Ki–din–*[d]*Hu–ut–ru–*DIŠ in Chronicle P iv 14, 17. This king is customarily identified with the Kitin–Hutran of the lists of Shilhak–Inshushinak (König, *Die elamischen Königsinschriften*, no. 48:46); see Cameron, *History of Early Iran*, pp. 104-105, and Hinz, *Das Reich Elam*, pp. 99-100, etc.

(446) Chronicle P iv 14-16.

(447) R. Labat, writing in 1963 (*CAH* II^2 xxix 12), says that the king in question was Adad–shuma–usur ("Adad–shum–naṣir"); but Chronicle P iv 17, the only passage referring to these events, quite clearly reads [[m]]⌜[d]⌝IM–MU–SUM.NA. W. Hinz, writing in 1964 (*Das Reich Elam*, p. 100), repeats Labat's mistake.

bylonia. Though the pertinent passage in Chronicle P is badly damaged, (448) it can be seen that the areas affected by his visit included Isin (449) and Marad. (450) Little else can be deduced from the text at this point. (451)

After the collapse of Tukulti–Ninurta's power in Babylonia, Adad–shuma–usur, son of Kashtiliash IV, came to the Babylonian throne. (452) During his reign, Babylonia managed to gain a temporary ascendancy over Assyria, (453) and a new dynasty came to the throne in Elam. (454)

The Kassite Dynasty, then, continued relatively vigorous down through the next two reigns, including that of Merodach–Baladan I, the thirty-fourth and third-last king of the dynasty, who reigned some thirteen years. (455) Up through this time, kudurrus show the king in control of the land in Babylonia. (456)

(448) Chronicle P iv 17-22.

(449) URU *I-šin* (iv 18).

(450) MARAD.DA[ki] (iv 19).

(451) There is no evidence for or against Wiseman's assertion (*CAH* II² xxxi 4) that Adad–shuma–iddina was killed or taken prisoner in this raid; this simply reflects an older, unsubstantiated opinion of Sidney Smith, *EHA*, p. 287. For further information on the reign of Kidin–Hutrutash, see Labat, *CAH* II² xxix 11-13. Smith, *EHA*, p. 287, suggested that these Elamite campaigns may have been directed in support of the Kassites and against any non-Kassite claimants to the throne.

(452) Chronicle P iv 7-9. That Adad–shuma–usur was the son of Kashtiliash, a fact suggested by Chronicle P iv 9, is now confirmed by the Luristan bronze dagger inscription published by Dossin, *Iranica Antiqua* II (1962) 151 no. 1.

(453) As attested in: (a) *ABL* 924 (last edited and translated by Weidner, *Tn. I*, p. 48, no. 42), an insulting and condescending letter which Adad–shuma–usur writes to Ashur–narara (=Ashur–nirari III) and Ilu–hadda of Assyria; (b) *CT* XXXIV 42 K. 4401b ii 3-8 (Synchronistic History) and the Khorsabad Kinglist iii 27-30 (=SDAS Kinglist iii 15-17, *JNES* XIII [1954] 218-219), in which Adad–shuma–usur assists Ninurta–apil–Ekur, father of Ashur–dan I, in gaining the Assyrian throne. Several authors (e.g., King in *A History of Babylon*, p. 244, Poebel in *JNES* II [1943] 58, Labat in *CAH* II² xxxii 4) have suggested that the Babylonian army of Adad–shuma–usur fought around Assur; Poebel believed that the Babylonians even held the city for a time. But in the pertinent passage of the Synchronistic History (K. 4401b ii 7), the logical subject of *ana kašādi ill*[*ika*] seems to be Ninurta–apil–Ekur (cf. the translation by Tadmor in *JNES* XVII [1958] 131; note, however, that Tadmor's imputation of the subsequent calamity to the camp of Adad–shuma–usur—rather than that of Ninurta–apil–Ekur—is based on restoration, as is the supposed Babylonian withdrawal from Assyria).

(454) The evidence for the new dynasty is summarized by Labat, *CAH* II² xxxii 1; see also Hinz, *Das Reich Elam*, p. 100.

(455) Kinglist A ii 13′. Wiseman's contention (*CAH* II² xxxi 39) that Merodach–Baladan I was a king of the Second Isin Dynasty is erroneous.

(456) Four kudurrus (*BBSt* no. 5, *MDP* VI 32-43), taken together with evidence of his building activity in Borsippa (*VAS* I 34), show Merodach–Baladan I still master in his own domain. The bricks recording the building of the temple of Eanna in Uruk, BM 90269–90271, assigned to Merodach–Baladan I by the British Museum's *A Guide to the Babylonian and Assyrian Antiquities* (3rd ed., 1922), p. 65, cannot now be readily located in the Museum for consultation; it is highly probable, however, that these bricks belong to Merodach–Baladan II (see *Studies Oppenheim*, p. 42 under 44.2.2; one of these bricks may have been published as I *R* 5 no. 17).

Economic texts from his reign have also been found at Ur, Dur–Kurigalzu, and Babylon; with the exception of *Iraq* XI (1949) 146 no. 7, these are still unpublished.

With the advent of the thirty-fifth Kassite king, Zababa–shuma–iddina, the situation seems to have rapidly deteriorated. Within the space of a single year, Babylonia was smitten first by the Assyrians under Ashur–dan I, (457) who marched south from Assur to raid the land between the Lower Zab and the Adhaim rivers, (458) and then by the Elamites under Shutruk–Nahhunte, who completed the vanquishing of the country by deposing Zababa–shuma–iddina and carrying off much booty from the cities of northern Babylonia. (459) Fragmentary inscriptions written in Elamite tell of Shutruk–Nahhunte's exploits in Babylonia and of considerable amounts of gold, silver, and other metals and woods taken from Dur–Kurigalzu, Sippar, Akkad, and Opis. (460)

At this point, according to later poetic tradition, Shutruk–Nahhunte appears to have handed over his throne to his eldest son, Kudur–Nahhunte. (461) The passage in question is terse and poorly preserved, and we cannot tell whether it means that Kudur–Nahhunte now became king in Elam or whether he was delegated merely to take charge of affairs in Babylonia. In either case, he was the Elamite who would deal with future events in Akkad.

Kassite resistance had not been entirely dissipated with the removal of Zababa–shuma–iddina. One last king, Enlil–nadin–ahi, (462) ascended the throne in Babylonia and for three years carried on the fight against Elam. (463) At the end of this time, the Kassite Dynasty was finally crushed, presumably by Kudur–Nahhunte. The Babylonian king was deposed and carried off as a prisoner, numerous

(457) Labat (*CAH* II² xxxii 4, 6) thinks that Babylonian domination over Assyria was maintained until the reign of Zababa–shuma–iddina. There is no evidence for any Babylonian political pre-eminence in that sphere after the accession of Ninurta–apil–Ekur; see note 453 above.

(458) *CT* XXXIV 42 K. 4401b ii 9-12 (Synchronistic History fragment). The towns of Zaban, Irrija, and Ugarsallu are mentioned.

(459) III *R* 38 no. 2:2′. The booty included such trophies as a statue of Manishtushu from Eshnunna (*MDP* X 1-3), the Victory Stele of Naram–Sin from Sippar (*MDP* III 40 ff.), and probably the famous Code of Hammurapi steles (*MDP* IV 11 ff.) likewise from Sippar. Cf. König, *Die elamischen Königsinschriften*, nos. 22-24c. There is no textual evidence for Olmstead's contention (*AJSL* XXXVI [1919-20] 145) that Shutruk–Nahhunte put Zababa–shuma–iddina to death.

(460) König, *Die elamischen Königsinschriften*, no. 28 C I; cf. nos. 28 B, 28 C I a, and 28 C II. The text (no. 28 C I) is badly broken and its exact purport uncertain. The names of Dur–Kurigalzu and Opis are the only ones that can be read with certainty here. The names of Eshnunna and Dur–Sharrukin might also be restored.

(461) III *R* 38 no. 2:3′, see Cameron, *History of Early Iran*, p. 110.

(462) The reading of this king's name is uncertain. Since the last two elements of the RN are always written -MU–ŠEŠ, the name could be read either as *Enlil–nādin–aḫi* or as *Enlil–šuma–uṣur*. The common reading of this name as Enlil–nadin–ahhe (most recently in several fascicles of the revised edition of the *Cambridge Ancient History*, vol. II) is undoubtedly incorrect. Note too that the text cited by Jaritz, *MIO* VI (1958) 262 no. 230, does not contain any mention of this king.

(463) Kinglist A ii 15′; cf. III *R* 38 no. 2:6′-7′. Hinz, *Das Reich Elam*, p. 104, thinks that Enlil–nadin–ahi was installed as an Elamite vassal; this is based on a restoration of III *R* 38 no. 2:6′-7′ suggested by Tadmor in *JNES* XVII (1958) 138, for which there is no supporting evidence.

important cities and cult centers were razed, and many people were deported to Elam. Not content with this display, Kudur–Nahhunte also took the opportunity to perpetrate the sacrilege for which he was to remain famous in the memory and in the poetic tradition of the Babylonians: the removal of the Marduk statue from Esagila and its deportation to Elam. (464) Babylon was soundly defeated, the nation bereft of its patron deity. (465) On this somber note, the long-lived Kassite Dynasty came to an end.

There is some evidence that the Elamites may have continued to occupy sections of Babylonia temporarily, (466) but the actual transition from the Kassite hegemony to that of the Second Dynasty of Isin is veiled in obscurity. Even if not in actual possession of northern Babylonia, (467) the Elamites continued to exert their influence in the land during the reign of their next king, Shilhak–Inshushinak. (468) A long document dealing with his campaigning tells of many towns and cities lying within the normal sphere of influence of Assyria or Babylonia which he visited, presumably during the fledgling years of the Second Isin Dynasty and the declining years of the aged Ashur–dan I. (469) The sites mentioned that are identifiable include Arrapha, Nuzi, (470) Halman, (471) and Ugarsallu (472) in the northeast,

(464) The collapse of Babylonia at the end of the Kassite Dynasty is described in III *R* 38 no. 2:8′-13′.

(465) Presumably the statue stolen by Tukulti–Ninurta I had either been returned by this time (by a Tukulti–Ashur early in the twelfth century) or had been replaced by another statue in the meantime. I hope to deal with this subject in detail in a separate article.

(466) See pp. 78-83 above.

(467) Labat (*CAH* II² xxxii 9) thinks that northern Babylonia was in vassalage to Elam until the death of Kudur–Nahhunte, c. 1140, which according to the chronology followed in *CAH* is roughly equivalent to the end of the reign of Marduk–kabit–ahheshu. There is no real evidence for or against this hypothesis. Tadmor (*JNES* XVII [1958] 138) suggests that a foreign governor was installed in Babylon; and in this he is followed by Labat (*CAH* II² xxxii 8). But the passage (III *R* 38 no. 2:14′) is heavily restored, including the crucial word "governor" and the verb "installed" in the sentence; so the assertion is speculation only.

(468) Since the order of the kings Kudur–Nahhunte, Shilhak–Inshushinak, Hulteludish–Inshushinak is known from Elamite inscriptions and the synchronisms Kudur–Nahhunte—Zababa-shuma-iddina/Enlil–nadin–ahi and Hulteludish–Inshushinak—Nebuchadnezzar I are known from Babylonian texts, Shilhak–Inshushinak's rule is to be placed in between Enlil–nadin–ahi and Nebuchadnezzar I.

(469) The text referred to is published as *MDP* XI no. 92 (=König, *Die elamischen Königsinschriften*, no. 54).

(470) AŠ *Ar–ra–ap–ḫa* ... AŠ *Nu–ú–za*: König, *Die elamischen Königsinschriften*, no. 54 ii 95. For Arrapha belonging to Assyria about this time, see Weidner's remarks in *AfO* X (1935-36) 20. Cameron, *History of Early Iran*, pp. 118-119, suggests that Shilhak–Inshushinak may have put an end to the reign of Ashur–dan around this time and that Elamite overlordship there may have caused the unrest after Ashur–dan's death.

Other places possibly in the Assyrian sphere of interest which are mentioned by Shilhak–Inshushinak are the land of Hashmar (König, *op. cit.*, no. 28 A:14) and Egallat (König, *op. cit.*, no. 48:191-197; identified with Ekallate by Cameron, *History of Early Iran*, p. 120), which was the site of building activity by the Elamite.

(471) König, *Die elamischen Königsinschriften*, no. 54b:3.

(472) König, *op. cit.*, no. 54 ii 85. Ashur–dan himself had just recently attacked this area (see note 458 above).

Epih, Bit–Riduti, and Jalman near the Diyala, (473) and even a Bit–Rapiqu, (474) presumably to be identified with the well-known Rapiqu at the northwestern tip of Babylonia on the Euphrates. Another inscription of Shilhak–Inshushinak mentions the Tigris, the town of Hussi, the Euphrates, and Nimittu–Marduk (probably the wall of Nippur). (475) The Elamite shadow continued to hang heavy over Babylonia during Shilhak–Inshushinak's years on the throne.

It was in such circumstances that the Second Dynasty of Isin commenced to reign. In an atmosphere psychologically supercharged by the loss of their primary tutelary deity, the Babylonians slowly began to rebuild their strength. Kudur–Nahhunte, an arch-malefactor, (476) had rudely shattered their national prestige. Only with the coming of an even greater champion for the cause of restoration could their national pride be redressed. Until that time, a humiliated Babylonia would recoup its forces and wait to strike the blow that would overthrow the enemy and restore the god to his land.

The Second Dynasty of Isin: A Political Prospectus (477)

The beginnings of this dynasty, which followed the Kassite Dynasty according to the tradition of Kinglist A, are relatively obscure. We may surmise, however,

(473) König, *op. cit.*, no. 54 iii 18, 55. For the location of Bit–Riduti, compare *CT* XXXIV 41 iv 4 (Synchronistic History) and Streck, *Asb.*, CCCLXXIX n. 3; Streck's proposal to connect the GN Bit–Riduti with the *šakin rīdûti* officials in the twelfth-century kudurrus (*BBSt* no. 4 i 6, no. 5 i 15, no. 6 ii 21, late Kassite and Second Isin dynasties) seems plausible, though the omission of the *Bīt* in the supposed gubernatorial title is unexpected. A Bit–Sin–shemi (König, *op. cit.*, no. 54 ii 82), presumably in the Diyala region, has been identified by Cameron (*History of Early Iran*, p. 115) with a place of the same name occurring in the Hinke Kudurru (ii 20 and *passim*).

(474) König, *op. cit.*, no. 54 iii 71.

(475) König, *Die elamischen Königsinschriften*, no. 55:7-10. For the location of Hussi, presumably somewhere near Opis (*Upî*) on the Tigris, see König, *op. cit.*, p. 134 no. 10 and note 589 below. Labat (*CAH* II^2 xxxii 13) suggests that Nimitti–Marduk was perhaps one of the walled fortifications protecting the southern approaches to Babylon; Cameron (*History of Early Iran*, p. 119) had earlier proposed that Nimettu–Marduk may have been meant for Nimitti–Enlil, the wall of Babylon.

(476) In the eyes of later Babylonian tradition, as attested in the Kedor-laomer texts, he was the evildoer par excellence, *[ē]piš lemnētum* (*MVAG* XXI [1916] 88 rev. 21). Another poetic text refers to him as one "whose crime was far greater than that of his fathers, whose guilt was heavier than theirs" *[ša] eli abbēšu arna šūturu šurbû ḫīṭušu kabtu* (III *R* 38 no. 2:4').

(477) The following procedure has been adopted for discussing individual kings and dynasties in this chapter. In an initial section, dealing with the dynasty as a whole, we shall discuss the name and origin of the dynasty (with full documentation) and briefly outline the history of the dynasty (without documentation). Then we shall devote separate sections to each of the kings of the dynasty together with full documentation and discussion of historical problems; the sections on the individual kings are each designed to be complete and independent in themselves—hence a certain amount of repetition between the various sections. The purpose of the initial prospectus for the dynasty as a whole is to set the scene of the action in perspective before proceeding to the myopic analysis of minute details.

on the basis of its name (478) that its first ruler probably came from the city of Isin and that the capital was shifted to Babylon only at a later date. (479) The temporary political pre-eminence of Isin continued even after the transfer of the principal seat of government, since the governor of Isin for some time enjoyed a favored role among the officials of the land. (480)

The opening years of the dynasty were singularly unspectacular. The land was undoubtedly smarting under the repeated campaigns of Shilhak–Inshushinak, especially in the north. There are no known documents from the reign of Marduk–kabit–ahheshu, the first ruler; and, from the time of Itti–Marduk–balatu, his successor, there are only a few commonplace texts dealing with economic matters and one fragmentary royal inscription. Under the third king, Ninurta–nadin–shumi, Babylonia began to make military advances outside its borders, reaching into Assyria. About this time too, Babylonia received the Assyrian king, Ninurta–tukulti–Ashur, as an exile during the struggle for power in Assyria around the end of the long reign of Ashur–dan I. The opening phase of the dynasty concluded with Nebuchadnezzar I, who effectively banished the Elamite shadow over the land (481) by defeating the king of Elam, Hulteludish–Inshushinak, and by restoring the purloined Marduk statue to Esagila.

The dynasty seems to have retained its power through the short reign of Nebuchadnezzar's son, Enlil–nadin–apli, and perhaps even augmented its prestige

(478) BALA PA.ŠE (Kinglist A iii 5′). This logographic spelling of the city's name is a paronomasia based on the word *išinnu*, "stalk," which is written PA.ŠE (*CAD* I 242). In the reign of Nebuchadnezzar I the name of the city of Isin begins to be written with a *š*: URU *I–ši–in* (*BBSt* no. 6 ii 17, no. 25:27; probably also in *BBSt* no. 12 ii 15); cf. the ninth-century writing *Ì–ši–in*[ki] (*BBSt* no. 28 rev. 20); the *s* is retained in the ninth-century URU *Ì–si–in* (*BBSt* no. 29 ii 9), while the writings (URU) *Ì–s/šin* (*BBSt* no. 9 top 16, iva 34) are ambiguous. There is no clear evidence for contemporary use of the logogram PA.ŠE for Isin, but compare the following passages in undated texts: 1 TÚG PA.ŠE–*a* (*PBS* II/2 127:9) and *šá–kìn* PA.ŠE.KI (*VAS* I 57 ii 2).

The name of the dynasty (PA.ŠE) was first identified as the (Second) Isin Dynasty by P. Jensen, *ZA* XI (1896) 90. Additional literature on early discussions of the name is presented in Hinke, *Boundary Stone*, pp. 126-130.

(479) The location of the capital in the early part of this dynasty cannot be ascertained with certainty from the available texts. Isin is supposed to be the original seat of the dynasty only because of the name of the dynasty (but see also note 486 below). Itti–Marduk–balatu, the second ruler of the dynasty, and Nebuchadnezzar I, the fourth ruler, are known to have ruled over most of Babylonia; but there is no clear information about their capital, save that a late poetic text—given to flights of fancy in other particulars—indicates that Nebuchadnezzar's residence was in Babylon (*CT* XIII 48:1). The capital was probably situated in Babylon by the reign of Marduk–nadin–ahhe, the sixth king, since Tiglath–Pileser I burnt that king's palace there.

(480) This is shown not only in documents written under the Second Dynasty of Isin, e.g., *BBSt* no. 6 ii 17, where the governor of Isin precedes the governor of Babylon in a list of witnesses. It is surprising how often the governor of Isin is named as the principal witness in kudurrus granted in Babylon (and not necessarily pertaining to the province of Isin) down through the tenth and early ninth centuries (*BBSt* no. 9 top 16; *BBSt* no. 28 rev. 20; *BBSt* no. 29 ii 9) or is listed as the first witness after the members of the royal family (*BBSt* no. 9 iva 34). See also note 799 below.

(481) Olmstead (*AJSL* XXXVI [1919-20] 146 and *History of Assyria*, p. 58) has suggested that the early kings of the Second Isin Dynasty may have been vassals of Elam. See also note 467 above.

under his successor, Marduk–nadin–ahhe, who was renowned for his military activity against Assyria, including his theft of the gods from Ekallate. Late in his reign, however, the Assyrians under Tiglath–Pileser I gained the upper hand and sacked Babylon, burning the royal palace.

At this point, semi-nomads from the middle Euphrates region interrupted the internal flow of Assyro-Babylonian history. Crop failures and famine in at least two separate years debilitated the inhabitants of the cultivated areas in Assyria and Babylonia; and the Arameans, unable to obtain food through regular channels, spilled into the civilized lands in search of food and plunder. The Assyrians in large numbers retired towards the mountains, and Tiglath–Pileser himself seems to have beaten a strategic retreat to a region in the neighborhood of the later Commagene. In Babylonia, the throne changed hands: Marduk–nadin–ahhe ceased to rule after a reign of almost two decades and the crown passed to Marduk–shapik–zeri. In the face of a common foe, Assyria and Babylonia made peace; but the Babylonians continued to be plagued by semi-nomads seeking food.

After the death of Marduk–shapik–zeri, the next king was Adad–apla–iddina, whom later Babylonian tradition linked with one of these semi–nomad groups. During his reign, the Arameans and Sutians living along the Euphrates irrupted into the land, devastating cult centers in Sippar, Nippur, Uruk, Der, and Dur–Kurigalzu and perhaps fomenting trouble in Babylon itself. Relations between the Assyrian and Babylonian kings remained friendly for the most part during this period of changing regimes in the south. Though Assyria may have assisted Adad–apla–iddina in gaining the throne, he paid the northern country back by later interfering in the Assyrian royal succession.

Both Babylonia and Assyria were soon on the decline, militarily speaking; and, for approximately the next century, they were occupied principally with keeping rampaging semi-nomads out of their ever-shrinking territories. After the reign of Adad–apla–iddina, the history of the end of the Isin Dynasty is quite uncertain. We know the names of two of the last three kings of the dynasty but little else about them. Whether they were successors to the Aramean Adad–apla–iddina or whether they represented the return of the old royal family to the throne cannot yet be ascertained. The Aramean and Sutian disturbances continued unabated through the closing decades of the dynasty; and, when the next attempt at stable government was made, the impetus came from the Sealand, a region less susceptible to invasions from the middle Euphrates region. By that time, the Dynasty of Isin had in all probability ceased to exist. ([482])

([482]) Though the possibility of an overlap or an interregnum between the Second Isin and Second Sealand dynasties cannot be ruled out. This is true of most changes of dynasty in this period, but the dynasties will be presumed here to be consecutive until more explicit evidence is available.

1. Marduk-kabit-ahheshu (483)

The first ruler of the Second Dynasty of Isin is at present a shadowy figure. Besides the fact that he was the initial monarch of the dynasty, we know only that he ruled for eighteen years (484) and that he was the father of his successor, Itti-Marduk-balatu. (485) Any attempt to identify either his capital or the extent of his realm on the basis of the sources presently available would be premature; but we may perhaps infer from the name of the dynasty in Kinglist A that he began his rule at Isin. (486) Probably by the end of his reign, he was in control of northern Babylonia, especially around Babylon itself, since his son could be designated simply as LUGAL.Ẹ already in his first year (487) and ruled over Dur-Sumulael (presumably quite near Babylon, to judge from the extent of that Old Babylonian king's kingdom) (488) likewise in his first year. (489)

(483) *Marduk-kabit-aḫḫēšu*: "Marduk is distinguished (among) his brothers." (Cf. J. J. Stamm, *Namengebung*, p. 225). The name type DN-kabit-ahheshu/ahishu is attested in the Kassite period (Clay, *CPN*, p. 74) and occurs rarely in later periods (e.g., *TCL* IX 58:35, 40; *ADD* 414 edge 3). As yet, only one other individual bearing the identical name Marduk-kabit-ahheshu is known to me—the Middle-Assyrian scribe who wrote documents nos. 17 and 44 (i.e., *KAR* 24 and *AfO* IV [1927] 71-73) in the library of Tiglath-Pileser I several decades later. (See Weidner, *AfO* XVI [1952-53] 204, for dating).

Writing of RN: ^{d}AMAR.UTU-DUGUD-ŠẸŠ.M[Ẹ̌Š-*x*] (*VAS* I 112:4, inscription of Itti-Marduk-balatu, his son), ^{md}AMAR.UTU-IDIM(=BẸ)-ŠẸŠ.MẸŠ-*šú* (Kinglist C, 1), possible traces of ^{md}AMAR.UTU-⌜x-x⌝ (Assur 14616c ii 12′). We would expect to find traces of ^{md}⌜ŠÚ⌝-[ ] in Kinglist A ii 17′, but my collation of the text in spring 1965 showed that the reading is uncertain because of the poor condition of the surface of the tablet.

(484) Kinglist C, 1. This is to be preferred to the seventeen years apparently listed for his reign in Kinglist A for reasons pointed out in the preceding chapter (p. 40). Because of the chronological uncertainties of the period, it is conceivable that the eighteen years of Marduk-kabit-ahheshu were reckoned as beginning at a time when he was still just a local ruler.

(485) *VAS* I 112:4. There is a badly broken line in a fragmentary Babylonian chronicle to be published by Grayson in his *Assyrian and Babylonian Chronicles* (BM 48498:12), which might refer to Marduk-kabit-ahheshu; but there are several difficulties attaching to that interpretation. The line itself reads (according to Grayson's preliminary transliteration): MU 13 *sar*(?) x *ka* [......]; the preceding section (lines 10-11) refers to the twenty-first year of Merodach-Baladan (I/II), the succeeding section (line 13) to the ninth year of Nebuchadnezzar (I/II). If the first ruler of each of these names is meant, then Marduk-kabit-ahheshu would be the most likely monarch referred to in line 12 (if any king is mentioned here at all), since he was the only king between Merodach-Baladan I and Nebuchadnezzar I who ruled for thirteen years or more; but Grayson has noted that the first two signs after the year date do not support a reading of Marduk-kabit-ahheshu here. But a real difficulty is posed by the reference in line 10 to the twenty-first year of Merodach-Baladan, since the first ruler by that name apparently reigned for only thirteen years (Kinglist A ii 13′). Though the twenty-second year of Merodach-Baladan II is probably attested (Brinkman, *Studies Oppenheim*, p. 16), one would not expect a leap in the chronicle from Kurigalzu (lines 8-9) to Merodach-Baladan II (lines 10-11) and Nebuchadnezzar II (line 13). We are not able to resolve this difficulty without further evidence, partially because of the poor preservation of the text.

(486) This is, of course, not the only possible inference from the name of the dynasty. It could mean simply that the first ruling family of the dynasty came originally from Isin.

(487) *AfK* II (1924-25) 56 rev. 7, 58 rev. 10, 61 rev. 11.

(488) See n. 520 below.

(489) *AfK* II (1924-25) 56:7, 61 rev. 5.

2. Itti-Marduk-balatu (490)

Son of his predecessor, Marduk-kabit-ahheshu, (491) and second ruler of the Second Dynasty of Isin, Itti-Marduk-balatu reigned but eight years. (492) Some contemporary Babylonian sources have survived from his reign: one royal inscription (fragmentary), one kudurru (fragmentary), and five economic documents. (493)

The royal inscription preserves only a section of his titulary:

Itti-Marduk-bala[tu],
King of kin[gs],
Favorite of the god[s],
Son of Marduk-kabit-ah[heshu],
Pio[us] (and) per[fect] prince,
Viceroy of Baby[lon],
Elect of A[nu] and D[agan],

(490) *Itti-Marduk-balāṭu*: "With Marduk (there is) life." For the name type, see Stamm, *Namengebung*, p. 230. The type began in Babylonia by at least the Old Babylonian period, when we find an Itti-Ea-balatum (H. Ranke, *EBPN*, p. 111). The name Itti-Marduk-balatu itself seems to have been used beginning in Kassite times (Clay, *CPN*, p. 94); see also *KBo* I 10, where an Itti-Marduk-balatu held a high position at the Kassite court in the time of Kadashman-Enlil II. In the period immediately preceding the Second Isin Dynasty, during the reign of Meli-Shipak, we find a man of the same name holding the position of *ša rēš šarri* and participating in the measuring of a field in the province of Bit-Piri'-Amurru (*BBSt* no. 4 i 17). Some years later, during the Second Isin Dynasty itself, besides the king, there was an Itti-Marduk-balatu of the family of Arad-Ea who was mentioned as the father of a surveyor (Hinke Kudurru iii 14) and, a decade or two later, probably the same Itti-Marduk-balatu as the father of another surveyor (*BBSt* no. 7 i 13). In the Broken Obelisk, probably to be dated to the reign of Adad-apla-iddina, Kadashman-Buriash, governor of Dur-Kurigalzu, is said to be the son of an Itti-Marduk-balatu (*AKA* 133 iii 7: DUMU KI-⌜dAMAR⌝. [UTU]-⌜TI⌝.LA—reading on the basis of personal collation of the text in the British Museum).

In addition to the surveyors' and governor's ancestor(s), one tradition about the origin of the same Adad-apla-iddina, eighth ruler of the Second Isin Dynasty, states that his father's name was Itti-Marduk-balatu (New Babylonian Chronicle, obv. 8′). Considering the popularity of the name, we need hardly consider an identification of this individual with our king a necessity—even if the space between the two kings' reigns did not render it a chronological improbability. The name Itti-Marduk-balatu continued to be extremely popular in later Babylonia (K. Tallqvist, *NBN*, pp. 82-83) and remained current until at least the year 94 of the Seleucid Era (*ZA* III [1888] 151 no. 13:4). It is also mentioned in what seems to be a list of ancestors: *JCS* XI (1957) 12:2; see the remarks of W. G. Lambert, *ibid.*, 6.

Writing of RN: in texts from his reign RN is always written KI-dAMAR.UTU-TI.LA (*VAS* I 112:1; *BBSt* no. 30 rev. 10, 24, both partially broken away; *AfK* II (1924-25) 53 rev. 17, 56 rev. 6, 58 rev. 9, 61:3, rev. 10). In Kinglist C, 2 the name is written mKI-dAMAR.UTU-DIN. There are no really legible traces in Kinglist A ii 18′ (though there is the beginning of a sign—KI is expected—after the masculine personal determinative) or in Assur 14616c ii 13′. For the interpretation of Assur 14616c ii 18′ see n. 179 above.

(491) *VAS* I 112:4.

(492) Kinglist C, 2.

(493) Royal: *VAS* I 112; kudurru: *BBSt* no. 30; economic: *AfK* II (1924-25) 49-64.

Governor for [Enlil] and Nin[lil],
King [...],
King of [...] (494)

To date there is little material for a comparative study of the titulary of Babylonian kings from the end of the First Babylonian Dynasty to the rise of the Chaldean Dynasty, but our brief observations are based on what little is available. The title "king of kings" (495) is attested in earlier Mesopotamia thus far only in the epithets of Tukulti–Ninurta I (496) and his son Ashur–nadin–apli, (497) who may have copied it from older Babylonian models. (498) "Favorite of the gods" is a rare royal title and apparently occurs only here. (499) "Pious (or obedient/submissive) prince" was first used in Old Babylonian times, (500) but "perfect" (*gitmālu*) seems to occur in this sequence only here. (501) This text offers the earliest attestation of "viceroy of Babylon," though the title recurs later. (502) The epithet "elect" (lit.: "naming") is perhaps an Akkadian rendering of the earlier Sumerian m u . p à d . a; there seems to be no instance of its use with Anu and Dagan (503) before this date, but Hammurapi used it with Enlil, (504) Kurigalzu with the "lord of the gods," (505) and Tukulti–Ninurta I simply with Anu. (506) The title "*iššakku* of [Enlil] and Ninlil"

(494) *VAS* I 112:1-13. In line 14, the votive section of the inscription begins *a–na* d[ ] and then breaks off after traces of one more line. Wiseman (*CAH* II² xxxi 8) thinks that two city names should be restored here (presumably in lines 12-13); but there are no parallels from this period to support such an assumption.

(495) Written LUGAL *šar–r*[*i*]. For additional references and a discussion of the use of the title in the Near East, see C. W. McEwan, *The Oriental Origin of Hellenistic Kingship*, pp. 32-34, and the bibliographical data there.

(496) Weidner, *Tn. I*, 18 no. 9 i 3, etc. Tukulti–Ninurta I died approximately seventy years before Itti–Marduk–balatu came to the throne.

(497) *AfO* VI (1930-31) 13:4. Ashur–nadin–apli died four years after his father.

(498) Considering that Tukulti–Ninurta was heavily influenced by things Babylonian, it is possible that this title ultimately goes back to a Babylonian prototype.

(499) The text reads *mi–gir* DINGIR.ME[Š (x–x)]. Because of the uncertain spacing of the copy, it is hard to tell whether or not GAL.MEŠ might be restored at the end of the line. The difference is insignificant for our purposes. See also M.-J. Seux, *Épithètes royales*, p. 167 n. 69. The title "favorite of the great gods" is much more common (*ibid.*, pp. 163-164).

(500) E.g., CH i 29-30, iv 32-33. Full references to its use may be found in Seux, *Épithètes royales*, pp. 254-255.

(501) According to the CAD files, there is no similar passage with *rubû na'du gitmālu*. It is not impossible that *gitmālu* is employed here as a separate substantival form. See also Seux, *Épithètes royales*, p. 97.

(502) GÌR.NITÁ DIN.T[IR.KI], here. Later: Nebuchadnezzar I in Hinke Kudurru ii 20 and as listed in Seux, *Épithètes royales*, p. 278.

(503) Seux, *Épithètes royales*, p. 205. The gods Anu and Dagan are again linked in the eleventh-century inscription of Simbar–Shipak: *JCS* XIX (1965) 123:7. Further references are collected by Goetze, *ibid.*, 128.

(504) *CH* i 52-53.

(505) *CT* XXXVI 6:4.

(506) *KAH* II 60 i 9. The issue is further complicated, since the restoration [Anu] here can hardly be regarded as certain.

is modelled on the older ensí/*išš(i)akku* DN, which was especially popular in Assyria after the beginning of the second millennium. (507) The final title could be restored in at least three different ways:

traces: LUGAL KI.[ ] (508)
possibilities: LUGAL KI.[EN.GI URI.KI]
LUGAL *ki–[ib–ra–at 4–im]*
LUGAL *ki–[iš–ša–ti]*

All three titles are attested for kings of the Second Dynasty of Isin, (509) but the most likely restoration would at present seem to be the first. (510) The inscription then continued with either a votive or building account, which is now totally broken away.

The chief significance of this inscription, besides telling us that the king was duly reverent to the gods in the best Babylonian tradition, is that Itti–Marduk–balatu, at some time in his reign, explicitly laid claim to being heir to the Kassite kingdom, i.e., ruling over Babylon. (511) He is the first ruler of the dynasty about whom this is known for certain.

The only kudurru dating from this reign deals with the sale of plots of land by a certain Eulmash–dinanni of the family of Sin–epiri. (512) The exact location of the places mentioned (513) is unknown, but there is some reason for supposing that they might be placed in the general area around Babylon itself. (514) The kudurru contains no politically significant information.

(507) Seux, *Épithètes royales*, pp. 110-116; cf. Hallo, *Early Mesopotamian Royal Titles*, pp. 47-48.

(508) *VAS* I 112:13.

(509) E.g., *SPA* I 283 no. VII: 4; *BE* I/2 148 i 6-7; *JRAS* 1856, pl. opp. p. 222 no. 2:2.

(510) The other titles, when spelled out syllabically in this period, are written with the *kib* and *kiš* signs initially rather than with *ki*. This does not rule out, however, the possibility of an alternative writing. The restoration of this title is also discussed by Seux in *RA* LIX (1965) 7 n. 1 and in *Épithètes royales*, p. 307, where he prefers the same restoration favored here.

(511) *VAS* I 112:7.

(512) *BBSt* no. 30. Contrary to Wiseman's statement in *CAH* II² xxxi 8, this is the sole kudurru as yet known from this reign.

(513) *Bīt–Ṣapri, Bīt–Nanijauti, Bīt–Udaši*. (*Bīt–Ṣapri* is probably to be viewed as a clan name, since *Ṣapru* at this time occurs only in it and in the patronymic *mār Ṣapri*, *BBSt* no. 6 ii 16; see note 1617 below).

(514) Names like Baba–aha–iddina (*BBSt* no. 30 rev. 22 and *AfK* II [1924-25] 61 rev. 2) and Rimutu (*BBSt* no. 30:7 and *AfK* II [1924-25] 51:7) occur in both the economic archive from Dur–Sumulael and in the kudurru; if these should prove not to be the same men (no patronymics are indicated in the economic archive) or if Dur–Sumulael were not near Babylon (see note 520 below), this argument would be invalidated. Another indication that the kudurru came from somewhere in the vicinity of Babylon is provided by the pre-Nebuchadnezzar prominence of Marduk and Sarpanitum in the text (*BBSt* no. 30 obv. 25, rev. 7); also in the kudurru Marduk occurs as the theophoric element in about thirty per cent of the personal names for which this element is preserved.

The five economic tablets which have survived from the reign of Itti–Marduk–balatu have already been dealt with at length by F. M. Th. Böhl. (515) They are administrative documents, treating of: (1) disposition of grain from the fields after harvest (Gron. 846); (2) provisions for the royal stables and officials located in the town of Dur–Sumulael (Gron. 847, 849); (3) hire paid for rented asses (Gron. 848); and (4) an inventory of slaves and their families (Gron. 850). (516) The texts seem to come from a single archive, and four of them are dated either in the accession year or the first year of Itti–Marduk–balatu's reign. (517) Other than Borsippa, (518) the only place name that can be approximately located is Dur–Sumulael itself, (519) which is around Babylon near the Imgur–Ishtar canal. (520) Although we cannot name Itti–Marduk–balatu's capital with certainty, it is probable that by the end of his reign it was at Babylon. (521)

These economic documents, as pointed out by Böhl, (522) show striking affinities with the Nippur economic texts published in *BE* XIV and XV. Though the Nippur texts come from a different region and are several generations earlier than those of Itti–Marduk–balatu, similarities in form and in phraseology are quite noticeable. Contrasted with the Nippur materials, however, we find that the shorter method for writing the month names is now used consistently (523) and that the written language is somewhat less strict in its use of case endings. (524) The population, to judge from the personal names, continues to use the Akkadian names popular during the latter half of the Kassite rule.

In the economic texts published by Böhl, the king is mentioned only in the date formulae and usually bears the simple title LUGAL.E. It is difficult to assign

(515) "Fünf Urkunden aus der Zeit des Königs Itti–Marduk–balâṭu," *AfK* II (1924-25) 49-64.

(516) Some minor improvements in the text readings: (a) Gron. 846 rev. 15: ...URU *šá–pa–di* (*šá–ḫaṭ–ṭi* ?) ⟨GAL⟩ 5–*ti* ^{m}[ ] (cf. following line); (b) Gron. 847:10 SAL–*su* can hardly be part of a proper name (are these signs to be read some other way such as *aššassu*?); (c) Gron. 848:2, rev. 1: for GIŠ.ḪAR.MEŠ read ANŠE.MEŠ; (d) Gron. 850 rev. 4 (at end of line): DAM–*su*; (e) Gron. 850 rev. 5: ^{f}*par–su* ^{f}*Man–nu–pi–it–ti–É–ul–maš* DUMU.SAL.NI "weaned female child (named) Mannu–pitti–Eulmash, his daughter."

(517) Gron. 846 is from the accession year, Gron. 847-849 from the first year; Gron. 850 is undated.

(518) *AfK* II (1924-25) 58 rev. 2, 5.

(519) *Ibid.*, 56:7, 61 rev. 5.

(520) *RLA* II 253b. Probably in northern Babylonia near Babylon to judge from the activities of Sumulael discussed by Edzard, *Die "Zweite Zwischenzeit" Babyloniens*, pp. 124-126. The site is also mentioned in a fragmentary text from Dur-Kurigalzu: O. R. Gurney, *Iraq* XI (1949) 149 no. 15:9.

(521) Based solely on his assumption of the title "viceroy of Babylon" in *VAS* I 112. Though it can be envisaged that the Babylonian ruler might have had his capital elsewhere, it is more likely that his claim to this title would indicate that he was in possession of the traditional capital.

(522) *AfK* II (1924-25) 51 and *passim*.

(523) The shorter forms seem to have begun sporadically in the thirteenth-century Kassite texts, e.g., *Iraq* XI (1949) 143 no. 1 and *UET* VII nos. 1, 8, 11. From the time of Itti–Marduk–balatu on, the abbreviated forms are the rule.

(524) E.g., *iškāri* (nominative singular, without pronominal suffix) in *AfK* II (1924-25) 59 rev. 6, *kalakki* (nominative) *ibid.*, 61:12.

any precise value to this title, but its very simplicity might speak for a translation like "the King" (i.e., of Babylonia). (525) This would then imply that Itti–Marduk–balatu was in effective control of the central remnants of the old Kassite kingdom of Babylonia as early as his first year of reign. (526)

We know nothing as yet of Itti–Marduk–balatu's activities outside of Babylonia. He might possibly have been the author of a letter to be discussed below, (527) but there is not enough evidence at present to attribute the events described in the letter to him. His successor on the royal throne, Ninurta–nadin–shumi, may have belonged to his family; but this cannot as yet be proven. (528)

3. Ninurta-nadin-shumi (529)

Ninurta–nadin–shumi, the third ruler of the Second Dynasty of Isin, reigned for six years. (530) As noted above, we are not as yet aware of any family relationship between him and his immediate predecessors. But he himself was succeeded by at

(525) See the discussion on pp. 166-168 below.

(526) The king bears the title in the economic texts dated from his first year in *AfK* II (1924-25) 56 rev. 7; 58 rev. 10; 61 rev. 9, 11; and also in the kudurru, *BBSt* no. 30 rev. 24.

(527) Pp. 101-104.

(528) The only definitely attested break in family succession on the throne during the dynasty is between kings no. 7 and 8 (Adad–apla–iddina, no. 8, is specifically labelled a usurper). But family relationship is attested only between kings nos. 1-2 and 3-4-5-6. Possible ties between 2-3 and between 6-7 can neither be ruled out nor proven.

(529) *Ninurta–nādin–šumi*: "Ninurta (is) giver of progeny." For *šumu* in the sense of "offspring," "progeny," see Stamm, *Namengebung*, pp. 40-41 and Gelb, *MAD* III 273-274. Names of the type DN-nadin–shumi are attested as early as the Old Babylonian period (Ranke, *EBPN*, p. 74). Other individuals named Ninurta–nadin–shumi are attested in Kassite times, e.g., *BE* XVII 75:4, *WZJ* VIII (1958-59) 569 H.S. 112:1. The king is the only person bearing this name during the Second Isin Dynasty, but in the early tenth century a Ninurta–nadin–shumi is a *sakrumaš* official (*BBSt* no. 9 iva 35). The name Ninurta–nadin–shumi is also attested in later periods in Babylonia, e.g., *TuM* II-III 42:7, 73:14, 79:8, 238:58.

The name should not be confused with Ninurta–shuma–iddina: "Ninurta has given progeny." (See Poebel, *OLZ* XXXI [1928] 697-698). This name was likewise popular during the Kassite and Neo-Babylonian periods; but the official named Ninurta–shuma–iddina, possibly dating around this time, who rebuilt the well at Nippur (*PBS* XV 69), is obviously not the same man as this king.

Writing of RN: in two contemporary documents, both Luristan bronze daggers, his name is written dNIN.IB–SUM–MU (*Iranica Antiqua* II [1962] 151 no. 3:1, two exemplars); it is written the same way in another Luristan dagger from the reign of his son Marduk–nadin–ahhe (*SPA* I 284 no. X:1). In Kinglist C, 3 the name is written mdMAŠ–*na–din*–MU (last sign written over an erased ŠEŠ). In two texts from the reign of Nabonidus the name is written variously as mdNIN.IB–SUM–MU (*CT* XLVI 48 ii 6') and mdNIN.IB–*na–din–šu–mi* (*YOS* I 45 i 30). In Assyrian texts, the synchronistic kinglist Assur 14616c ii 14' reads mdMAŠ–[x]–MU (according to Weidner's heavily shaded copy in *AfO* III [1926] 70; see Weidner's remarks in *AfO* XIX [1959-60] 138 and note 131 above) and the historical narrative published in *AfO* IV (1927) 215 rev. ii 11 has the unique reading: m[d]⌈NIN.IB⌉–SUM–MU.MEŠ.

(530) Kinglist C, 3.

least three lineal descendants: his son, Nebuchadnezzar I, (531) his grandson, Enlil-nadin-apli, (532) and then another son, Marduk-nadin-ahhe. (533) Whether or not the family then continued to hold the throne in the person of Marduk-shapik-zeri is matter for conjecture; but the following ruler, Adad-apla-iddiṇa, clearly stemmed from a different line. (534)

Ninurta-nadin-shumi was remembered by later generations chiefly as the father of the great Nebuchadnezzar I. (535) But a fragmentary Assyrian chronicle text (536) allows us to gauge something of the extent of Ninurta-nadin-shumi's own military exploits. At some time during his reign, (537) the Babylonian king and his army penetrated deep into Assyrian territory. (538) The Assyrian monarch, Ashur-resha-ishi I, who laid claim to being a significant military figure in his own right, (539) countered by moving with his soldiers and chariotry to Arbail. (540) Ninurta-nadin-shumi heard of the Assyrian move; (541) but here the Assyrian text becomes too broken for us to ascertain the next move of the Babylonian. Something is done with his forces (*emūqīšu*), and there is talk of the flight of more than one individual (*in-nabidū*) in connection with Babylonia (*māt Kardun*[*iaš*]). (542) One is tempted to

(531) *YOS* I 45 i 30; *CT* XLVI 48 ii 6′ (previously published by J. N. Strassmaier in *Hebraica* IX [1892-93] 5). We have no inscriptions of Nebuchadnezzar I in which he lists his own ancestry.

(532) Kinglist C, 5.

(533) Pope, *SPA* I 283 no. X.

(534) He is specifically branded as a "usurper" (New Babylonian Chronicle, obv. 8′).

(535) See the references in note 531 above.

(536) First published by Weidner, "Ein neuer assyrisch-babylonischer Synchronismus," *AfO* IV (1927) 213-217; latest translation of the pertinent section is given by Weidner, *Tn. I*, no. 70. See also Borger, *EAK* I 105-106 (where he states that the designations "obverse" and "reverse" for this tablet should be interchanged). Because so little is preserved of the tablet, it is difficult to tell what type of text it is. Weidner's suggestion that it might be "eine Art Annalenbericht" (*AfO* IV [1927] 214, repeated in Weidner, *Tn. I*, p. XVI) does not seem plausible for the reasons discussed in the following note.

(537) Wiseman (*CAH* II² xxxi 8) states that "according to the Assyrian annals it [the time of Ninurta-nadin-shumi's expedition to Assyria] was the accession year of Ashur-resh-ishi". This statement may be objected to on several grounds.

First and foremost, there is no basis in the text itself (Weidner, *Tn. I*, no. 70) for such an assertion. The only indication of time in the text is *ina šattimma šiāti* "in that (same) year," (rev. ii 7), for which there is no antecedent preserved in the text. Secondly, the description of the text as "annals" is questionable; Assyrian annals do not usually refer to their royal subject by full name and title (*šar māt Aššur*) in the narrative section. Thirdly, according to the chronology officially accepted by the new edition of the *CAH* and set forth by Rowton in 1962 (*CAH* I² vi), Ninurta-nadin-shumi would not yet have come to the throne in Ashur-resha-ishi's accession year.

(538) How far the Babylonian forces went is not preserved in the text, but they must have reached far into Assyria for an Assyrian move to Arbail to pose a threat to them.

(539) In his inscriptions, recently edited by Weidner, *Tn. I*, nos. 60-67, he called himself *šar kiššati* (no. 61:2) and "(he who) smote the Lullumi and Quti" (no. 60:7). As yet we have no detailed contemporary report of his exploits in the field.

(540) *AfO* IV (1927) 215 rev. ii 8-11. For Arbail as normally part of Assyria, see *RLA* I 141-142. (The cult of Ishtar of Arbail was also flourishing in Assur shortly before this time, as evidenced by an economic text from slightly earlier in the twelfth century published in *AfO* X [1935-36] 38 no. 76:6).

(541) *AfO* IV (1927) 215 rev. ii 11-14.

(542) *Ibid.*, rev. ii 15-17.

interpret the text as alluding to a Babylonian withdrawal homewards without engaging the enemy, (543) especially when one remembers a similar tale related in another Assyrian chronicle referring to a strategic withdrawal of Nebuchadnezzar I (without battle) before the advancing chariotry of the same Ashur–resha–ishi I. (544) Although this incident in all probability represented only a brief raid by Babylonia rather than an attempt at permanent expansion, we may look upon it as no small achievement that Ninurta–nadin–shumi penetrated so far north. (545)

As yet, we have only two brief texts written in the name of Ninurta–nadin–shumi, identical inscriptions on Luristan bronze daggers. (546) The titulary preserved on these daggers is grandiose: "king of the world, king of Babylon, king of Sumer and Akkad." This titulary is identical to that preserved on similar daggers (547) of other Second Isin kings: Nebuchadnezzar I, (548) Enlil–nadin–apli, (549) and Marduk–nadin–ahhe, (550) all descendants of Ninurta–nadin–shumi. The title *šar kiššati* ("king of the world") is not to be taken literally at this time, since many kings of Babylonia and of Assyria bear it—sometimes simultaneously—during these years: Ashur–resha–ishi I, Tiglath–Pileser I, Ashur–bel–kala, Eriba–Adad II, Shamshi–Adad IV, Ashurnasirpal I, and Shalmaneser II in Assyria and Ninurta–nadin–shumi,

(543) Note also that there are relatively few words missing in rev. ii 15-17 and there are no expressions referring to a battle.

(544) *CT* XXXIV 39 ii 4'-7', Synchronistic History.

(545) The episode connected with Arbail can be viewed in at least two totally different contexts. If we look at it in the light of the previous Assyrian recession and partial submission to Babylonia (as evidenced by the letter published in *AfO* X [1935-36] 2 ff.), then this "victory" could mark the beginning of an Assyrian resurgence which would continue in Ashur–resha–ishi's "victories" over Nebuchadnezzar I (*CT* XXXIV 39 ii 3'-13', Synchronistic History) and, despite minor setbacks, would culminate in Tiglath–Pileser I's burning of the palace(s) of Marduk–nadin–ahhe in Babylon. If we look at this contact from the Babylonian point of view, this is the deepest known Babylonian penetration into Assyria since the Old Babylonian period; and, however ephemeral the advance, it would show that Ninurta–nadin–shumi could send troops so far from home. The Assyrian point of view may look more plausible at present; but it must be remembered that most of the evidence available is presented as seen from Assyrian eyes and could be biased.

In interpreting these Assyrian and Babylonian maneuvers, Wiseman in *CAH* II² xxxi once places the initiative with the Babylonians (p. 8) and once with the Assyrians (p. 14).

(546) Noted by Langdon in Pope, *SPA* I 283 no. VI and recently published by Dossin in *Iranica Antiqua* II (1962) 151 no. 3 and pls. XV-XVI.

(547) This type of dagger has been discussed in detail recently by Nagel, "Die Königsdolche der Zweiten Dynastie von Isin," *AfO* XIX (1959-60) 95-104. See also pp. 9-12 above.

(548) *Iranica Antiqua* II (1962) 152 no. 4 and pl. XVII (three well-preserved inscriptions and possibly three more with the RN now missing); Pope, *SPA* I 283 no. VII.

(549) *Iranica Antiqua* II (1962) 153 no. 6 and pl. XIX (for the reading of the RN, see below, p. 117).

(550) Pope, *SPA* I 283 nos. VIII-IX; cf. *Iranica Antiqua* II (1962) 152 no. 5 and pl. XVIII (modern forgery?). Pope, *SPA* I 284 no. X omits "king of Sumer and Akkad" and inserts "son of Ninurta–nadin–shumi" after the title "king of the world." The only other published Luristan bronze daggers bearing an inscription of a ruler of the Second Dynasty of Isin belong to Marduk–shapik–zeri (*BASOR* LXXIV [1939] 7 ff.) and Adad–apla–iddina (E. Herzfeld, *Iran in the Ancient East*, pl. xxviii, no. 3). These list no ancestry for the rulers but just the simple title "king of the world" (*šar kiššati*).

Nebuchadnezzar I, Enlil–nadin–apli, Marduk–nadin–ahhe, Marduk–shapik–zeri, Adad–apla–iddina, and Nabu–shumu–libur in Babylonia. (551) The titulary is of little weight in estimating the significance of Ninurta–nadin–shumi. Of much more importance are the facts that he was able to carry on a military campaign reaching far into Assyria and that the monarchy under him became sufficiently stable to be handed down within his family for over forty years after his death. (552)

The "Ninurta-tukulti-Ashur" Letter(s) (553)

We are dealing here with two fragments of a letter or letters, extant only in Neo-Assyrian copies, which were written by a Babylonian king who ruled about this time to his Assyrian royal contemporary. Neither the name of the writer nor the name of the recipient of the documents is preserved; and attempts to establish their identity on the basis of the contents of the texts have proved inconclusive. (554) The evidence, both internal and external, is too slim to afford a solution to the puzzle at present.

The situation sketched in the documents is not altogether clear. The Babylonian king upbraids the Assyrian ruler for not keeping a rendezvous with him at the border town Zaqqu (*Zaqqa*). (555) The Babylonian further mentions that his own

(551) For references see Seux, *Épithètes royales*, pp. 309-312.

(552) Hinz, *Das Reich Elam*, p. 112, says that Ninurta–nadin–shumi lived in exile in Elam after his reign, presumably implying that the Elamites had taken him into captivity. This statement he bases on III *R* 38 no. 2 rev. 7′, last edited by Tadmor in *JNES* XVII (1958) 138-139; the text reads [ ]*-ia ša ina Elamti uššubu* and is translated by Tadmor as "my [predecessor] who lives in Elam." Since—according to Hinz—the carrying away of Enlil–nadin–ahi had taken place too long before Nebuchadnezzar I, this reference can only be to Ninurta–nadin–shumi.

There are several difficulties with this interpretation: (a) the text is anonymous, usually but not with certainty ascribed to Nebuchadnezzar, hence calculations of "too long before" are likewise uncertain; (b) the reference to an earlier Babylonian king is tendentious, since the key word "predecessor" is entirely restored; (c) the stative *uššubu* need not be translated as a present "lives" but could equally well be rendered as "was living" or "lived." Such objections make an Elamite exile of Ninurta–nadin–shumi quite hypothetical.

(553) Published most recently by Weidner, *AfO* X (1935-36) 2-6.

(554) The lengthy bibliography of publications and opinions offered by Weidner, *AfO* X (1935-36) 6 has been supplemented by Borger, *EAK* I 100 and *Handbuch der Keilschriftliteratur*, I, 395, 404, to which may be added Böhl's remarks in *MAOG* XI/3 (1937) 33-34 and Wiseman's in *CAH* II² xxxi 9.

(555) Shortly after this time, Zaqqu or Zanqu is known to have been a fortified town on the Assyrian border which Nebuchadnezzar I attempted unsuccessfully to wrest from Ashur–resha–ishi I (*CT* XXXIV 39 ii 3′, Synchronistic History). In the time of Adad–nirari II (911-891), the town, once again called a "fortress of Assyria," had to be reconquered by the Assyrians (*KAH* II 84:34). For the spelling and location of the town, see Forrer, *RLA* I 279, 295 and Weidner, *AfO* X (1935-36) 3 n. 16 and XXI (1966) 41. Though one would expect Zaqqu to be along the Tigris or to the east of it (to be a convenient meeting place for the Assyrian and Babylonian kings), yet its association with Hit (Idu) in the Synchronistic History and in the text of Adad–nirari II leads one to suspect that it may have been along the middle Euphrates (and hence a relatively neutral meeting ground for both parties).

father, presumably also a monarch, had received Ninurta–tukulti–Ashur [556] as an exile [557] from Assyria and seems to threaten that he will cross the border and set the former Assyrian ruler on the throne again unless his demands are complied with. [558] The Babylonian vaunts his own superiority by referring disparagingly to the Assyrian king and taunts the Assyrian with his weakness in his own royal court: "Who among you is giving the royal commands?" [559]

But the superiority of the Babylonian is largely apparent. The tone of his messages not only shows his insolence, which holds no fear of Assyrian chastisement, but also betrays his inability to punish the Assyrian ruler for defaulting on his word. [560] Instead, the Babylonian must resort to vituperative language and veiled threats and must complain about such minor matters as the bad manners of an Assyrian envoy [561]—a highly revealing situation in that the Assyrian delegate felt that he could exhibit his gaucherie with impunity.

The approximate date of the letter(s) is fixed by numerous references to Ninurta–tukulti–Ashur in a context whose freshness and urgency of treatment seem

[556] Ninurta–tukulti–Ashur, king number 84 in the Assyrian Kinglist, is assigned a *ṭuppišu* reign immediately after the forty-six-year reign of his father, Ashur–dan I. This may well mean that Ninurta–tukulti–Ashur and his *ṭuppišu* successor, Mutakkil–Nusku, acted as regents for their father in his declining years, perhaps even assuming the royal title; but the chronology of the period is far from clear. The most recent bibliography of inscriptions pertaining to Mutakkil–Nusku has been assembled by Borger, *EAK* I 100-102. For the reading of the RN as Ninurta–tukulti–Ashur, see Poebel, *JNES* II (1943) 66-70.

[557] The reason for the exile of Ninurta–tukulti–Ashur is unspecified in the sources. One may speculate that it may have been because he was too pro-Babylonian in his policies, as evidenced by:

(a) his repair of the temple of Erragal in Sirara (*YOS* IX 80, edited by Borger in *EAK* I 101; this Sirara, equated in *KAV* 183:17 with Me–Turnat in the Diyala region, is not to be confused with the Sirara around Lagash [Falkenstein, *AnOr* XXX/1 17-21, 162-164]; Borger has suggested that this building activity of Ninurta–tukulti–Ashur at Sirara implies a great expansion of Assyria to the south at this time [*EAK* I 100] but, though this seems a plausible interpretation at present, we are unable to establish a clear chronological picture of the shifting interests of Babylonia, Assyria, and Elam in this region about the middle of the twelfth century);

(b) the return of the Marduk statue to Babylonia during his time (Chronicle P iv 12-13, if Tukulti–Ashur is—as usually assumed—to be identified with Ninurta–tukulti–Ashur).

Ninurta–tukulti–Ashur certainly found a haven in Babylonia after his fall from power in Assyria.

[558] This may be inferred from the threats voiced in the letter: see Landsberger, *AfO* X (1935-36) 141ff.

[559] *Ina libbikunu mannu kî šarrimma ṭēma išakk[an]*? (*AfO* X [1935-36] 2:6). The plurality of rulers is likewise intimated by the reference to *šarrāni ša limītika* "the kings around you" (alluding to the members of the royal court, in whose eyes the Assyrian would be made ridiculous, *ibid.*, 2:1). The Babylonian king also accuses the Assyrian ruler of speaking in a manner unworthy of a king (*ibid.*, 3:14: "are these the words of a king?").

A similar plurality of persons at the Assyrian court bearing the royal title may be evidenced in *ABL* 924:2, written half a century earlier. Shortly after that time, a member of the Assyrian royal house, Ninurta–apil–ekur, who had been in exile in Babylonia, had with Babylonian aid taken over the throne in Assyria (*JNES* XIII [1954] 218 iii 27-30, 219 iii 15-17; *CT* XXXIV 42 K. 4401b 3-8, Synchronistic History). With this background the threat of Babylonian support for an Assyrian royal exile was not mere idle talk and would not be interpreted as such.

[560] The Babylonian must content himself with wishes like, "May the words of Assyria be like those of an evil demon" (*AfO* X [1935-36] 2:7, cf. 2:2), presumably alluding to the credibility of Assyrian statements.

[561] *Ibid.*, 2:8-3:11.

to point to a time shortly after that king had been dethroned and deported to Babylonia by Mutakkil–Nusku. ([562]) This in turn would indicate one of the following Assyrian kings as recipient of the letter: (1) Mutakkil–Nusku (1134), perhaps regent for Ashur–dan I towards the close of the latter's long reign; or (2) Ashur–resha–ishi I (1133-1116), but in that case the letter should have been written early in his reign close to the time of the expulsion of Ninurta–tukulti–Ashur and before his own "glorious" contacts with Babylonia at Arbail and Zaqqu (*Zanqi*). Neither monarch is ruled out by the contents of the letter.

On the Babylonian side, as possible candidates for writer of the letter(s) must be considered: (1) Itti–Marduk–balatu (1140*-1133*); (2) Ninurta–nadin–shumi (1132*-1127*); (3) Nebuchadnezzar I (1126*-1105*). Strictly speaking the only combination of writer-recipient (out of six possible combinations) that can be ruled out on chronological grounds is Nebuchadnezzar I—Mutakkil–Nusku, ([563]) a combination which was unlikely in any case. But certain other factors should be taken into consideration on the Babylonian side:

(1) Itti–Marduk–balatu: if he is to be identified with the sender of the letter, then we must suppose that the exile of Ninurta–tukulti–Ashur took place several years before the reign of Ashur–dan I officially ended, so as to fall during the reign of Marduk–kabit–ahheshu, the father of Itti–Marduk–balatu; ([564])

(2) Ninurta–nadin–shumi: may well have been the king in question, but then one of the first two rulers of the dynasty would have had to be his father (which is not otherwise attested);

(3) Nebuchadnezzar I: came to the throne at least three years after the exile of Ninurta–tukulti–Ashur, though his father, Ninurta–nadin–shumi, could have been on the throne at the time of the deportation; Zaqqu is known to have been close to the Assyro-Babylonian frontier at precisely this time (*CT* XXXIV 39 ii 3′, Synchronistic History); and, consequently, a one-day wait in relatively dangerous territory could provide a plausible subject for contention.

([562]) The dethronement and deportation are known principally from the Assyrian kinglist (references in note 559 above).

([563]) Mutakkil–Nusku and Nebuchadnezzar I could not have been contemporaries because Ashur–resha–ishi, Mutakkil–Nusku's successor, was already on the throne in the time of Ninurta–nadin–shumi, Nebuchadnezzar's predecessor.

([564]) Another factor which might argue for a regency of Ninurta–tukulti–Ashur early in the reign of Ashur–dan is the return of the Marduk statue under "Tukulti–Ashur," which should have preceded the Elamite spoliation of Babylon at the end of the Kassite Dynasty (see note 557 above).

None of these factors can be considered as probative evidence. The Ashur–resha-ishi I—Nebuchadnezzar I combination seems in some ways the least objectionable, since the available information fits these two individuals better than any other set of figures involved. But the question is best left open pending the discovery of further evidence.

4. Nebuchadnezzar I ([565])

Nebuchadnezzar succeeded his father, Ninurta–nadin–shumi, upon the throne of Babylon and reigned for twenty-two years. ([566]) He was in turn followed by his son, Enlil–nadin–apli, and then by his brother, Marduk–nadin–ahhe. As far as we know at present, this family held the throne longer than any other group of the Second Dynasty of Isin—in all some fifty years. ([567])

([565]) The royal name is given here in its customary English rendering, derived from the biblical references to the later Chaldean king Nebuchadnezzar II (see note 185 above). In Akkadian, the name is *Nabû–kudurrī–uṣur*: "O Nabu, protect my offspring." The name type with *kudurru* is treated by Stamm, *Namengebung*, p. 43. Late syllabary evidence substantiating the approximate equation *kudurru*=*aplu* is given in *TCL* VI 35 i 33-35 (*Erimḫuš* V):

p a b . š e š = *ra–bi a–a–ḫi*
b u – l u – u g BULUG = *ku–dúr–ru–um*
b u l u g . g a = *ap–lu*

On the basis of this passage and because of consistent use of the word in proper names, we may infer the approximate meaning of "offspring" for *kudurru*. (There is no reason for a word like "boundary" or "boundary stone" to occur so frequently in personal names; see also now von Soden, *AHw* 500a).

In Babylonia, the first names with *kudurru* occur in the Middle Babylonian period, e.g., Enlil–kudurri–usur, Kudur–Enlil (Clay, *CPN*, p. 178). These types of names continue to be popular down through the Second Dynasty of Isin and the Neo-Babylonian period (Tallqvist, *NBN*, pp. 318, 325). The only occurrences of Nabu–kudurri–usur as a non-royal name seem to be: (a) in *BBSt* no. 6 ii 24, where PN is the *nāgiru* of Namar during the reign of Nebuchadnezzar I; (b) in an unpublished economic text from the fifth year of Marduk–nadin–ahhe, the younger brother of Nebuchadnezzar I, which was found at Nippur—H.S. 157 i 19, iv 12. Three later kings, however, had the same name: the illustrious Nebuchadnezzar II (604-562) and the two Babylonian pretenders Nebuchadnezzar III (522) and Nebuchadnezzar IV (521), who led unsuccessful rebellions early in the Persian period. (For these last two rulers, see R. A. Parker and W. H. Dubberstein, *Babylonian Chronology*: 626 *B.C.-A.D.* 75, pp. 15-16 and Poebel in *AJSL* LVI [1939] 121-145). The name was also used in later Assyria (e.g., *ADD* 50:10; see also the remarks of Johns, *ADD* III 230).

Writing of RN: in contemporary texts as ᵈAG–*ku–dúr–ri*–ŠEŠ (*BiOr* VII [1950] 43:1; *Iranica Antiqua* II [1962] 152 no. 4:1, 158 no. 14:8; 2 N-T 483:4; *BBSt* no. 6 i 1, 23, 42, 49, ii 7; *BBSt* no. 24:4, 7; *BRM* I 1:14, 1A:14) and as ᵈAG–NÍG.DU–ŠEŠ (Hinke Kudurru i 23, ii 23, v 26; *BBSt* no. 24:15, 27; *SPA* I 283 no. VII:1); in later texts as ᵈAG–*ku–dúr–ri*–ŠEŠ (*BE* I/1 83:7; *UET* IV 143:11, 13), as ᵈAG–NÍG.DU–ŠEŠ (*CT* XIII 48:1, 11), as ᵈ*Na–bi–um–ku–dúr–ri–ú–ṣur* (*YOS* I 45 i 29, inscription of Nabonidus), as ᵐᵈAG–NÍG.DU–ŠEŠ (Kinglist C, 4; *JCS* XIX [1965] 123:9, inscription of Simbar–Shipak; *CT* XLVI 48 ii 6′, inscription of Nabonidus), as ᵐᵈPA–*ku–dúr*–PAB (*CT* XXXIV 39 ii 6′, 8′, Synchronistic History, cf. *ibid.* ii ⌜2′⌝; *RMA* 200 rev. 5). Other fragmentary writings: [ ]–NÍG.DU–PAB (*KAV* 12:1) and uncertain traces in Assur 14616c ii 15′.

([566]) Kinglist C, 4. We have as yet no inscription in which Nebuchadnezzar I cites his own ancestry; this information is obtained from texts of Nabonidus (*YOS* I 45 i 30, *CT* XLVI 48 ii 6′).

([567]) New documentation could conceivably show the reign of the family to extend—through presently unknown ancestral connections—from the beginning of the Second Dynasty of Isin down through king no. 7, Marduk–shapik–zeri. See note 528 above.

Nebuchadnezzar I seems to have been the only king of this dynasty who achieved heroic stature in the eyes of Babylonian posterity. His claim to fame seems to have derived principally from his triumph over the Elamites, an event that so impressed his contemporaries and their descendants that he became the center of a literary tradition, which found expression in song, narrative poetry, and omens, some of them still in vogue even in seventh-century Assyria.

In dealing with the reign of Nebuchadnezzar, we shall group our discussion under three principal headings: (1) relations with Elam, (2) relations with Assyria, (3) activities within Babylonia. Under the final category we shall include a brief note on Nebuchadnezzar's royal titulary.

Relations with Elam. In the beginning of this chapter, we discussed the Elamite campaigns in Babylonia around the close of the Kassite Dynasty. In devastating the land of Akkad and especially by removing the statue of the patron deity of Babylon, the Elamites had lowered the morale of the country to a state seldom equalled throughout its long history. Now, with the coming of Nebuchadnezzar I to the throne of Babylonia, the stage was set for the rise of Akkad once more.

In comparison with other sections of the Post–Kassite period, there is an abundance of available materials pertaining to this event. The sources range from detailed contemporary description of the crucial battle in Elam to late fanciful theological interpretation of the event (depicted almost as historical romance). Some of the sources—or at least their preserved portions—do not mention Nebuchadnezzar I by name; but they may be assigned here on the basis of their contents. ([568]) It is impossible to tell from the texts alone whether they are all describing a single, masterful stroke of military genius or a series of separate campaigns conducted over a number of years against the Elamites.

In the next few paragraphs, I am going to set forth a speculative reconstruction of the Elamite campaign(s) of Nebuchadnezzar I. It should be clear from the outset that this montage of military activities is hypothetical and that the evidence may be interpreted in other ways. Some other interpretations will be suggested following the integrated presentation here.

Early in his reign ([569]) Nebuchadnezzar conceived a plan for ridding Babylonia of fear of the Elamites and for restoring the cult statue of Marduk to its rightful

([568]) Chiefly because they deal with the recovery of the Marduk statue from Elam, which took place at this time.

([569]) We have no clear evidence as to when in Nebuchadnezzar's reign the Elamite campaign should be placed. From a reference in the Hinke kudurru, written in his sixteenth year, "(Enlil) shattered the weapon of (Nebuchadnezzar's) enemy and placed the reins of his enemy in his hand," (ii 4-5) it might be inferred that the subduing of the Elamites had taken place before that time; but this is hardly a necessary conclusion.

place in Esagila. (570) But his first attempt to cast off the Elamite pall by striking a decisive blow deep in Elamite territory failed at the last moment, due to a sudden outbreak of plague among his troops after they had already arrived in Elam. (571) Nebuchadnezzar hastily retreated with his debilitated army to Kar–Dur–Apil–Sin, (572) but eventually was forced to flee from there as well. (573)

After this initial failure of the Babylonian king, the Elamites continued to menace the lands east of the Tigris. (574) Finally, after receiving favorable omens from the gods, (575) Nebuchadnezzar summoned up enough courage to make another attempt at freeing the land from the Elamite threat. (576) Gathering chariotry from

(570) Labat (*CAH* II² xxxii 22), followed by Hinz (*Das Reich Elam*, p. 112), claims that Hulteludish–Inshushinak, the contemporary king of Elam, controlled the Sealand during part of his reign and uses as evidence the mention of the town Shalulikki in his inscriptions (König, *Die elamischen Königsinschriften*, no. 64:10). But the *Šallukkēja* people in the Bel–ibni correspondence (*ABL* 281:21, rev. 17; 789:7; 1311: 24), with whom Shalulikki has usually been compared, occur only in news reports from Elam; and there is no indication that they should be located anywhere outside Elam.

(571) III *R* 38 no. 2 rev. 10′-11′. The outbreak took place while the army was awaiting the Elamite king *ina rēš Uknê*. Tadmor in *JNES* XVII (1958) 139 (followed by Wiseman, *CAH* II² xxxi 15) translates this phrase "at the upper Kerkha river"; but "alongside the Kerkha" or "at the mouth of the Kerkha" would be more accurate renderings.

(572) Probably not to be identified with the Dur–Apil–Sin in Hallo's Old Babylonian itinerary, which is decidedly west of modern Baghdad (*JCS* XVIII [1964] 66-68). E. Ebeling in his article "Dûr–Apilsin," *RLA* II 242 is undoubtedly closer to the truth in seeing this region east of the Tigris; but whether or not it lay close to the Uknu river cannot at present be proven.

(573) III *R* 38 no. 2 rev. 14′-16′.

(574) *BBSt* no. 24:3.

(575) *I–na an–ni [ki–ni ...]*: *BiOr* VII (1950) pl. III 16—restoration suggested by Professor T. Jacobsen. Similar recourse to divine encouragement is mentioned in III *R* 38 no. 2 rev. 5′ (for an earlier occasion; Tadmor's edition of the text, made from photos, in *JNES* XVII [1958] 138-139 should be corrected to read *Marduk*, ᵈAM[AR.UD], instead of *Šamaš*, ᵈU[D], in this line—based on my collation of the tablet in the British Museum), IV *R* 20 no. 1:5-11, and *CT* XIII 48:5 ff., where Marduk answers Nebuchadnezzar's anguished plea by a personal appearance from the heavens. Nebuchadnezzar's divine mission against Elam is ascribed to Marduk's behest in a semi-official account of the campaign (*BBSt* no. 6 i 12), while the king's successes against an unnamed enemy are attributed to Enlil in a kudurru from Bit-Sin-sheme (Hinke Kudurru ii 4-5).

A recently published votive hatchet from the reign of Nebuchadnezzar (Dossin, *Iranica Antiqua* II [1962] 158 no. 14) extols the power of Marduk over the king's enemies. I cannot as yet read all of the text, but offer some emendations below:

te–le–'e–e ᵈAMAR.UTU	Marduk, you are able
mut–nen–na–a e–te–na	to make the pious (man) ...,
muš–te–'u–ú aš–ra–ti–ka	who frequents your shrines,
UGU *na–ki–ri šu–zu–uz–za*	stand over (his) enemies.
i–zi x–(x)–ra–ka a–si–i' (or *a–ru!–uḫ*) *na–ak–ri–ia*	...(*devour*) my enemies.
(rev.) *du–un–ni–in kak–ki–ia–ma*	Strengthen my weapons so
lu–šam–qi–ta ge–ri–ia	that I may cause my foes to fall.
ša ᵈAG–*ku–dúr–ri*–ŠEŠ LUGAL ŠÁR	Belonging to Nebuchadnezzar, king of the world.

For a recent discussion of the idiom *šite'û ašrāti*, see Seux, *RA* LX (1966) 172-174.

(576) The campaign against Elam is pictured as aiming to avenge Babylonia (*ana turri gimilli māt Akkadî*: *BBSt* no. 6 i 13), a sentiment probably echoed in the obscure phrase *tuqtû uttarru* in III *R* 61 no. 2:22′ (=C. Virolleaud, *Sin*, IV 22) and *LBAT* 1526 rev. 3. See note 585 below.

his own land as well as from the traditionally Babylonian villages in the east, (577) he launched a surprise offensive in the extremely hot summer months, when the Elamites would hardly have been expecting an attack from Babylonia. A poetic passage in a royal land grant describes the sweltering heat encountered on the march:

> In the month of Dumuzu, he launched the campaign. ...The axes (in the soldiers' hands) burnt like fire, and the surface of the roads scorched like flame. In the wells, there was no water; the drinking supply was cut off. The strength of the powerful horses gave out, and the legs of even the strong warrior sought for respite. (578)

The army struck farther into the Elamite homeland this time and penetrated as far as the bank of the Eulaeus River (579) before it encountered the Elamite troops. The two kings joined battle; and, according to a contemporary inscription, the dust which their armies raised blotted out the light of day. (580) If we can believe the account of LAK–ti–Marduk, (581) the captain of the right-wing chariotry, it was his forces which eventually won the day for Nebuchadnezzar. (582) At any rate, a decisive victory seems to have been gained by the Babylonian king; (583) and the

(577) I.e., in Bit–Karziabku in the province of Namar (*BBSt* no. 6 i 47 and *passim*). Cameron, *History of Early Iran*, pp. 133-134 suggested that LAK–ti–Marduk had been an Elamite subject; but it is clear from *BBSt* no. 6 that Bit–Karziabku had been under Babylonian jurisdiction and that Babylonian tax collectors and official soldiery had already made themselves unpopular there (i 48-ii 5). When *BBSt* no. 6 refers to Bit–Karziabku's loss of freedom "through enemies" (*ina nakrūti*: i 48), it does not allude to the Elamites since the loss of freedom involved had only the effect of bringing the villages under the jurisdiction of the local Babylonian governor of Namar (i 48).

(578) *BBSt* no. 6 i 16-21. The beginning of line 18 should be read *ù tu–šá gir–ri–e–ti*....

(579) Written ÍD *Ú–la–a* (*BBSt* no. 6 i 28). Smith (*EHA*, p. 296) places the site of the battle in the Namar region near the Tigris; the text, however, speaks explicitly of the Eulaeus.

(580) *BBSt* no. 6 i 29-34. Weidner (*MAOG* IV [1928-29] 239) interpreted *BBSt* no. 6 i 17-18 and 30 ff. as referring to meteorological phenomena and related it to the omen series regarding Nebuchadnezzar's Elamite campaign which is mentioned in *RMA* 200 rev. 4-5. But these passages are more likely to be poetic descriptions of the hardships of the march and the fierceness of the battle.

(581) In *OLZ* XVII (1914) 156-157, G. Hüsing proposed reading *Lakti–Šipak* from *Bit–Karziašku* in place of *Ritti–Marduk* from *Bit–Karziabku*. Labat in *CAH* II² xxxii 23 and n. 1 (followed by Wiseman in *CAH* II² xxxi 15) has accepted a slightly modified form of Hüsing's reading: *Lakti–Šiḫu*. It is true that the signs LAG (e.g., *BBSt* no. 6 i 25, 35, 45; Hinke Kudurru i 18) and RID (e.g., *BBSt* no. 6 i 23) are distinguished at this time and that the reading Ritti–Marduk should be abandoned. But Lakti–Shihu is likewise a questionable reading since: (a) no PN form *lakti* is attested in either Akkadian or in Kassite (and PN's beginning with L in Kassite are extremely rare: Balkan, *Kassitenstudien*, I, 68), (b) ᵈAMAR.UTU in personal names is read Marduk not Shihu (the two gods are equivalent in their respective pantheons, but the two divine names do not serve as interchangeable readings for the same logogram; Balkan, *Kassitenstudien*, I, 114), and *Ši–(i)–*ḪU is always written syllabically in personal names. The name is probably, therefore, to be considered as Akkadian, possibly even to be read *Šitti–Marduk* (no strict parallels). Hüsing's second suggested reading, Bit–Karziashku, has not received even slight modern support.

(582) *BBSt* no. 6 i 35-41. The account may be slightly colored for LAK–ti–Marduk's benefit, since it is inscribed on a stone erected in his locality.

(583) A poetic description of the havoc wrought in Elam on this occasion may be given in IV *R* 20 no. 1:1-4.

Elamite monarch, Hulteludish–Inshushinak, disappeared permanently. [584] The Babylonians returned home in triumph, and it was a long while before Elamite invaders set foot in Babylonia again.

Among the rich booty brought back after this victory in Elam were two honored cult statues. [585] One was the famous Marduk statue, the loss of which the Babylonians had felt so keenly when it was stolen at the end of the Kassite Dynasty and which was now restored amidst great popular rejoicing and with lavish ceremonies to its proper place in Esagila. [586] The other was the statue of Erija, [587] a minor deity from an Elamite city named Din–Sharri, [588] which Nebuchadnezzar brought back to Babylon with Marduk and subsequently established in a new location more apt to afford protection from Elamite raids. [589] The priests of this deity were at the same time endowed with lands in several localities to provide revenue for their support in the new country. [590]

Quite probably the results of this campaign, militarily speaking, were not far-reaching. [591] Since Nebuchadnezzar found it necessary to re-establish the god

[584] *ītemid šadâšu* (*BBSt* no. 6 i 41). The correct reading of this line, including the name of the Elamite king, was first proposed by F. Thureau-Dangin, *RA* X (1913) 98.

[585] *BBSt* no. 24:11-12. Were other Babylonian gods as well as Marduk rescued from Elam? An astrological omen text gives as an apodosis: "The Umman–manda will arise and rule the land. The great gods will arise ⟨from?⟩ their daises [or: the daises of the great gods will arise]. Bel will go to Elam and—it is said—vengeance will be taken after thirty years and the great gods will return ⟨to⟩ their places." (III *R* 61 no. 2:21′-22′ = Virolleaud, *Sin*, IV 21-22; the parallel text *LBAT* 1526 rev. 1-3 has the word "to" in the last phrase). This text undoubtedly refers to this time, since Marduk's Elamite captivity was unique and the thirty years mentioned would be roughly the time intervening between the last Kassite ruler and Nebuchadnezzar I (18 + 8 + 6 = 32 years, allowing even for a slight overlap between Enlil–nadin–ahi and Marduk–kabit–ahheshu). The text certainly hints that other gods were carried into exile or at least displaced at the same time.

[586] Description in IV *R* 20 no. 1.

[587] Written ᵈURU–*ia*. The exact reading of this divine name is uncertain, but it is a true proper name and should be distinguished from the generic *il āli*(*ja*), "(my) city god" (*CAD* I 93a-b). The same proper divine name also occurs on the dedication of a Luristan votive dagger (Dossin, *Iranica Antiqua* II (1962) 153 no. 7:1), which was offered by a *Marduk–nāṣir* for his life (*ana balāṭ napšātišu*). For a possible identification of this Marduk–nasir, see p. 12 and n. 45 above.

[588] *BBSt* no. 24:2-3. Despite the Akkadian(ized) name of the city, Din–sharri was definitely in Elamite territory because: (a) its priests fled "to Karduniash," i.e., into Babylonia, to ask for aid (*BBSt* no. 24:5-6); (b) Ashurbanipal later referred to it as a city conquered during his campaign within Elam (Streck, *Asb.*, 48 v 85).

[589] URU *Ḫuṣṣi* (*BBSt* no. 24:14). *CAD* Ḫ 260a interprets this as a generic name for "rural settlement." It should be noted, however, that the other examples of URU *ḫuṣṣu* or URU *ḫuṣṣē/āti* occur centuries later than the *BBSt* no. 24 reference and are always further specified by a personal or occupational name immediately following. Von Soden, *AHw* 361a, distinguishes between the use of *ḫuṣṣu* as "reed hut" and in geographical names. Cf. also the town *Ḫu–us–si* in an inscription of Shilhak–Inshushinak (König, *Die elamischen Königsinschriften*, no. 55:8).

[590] *BBSt* no. 24:15-30.

[591] Nebuchadnezzar is said to have "triumphed, captured the land of Elam, and despoiled its property": *šarru* RN *ittašiz ina līti iṣṣabat māt Elamti ištalal makkūrša* (*BBSt* no. 6 i 42-43). Labat (*CAH* II² xxxii 23) believes that this conquest of Elam was quite extensive.

The reading *i–ša–ta–lal* in line 43 by L. W. King, *BBSt*, p. 33, should be changed to *i–iš–ta–lal*; cf. the form of the sign *iš* in line 40. The writing of initial *i–iš* is uncommon in this period, though it is paralleled in the writing *i–ik–nu–uk–ma* in *BBSt* no. 8 B 5.

Erija well within central Babylonia and since there was also still question of quartering royal troops in number in the eastern frontier settlements, [592] it seems likely that his victory in that region was not overwhelming. He had struck a blow at the declining Elamite monarchy, but he does not seem to have retained any authority over Elam. Nonetheless, the raid against Elam, however short-lived its military advantages may have been, had a salutary effect on the morale of the Babylonian people; the great god Marduk had clearly relented in his anger against his land and had returned to take care of the nation once again. The dreaded Elamite, who had so humbled Babylon, had at last been bested. What may actually have been little more than a tactical raid carried out with quick and not especially perduring success was nonetheless regarded as a vindication of the land; and the agent of this vindication, a man upon whom the gods smiled, the brave and pious Nebuchadnezzar, became a national hero and a popular subject for later eulogies.

This is my interpretation of the circumstances surrounding Nebuchadnezzar's Elamite campaign, and it is only fair to point out here some shortcomings of this particular reconstruction. We have already mentioned the uncertainty created by the anonymity of two of the more important sources, [593] which mention no Babylonian king by name. The question is further complicated by the fact that other sources, although definitely referring to activities by Nebuchadnezzar, may not refer to the same event at all; and we might distinguish several separate campaigns among them: (1) the campaign with LAK–ti–Marduk, the frontier chariotry commander, in which Hulteludish–Inshushinak was soundly defeated on the banks of the Eulaeus; [594] (2) a second campaign, waged on the pretext of helping the fugitive priests of Erija who had been menaced by the Elamite king, in which the statue of Marduk was recovered and brought back together with the statue of Erija to Babylon; [595] (3) a third campaign, for the success of which Adad was later thanked and a building (re)constructed at Babylon in his honor. [596] There is no conclusive evidence that the texts referring to an anonymous king who lived about this time or that the texts narrating the military activities of Nebuchadnezzar I should all be referred to one and the same glorious campaign. The reader may choose to reject the assignation of the two anonymous texts to Nebuchadnezzar and may prefer to break down Nebuchadnezzar's military accomplishments into two or three separate campaigns; the question is still open.

[592] *BBSt* no. 6 ii 3-4.

[593] I.e., III *R* 38 no. 2 and IV *R* 20 no. 1, dealing principally with events prior to or subsequent to the main campaign against Elam.

[594] Recounted in *BBSt* no. 6 i 14-43. If the statue of Marduk was recovered on this campaign, why was such an outstanding accomplishment not mentioned in the inscription?

[595] *BBSt* no. 24:7-10.

[596] *BiOr* VII (1950) 43-45.

One further text should be noted before we close this section on the Elamite campaign(s). In later years, besides the poetic narrative tradition which grew up around Nebuchadnezzar's feats, (597) there also flourished a branch of omen literature compiled on the basis of portents connected with his Elamite campaign(s). (598) One of the Assyrian court astrologers of the early seventh century in dealing with celestial phenomena refers to an omen series entitled "How Nebuchadnezzar Shattered Elam." (599)

Relations with Assyria. Nebuchadnezzar's contacts with Assyria, on the other hand, are known only from the Synchronistic History, (600) which was written from the Assyrian point of view. According to this account, Nebuchadnezzar, at an unspecified time during his reign, decided to relieve Assyria of two of its fortified border outposts, Zanqu and Idu. (601) He attacked Zanqu first but, according to the Assyrian text, was obliged to raise the siege and burn his siege engines (602) when Ashur–resha–ishi approached with chariotry to reinforce the defenders. On the second occasion, Nebuchadnezzar sent a detachment of chariots and infantry against Idu. Ashur–resha–ishi marched out with a similar contingent and defeated the Babylonian forces, routing the entire Babylonian camp and capturing the leader of the Babylonian expedition (603) and forty chariots with full equipment. (604)

(597) Note, however, that the supposed reference to Elam in tablet I of the Era Epic (F. Gössman, *Das Era–Epos*, 97:87) has been disproved by W. G. Lambert in *AfO* XVIII (1957-58) 401.

(598) See *RMA* 200 rev. 4-5 and note 580 above. Cf. also the isolated omen cited in note 585.

(599) Akkadian: *kî Nabû–kudurrī–uṣur Elamta iḫpûni* (*RMA* 200 rev. 5; see the comments of Weidner on this passage in *MAOG* IV [1928-29] 238-239 and in *AfO* XIV [1941-44] 176). The same phrase, *Elamta iḫpi*, is used also in the contemporary twelfth-century kudurru, *BBSt* no. 24:10.

(600) *CT* XXXIV 39 ii 1'-13'. Immediately before the two border raids of Nebuchadnezzar, lines 1'-2' of this passage mention conclusion of peace (between Babylonia and Assyria). Since no horizontal dividing line on the tablet separates this section (lines 1'-2') from what follows, it may be inferred that Ashur–resha–ishi and Nebuchadnezzar were involved in the peace treaty and that a period of good relations had preceded Nebuchadnezzar's border raids.

Another chronicle reference to Nebuchadnezzar I may be contained in BM 48498:13, where the ninth year of a Nebuchadnezzar is mentioned (for the difficulties in interpreting this text, see Grayson's forthcoming edition in *Assyrian and Babylonian Chronicles* and my remarks in note 485 above).

(601) For opinions concerning the location of Idu and Zanqu, see Weidner, *Tn. I*, p. 59 note; for Zanqu, see note 525 above. They might both be located in the Hit region on the middle Euphrates, though this is not certain. Olmstead (*AJSL* XXXVI [1919-20] 150) believed that Ashur–resha–ishi I took the initiative in these hostilities with Babylonia; but there is no textual evidence for this.

(602) To prevent them from falling into the hands of the Assyrians (*CT* XXXIV 39 ii 6', Synchronistic History).

(603) *40 narkabātišu ḫalluptu(m)* (*CT* XXXIV 39 ii 12', Synchronistic History). The precise meaning of *ḫalluptu(m)* is uncertain (but cf. *CAD* Ḫ 46b, *AHw* 312b). A generic meaning like "equipment" (rather than "harness") is called for by the passage *ḫallupti ṣābē ḫallupti sīsê* (*AKA* 352 iii 22), where the word is used to refer to the paraphernalia of both the soldiers and the horses of chariotry corps. The Synchronistic History and the annals of Tiglath–Pileser I and of Ashurnasirpal II use it in the same sense.

Later Neo-Assyrian references cited in *AHw* deal with a subsequent, more specific use of the same word; *ša ḫalluptišunu* (*ADD* 953 iv 8) refers to an occupation (parallel to *ša ṣallišunu* and *išpar ṣiprāt* in the preceding lines of the text) and TÚG *ša ḫallupte* (*Iraq* XXIII [1961] 21 ND 2312:2) refers to a type of cloth garment.

(604) mKARAŠ.TU *ālik pān ummānišu* (*CT* XXXIV 39 ii 13', Synchronistic History).

These, of course, were minor skirmishes, and the Babylonian king did not participate personally in at least the second of them. Through the Assyrian narrative can be glimpsed the story of contemporary Assyria troubled by Babylonian border raids, which she claims to have beaten off. (605) The capture of forty chariots may have represented a sizable booty for a small engagement in those days, (606) though historians have generally come to view Assyrian statistics of this type with some scepticism. Assyria and Babylonia seem to have confined their hostilities at this time to small, intermittent clashes, with the weaker Assyria mostly on the defensive. (607)

Activities within Babylonia. Nebuchadnezzar left his imprint over quite an extensive area for his time. Including both military and peaceful activities, his power was felt from the Eulaeus river in Elam on the east to Hit on the Euphrates in the west and from Opis (608) and Namar in the north to Ur in the south. (609) He hints at military activities over an even wider area in his titulary. "Conqueror of

(605) It is always possible that there were other border disturbances (less successful from the Assyrian point of view) that eluded the pen of the ancient narrator.

(606) Especially if we compare the twenty-two horses in Itti-Marduk-balatu's stables at Dur-Sumulael (see the calculations of Böhl in *AfK* II [1924-25] 56-58). During the reign of Tiglath-Pileser I, the next Assyrian king, 120 chariots were captured in a battle with the Nairi chieftains (*AKA* 68:94-96).

(607) Cf. also Ashur-resha-ishi's defensive action against Ninurta-nadin-shumi, Nebuchadnezzar's father, near Arbail (see p. 99 above). It should be noted that both Ashur-resha-ishi and Nebuchadnezzar claimed to have been active against the Lullubi (Weidner, *Tn. I*, no. 60:7; *BBSt* no. 6 i 9), which mutual interest might also have led to some friction.

(608) URU *Ú-pi-i* in *BBSt* no. 24:19 is presumably to be identified with the later Opis. *Upî* is also attested in this period in the time of Marduk-nadin-ahhe (*AfO* XVIII [1957-58] 351:46, inscription of Tiglath-Pileser I; *CT* XXXIV 39 ii 20′, Synchronistic History) and possibly in the time of Adad-apla-iddina ([URU *Ú-p*]*i-i* in VA 5937 rev. 6′, unpublished kudurru dated in RN's first year). The city likewise paid tribute to Shutruk-Nahhunte towards the end of the Kassite period (König, *Die elamischen Königsinschriften*, no. 28 C I 10).

The exact site of Upi along the Tigris in northern Babylonia is still unknown, but presumably somewhere near later Seleucia. The town is connected with Akshak (e.g., the gloss *Ú-pi-e*ki for UD.KUŠÚ in *TAPS* XLVI [1956] 312 y+11, Assyrian Dream-Book); and the two sites, if not identical, were presumably near each other. Upi-Opis was once thought to be identical with Tell Umar (e.g., L. Waterman, *Tell Umar*, I, 1-8; Kraus, *ZA* LI [1955] 62-64), but this is as yet unproven. Select bibliography on the location of Upi-Opis: C. Hopkins, *Antiquity* XIII (1939) 440-448; *Iraq and the Persian Gulf* (British Admiralty, Geographical Handbook Series, B.R. 524, September 1944), pp. 45-46; Weidner, *AfO* XVIII (1957-58) 354; R. D. Barnett, *JHS* LXXXIII (1963) 18-20 and especially note 90; Adams, *Land behind Baghdad*, pp. 173-174 n. 20; G. Gullini, *Mesopotamia* I (1966) 7-38. For the reading of the logogram ÚḪ.KI for Akshak, see Jacobsen, *AS* XI 106 n. 204. A full study of the inscriptional materials pertaining to Akshak, Upi, and Opis (which materials go back to at least the middle of the third millennium B.C.) and of the archeological data is badly needed.

(609) Sources for the extent of Nebuchadnezzar's activities: (a) east: *BBSt* no. 6 i 28; (b) west: *CT* XXXIV 39 ii 8′ (Synchronistic History); (c) north: *BBSt* no. 24:19 and *BBSt* no. 6, *passim*; (d) south: *UET* IV 143:11, 13 and *YOS* I 45 i 29-30, etc.

the Amorites" ([610]) would imply some activities further west on the Euphrates in the direction of Syria. "Despoiler of the Kassites" ([611]) and "(the one) who smote the mighty Lullubi with the sword" ([612]) refer to actions in the foothills on the north-eastern periphery of Babylonia. But no detailed records of such campaigns have survived. Nebuchadnezzar did not attempt to govern either the eastern or western limits that his armies reached, but his military achievements were outstanding in a period of relative Babylonian weakness.

It is interesting to note that Nebuchadnezzar's conception of himself as a "pious prince" (*rubû na'du*, Sumerian: n u n n í . t e n . a) ([613]) was in keeping with the royal tradition in Babylonia, where kings were eager to express their relationship with the gods and liable to neglect the recording of their mundane military activities. ([614]) Nebuchadnezzar was at pains to assert that his commission to free the land from the Elamite menace was of divine origin ([615]) and avowed his recourse to prayer and his seeking of divine guidance before setting out on his military missions. ([616]) Similarly, after his singular success on the battlefield, the gods were amply rewarded for their display of divine favor; and in Babylon, Nippur, and Ur, suitable offerings were made. ([617])

During Nebuchadnezzar's reign, Babylon witnessed the joyful return of Marduk from exile. After the fierce battle in "wicked Elam," the god returned amidst great

([610]) *kāšid (māt) Amurrî* (*BBSt* no. 6 i 10). This may indicate that Babylonia had trouble in this region with the Ahlamu, as did Ashur–resha–ishi I and Tiglath–Pileser I. One need hardly interpret this reference as alluding to latter-day Amorites (*sic* Wiseman, *CAH* II² xxxi 16) or as a campaign against the (neo-)Hittites (*sic* Olmstead in *AJSL* XXXVI [1919-20] 149-150 and *History of Assyria*, p. 59). See also the possibility mentioned by Weidner in *AfO* XVI (1952-53) 18 n. 134.

([611]) *šālilu Kaššî* (*BBSt* no. 6 i 10).

([612]) *ša danna (māt) Lullubî ušamqitu ina kakki* (*BBSt* no. 6 i 9). An oracle from about this time concerning the campaign of an unnamed Babylonian king against the Lullubi, K. 2617 III (unpublished), is mentioned by W. G. Lambert in *JCS* XIII (1959) 132. H. Klengel has commented on these references to Lullubi by Nebuchadnezzar I and by his older and younger Assyrian contemporaries, Ashur–resha–ishi I and Tiglath–Pileser I, in *MIO* XI (1965) 361-362.

([613]) *BBSt* no. 6 i 1; cf. restoration in *BiOr* VII (1950) 43:1. The Sumerian occurs in a brick recently unearthed at Nippur (see n. 624 below). For other references to this old title, see Seux, *Épithètes royales*, pp. 254-255. Nebuchadnezzar elsewhere gives himself such religious epithets as "submissive" (*kanšu*, Sumerian: g ú – k i – g á l ; *BiOr* VII [1950] 43:4), "humble" (*ašru*, Sumerian: s u n$_x$ – n a , *BiOr* VII [1950] 43:3), "pious" (*mutnennû*, Sumerian: n í b í – i n – t u r – [t u r] ; *BiOr* VII [1950] 43:4, *Iranica Antiqua* II [1962] 158 no. 14:2, cf. IV *R* 20 no. 1:5-6), and "who seeks after your (i.e., Marduk's) places" (*mušte'û ašrātika*, *Iranica Antiqua* II [1962] 158 no. 14:3, cf. Hinke Kudurru i 24; for the meaning of this phrase, see Seux, *RA* LX [1966] 172-174), "favorite of Enlil" (Hinke Kudurru ii 15), "beloved of Marduk" (*BBSt* no. 6 i 11), etc.

([614]) Especially noticeable in the Neo-Babylonian period proper, when kings in their royal inscriptions concentrated on building activities for the gods almost to the exclusion of other events.

([615]) *BBSt* no. 6 i 12.

([616]) See note 575 above.

([617]) As attested by votive inscriptions there (see succeeding paragraphs).

rejoicing to Babylon, where he took up residence in his shrine again. His temple was once more endowed with lavish offerings and with all products of the earth, sky, sea, and mountains; and happy music was heard in its courts once again. (618) W. G. Lambert has suggested that it was on this joyous occasion that Marduk was finally elevated to the supreme authority in the Babylonian pantheon, since the first formal statement of Marduk's divine supremacy occurs at this time. (619)

Also in Babylon, Nebuchadnezzar reconstructed for the god Adad, another of his divine patrons in war, (620) one of his shrines, the Ekidurhegaltila, (621) probably a section of the older Enamhe temple in Babylon-West. (622) The city of Babylon seems likewise to have been the site of Nebuchadnezzar's royal residence, if a later poetic narrative may be believed. (623)

In Nippur, the famous Ekur temple was partially restored; (624) and the throne of Enlil in the Ekurigigal was built. (625) The temple revenues of the Ekur were once again regulated, and rich gifts were offered in the name of the king. (626) The chief priest of Enlil, who was also the mayor of Nippur, was given a grant of land along the Tigris in the province of Bit–Sin–sheme. (627)

At Ur, as a later inventory informs us, (628) Nebuchadnezzar gave to a temple two bowls fashioned of red gold (629) and two imitation reed-baskets of the same

(618) The preceding two sentences paraphrase the account in IV *R* 20, no. 1.

(619) Lambert, "The Reign of Nebuchadnezzar I: A Turning Point in the History of Ancient Mesopotamian Religion," *The Seed of Wisdom*, p. 10.

(620) *BiOr* VII (1950) 43; cf. *BBSt* no. 6 i 40.

(621) *BiOr* VII (1950) 43:11. Lines 23ff. of the text probably refer to the actual building activity.

(622) Note how the two names are coupled in *BiOr* VII (1950) 43:11. For Enamhe see *RLA* II 368 and see also the comments of Böhl in *BiOr* VII (1950) 42.

(623) *CT* XIII 48:1. Nebuchadnezzar may have been a native of Babylon (*ṣīt Bābili*: *BBSt* no. 6 i 2).

(624) According to unpublished bricks stamped with a Sumerian inscription of Nebuchadnezzar I found by the recent joint Oriental Institute-University of Pennsylvania Nippur expedition. (The only text number available to me at present is 2 N-T 483, found in room EN-13 of the Enlil Temple, level III, on January 31, 1950). The bricks were found in room 13 in the pavement or as part of a sump pit and in a socle in street 20 (see McCown and Haines, *OIP* LXXVIII, 13-14, 17). The inscription reads: (1) ᵈen–líl–lá (2) umun–kur–kur–ra (3) lugal–a–ni–ir (4) ᵈAG–*ku–dúr–ri*–ŠEŠ (5) nun ní–te–na (6) sig_4–al–ùr–ra (7) mi–ni–in–du_8–àm (8) ki–gar unu–maḫ–a (9) mi–ni–in–dù–dù: "For Enlil, lord of the lands, his king, Nebuchadnezzar, reverent prince, having fashioned baked bricks, built the base of the Unu–mah (with them)." (This text was called to my attention by Professor Jacobsen).

(625) *JCS* XIX (1965) 123:9. For Ekurigigal, see note 920 below.

(626) Hinke Kudurru ii 2-3, 8-9.

(627) Hinke Kudurru, *passim*.

(628) *UET* IV 143. The text records gifts of gold and silver objects of kings Burnaburiash, Kurigalzu, Meli–Shipak, Nebuchadnezzar I, Marduk–shapik–zeri, and possibly several later kings (in the broken sections).

(629) 2 SAB.MEŠ: *UET* IV 143:9. One of the bowls was later broken and one stolen (?) by a courtier named Ninazu–iqisha.

precious metal. (630) He also erected a stele in the giparu which depicted the *entu* priestess in her ceremonial dress and described her duties and rituals. The antiquarian Nabonidus was overjoyed when this stone was found during his reign, as it enabled him to revive the old religious practices. (631) It is possible that the erection of such a stele indicates that Nebuchadnezzar I had installed his own daughter as chief priestess there, since that normally provided the occasion for setting up steles on the spot. (632)

In other areas in the realm, Nebuchadnezzar was also active. (633) East of the Tigris, in the region of Namar, he exempted LAK–ti–Marduk, a local chieftain who had served as his trusted assistant on the Elamite campaign, and his villages from payment of royal and provincial taxes and from forced labor on public projects. (634) Near Opis and in several other areas in northern Babylonia which we have been unable to locate as yet, (635) Nebuchadnezzar granted plots of public land to the priests of Erija and released them from certain taxes. (636) We likewise possess two economic texts from his reign, dated in the eighth and eleventh years, both administrative documents dealing with the disposition of grain. (637) In neither of these texts has the geographical name been read successfully. (638)

Also during these years in Babylonia a notable literary revival took place. The poetic language of the royal inscriptions and of the famous LAK–ti–Marduk kudurru mark the literary highpoint of the era. It is likely that this burst of creativity sprang from the desire to glorify fittingly the spectacular achievements of Nebuchadnezzar I and to enshrine his memorable deeds in lasting words. These same deeds were also to provide inspiration for later poets who sang the glories of the era. (639) The scribes of Nebuchadnezzar's day, reasonably competent in both Akkadian and Sume-

(630) 2 GI.GUR.SAL.LA.MEŠ *UET* IV 143:12. (See *MSL* VII 69:42a). These also seem to have been damaged: TAR.MEŠ. (See *CAD* Ḫ sub *ḫepû*, v., lexical section). [See addendum, p. 395.]

(631) *YOS* I 45 i 29-33; see also *CT* XLVI no. 48 ii 5'-8'. No trace of Nebuchadnezzar's work on this site has been found (Woolley, *UE* VIII 18-19).

(632) E.g., *UET* I nos. 12, 23, 24B, 25, 48, 51, 64, 103-105, 297; *UET* VIII 12 (=*AfO* XVII [1954-56] 27), 64; *ITT* I 1094 (=*RT* XIX [1897] 187); *SAKI* 206 1b; *Iraq* XIII (1951) 27-39. But in these dedications—as opposed to simple royal building inscriptions on the site—the *entu* priestess herself usually erected the stele, sometimes mentioning the name of her father or royal benefactor.

(633) Labat's theory that the Sealand was under Elamite control until approximately this time (*CAH* II² xxxii 22) can neither be proven nor disproven because of the lack of pertinent evidence from the reigns of the first three kings of the Second Isin Dynasty. See also note 570 above.

(634) *BBSt* no. 6 i 51-ii 10.

(635) I.e., Dur–Sharrukin, Hussi (*Ḫuṣṣi*), Bit–Bazi, Bit–Ugarnakkandi.

(636) *BBSt* no. 24:15-30.

(637) *BRM* I 1 and 1A.

(638) *BRM* I 1:12 reads URU *šá* DUMU?-*za-a*'-BAR?. *BRM* I 1A:10-12 might contain a geographical name, but it is unclear.

(639) It is difficult to say whether such texts as III *R* 38 no. 2 or IV *R* 20 no. 1 were originally composed now or later.

rian,[640] produced works of an astonishing vigor, even though these may have lacked the polish of a more sophisticated society. The name of Esagil-kini-ubba, *ummânu* or "royal secretary" during the reign of Nebuchadnezzar I, was preserved in Babylonian memory for almost one thousand years—as late as the year 147 of the Seleucid Era (=165 B.C.). [641] Nor was the tradition of the sciences dead in his reign, since texts containing chemical recipes for the manufacture of artificial gems were being copied at this time. [642]

Nebuchadnezzar's titulary is somewhat problematic. In some instances his titles reflect the poetic character of the document in which they are imbedded rather than any politically significant realities. In the LAK-ti-Marduk kudurru, Nebuchadnezzar was extolled as the "prince of kings," [643] as "fearless in battle," [644] as "bearer of an awesome bow," [645] as "the warlike male whose strength is devoted to waging battle." [646] Like the illustrious Hammurapi of the distant past, Nebuchadnezzar too claimed to be the "sun" of his land; [647] he regarded himself as the shepherd of his people [648] and was much concerned with the administration of justice. [649] We have already noted his claim to the title of "pious prince" [650] in the best Babylonian tradition. Adverting to his more prosaic titulary, we find him designated

[640] Besides the Sumerian bricks at Nippur, they produced at least *BiOr* VII (1950) 43-45, of which the preserved Sumerian—even though influenced by the Akkadian word order—seems, if anything, somewhat pretentious. See Falkenstein's comments on the style of this text in *BiOr* IX (1952) 91-92 and in *MDOG* LXXXV (1953) 4.

[641] J. J. A. van Dijk, *UVB* XVIII 45 rev. 18. Note (*ibid.*, rev. 17) that Esagil-kini-ubba served as *ummânu* also under Adad-apla-iddina and, therefore, his career extended over at least thirty-five years. The chronological order of the royal names has become reversed in these lines. See note 852 below.

[642] Colophon to a chemical text from Babylon: "(according to) an old original (tablet) from Babylon; (property of the) palace of Nebuchadnezzar, king of Babylon" (GABA.RI LIBIR.RA KÁ.DINGIR.RA.KI É.GAL ᵈAG-NÍG.DU-ŠEŠ LUGAL KÁ.DINGIR.RA.KI). For the meaning of *gabarû labīru*, see *AHw* 271b. The text has been published by Oppenheim in *RA* LX (1966) 30-35.

Contrary to the statement in *RA* LX (1966) 29, the text was purchased by R. Koldewey in Babylon in 1905 as part of a lot of five texts (Weidner, *AfO* XVI [1952-53] 71-72). One of the other texts, a fragmentary royal inscription (the present A. 3647 in the Oriental Institute, Chicago), also belonged to Nebuchadnezzar I.

[643] *BBSt* no. 6 i 2; the same title was borne before him by Hammurapi and after him by Nabonidus (Seux, *Épithètes royales*, p. 91).

[644] *BBSt* no. 6 i 8.

[645] *BBSt* no. 6 i 8. The same title was later borne by Nabu-apla-iddina (*BBSt* no. 36 ii 25).

[646] The title "warlike male" apparently occurs first here. It was later claimed by Nabu-apla-iddina and several Assyrian kings (Seux, *Épithètes royales*, p. 378). The rest of the quoted epithet is unique (*ibid.*, p. 136).

Nebuchadnezzar also bore the title "warlike viceroy" (*iššakku qardu*, *BBSt* no. 6 i 3).

[647] *BBSt* no. 6 i 4; cf. *CH* v 4-5, etc.

[648] *BiOr* VII (1950) 43:5; cf. Hinke Kudurru ii 15.

[649] *BBSt* no. 6 i 5-6, cf. *BiOr* VII (1950) 43:6. He was also termed the "establisher of the foundation(s) of the land" (Hinke Kudurru ii 24; see Seux, *Épithètes royales*, pp. 131-132).

[650] References in n. 613 above.

simply as king, (651) king of Babylon, (652) viceroy of Babylon, (653) king of the world, (654) king of Sumer and Akkad. (655) It is evident that he was laying claim to hegemony over all of Babylonia and to the full political heritage of the Kassite rulers. (656) It is regrettable that there is such a limited corpus of royal titles from contemporary Babylonia with which these may be compared.

5. Enlil-nadin-apli (657)

The son and successor of Nebuchadnezzar I, (658) Enlil–nadin–apli was the fifth king of the Second Dynasty of Isin and ruled for four years. (659) Presumably he

(651) *BBSt* no. 24:4, 7, 27 (LUGAL); *BRM* I 1:15, 1A:14 (LUGAL.E).

(652) *SPA* I 283 no. VII:3; *Iranica Antiqua* II (1962) 152 no. 4:3; and also in the colophon of a contemporary glass text (Babylon, Photo Konst. 713, rev. 10′) and in an inscription written during the reign of his son (*BE* I/1 83:7).

(653) GÌR.NITÁ URU.DÙG (*BBSt* no. 6 i 3). Though L. W. King attempted to read this as *šakkanak Eridu* (*BBSt*, p. 31 and n. 3; also Seux, *Épithètes royales*, p. 278), such a title is not attested elsewhere, while the title *šakkanak Bābili* is common for kings (e.g., D. G. Lyon, *Sargon*, p. 13:2; R. C. Thompson, *Esarhaddon*, pl. 1 i 2; *VAB* IV 60 i 10; see Seux, *Épithètes royales*, p. 278). Nebuchadnezzar I himself is referred to under the title *šakkanak Bābili*, with the geographical name written unambiguously as KÁ.DINGIR.RA.KI, in another contemporary text (Hinke Kudurru ii 20). The equation URU.DÙG=*Ba–bi–il–ú* is known from *Erimḫuš* tablet V (*TCL* VI 35 i 25); cf. also IV *R* 20 no. 1:9, 11, 12, 14, a bilingual text probably relating to the time of Nebuchadnezzar I, where URU DÙG.GA seems to be a synonym for *Šuanna* (pointed out by Thureau-Dangin, *RA* XXIV [1927] 185). Winckler, Hinke, and others read the city name correctly as "Babylon" (bibliography: *BBSt*, p. 31 n. 3 and *AJSL* XXIX [1912-13] 220).

(654) *SPA* I 283 no. VII:2; *BBSt* no. 6 ii 7; *BBSt* no. 24:15; Hinke Kudurru ii 23; *Iranica Antiqua* II (1962) 152 no. 4:2, 158 no. 14:8.

(655) *SPA* I 283 no. VII:4; *Iranica Antiqua* II (1962) 152 no. 4:4.

(656) He is the only post-Kassite Babylonian king to express hostility towards Kassites, and this he does merely in the title "despoiler of the Kassites" (*šālilu Kaššî*, *BBSt* no. 6 i 10), probably alluding to military activity in the Zagros foothills rather than to any vaunted rivalry with the earlier dynasts or their descendants. See p. 258 below.

(657) *Enlil–nādin–apli*: "Enlil (is) giver of an heir." For the name type, see Stamm, *Namengebung*, p. 217. It should be noted, however, that Stamm's statement "die Form *–nadin–apli* findet sich erst neuassyrisch und neubabylonisch" is inaccurate. Earlier occurrences of the type may be found in the Kassite period (e.g., Sin–nadin–apli in *BE* XV 199:5 and *BE* XVII 68:32) and in the Middle Assyrian period (e.g., *KAJ* 107:17). It is quite possible in view of the fact that both elements of this name type occur in the Old Babylonian period in such names as Sin–nadin–shumi and Nanna–apla–iddinam, that we shall discover that this type dates back even earlier than presently attested.

Other individuals bearing the identical name include the thirteenth-century Assyrian limmu official in *KAJ* 107 (=*KAJ* 117):17, 133:17, 319:15-16, and the ninth-century Babylonian in *BBSt* no. 29 ii 17, who held the post of *bēl* [*pīḫati*].

Writing of RN: in contemporary texts, a Luristan bronze dagger and a kudurru, the name is written ^{d}EN.LÍL–SUM–IBILA (=DUMU.NITA) (*Iranica Antiqua* II [1962] 153 no. 6:1; *BE* I/1 83:9, 18). In Kinglist C, 5 the name is written ^{md}EN.LÍL–*na–din*–IBILA. In Assyrian synchronistic kinglists the name is written ^{md}BE–MU–A (Assur 14616c ii 16′, uncertain reading of copy made from photo) and [ ]–A (*KAV* 12:4).

(658) Kinglist C, 5 (note that A–*šú* in the copy is omitted in Poebel's transliteration in *AS* XV 3).

(659) Kinglist C, 5.

came to the throne while still a minor [660] and died without offspring. His uncle, Marduk-nadin-ahhe, succeeded him as king.

Information concerning his short reign is quite sparse at present. All that can be assigned with certainty to these years are an inscribed Luristan dagger and a kudurru.

The Luristan bronze dagger, recently published by Prof. Georges Dossin, [661] bears the first known royal inscription of this king. Although Dossin hesitated between reading [*Enlil-nādin*]-*apli* or [*Nabû-mukīn*]-*apli*, [662] the photograph provided of the inscription [663] shows clearly that the reading should be:

šá ᵈEN.LÍL-SUM-DUMU.UŠ
LUGAL ŠÁR
(rev.) LUGAL KÁ.DINGIR.RA.KI
LUGAL KI.IN.GI URI.KI

The titulary is common on daggers of this type, occurring also on daggers of Ninurta-nadin-shumi, [664] Nebuchadnezzar I, [665] and Marduk-nadin-ahhe. [666]

In the fourth and last year of Enlil-nadin-apli [667] a kudurru was drafted concerning land in southern Babylonia which had belonged to a temple for 696 years, [668] the original grant dating from the reign of Gulkishar during the First Dynasty of the Sealand. [669] From this kudurru we learn that Ekarra-iqisha, governor of the province of Bit-Sin-magir, after a new survey of boundaries had by a judicious rearrangement of the boundary markers appropriated a strip of temple land along the Tigris and had claimed it as province land. Nabu-shuma-iddina, priest of the temple, [670] had gone before the king and complained of this injustice. The king

(660) His father and grandfather had both died within the preceding twenty-three years, and his uncle who was to succeed him lived to reign for eighteen years and was an active monarch. Although the youthfulness of Enlil-nadin-apli is not a necessary conclusion from the chronological data, it seems highly plausible.

(661) *Iranica Antiqua* II (1962) 153 and pl. XIX, no. 6.

(662) *Ibid.*, 153.

(663) *Ibid.*, pl. XIX.

(664) *Ibid.*, 151 no. 3.

(665) References in note 548 above.

(666) References in note 550 above.

(667) *BE* I/1 83:9.

(668) *Ibid.*, line 8. On the calculation of the number 696, see pp. 83-84 above.

(669) *Ibid.*, line 6; fragmentary end of [*Gul-ki-š*]*ár* also preserved in line 3.

(670) *šangû* of the gods Nammu and Nanshe (gods originally associated with Ea/Enki and Eridu) according to *BE* I/1 83:16.

bade Ekarra–iqisha and Eanna–shuma–iddina, governor of the province of the Sealand, to institute inquiries into the ownership of the land. (671) When this investigation had been completed, the claim of the priest was upheld; and the land under dispute was restored to the temple estate. A new boundary stone was then erected, bearing the significant name: "Do-not-Overstep-the-Boundary-Do-not-Efface-the-Border-Line." (672) The document shows at least that the governors of both these provinces in southern Babylonia were at this time subject to Enlil–nadin–apli.

Another document coming from approximately the same time is the kudurru *BBSt* no. 11. It too mentions Eanna–shuma–iddina as governor of the Sealand and depicts him as instrumental (673) in obtaining a grant of land near the town of Edina (674) for one of his subordinates. (675) The text mentions no king by name (676) and could plausibly be assigned either to this reign or to the reigns of the immediately preceding or succeeding monarchs. (677)

The circumstances surrounding the demise of Enlil–nadin–apli are unknown. It is possible that his uncle, who succeeded him, may have deposed him before he reached his majority. Overshadowed by the powerful monarchical figures of his predecessor and successor, Enlil–nadin–apli does not as yet emerge with any clarity upon the page of history. (678)

(671) The fields are described as *eqlēti ša Bīt–Sîn–magir ša māt Tâmtim* (*BE* I/1 83:12-13). The phrase could be translated and interpreted in several ways, though the literal translation would read "fields of Bit–Sin–magir of the Sealand." Possibly Bit–Sin–magir was a province belonging to a larger region described as the "Sealand"; but both areas were presided over by governors of equal rank (*šaknu*, *BE* I/1 83 rev. 6-7). Perhaps Bit–Sin–magir had originally had some claim to fields that now lay within the borders of another province and was simply attempting to repossess them. Or, conceivably, the plot in question was near the common border between the two provinces; and so both governors were called in to supervise the investigation.

(672) *šumu ša abni annî: ē tētiq itâ ē tusaḫḫi miṣ[ra]* (*BE* I/1 83 rev. 21-23).

(673) Because of the undefined antecedent of *rubû* in i 3, it is uncertain whether Eanna–shuma–iddina presented the land on his own initiative or not.

(674) Location uncertain, but possibly to be connected with the town and canal bearing the same name in the Old Babylonian period (see Ebeling, *RLA* II 273).

(675) Exact title uncertain, but apparently ÌR.KA.KAL–*šu*. Note in the same kudurru that the title *gu–za–an–nu* (i 11, ii 2) should be read *ḫa–za–an–nu*.

(676) It is possibly a king who is referred to in i 3 as *rubû* (cf. *BBSt* no. 6 i 1, etc., where *rubû* serves as a royal title). The omission of the RN might be explained by a state of affairs in which the kudurru would be issued by the governor of the province at the beginning of Marduk–nadin–ahhe's reign on the authority of the recently deceased king, but this is quite uncertain.

(677) As already noted by King, *BBSt*, p. 76, n. 1.

(678) Wiseman's proposal that Marduk–nadin–ahhe may have been a co-regent towards the end of Nebuchadnezzar's reign or during the reign of Enlil–nadin–apli is discussed in note 438 above.

6. Marduk-nadin-ahhe (679)

Marduk–nadin–ahhe may have been the last of his family to hold the royal power in Babylonia. The son of Ninurta–nadin–shumi, (680) he succeeded his young nephew, Enlil–nadin–apli, as king and reigned for eighteen years. (681) One of his sons was witness to a kudurru in the tenth year of his reign, (682) but apparently did not succeed him on the throne. His connection with his successor, if any, is at present unspecified in our sources. (683)

Marduk–nadin–ahhe seems to have been a successful monarch for the greater part of his reign. Inheriting extensive territory relatively intact from the days of his brother, Nebuchadnezzar I, he probably kept Assyria at bay until late in his reign—no mean feat when we consider that Marduk–nadin–ahhe reigned entirely during the days of Tiglath–Pileser I, by whom he is usually overshadowed. (684) Towards the end of his rule, Marduk–nadin–ahhe saw Babylon itself the target of a successful raid by the powerful army of Tiglath–Pileser I. Not long after that, in the midst of disturbances caused by the invasion of hungry tribes from the west seeking food, Marduk–nadin–ahhe disappeared from power.

(679) *Marduk–nādin–aḫḫē*: "Marduk (is) giver of brothers." The name is usually borne by a third or later son. For the name type, see Stamm, *Namengebung*, pp. 139, 217. The name begins to be used in Mesopotamia in the Middle Assyrian and Middle Babylonian periods (e.g., *AfO* X [1935-36] 38 no. 80 rev. 8; Clay, *CPN*, p. 105). The last element of the name may also occur in the singular, *–aḫi*, "Marduk (is) giver of a brother," e.g., the name of a son of Nebuchadnezzar II (*Nbk*. 382:5). To date, the name is attested for less than ten individuals in Mesopotamia (including both singular and plural forms of the final element).

Writing of RN: in contemporary Babylonian inscriptions—or copies of them—as ^{d}AMAR.UTU–SUM–ŠEŠ.MEŠ (*UET* I 306:2; *UET* VIII 101:12, 52-53; *SPA* I 284 no. X 1; *Iranica Antiqua* II [1962] 152 no. 5:1-2; *BBSt* no. 25:3, 38; *BBSt* no. 8 i 4, i ⸢22⸣, i ⸢28⸣, B 4; *PSBA* XIX [1897] 71 ii ⸢1⸣, 4, 19; *YOS* I 37 iv 32), ^{d}AMAR.UTU–MU–ŠEŠ.MEŠ (*SPA* I 283 no. VIII 1, no. IX 1), ^{d}AMAR.UTU–*na–din–aḫ–ḫe* (H.S. 157 iv 31, unpublished; iv 16 has *di–in* for *din*). In contemporary Assyrian texts, the final element of the RN is sometimes apparently written in the singular: ^{md}AMAR.UTU–SUM–*a–ḫi* (*KAH* II 63:9d; *KAH* II 71:29, 32 var.); but Assyrian writings with the final element obviously in the plural also occur: ^{md}AMAR.UTU–SUM–ŠEŠ.MEŠ (*KAH* II 71:29 var., 32; King, *Records of the Reign of Tukulti–Ninib I*, 118:49 var.; cf. *AfO* XVII [1954-56] 384:9′), ^{md}AMAR.UTU–SUM–PAB.MEŠ (*CT* XXXIV 39 ii 14′, Synchronistic History; King, *Records of the Reign of Tukulti–Ninib I*, 118:49, Bavian Inscription), ^{md}ŠID–SUM–PAB.MEŠ (*ABL* 1391 rev. 7). Incompletely preserved writings: ^{md}AMAR.UTU–SUM–P[AB?.(MEŠ?)] (*KAH* II 66:23), ^{md}⸢AMAR.UTU–X⸣–ŠEŠ.MEŠ (Broken Obelisk i 17, personal collation), [ ].MEŠ (*KAV* 12 i 5). Erroneous writing: ^{md}AMAR.UTU–*na–din*–MU (Kinglist C, 6; discussed above on p. 42).

(680) *SPA* I 284 no. X 3.

(681) Kinglist C, 6.

(682) ^{m}KÁ.GAL–*te–ta–par–a–a–ú* DUMU LUGAL.E in *BBSt* no. 8 ii 26-27. The signs are clear on the photo in *BBSt*; the name is not yet explained.

(683) Despite Tadmor's restoration of line 9′ of VAT 10453+10465 in *JNES* XVII (1958) 134. The fact that Marduk–nadin–ahhe was the father of Marduk–shapik–zeri cannot as yet be demonstrated, nor can it be disproved.

(684) Tiglath–Pileser I is certainly better known, partially because of the multitude of surviving records written in his name (bibliography in Borger, *EAK* I 108-134).

Our discussion of this king and his reign will be divided as follows: (1) internal affairs in Babylonia, (2) royal titulary, (3) Assyria and the Aramean invasions.

Internal Affairs in Babylonia. Many documents have survived from the reign of Marduk–nadin–ahhe, but few of them give much pertinent political information. There are four Luristan Bronze daggers with brief standard inscriptions. (685) There are two building inscriptions, both written in Sumerian, from Ur. (686) There are five kudurrus which can definitely be assigned to this reign, (687) and two more kudurrus can be dated to approximately this time on the basis of internal evidence. (688) The single economic text, long known only from a brief mention by H. Hilprecht in his *Excavations in Babylonia and Assyria*, p. 519, can now possibly be identified with H.S. 157, an unpublished text in the Jena collection. (689)

From these documents we learn of activities taking place in years 1, 5, 8, 10, and 13 of the king's reign. (690) The Babylonian government was still intact and undisturbed as late as the year 13—a good reason for dating the Assyrian raid on Babylon after that time. The realm reached from Ur in the south (691) to the Lower Zab in the northeast (692) and to Rapiqu on the Euphrates in the northwest. (693) Unfortunately, the borders of the land cannot be drawn in more detail; but these

(685) *SPA* I 283-284 nos. VIII-X; *Iranica Antiqua* II (1962) 152 no. 5.

(686) *UET* I 306, *UET* VIII 101.

(687) *BBSt* no. 8; *BBSt* no. 25 and *MDOG* VII (1901) 25-29; *PSBA* XIX (1897) 71-73; *YOS* I 37 iv. For the relationship between *BBSt* no. 25 and the *MDOG* VII kudurru, see *RA* LXI (1967) 70-74 and also note 2133a below.

(688) (a) I *R* 70 is assigned here because Tab–ashab–Marduk, son of Ina–Esagila–zeru (i 15), occurs also in *BBSt* no. 25:31 as a *sukkallu*; he also occurs a few years earlier in *BBSt* no. 6 ii 22. (b) *BBSt* no. 7 is assigned here because the surveyor of the land in i 13 is identical with the scribe in *YOS* I 37 iv 29, Shapiku of the family of Arad–Ea, and because its decoration—especially the figure of the king—is strikingly similar to that of the kudurru published in *MDOG* VII (1901) 25-29 (see King, *BBSt*, p. 38 n. 1). Ungnad's opinion (*Orientalia N.S.* XIII [1944] 101) that Shapiku's father, Itti–Marduk–balatu, was identical with the Babylonian king of that name was based largely on the erroneous reconstruction of the sequence of kings in the Second Dynasty of Isin that obtained prior to the publication of Kinglist C. The identification is still possible from a chronological point of view, since the *BBSt* no. 7 kudurru dates about 35 years after the death of the king, but is unlikely (the family of Arad–Ea serves largely in official scribal posts: Lambert, *JCS* XI [1957] 1-14 and 112).

(689) Especially since they both date from the king's fifth year and the Jena text from internal evidence can clearly be seen to originate from Nippur. But see Appendix A under 6.2.8.

(690) Year 1: *BBSt* no. 25:37-38; year 5: see note 689; year 8: *YOS* I 37 iv 31-32; year 10: *BBSt* no. 8 i 27-28; year 13: *PSBA* XIX (1897) 71 ii 19.

(691) *UET* I 306 and *UET* VIII 101.

(692) The border between Assyrian and Babylonian territory is clearly the Lower Zab at this time: Tiglath–Pileser enters into enemy territory when he crosses it (*AfO* XVIII [1957-58] 350:37) and operative Babylonian provinces are in this area. (See n. 738 below). The northern boundary west of the Tigris was probably defined by the desert north of Dur–Kurigalzu, which is attested as under Babylonian rule at this time by *CT* XXXIV 39 ii 18′ (Synchronistic History), *AfO* XVIII (1957-58) 351:45, and slightly later by the "Broken Obelisk" of Ashur-bel-kala, *AKA* 133:6.

(693) *AfO* XVIII (1957-58) 344:33.

few geographical points can help us to visualize the extent of territory under Marduk-nadin-ahhe in his early years.

The only building activity known from Marduk-nadin-ahhe's reign took place at Ur, where the E(ga)nunmah shrine was restored (694) and repairs were made on the "kitchen complex" on the northwest side of the ziggurat terrace. (695) Marduk-nadin-ahhe's rule in northern Babylonia is known chiefly from the kudurru inscriptions, which mention sites like Irrea and the province of Bit-Ada, (696) Dindu-Ek[allim], (697) Bit-Habban, (698) Hudadu, (699) Kar-Nabu, (700) Bit-Tunamissah, (701) and Bit-Hanbi; (702) the annals of Tiglath-Pileser and the Synchronistic History contribute the names of other sites under Babylonian control: Dur-Kurigalzu, Sippar of Shamash, Sippar of Annunitum, Opis, and the region of Ugarsallu (including the city of Lubdu). (703) From these geographical names we can see that even the tribal regions between the Radanu and the Lower Zab rivers were under Babylonian control during the early part of Marduk-nadin-ahhe's reign. From Babylon itself (Amran-ibn-Ali) comes a fragmentary boundary stone probably from early in the

(694) Four limestone gate-sockets (U. 7818=*UET* I 306) were found *in situ* at the entrance to the sanctuary and also at the entrance to the three southwesterly chambers of the E(ga)nunmah. The find spots of the gate-sockets are described in the preliminary excavation reports in *AJ* VII (1927) 406 and 409-410; the approximate positions of the finds may be gauged from the rough plan published in *AJ* VII (1927) pl. LI. In the four identical Sumerian inscriptions on the gate-sockets, Marduk-nadin-ahhe adds to his usual titulary the epithets "nourisher of Ur" (ú - a š e š . u n u g . k i) and "builder of Ekishnugal" (m ú - m ú é - k i š - n u - g̃ á l) and tells how he (re)built É-g̃á-nun-maḫ, a "very old temple," restoring the building and repairing its door sockets.

(695) BM 123124 (=1932-10-8,8=U. 17627a, text published as *UET* VIII 101), a solid copper cylinder found together with a Larsa period foundation deposit (cylinder of Nur-Adad, published as *UET* VIII 67C) in a brick box dug into the Ur III level walls at the south corner of room 3 of the so-called "kitchen block" in the northwest section of the ziggurat terrace at Ur. A corresponding foundation deposit with two copper cylinders of Nur-Adad (published as *UET* VIII 67A-B), found at the west corner of room 6 of the same complex (*UE* V, p. 38), strongly suggests that Marduk-nadin-ahhe substituted one of his own cylinders for a Nur-Adad cylinder when repairing the earlier building. Contrary to Woolley's statements (*UE* V, p. 38; *UE* VIII, p. 69 and n. 1), the Marduk-nadin-ahhe text is not a virtual duplicate of the Nur-Adad texts; see also E. Sollberger, *UET* VIII, p. 21, and Gadd, *BMQ* VII (1932) 44.

Description of the find spot of the Marduk-nadin-ahhe cylinder: *UE* V, pp. 38, 46-47 and *AJ* XII (1932) 375. Plan showing find spot: *UE* V, pl. 70. Photograph of the Nur-Adad cylinders in the matching deposit at the corner of room 6: *UE* V, pl. 18a (=*AJ* XII [1932] pl. LXIV no. 2). This cylinder is mistakenly attributed to Adad-apla-iddina in *UE* VIII, p. 4.

The text of the cylinder is in Sumerian, but little is legible save for the king's name (lines 12, 52-53) and a few titles of the king. The dedication (lines 1-11) is clearly to Nanna-Sin (d⌜š e š . k i⌝, line 1).

(696) *BBSt* no. 8 i 2-3 and *passim*. See n. 738 below.

(697) *BBSt* no. 8 i 27 (see E. Unger, *Babylon*, p. 64).

(698) I *R* 70 i 3, etc.

(699) I *R* 70 i 6. See note 1745 below.

(700) I *R* 70 i 2.

(701) I *R* 70 i 8.

(702) *BBSt* no. 7 i 3, etc. (and Bit-Imbiati nearby: *BBSt* no. 7 i 5).

(703) *CT* XXXIV 39 ii 18′-23′, Synchronistic History; *AfO* XVIII (1957-58) 350-51:37-47.

king's reign. (704) Some witnesses to this text are also mentioned on a stone tablet (without pictures or symbols) found at Za'aleh, twelve miles to the northwest of Babylon, and seems to have been the copy of the document issued to the people who were granted the tax exemption. (705) From Kar–Bel–matati, a small town perhaps just to the south of Babylon, (706) there is a partially preserved kudurru recording a royal land grant to a leather worker in the king's thirteenth year. (707) From Nippur comes a garment inventory, listing clothes brought from Babylon (708) to Nippur by Napsamenni, a seer and high priest of Enlil, (709) on the occasion of a marriage (710) in the second year of Marduk–nadin–ahhe. (711) Likewise from central Babylonia a governor of Isin is attested as chief witness in one of the contemporary kudurrus. (712) Except for Ur, we have no references to southern Babylonia at this time.

The kudurrus from northern and northeastern Babylonia present the usual picture of internal administration: granting of tax exemptions, sale of privately owned land, transfer of province lands to individual ownership. We do not discuss them here, since Chapter V will deal in detail with the provincial administration in Babylonia during this period. (713)

(704) Found in a pile of stones in a Parthian building in the mound Amran–ibn–Ali at Babylon and published in the preliminary excavation report by Koldewey, *MDOG* VII (1901) 25-29; photos of the stone were published in D. K. Hill, *The Fertile Crescent*, p. 12. For the date of the text, see Brinkman, *RA* LXI (1967) 70-74 and note 2133a below.

(705) *BBSt* no. 25. The document contains a grant of freedom (*zakûtu*) from taxes and forced labor to some minor officials in the neighborhood of Babylon.

(706) *PSBA* XIX (1897) 71 ii 18. The capture of a gate of this town by the Arameans some 116 years later was thought worthy of mention in the Religious Chronicle (iii 7′). W. G. Lambert in *JSS* IV (1959) 14 has collected a series of Kassite and later references to the town, which also occurs in his "Divine Love Lyrics" (Col. B 10, 13). To the references assembled there may be added "the fortress of the city of Kar–Bel–matati" in the royal inscriptions of Tiglath–Pileser III (II *R* 67:8, and possibly to be restored in *Iraq* XXVI [1964] 120:7), a reference in the Middle Babylonian letter H.S. 108:13 (*WZJ* VIII [1958-59] 565), and in the temple-list DŠ 32-14 (*Orientalia N.S.* XXIX [1960] 103 n. 1). See also Unger, *Babylon*, p. 138, and Winckler, *OLZ* X (1907) 592.

(707) The text is published in *PSBA* XIX (1897) 70-73. For the reading of the man's profession, see Steinmetzer, *OLZ* XXIII (1920) 199, and Oppenheim, *JCS* IV (1950) 192. As pointed out by Steinmetzer, *OLZ* XXIII (1920) 198-199, this text may be compared to a similar grant made by Kashtiliash (IV) to a leather worker (*MDP* II 95).

(708) The text is H.S. 157 (unpublished tablet in the Jena Hilprecht Sammlung, information courtesy of J. Aro). The bringing of the garments from Babylon (ŠU.AN.NA.KI) is mentioned in iv 18′ of the text.

(709) *bārû nišakku Enlil* (H.S. 157 iv 14′). The Oriental Institute expedition to Nippur in its excavations in December 1964 found a duck weight (9-N-99) bearing an inscription of the same Napsamenni, but written during the reign of the next king, Marduk–shapik–zeri, when Napsamenni is entitled "chief of the seers" (PA UZÚ). (Information courtesy of R. Biggs and M. Gibson).

(710) *ina šakān ḫa–da–šu–ti* (H.S. 157 iv 9′).

(711) H.S. 157 iv 15′-16′. The text itself is dated in the fifth year of Marduk–nadin–ahhe.

(712) *BBSt* no. 25:27. The kudurru is dated at Babylon.

(713) Pp. 296-311 below.

In the letter *ABL* 1391, ([714]) dated by L. F. Hartman to around May 15, 657 B.C., ([715]) an astrologer attached to the court of Ashurbanipal cites a tablet which "Ea–mushallim wrote to Marduk–nadin–ahhe, his lord." ([716]) The astrologer alludes to an astronomical omen (*ittu ina šamê*), which has no clear interpretation, but is apparently connected in some way with lack of rainfall (*maqāt zunnē*) and also with campaigns against the enemy. ([717]) This text at least serves to show that the practice of interpreting astronomical omens was flourishing in Babylonia during Marduk–nadin–ahhe's reign.

Titulary. The following table presents schematically the titulary borne by Marduk–nadin–ahhe: (a) in his own inscriptions, ([718]) (b) in date formulae or kudurrus from his reign, (c) in later texts.

1. "king"	LUGAL	(a-b)	*Iranica Antiqua* II (1962) 152 no. 5:2; *YOS* I 37 iv 32.
	LUGAL.E	(b)	*PSBA* XIX (1897) 71 ii 19 (and possibly ii 4); *BBSt* no. 25:3, 38; *BBSt* no. 8 i 4, 10, 23, 28, ii 27.
2. "king of Babylon"		(a)	*SPA* I 283 nos. VIII-IX:1, 284 no. X:2; *Iranica Antiqua* II (1962) 152 no. 5:3; *UET* I 306:5.
3. "king of Sumer"		(a)	*Iranica Antiqua* II (1962) 152 no. 5:4.
4. "king of Sumer and Akkad"		(a)	*SPA* I 283 no. VIII:2, no. IX:2; *UET* I 306:6; *UET* VIII 101:22.
5. "king of the four quarters"		(a)	*UET* VIII 101:23.
6. "king of the world" LUGAL ŠÁR: *šar kiššati*		(a-b)	*SPA* I 283 no. VIII:2, no. IX:2, 284 no. X:2; *UET* I 306:3; H.S. 157 iv 17′.

([714]) Also published by King in *CT* XXXIV 10-11.

([715]) *JNES* XXI (1962) 37.

([716]) *ABL* 1391 rev. 6-7.

([717]) Though one can hardly present such a proposal very strongly, it would be possible to speculate on connections between the cessation of rainfall and the famine mentioned in *AfO* XVII (1954-56) 384:2′. Marduk–nadin–ahhe is also known to have beaten Assyria in battle (see pp. 124-128 below). Is it mere coincidence that the successes of the *Aḫlamû*, likewise active at the time of the downfall of Marduk–nadin–ahhe, are mentioned in the following section in *ABL* 1391 rev. 12-13?

([718]) Ghirshman, *Iranica Antiqua* II (1962) 153 suggests that the inscription on a Luristan Bronze dagger (*ibid.*, 152 no. 5) may have been engraved in modern times on the ancient dagger. Yet, despite the omission of expected signs at the end of lines 2, 3, 4 (i.e., ŠÁR, KI, URI.KI), one should note that (a) the royal name is entire (though a runover into line 2) and its last few signs could have been omitted, (b) despite omissions and shortening of the customary formulae, the lines make complete sense as they stand. These facts would not argue for the text being a modern copy.

7. "king of Ur" (a) *UET* I 306:4. ([719])
8. "shepherd..." (a) *UET* VIII 101:15, 55. ([720])
9. "king of Akkad" (c) *OIP* II 83:49 (Sennacherib).
10. "king of Karduniash" (c) *CT* XXXIV 39 ii 14′, Synchronistic History; *AfO* XVII (1954-56) 384:⌜8′⌝ (Assyrian chronicles). ([721])

The titulary is relatively uninformative. "King of Babylonia" and "king of Sumer and Akkad" had been claimed by Nebuchadnezzar I before him. ([722]) "King of the world" was also a title of Nebuchadnezzar ([723]) and was to be claimed after him by Marduk–shapik–zeri, Adad–apla–iddina, and Nabu–shumu–libur ([724]) among the members of his own dynasty. "King of the four quarters" is a title borne only by Marduk–nadin–ahhe and Marduk–shapik–zeri in this dynasty. ([725]) Even "king of the world" (*šar kiššati*), the most far-reaching of any of the titles, was relatively meaningless at this time, since both Marduk–nadin–ahhe and his Assyrian contemporary, Tiglath–Pileser I, could claim it at the same time. ([726]) He alone in this dynasty claimed the title "king of Ur." ([727])

The titulary, therefore, is typical of a Babylonian ruler of this time, containing some pretense to kingship on a relatively grand scale. It is certainly an apt description of the power of his early years, though the epithet "king of the world" has only restricted significance. From his declining years we have as yet no inscriptions.

Assyria and the Aramean Invasions. Four major episodes of Marduk–nadin–ahhe's reign were connected with Assyria or the Arameans: (1) his theft of the Assyrian gods Adad and Shala from Ekallate, (2) a military victory over As-

([719]) Cf. *UET* VIII 101:18. Marduk–nadin–ahhe also gives himself epithets like "nourisher of Ur, builder of Ekishnugal" (*UET* I 306:7-8).

([720]) Plus many other pious epithets, especially in *UET* VIII 101 (e.g., ⌜n u n n í t u k u⌝ line 13).

([721]) Note that titles in sections 9-10 are conferred in later Assyrian sources only.

([722]) *SPA* I 283 no. VII. "King of Babylonia" was also claimed by Marduk–nadin–ahhe's two immediate successors, e.g., *BE* I/2 148 i 3 and *UET* I 167:3.

([723]) *SPA* I 283 no. VII:2.

([724]) E.g., *BE* I/2 148 i 5; *BBSt.* no. 12 ii 5; *JRAS* XVI (1856) pl. opp. p. 222, no. 2:2. Additional documentation by Seux, *RA* LIX (1965) 7.

([725]) *UET* VIII 101:23; *BE* I/2 148 i 6-7.

([726]) *AfO* XVIII (1957-58) 343:1, 349:1. For the widespread use of the title at this time in both Assyria and Babylonia, see Seux, *Épithètes royales*, pp. 308-312.

([727]) Though "provider for Ur" (*UET* I 306:7) is also used by Adad–apla–iddina (*UET* I 166:6, 167: 6-7), the only other monarch of the time whose building inscriptions have been recovered from that site.

syria, (728) (3) two chariotry battles with the forces of Tiglath–Pileser I, which led to the burning of Marduk–nadin–ahhe's palace in Babylon, and (4) Marduk–nadin–ahhe's disappearance from power during the Aramean invasions of Assyria and Babylonia. (729) Before proceeding to discuss and interpret these events in any unified fashion, we must prefix a few remarks about the date of each of these occurrences.

The removal of the divine statues of Adad and Shala from Ekallate is mentioned only in the Bavian inscription of Sennacherib:

> In the time of Tiglath–Pileser, king of Assyria, Marduk–nadin–ahhe, king of Akkad, had taken Adad and Shala, the gods of Ekallate, and carried (them) off to Babylon. Four hundred and eighteen years later, I brought (them) out of Babylon and returned them to their places in Ekallate. (730)

In the second chapter, we saw how Marduk–nadin–ahhe's theft of these gods may well be dated in one of the first years of his reign. (731) This, though the most likely opinion, raises another question: if the gods were taken early in the reign of Marduk–nadin–ahhe, why were they not recovered by Tiglath–Pileser I when he later took Babylon?

Two basic solutions have been proposed to this problem of the relative dates of the Ekallate theft and Tiglath–Pileser's attack on Babylon. The first solution (732) accepts the chronological priority of the Ekallate theft and suggests that the statues were removed for safety to Nippur or some other place to the south when Tiglath–Pileser's army visited Babylon. The second solution (733) asserts that the statues could have been captured only after Tiglath–Pileser's sack of Babylon and, therefore, rejects any literal or nearly literal interpretation of the Bavian date. (734) A third alternative should also be mentioned. Tiglath–Pileser's burning of the palace in Babylon has all the earmarks of a quick raid on the city, and his soldiers might not have had either time or opportunity to locate the missing statues before they had to retire. In any case, the fact that Tiglath–Pileser I did not recapture the missing

(728) This could conceivably have been on the same occasion as the theft of Adad and Shala (1) or have been identical with the first chariotry battle with Tiglath–Pileser I (3); there is no real evidence for or against either alternative.

(729) Marduk–nadin–ahhe is also mentioned in uncertain context in a damaged portion of the Broken Obelisk (i 17) of Ashur–bel–kala. Despite Wiseman's collation of the text noted in *JSS* IV (1959) 204 n. 4, the text in 1965 still had a clear –ŠEŠ.MEŠ with traces preceding that definitely favored the reading ⌜*Marduk–nādin*⌝– (based on personal collation).

(730) *OIP* II 83:48-50.

(731) P. 84 above.

(732) Held, e.g., by Smith, *EHA*, p. 302, followed by Wiseman, *CAH* II² xxxi 22.

(733) Held, e.g., by Weidner, *MVAG* XX/4 (1915) 84 and Borger, *EAK* I 120; cf. also Schnabel, *MVAG* XIII/1 (1908) 62.

(734) See note 745 below for the calculation of the date of Tiglath–Pileser's visit to Babylon.

gods on this occasion does not mean that the idols were removed from Ekallate only later. (735) Hence, we prefer to date Marduk–nadin–ahhe's raid on Ekallate towards the beginning of his reign.

The second encounter between Marduk–nadin–ahhe and the Assyrians is mentioned in a kudurru dating from the king's tenth year, where there are cryptic references to "the king of Babylonia (who) defeated Assyria," (736) and "the victory over Assyria." (737) No explicit mention is made of either the time or the place of the victory, but these may be inferred on other grounds. Since the soldier who was granted land in the kudurru was associated with the northernmost region of Babylonia east of the Tigris, (738) and since the document was dated in the sixth month of the king's tenth year, (739) we may presume that the battle in which the man distinguished himself probably took place close to the Babylonian-Assyrian border around the ninth year or early in the tenth year of Marduk–nadin–ahhe's reign. (740)

A third account of Babylonian-Assyrian relations at this time is provided in the royal inscriptions of Tiglath–Pileser I, echoed by the Synchronistic History. (741) These texts tell of clashes between Assyrian and Babylonian chariotry in two successive years. In the first year, the eponymy of Ashur–shuma–eresh, Tiglath–Pileser conducted a double campaign, first against the northeastern provinces of Babylonia between the Lower Zab and the Diyala rivers, (742) then against the land of Suhi on the middle Euphrates. (743) In the second year, the eponymy of Ninuaju, the Assyrians attacked the main cities of northern Babylonia proper, including

(735) One should also note that in the eighth century (before the days of Sennacherib) Tiglath–Pileser III, Shalmaneser V, and Sargon II would have had opportunities to return the statues but did not do so.

(736) *BBSt* no. 8 ii 27.

(737) *BBSt* no. 8 i 5. For the difficulty in interpreting this and the preceding passage, see Ungnad, *Orientalia N. S.* XIII (1944) 77-78.

(738) Land was granted him in the territory of KUR (URU) NI–*ri–e–a* (*BBSt* no. 8 i 2, top 2, 6, 7, 11). This is almost certainly identical with the similarly spelled (KUR) URU *Ir–ri–e–a* and *Ir–⟨ri?⟩–e–a* mentioned in *MDP* VI 44 i 7, 10, 12 and with the URU *Ir–ri–ja* in the Synchronistic History (*CT* XXXIV 42 K. 4401b ii 11) which was in the same general border region between Assyria and Babylonia east of the Tigris; cf. also KUR *Ir–ri–ja* in K. 2667 (Bezold, *Catalogue*, II, 464). This proposed identity is further bolstered by the fact that both cities mentioned in the kudurrus were known as provincial centers (*MDP* VI 44 i 7, *BBSt* no. 8 top 7). I would therefore propose that the *BBSt* no. 8 occurrences be read as *Ì–ri–e–a* (cf. *Ì–ši–in* in *BBSt* no. 28 rev. 20, etc.). Prof. Fuad Safar has suggested to me orally that Irrea might be identified with the site Ṣātu Qālā in the neighborhood of Taqtaq on the Lower Zab. (For collations of the texts discussed here, see my previous treatment in *JESHO* VI [1963] 235 n. 2).

(739) *BBSt* no. 8 i 27-28.

(740) These dates, as Ungnad has pointed out in *Orientalia N.S.* XIII (1944) 78, represent only the latest possible dates for the battle.

(741) *AfO* XVIII (1957-58) 350-351:37-51; *CT* XXXIV 39 ii 14'-24'.

(742) *AfO* XVIII (1957-58) 350-351:37-40; cf. *CT* XXXIV 39 ii 15'-16', 22'-23'.

(743) *AfO* XVIII (1957-58) 351:44-51; cf. *CT* XXXIV 39 ii 24'. King, *A History of Babylon*, p. 256 n. 3, suggested that the statues of Adad and Shala were removed from Ekallate in this first year of campaigning.

Babylon. (744) Though no absolute date can be assigned to these two attacks, they probably took place during the third decade of Tiglath–Pileser's reign sometime before his twenty-eighth year, i.e., between 1095 and 1089. (745)

The fourth and final episode mentioned above is the disappearance of Marduk–nadin–ahhe during the Aramean raids on Mesopotamia. This is to be dated in 1083*, as has been established in the preceding chapter.

Having thus discussed the dating of the four major events of Marduk–nadin–ahhe's reign which were connected with the Assyrians or Arameans, I wish to propose a chronologically ordered but admittedly hypothetical account of Babylonian foreign relations at this time. After the first five years of his reign, Tiglath–Pileser I was largely concerned with campaigns against his enemies to the west, especially the Ahlamu Arameans. (746) In his inscriptions he noted that he crossed the Euphrates twenty-eight times (747) to do battle against these Arameans and that he defeated them over a wide area ranging from Carchemish and the foot of the Lebanon to Rapiqu on the northwestern border of Babylonia. (748) Save for a battle in his second year against mountaineers south of the Lower Zab, (749) he left the region east of the Tigris pretty well alone. Marduk–nadin–ahhe, on the other hand, in the early years of his reign consolidated the provincial holdings of Babylonia between the Lower Zab and the Diyala. He defeated Assyria in a minor battle in the

(744) *AfO* XVIII (1957-58) 351:44-51; cf. *CT* XXXIV 39 ii 18′-21′.

(745) The campaigns of Tiglath–Pileser during his accession year and his first five regnal years are described in detail in his prism inscriptions. After this time, we know that he conducted more campaigns against the Nairi and probably at least fourteen campaigns (possibly twenty-eight, see n. 747 below) against the Ahlamu Arameans, not to mention other, minor encounters. This would occupy him down through at least his twentieth year. We have an eponym list for the last eleven years of his reign (*KAV* 21 iii), and the eponymates during which the chariot battles with Babylonia took place and the eponymate during which the final battle account was written do not occur in that list. So, as far as we can judge at present, the campaigns probably took place somewhere between the twenty-first and twenty-seventh years of Tiglath–Pileser, which would correspond (at the earliest) to the first through seventh years of Marduk–nadin–ahhe or (at the latest) to that king's eleventh through seventeenth years. These vague determinations do not help to place the battles within the reign of the Babylonian king.

(746) For the Ahlamu Arameans, see note 1799 below.

(747) *AfO* XVIII (1957-58) 350:34, etc. Was each campaign represented by a single or by two crossings of the Euphrates? The phrasing of the text is ambiguous, but it could be taken to mean "Twenty-eight times, I crossed the Euphrates in pursuit of the Ahlamu Arameans, twice each year" (thus, e.g., Schroeder, *JSOR* X [1926] 291, and Weidner, *AfO* XVIII [1957-58] 350; Borger, *EAK* I 117, disagrees).

(748) *AfO* XVIII (1957-58) 344:31-35, 350:34-36; *AKA* 73 v 48-50. The approximate location of Rapiqu near the modern city of Ramadi (33°26′ N., 43°18′ E.) on the middle Euphrates is reasonably certain, though modern authors disagree as to the exact site. Forrer (*Provinzeinteilung*, p. 13) placed it where the Nahr Ṣeqlawîje takes off from the Euphrates. A. Musil attempted to identify it variously as ar–Raḥâja (*The Middle Euphrates*, p. 34 n. 24) or as Ramadi (=ar–Rumadi, *The Middle Euphrates*, p. 202; this identification had been denied earlier by Albright in *JAOS* XLVI [1926] 224). Further literature on the location of the site: S. Horn, *ZA* XXXIV (1922) 128; Weidner, *AOB* I 59 n. 5; Weissbach in *RLA* I 218, 241 and in *ZA* XLIII (1936) 281-282; Goetze, *JCS* IV (1950) 95. The city is amply attested in texts from the Old Babylonian period on.

(749) *AKA* 52 iii 35-63 iv 39.

border regions there about his ninth year (750) and had earlier dared a raid into the Assyrian homeland against Ekallate, north of Assur itself, (751) when he had stolen the statues of the gods Adad and Shala from the town. (752) Probably sometime during Marduk–nadin–ahhe's last years of reign, (753) Tiglath–Pileser tried to even the score. On his first attempt, Tiglath–Pileser mustered all the chariotry he had available in the region of the Lower Zab (754) and drew up his forces in battle formation opposite the city of Arzuhina. (755) The outcome of the battle is unstated, but Tiglath–Pileser had to content himself with despoiling the area between the Lower Zab and the Adhaim and a few villages across the Adhaim. (756) Thwarted in his attempts in the northeastern provinces of Babylonia, Tiglath–Pileser then spent the rest of his campaign despoiling the land of Suhi on the middle Euphrates. (757)

In the next year, Tiglath–Pileser bypassed the Babylonian provincial strongholds around Lubdu and marched down the Tigris into northern Babylonia. His chariotry fought a victorious battle against the outflanked forces of Marduk–nadin–ahhe at a place which the Synchronistic History calls *Gur–mar–ri–ti*. (758) Tiglath–Pileser then captured the principal cult centers (759) of northern Babylonia: Dur–Kurigalzu, the Sippars of Shamash and Annunitum, Babylon, and Opis. (760) At

(750) See p. 126 and nn. 739-740 above.

(751) For the location of the site, see Finkelstein, *JCS* VII (1953) 119 and Hallo, *JCS* XVIII (1964) 72; but note that there is no question of anything more than a raid of Marduk–nadin–ahhe against the city. Much still remains to be said about the location of Ekallate in the light of all the available sources. Cf. also the building activity of Shilhak–Inshushinak in a place called *E–gal–la–at* (König, *Die elamischen Königsinschriften*, no. 48:191-197).

(752) *OIP* II 83:48-50.

(753) Placed between his fourteenth and seventeenth years simply because there is as yet no documentation from Babylonia after his thirteenth year.

(754) *CT* XXXIV 39 ii 15′-16′, Synchronistic History. The determinative URU before *Zaban šupalê* is a mistake for ÍD, as the parallel ÍD *Za–ba šu–pa*(var.: *ba*)*–li–e* (*AfO* XVIII [1957-58] 350:37) clearly shows.

(755) *CT* XXXIV 39 ii 15′-16′, Synchronistic History.

(756) *AfO* XVIII (1957-58) 350:37-351:39. The area conquered between the Lower Zab and the Radanu reached from the city of Arman in the district Ugarsallu to the city of Lubdu. (For the location of Arman and Lubdu, see notes 1195 and 1096 below; Arman in the district Ugarsallu is also mentioned in *CT* XXXIV 38 i 30′, Synchronistic History). Ugarsallu, which is written sometimes with an URU determinative before Ugar (e.g., *CT* XXXIV 39 ii 22′; *ibid.*, 42 K. 4401b ii 11) and sometimes with an URU determinative before Sallu (e.g., *AfO* XVIII [1957-58] 351:38; *KAH* II 84:28), was a district east of the Tigris and just south of the Lower Zab (cf. its association with Zaban and Irrija in *CT* XXXIV 42 K. 4401b ii 11); Shilhak–Inshushinak campaigned in this area (König, *Die elamischen Königsinschriften*, no. 54 ii 85). For the identification of the ancient Radánu river with the modern Adhaim, see note 874 below.

(757) *AfO* XVIII (1957-58) 351:41-43.

(758) The place is to the north of Akkad (*ša eliš māt Akkadî*[ki], *CT* XXXIV 39 ii 17′, Synchronistic History). Its name has been much pondered over, with various scholars attempting to read URU instead of *Gur*. Weidner in *AfO* XVII (1954-56) 309 gives a bibliography of the earlier attempts at emendation and suggests that Surmarriti (=Samarra) may have been meant instead. (For the location of Surmarriti, see Grayson in *AfO* XX [1963] 88).

(759) *māḫazī rabûti* (*AfO* XVIII [1957-58] 351:46; *CT* XXXIV 39 ii 20′, Synchronistic History). For a recent discussion of the meaning of the word *māḫazu*, see Seux, *Épithètes royales*, p. 77 n. 16 (with earlier bibliography).

(760) *AfO* XVIII (1957-58) 351:45-48; *CT* XXXIV 39 ii 18′-21′, Synchronistic History.

Babylon he burnt the palace (761) of Marduk–nadin–ahhe, (762) but retired without recapturing the purloined gods of Ekallate. (763)

Not too long after this, Babylonia and Assyria were afflicted with a common scourge, famine. This hardship drove the semi-nomad Arameans, who relied on

(761) Literally plural: "palaces" or "palace rooms"; cuneiform: É.GAL.MEŠ (cf. [É].GAL.MEŠ–*te–šu ma–a–a'–da–[te]* in *AfO* XVIII [1957-58] 351:49-51, var.

(762) It is reasonably certain now that Marduk–nadin–ahhe was not killed at this time, as was once supposed, e.g., by Meissner (*OLZ* XXVI [1923] 157) and Schroeder (*JSOR* X [1926] 292). The word *adūkšu* in the inscriptions of Tiglath–Pileser I (latest edition in *AfO* XVIII [1957-58] 351:51) may be translated "I defeated him"; and the chronicle published by Weidner in *AfO* XVII (1954-56) 384 does not even mention Tiglath–Pileser in connection with the disappearance of Marduk–nadin–ahhe.

Hallo in *IEJ* XVI (1966) 231-242 has proposed identifying five kings mentioned in an Akkadian prophecy (*JCS* XVIII [1964] 13, Text A, col. ii) with Marduk–nadin–ahhe and his four successors. Hallo presumes that the reigns mentioned in the prophecy were successive and then points out (a) that an 18-year reign followed immediately by a 13-year reign occurs only once in Babylonian history (Marduk–nadin–ahhe and Marduk–shapik–zeri), (b) that at least the beginning of Marduk–nadin–ahhe's reign was quite successful (because of his triumph over Assyria), (c) that a usurper (Adad–apla–iddina) succeeded the king who ruled 13 years (Marduk–shapik–zeri), (d) that the king who followed the usurper (Marduk–ahhe–eriba) ruled but a short time (one year and/of six months), (e) that the Luristan bronze daggers inscribed with the names of Babylonian kings down through Adad–apla–iddina which have been found near Kermanshah suggest strongly that "Elam was able to despoil Babylon at least this long" (pp. 237-238). Nonetheless, even if one does accept that the "prophecy" in question is to be interpreted as a *vaticinium ex eventu* and that the kings described are to be viewed as five successive rulers (an opinion neither supported nor refuted by the text), there are still major difficulties with this position:

(a) the principal foreign adversaries of Assyria and Babylonia in the period between Marduk–nadin–ahhe and Adad–apla–iddina were the Arameans and Sutians; it is strange that neither of these groups, often occurring in chronicles relating to this period, would be mentioned in this text dealing with crucial political events;

(b) on the other hand, the principal adversaries of Babylonia as described in the text are the Elamites, who—as already noted by Hallo—do not occur in Babylonian sources between the twelfth and tenth centuries; in addition, a major devastation of Akkad and its shrines is assigned to the thirteen-year reign (Marduk–shapik–zeri); yet none of the dozen documents referring to the reign of Marduk–shapik–zeri mentions either the Elamites or a major devastation of the land;

(c) the Luristan bronze daggers inscribed with the names of Babylonian kings of the twelfth and eleventh centuries can hardly be used to prove Elamite ability to invade Babylonia until the middle of the eleventh century; there is no evidence to connect these daggers with contemporary Elamites (much less to prove contemporary Elamite activity in either Luristan or Babylonia);

(d) there is no mention of Elamite attacks on Babylonia in the Era Epic; the sole context in which Elamites occur there is in IV 131-136, where the various lands surrounding Babylonia are described as engaging in civil war (e.g., Elamite against Elamite) prior to the golden age when Akkad would rule over all of them;

(e) there is no tradition that Marduk–nadin–ahhe died in a revolt (Text A ii 8);

(f) there is no evidence that the tenth king of the Second Isin Dynasty reigned for only three years (*ibid.*, ii 20).

The best argument for Hallo's position is the numerical correspondence between the length of reigns of three rulers in the prophecy with the reigns of three kings of the Second Isin Dynasty. The strongest arguments against his position are the total omission of the Arameans and Sutians in the text and the unexpected reference to the Elamites, who were not known to be militarily active at this time (and certainly not to the extent of devastating Akkad and its shrines). The question must be left open pending further evidence.

(763) As noted above, the dates in this account are largely hypothetical; and the revision of the account will depend almost exclusively on new evidence. There is always the possibility that the Bavian Date should not be considered as even approximately accurate chronologically and that the Ekallate raid should be placed after the burning of Marduk–nadin–ahhe's palace (see note 735 above).

trade with the settled peoples of Mesopotamia for some of their food, into the cultivated lands to seek sustenance by force. This famine is dated in the eighteenth year of Marduk–nadin–ahhe, ([764]) and it became so severe that people resorted to eating human flesh. ([765]) In the midst of this crisis, Marduk–nadin–ahhe disappeared from power; and his vanishing from the political scene is recorded in an Assyrian chronicle with the cryptic phrase *šadâ ēmid*, ([766]) for which the best translation seems simply to be "he disappeared." ([767]) Subsequently, another famine and Aramean invasion were to force Tiglath–Pileser to retire to the outlying region of Katmuhi for safety. ([768]) In these days, the Arameans, who had long been the object of military campaigns by Tiglath–Pileser, became for the first time a direct menace to the heartlands of Assyria and Babylonia. The Arameans and their semi-nomadic confreres were to prove a major factor in the political decline of Babylonia and Assyria over the next two centuries.

7. Marduk-shapik-zeri ([769])

Marduk–shapik–zeri succeeded Marduk–nadin–ahhe on the throne and reigned for thirteen years; ([770]) no family relationship between the two is yet attes-

([764]) The account of the famine is given in the Assyrian chronicle published by Weidner in *AfO* XVII (1954-56) 384 and transliterated and translated by Tadmor in *JNES* XVII (1958) 133-134.

([765]) [*a'il*]⌈*uttu*⌉ UZU.MEŠ *a–ḫa–iš e–*⌈*ku–lu*⌉ (*AfO* XVII [1954-56] 384:2′).

([766]) *AfO* XVII (1954-56) 384:8′.

([767]) *CAD* E 140.

([768]) *AfO* XVII (1954-56) 384:13′.

([769]) *Marduk–šāpik–zēri*: "Marduk (is) the outpourer of seed." For the name type, see Stamm, *Namengebung*, p. 218. DN–shapik–zeri is not attested in Babylonia before this time, but it is used in the later Neo-Babylonian and Neo-Assyrian periods (Tallqvist, *APN*, p. 309; Tallqvist, *NBN*, p. 334). The second element is always attested in combination with the third, i.e., *šāpik* does not occur without *zēri* in PN's, and it always occurs in the G active participle.

Private individuals bearing the same name as the king are attested in the ninth century (*BBSt* no. 36 vi 22; *BBSt* no. 28 rev. 23) and throughout the Neo-Babylonian period (e.g., *VAS* IV 18:15) and into Persian times (e.g., *TCL* XIII 152:22). A scribe named Marduk–shapik–zeri also figures prominently in Seleucid period astronomical texts (e.g., *ana tarṣa* PN, "at the time of PN," not "opposite PN" in *ACT* I 22 no. 122). Van Dijk's attempt to identify this individual as the Second Isin king (*UVB* XVIII 46) is to be discounted since (a) this king would antedate by some seven centuries other monarchs mentioned in the *ACT* colophons; (b) there is already a well-known Marduk–shapik–zeri occurring as a scribe in these texts (*ACT* I 24 nos. 207ca, 811); (c) this Marduk–shapik–zeri—in contrast to the Seleucid kings mentioned in the same colophons—bears no royal title, but is called "scribe of the Enuma–Anu–Enlil series" and has a father whose name begins with Nabu–[ ].

Writing of RN: ^{d}AMAR.UTU–DUB–NUMUN (*UET* VII 6:5′; *YOS* I 37 ii 4, 6; in later texts the same writing is sometimes used, but with the masculine personal determinative prefixed: Kinglist C, 7, 9; New Babylonian Chronicle, obv. 4′; *ABL* 1237 rev. 24), ^{d}AMAR.UTU–*ša–bi–ik*–NUMUN (ROM 938.35:1 [published in transcription in *BASOR* LXXIV (1939) 7]; *BBSt* no. 12 ii 5; 9 N 99:4), ^{d}AMAR.UTU–*ša–bi–ik–ze–ri–im* (*BE* I/2 148 i 1-2; *LIH* I 70:10-11, copy of earlier text), ^{d}AMAR.UTU–*ša–pi–ik–ze–ri* (*UET* IV 143:15), ^{md}AMAR.UTU–*šá–pi–ik*–NUMUN–≪KUR≫ (*CT* XXXIV 39 ii 26′, Synchronistic History; the KUR may be omitted *ibid.*, ii 30′). Passages containing the royal name, but too broken to be read in full are Assur 14616c ii 20′ (less probably 19′) and *AfO* XVII (1954-56) 384:8′.

([770]) Kinglist C, 7.

ted. (771) The circumstances surrounding this king's accession have been described in the preceding paragraph. (772) His reign seems to have been peaceful compared with that of his predecessor, and during it there is no evidence of hostility with Assyria. However, the seeds of chaos implanted by the surge of Arameans in the last year of Marduk–nadin–ahhe did not lie dormant: semi-nomads continued to pour into Babylonia during the reign of Marduk–shapik–zeri and, after his death, one of their number succeeded him on the throne.

The titulary attested for this king is scanty. The only complete Akkadian titulary is preserved in the brief dagger inscription: "Belonging to Marduk–shapik–zeri, king of the world." (773) The only other Akkadian royal inscription published to date begins: "Marduk–shapik–zeri, king of Babylon, mighty king, king of the world, king of the four quarters ..."; (774) but the rest of the text is fragmentary. (775) He is the only king of the dynasty thus far to call himself "mighty king"; (776) and only his predecessor in this dynasty also called himself "king of the four quarters"; (777) but "king of the world" was claimed by at least six other monarchs of this dynasty (778) and "king of Babylon(ia)" by five. (779) Epithets claimed in his sole Sumerian inscription express only personal piety and are of no political significance. (780) Taken as a whole, the titulary shows that Marduk–shapik–zeri retained some pretense to glory in the tradition of his predecessors, regardless of what his political limitations may have been.

(771) See note 683 above.

(772) Wiseman (*CAH* II² xxxi 25-26) makes the interesting suggestion that, since a later text (*ABL* 1237 rev. 24) compares the accession of Marduk–shapik–zeri with that of Esarhaddon, Marduk–shapik–zeri may have been a younger son of Nebuchadnezzar or of Marduk–nadin–ahhe who succeeded in gaining the throne only after a struggle.

(773) T. J. Meek, "Bronze Swords from Luristan," *BASOR* LXXIV (1939) 7-11, with photo of this dagger on p. 1. The text on the dagger (now number 938.35 in the Royal Ontario Museum collection) reads: *ša* ᵈAMAR.UTU–*ša–bi–ik*–NUMUN (rev.) LUGAL ŠÁR.

(774) *BE* I/2 148 i 1-7.

(775) Towards the end, we can distinguish such pious epithets as *ašru*, *šaḫtu* (i 1 f.e.).

(776) *šarru(m) dannu(m)* (*BE* I/2 148 i 4). The same title, however, was used to refer to Nebuchadnezzar I in a poetic kudurru (*BBSt* no. 6 i 28).

(777) *BE* I/2 148 i 6-7, cf. *UET* VIII 101:23.

(778) I.e., Ninurta–nadin–shumi, Nebuchadnezzar I, Enlil–nadin–apli, Marduk–nadin–ahhe, Adad–apla–iddina, Nabu–shumu–libur, and possibly Itti–Marduk–balatu (see p. 96 above), not to mention their Assyrian contemporaries. References for the above and for Marduk–shapik–zeri are listed by Seux in *Épithètes royales*, pp. 311-312.

(779) I.e., Ninurta–nadin–shumi, Nebuchadnezzar I, Enlil–nadin–apli, Marduk–nadin–ahhe, and Adad–apla–iddina (references under the individual monarchs); references for Marduk–shapik–zeri: *BE* I/2 148 i 3, ii ⌜6⌝. It is interesting that Marduk–shapik–zeri bears so many of the titles claimed by his four immediate predecessors on the Babylonian throne. According to a transliteration made by Prof. Oppenheim, Marduk–shapik–zeri bears the simple title "king" (LUGAL.[E]) in an unpublished economic text from Ur, *UET* VII 6:5′.

(780) M e – a – a m ! g ù – d é – a – n i n u n – š u – d ù – d ù – a – n i : *LIH* I 70:12-13.

From our chronological considerations in the second chapter, we know that Marduk–shapik–zeri's rule in Babylonia was concurrent with the reigns of three kings in Assyria. He witnessed the last part of Tiglath–Pileser I's thirty-nine year reign, the whole of Ashared–apil–Ekur's two years, and the beginning of Ashur–bel–kala's eighteen-year rule. We know nothing of his relations with the first two of these monarchs and will discuss here only the evidence for his dealings with Ashur–bel–kala.

There are two passages which mention diplomatic relations between Marduk–shapik–zeri and Ashur–bel–kala. The first of these, from the Synchronistic History, presents no difficulties:

> At the time of Ashur–bel–kala, king of [Assyria], and Marduk–shapik–zer–« mati », king of Kardu[niash]: they (i.e., the two kings) pledged mutual pea[ce] and good will. At the time of Ashur–bel–kala, Marduk–shapik–zeri [m]et his end. (781)

This text is simply interpreted: the two kings concluded a peace treaty, and the reign of Marduk–shapik–zeri terminated while Ashur–bel–kala was still on the throne.

The passage in the New Babylonian Chronicle is less clear and, for that reason, is given here in detail:

(4′) *Marduk–šāpik–zēri* x[ ]x *īpuš*
(5′) ⌜105⌝ *šarrāni ša mātāt A*[*ḫlamê ina māti illikūma nuḫša*] *u ḫegalla īmurū*
(6′) *ṭubtu u sulummû itti* ⌜*Aššur–bēl–k*⌝[*ala ša*]*r māt Aššur iškun*
(7′) *ina ūmišūma šarru ultu māt Aššur ana Sippar illikam* (782)

(4′) Marduk–shapik–zeri *built* [ ]. (783)
(5′) *105* kings of the lands of the A[hlamu came into the land] and enjoyed abundance and [prosperity].
(6′) (Marduk–shapik–zeri) established friendly relations with Ashur–bel–ka[la kin]g of Assyria.
(7′) At that time, the king came from Assyria to Sippar.

(781) *CT* XXXIV 39 ii 25′-30′. The reading of the king's name has been discussed above on p. 43.

(782) Transliteration: (4′) mdAMAR.UTU–DUB–NUMUN x[ ]x DÙ–*uš* (5′) ⌜105⌝ LUGAL.MEŠ *šá* KUR.KUR *A*[*ḫ–la–me–e ina* KUR GIN.MEŠ–*ma* ḪÉ.NUN] *u* ḪÉ.GÁL IGI.MEŠ (6′) DÙG–*tú u su–lum–mu–ú* KI m⌜dŠÁR–EN–*k*⌝[*a–la* MA]N KUR *Aš*+*šur iš–kun* (7′) *ina* u_4*–mi–šú–ma* MAN TA KUR *Aš*+*šur ana Sip–par* DU–*kam*.

Notes on restorations: (4′) about six to ten signs are missing in the gap, depending on the spacing of the line; (5′) the number should end in 5 ( ), since all other fours in the text have only one wedge in the bottom row (lines 15, 16:)—so King's reading in *CCEBK* II, p. 58 must be altered; the traces as copied could fit either 105 (i.e., 60+40) or 145 (100+40), but the usual writing of 100 as 1 ME rather than ME alone would speak against the latter alternative. See also p. 133 and Appendix C below.

(783) Note on translation: *built* in line 4′ is adopted as a tentative translation for *īpuš*. Reconstruction of cult objects is narrated elsewhere in the chronicle (obv. 13′, rev. 13, and possibly in obv. 11′, negatively), and the only other occurrence of the verb in this text is in the first of these examples.

The passage is not clear as it stands. The opening line might indeed allude to construction activity of the king; but it might also be interpreted in some other way, e.g., winning a victory. (784) Since the verb *epēšu* can be used in so many highly idiomatic contexts, (785) no restoration can be regarded as entirely satisfactory.

The second line of the passage refers to a large number of "kings," who "experienced prosperity." (786) Remembering the conditions of famine in Mesopotamia which prevailed at the time of Marduk–shapik–zeri's accession and which caused the Arameans to irrupt into the land, (787) we have proposed this restoration. There would be no need to mention the semi-nomad chieftains in the chronicle unless they were in some way affecting Babylonia; and, on the basis of other contacts with semi-nomads mentioned in the same chronicle (788) and the prevailing conditions at this time, this or some similar restoration seems called for. It is likely that the petty chieftains were overcoming famine conditions and that they were accomplishing this with willing or unwilling Babylonian aid. (789)

The third line of the passage tells of the Assyro-Babylonian peace treaty, already known from the Synchronistic History. The "king" mentioned in the fourth line is presumably the king of Babylonia (790) returning from concluding the treaty with Assyria. (791) This interpretation would fit in well with the general picture of

(784) I.e., [*ṣaltam*] *īpuš*.

(785) *CAD* E 201-225.

(786) Note, however, that *ḫegalla* as the object of *amāru* is unattested elsewhere.

(787) *AfO* XVII (1954-56) 384:2′-5′.

(788) E.g., New Babylonian Chronicle obv. 10′-11′, rev. 10-12.

(789) King, *A History of Babylon*, p. 256 n. 4, interprets this reference in the chronicle as alluding to Marduk–shapik–zeri's establishing his suzerainty over a large number of petty rulers.

(790) The simple designation "king" (MAN) in a Babylonian chronicle should refer to the reigning sovereign of Babylonia; elsewhere in this chronicle Assyrian kings are always called explicitly "king of Assyria" (*šar māt Aššur*: obv. 6′, rev. 1, 2, 18). Weidner (*AfO* VI [1930-31] 77) and J.-R. Kupper (*Les nomades*, p. 117 n. 1) seem to think that the king involved here is Ashur–bel–kala of Assyria. Weidner explains Ashur–bel–kala's presence in the south by the Assyrian hegemony over Babylonia at this time, which extended into the reign of Adad–apla–iddina (probably an Assyrian appointee according to *CT* XXXIV 39 ii 31′-32′, Synchronistic History). Ashur–bel–kala may also have come down into Babylonia to conclude a treaty with Adad–apla–iddina and to fetch the latter's daughter home as his wife to Assyria, but these would hardly be mentioned in a chronicle under the reign of Marduk–shapik–zeri. The arguments brought forward by Weidner and Kupper are possible; but it seems to me equally possible that Marduk–shapik–zeri may have journeyed to Assyria to conclude a treaty there with his "overlord," and the general style of the use of the unqualified designation "king" within a Babylonian chronicle seems to speak against the interpretations of Weidner and Kupper as "king (of Assyria)." (The political preeminence of Assyria at this time is asserted only by the pro-Assyrian Synchronistic History, which indicates that the next Babylonian king may have been appointed by Assyria).

Sippar around this time was particularly vulnerable to the Aramean onslaughts (see n. 830 below).

(791) An inference from the use of the ventive *illikam*, which would imply that the king was returning from a foreign land. The ventive, however, need not be interpreted in the strict sense in this period.

Sidney Smith (*EHA*, p. 307), followed by H. W. F. Saggs (*The Greatness That Was Babylon*, p. 90), suggested that the reason that the Babylonian king stopped at Sippar was that Adad–apla–iddina had already usurped the throne at Babylon. Olmstead (*AJSL* XXXVI [1919-20] 151) believed that the capital had been shifted to Sippar after Babylon lost prestige by concluding a treaty recognizing Assyrian overlordship.

a weakened Babylonia—its capital sacked by Assyria in the preceding reign, and now generally overrun by semi-nomads—seeking some sort of understanding with its northern neighbor lest it be forced to wage defensive action on more than one front.

The borders of Babylonia at this time are not known with certainty. Besides the mention of Sippar in the New Babylonian Chronicle, (792) we also know that Marduk–shapik–zeri was sufficiently in control of Borsippa at some point during his reign to further repairs on Ezida. (793) In recent excavations at Nippur (1964-65), a duck weight was found bearing an inscription of Napsamenni, chief of the seers and high priest of Enlil there during the reign of Marduk–shapik–zeri. (794) In the south, we know of activities at Ur: the dedication of gold votive offerings in a temple (795) and the writing of a private economic tablet in the king's third year. (796) The obverse of a kudurru (presumably also from the south) mentions the provinces of Bit–Sin–magir and the Sealand. (797) The only other kudurru dating from his reign is very fragmentary; four personal names and one (partial) geographical name are preserved in the text. (798) The title of the first witness in this document can plausibly be restored: [LÚ *šá–kin* URU *I*–]*ši–in*; (799) and we may consequently infer that that city was under the sway of Marduk–shapik–zeri. In the northern sections

(792) Obv. 7′.

(793) *LIH* I 70 is a seventh-century copy (made in the fifteenth year of Kandalanu) of a Sumerian text concerning Marduk–shapik–zeri's construction work on Ezida. The copy was made by Nabu–shumu–lishir, a member of the family of m*Huṣābu*, which was well known at Borsippa beginning in the seventh century (e.g., *TuM* II-III 32:5, 67:8, 103:16; *TCL* XII 81:14, XIII 143:10; *BRM* I 71:14; *VAS* IV 32:15, etc.).

(794) The black stone duck weight, excavation number 9-N-99, was found on Dec. 3, 1964, on the southeast of the expedition house site at Nippur in a mud-mortar pit within a thick and extensive ash layer. It originally weighed 10 minas and bears a five-line inscription in Sumerian in the name of Napsamenni, who claims the titles p a u z ú (*akil bārê*) and n u . è š d5 0 . l á (*nišakku Enlil*). The weight is now in the Iraq Museum, Baghdad. If the ash layer in which the weight was found should prove relatively contemporary to the weight itself, one could connect this layer with the sack of Nippur by Arameans and Sutians during the reign of Adad–apla–iddina, the successor of Marduk–shapik–zeri (*JCS* XIX [1965] 123:10-14).

(795) *UET* IV 143:14-15.

(796) *UET* VII 6 (unpublished) is dated at Ur (URU *Ú–ri*) on the thirtieth day of Ajar in the third year of Marduk–shapik–zeri (information courtesy of Prof. Oppenheim). This text is dated a century later than the other documents in the late-second-millennium economic archives from Ur (*Orientalia N.S.* XXXIV [1965] 242 n. 2).

(797) *YOS* I 37 ii 10, 13. The text mentions the delivery of animals in the twelfth year of Marduk–shapik–zeri (ii 4, 6) to the "keeper of the horses" (*rē'ī sīsê*) of Bit–Sin–magir, and each animal is listed with a monetary evaluation in silver. As in *BBSt* no. 9 iii 1-15, this terminology probably refers to the collection of taxes, especially since the office of "keeper of the horses" seems to be province-wide.

(798) *BBSt* no. 12.

(799) Four other kudurrus of the early post-Kassite period include the governor of Isin either at or towards the beginning of the list of witnesses: *BBSt* no. 28 rev. 20, *BBSt* no. 29 ii 9, *BBSt* no. 6 ii 17, *BBSt* no. 25:27, to which may now plausibly be added *BBSt* no. 12 ii 15. For the writing of the GN, see note 478 above.

of Babylonia, we have no evidence as to how far the borders went. (800) That the land was not secure at this time may be indicated by the fact that Marduk–shapik–zeri felt compelled to repair the walls and gates of Babylon during his reign. (801)

We do not as yet know under what circumstances the reign of Marduk–shapik–zeri drew to a close. The Synchronistic History tells us quite simply that he met his end during the reign of Ashur–bel–kala. (802) Perhaps, in view of the fact that he was succeeded by an Aramean (803) and the probability that his years were troubled by semi-nomad advances, (804) we might suppose that the Arameans had finally gained enough strength to impose their will on Babylon itself. In any event, after his death, one of their number succeeded to the Babylonian throne. (805)

8. Adad-apla-iddina (806)

The family background of Adad–apla–iddina and the manner in which he came to the throne are disputed in the sources, which preserve three apparently different

(800) Save for the mention of Bit–Sin–magir in *YOS* I 37 ii 10. The location of Bit–Sin–magir is unknown. The grouping of the Sealand and Bit–Sin–magir in *YOS* I 37 ii and in *BE* I/1 83 might indicate a southern locale, but the grouping in the Kassite kudurru *MDP* II 86-92 points towards the northeast (Tupliash, Opis, Dur–Papsukkal, Hudadu, etc.). Neither alternative can be definitely ruled out.

(801) *BE* I/2 148 ii 7-2 f.e. The inscription is broken, but it could be read: (7) *in qí–ri–[ib]* (6) KÁ.DINGIR.[RA.KI] (5) *ba–ba–[ni]* (4) . . . (3) BÀD *Im–gur–*[^{d}EN.LÍL] (2) BÀD X [ ] . . . Imgur–Enlil was the inner wall of the city (Unger, *Babylon*, pp. 59ff.).

(802) *CT* XXXIV 39 ii 30′: *šadâšu ē[mid]*.

(803) New Babylonian Chronicle, obv. 8′.

(804) See above, p. 133.

(805) It is chronologically possible that some of Ashur–bel–kala's campaigns against the Arameans and even his attack on Dur–Kurigalzu may have occurred towards the end of Marduk–shapik–zeri's reign. These events are discussed under Adad–apla–iddina below.

(806) *Adad–apla–iddina*: "Adad has given me an heir." For the name type, see Stamm, *Namengebung*, pp. 39-40. Names of this type, DN-apla(m)–iddina(m) are attested as early as the Old Babylonian period (Ranke, *EBPN*, p. 128). They continue through the Kassite era and down into Neo-Assyrian and Neo-Babylonian times (Clay, *CPN*, p. 124; Tallqvist, *APN*, p. 7; Tallqvist, *NBN*, p. 2). This king seems to represent one of the earliest presently known occurrences of the name Adad–apla–iddina; the only earlier instances seem to be a name in text no. 40:11 of the archive of Ninurta–tukulti–Ashur (*AfO* X [1935-36] 45, reading possible, not certain), which dates from the century preceding this king, and an eponym official from the time of Tiglath–Pileser I (*AfO* XVI [1952-53] 215 no. 9, VAT 14472). The name Adad–apla–iddina was more popular in the later periods.

Writing of RN: in contemporary documents as ^{d}IM–IBILA–SUM-*na* (*BBSt* no. 13:1; Herzfeld, *Iran in the Ancient East*, pl. XXVIII; VA 5937 rev. 7′, unpublished kudurru; unpublished economic text from Nippur as cited in Hilprecht, *Excavations in Assyria and Babylonia*, p. 519 n. 1), as ^{d}IM–IBILA–*i–din–nam* (*MDOG* LIII [1914] 28, transcription only; I *R* 5 no. XXII 1-2; *UET* I 166:1; *UET* I 167:1), as [$^{m?}$]^{d}IM–IBILA–*i–di–nam* (*Studia Orientalia* I [1925] 32:6, later copy), as ^{d}IM–IBILA–*i–di–na–am* (Place, *Ninive et l'Assyrie*, II, 308:1-2), and only partially preserved in *BBSt* no. 26 rev. 3 (^{d}IM–IBIL[A–]); in later documents as ^{d}IM–IBILA–SUM-[*na*] (K. 6156, colophon, according to Bezold, *Catalogue*, II, 767), ^{md}IM–IBILA–SUM-*na* (*UVB* XVIII 45:17), ^{md}IM–IBILA–MU (*JCS* XIX [1965] 123:10), ^{md}IM–A–SUM-*na* (*CT* XXXIV 39 ii 31′, 34′, Synchronistic History), ^{md}IM– [illegible] –MU (New Babylonian Chronicle, obv. 8′). Fragments of

accounts of his parentage and two of his mode of succession. The pertinent documents, one of his royal inscriptions, a later Babylonian chronicle, and the Synchronistic History, read as follows:

own royal inscription

Adad–apla–iddina, son of Nin–Duginna, (807) king of Babylon... (808)

New Babylonian Chronicle

Adad–apla–iddina, son of Itti–Marduk–balatu, an Aramean, (809) a usurper... (810)

Synchronistic History

He (i.e., Ashur–bel–kala) (811) appointed Adad–apla–iddina, son of Esagil–shaduni, son of a nobody, to rule over them. (812)

The lineage set down in the royal inscription, as already observed by Poebel, (813) refers to divine rather than human descent. In the following lines of the same text, the king goes on to describe himself as "son-in-law of (the god) Nanna(r)" (814)—clear evidence that natural descent was not meant.

The other two accounts, however, present discrepancies which are less easily resolved. First, was the name of Adad–apla–iddina's father Itti–Marduk–balatu or was it Esagil–shaduni? It is always possible that one of these men referred to as the king's father was actually a slightly more distant forbear, since calling a man "son" of PN in this period can designate simply ancestry (without implying whether

---

the name are possibly preserved in Assur 14616c ii 21′ (mdIM–[ ]), in K. 10802 rev. 2 ([ ]–⌜A(?)⌝–SUM; see *JCS* XVI [1962] 62); and in Kinglist A iii 1′ the masculine personal and divine determinatives are partially visible.

(807) dNIN.EZEN×⌜TÙN⌝KI.NA (=Nin–Duginna/–Isinna/–Gubla?). The reading of this name is not certain, but see Seux, *Épithètes royales*, p. 160 n. 30. Cf. *MSL* II 88:782,

(808) *UET* I 166:1-3 (Sumerian) = *UET* I 167:1-3 (Akkadian).

(809) Written KUR *A–ra–mu–u*. For other gentilics written with the determinative for land (KUR) rather than the determinative for people (LÚ), cf. *AfO* XVIII (1957-58) 350:34, etc.

(810) Obv. 8′.

(811) The verb *iškun* is in the singular, and the only probable subject in the singular is the Assyrian king (understood). The identical phrase PN *ana šarrūti iškun* is employed earlier in the Synchronistic History (i 17′) to describe Ashur–uballit's installation of Kurigalzu II as king of Babylonia. See also Weidner, *AfO* VI (1930-31) 76 n. 9.

F. E. Peiser in *OLZ* X (1907) 616 suggested that, rather than viewing the subject of *iškun* as unexpressed, one should consider the patronymic of Adad–apla–iddina as having been omitted from the text. He thus interpreted the lines as "Esaggil–shaduni, son of a nobody, appointed Adad–apla–iddina, son of 〈 〉, as king over them." He then identified Esagil–shaduni with the Aramean usurper (or "King of IM.GI," as the epithet was read at that time) mentioned in the New Babylonian Chronicle, obv. 8′. These passages are both broken and their phraseology difficult to interpret; but Peiser's theories seem quite improbable at present.

(812) *CT* XXXIV 39 ii 31′-32′.

(813) Poebel, "Kein neuer Vater Adad–apla–iddinas!" *AfO* V (1928-29) 103-104.

(814) *UET* I 166:4-5 and 167:4-5.

one or several generations were involved). (815) But there is not sufficient evidence here to determine whether either of these "fathers" was in reality a more remote ancestor. Neither of the men bears a name that would be improbable for individuals living during the Second Isin period; (816) and both names are attested as possible "ancestral names" in a list edited by W. G. Lambert. (817) Hence, we cannot yet arrive at a satisfactory solution, though it may be remarked that the version of the New Babylonian Chronicle is generally more reliable (because of the Synchronistic History's inaccuracy in the transmission of proper names elsewhere). (818) It is noteworthy that, although Adad-apla–iddina was supposed to be an Aramean, neither his own name nor the name of either of his "fathers" was Aramean; (819) and, apart from the statement of the New Babylonian Chronicle, we have no real evidence to connect him with the Arameans. (820)

Secondly, was Adad–apla–iddina a usurper or was he installed by Ashur–bel–kala on the Babylonian throne? The two alternatives are not necessarily mutually exclusive. A Babylonian king who was either directly appointed or indirectly sanctioned by the reigning Assyrian monarch could be described as a "usurper," if his accession were effected in a manner differing from the usual procedure in Babylonia. Both sources agree in stressing that he was not of royal descent and came to the throne in an extra-legal manner.

Besides his "relationships" with the gods, i.e., as son of Nin–Duginna and son-in-law of Nanna, (821) Adad–apla–iddina also laid claim to the following titles:

(1) "king of Babylon" (822)—a title borne also by his five immediate predecessors;

(815) E.g., Hinke Kudurru v 24 (cf. *ibid.*, iii 13-14).

(816) The number of individuals bearing the name Itti–Marduk–balatu has been discussed in note 490 above. Though I have found individuals named Esagil–shaduni/u only later in the Neo-Babylonian period (*Nbn*, 13:13, 1102:5), other proper names with Esagila in them (e.g., Esagil–bunua, *BBSt* no. 8 ii 24) occur at this time.

(817) Itti–Marduk–balatu in *JCS* XI (1957) 12:2 and Esagil–shaduni *ibid.*, 13:60. For the possibility that this list catalogues family or ancestral names, see Lambert's remarks *ibid.*, 6.

(818) See note 150 above.

(819) This need not be an argument against the king's Aramean origin since many members of the foreign populations groups settling in Babylonia, e.g., the Kassites and the Chaldeans, were rapidly assimilated and bore Babylonian names.

(820) Doubt on the point of Adad–apla–iddina's Aramean affiliation has recently been expressed by Kupper, *Les nomades*, pp. 116-117. See also note 840 below.

(821) Contrary to the opinion expressed in *CAD* E 156, *emu* can very well mean "son-in-law" here, considering the king's symbolic marriage to Ishtar, the daughter of Sin (see Poebel, *AfO* V [1928-29] 103-104; Van Buren, *Orientalia N.S.* XIII [1944] 55 and n. 7; Tallqvist, *Akkadische Götterepitheta*, p. 332). Therefore, *CAD*'s unique reference for a meaning "son of wife's sister" for *emu* disappears; and the pertinent heading should be deleted. (Seux, *Épithètes royales*, pp. 82-83 n. 41 discusses the problem at greater length and arrives at the same conclusion).

(822) Contemporary texts: *Studia Orientalia* I (1925) 32:6; *MDOG* LIII (1914) 28:2 (transcription only); I *R* 5 no. XXII:3; Place, *Ninive et l'Assyrie*, II, 308:3 (the cuneiform sign for "king" is missing in printed copy); *UET* I 166-167:3. Later texts: *JCS* XIX (1965) 123:10.

(2) "provider for Ur" ([823])—an epithet whose Sumerian equivalent was likewise attributed to Marduk–nadin–ahhe;

(3) "king of the world" ([824])—used also by his five predecessors (and possibly the sixth as well) and relatively meaningless by this time; it was also used by Nabu–shumu–libur about fifteen years after Adad–apla–iddina's reign;

(4) strictly *ad hoc* epithets, such as "prince, revering (Nabu)" ([825]) and "builder of Nemed–Marduk." ([826])

These titles indicate little save that Adad–apla–iddina, if he was an Aramean and a usurper, was nonetheless anxious to retain the Babylonian royal titulary employed by previous members of the dynasty.

But, even if there were an Aramean on the throne, Babylonia did not escape further depredations from invading semi-nomads. ([827]) During the reign of Adad–apla–iddina, Sutians, aided on occasion by Arameans, assailed the land and "took home the spoils of Sumer and Akkad." ([828]) Old cult centers were sacked, as a later inscription narrates:

> Shamash, the great lord, who dwells in Ebabbar in Sippar, the foundation lines of which the Sutians, an evil foe, had obliterated and destroyed during the troubles and disorders in Akkad... ([829])

The cult statue of Shamash was lost, the regular offerings ceased, and the major religious ritual of the temple stopped for over a century and a half, despite occasional attempts to renew it. ([830]) In Nippur, the temples were sacked and the property

([823]) *UET* I 166:6; *UET* I 167:6-7.

([824]) Herzfeld, *Iran in the Ancient East,* p. 134:2 (transcription only).

([825]) *Studia Orientalia* I (1925) 32:6.

([826]) Place, *Ninive et l'Assyrie,* II, 308:4-5.

([827]) Compare the later reign of Eriba–Marduk, a Chaldean, which was troubled by Aramean disturbances.

([828]) New Babylonian Chronicle, obv. 10′-11′; cf. *JCS* XIX (1965) 123:10-13.

([829]) From a stone inscription of Nabu–apla–iddina, relating the restoration of the Sippar cult and its regular offerings, published as *BBSt* no. 36. The section quoted (i 1-8) does not mention the reign of a specific king; but comparison with the New Babylonian Chronicle, obv. 10′-11′ and with an inscription of Simbar–Shipak (*JCS* XIX [1965] 123:12) shows that it is probably to be assigned around this time.

([830]) *BBSt* no. 36 i 20-23. Another item found at Sippar, which dates from about this time, is an oblong stone and bronze object, now BM 93077, dedicated to Shamash by Tukulti–Mer, king of Hana. The short votive inscription on it was first published by T. Pinches in *TSBA* VIII (1885) 351-353 and most recently edited by Weidner in *AnOr* XII 336-338 (with additional bibliography and arguments for dating at around this time); a picture of the object was published in S. Smith, *EHA*, pl. XVIIIa. Does this dedication by a king ruling over Aramean territory imply that Sippar was for a while under foreign jurisdiction about this time? (Wiseman's contention in *CAH* II² xxxi 29 that Tukulti–Mer claimed to be king of Assyria was obviated by Weidner's observations in *AnOr* XII 336-338).

of the god Enlil carried off. (831) Similar outrages were perpetrated throughout Babylonia. (832)

The raids of the Sutians and Arameans evidently continued for some time, if one can believe the account of Nabu-apla-iddina, who considered himself the effective avenger of Babylonia against the Sutians in the early ninth century. (833) Their frenzied attacks upon the settled land became the background against which the Era Epic was written. In this epic, the author, Kabti-ili-Marduk, (834) sketched the theological causality behind the Sutian raids (835) and then the raids themselves: the destruction in Dur-Kurigalzu (Parsa), (836) Sippar, and Der, and male and female Sutians howling in the city of Uruk. (837) Babylon became the scene of civil war: the peaceful citizens rose in arms, and the king sent his army against them with orders to plunder the city. (838)

W. G. Lambert has proferred an explanation of the background of the fourth tablet of the Era Epic:

> ...the reign of Adad-apal-iddina fits the account in the epic exceedingly well. The curious phenomenon is the civil war in Babylon, while other cities suffer from outside attacks. Adad-apal-iddina was himself an Aramaean usurper. This fact alone could easily lead to friction between the court and the townspeople. The invading Aramaean Sutû may well have regarded him as an ally, so that they spared his city, but the citizens would obviously not stay quiet under a ruler who was abetting barbarous tribes in their pillage of other cities of the country. This explains the rise of the citizens to arms, and why the king was forced to use his troops on them. (839)

In some respects, this is a plausible explanation of the data, since it takes into account the later unpopularity of Adad-apla-iddina in Babylonian tradition (840)

(831) *JCS* XIX (1965) 123:11, 14. For possible traces of a contemporary destruction of Nippur, see note 794 above.

(832) The whole country had to be "avenged" and reconstructed according to *BBSt* no. 36 ii 29-iii 10. Cf. *JCS* XIX (1965) 123:13, which says that the hostile Arameans and Sutians sacked the land of Sumer and Akkad and levelled all temples (*ušamqitū gimir ekurrāti*).

(833) *BBSt* no. 36 ii 29-30.

(834) Era Epic V 42.

(835) I.e., Era persuading Marduk to leave his statue temporarily, which resulted in withdrawal of divine protection from Babylonia and consequent general chaos in the land.

(836) For this reading, see W. G. Lambert, *AfO* XVIII (1957-58) 396-397, and W. L. Moran, *Orientalia N.S.* XXIX (1960) 103-104.

(837) Era Epic IV 50 ff.

(838) Era Epic IV 6-35.

(839) *AfO* XVIII (1957-58) 398.

(840) As expressed in the New Babylonian Chronicle, obv. 8′-11′, where he was charged with being an Aramean, a usurper, a man who did not protect his country, and probably with not completing existing building projects (i.e., [*la*] restored before *ušaklil* in keeping with the rest of the negative reports). One cannot help wondering whether the king's ineffective defense of the land might not have led to his being branded as an Aramean. See also Goetze's suggested translation (stylistically unlikely) of the New Babylonian Chronicle obv. 8′ in *JCS* XIX (1965) 134.

and the king's apparent disregard in the epic for the fate of other Babylonian cities.

On the other hand, there is contemporary evidence from Babylonia which contradicts the later poetic description of the Era Epic as well as the unfavorable impression left by the New Babylonian Chronicle and shows that Adad–apla–iddina did not neglect his duties as a Babylonian monarch. (841) Besides claiming the usual titulary of his royal predecessors, (842) he contributed much to the general well-being of the land. At Babylon, he repaired Imgur–Enlil, the inner wall of the city. (843) At Borsippa, he gave a belt made of gold and precious stones to the statue of the god Nabu. (844) In Kish, he constructed a large retaining wall on the southern side of the temple Emeteursag. (845) At Nippur, he renewed Nemed–Marduk, the city's outer wall; (846) and, in Ur, he made repairs in the great Nanna courtyard and in

(841) Of course, one must always remember that the allusion in the Era Epic is anonymous and may not apply here at all.

(842) See pages 100, 116, 117, 123-124, 131 above.

(843) The German excavators at Babylon in the 1913-1914 season found a brick fragment (excavation no. Bab. 59431), poorly stamped with a four-line inscription of Adad–apla–iddina. The inscription, partially legible and published in transliteration only (*MDOG* LIII [1914] 28), reads: "Adad–apla–iddinam, king of Babylon, [builder of?] Imgur–Enlil, ..." The brick was found among refuse near the Southeast Gate on the east side of the inner city wall (*MDOG* LIII [1914] 28; *WVDOG* XLVIII 64, 79, with the exact find spot shown in the plan on pl. 37). Unger has identified the gate near which this brick was found as the Zababa Gate, through which passed the road to Kish (*WVDOG* XLVIII 105-106). Fr. Wetzel remarked concerning this brick: "Will man der Stelle des Fundes einiges Gewicht beilegen, so könnte man annehmen, daß zu Adadapaliddins Zeit der Mauerumfang Babylons schon der gleiche war wie zur neubabylonischen Zeit" (*WVDOG* XLVIII 64).

In his work on Imgur–Enlil, Adad–apla–iddina was continuing the work of his predecessor, Marduk–shapik–zeri (*BE* I/2 148 ii 3 f.e.), though no inscribed bricks of the latter have been recovered from the wall area. After the time of Adad–apla–iddina, the next work on the wall attested by inscribed bricks dates from the reign of Sargon II (*WVDOG* XLVIII 64-65).

(844) A copy of the inscription on the gold belt of the statue of Nabu was made by the scribe Arad–Gula in the time of Esarhaddon, when the text was already in slightly damaged condition. It is this clay-tablet copy, BM 79503, acquired by the British Museum in 1889, that has come down to us. The text, published by Gadd in *Studia Orientalia* I (1925) 29-33, is written interlinearly in Sumerian and Babylonian, with each pair of lines divided by a horizontal stroke drawn across the tablet. In so far as the text is intelligible, it contains a dedication to Nabu with suitable epithets (lines 1-5), the king's name and titulary with a brief prayer for his well-being (lines 6-8), and a description of the belt given by the king to the god (lines 9-11).

The word *nēbeḫu*, "belt," is sometimes preceded by the determinative TÚG (as here in the Sumerian) and was often made of cloth. Here the belt is described as being made of reddish gold (*ḫurāṣi ruššî*), studded with precious stones (*abni aqarti*), decorated with a picture of wild bulls (*rīmū kadrūtu*) looking towards the four winds.

(845) Langdon, *Excavations at Kish*, I, 16-17 and 65. Copies of the stamped-brick inscription have been published in R. Ker Porter, *Travels*, II, pl. 77(a) and in I *R* 5 no. XXII; and a transliteration and translation of the text were published by Langdon, *op. cit.*, pp. 16-17. One stamped brick with an identical inscription is on exhibit in the Field Museum, Chicago, number 156011.

(846) As known from an inscription on a truncated clay cone found at Khorsabad by the French in the nineteenth century (Place, *Ninive et l'Assyrie*, II, 308). The inscription reads: "Adad–apla–iddinam, (king) of Babylon, who built Nemed–Marduk, the outer wall, the wall of Nippur, for Enlil, his lord."

the pavement against the northeast face of the ziggurat. (847) As a matter of fact, we have record of more building from his reign than from the reign of any other monarch of the Post–Kassite period down through Shalmaneser V. This hardly corresponds with the picture of a monarch derelict in his royal duties which we might be tempted to postulate on the sole basis of later written evidence. (848)

At least three fragmentary kudurrus survive from this reign, showing that the king continued this old tradition as well. (849) Unfortunately, the published kudurrus preserve neither dates nor identifiable geographical names. (850)

There is some evidence for literary activity in Babylonia during his reign. Royal inscriptions continued to be composed in Sumerian; (851) and the name of Esagil-kini–ubba, *ummânu* under Adad–apla–iddina, was remembered down into Seleucid times. (852) Beginning with Bezold, (853) it has often been suggested that some colophons of scientific texts, in which a royal name [D]N/[DN]–apla–iddin(a) is preserved, refer to this king. (854)

Adad–apla–iddina's relations with Assyria are known only from the Assyrian point of view as expressed in the Synchronistic History, the Broken Obelisk, and the Assyrian Kinglist (though Adad–apla–iddina is mentioned by name only in the Synchronistic History). The Synchronistic History tells that Ashur–bel–kala in-

(847) Description of his building activities in the excavation reports: *UE* V pp. 74, 77 n. 1, 81, 92-93, 95, 124; *UE* VIII pp. 4, 69 (largely repeated from *AJ* V [1925] 7, 15; VII [1927] 409; VIII [1928] 416; IX [1929] 335). Texts inscribed on bricks: *UET* I 166 (found in the great courtyard of Nanna; catalogued as U. 3130 in *UE* VIII p. 103), *UET* I 167 (find spot unstated; catalogued as U. 2877 in *UE* VIII p. 102). The bricks bear almost identical texts, *UET* I 166 in Sumerian, *UET* I 167 in Akkadian.

The copper cylinder attributed by Woolley (*UE* VIII p. 4) to Adad–apla–iddina is actually a cylinder of Marduk–nadin–ahhe, now BM 123124 (published as *UET* VIII 101); see also *UE* VIII 69 n. 1.

(848) Because his building activities cannot be dated precisely, it is impossible to tell whether they represent routine repairs, fortifications against threatening invaders, or restoration of brickwork damaged by invaders.

(849) Two of these kudurrus have been published (as *BBSt* nos. 13 and 26). Prof. Weidner generously called my attention to a fragmentary kudurru found at Assur, Assur S 16562=VA 5937, photos of which were kindly furnished by Prof. G. R. Meyer. This unpublished text is dated in the fourth month of the first year of Adad–apla–iddina and was possibly drawn up at *Upî* (see the following note).

(850) With the exception of VA 5937 which is dated at [URU *Ú*]–⌜*pi*⌝–*i* in the first year of the king's reign.

(851) *Studia Orientalia* I (1925) 32-33, I *R* 5 no. XXII, *UET* I 166. Falkenstein has commented on the inferior quality of this Sumerian (occasional use of Emesal forms, word order influenced by Akkadian versions) in *MDOG* LXXXV (1953) 4-5.

(852) *UVB* XVIII 45:17. Note, however, that Nebuchadnezzar I and Adad–apla–iddina are listed in inverse chronological order and share the same *ummânu* (or had similarly named *ummânus*). (E)sagil-kinam–ubbib was the author of the "Babylonian Theodicy" (latest edition by Lambert, *BWL*, pp. 63 ff.) according to K. 10802 rev. 1-2 (*JCS* XVI [1962] 62, see note by Lambert, *ibid.*, 71).

(853) Bezold, *Catalogue*, II, 767 for K. 6156 (now joined also to K. 6141, 6148, and 9108).

(854) None of the royal names in these colophons can be read with certainty. See my remarks in *JCS* XVI (1962) 96 under 24.3.3 and n. 19 and in *Studies Oppenheim*, pp. 37 and 48 under 44.3.6-7. The case for reading Adad–apla–iddina in various colophons has recently been set forth by van Dijk, *UVB* XVIII 46, 51.

stalled Adad–apla–iddina, an upstart ("son of a nobody"), as king of Babylonia. (855) Adad–apla–iddina in turn gave his daughter in marriage together with a large dowry to Ashur–bel–kala. (856) The account in the Synchronistic History concludes with the formula: "the people of Assyria and Babylonia mingled (peacefully) with one another." (857)

The Broken Obelisk records many campaigns of Ashur–bel–kala against the Arameans. (858) According to the presently accepted theory, it dates from about the fifth or sixth year of Ashur–bel–kala's reign. (859) It describes a campaign in the

(855) *CT* XXXIV 39 ii 31′-32′ (see note 811 above for interpretation of this section).

(856) *CT* XXXIV 39 ii 33′-35′. Olmstead (*History of Assyria,* p. 70) suggested that this marriage indicated that Adad–apla–iddina had become the suzerain of Ashur–bel–kala. But in point of fact, diplomatic marriages of this sort do not imply the suzerainty of either party, groom or father-in-law. In the Kassite period, Babylonian princesses had been married to the Egyptian pharaoh (*EA* 1:12, etc.) and to the Hittite king (H. G. Güterbock, *Siegel aus Boğazköy,* I, 6-9; Claude F. A. Schaeffer, *Ugaritica,* III, 3-4, 99-103); and there is no indication that Egypt or Hatti was either suzerain of or vassal to Babylonia. Marriages between the royal families of Babylonia and Assyria were uncommon: the daughter of Ashur–uballit I married a Babylonian king (name disputed; *CT* XXXIV 38 i 8′-10′, Synchronistic History; Chronicle P i 5′-6′), the daughter of Adad–apla–iddina married Ashur–bel–kala (*CT* XXXIV 39 ii 33′-34′), and Adad–nirari II and Nabu–shuma–ukin I exchanged daughters in marriage (*CT* XXXIV 40 iii 17); there is slight evidence that the royal grooms in the first two of these instances may have been politically more powerful at one time (*EA* 9:31; *CT* XXXIV 39 ii 31′-32′), but they were hardly suzerains at the time of their marriage. Further instances of real or projected diplomatic marriages in and around Mesopotamia show how difficult it is to attempt to see a uniform vassal or suzerainty pattern in such unions:

(a) Shulgi married his daughter to the ensi of Anshan, who was nominally his vassal (*An.Or.* XIII 15 no. 28);

(b) Ishme–Dagan took the daughter of a Turukkian chieftain as wife for his son Mut–Ashkur (*ARM* II 40);

(c) Esarhaddon contemplated marrying his daughter to a Scythian chieftain (*PRT* 16).

In the Neo-Assyrian period, daughters of vassals (especially from Syria and Palestine) were sometimes sent to the Assyrian court to act as servants (*ana abrakkūti*: Streck, *Asb.*, 16:57, etc.; *ana epēš ardūtija*: *ibid.*, 18:59). The princesses sent to perform such services were often accompanied by means for their support (usually described as *nudunnû* or *terḫatu*: Streck, *Asb.*, 18:61, 65, etc.); cf. the princesses with financial support sent to Shalmaneser III by five western rulers: III *R* 7-8 i 40-41, ii 21-29 and *WO* I/2 (1947) 58 iii 7-8—there is no mention of any royal marriage in such cases.

In general, this kind of diplomatic marriage proves only that amicable relations existed between the two countries at the time of the marriage and that there was some interest in insuring the continuance of this mutual benevolent disposition.

(857) UN.MEŠ KUR *Aš+šur* KUR *Kar–du–ni–á[š] it–ti a–ḫa–meš ib–ba–[lu]* (*CT* XXXIV 39 ii 36′-37′). For the restoration of the final word, see Borger, *AfO* XVIII (1957-58) 112.

(858) Principal publication by King, *AKA* 128-149; additional bibliography and commentary by Borger, *EAK* I 135, 138-142. Further information on the campaigns is given by various fragments of the annals of Ashur–bel–kala (bibliography by Borger, *EAK* I 135-144).

See Appendix B for a brief excursus on the presently accepted attribution of the Broken Obelisk to Ashur–bel–kala and on the internal chronology of the inscription.

(859) The eponymate of Ashur–ra'im–nisheshu, in which an edition of the annals of Ashur–bel–kala was made (*AfO* VI [1930-31] 87 Teil IV), was either the fourth or fifth year of the king's reign (cf. Borger, *EAK* I 140). It occurs also as the second named eponymy in the Broken Obelisk (*AKA* 133 iii 3). Since the Broken Obelisk treats of events in at least two earlier eponym periods (before ii 13 and from ii 13 to iii 2) and one later eponym period (iii 20ff.), this means that the events described in that text cover the

eponymate of Ashur–ra'im–nisheshu (probably the fourth year of his reign) against two cities—whose names are not fully preserved—in the province of Dur–Kurigalzu. (860) The Babylonian governor of the province, Kadashman–Buriash, son of Itti–Marduk–balatu, (861) was captured. Later, in a summary of his exploits, Ashur–bel–kala mentions that he had conquered all people "from the city of Babylon in the land of Akkad [to the sea of] the land of Amurru ..."; (862) but this is the only hint that we have that he may have penetrated as far as Babylon itself. (863) The reigning Babylonian monarch at the time is not mentioned by name, but these events would fall either late in the reign of Marduk–shapik–zeri or early in that of Adad–apla–iddina. (864) They could conceivably have been part of the pattern of Assyrian intervention in northern Babylonia which culminated in Ashur–bel–kala's support for Adad–apla–iddina as king. Alternately, if dated later within the present range of possibilities, they may have marked the deterioration of good relations between Ashur–bel–kala and Adad–apla–iddina which would eventually lead to Babylonia's part in ousting Ashur–bel–kala's branch of the royal house from the Assyrian throne. (865)

The Assyrian Kinglist preserves the memory of this ouster, an event which happened two years after the death of Ashur–bel–kala. (866) His son, Eriba–Adad II, was removed from the throne in 1055 by Ashur–bel–kala's brother, Shamshi–

---

years 2-5 or 3-6 of Ashur–bel–kala's reign. Yet one cannot help being struck by the difference in style between the annals and the Obelisk account; and, though their accounts of events should overlap for years 2-4 or 3-5, no definite statements can yet be made on the subject because of the many lacunae in both texts.

(860) *AKA* 133 iii 5-6: URU *x*[...]*–in–di–šu–la* and URU *x*[...]*–sa–an–di–e*. No plausible restorations have been suggested to date.

(861) *AKA* 133 iii 7. The name of the governor's father reads KI–⌜dAMAR⌝.[UTU]–⌜TI⌝.LA (personal collation). Jaritz's comment on the missing masculine personal determinative before this name (*JSS* IV [1959] 205 n. 2) is obviated by the relatively common writing at this time of personal names beginning with *Itti–* without preceding determinatives (cf. note 490 above). Could Kadashman–Buriash and Adad–apla–iddina have been related (cf. the king's parentage according to the New Babylonian Chronicle, obv. 8')?

Jaritz's attempts (*MIO* VI [1958] 257 no. 206; *JSS* IV [1959] 209 n. 5) to connect this Kadashman–Buriash with Kadashman–Harbe (II) are unconvincing. Even were the approximate equivalent Buriash = Harbe in the Kassite pantheon to prove accurate, it is unlikely that Kadashman–Buriash and Kadashman–Harbe would be interchangeable names for a single individual. There can be no question of Kadashman–Harbe II himself being mentioned in the Broken Obelisk under the name Kadashman–Buriash, since the Kadashman–Buriash of the Broken Obelisk lived 150 years after the aforementioned Kassite king.

(862) *AKA* 144 iv 38-39. For the restoration, see Borger, *EAK* I 141.

(863) Which arouses a suspicion that the statement may be formulaic or exaggerated. This, however, can be determined only by further evidence.

(864) If we accept the date of the campaign as the fourth year of Ashur–bel–kala (=1071), the campaign could fall either during the reign of Marduk–shapik–zeri (1082*-1070*) or Adad–apla–iddina (1069*-1048*)—since the margin of error for these dates is five years.

(865) Because of the uncertainty of dating the campaign within the scheme of Babylonian chronology, it is possible to envisage it in very different contexts within the presently allowable limits.

(866) Ashur–bel–kala himself apparently died peacefully. His royal sarcophagus at Assur was the earliest sarcophagus of a named king to be recovered there (A. Haller, *WVDOG* LXV 176-177).

Adad IV, who returned from exile in Babylonia to accomplish this coup, presumably with the aid or at least the connivance of the Babylonians. (867) Although not explicitly stated in the account, the king of Babylonia at the time of this revolt in Assyria—as determined from our previous chronological calculations—must have been Adad–apla–iddina. (868) Adad–apla–iddina's motivation for assisting the coup is unknown; it could have been revenge for the attack on Dur–Kurigalzu or simply desire to extend his power into Assyria. (869)

Not long after this event, Adad–apla–iddina died. We do not know as yet whether he was succeeded as king by members of his own family, but there is no internal political upheaval attested in Babylonia at the time.

9. Marduk-ahhe-eriba (870)

The ninth king of the Second Dynasty of Isin, whose name is known only from a kudurru, (871) reigned for six months, which were counted in the official chronological reckonings as one regnal year. (872) We do not know whether he was related to any of his predecessors or successors.

(867) *JNES* XIII (1954) 220-221: Khorsabad Kinglist iv 1-4=SDAS List iii 33-36. Compare also the entries in the Assyrian Kinglist for Shamshi–Adad I and Ninurta–apil–Ekur, who both gained the throne in Assyria after "coming up" from Babylonia.

(868) The highest date for his last regnal year is 1053; Shamshi–Adad IV's first official year was 1054.

(869) Ashur–bel–kala was also Adad–apla–iddina's son-in-law. Perhaps the Babylonian king's daughter had not fared well in the north, but we have no real clue as to what had happened to change Adad–apla–iddina's attitude towards Assyria.

(870) *Marduk–aḫḫē–erība*: "Marduk has replaced the brothers for me." For the name type, see Stamm, *Namengebung*, pp. 289-290. It was usually given to a son born after at least two of his older brothers had died.

The name type DN-ahhe-eriba begins in at least the Middle Babylonian period (e.g., *BE* XVII 26:13); but the verbal root RIB occurs in personal names in the Old Akkadian period (Gelb, *MAD* III 229-230) and in names like Sin–eriba(m) in the Old Babylonian period (Ranke, *EBPN*, p. 155). The king seems to be the earliest individual to bear the name Marduk–ahhe–eriba, though it is attested in later Babylonia, e.g., *CT* XXII no. 197:20.

Writing of RN: md AMAR.UTU–ŠEŠ.MEŠ–SU (*BE* I/2 149 i 14, contemporary?) and md ŠÚ–ŠEŠ(?)–[x–(x)] (Kinglist A iii 2′).

(871) *BE* I/2 149. For the probable dating of the kudurru about this time, see Hinke, *Boundary Stone*, pp. 188-189; but it may be doubted whether the document itself was drawn up and finished during this short reign (especially since the names of living monarchs are practically never prefixed with a masculine personal determinative in this period, see note 1871 below), and it may have been completed during the early part of the reign of this king's successor. For further strengthening of the approximate dating of this text to the late Second Dynasty of Isin, it may be remarked that the provincial administration described fits in well with what is known about the *šaknu* ("governor") and other officials during the Second Isin Dynasty. The epithet *Ḫa–pir–a–a* borne by Kudurra, the recipient of the land grant, is paralleled in the twelfth-century letter *AfO* X (1935) 2:5, etc., where the gentilic refers to a man with the Kassite name Harbi–Shipak. To date, Bit–Piri'–Amurru occurs only in documents of the twelfth and eleventh centuries. But compare PN *mār Piri'–Amurru* in *BBSt* no. 29 ii 14 (ninth century).

(872) Kinglist A iii 2′. See p. 67 above.

The kudurru reveals little information about Marduk–ahhe–eriba. He is given the simple title LUGAL.E, [873] customary titulary for kings in Babylonian economic texts of this period. He was obviously in sufficient control of the province of Bit–Piri'–Amurru in northern Babylonia [874] to bestow land there as an indirect royal gift. [875] It is worth noting that this kudurru, in contrast with the late Kassite documents from the same region, shows Marduk now elevated to a position immedi-

[873] *BE* I/2 149 i 14.

[874] The precise location of the province of Bit–Piri'–Amurru within the territory of northern Babylonia is uncertain. Indirect evidence would connect it with:

(a) the Radanu river, east of the Tigris and north of the Diyala (cf. *KAH* II 69:16, *AKA* 312 ii 52, Nimrud Letter XLI 18; in Abbasid times, the name probably survived in the administrative district known as Upper and Lower Rādhān and in modern times a dry branch of the Adhaim river was called the Nahr Rathan: see Adams, *Land Behind Baghdad*, p. 78); the Radanu is probably to be identified with the Shatt el Adhaim and its continuation in the Tauq. In the reign of Merodach–Baladan I, according to *MDP* VI 39 i 5-11, a local official, the *ḫazannu* of Bit–Piri'–Amurru, was involved in measuring a field whose eastern boundary was the Radanu. Such a field would normally be expected to fall within the local official's purview; and this is bolstered by the curse formulae of the text, in which both the *ḫazannu* and *šaknu* of Bit–Piri'–Amurru are referred to as having jurisdiction over the field (*MDP* VI 40 ii 2, 4).

(b) the city of Agade. A field belonging to Bit–Piri'–Amurru—whether the name is to be interpreted here as a province or as a clan is not altogether certain—is described as connected with a village (in) the Agade meadow region (*ugar* URU *A-ga-dè* KI: *MDP* II 99 i 4). The same field is described as bordering on the land of Ishtar of Agade (*MDP* II 100 i 47-48, cf. *ibid.* 101 ii 26). The *šakkanakku* of Agade served as a witness to another kudurru involving land in the province of Bit–Piri'–Amurru (*A-ga-dè* KI, *BBSt* no. 4 ii 9-10). It should be noted that there was a royal residence in Agade at this time in the late Kassite period (URU *Ak-ka-di*, *BBSt* no. 3 v 19-21). [One cannot help wondering whether the references just cited to *Agade* in *BBSt* nos. 3-4 might not be interpreted as synonyms for "Babylon," similar to the usage of the later Neo-Assyrian period (e.g., Landsberger, *Bischof*, pp. 46-51). The interpretation is uncertain].

Bit–Piri'–Amurru is also connected with the *nār šarri* (*MDP* II 99 i 5, probably not to be identified with the *nār* URU *ša-šar-ri* KI(*di?*) in *BE* I/2 149 i 6, 11), but there were several waterways of that name in Babylonia. A field in the province of Bit–Piri'–Amurru was owned by a porter (*āpil bābi*) from Dur–Kurigalzu (*MDP* II 100 i 18-20); but this need hardly imply that the province of Bit–Piri'–Amurru included the area of Dur–Kurigalzu. Dur–Kurigalzu and Bit–Piri'–Amurru comprised separate provinces under the Second Dynasty of Isin (*AKA* 133 iii 6 and *BE* I/2 149 i 4; cf. my remarks in *JESHO* VI [1963] 234-235); and both areas were provinces also in the Kassite period (e.g., *BBSt* no. 4 i 3, *BE* XIV 12:42).

The chief difficulty of interpretation is that the Radanu is east of the Tigris, while Agade is usually presumed to be some distance to the west of that river. This need not be an insoluble impasse, since Bit–Piri'–Amurru could have straddled both banks of the river. But the references connecting Bit–Piri'–Amurru with the Radanu are of more weight for the localization of the area since they deal with Bit–Piri'–Amurru as a geographical and jurisdictional entity (i.e., as part of a specific province of Bit–Piri'–Amurru), while the Agade references could conceivably refer to clan possessions. Further evidence is needed before this question can be satisfactorily resolved.

To Ebeling's collection of references for the region of Bit–Piri'–Amurru in *RLA* II 48 may be added *MDP* VI 39f. i 11, ii 4; *BBSt* no. 4 i 3, 4, 9; *BBSt* no. 15 ii 2. The *RT* XVI text was published in a better edition as *BE* I/2 149.

[875] The king made the gift through the agency of the local governor, Sin–bel–ili (*BE* I/2 149 i 3-4) and sent out other local officials to do the surveying (*ibid.*, i 15-19). The reason for the king's gift is not stated in the text.

ately behind the Anu–Enlil–Ea triad in the curse formulae, (876) a position formerly held by Shamash (877) or Ninhursag. (878)

10. Marduk-zer-[x]

The full form of this king's name has not survived in any of the available sources. But several possibilities for restoration may be suggested on the basis of other names attested with the same first two elements:

(1) *Marduk–zēra–ibni*: by far the most popular name with these first two elements. It is attested throughout the Neo–Assyrian, Neo-Babylonian, and Persian periods (e.g., Tallqvist, *APN*, p. 134; Tallqvist, *NBN*, pp. 109-110). In the Chicago Assyrian Dictionary files, over one hundred entries listing individuals with this name may be found. (879)

(2) *Marduk–zēra–iddina*: occurs in Neo-Babylonian and Persian times, e.g., *YOS* VI 196:20, *Dar.* 330:3.

(3) *Marduk–zēra–iqīša*: occurs in the Neo-Babylonian period, *Nbk.* 381:9. (880)

(4) *Marduk-zēra-uballiṭ:* (uncertain; see *Studies Oppenheim*, p. 28)

(5) *Marduk–zēra–ukīn*: in *VAS* III 53:10 (Neo-Babylonian).

(6) *Marduk–zēra–uṣur*: possibly in *VAS* V 105:5 (Persian) and in *Coll. de Clercq*, II, tablet B, p. 120 II 17 (Neo-Babylonian).

(7) *Marduk–zēra–ušallim*: *CT* XXII no. 112:1 (Neo-Babylonian letter).

(8) *Marduk–zēru–līšir*: *YOS* III 149:3 (Neo-Babylonian/Persian), *AnOr* VIII 52 rev. 18 (Persian).

It should be noted that these names come from the later periods and chiefly from Babylonia. If the first two elements of the king's name have been read correctly here, (881) it would be the earliest occurrence of a *Marduk–zēr–* name.

(876) *BE* I/2 149 ii 18, 21.

(877) *BBSt* no. 4 iii 9-12. At least Anu, Enlil, and Ea are to be restored before Shamash in *MDP* VI 40 as subjects of the verb in iii 2 (cf. *MDP* II 108-109 vi 16-28, *BBSt* no. 5 iii 26-34); in any case Shamash (*MDP* VI 40 iii 3) precedes Marduk (iii 14) in this text.

(878) *MDP* II 108 vi 16-19.

(879) The personal name files of the *CAD* are roughly complete for major publications of Neo-Babylonian texts up to 1934 (with the notable exception of the two volumes of *GCCI*).

(880) Ungnad, *Orientalia N.S.* XIII (1944) 74 tentatively suggested restoring the name in this fashion; other possible restorations were mentioned *ibid.*, p. 76.

(881) The reading of the second element of the king's name is not altogether certain: see p. 45 above.

The only definite information presently available on this monarch is that he ruled for twelve years. (882)

11. Nabu-shumu-libur (883)

Very little is known of this last king of the Second Dynasty of Isin save his name (884) and that he ruled for eight years. (885) On a large (886) duck weight made of fine-grained white marble and inscribed during the reign of Nabu–shumu–libur, the monarch is called "king of the world" (*šar kiššati*); (887) but there is no evidence to indicate that this grandiose title was deserved. Instead, the fragmentary list of portents pertaining to his reign which is preserved in the Religious Chronicle could be interpreted as indicating that the land suffered from political weakness under him. (888)

(882) The first two elements of his name and his regnal years are known only from Kinglist A iii 3′.

(883) *Nabû–šumu–libūr*: "O Nabu, may (my) progeny stay in good health." For the comparatively rare name type DN–shumu–libur, see Stamm, *Namengebung*, pp. 155-156; the name of this king is its first attested occurrence. The name Nabu–shumu–libur was also borne by a judge in the reign of Nabonidus (*TCL* XIII 219:33; *Nbn.* 776:13; probably to be restored also in *Nbn.* 720:20) and possibly one other individual in the NB-Persian period (*VAS* IV 190 rev. 14). The verb *bâru* first occurs in personal names in the Old Akkadian period (Gelb, *MAD* III 91) and continues in Babylonia down till at least the Persian period (Ranke, *EBPN*, p. 238; Clay, *CPN*, p. 149; Tallqvist, *NBN*, p. 301; these authors, however, incorrectly derived the form from a verb *abāru* or *ebēru*). For the translation of *bâru* in personal names, see now *CAD* B 126.

Writing of RN: in a contemporary Babylonian inscription as ᵈAG–MU–*li–bur* (*JRAS* XVI [1856] pl. opp. p. 222 no. 2:2), in the Religious Chronicle as [ᵐᵈA]G–MU–*li–bur* (i 16, though [P]A could just as well be read as [A]G), and in Kinglist A as ᵐᵈAG–MU–[x] (iii 4′). Traces of a personal determinative appear in Assur 14616c ii 24′, where the name of this king would be expected. Poebel in *AS* XV 23 read the second element of this name as *–šumi–*, but the syllabic writing of the same name as *–šu–mu–* in *Nbn.* 776:13 makes Poebel's reading less likely.

(884) For about sixty years Nabu–shumu–libur was thought by scholars to have been an Assyrian king because his only inscription had been found at Nimrud (see note 889 below), though E. Norris had early noted that the script was Babylonian rather than Assyrian (*JRAS* XVI [1856] 218). This difficulty, however, was cleared up by King in *PSBA* XXIX (1907) 221 and Winckler in *OLZ* X (1907) 592.

(885) Kinglist A iii 4′.

(886) The "thirty-mina" weight weighs more than 39 pounds; see Weissbach, *ZDMG* LXI (1907) 394-395. A sketch of the weight was published by A. H. Layard in *The Monuments of Nineveh, First Series* (London: John Murray, 1853), pl. 95a no. 11.

(887) The inscription on the weight was first published by Layard in *ICC*, pl. 83 F. Better editions of the text were subsequently made by Norris, *JRAS* XVI (1856) plate opposite p. 222 no. 2 and by King, *PSBA* XXIX (1907) 221. The inscription reads:

30 MA GI.NA
šá ᵈAG–MU–*li–bur* LUGAL ŠÁR

The first line need not be read MA.⟨NA⟩, since the single sign was an acceptable abbreviation in the early Neo-Babylonian period (cf. *BBSt* no. 30 rev. 3-6, *UET* IV 143:3, and *passim*).

(888) Religious Chronicle i 16 ff.

How the Second Dynasty of Isin came to an end is uncertain. But, since northern Babylonia had been overrun by western tribesmen during the preceding decades, it is conceivable that, under the pressure of these invaders, effective government in the north finally died out and that the hegemony shifted to the south, perhaps with the assistance or at least the tacit approval of Assyria. ([889])

THE TURN OF THE MILLENNIUM: THREE SHORT DYNASTIES

Within the span of half a century, between the years 1026* and 980*, a total of three dynasties and seven rulers came and went in Babylonia. ([890]) Political stability in this age was a rarity, as various local groups in the peripheral regions of Babylonia vied for power. The initial impetus to establish stable rule in the land came from the Sealand, when Simbar–Shipak, previously a military official of humble rank, seized the throne and reigned for almost two decades. In his eighteenth year, however, he was assassinated; and Ea–mukin–zeri, a tribesman from eastern Babylonia, usurped the throne for five months. He in turn was supplanted by Kashshu–nadin–ahi (possibly the legitimate successor of Simbar–Shipak), whose reign sputtered out after three years in the midst of hard times and continuing semi-nomad attacks.

([889]) The Nabu–shumu–libur duck weight was found in Assyria in the rubbish covering the Northwest Palace at Nimrud (Layard, *Nineveh and Its Remains*, 3rd ed. [London: John Murray, 1849], II, 316), where it had been preserved as an antique (R. D. Barnett, *A Catalogue of the Nimrud Ivories*, p. 4). How did it get to Assyria? We cannot rule out the possibility that it was carried there at the end of or shortly after Nabu–shumu–libur's reign, especially since Assyria was known to be on friendly terms with the first ruler of the new dynasty which supplanted the Isin kings (*JCS* XIX [1965] 124:19, cf. *ibid.*, 134-135). The evidence for this, however, is hardly convincing, because the weight could have been taken north at any time. Since Nimrud itself became the capital only about a century and a half after Nabu–shumu–libur's death, the weight could have been brought there much later, at the same time as the eighth-century weight of Eriba–Marduk (see note 1399 below).

For a still unpublished duck weight (supposedly bearing an Assyrian inscription) found in the early Post-Kassite level at Babylon, see Reuther, *WVDOG* XLVII 22 and pl. III (26n1), excavation number 35802. For a bureau of weights maintained at Nimrud in the eighth and seventh centuries, see Mallowan, *Nimrud and Its Remains*, I, 109.

([890]) Olmstead (*AJSL* XXXVI [1919-20] 153 and XXXVII [1920-21] 212) claimed that Babylon after the Second Isin Dynasty ceased to have an independent history and became an Assyrian dependency. This is unlikely. According to the evidence presently available, after the Assyrians had returned stolen goods to Nippur about the time of Simbar–Shipak (*JCS* XIX [1965] 124:19), they had no further contacts with Babylonia until about the time of Shamash–mudammiq, approximately a century later. Furthermore, Assyria's power was severely limited in the days between Eriba–Adad II (1056-1055) and Ashur–dan II (934-912). Nor did any Assyrian king claim that Babylonia was subject to him until the time of Shamshi–Adad V.

At this point, the eastern tribe of Bazi took the reins of government into its hands. Eulmash–shakin–shumi, descendant of a tribe that had held high office during the Second Dynasty of Isin, ascended the throne and reigned for seventeen years. But, after his powerful presence had vanished from the political scene, two more of his fellow clansmen were less successful in holding the country in check. Ninurta–kudurri–usur I and Shirikti–Shuqamuna reigned for three years and three months respectively, and then the Bazi Dynasty came to an end.

The next dynasty consisted of a single king, Mar–biti–apla–usur, who was of Elamite descent and reigned for six years. We know practically nothing about his term in office.

A noteworthy feature of this age is its almost utter dearth of primary documentation. Until 1962, only two Babylonian inscriptions dating from these three dynasties had been published, one a kudurru of moderate length and the other a bronze arrowhead with a two-line text. (891) These inscriptions came from the two most stable reigns of the period: the kudurru from that of Simbar–Shipak, founder of the Sealand Dynasty, and the arrowhead from that of Eulmash–shakin–shumi, founder of the Bazi Dynasty. Since 1962, several further texts have been published: a royal inscription of Simbar–Shipak, (892) thirteen additional duplicates to the arrowhead inscription of Eulmash–shakin–shumi, (893) two identical two-line arrowhead inscriptions of Ninurta–kudurri–usur (I), (894) and four identical two-line arrowhead inscriptions of Mar–biti–apla–usur. (895) With the exception of the two long texts from the reign of Simbar–Shipak, all these inscriptions are on Luristan bronze arrowheads and contain only the royal name and the title "king of the world." So almost all information about these three dynasties must still be garnered from the kinglists and chronicles.

The Second Sealand Dynasty

Historians commonly refer to this small dynasty by the title given it in Kinglist A, "Dynasty of the Sealand," (896) and call it the second of that name. It should be noted, however, that Kinglist A apparently does not refer to the earlier second dynasty of Babylon—the First Sealand Dynasty of the historians—as a dynasty

(891) Also a legal document drawn up under the Bazi Dynasty is cited in its entirety in a kudurru written under Nabu–mukin–apli (*BBSt* no. 9, top). For another text possibly dating from about this time (*RA* XIX [1922] 86-87), see p. 257 below.

(892) Goetze, "An Inscription of Simbar–Šiḫu," *JCS* XIX (1965) 121-135.

(893) Dossin, *Iranica Antiqua* II (1962) 160 no. 17.

(894) *Ibid.*, no. 18. (See note 993 below).

(895) Dossin, *Iranica Antiqua* II (1962) 160 no. 19.

(896) BALA KUR *Tam–tim* (Kinglist A iii 9′).

of the Sealand but rather as BALA ŠEŠ.ḪA (interpretation uncertain). (897) But this earlier dynasty is usually called "First Sealand Dynasty" because: (a) Gulkishar, one of its rulers, is called "King of the Sealand" (LUGAL KUR A.AB.BA) in a late-twelfth-century kudurru; (898) (b) Ea–gamil, another of its monarchs, is referred to in a chronicle as "King of the Sealand" (LUGAL KUR *Tam–tim*). (899) For these reasons, it is regularly assumed that the BALA ŠEŠ.ḪA of Kinglist A was a dynasty of the Sealand.

For several centuries prior to the rule of the Second Sealand Dynasty, the Sealand had been subject to Babylonia. (900) After the collapse of the Second Dynasty of Isin, the hegemony of Babylonia passed to the south; and the first ruler of the new dynasty was a military official of the Sealand, who had some remote connection with one of the kings of the First Dynasty of the Sealand. The jurisdiction of the new dynasty, however, was not confined to the south, as may be seen from the activities of its first king at Nippur and Sippar.

12. Simbar-Shipak (901)

Simbar–Shipak was the first ruler of the Second Sealand Dynasty (902) and reigned for eighteen years. (903) To judge from the length of his reign—the longest

(897) Kinglist A i 15′. See Landsberger, *JCS* VIII (1954) 71 n. 182, and cf. the designation of this dynasty as that of ŠEŠ.KÙ.K[I] in Kinglist B.

(898) *BE* I/1 83:6.

(899) *CCEBK* II 22 rev. 11 ("Chronicle of Early Kings").

(900) The Sealand is attested as a province in the kudurrus, e.g., *MDP* X 93 viii 10 (late Kassite period) and *BBSt* no. 11 i 3 (Second Dynasty of Isin); and Kassite kings had built at Ur and Uruk.

(901) *Simbar–Šipak*: "offspring of Shipak." For the equation Simbar–Shipak = Lidan–Marduk (V *R* 44 i 24), see Balkan, *Kassitenstudien*, I, 77. The name of the god Shipak is common in Kassite personal names (Balkan, *ibid.*, I, 114-115; for the reading of the divine name as Shipak rather than Shihu, see Eilers' review of Balkan's book in *AfO* XVIII [1957-58] 137 and n. 12). The first element of the name appears also as Sibar and Sibbar (Balkan, *op. cit.*, I, 76 and 206) and possibly also as Sibir; but there is no reason for postulating an original *Singbar (Balkan, *ibid.*, I, 206), which is phonetically unlikely. No one else bearing this name is as yet attested from Babylonia.

Writing of the name: *Si–im–bar–ši*–ḪU (*BBSt* no. 27 edge 3; *BBSt* no. 36 i 13), m*Sim–bar–*d*Ši–i*–ḪU (*JCS* XIX [1965] 123-124:7, 20, ⌜26⌝), m*Sim–bar–ši–i*–ḪU (New Babylonian Chronicle, obv. 12′), m*Sim–bar–ši*–ḪU (Dynastic Chronicle v 2′; cf. V *R* 44 i 24, a Kassite name list). An abbreviated form, m*Sim–bar–ši*, occurs in Kinglist A iii 6′ and a possible hypocoristic, m*Si–bir*, in an inscription of Ashurnasirpal II (*AKA* 325:84). A history of the reading of this RN has been given by Goetze in *JCS* XIX (1965) 133 and nn. 85-87; but he overlooked the contribution of Eilers cited above. The reading of the theophoric element of the name must still be regarded as uncertain.

The text tentatively assigned to Simbar–Shipak by Koldewey (*MDOG* X [1901] 12) belongs really to Sin–magir (*WVDOG* IV 1 no. 1).

(902) For the time being, we presume that the reigns of Nabu–shumu–libur and Simbar–Shipak were consecutive, since there is no evidence to the contrary. But there is always the possibility that the dynasties overlapped or that there was a chronological hiatus between them.

(903) Kinglist A iii 6′. (Seventeen years according to the Dynastic Chronicle v 3′).

in his dynasty—and from his position as founder of the dynasty, it may safely be asserted that he was its most notable king. (904) As far as we now know, he was not descended from any ruler of the previous dynasty; and, in fact, a chronicle indicates that before his accession he was a soldier of not very high rank who was living in the Sealand. (905) Though the king himself bore a Kassite name, his father, according to two chronicles, was a man with the Babylonian name Eriba-Sin; (906) and the king's designation as a "soldier(?) of the dynasty of Damiq-ilishu" (907) may bespeak some remote family connection with the ruler of the First Sealand Dynasty who bore that name. (908) Thus the evidence available suggests that he came originally from the Sealand, regardless of the high or low connections of his family.

From his reign dates the lone kudurru of the dynasty, the stone tablet BM 90937 (published as *BBSt* no. 27). It was written in the city of Sahritu (909) in the intercalary Ululu of his twelfth year. (910) It records two transactions: (1) the apprenticing (911) of three brothers to men in sundry occupations, (2) a private purchase. The document—or at least the transaction recorded in the second half—was then witnessed by several high officials of the Sealand, including the *ša rēši ša māt Tâmti(m)*, (912) the *sakrumaš Tâmti(m)*, and the *šangû* of Eridu. (913) The only clearly legible geographical name, besides Sahritu and Eridu, is the city Kissik, (914) which is

(904) A conclusion bolstered by his restorations at Sippar and Nippur, as discussed below. At Sippar these improvements did not last much beyond his own reign.

(905) UKU.UŠ LÚ KU.A ⌈KUR.A.A⌉B.BA.KE$_4$ (Dynastic Chronicle v 2′). Cf. New Babylonian Chronicle, obv. 12′.

Olmstead (*AJSL* XXXVII [1920-21] 212), following Johns (*PSBA* XL [1918] 126-127), said that Simbar-Shipak was a priest before coming to the throne. This was based on a misinterpretation of the beginning of the Dynastic Chronicle fragment *ADD* 888, which actually refers to the predecessor of Marduk-apla-usur.

(906) Dynastic Chronicle v 2′; New Babylonian Chronicle, obv. 12′.

(907) ERÍN BALA SIG$_5$-DINGIR-*šú* (Dynastic Chronicle v 3′). Cf. ERÍN *Ḫa-bi* said of Merodach-Baladan II (Kinglist A iv 14) and my discussion of this term in *Studies Oppenheim*, p. 36. Goetze, *JCS* XIX [1965] 133) attempts to emend the first two signs to ŠÀ(?).BAL, but this seems quite unlikely from photographs of the text.

(908) More likely than referring to the Damiq-ilishu who reigned as the last king of the First Dynasty of Isin. For the surviving fame of Damiq-ilishu in later Babylonia, compare the "Processional Way of Damiq-ilishu," the name of a thoroughfare in Babylon (Unger, *Babylon*, p. 47). For the writing of the RN Damiq-ilishu, see Landsberger, *JCS* VIII (1954) 69 n. 178.

(909) Written URU NIGIN-*tu* in *BBSt* no. 27 bottom edge 3. The city is probably to be placed in the south; cf. Sennacherib's reference to the *agammē ša* URU *Sa-aḫ-ri-ti* ("the swamps of Sahritu") in *OIP* II 157 XXX 3). It occurs also in Neo-Babylonian economic texts, e.g., *ZA* IV (1889) 143 no. 14:13 and 147 no. 20:15.

(910) *BBSt* no. 27 bottom edge 3. According to Layard, *ICC*, pl. 53, the text was found at Nimrud.

(911) For this translation of *patāqu*—still unparalleled—see the remarks of King, *BBSt*, p. 102, n. 4.

(912) Written SAG *šá* KUR A.AB.BA (*BBSt* no. 27 rev. 15). For the writing of *ša rēši* as SAG, see note 2062 below.

(913) *BBSt* no. 27 rev. 15 and bottom edge 1.

(914) The tax collector (*mākisu*) of Kissik is mentioned in *BBSt* no. 27 obv. 10.

also in the Sealand area. ([915]) The title ascribed to the king in this text is LUGAL.E, ([916]) the usual royal title which had been given to kings of the Second Isin Dynasty in economic texts.

Simbar–Shipak attempted to repair the ravages wrought on the cult centers of Sippar and Nippur by Aramean and Sutian invaders over twenty years before. At Sippar he reestablished regular food offerings for the god Shamash, though he searched in vain for the vanished statue of the god. ([917]) He also installed Ekur–shuma–ushabshi, a seer (*bārû*), as chief priest (*šangû*) of the city. ([918]) At Nippur, as has long been known from the New Babylonian Chronicle, he had the throne of Enlil ([919]) in the Ekurigigal shrine restored. ([920]) A later copy of an inscription of Simbar–Shipak, recently published by Goetze, ([921]) tells the story of the old throne of Enlil made in the time of Nebuchadnezzar I, which had been lost when the property of Enlil was carried off by the Arameans. This property was subsequently recovered by the Assyrians, ([922]) who allowed it to be returned from Assur to

([915]) As may be seen from the Harper Letters, especially *ABL* 521 rev. 8, 10; 1241:16.

([916]) *BBSt* no. 27 bottom edge 3. He bears the same title in the ninth-century text *BBSt* no. 36 i 13.

([917]) *BBSt* no. 36 i 13-20. The disruption of cultic activities at Sippar is described *ibid.*, i 1-12 and in *JCS* XIX (1965) 123:12.

Though Simbar–Shipak could not find the cult statue of Shamash, he did re-erect the image of the sun disk which was on a table before the shrine of Shamash (*nipḫa ša pān Šamaš ušatriṣamma, BBSt* no. 36 :18-19). For a picture of this sun disk in its position before the shrine, see *BBSt*, pl. XCVIII.

([918]) *BBSt* no. 36 i 21-23.

([919]) Written here as dEN NIGIN (New Babylonian Chronicle, obv. 13′, checked from photo) not dEl-lil(!) as recently conjectured by Goetze (*JCS* XIX [1965] 134 and n. 98). Despite the writing, the reference to Enlil is now clear because of the text published by Goetze, *JCS* XIX (1965) 123-124.

([920]) New Babylonian Chronicle, obv. 13′. Its location in Nippur and its epithet "storehouse" (of Enlil) are known chiefly from the Tummal Chronicle (*JCS* XVI [1962] 46:31; for é.GI.NA.AB.TUM (var.: DU_7), see Deimel, *ŠL* 85.161, 324.40-41, and Falkenstein, *NSG*, I 125 n. 2). The Ekurigigal was presumably a shrine within the Ekur (cf. *JCS* XIX [1965] 123:9 and 124:22-24), probably where the cult statue of Enlil was solemnly enthroned.

([921]) Goetze, "An Inscription of Simbar–Šīḫu," *JCS* XIX (1965) 121-135.

([922]) Goetze, *ibid.*, nn. 101 and 106 implies that the Subarians are to be included with (and perhaps identified with) the Arameans as the original thieves. The line in question (14) can also be interpreted "the goods (and) property of Enlil, which the Arameans had carried off and (which) Subartu had (subsequently) taken (from them)." This, of course, is supported by the well-known equation of Subartu with Assyria in the first millennium (e.g., *RMA* 62:4) as well as by the events recorded later in this inscription (lines 18-19), which reveal that it was the Assyrians who gained possession of the goods after the Arameans and restored them to Babylonia. (For the use of "Subartu" for Assyria in first-millennium Babylonia, see Gelb, *Hurrians and Subarians*, p. 45 and cf. *Iraq* XV [1953] 133:9 for a late-eighth-century reference and *MDP* II 93 i 5 for a possible reference in the late second millennium in Babylonia).

In the inscription, several distinct steps in the disposition of the property of Enlil may be recognized. First, the property was stolen from Nippur by the Arameans (*ša Aramu itbaluma*, line 14). Then, it was taken from the Arameans by "Subartu," i.e., the Assyrians (*ša ...īkimu Subarti*, line 14). Fortunately "an Assyrian" (*Aššurû*), presumably an unnamed king or high official, recognized the property as belonging to Enlil (*bušâ makkūr Enlil ... īdûma*, line 18) and saw that it was brought back safely to Assur (*ušērib qereb* BAL.TIL.KI, line 18). From Assur it was then returned to its proper place in "Duranki," i.e., Nippur (*ultu qereb* BAL.TIL.KI *ana Duranki itūru ašrušš[u*], line 19). In line 19, one may either interpret the

Nippur. (923) A new throne made from *mēsu*–wood and ornamented with red gold was then constructed, and the god who would occupy the throne was asked to bless the king in these words:

> Therefore may Marduk, the great lord, the Enlil of the gods, look joyously (upon the king) and, when he (i.e., Marduk/Enlil) is seated on that throne, may the fate of Simbar–Shipak, the king of justice, the shepherd dear to his heart, be determined favorably. (924)

We must now mention briefly two passages which may refer to the reign of Simbar–Shipak. The first is a section of the Religious Chronicle, dealing with portents such as floods, the appearance of wild animals in the cities, and a possible eclipse. (925) This passage should refer either to Simbar–Shipak or to his third successor, Eulmash–shakin–shumi, (926) but no royal name has been preserved in this

---

final –*u* of *itūru* as written, but unpronounced (see Hyatt, *Final Vowels,* which applies to this time) and the *bušû makkūr* DN as a collective, or one may interpret the form as *itūrū* (a grammatical plural after a logically plural subject) and restore the final part of the phrase as *áš–ru–uš–š[u–un/–nu*).

(923) *JCS* XIX (1965) 124:19, see the preceding note for the precise phraseology. Goetze, *ibid.*, 134-135, speculates on this "astonishing change in Assyrian policy towards Babylonia" and postulates as the only possible reason for it that both countries were now confronted by a common crisis in the attacks of the Arameans.

The question of Assyro-Babylonian relations in the eleventh century is not a simple one. Tiglath–Pileser I and Marduk–nadin–ahhe had carried on raids against each other's territory, culminating in the sack of Babylon on the one hand and in the theft of the gods from Ekallate on the other. Over fifty years before the beginning of Simbar–Shipak's reign, Assyria and Babylonia had been confronted by a common Aramean menace; and, during the Aramean invasions in 1083* and slightly later, Tiglath–Pileser had to flee from Assyria and Marduk–nadin–ahhe lost his throne. Within the next thirteen years, diplomatic relations were resumed between Assyria and Babylonia under Ashur–bel–kala and Marduk–shapik–zeri. The era of good will persisted even after Adad–apla–iddina's usurpation of the Babylonian throne, and the usurper's daughter was married to Ashur–bel–kala. Then came a change in Assyro-Babylonian relations. Ashur–bel–kala attacked northern Babylonia (Dur–Kurigalzu); and Babylonia harbored Shamshi–Adad IV, an exiled member of the Assyrian royal family, who came out of exile and removed Eriba–Adad II, son of Ashur–bel–kala, from the Assyrian throne. Thus the currently reigning branch of the Assyrian royal house had been installed with Babylonian support less than thirty years before Simbar–Shipak's accession, and it is not strange to see Assyria on friendly terms with the first ruler of a new dynasty.

(924) *JCS* XIX (1965) 124:25-27. "Therefore": i.e., because of the restoration of the throne, related in the preceding lines. "When he is seated" (*ina ašābišu*) rather than "while letting him sit down" (which would be causative). *bibil libbišu*: "dear to his heart" rather than "his offspring" (see *AHw* 125a; *CAD* B 221; Seux, *Épithètes royales,* p. 61). *liššakin*: "be determined" (N stem and therefore passive). In lines 25-27 here, a certain—at least verbal—syncretism appears, in that Marduk in his function as "Enlil of the gods" is conceived of as sitting on Enlil's throne in Nippur to decree the fates.

(925) Religious Chronicle, col. ii; the supposed eclipse is discussed in note 345 above.

(926) The king in question reigned at least 17 years (Religious Chronicle, ii 19), and only Simbar–Shipak and Eulmash–shakin–shumi had reigns of this length between Nabu–shumu–libur (i 16) and Nabu–mukin–apli (iii 6′). It is also conceivable that column ii might refer to more than one ruler: Simbar–Shipak might be meant in the section up to ii 25 and Eulmash–shakin–shumi thereafter. But events in this chronicle are not always listed in strictly chronological order (e.g., iii 10′ ff.). Poebel (*AS* XV 23-24 n. 80) referred them to Simbar–Shipak, while Olmstead (*AJSL* XXXVII [1920-21] 213-214) assigned them to Eulmash–shakin–shumi.

section. The second passage is in an inscription of Ashurnasirpal II, which raises the possibility that Simbar–Shipak may have ruled in the Kifri region or even farther north. The text describes some building activities of Ashurnasirpal II as follows:

> At that time in the land of Zamua, the city Atlila—which Sibir, king of Karduniash, had captured (927) and (which) had then collapsed and turned into mounds and ruin hills—he (Ashurnasirpal) reorganized. (928)

If Sibir is to be identified with Simbar–Shipak, (929) the king was militarily active in this area; (930) but the region fell into a subsequent decline and did not remain under Babylonian control. These texts must be mentioned as containing possible allusions to this time; but, because of the uncertainty of their references, they can hardly be incorporated into the main account of this reign.

The extent of the royal power of Simbar–Shipak may be inferred from the various documents already cited. He is referred to twice as LUGAL.E, (931) implying that he was considered king of Babylonia in the same sense as the kings of the Second Dynasty of Isin. (932) His jurisdiction in Sippar in the north and in Sahritu, Eridu, and Kissik in the south indicates that he ruled approximately the same area as his predecessors. To date, we have no evidence as to whether he made Babylon or some other site his capital.

(927) Text: DIB–*šú–ni*. King's proposed emendation to *ib–ni–šú* (*AKA* 325 n. 4) is unlikely.

(928) *AKA* 325 ii 84-85.

(929) With the possible exception of some very early Kassite monarchs, the names of all Babylonian kings after the Old Babylonian period down to the time of Ashurnasirpal II (883-859) are known. Simbar–Shipak is the only king whose name is close to the form "Sibir." The question of the identification of Sibir has been discussed by Streck in *ZA* XV (1900) 285 n. 3, with abundant citation of earlier literature. (The "Kassite" text containing the name "Sibir" mentioned by Streck, *ibid.*, 286 in the continuation of n. 3, has to my knowledge never been published). See also Weissbach, *RLA* I 375b.

King, *A History of Babylon*, pp. 258-259 n. 2, suggested that Sibir had probably ruled at some time between Nabu–mukin–apli and Shamash–mudammiq; but the gap in the kinglists at this point was shortly thereafter filled by the publication of the synchronistic kinglists found at Assur (*KAV* 10 and 182), which ruled out that possibility. Wiseman in *CAH* II² xxxi 32 reiterates King's old proposal, without advancing further evidence. But it is clear that Sibir could not have been a ruler of the little-known eighth dynasty, since we now know the names of all rulers of the dynasty before the reign of Ashurnasirpal II and none of these will fit. Also Wiseman's calculation (*ibid.*) of 250 years between Simbar–Shipak and Ashurnasirpal II is about a century too high.

D. D. Luckenbill, *ARAB* I 458, translated *sibir* as "scepter" rather than as a personal name. While it is true that *šibirru*, "scepter," has an Assyrian form *sibirru* (*STT* 28 ii 27′, 30′, and possibly *AS* VII 25: 266, following *šibirrum* in the preceding line), the translation "Atlila, which for the scepter of the king of Karduniash they had seized" makes no sense here, since the idiom is foreign to Akkadian.

(930) Atlila, renamed Dur–Ashur by Ashurnasirpal, has been identified with Bakrawa by Speiser, *AASOR* VIII (1926-27) 28. For additional remarks and other bibliography, see Olmstead in *JAOS* XXXVIII (1918) 233 n. 53, Ebeling in *RLA* I 311, and Klengel in *MIO* XI/3 (1966) 366 n. 93.

(931) *BBSt* no. 27 bottom edge 3 and *BBSt* no. 36 i 13. The title is not borne, to my knowledge, by any ruler who was not considered at least nominal head of Babylonia.

(932) His other titulary is generic or religious: "king of justice, humble servant, who maintains aright the ways of Anu and Dagan and assures the perfection of their lustral rites" (*JCS* XIX [1965] 123:7-8).

After a reign of eighteen years, Simbar–Shipak died a violent death, presumably assassinated during a revolt. (933) He received a burial befitting a legitimate king. (934) His immediate successor was a usurper, Ea–mukin–zeri, who reigned but a few months. (935)

13. Ea-mukin-zeri (936)

The theory that Simbar–Shipak was assassinated becomes more plausible when we consider that his successor on the royal throne was designated as a "usurper" (LUGAL IM.GI = *šar ḫammā'i*). (937) As may be surmised from the theophoric element in his name, (938) he probably came from southern Babylonia; and he may have been a priest (*šangû*) at Eridu before his accession. (939) Like other revolutionaries in Babylonia, (940) he reigned only a short time—a scant five months—and did not merit an official regnal year. The contention that his reign interrupted the normal

(933) GIŠ.TUKUL.TA BA.AN.SÌG.GI.IN (Dynastic Chronicle v 3'). As noted by Goetze, *JCS* XIX (1965) 133 n. 93, the verb form is "present" (durative). The rough sense of the phrase is clear: the king was smitten with a weapon. Simbar–Shipak's violent death plus the fact that his successor was designated as a usurper suggest that the king died during a revolt.

(934) *Ina* É.GAL LUGAL GI.NA *qé–bir* (Dynastic Chronicle v 4'). LUGAL GI.NA can be translated either as "legitimate king" or as a royal name, "Sargon" (the lack of a masculine personal determinative before the name does not preclude the latter translation, since the name of Damiq–ilishu in the preceding line also has no personal determinative). One may contrast LUGAL GI.NA with LUGAL IM.GI ("usurper") in the succeeding line and therefore prefer the translation "legitimate king." But whether one interprets the phrase as meaning that Simbar–Shipak was buried "in the palace of Sargon" or "in the palace of the legitimate king," it is plain that he received a burial becoming a rightful monarch.

Unlike other Babylonian and Assyrian chronicles (which sometimes tell the place of death of royal personages, but never the place of entombment), the Dynastic Chronicle was concerned with recording the burial places of kings. A similar interest is reflected in the later text of Sennacherib, K. 4730:9 ("The Sin of Sargon" in *Eretz Israel* V [1958] 154) and in the biblical books of Kings.

(935) The remote possibility that his second successor, Kashshu–nadin–ahi, may have been his son is discussed below, note 944.

(936) *Ea–mukīn–zēri*: "Ea (is) the establisher of offspring." For the name type, see Stamm, *Namengebung*, p. 219. The second and third elements of the name are both found in Middle Babylonian PN's but as yet they are not attested together in a single name before the late eleventh century. No other person bearing this name is known, unless the official in *BBSt* no. 27 (see note 939 below) should prove to be different from the later king.

Writing of the RN: mdÉ*–a–mu–kin–*NUMUN (Dynastic Chronicle v 5') and in an abbreviated form mdBE*–mu–kin* (Kinglist A iii 7'). [*BBSt* no. 27 edge 1 writes the same name md*É–a–mu–kin–*NUMUN.]

(937) Dynastic Chronicle v 5'. Cf. *CAD* Ḫ sub voce *ḫammā'u*, where this reference may be added.

(938) There are only two Babylonian royal names with Ea as the theophoric element: this king and Ea–gamil, the last ruler of the First Sealand Dynasty. This would likewise point to a southern origin for this king.

(939) *BBSt* no. 27 bottom edge 1: dated six years before this king came to the throne. It would be a surprising coincidence—considering the paucity of sources from the period—if the only two men attested with this name throughout the whole of Mesopotamian history lived in the same region only six years apart.

(940) E.g., Nabu–shuma–ukin II, who reigned for little over a month in 732.

succession is supported by the fact that his burial took place in the swamp of Bit-Hashmar, (941) in contrast to the other two rulers of his dynasty, who were entombed in the official royal burial place.

We have no contemporary documents from this reign. The king's death may well have occurred when the rebellion which he led was suppressed.

14. Kashshu-nadin-ahi (942)

We know nothing about the origin of this king, save that in the Dynastic Chronicle (943) he is designated simply as the son of ^m^SAP-*pa-a-a*. (944) The history of the

(941) The location of the tribal lands of Bit-Hashmar is uncertain. In the Dynastic Chronicle v 5'-6', part of the area is referred to as swamp (*raqqatu*); this would fit in well with a location in southern or southeastern Babylonia and would moreover be bolstered by the alleged southern origin of Ea-mukin-zeri (notes 938-939) and his connection with a Sealand Dynasty. [For the meaning of *raqqatu*, "swamp," see Ebeling, *Glossar zu den neubabylonischen Briefen*, p. 198]. Unger in *RLA* II 42, with earlier bibliography, opted for the location of this Bit-Hashmar in southern Babylonia.

There is, however, a land of Hashmar or Hashimur which occurs in the inscriptions of ninth-century Assyrian kings (Ashurnasirpal II, Shalmaneser III, Shamshi-Adad V). Streck in *ZA* XV (1900) 286-287 identified this Hashmar, which is near Zamua, with the earlier Bit-Hashmar and placed it somewhere between Sulaimaniya and Zohab. With minor variations, Streck's localization of Hashmar was usually followed until Weidner's publication of a new fragment of the annals of Shamshi-Adad V, which showed that Hashmar should probably be sought in the southeastern part of the Jebel Hamrin (*AfO* IX [1933-34] 97 and nn. 42-43). This opinion has generally been accepted, though Balkan (*Kassitenstudien*, I, 94) suggested that Ea-mukin-zeri might have come from a branch of the Hashmar tribe which had wandered south.

The evidence for identifying the ninth-century Hashmar/Hashimur with the earlier Bit-Hashmar does not seem to be very strong. Sargon's mention of Hashmar (Lie, *Sargon*, 8) as one of the limits of his conquests does not support the theory that there is only one Hashmar and that it is in the Diyala region; Sargon conquered far to the east and to the south of this area. Furthermore, there is an often overlooked reference to a Hashmar in the texts of the twelfth-century Elamite king Shutruk-Nahhunte (König, *Die elamischen Königsinschriften*, no. 28 A § 8), which has yet to be satisfactorily localized. The location of a Bit-Hashmar in southern or southeastern Babylonia has yet to be ruled out, though evidence for it at present is only circumstantial.

(942) *Kaššû-nādin-aḫi*: "Kashshu (is) the giver of a brother." For the name type, see Stamm, *Namengebung*, p. 139. This form usually designates the second son born in a family. The type DN-nadin-ahi appears first in the Kassite period (e.g., *BE* XIV 116:3). No other person in Babylonia is yet known who had exactly the same name as this king, but a Kashshu-nadin-ahhe appears some thirty years after this reign as a private citizen (*BBSt* no. 9 i 13, iva 34).

Kashshu, "the Kassite (god)," is an Akkadian designation for one of the Kassite deities (Balkan, *Kassitenstudien*, I, 108-110); so the name is to be considered a Semitic formation, albeit with Kassite overtones. This god should not be confused with the Akkadian Sin, as noted already by Purves, *NPN*, p. 231.

No contemporary writings of the RN survive. Later documents preserve it as ^d^*Kaš-šú-ú*-SUM-ŠEŠ (*BBSt* no. 36 i 25), ^md^*Kaš-šú-ú*-SUM-ŠEŠ (Dynastic Chronicle v 7'), ^m^*Kaš-šú-u*-MU-ŠEŠ (Kinglist A iii 8'), and ^md^*Kaš-šu*-[x-x-x] (Assur 14616c iii 4). [For the revised reading of this RN, see p. 395 below].

(943) Dynastic Chronicle v 7'.

(944) In the original draft of this history (1962), I proposed a theory that would have seen in the reign of this king a return of the family of Simbar-Shipak to the throne. (Wiseman subsequently followed this theory in *CAH* II² xxxi 32). This hypothesis rested on three admittedly slim pieces of evidence: (1) the

Ebabbar temple endowments at Sippar recounted in the ninth-century document *BBSt* no. 36 (945) relates that during Kashshu–nadin–ahi's reign hard times and famine forced suspension of the regular food offerings in the temple. (946) The circumstances of this time were probably similar to those prevailing at the time of Marduk–nadin–ahhe and Marduk–shapik–zeri of the previous dynasty, when crop failure caused famine in the land and the hungry semi-nomads poured in to create havoc everywhere. This would help to explain why the king's reign ended after only three years. (947)

The section of the Dynastic Chronicle dealing with Kashshu–nadin–ahi terminates with the cryptic remark "in the palace". (948) Without doubt, as was pointed out by L. W. King long ago, (949) the word *qebir* should be supplied here by analogy with the preceding entries in the chronicle. This reference would then allude to the burial of Kashshu–nadin–ahi, which was accomplished in a manner suitable for a legitimate ruler—identical with the burial of the founder of the dynasty, Simbar–Shipak, (950) and in contrast to the burial accorded the usurper, Ea–mukin–zeri.

The Bazi Dynasty

This dynasty was composed of three kings, who ruled for a total of twenty years. Having begun with Eulmash–shakin–shumi, founder and most powerful

---

Dynastic Chronicle lists the father of Kashshu–nadin–ahi as mSAP(=Sip_4)–*pa–a+a*, which—as Sippaju—might be construed as a hypocoristic for Simbar–Shipak; (2) Simbar–Shipak bore a Kassite name, and his second successor had a name honoring a Kassite god; (3) the two kings were accorded similar burials.

In regard to the linguistic possibility of Simbar becoming *Sippaju*, it should be remarked: (a) the first element of the RN, *Simbar*, could represent a dissimilation from Sibbar (forms listed in Balkan, *Kassitenstudien*, I, 206); (b) consonants that appear as voiced in the writing of Kassite may actually have been unvoiced in common speech (the signs could also be read as *Sip–pár* or *Si–pár* in all instances cited by Balkan); (c) CVC signs like SAP can be indifferent to vowel quality (Gelb, *BiOr* XII [1955] 98b). For dissimilation of unvoiced consonants (relatively rare), see the late-second-millennium examples cited in Aro, *Studien zur mittelbabylonischen Grammatik*, p. 36.

This evidence is tenuous, but does hold out the slight possibility that the Second Dynasty of the Sealand may prove to be not merely a collection of three unrelated rulers but a family sequence interrupted briefly by a usurper.

(945) Wiseman's calculation (*CAH* II^2 xxxi 32) that this reference by Nabu–apla–iddina dates from about a generation after the narrated events is far too short. Nabu–apla–iddina's thirty-first year (*BBSt* no. 36 vi 28) comes sometime towards the end of the first half of the ninth century and would therefore be about a century and a half after the reign of Kashshu–nadin–ahi (1008*-1006*).

(946) *BBSt* no. 36 i 24-28. He bears the simple title *šarru* (LUGAL) in this text.

(947) Kinglist A iii 8′; Dynastic Chronicle v 7′.

(948) *ina* É.GAL (v 7′).

(949) *CCEBK* II 53.

(950) See note 934 above.

monarch of the dynasty, who made some attempt to remedy the chaos and confusion that had attended the demise of the preceding ruler, the dynasty survived for only three years after his death, when it was replaced by the Elamite Dynasty. As with the Second Sealand Dynasty, the first king of the Bazi Dynasty was its only strong ruler. There is practically no primary documentation from this time, (951) and it is difficult to characterize this period by any adjective other than little-known.

The name of this dynasty is written in two different ways in the chronological sources: BALA ⌈*Ba-zum*(?)⌉ in Kinglist A, (952) and BALA É ᵐ*Ba-zi* in the Dynastic Chronicle. (953) These variant writings may be clarified if we review briefly the history of the tiny but ancient settlement of Baz. (954)

The first appearance of Baz seems to be in the Manishtushu Obelisk, where we find references to a GÁN *Ba-az*[KI], which lies in the larger district of Dur-Sin. (955) Then the sources do not mention the area for about a millennium; (956) but in the Kassite period, when many regions came to be designated by tribal or clan names in accordance with the prevalent practice, Baz seems to have been made over into Bit-Bazi, (957) while its citizens were referred to as "sons" of an eponymous and fictitious ᵐ*Ba-zi*. (958) We find references to Bit-Bazi in two kudurrus, one from late Kassite times (959) and one from the Second Dynasty of Isin. (960) From the

(951) Save for several Luristan bronze arrowheads (*RA* XXIX [1932] 29; *Iranica Antiqua* II [1962] 160 nos. 17-18) and an old record cited in a later kudurru (*BBSt* no. 9 top).

(952) Kinglist A iii 13′. See note 165 above.

(953) Dynastic Chronicle v 12′.

(954) As is the case for most names of dynasties in Kinglist A, the Bazi Dynasty derives its title from a geographical name.

(955) *MDP* II 12 A x 1 and 17 A xvi 20. Dur-Sin is written BÀD-EN.ZU[KI]; its location is unknown (*Unger*, *RLA* II 252-253).

(956) The city whose name is written in Old Babylonian texts as URU.KI *ša Ba-zi* (letter, *PBS* VII 130:30), URU *Ba-zi*[KI] (date list, *RLA* II 179 no. 123, var.), URU *Ba-zum*[KI] (date list, *RLA* II 179 no. 123; date formulae in economic texts, *VAS* XIII 15 rev. 4, 16 rev. 3, and possibly in the letter *LIH* II 102:8), URU *Ba-zum* (letter, *CT* II 20:5-6 [= *VAB* VI no. 233]; date formulae in economic texts, *BE* VI/1 18:22, *BE* VI/2 72:21), (*ina*) *a-li* URU *Ba-zum* (letter, *CT* II 48:33 [= *VAB* VI 158]) is not to be identified with Baz or the later Bazi. According to the letter *CT* II 20 (BM 80175, formerly Bu. 91-5-9, 294), URU *Bazum* was a walled town serving as a checkpoint for boat traffic passing along a waterway near the northwestern frontier of Babylonia; the waterway was presumably the Euphrates, since one of the boat inspectors from URU *Bazum* went to Sippar for grain (*ibid.*, line 19). This conclusion is supported by a passage in a later geographical list which connects URU *Bazum* with Shuruppak (*KAV* 183:25-26), also on the Euphrates. The name of this city is to be read *āl-Bazi/Baṣum*, i.e., with the determinative pronounced, as may be seen from the gloss *a-la-ba-ṣi* in *KAV* 183:25. See Forrer in *RLA* I 431 and J. Lewy in *HUCA* XXXII (1961) 57 n. 156.

(957) The identity of Akkadian Baz and Kassite Bit-Bazi is assured by the fact that both are located in the region Dur-Sin (*MDP* II 17-18 A xvi 20-21 and *BE* XIV 16:2-3).

(958) The personal name Bazi does occur, however, in texts written under the Ur III Dynasty: *UDT* 54:19, 25 (as e n$_5$. s i . g a l), Pinches, *Berens Collection*, no. 22 rev. ii 2, no. 31:3, etc. Cf. a possible earlier occurrence of Bazi as a PN mentioned by Langdon, *Excavations at Kish*, IV, 61 (W. 1928, 428).

(959) *MDP* VI 42 i 14 (time of Merodach-Baladan I).

(960) *BBSt* no. 24:24 (reign of Nebuchadnezzar I).

first of these references, we learn that Bit–Bazi bordered on the Tigris. (961) Beginning in the thirteenth year of Kurigalzu II (c. 1333), we find references to the following natives of the region: (962)

(1) Emid–ana–Marduk, DUMU mBa–a–zi (*BE* XIV 16:3); (963)

(2) ME.NA.RU.UB.TUM, DUMU.SAL *Ba–a–zi* (*Old Testament Studies in Memory of William Rainey Harper*, I, 389, no. 4:1-2); (964)

(3) Eulmash–shakin–shumi, DUMU m*Ba–zi* (*BBSt* no. 8 i 30 and *PSBA* XIX [1897] 71 ii 12); (965)

(4) Kashshu–mukin–apli, DUMU m*Ba–zi* (*BBSt* no. 9 top 17); (966)

plus the three kings of the Bazi Dynasty, whom the Dynastic Chronicle refers to individually as DUMU m*Ba–zi* and collectively as BALA É m*Ba–zi*. (967)

In the Neo-Babylonian building inscriptions of Nebuchadnezzar II, the city name appears once more as Baz: URU *Ba–az*KI (*VAB* IV 74:30, 170:70, 182:8) and URU *Ba–az* (*ibid.*, 92:48, 108:60). It is the site of a temple built by Nebuchadnezzar to the god *Bēl–ṣarbi*. (968)

The writing of the name of the dynasty alternately as Bazi and Bazum (969) probably reflects an attempt to normalize the original Baz with Akkadian case endings. The return to the older form of the name in the Neo-Babylonian period could reflect either the dropping of all case endings in current speech or a persisting tradition of the original form. Despite the incidental changes in nomenclature, the city was the same. It is unfortunate that it cannot be localized more definitely than somewhere along the Tigris.

(961) *MDP* VI 42 i 16-17. The Tigris is also mentioned in the Manishtushu Obelisk in a passage near where Baz occurs: *MDP* II 12 A ix 21.

(962) There is no question of Bazi being a simple personal name here, since it occurs only in patronymics in Kassite and later times. Compare also the gentilic m*Ba–za–a+a*, the name of Assyrian king no. 52 (*JNES* XIII [1954] 214 ii 20, 215 ii 18).

(963) Dated in the thirteenth year of Kurigalzu (II).

(964) Kassite seal of unknown date.

(965) Dated respectively in the tenth and thirteenth years of Marduk–nadin–ahhe, 1091* and 1088*.

(966) In a business transaction taking place in the second year of Ninurta–kudurri–usur I, 987*. Both Eulmash–shakin–shumi and Kashshu–mukin–apli (nos. 3-4) bore the title of *sakrumaš*.

(967) Dynastic Chronicle v 9′-12′.

(968) One should note, however, that there is no direct evidence to link the NB Baz with the earlier city of the same name; and it is possible that the two were not identical.

A doubtful reference, slightly earlier than these, occurs in *ABL* 1283 rev. 15: LÚ *Ba–az–*[ ]; but this could refer to another locale.

(969) See notes 952-953 above.

There is no evidence that this city is to be identified with the Assyrian *Baz(z)u*, of which there appear to be at least two. (970)

15. Eulmash-shakin-shumi (971)

Eulmash–shakin–shumi of the Bazi tribe (972) came to the throne amidst the chaos that had reigned at the close of the Second Sealand Dynas-

(970) The location of the Bazu mentioned in the Neo-Assyrian sources has been much discussed. Besides the standard reference articles in *RLA* I 439-441 and the handy summary of the chief earlier opinions by Bauer in *ZA* XLII (1934) 182-184, one should note also the contributions by J. Schawe (*AfO* IX [1933-34] 59), Weidner (*AfO* XV [1945-51] 169-170, XVI [1952-53] 4-6), and Wiseman (*Iraq* XVIII [1956] 128).

There are at least two and perhaps three separate regions named *Bazu/Bāzu* (*Bazzu*), etc. in the Neo-Assyrian sources:

(a) the famous desert region in eastern or northeastern Arabia mentioned in the inscriptions of Esarhaddon (references in Borger, *Asarhaddon*, p. 130); this is described as being in the region of the road to Meluhha (*Ba–za*KI *ša pāṭ ḫarrān māt Meluḫḫ*[*a*], *AfO* XVI [1952-53] 4:1) and is possibly to be connected with the (LÚ) *Bezu*, presumably near the Sealand, mentioned in *ABL* 839 rev. 9; this area is prefixed with the determinatives for "country" or "city" (Borger, *Asarhaddon*, p. 130) and so might have had a capital bearing the same name;

(b) the country northwest of Assyria mentioned in a fragmentary inscription of Tiglath–Pileser III (ND 4301+4305:20′, published in *Iraq* XVIII [1956] pls. XXII-XXIII); the city of Ura was located in this region, which lay along the upper part of the Euphrates; with this land might be connected the gentilic personal name m*Ba–zu–a+a* attested at Tell Halaf (Ungnad, *Die Inschriften vom Tell Halaf*, no. 114:7);

(c) the country of (KUR) *Ba–a–za* located near the region of Habhi, which was attacked by Adad–nirari II (*KAH* II 83 rev. 7); this area has generally been located in the mountains northeast of Assyria proper, but might be identical with (b) above and therefore to be located near the western lands of the Nairi.

At one time Sidney Smith (*BHT*, pp. 17-18) and Landsberger and Bauer (*ZA* XXXVII [1927] 74-77) identified the regions of Bazu mentioned by Esarhaddon and Adad–nirari II and located the area in Iran (in Ardistan and in the desert of Kewīr [Kavir] respectively). Subsequently, Bauer showed the unlikelihood of these opinions in *ZA* XLII (1934) 183.

It is quite clear from the Neo-Assyrian contexts that none of these lands can be identified with the Bazi east of the Tigris in Babylonia.

(971) *Eulmaš–šākin–šumi*: "Eulmash (is) the establisher of offspring." The name type DN–shakin–shumi begins in the Kassite period (Clay, *CPN*, p. 198). Personal names containing Eulmash begin by the Old Babylonian period (e.g., VAT 819:5 and VAT 1176:14 in *JNES* XXI [1962] 75; names with the form Ulmash begin in the Old Akkadian period (*MAD* III 140, 195). For Eulmash as the name of both the temple of Ishtar in Agade and of the temple of Annunitu in Sippar, see *RLA* II 484.

Another individual named Eulmash–shakin–shumi occurs in *BBSt* no. 8 i 29 and in *PSBA* XIX (1897) 71 ii 12, kudurrus from the reign of Marduk–nadin–ahhe, sixth king of the Second Isin Dynasty. For discussion of a possible relationship between this individual and the later king, see note 972 below.

Writing of RN: *É–ul–maš*–GAR–MU in the contemporary arrowheads, a ninth-century kudurru, and a Babylonian chronicle (*RA* XXIX [1932] 29:1; *Iranica Antiqua* II [1962] 160 no. 17:1; *BBSt* no. 36 i 29, iv 50; New Babylonian Chronicle, obv. 14′); Kinglist A iii 10′ prefixes a masculine personal determinative before the name (the Dynastic Chronicle v 9′ probably did the same). In the Assyrian synchronistic kinglist Assur 14616c iii 5, the name is written md*Ul–maš*–[x–x] (for an explanation of this writing, see pages 46-47 above); and the same determinatives—and perhaps the same writing—may have been used in another Assyrian synchronistic kinglist, *KAV* 182 iii 2′, where all that is preserved according to the copy is the masculine personal determinative and the first horizontal wedge of what may have been a divine determinative.

(972) Eulmash–shakin–shumi may have had an ancestor of the same name who held the position of *sakrumaš ša mātāti* under Marduk–nadin–ahhe. This possible ancestor of the king is mentioned in texts

ty. (973) He succeeded in creating peace in the land and reigned for seventeen years. (974)

Fourteen arrowheads with identical brief royal inscriptions date from this time and give the king the title "king of the world" (*šar kiššati*), (975) an impressive epithet but relatively meaningless even under the more powerful Second Isin Dynasty. The ninth-century stone stele relating the history of the temple endowments at Sippar tells how Eulmash-shakin-shumi restored food offerings for Shamash and entrusted a garden plot in the section of Babylon known as the New City (976) to Ekur-shuma-ushabshi, the high priest in Sippar. (977)

The New Babylonian Chronicle contains enigmatic abbreviated statements: "in Nisan of the fifth year of King Eulmash-shakin-shumi" (978) and "year 14" (979)

---

dating from the tenth and thirteenth years of Marduk-nadin-ahhe's reign: *BBSt* no. 8 i 29 and *PSBA* XIX (1897) 71 ii 12. In King's edition of *BBSt* no. 8, his name was misread as Eulmash-shurki-iddina; this is wrong for two reasons: (1) the same man's name is written ᵐ*É-ul-maš*-GAR-MU in the other kudurru (he is known to be the same person because he is also a "son of Bazi" and the kudurrus have two other witnesses in common); (2) *šakin* is also written GAR.KI elsewhere in the same document (*BBSt* no. 8 top 7).

The possible ancestry is postulated on the basis of the high position of these two men in the same "tribe" (Bazi). The distance of over eighty years between the attestation of the first Eulmash-shakin-shumi and the accession of the later one to the throne would allow ample time for the repetition of the same name in the same family in a society which occasionally observed papponymy (i.e., naming the eldest male child after his grandfather); cf. Ninurta-kudurri-usur I and II below. Olmstead (*AJSL* XXXVII [1920-21] 214 n. 2) seemed to identify the two individuals named Eulmash-shakin-shumi, but the time gap involved is too great.

(973) *BBSt* no. 36 i 24-25.

(974) Kinglist A iii 10′; variants in the kinglist-chronicle tradition were discussed on p. 47 above.

(975) *RA* XXIX (1932) 29; *Iranica Antiqua* II (1962) 160 no. 17.

(976) *ālu eššu ša qereb Bābili* (*BBSt* no. 36 ii 12-13).

(977) *šangû Sippar* (*BBSt* no. 36 ii 9); Ekur-shuma-ushabshi was also a seer (*bārû*: *ibid.*, ii 10). The whole story of Eulmash-shakin-shumi's dealing with Sippar is given *ibid.*, i 29-ii 17, iv 49-53.

(978) New Babylonian Chronicle, obv. 14′. The line reads *ina* BÁR MU 5 *É-ul-maš*-GAR-MU LUGAL. King, *CCEBK* II 61, followed by Grayson in his new edition of this chronicle, read the beginning of the line as *ina parakki*, "in the shrine" (Grayson: "on the dais"); but it would seem unlikely that a chronicle would refer simply to a temple locale without specifying which temple was involved. Therefore, I prefer the reading *ina Nisanni*, which (despite the omission of the month determinative) would go well with the year number following; as far as I can ascertain, this reading was first proposed by Winckler in *OLZ* X (1907) 589. Neither reading can be regarded as certain; and one may compare the equally brief statement "the eighth year (of Nabonidus)" in *BHT* 112 ii 9, which might also allude to the non-celebration of the New Year's festival (cf. *ibid.*, 111 ii 5-6, 112 ii 10-11, ii 19-20, ii 23-24).

Wiseman has adopted each of these suggestions in different places in *CAH* II² xxxi. On p. 33, he interprets the phrase as meaning "within the shrine"; but, on p. 34, he takes the same set of signs occurring two lines later in the text as meaning "in Nisan".

(979) New Babylonian Chronicle, obv. 15′.

(evidently referring to the same ruler). (980) These may allude to times at which the New Year's festival could not be celebrated, but this is debatable. (981)

The king is reputed to have been buried in the palace of Kar–Marduk. (982) Though the name of this city has been read as *Eṭir–Marduk* and interpreted as deriving from a personal name, (983) the city of Kar–Marduk is attested as the site of an economic transaction in the reign of the following king. (984) We take the two references as pertaining to the same place, which could conceivably have been the capital of the Bazi Dynasty. (985)

16. Ninurta-kudurri-usur I (986)

This king, who reigned for three years, (987) is also designated by the Dynastic Chronicle as belonging to the tribe of Bazi. (988) The only other information which we have at present concerning his term of office comes from a lawsuit recorded in *BBSt* no. 9, where from geographical names mentioned it may be inferred that he

(980) The king mentioned in the line immediately following the reference to the "fourteenth year" is Mar–biti–apla–usur. Since no king between Eulmash–shakin–shumi and Mar–biti–apla–usur reigned so long, the line should refer to Eulmash–shakin–shumi.

(981) The New Year's festival is not one of the preoccupations of this chronicle, as it is with the Religious Chronicle. The only certain reference to anything connected with this festival occurs later in the text, rev. 9. But the festival is the major event occurring in Nisan according to the Babylonian calendar.

(982) Dynastic Chronicle v 9′.

(983) E.g., King in *CCEBK* II 54. Neo-Babylonian names written as mKAR–dAMAR.UTU (e.g., *CT* XXII 94:2, 178:2; *Nbn.* 586:5, etc.) are presumably to be read *Eṭir–Marduk*, though a similar writing (mKAR–dŠÚ) is also used for *Mušēzib–Marduk* (Kinglist A iv 18).

(984) *BBSt* no. 9 top 23 in the second year of Ninurta–kudurri–usur I. The place is not clearly attested elsewhere. (A possible reference in a later economic text, *VAS* III 226:1′, cited in the 1962 edition of this manuscript, should more likely be interpreted as a PN, judging from other personal names in the surrounding context; but, since neither a personal nor a geographical determinative has survived before the word—because of the broken condition of the tablet—, the question cannot definitely be settled).

(985) Seeing that a palace is there and that many of the kudurrus after the Kassite period are dated in the capital even though pertaining to outlying regions. This proposal has been followed by Wiseman, *CAH* II² xxxi 33.

(986) *Ninurta–kudurrī–uṣur*: "O Ninurta, protect my offspring." For further references concerning the name type DN–kudurri–usur, see note 565 above. This particular name is not yet attested for persons outside the royal family.

The RN is written variously as dNIN.IB–NÍG.DU–ŠEŠ (*BBSt* no. 9 top 1, 24), dNIN.IB–NÍG.DU–PAB (*BBSt* no. 9 ii 36, iii 13 and *Iranica Antiqua* II [1962] 160 no. 18). The name is abbreviated as mdMAŠ–⌜NÍG.DU⌝ in Kinglist A iii 11′; and broken forms occurring are mdMAŠ–*ku*–[ ] in Assur 14616c iii 6 and [NÍG.] DU–ŠEŠ in Dynastic Chronicle v 10′, while only the determinatives md are preserved in *KAV* 182 iii 3′. As discussed below (note 995), the theophoric element of the name is incorrectly written as dAG (i.e., Nabu) in BM 96273:21 (*Iraq* XXVI [1964] 15, the Shamash–shuma–ukin Chronicle published by Millard).

(987) Kinglist A iii 11′. For a divergent tradition in the Dynastic Chronicle v 10′, see p. 47 above.

(988) DUMU m*Ba–zi* (Dynastic Chronicle v 10′).

ruled over at least the cities of Isin and Kar–Marduk. (989) The record of the suit is dated in the month Simanu of the king's second year, and the king bears the simple title LUGAL. (990)

There are also brief inscriptions on Luristan bronzes which contain the name of Ninurta–kudurri–usur; but it is difficult to determine whether they refer to the first or the second king of that name. There are two inscribed arrowheads which have identical inscriptions ("Belonging to Ninurta–kudurri–usur, king of the world") (991) and an inscribed situla on which Ninurta–kudurri–usur bears only the title prince (A LUGAL). (992) For the time being, we are tentatively assigning the first two inscriptions to Ninurta–kudurri–usur I and the third to Ninurta–kudurri–usur II, (993) although each of them could be referred to either monarch.

According to a brief entry in the chronicle recently published by A. R. Millard, (994) it is likely that Shirikti–Shuqamuna, the successor of Ninurta–kudurri–usur I, was his brother. (995) For a discussion of the possibility of relationship of this king to Ninurta–kudurri–usur II, see p. 175 below.

(989) *BBSt* no. 9 top 16 mentions a governor of Isin during the reign; the transaction takes place in Kar–Marduk (top 23). For Kar–Marduk, see notes 982-985 above.

CAD Z 75a, in its article on *zazakku*, section b, quotes the passage *BBSt* no. 9 top 23 as: PN *za–za–ku* URU GN. This interpretation is erroneous for two reasons: (1) no other *zazakku* reference is followed by a place name qualifying the office, (2) in this context, immediately before the date of the document (cf. *BBSt* no. 9 ivb 7), the place where the document is written is naturally expected.

(990) *BBSt* no. 9 top 1, 24-25; the title is also given to Ninurta–kudurri–usur in a later transaction recorded in the same document ii 37, iii 13.

(991) Dossin, *Iranica Antiqua* II (1962) 160 no. 18.

(992) Amandry, *Antike Kunst* IX/2 (1966) 59, 66, and pl. 13 nos. 3a-3b.

(993) The first two inscriptions are assigned to the first king principally because the second ruled for just a few months. The third inscription is assigned to Ninurta–kudurri–usur II because he certainly bore the title prince before his accession (*BBSt* no. 9 iva 30) and because he was probably prince for a long time (his father ruled for 36 years). Note too that the inscribed Luristan bronze arrowheads date generally before the inscribed situlae. (See further the stylistic comments and dating by Amandry, *Antike Kunst* IX/2 [1966] 67-68).

(994) *Iraq* XXVI (1964) 15:21.

(995) Despite the *lapsus calami* that presents the royal name as Nabu–kudurri–usur rather than Ninurta– (i.e., dAG for dMAŠ). Millard (*Iraq* XXVI [1964] 30) has explained this lapse as a possible confusion with the Nebuchadnezzar who lived closer to the scribe's own time; and this seems a likely explanation. Despite the apparently similar lapse in the *apkallu* list written in the Seleucid period (*UVB* XVIII 45:18), which places a "Nebuchadnezzar" after Adad–apla–iddina and before Esarhaddon, the present evidence does not seem to warrant the insertion of an additional Nebuchadnezzar somewhere between the eleventh century and the early seventh century in the Babylonian kinglists—although the possibility cannot be regarded as entirely speculative. (It is more likely that Nebuchadnezzar I occurs out of order in the list because he is closer to Adad–apla–iddina in time and could have had the same *ummânu*; if the text should eventually have to be corrected to read Ninurta–kudurri–usur [I] or [II], then we could be dealing with an *ummânu* in the same family and with the same name, but hardly with the same individual because of the distance in time).

17. Shirikti-Shuqamuna (996)

This king, who ruled for only three months and not long enough to merit an official regnal year, is attested to date only in kinglists and chronicles. (997) The Dynastic Chronicle states that he was a "son" of Bazi; (998) but the spot in that document where his place of burial should be recorded is broken away. Since he was the last king of his dynasty, it may be suspected that the new ruler of the Elamite Dynasty had something to do with his quick removal.

The most recently published passage referring to Shirikti–Shuqamuna was presented by Millard in his "Another Babylonian Chronicle Text," *Iraq* XXVI (1964) 14-35. It reads as follows:

> ⸢3⸣ ITI.MEŠ ^{m}*Ši–rik–ti–*^{d}*Šu–qa–m[u]–nu*
> ŠEŠ ^{d}AG–NÍG.DU–ŠEŠ LUGAL–*ut* DIN.TIR.KI *i–p[u–u]š* (999)
> Shirikti–Shuqamunu, brother of Nebuchadnezzar,
> ruled as king over Babylon for three months.

A problem is raised by reference to an otherwise unknown Nebuchadnezzar as Shirikti–Shuqamuna's brother; (1000) Millard is undoubtedly correct in seeing this writing as a scribal confusion for Ninurta–kudurri–usur, his predecessor. (1001)

(996) *Širikti–Šuqamuna*: "gift of Shuqamuna." In Babylonia, *širikti* first occurs in personal names of the Kassite era (Clay, *CPN*, p. 132), but it was not in common use in names before the Neo-Babylonian period (Tallqvist, *NBN*, p. 203). The god Shuqamuna and his possible Akkadian equivalents have been discussed by Balkan, *Kassitenstudien*, I, 118-122. (The name is not derived from a nominal form of the verb *šarāqu*, "to steal," and hence misspellings like Shiriqti [e.g., Wiseman, *CAH* II^{2} xxxi 33] for the first element should be allowed to die out.) The king is the only man bearing this name thus far attested from Babylonia.

The only complete writing of the name that has survived is in the chronicle published by Millard: ^{m}*Ši–rik–ti–*^{d}*Šu–qa–m[u]–nu* (*Iraq* XXVI [1964] pl. VII 20). Other fragmentary writings are: ^{m}*Ši–rik–tú–*^{d}[*x–x–*(*x*)] (Assur 14616c iii 7), ^{m}*Ši–⸢x–*(*x*)*–šu–qa⸣–mu* (Kinglist A iii 12′), ^{m}*Š*[*i–*. . .] (*KAV* 10 ii 1′, *KAV* 182 iii 4′), and [. . .]–^{d}*Šu–qa–mu–na* (Dynastic Chronicle v 11′).

(997) See the references at the end of the preceding note.

(998) Dynastic Chronicle v 11′. The actual phrase used is KI.MIN, "ditto," but its place in the line clearly indicates that it refers to the DUMU ^{m}*Ba–zi* occurring after the names of the two preceding kings of the dynasty.

(999) *Iraq* XXVI (1964) 15:20-21. As a result of personal collation of the text (June 1965), I saw that the reading *i–p*[*u–u*]*š* is probably to be preferred to Millard's *i–te–p*[*u–u*]*š*. The supposed head of the vertical to TE is in reality just a pit in the clay and has no tail. The surface of the tablet is pitted between the and the at the end, but there is only room enough for in between them. The perfect tense, in any case, would be suspect because of the preterites occurring elsewhere in this idiom (*šarrūta īpuš*) in the chronicles.

(1000) See note 995 above.

(1001) *Iraq* XXVI (1964) 30.

The Elamite Dynasty

18. Mar-biti-apla-usur (1002)

This short-lived dynasty consisted of a single king, who ruled for six years. (1003) Though bearing an obviously Akkadian name, he is referred to as ŠÀ.BAL.BAL LIBIR. [RA] NIM.MA.KI (=*liplippi Elamti labīru*): "remote(?) descendant of Elam." (1004) Since it is unlikely that an Elamite king would have such a Semitic name, (1005) we should probably view this individual as a Babylonian who could claim an Elamite (and possibly an Elamite king) among his ancestors. On four Luristan bronze arrowheads which bear his inscriptions, (1006) Mar-biti-apla-usur calls himself "king of the world" (*šar kiššati*), a title borne by many Babylonian rulers, (1007) but of only nominal significance at this time. (1008) Despite his Elamite ancestry, Mar-biti-apla-usur does not seem to have been regarded as a foreign oppressor by later ages;

(1002) *Mār-bīti-apla-uṣur*: "O Mar-biti, protect the heir". For the name type DN-apla-usur, see Stamm, *Namengebung*, p. 158. This type may have begun as early as the Kassite period, since both the second and third elements of the type are then attested (Clay, *CPN*, pp. 159, 189), although to my knowledge not as yet together.

The divine name is written both DUMU.É and A.É in both this RN and in subsequent Neo-Babylonian personal names (e.g., Tallqvist, *NBN*, p. 3; *VAS* III 84:8; and *passim*). In the Post-Kassite period, the god Mar-biti is connected with Der, where he was known under two manifestations, *Mār-bīti ša pān bīti* and *Mār-bīti ša birīt nāri* (*AfO* IX [1933-34] 92 iii 43-44; cf. *BBSt* no. 6 ii 49, where *mār bīti* seems to be an epithet, possibly to be interpreted as the origin of the later DN), with Maliki (references in note 1320 below), and with Borsippa, where he had a shrine (*VAS* I 36 iii 26). Confusion of Mar-biti with the god dA.MAL may occasionally have arisen because of the similarity of the signs with which their names were sometimes written (dA.É and dA.MAL); but this is difficult to determine on the basis of present limited evidence.

The RN is preserved in contemporary writing only on the Luristan bronze arrowheads: dDUMU.É-A-PAB (*Iranica Antiqua* II [1962] pl. XXVII no. 19a is the only really legible photo of an exemplar; no. 19b might read dA.É-A-PAB, but the photo does not permit a certain reading). The New Babylonian Chronicle has the only other complete writing of the RN: dA.É-A×A-ŠEŠ (obv. 16′). The name is partially preserved as mDUMU.⌈É⌉-[x-x] (Kinglist A iii 14′), mdDUMU.É-[x-x] (Assur 14616c iii 8), mdDU[MU?.É-x-x] (*KAV* 10 ii 2′), m[ ]-⌈A⌉-PAB (*KAV* 182 iii 5′), [Š]EŠ (Dynastic Chronicle v 13′).

(1003) Kinglist A iii 14′; Dynastic Chronicle v 15′.

(1004) Dynastic Chronicle v 13′. The restoration of LIBIR.RA is not altogether certain.

(1005) No other Elamite king now known bore a Semitic name. Note however that König, *Die elamischen Königsinschriften*, p. 7 considers Mar-biti-apla-usur as a king of Elam, but retains approximately the old dates given by Cameron, *History of Early Iran*, p. 137. Cameron himself, *ibid.*, called Mar-biti-apla-usur only a "descendant of Elam" and referred to the political history of Elam after the time of Hulteludish-Inshushinak as three centuries of silence. Labat (*CAH* II² xxxii 24) and Hinz (*Das Reich Elam*, p. 115) follow Cameron in his judgment of three centuries of silence, but do not even mention Mar-biti-apla-usur.

(1006) Dossin, "Bronzes inscrits du Luristan de la Collection Foroughi," *Iranica Antiqua* II (1962) pl. XXVII and p. 160 no. 19.

(1007) See Seux, *Épithètes royales*, pp. 310-312.

(1008) Compare enfeebled monarchs like Nabu-shumu-libur, who claimed the same titulary.

and his burial was that regularly accorded a legitimate Babylonian ruler. (1009) Save for a cryptic reference in the New Babylonian Chronicle to "the fourth year of Mar–biti–apla–usur," (1010) we know nothing about his activities as king. He brings to a close the half century of short reigns and brief dynasties in Babylonia.

UNCERTAIN DYNASTIES

Under this heading, we shall deal with the next twenty rulers of the Post–Kassite period, from Nabu–mukin–apli to Shalmaneser V (Ululaju). We know the dynastic affiliation of only eight of these twenty kings for certain: the kings from Eriba–Marduk to Nabu–shuma–ukin II (nos. 31-35) belonged to the E Dynasty, the Chaldean Mukin–zeri (no. 36) was said to belong to the Shapi Dynasty, and Tiglath–Pileser III and Shalmaneser V (nos. 37-38) were Assyrians. The E Dynasty may have contained at least several more earlier kings, but this cannot as yet be established definitely. (1011)

Thus we cannot state the dynastic designations for kings 19-30. Kings 19-21 belonged to the same family and therefore to the same dynasty; (1012) but how long this dynasty endured is uncertain. Kings 23-26 were four generations of a single family and also presumably belonged to one dynasty, but this dynasty could have embraced several earlier and later kings as well. Beyond these rather general statements we cannot at present safely go.

Our next problem is posed by the name of the E Dynasty. (1013) Though the name is applied only once to this group of kings (nos. 31-35), we know that BALA E was not simply a slip of the stylus since the same designation is used in Kinglist A of two later Babylonian monarchs. (1014) The question here is not so much whether the name was accurate or not, (1015) but rather what did Kinglist A mean by it.

(1009) *Ina* É.GAL LUGAL GI.NA *qé–bir* (Dynastic Chronicle v 14'). For the interpretation of this phrase see note 934 above.

(1010) New Babylonian Chronicle, obv. 16', possibly but not necessarily referring to the non-celebration of the New Year's festival in that year. The line in question may have nothing missing before MU *4* (compare the immediately preceding line 15') and therefore *ina* BÁR is probably to be understood as repeated from line 14'.

(1011) See pp. 52-59 above.

(1012) They also occur in a single dynastic grouping in Kinglist A iii 15'-17'.

(1013) Kinglist A iv 6.

(1014) *Ibid.*, iv 15, 18 (said of Bel–ibni and Mushezib–Marduk).

(1015) Kinglist A and the Dynastic Chronicle (*ADD* 888) disagree on the dynastic divisions of the early-eighth-century Babylonian rulers (see notes 163 and 287 above); and it is difficult to speak of one tradition being more accurate than the other.

Though we cannot pretend that this question can now be answered with absolute certainty, the most probable origin of the E in BALA E is in the formula LUGAL E, which was used as a royal title in contemporary legal and administrative documents. (1016) This formula, in turn, was handed down from the economic text tradition of the Kassite period (1017) and probably derived ultimately from a misunderstanding of l u g a l . e in the Sumerian date formulae of the Old Babylonian period. (1018) LUGAL E continued to be used as an epithet for Babylonian kings down into the early days of the Chaldean Dynasty, (1019) when the Neo-Babylonian scribes seem to have reinterpreted E as a geographical name referring to Babylon (1020) and to have added the determinative KI behind it. (1021)

It is difficult to say what LUGAL E meant to the scribes during Kassite and later times before scribes of the Chaldean Dynasty clarified their own interpretation of the expression through the addition of KI. It does not seem to have been a substitute for the simple LUGAL, since this also occurs throughout these periods. (1022) The scribes had more explicit ways of expressing "king of Babylon" when they wished to do so. (1023) It seems likely that the phrase, at the time of its initial adoption, was used simply for "king"; but then later scribes, unaware of the original intent of the phrase and of its origin in the Sumerian formulary of the Old Babylonian period, reinterpreted its meaning and eventually added the determinative to suit their interpretation. When E first came to stand for "Babylon" is uncertain, but the adding of

(1016) E.g., *AfK* II (1924-25) 56 rev. 7, *BRM* I 12 rev. 7, and *passim*.

(1017) The phrase occurs frequently in Nippur texts (e.g., *BE* XIV 7 rev. 39), Ur texts (e.g., *UET* VII 3:34, unpublished), Dur-Kurigalzu texts (e.g., *Iraq* XI [1949] 144 no. 4:47), and texts of unknown origin (e.g., *TCL* IX 48:26). The earliest occurrence known to me is the eighth (ninth?) year of Burnaburiash II (c. 1368) in *BE* XIV 7. Thus the use of the formula in the Kassite period is practically coextensive in time with the surviving economic documents.

(1018) A transitional stage may be seen in the retention of l u g a l . e in Akkadian date formulae in the late Old Babylonian period (Hana), e.g., MU RN LUGAL.E *me-ša-ra-am iš-ku-nu* (*Syria* V [1924] 270:24-25), where it contrasts with simple LUGAL used in similar context in other texts (*Syria* V [1924] 271 rev. 9′, *Syria* XXXVII [1960] 206:32, *TCL* I 237:36, *VAS* VII 204:57, *BRM* IV 52:31). The same inchoative tendency to regard e as part of the royal title may be seen in some summaries in late Old Babylonian datelists, e.g., "38 m u s a - a m - s u - i - l u - n a l u g a l - e" (*RLA* II 168, BM 92702 iv 33) as contrasted with "10 m u a m - m i - s a - d u - g a l u g a l (*RLA* II 169, BM 16924 vi 7).

(1019) E.g., *TuM* II-III 43:15, 134:23 (both Nabopolassar).

(1020) E.KI for Babylon also occurs in such documents as the Kedor-laomer texts (Sp. III, 2:10′), which may have been written slightly earlier in the seventh century, but cannot be dated as precisely as the economic texts. (This date refers to the originals of the Kedor-laomer texts, not to the Spartoli copies).

(1021) This changeover takes place about the time of the first year of Nebuchadnezzar II, when two texts dated in succeeding months from Borsippa exhibit the writings LUGAL E (*TuM* II-III 195:16) and LUGAL E.KI (*TuM* II-III 150:18).

(1022) LUGAL was much less common than LUGAL E in the economic texts of the Kassite period, but seemed to gain in relative popularity after that time until in the reign of Nabonassar (*BRM* I 4-21) it had become more common than LUGAL E. After the accession of Nebuchadnezzar II, it rapidly became extinct.

(1023) LUGAL KÁ.DINGIR.RA.KI (*BE* I/1 83:7, etc.), LUGAL DIN.TIR.KI (*BRM* I 10:8, etc.).

the determinative seems to have originated in the late seventh century. The new interpretation may have begun somewhat earlier.

In line with these observations, what can we say about the meaning of the phrase BALA E? Kinglist A, the only document to use it, was probably composed during the time when the determinative KI was consistently added to E in the formulae of the economic texts. (1024) It is not inconceivable that a contemporary scribe, on seeing an earlier document with the simple title LUGAL E, may have interpreted the E as a dynastic designation, since the simpler form of the title (i.e., without KI) had become obsolete in his day. (1025) Alternately, the compiler of the list may have meant simply to assign this dynasty to Babylon (E.KI) and have omitted the geographical determinative as he did in other cases. (1026) At any rate, considering the time of composition of Kinglist A, it is likely that E.(KI) was intended as a reference to Babylon. Despite its probable origin in late Sumerian and the alteration of its meaning in later tradition, the E here may plausibly be interpreted as alluding to that city. (1027)

Our study concludes with the three rulers who immediately followed the E Dynasty. Kinglist A explicitly assigns two of these rulers to dynastic groups: Mukin–zeri to BALA *Šá–pi–i* and Ululaju to BALA BAL.TIL. (1028) First, we should remark that the dynastic designations in this section of the kinglist (iv 7-18) need not always be taken literally, since Merodach–Baladan II could alternately be connected with BALA KUR *Tam* or described as ERÍN *Ḫa–bi*. (1029) In the cases of Mukin–zeri and Ululaju, however, the allusions are to principal cities of their realms: Shapi referring to Mukin–zeri's capital of Shapija (1030) and BAL.TIL to the city of Assur, (1031) over which Ululaju (Shalmaneser V) ruled.

Before proceeding to the treatment of the individual monarchs of this time, we present the following brief historical prospectus of the period between 979* and 722. Immediately after the one-man Elamite Dynasty, Nabu–mukin–apli came to the throne and ruled for thirty-six years, longer than his six immediate predecessors

(1024) I.e., during the reign of Nebuchadnezzar II or later; see p. 16 above.

(1025) The title LUGAL.E was still being used in economic texts during the reigns of Nabu–shuma–ishkun (*BRM* I 3:14) and Nabonassar (*BRM* I 12:7, 18:7, 19:15), both of whom belonged to the E Dynasty according to the tradition of Kinglist A.

(1026) E.g., PA.ŠE (iii 5′), ⌜*Ba–zum*(?)⌝ (iii 13′), BAL.TIL (iv 9), *Ḫa–bi–gal* (iv 12, 16).

(1027) The lack of references to Babylon as E in the geographical and lexical lists speaks strongly for an artificial origin such as that suggested here.

(1028) Kinglist A iv 7, 9.

(1029) *Ibid.*, iv 10, 14. For an explanation of these expressions, see my remarks in *Studies Oppenheim*, pp. 35-37.

(1030) For the reading of the GN, see notes 1494-1495 below.

(1031) BAL.TIL.KI=ŠU=URU ŠÀ URU (*KAV* 183:19). For discussions of BAL.TIL, see Poebel, *JNES* I (1942) 263-267, 469-470; J. Lewy, *HUCA* XIX (1946) 467-473; Goetze, *JCS* XIX (1965) 134 n. 108. Note that Sargon II, the successor of Shalmaneser V, called himself *zēr* BAL.TIL.KI (*TCL* III 113).

together. Babylonia was still weak after the quick succession of rulers in the previous half century; and, during much of Nabu–mukin–apli's reign, the country was troubled with Aramean invasions, which came quite near to Babylon itself on several occasions. Nabu–mukin–apli was succeeded by two of his sons: Ninurta–kudurri–usur II, who died after a reign of a few months, and Mar–biti–ahhe–iddina, of whom little more is known than his name.

With the accession of Shamash–mudammiq, the next ruler, there began a century of close contact with Assyria: battles, alliances, shifting of borders, and diplomatic marriages, most of which seem to have bound the two countries closer together. Under Shamash–mudammiq, Babylonia seems to have received a temporary setback, if Assyrian accounts of the regaining of Arrapha and Lubdu are true. Nabu–shuma–ukin I, his successor, restored the former border of Babylonia to the Lower Zab, concluded a lasting peace with Assyria, and exchanged daughters in marriage with Adad–nirari II. Under Nabu–apla–iddina, son of Nabu–shuma–ukin, Babylonia seems to have reached the height of her power for this time: the Aramean–Sutian invasions were ended and their effects effaced, while Babylonian aid to Assyrian tributaries in Suhi inspired widespread rebellion against the Assyrian government at Calah. Literary activity in the land swelled to sing the praises of the king "who had avenged Akkad." ([1032]) After the disagreement with Babylonia in the Suhi area, Ashurnasirpal II seems to have left that country in peace for the remainder of his reign; and Shalmaneser III, on his accession, took steps to insure continued friendliness between the two lands.

Unfortunately, this halcyon era in Babylonia did not long survive the king who created it. And Marduk–zakir–shumi I, the legitimate heir of Nabu–apla–iddina, found himself in disputed possession of his kingdom. His brother and rival, Marduk–bel–usati, was driven out of the land only after Shalmaneser III, his father's old friend, had conducted two extensive campaigns against the rebels. In the course of these campaigns, the powerful Chaldean tribes living in southern Babylonia—Bit–Dakkuri, Bit–Jakin, and Bit–Amukani—make their first extended appearance in history. At this juncture, they seem to have acknowledged the nominal sovereignty of the Babylonian king; but it would not be many years before they would themselves gain control of the throne of Babylon and be ruling the more settled people of northern Babylonia.

Marduk–zakir–shumi I reigned for about three decades and lived to help Shamshi–Adad V, the son of his former benefactor, put down a revolt in Assyria even more widespread than that which Marduk–zakir–shumi had faced in Babylonia in his early years. The treaty which resulted from this Babylonian aid was hardly

([1032]) Cf. *BBSt* no. 36 ii 29-30.

flattering to Assyria; and, after the death of Marduk–zakir–shumi I, Shamshi–Adad V amply revenged himself on Babylonia for the humiliating terms of the agreement. Marduk–balassu–iqbi, the son of Marduk–zakir–shumi, ruled for at most a decade before Shamshi–Adad thoroughly defeated him and his allies (Elamites, Chaldeans, Kassites, and Arameans) and led him away captive to Assyria. Baba–aha–iddina, who followed Marduk–balassu–iqbi on the throne, met a similar fate and was taken off to Assyria in his very first year.

A period of anarchy followed in Babylonia. Various sources indicate that there was a period of 12(+x) years when there was no king in the land or that there were several minor kings whose names cannot always be wholly restored. ([1033]) Eriba–Marduk, a Chaldean chieftain, was the man who drew order out of this chaos. We know little about his rise to power, but during his reign he furthered old religious cults and provided protection for private property against Aramean raiders. He was succeeded by Nabu–shuma–ishkun, who was unable to defend even nearby Borsippa from marauders. This ineffectiveness of the central administration continued under Nabonassar, who could do little to check the activities of the Aramean tribes living in the south and east of Babylonia (who had begun to bother even the Assyrians). At this point, however, Assyria revived from a long languor; and, after a revolution in Calah, Tiglath–Pileser III emerged as a strong monarch ready to assert his country's might over much of western Asia. His first campaign, conducted in his accession year, was aimed at quelling the disturbances in Babylonia; and, at that time, he seems to have succeeded in policing the country so well that neither Arameans nor Chaldeans caused noteworthy trouble there for better than a decade. Nabonassar continued to exercise a weakened control over most of the country; and Tiglath–Pileser contented himself with placing the more troublesome Arameans and Chaldeans under Assyrian officials and claiming a nominal suzerainty over "Sumer and Akkad."

Nabonassar, despite his military ineffectuality, managed to hand over his realm intact to his son at his death. But Nabu–nadin–zeri reigned for only two years before the crown was usurped by the rebellious Nabu–shuma–ukin II, a former provincial official. Nabu–shuma–ukin in turn was replaced on the throne after little more than a month by a Chaldean chieftain of the Amukanu tribe, Mukin–zeri.

Mukin–zeri held a tenuous control over the land for about three years before the Assyrians managed to confine him to a small area around his capital at Shapija. Then Tiglath–Pileser himself assumed the crown of Babylonia for two years; and, at his death, the kingship of Assyria and Babylonia passed to his son Shalmaneser V, who reigned for five years. We know little about this period of Assyrian rule over Babylonia; but the Assyrian dynasty was unable to gain a permanent hold. Upon

([1033]) E.g., Ninurta–apl?–[x], Marduk–bel–[zeri].

Shalmaneser's death, when Sargon took up the reins in Assyria, Babylonia set up an independent government again under Merodach–Baladan II, a Chaldean who was to prove one of the most effective antagonists that the Assyrian military machine was ever forced to face.

19. Nabu-mukin-apli (1034)

This first ruler of the new dynasty ruled for thirty-six years. (1035) The relative length of his reign is substantiated by a kudurru mentioning a legal action in his twenty-fifth year and by a chronicle relating a portent in his twenty-sixth year. (1036) We know nothing of his background before he became king, (1037) but the throne continued in his family after his death, since his two immediate successors were his sons. (1038)

Nabu–mukin–apli's reign, though long, was hardly peaceful, to judge from most of the sources. The Arameans were on the rampage in western areas of the country from at least his seventh through his twentieth years and perhaps even longer. The sources hardly permit us to reconstruct a continuous narrative; so the pertinent documents shall be treated here separately.

(1034) *Nabû–mukīn–apli*: "Nabu (is) the establisher of a legitimate heir." For the name type, see Stamm, *Namengebung*, pp. 85, 218-219. The form DN–mukin–apli begins in the Kassite period (Clay, *CPN*, p. 178) and is especially popular in Neo-Babylonian and Persian times. This king seems to be the first individual to bear this particular name; but there are other private individuals with the same name later, e.g., *TCL* XIII 196:6, *Nbn.* 16:6.

The Nabu–mukin–apli who dedicated a blue chalcedony macehead to Nabu (C. J. Ball, *Light from the East*, pp. 216-217 = L. Speleers, *Les Arts de l'Asie antérieure ancienne*, pl. XXIV, fig. 518 = *RA* XLV [1951] 22 no. 24) was another person, who may have lived around the seventh century B.C. From the photograph of the macehead published by Ball (p. 217), we can see that this individual (name not visible on the photograph) was *šākin ṭēmi* of Babylon (line 2) and that he dedicated the macehead "for his own life, for the length of his days, for his happiness, (and) for the security of his position (*ana kun išd šu*)."

Writing of RN: in a contemporary kudurru as ᵈAG–DU–A (*BBSt* no. 9 i 18 and *passim*) and ᵈAG–GI.NA–A (*BBSt* no. 9 i 10, ivb 9); on Luristan bronze arrowheads as ᵈAG–DU–A, ᵈPA–DU–A, and ᵈPA–GI.NA–A (*Iranica Antiqua* II [1962] 161 nos. 21a-21c:1, from photos; in Babylonian chronicles as ᵈAG–DU–A (Religious Chronicle iii 6′, 10′, 13′, 15′, 19′), ᵈAG–DU–IBILA (Religious Chronicle iv ⌜4′⌝, 5′), and with a broken ᵈAG–DU–[ ] (New Babylonian Chronicle, obv. 17′); in Assyrian synchronistic kinglists: ᵐᵈPA–D[U–X] (*KAV* 10 ii 3′), ᵐ[ ]–DU–A (*KAV* 182 iii 6′), [ ] ⌜x⌝[ ]–A (Assur 14616c iii 9).

A picture of Nabu–mukin–apli appears on top of *BBSt* no. 9 (*BBSt*, pls. LXVII and LXXIV).

(1035) Kinglist A iii 15′.

(1036) *BBSt* no. 9 i 18; Religious Chronicle iii 19′.

(1037) Forrer in *MVAG* XX/3 (1915) 20 speculated that Nabu–mukin–apli had been installed by an Elamite king as successor to the Elamite Dynasty.

It will be suggested below (p. 175) that Ninurta–kudurri–usur II may have been related to Ninurta–kudurri–usur I. If this theory should prove correct, the founder of this dynasty (as father of Ninurta–kudurri–usur II) would have been related to one of the last rulers of the Bazi Dynasty.

(1038) The family relationship of Nabu–mukin–apli with Ninurta–kudurri–usur II and Mar–biti–ahhe–iddina is known from *BBSt* no. 9 iva 30, 32.

The first reference to his reign is contained in the New Babylonian Chronicle in one of its abbreviated passages: "(in Nisan of) the first year of Nabu–mukin–[apli]." (1039) As noted above (p. 162), we cannot ascertain the meaning of the cryptic allusions in this chronicle, though the most likely interpretation would be that the New Year's festival was not celebrated in the king's first year (thereby implying that Nabu–mukin–apli won control of the land only gradually).

The preserved portions of the Religious Chronicle deal almost exclusively with the reigns of two Babylonian kings. (1040) The name of the first is not preserved; (1041) but the second, whose reign is described through two columns of portents, is Nabu–mukin–apli. Prescinding from the references to wild animals appearing in settled areas, with which the Religious Chronicle seems to be preoccupied and which are of little relevance for political history, (1042) we find numerous statements dealing with the turmoil in the land caused by contemporary Aramean invasions. In no fewer than eleven of Nabu–mukin–apli's first twenty years, (1043) the procession of Marduk outside the city of Babylon in the New Year's festival could not take place because of the proximity of the hostile semi-nomads. Even though offerings were made to rectify these bad omens, (1044) the disturbances continued for some time. (1045) In his seventh year, Nabu–mukin–apli was prevented from coming upstream to Babylon at all; (1046) and, in his eighth year, the crossing gate (*bāb nēberi*) at Kar–Bel–matati, just south of Babylon, was in the hands of the Arameans, so that the king could not cross the river. (1047) During these difficult times, lasting at least from Nabu–mukin–apli's seventh through twentieth years, the land was often disrupted by semi-nomad incursions.

(1039) New Babylonian Chronicle, obv. 17′. The spacing at the beginning of lines 14′-17′ indicates that *ina* BÁR is to be understood at the beginning of line 17′.

(1040) The very fragmentary first column dealt with earlier ruler(s), e.g., Nabu–shumu–libur (i 16).

(1041) It could have been either Simbar–Shipak or Eulmash–shakin–shumi; see note 926 above.

(1042) Other than that they might indicate the unsettled condition of the land at the time. Animal portents in this reign are listed in the Religious Chronicle iii 2′-3′ (probably before Nabu–mukin–apli's seventh year), 11′ (sixteenth year), possibly in 15′-17′ (twenty-fourth year); and a meteorological or astronomical portent is recorded in 19′ (twenty-sixth year).

(1043) Besides the seventh and eighth years of his reign (iii 4′-9′), the chronicle also mentions immediately after its recording of the omission of the procession in the twentieth year that nine consecutive years elapsed in which no procession was held: *9 šanātu arki aḫāmeš Bēl ul uṣâ u Nabû ul illiku* (iii 14′-15′). It is more likely that these nine years are to be reckoned from the twelfth through the twentieth year (the same style of reckoning a total of preceding years is used in ii 16′ of this document), but this cannot be regarded as certain.

(1044) Religious Chronicle iii 9′, 11′.

(1045) See note 1043 above. Portents continued to be recorded also in the twenty-fourth and twenty-sixth years of the reign (Religious Chronicle iii 15′, 19′).

(1046) Religious Chronicle iii 5′. From this passage it may be inferred that his royal residence was further south, out of reach of the invading semi-nomads.

(1047) Religious Chronicle iii 7′-8′. For literature on Kar–Bel–matati, see note 706 above.

A complementary picture is painted by the kudurru *BBSt* no. 9, which dates from the same reign. (1048) Dealing principally with the affairs of the clan of Abirattash (1049) in the township of Sha–mamitu, (1050) this document gives information on the payment of taxes by the family between the second year of Ninurta–kudurri–usur I (987*) and the twenty-fifth year of Nabu–mukin–apli (955*). (1051) The taxes were paid in asses to be delivered to the "keeper of horses (received) as income"; (1052) and the twenty-fifth year of Nabu–mukin–apli seems to have marked an attempt to reenforce the collection of the taxes. The account as preserved in the kudurru indicates that there was no written record concerning the payment of taxes in the third and fourth years of Nabu–mukin–apli, but only the oral statement of Arad–Sibitti, member of the clan of Abirattash; (1053) these years fell during the term of Bel–iddina as "keeper of the horses." (1054) During the term of the next "keeper," Eanna–mudammiq, who held office from the fifth to the twenty-fourth year of Nabu–mukin–apli, (1055) only four asses were received (as compared with two asses in the third and fourth years alone); and we can surmise that tax collection during these years, when Arameans were harassing the land, was at best irregular. (1056) In the twenty-fifth year, then, a new "keeper," Kuddaju, (1057) was installed; a reckoning of the preceding thirty-three years was made and the taxes settled. (1058)

The only other primary sources presently known from the reign are a brief inscription of the king on Luristan bronze arrowheads, (1059) two Luristan bronze situlae inscribed with names of his sons, (1060) and an unpublished economic text. (1061)

(1048) The document seems to be dated in the twenty-second year of the king (ivb 8-9), but events as late as the twenty-fifth year are mentioned in the text (i 18, iii 6, 14). Poebel (*AS* XV 18 n. 64) suggested that the date 22 was a mistake of the stone-cutter for 25 or an even later year.

(1049) Read formerly as Atrattash by King in his edition of *BBSt* no. 9.

(1050) Written URU *šá* SAG.BA (*BBSt* no. 9 ivb 7, cf. i 2), but otherwise unknown.

(1051) *BBSt* no. 9 iii 1-15.

(1052) *rē'ī sīsê ša isqi* (*BBSt* no. 9 iii 3, 5-6, 7, 15); these references may be added to the *isqu* articles in both *CAD* and *AHw*.

(1053) *BBSt* no. 9 iii 2.

(1054) *Ibid.*, iii 2-3.

(1055) *Ibid.*, iii 3-5.

(1056) Economic insecurity in the land is also shown by the high prices for grain at this time (*BBSt* no. 9 iva 13-15; cf. King, *ibid.*, p. 67 n. 5, and *ibid.*, no. 7 i 21).

(1057) *BBSt* no. 9 iii 6-7.

(1058) *Ibid.*, iii 11-15.

(1059) *Iranica Antiqua* II (1962) 161 no. 21. Another bronze arrowhead which may date from about this time is the one inscribed with the name of Mar–biti–shuma–ibni, a *sakrumaš* official (*Iranica Antiqua* II [1962] 161 no. 20); see note 46 above.

(1060) See notes 1071-1072 below.

(1061) *JCS* V (1951) 19: "2.9 Eighth dynasty of Babylon: 1 tablet from the reign of Nabu-mukin–apli(?)." I have been unable to verify this statement or to learn anything concerning the contents of the text (in the Musée d'art et d'histoire, Geneva).

We can tell little about the extent of Nabu–mukin–apli's kingdom at this time. Certainly the western regions of Babylonia around the Euphrates were troubled by semi-nomads for a good part of his reign, but this state of affairs was hardly new in Babylonia. [1062] Since the towns mentioned in the kudurru (*BBSt* no. 9) have not been identified, we cannot say over how large an area Nabu–mukin–apli ruled; but we know at least, from the title of a witness in the kudurru, that there was a governor at Isin during his reign. [1063] As already noted, his own residence was located south of Babylon. [1064]

Little titulary of this king has survived. He claims the usual "king of Babylon" [1065] and also the vapid "king of the world" (*šar kiššati*). [1066] There is little significance in these titles, save that he wished to be considered a Babylonian monarch in the old tradition.

Nabu–mukin–apli was followed on the throne by two of his sons in succession. These princes and a third son were the primary witnesses to the kudurru *BBSt* no. 9:

(1) Ninurta–kudurri–usur, son of the king (DUMU LUGAL);

(2) Rimut–ili, [1067] son of the king, *šatammu* official of the temples; [1068]

(3) Mar–biti–ahhe–iddina, son of the king. [1069]

The first and the third of these princes succeeded Nabu–mukin–apli; the second, satisfied with a lucrative position for life, seems to have been left out of consideration. [1070] Both Ninurta–kudurri–usur and Rimut–ili left inscriptions on Luristan bronze situlae dating from this reign; in these Ninurta–kudurri–usur bears the title "prince" [1071] and Rimut–ili the title "*šatammu* official of the temples." [1072]

(1062) Compare the Sutian disturbances under Adad–apla–iddina and Kashshu–nadin–ahi.

(1063) *BBSt* no. 9 iva 34.

(1064) See note 1046 above.

(1065) LUGAL DIN.TIR.KI (*BBSt* no. 9 Face B 3).

(1066) *BBSt* no. 9 ivb 9, Face B 2; *Iranica Antiqua* II (1962) 161 no. 21:2. He bears the simple title "king" (LUGAL) in *BBSt* no. 9 i 10, 18 and *passim* in this inscription.

(1067) Previously read *Rīḫu–ša-ilī*. Borger (*Handbuch der Keilschriftliteratur*, I, 220 and 415) has suggested *Rīmūt-ilī* as a more likely reading. That this suggestion is correct may be seen by comparing forms of the sign *šá* which occur in *BBSt* no. 9 and in *SPA* I 284 no. XIII (photo in *SPA* IV pl. 70A) with the right half of the *mut* sign: *šá* in these texts has only two wedges in its upper row, while the *mut* sign has three. Thus the sign form should be viewed as a tenth-century form intermediate between the twelfth-century and the eighth-century . Cf. also *BBSt* no. 8 iv 14.

(1068) For this title, see p. 300 below.

(1069) *BBSt* no. 9 iva 30-32.

(1070) Or he may have predeceased his elder brother.

(1071) A LUGAL (Amandry, *Antike Kunst* IX/2 [1966] 59 fig. 3). For the tentative dating of this inscription to Ninurta–kudurri–usur II rather than Ninurta–kudurri–usur I, see note 993 above.

(1072) ⸢ŠÀ.TAM É.KUR(?).⸣MEŠ (*SPA* I 284 no. XIII).

20. Ninurta-kudurri-usur II (1073)

The name of this ruler is furnished us by the synchronistic kinglists and the length of his short reign, 8 months 12 [days], by Kinglist A. (1074) Nothing is known about him except that he succeeded his father on the throne, was listed first among the three royal princes in a kudurru dated under his father's rule, (1075) and that a Luristan bronze situla was inscribed with his name during his father's reign. (1076)

Because this king took the same name as Ninurta-kudurri-usur I relatively soon after that king's reign, some family connection between them might be suspected. Ninurta-kudurri-usur I was not a noteworthy monarch, and there would be little glory in adopting his name. Furthermore, his reign (988*-986*) would be just far enough removed from this time (944*) to make it possible for him to be the later king's grandfather. (1077) This proposal is obviously hypothetical; but another connection between the same two dynasties could be seen in the continuity of the legal actions sketched in *BBSt* no. 9, which began under Ninurta-kudurri-usur I and ended in the reign of Nabu-mukin-apli, father of Ninurta-kudurri-usur II.

21. Mar-biti-ahhe-iddina (1078)

Mar-biti-ahhe-iddina, the second of Nabu-mukin-apli's sons to occupy the throne, is almost completely unknown. Part of his name is preserved in the New

(1073) For a discussion of the meaning of the name and its occurrence in Babylonian documents, see above under Ninurta-kudurri-usur I (note 986). Writing of RN: in documents when he was prince as mdNIN.IB-NÍG.DU-PAB (*BBSt* no. 9 iva 30) and as mdMAŠ-NÍG.DU-PAB (Luristan bronze situla published by Amandry, *Antike Kunst* IX/2 [1966] 59 fig. 3; see note 993 above); in Assyrian synchronistic kinglists as mdMAŠ-NÍG.DU-PAB (*KAV* 10 ii 4'; NÍG and part of DU must be restored in *KAV* 182 iii 7'; only last sign preserved in Assur 14616c iii 10). Note that the second element of the name was erroneously restored in *JCS* XVI (1962) 94 under 20.1.3 (*KAV* 182).

(1074) *KAV* 10 ii 4', *KAV* 182 iii 7', Assur 14616c iii 10; Kinglist A iii 16'. For the reading of the number in Kinglist A, see p. 48 above.

(1075) *BBSt* no. 9 iva 30.

(1076) See note 1071.

(1077) The taboo in Mesopotamia against giving members of successive generations the same name (probably a practical matter as well) did not extend to the second generation; and grandfathers and grandsons could bear the same name (papponymy). Eulmash-shakin-shumi (note 972 above) could be another case in point.

(1078) *Mār-bīti-aḫḫē-iddina*: "Mar-biti has given me brothers." For the meaning of the name, see Stamm, *Namengebung*, pp. 44-45. In this case, the nuance of the name stands out clearly, since it is known that this king had two older brothers (*BBSt* no. 9 iva 30-31) and this name is worded as though spoken by the eldest brother upon the arrival of his second younger brother. For the use of the god Mar-biti in proper names, see above under Mar-biti-apla-usur (note 1002).

Names of the type DN-aham-iddinam occur as early as the Old Babylonian period (Ranke, *EBPN*, p. 153), but the first attestation of the second element of the name in the plural comes in Kassite times

Babylonian Chronicle but without any mention of activity. (1079) He is also mentioned in various synchronistic kinglists, (1080) and is listed as a witness in a kudurru drafted while he was still prince. (1081) We have no idea of the length or extent of his reign nor do we know whether his successors on the throne were related to him. (1082)

Early in the annals of Ashur–dan II (934-912), there is a brief, but badly broken passage referring to Assyrian interest or activities in the land of Ruqahu, (1083) probably to be located somewhere near where the Lower Zab flows into the Tigris. (1084) Since this land otherwise is part of the central province of Assur itself, (1085) it is surprising to see it mentioned in a context which would suggest its having lapsed from Assyrian royal control. (1086) There is no direct evidence that would suggest that Ruqahu had fallen into the hands of either the Arameans (1087) or the Babylonians; but its defection from the jurisdiction of the Assyrian central government would point up the grave territorial limitations of Assyria at this time. These Assyrian troubles in the region east of the Tigris could be dated during the reigns of either Mar–biti–ahhe–iddina or Shamash–mudammiq in Babylon.

(Clay, *CPN*, p. 152). Private individuals in the Neo-Babylonian and Persian periods sometimes bore the same name as this king, e.g., *VAS* IV 25:19, *VAS* III 91:9.

Writing of RN: in a kudurru (before he became king) as mdDUMU.É–ŠEŠ.MEŠ–SUM–*na* (*BBSt* no. 9 iva 32); in the Assyrian synchronistic kinglists with the element *–aḫa–* in the singular as mdDUMU.É–PAB–AŠ (*KAV* 10 ii 5′), mdA.É–⌈PAB–SUM⌉–*na* (*KAV* 182 iii 8′), and [ ]–PAB–AŠ (Assur 14616c iii 11); partially preserved in the New Babylonian Chronicle, edge as [ ].ME–MU.

(1079) New Babylonian Chronicle, edge.

(1080) References in note 1078 above.

(1081) *BBSt* no. 9 iva 32.

(1082) Immediately after the name of Mar–biti–aha(sic)–iddina in Assur 14616c occur traces of the name of his *ummânu* official (iii 12). All that is legible of these traces are the masculine personal determinative and the divine determinative (preceding the name proper).

(1083) *AfO* III (1926) 156:22.

(1084) Forrer, *Provinzeinteilung*, pp. 12 and 47, places Ruqahu on the east bank of the Tigris between the Lower Zab and the Jebel Hamrin. Weidner in his edition of the Ashur–dan text (*AfO* III [1926] 156 n. 9) concurred in this opinion.

(1085) W. Andrae, *Stelenreihen*, nos. 37:6, 38:6; cf. *ABL* 94 rev. 1 ("royal troops of the land of the *Ruqaḫaju*").

(1086) The verb is missing in the sentence, however, so one cannot say definitely why Ruqahu was mentioned here. Most of the lands and cities referred to in the Ashur–dan text were objects of attack of the Assyrian army.

(1087) Albright in *CAH* II² xxxiii 50 has stated that "Ashur–dan II (934-912) informs us that the Aramaeans had occupied part of the region between the Lower Zab and the Ḥamrin mountains, in the East–Tigris country between Assyria and Babylonia, during the reign of Ashur–rabi II (1012-972 B.C.)." The annals of Ashur–dan, however, allude to Ruqahu and the (Lower?) Zab in a passage mentioning only Shalmaneser II (*AfO* III [1926] 156:16-22) and containing no reference to Arameans. The following section (*ibid.*, 23-32) mentions [Ashur–ra]bi and the land of Arumu, but in a context which strongly suggests the Upper Euphrates (Weidner, *AfO* III [1926] 156 nn. 10-12).

22. Shamash-mudammiq (1088)

Mar–biti–ahhe–iddina was succeeded by Shamash–mudammiq, who is known thus far only for his relations with Assyria. (1089) We know nothing about his ancestry or the length of his reign and can state definitely only that his contacts with Adad–nirari II took place during the last decade of the tenth century. (1090)

Shamash–mudammiq, if we can believe the Assyrian sources at this point, seems to have been a singularly unlucky ruler. During his reign, the whole of Babylonia was supposedly overrun by the Assyrian armies; (1091) and the official borders of the land receded in both the northwest and northeast. In the northeast, he was defeated by Adad–nirari II at the foot of Mt. Jalman (probably towards the southeastern end of the Jebel Hamrin range). (1092) The Assyrians then annexed

(1088) *Šamaš–mudammiq*: "Shamash (is the one who) makes happy." Lit.: Shamash is the one who makes good—i.e., brings prosperity, luck, or good fortune. Names of this type are discussed in Stamm, *Namengebung*, p. 220. The form DN–mudammiq begins to appear in Old Babylonian personal names (Ranke, *EBPN*, p. 240). Private citizens with the name Shamash–mudammiq are attested in the Middle Babylonian (e.g., *BE* XIV 73:36) and the Middle Assyrian (e.g., *KAJ* 71:4, 244:13) periods; and the name continues in use through the Neo-Babylonian (e.g., *Nbn.* 1113:5, *CT* XXII 155:4) and Persian (e.g., *YOS* VII 79:2) periods. The Shamash–mudammiq in *BBSt* no. 9 top 22 (dated 987*) is undoubtedly too early to be this king, but might have been an ancestor of his.

Writing of RN: with the exception of a fragmentary [*i*]*q* preserved in the New Babylonian Chronicle, the name of Shamash–mudammiq occurs only in Assyrian sources. The contemporary annals of Adad–nirari II write the name as ^{md}*Šá–maš–mu*–SIG$_5$ (*KAH* II 84:27). The Assyrian synchronistic king-lists write it uniformly as ^{md}UTU–SIG$_5$ (Assur 14616c iii 13, *KAV* 182 iii 9′, *KAV* 10 ii ⌜6′⌝) and the Synchronistic History as ^{md}UTU–*mu*–SIG$_5$ (*CT* XXXIV 40 iii 2, ⌜4⌝, 8).

(1089) The sole Babylonian passage referring to this king (New Babylonian Chronicle, rev. 1, only faint traces of RN) also mentions Adad–nirari II in a broken and abbreviated context.

The name of the *ummânu* official of Shamash–mudammiq, ^{m}*Qa–li–ia–a*, is preserved in Assur 14616c iii 15.

(1090) The events described in *KAH* II 84:26-29, 34 took place before the eponym year of Dur–mat–Ashur (*KAH* II 84:39). They also took place after the eponym year of She'i–Ashur, since a preceding edition of the exploits of Adad–nirari II was written in the ninth month of that eponymate (*KAH* II 83 rev. 19) and no mention is made of a campaign against Babylon. The eponymate of She'i–Ashur should be dated in 909, immediately after the eponym year of Adad–nirari himself, as may be seen from the new Sultantepe eponym list (*STT* 47 i 1-2; cf. likewise K. 4329b 1′[=C^{a}1, checked from photo]). The eponym year of Dur–mat–Ashur should be dated in 901 (*STT* 47 i 10, as restored from *KAH* II 84:39; this is the latest possible date for this eponymate since four eponym officials—Illeqaju [*KAH* II 84:42], Ninuaju [*ibid.*, 45], Liqberu [*ibid.*, 49], Adad–aha–iddin [*ibid.*, 61]—served between Dur–mat–Ashur [*KAH* II 84:39] and Adad–dan [*KAH* II 84:62, *STT* 47 i 15]). Thus the campaign of Adad–nirari against Shamash–mudammiq should probably be dated between the years 908 and 902.

(1091) Adad–nirari calls himself *kāšid māt Karduniaš ana pāṭ gimriša*, "conqueror of Babylonia in its entirety," (*KAH* II 84:26).

(1092) *CT* XXXIV 40 iii 3-5, Synchronistic History. The annals of Adad–nirari say that he defeated Shamash–mudammiq "from Mt. Jalman to the river Dur–ili" (*KAH* II 84:26-27). The *Dūr–ili* has been identified with the Diyala by Forrer (*RLA* I 294) and Poebel (*ZA* XXXVIII [1929] 94).

Mt. Jalman is also attested in the annals of Shamshi–Adad V (I *R* 31 iv 11), where a location to the southeast of the Diyala is indicated. It may also be mentioned in an inscription of Shilhak–Inshushinak (König, *Die elamischen Königsinschriften*, no. 54 iii 55; cf. *ibid.*, iii 25-26), possibly as the name of a district.

Babylonian territory from Lahiru to Ugarsallu into their country. (1093) The whole of the land of Der (1094) was conquered; and the fortified cities of Arrapha (1095) and Lubdu, (1096) which had served as outposts for the northern border of Babylonia,

(1093) *KAH* II 84:27-28. Ugarsallu was between the Lower Zab and the Radanu (*AfO* XVIII [1957-58] 350-351:38, see note 756 above). Lahiru is presumably to be located further to the southeast, towards the Babylonian-Elamite frontier.

Assyrian conquests of Lahiru from the late tenth through the early eighth century were ephemeral. After the first conquest of the area by Adad–nirari II, it had to be reconquered by Shalmaneser III in 850 (*WO* IV/1 [1967] 30 iv 6) and again by Shamshi–Adad V about 811 (*CT* XXXIV 41 iv 3-6, Synchronistic History). Tiglath–Pileser III incorporated the city within the border of Assyria and referred to it as being in the region of *I–di–bi–ri–i–na* (II *R* 67:13). Sargon referred to the area as being variously in the land of *Ia–ad–bu–ri* (Lie, *Sargon*, 52:2) or *Ia–a–di–bi–ri* (*ibid.*, 52:3), and received obeisance and tribute (horses, mules, oxen, sheep, goats) from the sheikhs (*nasīkāte*) of the region in the year 710 (*ibid.*, 52:2-3); Sargon reincorporated the same area into Assyria (*ibid.*, 52:4), with more effect than Tiglath–Pileser. Though the area had its own tribal sheikhs (*ibid.*, 52:2; *ABL* 280:20), it was made into an Assyrian province under the Sargonids (e.g., *ADD* 774:8, *ABL* 558 rev. 4, and *passim*). Sennacherib on a subsequent occasion stated that Shuzubu the Chaldean (=Mushezib–Marduk) was subject to the governor (*bēl pāḫiti*) of Lahiru (*OIP* II 41-42 v 20-22); and the governor (*bēl pāḫiti*) of Lahiru was eponym official under Esarhaddon in 673; also Esarhaddon's mother seems to have owned property near there (see H. Lewy, *JNES* XI [1952] 274). By the time of Ashurbanipal's campaigns against Elam, the area had once more become independent but, according to Ashurbanipal (Streck, *Asb.*, 42:116-123), submitted to Assyrian overlordship once again.

Forrer, *Provinzeinteilung*, p. 47 (following Delitzsch, *Wo lag das Paradies?*, pp. 204 and 323, and other scholars) postulated the existence of two separate Lahirus: one north of the Jebel Hamrin and one southeast of Der. This opinion is still possible, but seems somewhat less likely. When Shalmaneser III attacked Gannanate in 850, he may have done so from the south, especially since Marduk–bel–usati was forced to flee north to Arman (Halman, see note 1195 below). Note too that Lahiru is mentioned between Der and Gannanate in *CT* XXXIV 41 iv 3 (Synchronistic History). Billerbeck (*Das Sandschak Suleimania*, pp. 55-56) located the city in the region where the Diyala cuts through the Jebel Hamrin. Streck (*Asb.*, CCXXVIII n. 4) referred to further examples of the occurrence of Lahiru in Neo-Assyrian economic texts, etc., and also stated that he considered the postulating of two places named Lahiru unnecessary.

The name Lahiru is to be transcribed as *Laḫīru* or *Laḫēru*, i.e., with the second vowel long. Cf. the writings URU *La–ḫi–i–ri* (*Camb.* 13:5), URU *La–ḫi–i–ri–a+a* (*YOS* III 76:35).

(1094) Surrounding the city of Der, located at modern Badrah. See Smith, *JEA* XVIII (1932) 28.

(1095) For the history of Arrapha, see Unger, *RLA* I 154.

(1096) Lubdu was a city considered as one of the boundaries of the Arrapha territory according to the geographical treatise of Sargon (*KAV* 92:10). Albright in *JAOS* XLV (1925) 211-212 considered it to be the southern boundary; and this is now even more likely since it is the last place Tiglath–Pileser I mentions before crossing the Radanu river (*AfO* XVIII [1957-58] 351:38). Finkelstein (*JCS* IX [1955] 2) has suggested an approximate location near the modern town of Tauq, about twenty miles south of Kirkuk.

Lubdu occurs in the Mari letters as a locale in which soldiers subject to the Shamshi–Adad dynasty were stationed (*ina Lu–ub–di–im*KI: *ARM* V 50:7); and, in a late Old Babylonian contract, a female slave from Lubdu (URU *Lu–ub–da*KI) was sold (*JCS* IX [1955] 1 MLC 606:4-6). The site is also frequently mentioned in the Nuzi texts: there was a palace there (JENu 526:⸢5⸣, Tu 313:⸢5-6⸣), and Ishtar of Lubdu was invoked in curses (*HSS* X 231:19). Further references, including the use of the city in personal names, are collected by Purves in *NPN*, p. 232 (s.v. *lumti*), by Weidner in *AfO* XV (1945-51) 79 n. 38, and by Finkelstein in *JCS* IX (1955) 1-2; see also *HSS* V 14:2. In the later Kassite period, from at least the last half of the fourteenth century on, the area was subject to Babylonia; Lubdu is mentioned in a gold-inventory text from the fifth year of Nazimaruttash (*PBS* XIII 80 rev. 2) and in several MB letters (*PBS* I/2 63:5, *BE* XVII 99:6, *PBS* VII 29:7—for the date of the last, see Ungnad, *PBS* VII, pp. 7-8). The mayor of Lubdu occurs in an undated MB text from Dur–Kurigalzu (*Iraq* XI [1949] 133 no. 3:4, 12). It was regarded as the northern boundary of Babylonia by Adad–nirari I (*KAH* I 3:7, II 35:6) and was part of the Babylonian territory between the Lower Zab and the Radanu ravaged by Tiglath–Pileser I (*AfO*

were reincorporated into Assyria proper. (1097) Babylonian prestige east of the Tigris had sunk to a new low.

From another brief episode recorded in the annals of Adad–nirari II, we learn that Assyria was also expanding along the Euphrates towards Babylonia once again. The towns of Hit and Zanqu, (1098) formerly border fortresses of Assyria, (1099) were once more restored to that country. (1100) In the context of Babylonia's previous interest in those two towns and the interest that she would show in this region a generation later under Nabu–apla–iddina, it seems likely that Assyria was taking advantage of the temporary weakness of Babylonia. (1101)

It has sometimes been asserted, on the basis of a passage in the Synchronistic History, that Shamash–mudammiq was killed by his successor (Nabu–shuma–

XVIII [1957-58] 351:38; cf. *CT* XXXIV 39 ii 23′, Synchronistic History). The gentilic personal name *ᶠLu–ub–da–it–tu* occurs in a MA economic text from the archive of Ninurta–tukulti–Ashur (*AfO* X [1935-36] 43 no. 100:13).

Adad–nirari II conquered the area and restored Lubdu (here called a "stronghold" or "fortress," i.e., *birtu*, of Babylonia) to Assyria proper for the first time in more than half a century (*KAH* II 84:29); note that the verb *utīr* (*ibid.*) must be taken literally as "return"—and not as J. Seidmann translates it, "schlug," in *MAOG* IX/3 (1935) 15—since the territory had belonged to Assyria earlier. Some twenty-five years later, the governor (*šaknu*) of Lubdu and the governor of Suhi were to present five live elephants to Ashurnasirpal on the occasion of the great dedicatory banquet at Calah (*Iraq* XIV [1952] 34:96; the leg bones of an elephant found at Nuzi in a second-millennium level [R. F. S. Starr, *Nuzi*, I, 493 and II, plate 28C] show that elephants were known in this area in a slightly earlier period; see also B. Brentjes, "Der Elefant im Alten Orient," *Klio* XXXIX [1961] 8-30).

Lubdu was one of the 27 important Assyrian cities which revolted against Shalmaneser III at the end of his long reign (I *R* 29:49). The city is mentioned briefly once more in a badly broken Harper letter (*ABL* 1191:14), in which the city Zaban also occurs (line 12). Lubdu (*Lu–úb–da*KI) is likewise mentioned in Tablet IX of the Assyrian Dream-Book: "if a man goes to Lubdu, imprisonment will seize [him]" (Oppenheim, *TAPS* XLVI [1956] 312 obv. ii y+13).

Luckenbill's rendering of Lubdu in *ARAB* I 785 among the cities of Urartu must be discounted; the copies read URU *Lu–ub–[x]* (Layard, *ICC* pl. 18:31) and URU *Lu–ub–ba* (Rost, *TP III*, pl. XXXIII 30). The reading of *Lubdi* (for *Urarṭi*) as the seat of Andaria in K. 2732 (Ashurbanipal) has been shown to be erroneous by A. Piepkorn, *AS* V 57 n. 8.

Literature on Lubdu: Albright, *JAOS* XLV (1925) 211-212; Weidner, *AOB* I 58 n. 4; Meek, *HSS* X p. xxvi; E. Speiser, *JAOS* LV (1935) 443; Seidmann, *MAOG* IX/3 (1935) 64; Oppenheim, *RA* XXXV (1938) 152; Purves, *NPN*, p. 232; Weidner, *AfO* XV (1945-51) 79 n. 38 (with additional bibliographical citations); Weidner, *AfO* XVI (1952-53) 12; Finkelstein, *JCS* IX (1955) 1-2.

(1097) *KAH* II 84:28-29.

(1098) Previously fought over by Nebuchadnezzar I and Ashur–resha–ishi I. For the location of these fortresses, see note 601 above.

(1099) *CT* XXXIV 39 ii 3′, 8′-9′, Synchronistic History; *KAH* II 84:34.

(1100) *KAH* II 84:34.

(1101) A block of granite bearing an inscription of Adad–nirari II (titulary and ancestry only) was found at Babylon and published by F. H. Weissbach (*WVDOG* IV 15+pl. 6 no. 1), who thought that Adad–nirari might have built at Babylon; this would fit well with the Assyrian king's claim to have conquered all of Babylonia (*KAH* II 84:26). However, Weissbach's alternate theory—that the stone was brought as booty from Assyria—could also be correct, since the brick was found in the "Schlossmuseum" of Nebuchadnezzar II along with other relics of bygone ages, including spoil from the Mari region (Unger, *Babylon*, p. 224).

ukin). (1102) However, the traces in the text clearly speak for his dying the usual death of defeated monarchs: [KUR–šú] ⌜e–mid⌝ (1103)—a phrase which, whatever its precise nuance, does not imply assassination. We do not yet know of any family relationship or other connection between Shamash–mudammiq and his successor. (1104)

23. Nabu-shuma-ukin I (1105)

This king, like his predecessor, is known almost entirely from his contacts with Assyria. (1106) Though his name is preserved in the synchronistic kinglists and the total of his regnal years is now completely lost, we know from chronicles that he was a contemporary of both Adad–nirari II and Tukulti–Ninurta II.

The Synchronistic History is the source for our knowledge of Nabu–shuma–ukin's relations with Adad–nirari II. (1107) According to this Assyrian document, Adad–nirari defeated the Babylonian king, (1108) despoiled several Babylonian towns, (1109) and brought the booty home to Assyria. (1110) Then, following a brief

(1102) E.g., Forrer in *MVAG* XX/3 (1915) 20, Olmstead in *AJSL* XXXVII (1920-21) 216 and in *His ory of Assyria*, pp. 75.

(1103) *CT* XXXIV 40 iii 8. The *ni–ri–šú* in the preceding line, because of the chariots mentioned before it, clearly refers to battle apparel, not slaughter.

(1104) Though the traces after the name of Nabu–shuma–ukin! in *CT* XXXIV 40 iii 9 might possibly be read as DU[MU–šú], thereby indicating that Nabu–shuma–ukin was the son of Shamash–mudammiq.

(1105) *Nabû–šuma–ukīn*: "Nabu has established legitimate progeny." For the name type, see Stamm, *Namengebung*, p. 41. Both the second and third elements of this name are used frequently in the Kassite period, though no combination DN–shuma–ukin has yet been discovered from that time. This king seems to be the earliest individual attested bearing this name; king no. 35 of the Post-Kassite period was to assume the same name. It was extremely popular among private persons in the Neo-Babylonian and Persian periods (Tallqvist, *NBN*, pp. 147-148).

Writing of RN: in the New Babylonian Chronicle as mdAG–MU–*ú–kin* (rev. 3, partially restored from rev. 2), in the Assyrian synchronistic kinglists as mdPA–MU–*ú–kin* (complete only in *KAV* 182 iii 10′, the last element of the RN is missing in *KAV* 10 ii 7′ and Assur 14616c iii 16), and in the Synchronistic History erroneously as mdPA–MU–GAR–*un* (*CT* XXXIV 40 iii 9, ⌜10⌝).

(1106) The possibility that he might have been a son of Shamash–mudammiq is mentioned in note 1104. The assertion of Unger that Nabu–shuma–ukin I came from Bit–Dakkuri (*RLA* II 39) is based on a later text referring to Nabu–shuma–ishkun (published in *JRAS* 1892 350-368, transliterated and translated also by Winckler in *AOF* I/3 [1895] 254-259); Unger, following the Synchronistic History, confused the names Nabu–shuma–ishkun and Nabu–shuma–ukin.

(1107) For the writing of this king's name as Nabu–shuma–ishkun in the Synchronistic History, see pp. 49-50 above.

(1108) *Adad–nīrārī šar m[āt Aššur itti] Nabû–šuma–iškun šar māt Kard[uniaš imd]aḫiṣ dabdāšu išk[un]* (*CT* XXXIV 40 iii 10-11, Synchronistic History).

(1109) The names are broken: [... URU] ⌜*Ban?*⌝*–ba–la* URU *Ḫu–da–d[a/d[u]* (*CT* XXXIV 40 iii 12). A city Banbala is known from *ADD* 1096 rev. 7, 8; and Hudada seems the natural restoration for the other name. Neither restoration should be regarded as certain. (Panbalu is known elsewhere as the Kassite name for Babylon: Balkan, *Kassitenstudien*, I, 90-91; for Hududu, see note 1745 below).

(1110) *CT* XXXIV 40 iii 14-15 (Synchronistic History).

broken passage that is at present unintelligible, we learn that the two kings exchanged daughters in marriage and established amicable relations between the two lands. (1111) The borders were then re-aligned east of the Tigris "from Til–Bit–Bari, which is north of the city of Zaban, to the tells of Sha–Batani and Sha–Zabdani." (1112)

The very record of the Synchronistic History speaks against the Assyrian claim of victory in this instance. The border was shifted north once again, and Babylonia definitely gained back territory it had lost in the time of Shamash–mudammiq. (1113) The exchange of royal brides would argue more for equality between the two nations than for a humbled Babylonia.

The date of this battle between Nabu–shuma–ukin and Adad–nirari may be fixed with reasonable probability late in the reign of the latter. Since Adad–nirari's campaigns are recounted in summary fashion between 911 and 902 and then year by year from the eponymate of Dur–mat–Ashur (901) (1114) through the eponymate of Shamash–abua (894), (1115) his second encounter with Babylonia must be dated between 893 and the end of his reign in 891. The power of the Assyrian may well have failed during his declining years.

The era of peace and good will between Babylonia and Assyria which was inaugurated at this time lasted, with only minor unpleasant intervals, for more than eighty years—truly a phenomenon in Assyro-Babylonian relations. Although Assyria at this time was beginning to expand her empire once again, her contacts with Babylonia do not indicate a weakened land in the south. After the time of Shamash–mudammiq, though we have little specific information on Babylonian power, the next Babylonian kings were able to maintain the old boundaries of the Second

(1111) *Ibid.*, iii 17-19.

(1112) *Ibid.*, iii 20-21. The tells of Sha–Batani and Sha–Zabdani occur only here and in the inscriptions of Ashurnasirpal II, where they are also mentioned as being near the northern border of Babylonia (*AKA* 344 ii 130, 383 iii 123-124, etc.). Til–sha–Zabdani, the last element of which is sometimes preceded with a masculine personal determinative (*AKA* 181:27), bears a name similar to that of a brother of Nabu–shuma–ukin I, m*Za–ab–da–a–nu* (*AKA* 351:20). Compare the city Zabdanu, mentioned in the seventh-century letter *ABL* 280:7, which was used as a base for raids against Elam; this might not have been the same place, since it could be located further south.

(1113) Til–Bit–Bari, because north of the city Zaban, was quite close to the Lower Zab; and therefore Arrapha and Lubdu would once more be within Babylonian territory. For the location of Til–Bit–Bari, see Speiser, *AASOR* VIII (1926-27) 19 n. 36; and cf. note 1150 below.

As Grayson has suggested in *AS* XVI 340 n. 25, it is possible that Assyria may have lost more territory since the time of Shamash–mudammiq and may thus actually be advancing again. This, however, seems less likely, since an advancing Assyria would hardly be eager to conclude a parity treaty (such as Adad–nirari made with Nabu–shuma–ukin).

(1114) See note 1090 above.

(1115) The eponym mentioned in *KAH* II 84:94, despite its ending in *–ia*, must be identical with the eponym named in *STT* 47 i 17.

Dynasty of Isin (1116) and stopped most Assyrian advances cold at these lines. (1117) Assyria refrained from subjugating Babylonia at this time not because she revered the old cultural center of Mesopotamia, but because she did not have sufficient strength until later to overcome the by then debilitated Babylonians.

Nabu–shuma–ukin's reign extended down into the time of Tukulti–Ninurta II of Assyria (890-884). At this point, the New Babylonian Chronicle provides us with an abbreviated synchronism, but no further information. (1118) An expedition of Tukulti–Ninurta which may have occurred during Nabu–shuma–ukin's reign, but more probably during the reign of his son, Nabu–apla–iddina, will be treated below under the latter king.

Nabu–shuma–ukin's descendants continued to hold the throne in Babylonia during most of the ninth century. He was succeeded by his son, his grandson, and finally his great-grandson before trace of the family is lost. He had strengthened Babylonia more than any of his immediate predecessors and had paved the way, by enlarging the borders and making pacts with Assyria, for the cultural renaissance that would follow in the reign of his son.

24. Nabu-apla-iddina (1119)

The son of his predecessor, (1120) Nabu–apla–iddina came to the throne after his father's death and ruled Babylonia for at least thirty-three years. (1121) Under

(1116) After the middle of the ninth century, however, some of the regions south of Nippur were more independent than they had been during the Second Isin Dynasty.

(1117) The sole exception in the ninth century was when Marduk–zakir–shumi I requested the aid of Shalmaneser III in putting down the Babylonian rebels.

(1118) [...M]U–*ú*–*kin* ^{m}TUKUL–[^{d}NIN.I]B ⌈MAN KUR⌉ *Aš*+*šur* (rev. 2). The traces in this section of the chronicle can fit only these two kings.

(1119) *Nabû–apla–iddina*: "Nabu has given me an heir." For the name type, see Stamm, *Namengebung*, pp. 39-40. The development of the form DN–apla–iddina in personal names has been sketched above under Adad–apla–iddina (note 806).

This particular name seems to occur for the first time here, though a private person from the same time as the king bears the same name (*BBSt* no. 28 obv. 1). The name is quite common in both later Assyria and Babylonia (Tallqvist, *APN*, pp. 144-145; Tallqvist, *NBN*, pp. 122-123).

Writing of RN: in contemporary Babylonian texts as ^{d}AG–A–SUM–*na* (*BBSt* no. 28 rev. 4, 16, 26; *BBSt* no. 36 ii 18, iii 15, iv 3, 36, v 3, vi 9, 28, 36; *VAS* I 35:30, slightly later copy), as ^{d}PA–A–SUM–*na* (*BBSt* no. 28, label), as ^{d}AG–IBILA–SUM–[*na*] (*BBSt* no. 36 iv 1); in a contemporary Assyrian text it is written ^{md}AG–A–SUM–*na* (*AKA* 351 iii 19). In later texts it is written as ^{md}AG–A–SUM–*na* (*CT* XVI 38 iv ⌈20⌉); *Iraq* XVIII [1956] pl. 24 rev. 10, DN uncertain, cf. *Iraq* XVIII [1956] 136, *JCS* XI [1957] 13, *JCS* XVI [1962] 96 n. 19), ^{md}AG–IBILA–MU (*OECT* I pl. 20 obv. 6, ⌈19⌉, second element of RN unclear), ^{md}PA–A–SUM–[*na*] (Assur 14616c iii 18), ^{md}PA–A–AŠ (*KAV* 182 iii 11′); fragmentary writings: ^{md}PA–A–[x] (*KAV* 10 ii 8′), [ ]–IBILA–SUM–*na* (*CT* XXXIV 40 iii 26, cf. iii 23, Synchronistic History), [IBIL]A–MU (New Babylonian Chronicle, rev. 3), ^{d}AG–[x–(x)–S]UM–*na* (unpublished and unnumbered kudurru in the Louvre, information courtesy of Douglas Kennedy).

A picture of the king appears at the top of *BBSt* no. 28 (pl. CIII).

(1120) New Babylonian Chronicle, rev. 3.

(1121) An unpublished and unnumbered kudurru in the Louvre dated in the thirty-third year of ^{d}AG–[x–(x)–S]UM–*na* has kindly been called to my attention by Douglas Kennedy. The traces of the RN will

his capable guidance, the land retained its military eminence—keeping Assyria at bay and even fomenting difficulties in Assyrian-claimed territory on the middle Euphrates—and enjoyed a religious and cultural rebirth.

The Assyrian kings of this time occasionally toured the lands of the Habur and the middle Euphrates with their armies to collect tribute in person. (1122) One such tour which took place towards the close of the reign of Tukulti–Ninurta II probably fell during the early years of the reign of Nabu–apla–iddina. (1123) The Assyrian king left Assur on the twenty-sixth of Nisan in the year 885 (1124) and proceeded along the Wadi Tharthar until he reached its southern end. Then he turned east to the Tigris, descended to the region of Dur–Kurigalzu, and crossed over to Sippar of Shamash before beginning his tour up the Euphrates. It should be noted that Tukulti–Ninurta travelled for over a week within territory that was Babylonian, apparently presuming on the earlier treaty of friendship between Babylonia and Assyria. (1125) The Assyrian king's itinerary was recorded in detail throughout the journey; and it is obvious that Tukulti–Ninurta was journeying in foreign or non-subject territory at least as far as the city of Anat, which was the first place at which he received tribute. (1126) Even there the official, Ilu–ibni, who was called the governor (*šaknu*) of the land of Suhi and who offered the king "tribute" (*nāmurtu*), was a vassal in an isolated outpost, the loyalty of which was vacillating. (1127) It was

---

fit only this king, since he is the only known king with these first and third elements in his name and there is no room in Babylonian chronology for any presently unknown king to have ruled so long. (The latest date previously known, his thirty-first year, was recorded in *BBSt* no. 36 vi 28).

The earliest possible date for Nabu-apla-iddina's first regnal year is 890 (because of his father's synchronism with Tukulti–Ninurta II). The latest possible date for his death is in early 851 (the year in which Shalmaneser III first aided Marduk–zakir–shumi I). Thus the maximum reign possible for Nabu–apla–iddina is forty official regnal years.

(1122) Adad–nirari undertook such a journey down the Habur to the middle Euphrates in 894 (*KAH* II 84:97-119).

(1123) It might also have occurred during the last years of Nabu–shuma–ukin I, because the regnal years between 890 and 884 in Babylonia could be assigned either to him or to his son, Nabu–apla–iddina. It is tentatively assigned here in the reign of the latter because Nabu–apla–iddina is known to have ruled closer to the actual year of the campaign, 885.

(1124) V. Scheil, *Annales de Tn. II*, obv. 41. The trip was begun in the eponymy of Na'id–ili, which is now known from *STT* 47 i 26 to have been 885. This eponymate was inadvertently omitted from Ca2 between the eponymates of Ilu–milki and Jari (*RLA* II 418).

(1125) Between Nabu–shuma–ukin I and Adad–nirari II (*CT* XXXIV 40 iii 18-19, Synchronistic History). Weidner (*MVAG* XX/4 [1915] 95) suggested that the treaty gave the Assyrian king the right to march unhindered through Babylonian territory.

(1126) Scheil, *Annales de Tn. II*, obv. 69 ff.

(1127) The land of Suhi, with its capital at various times at Anat (Scheil, *Annales de Tn. II*, obv. 69-73) or at Suru (*AKA* 350-351 iii 16-17), stretched from the border of Babylonia at Rapiqu (*AKA* 180 obv. 23, etc.) to about Hindanu on the middle Euphrates. It was strategically located near the northwestern border of Babylonia and was an important commercial center in the trade which furnished ivory (Scheil, *Annales de Tn. II*, obv. 70; *WO* II/2 [1955] 142 D; cf. the five live elephants presented by the governors

four more days' journey before the king reached the next place for exacting tribute on his triumphal march, which then continued up the Euphrates and the Habur.

Seven years later, in the year 878, Ashurnasirpal II made the same tour from the opposite direction. Beginning towards the northern end of the Habur, the Assyrian king marched down along that river and then along the Euphrates until he reached Anat. After leaving Anat, however, he no longer found the same peaceful conditions that his father had experienced. Suhi had revolted in 882; and Ilu-ibni, the governor who had paid tribute to Tukulti-Ninurta in 885, had been forced to

---

of Suhi and Lubdu: *Iraq* XIV [1952] 34:95) and cloth (Scheil, *Annales de Tn. II*, obv. 72; *WO* II/2 [1955] 142 D; cf. *KAV* 106:5) to Babylonia and Assyria.

Suhi as a region tributary to Babylonia is attested in the OB period (*VAB* VI 238:2, 3, 18), when it already had a governor (*šāpir Sūḫi*). In the MB period, a group of troops from the Hiranu tribe was stationed there (*Iraq* XI [1949] 139:21-24). Tiglath-Pileser I was the first Assyrian king to mention explicitly his conquest of the land of Suhi, then part of the territory of the Ahlamu Arameans (*AfO* XVIII [1957-58] 351:41-43, etc.; cf. *ibid.*, 350:35). Adad-nirari II also claimed to have defeated the Ahlamu Arameans and to have received the tribute of Suhi (*KAH* II 84:33). In 885 Ilu-ibni, governor (*šaknu*) of Suhi, paid tribute to Tukulti-Ninurta II (Scheil, *Annales de Tn. II*, obv. 69-73); but three years later Ilu-ibni was forced to flee with his family to Assyria to save their lives (*AKA* 289:100). In 878 and in a later year (sometime between 877 and 869), Ashurnasirpal was obliged to march to Suhi to deal with rebels (*AKA* 350-353 iii 16-26, 353-357 iii 26-38), and in his standard titulary he claimed to have caused "Suhi as far as Rapiqu" to submit to him (*AKA* 344 ii 128). At the solemn inaugural banquet for Ashurnasirpal's new capital city of Calah, envoys from Suhi were present, elephants were presented from the ruler of Suhi, and some native Suhians subsequently settled in the city (*Iraq* XIV [1952] 33:33, 34:95-96, 35:143). Shalmaneser III collected "tribute" from Marduk-apla-usur, who was governor there (WO II/2 [1955] 142 D; see also note 1232 below). Shamshi-Adad V claimed that the land of Suhi had submitted to him (I *R* 30 ii 13-16), and Nergal-eresh was a nominally loyal but extremely powerful governor of Suhi and adjacent regions under Adad-nirari III (Saba'a stele and *AAA* XX [1933] 113 ff.). Shamash-resha-usur ruled Suhi as an independent governor, dating by his own regnal years, performing building activities in his own name, and introducing apiculture to the area (*WVDOG* IV no. 4, probably to be dated to the early eighth century). Another text, presumably dating from some independent ruler of Suhi in the first half of the first millennium, has been published in E. Schmidt, *Persepolis*, II, 59 PT4 942.

Suhi came under the closer domination of Assyria in the late eighth century (Nimrud Letter XVII) and remained in the Assyrian sphere of influence until late in the Neo-Assyrian period. Then, although paying tribute to Nabopolassar in 616 (Wiseman, *Chronicles*, 54:2), Suhi supported Assyria against him three years later (*ibid.*, 58:31). Under Nebuchadnezzar II, Suhi was listed as one of the regions furnishing wine to the temples of Marduk and Sarpanitum (*VAB* IV 90 i 24, 154 iv 52).

In 885, the tribute of Suhi to Tukulti-Ninurta II is specified as three talents of silver, twenty minas of gold, various objects made of ivory and of *meskannu* wood, quantities of tin, cloth, animals, and foodstuffs; and it was the most valuable tribute received by Tukulti-Ninurta in the course of his journey. The wealth of the land is further attested by the booty taken from there by Ashurnasirpal (*AKA* 352 iii 21-23, including gold, silver, and precious stones), by the "tribute" received from there by Shalmaneser III (*WO* II/2 [1955] 142 D, similar in many respects to that received by Tukulti-Ninurta II), by the extensive building and planting operations undertaken there by Shamash-resha-usur (*WVDOG* IV no. 4), and by levies of animals and soldiers in the late eighth century (Nimrud Letter XVII). Suhian date-palms (*TuM* II-III 152:2, cf. *WVDOG* IV no. 4 ii 37, iv 1-4), and clothing (*KAV* 106:5) were referred to. Pottery (*YOS* III 138:8) and wine (*VAB* IV 90 i 24, 154 iv 52; *VAS* VI 121:1) are likewise known from there in later periods.

Select bibliography of earlier writings on Suhi: Forrer, *Provinzeinteilung*, pp. 13-17; Horn, *ZA* XXXIV (1922) 129-141; Musil, *The Middle Euphrates*, pp. 205-213. [For *Sūḫum* as an OB nominative form for the later *māt Sūḫi*, see F. R. Kraus, *Ein Edikt des Königs Ammi-ṣaduqa von Babylon*, p. 36 iv 31.]

flee to Assyria to save his life. (1128) Now in 878, Kudurru, (1129) the new governor of Suhi, backed by Babylonian aid, refused tribute to Ashurnasirpal; and a battle was fought at Suru, Kudurru's stronghold. (1130) Ashurnasirpal claimed a victory in the best Assyrian tradition: a complete rout of the opposition, capture of many troops—including a contingent under Zabdanu, brother of Nabu–apla–iddina, king of Babylonia—and considerable booty. (1131) The Assyrian king then monumentalized his triumph by erecting at Suru a statue of himself inscribed with the following legend: "King Ashurnasirpal, whose glory and might are everlasting, whose face is set towards the desert, whose heart delights in casting the *ḫutennu*-weapon." (1132)

Once again subsequent events give the lie to the Assyrian assertion of victory. The city of Suru was the terminus of Ashurnasirpal's march in the year 878, and he could advance no farther down the Euphrates after his "great victory." (1133) Furthermore, encouraged by the same "great victory," all the previously submis-

(1128) *AKA* 289:100-101. Ashurnasirpal shows how independent a vassal Suhi had been until this time by saying "in the time of my royal ancestors, no governor of Suhi had ever come to Assyria."

(1129) Reading mNÍG.DU LÚ! *šá–kìn mat Su–ḫi* (*AKA* 351 iii 17). The old reading of this name as Shadudu (e.g., King, *AKA* 351, defended by Olmstead in *JAOS* XXXVIII [1918] 240-241 n. 61) is unlikely. The name is clearly written as mNÍG.DU (Kudurru) in *AKA* 351 iii 18. Furthermore, the second DU sign copied by King in iii 17 and here interpreted as LÚ! is very close in form to a Neo-Assyrian LÚ (cf. King's copy of a LÚ in *AKA* 181:31). The most convincing argument, however, comes from the same text of Ashurnasirpal in the writing of the identical title for Kudurru's predecessor, Ilu–ibni; his title is written LÚ *šá–kìn* (var.: GAR) *mat Su–ḫi* (*AKA* 289:100) and here the LÚ is practically identical in form to the supposed DU copied by King in iii 17. The correct reading of the personal name was proposed already by Streck in *ZA* XIX (1905-06) 252, but without the pertinent parallels.

(1130) Not to be confused with Suru in Bit–Halupe (or –Hadippe) along the Habur (*AKA* 280 i 75, 354 iii 28-29, etc.), for the location of which see Horn, *ZA* XXXIV (1922) 147.

(1131) The fight at Suru is related in *AKA* 350-353 iii 16-26. The captured forces are described as "50 cavalry (*pitḫallu*) together with the soldiers of Nabu–apla–iddina, king of Karduniash, Zabdanu, his brother, plus 3000 soldiers, their warriors (*tidūkīšunu*) (and) Bel–apla–iddin, a seer, who led their troops." These same troops were earlier described as the *ummānāt māt Kaššî rapšāti* "the widespread hosts of the Kassite land" (*AKA* 351 iii 17), which led Sidney Smith (*EHA*, p. 295 and n. 2) followed by Wiseman (*CAH* II² xxxi 7), to postulate that the Kassites provided the chief element in the Babylonian armed forces till the ninth century. The "Kassite land," however, refers to Babylonia, not to the ethnic character of the troops.

Olmstead (*JAOS* XXXVIII [1918] 241-243 and *History of Assyria*, p. 92) has called attention to reliefs which may illustrate the flight of Kudurru across the Euphrates described in *AKA* 351 iii 18-19. One relief portrays three fugitives, two on inflated skins, swimming across a river to a friendly fortress while Assyrian archers shoot arrows at them (pictured in E. A. Wallis Budge, *Assyrian Sculptures in the British Museum, Reign of Ashur–nasir–pal*, 885-860 *B.C.*, pl. XIII no. 2; earlier portrayal of the same relief in Layard, *The Monuments of Nineveh* [First Series], pl. 33).

(1132) *AKA* 352-353 iii 24-26. The last two phrases in the inscription commemorate Ashurnasirpal's fondness for hunting in desert terrain.

(1133) His armies were effectively stopped at this point, but that did not prevent Ashurnasirpal from proclaiming: "Fear of my rule reached as far as Babylonia (Karduniash). The awesomeness of my weapons overwhelmed Chaldea. I poured out terror over the mountains along the banks of the Euphrates." (*AKA* 352 iii 23-24) More than once during the long history of the Assyrian annals, the Neo-Assyrian kings resorted to the face-saving claim that lands which their arms were powerless to touch cringed in abject terror at the thought of Assyrian might.

sive tribes at the junction of the Habur and the Euphrates were soon in revolt against the Assyrian king. (1134) The only probable explanation of this phenomenon is to see in the battle of 878 a decisive checking of the Assyrian advance along the Euphrates through native resistance and Babylonian help, which encouraged other local tribesmen to throw off the yoke of Assyria. When Ashurnasirpal attempted to retake Suhi shortly thereafter, (1135) he could capture only cities on the northern bank of the Euphrates, (1136) though his efforts seem to have been more effective in the region of Ḫindanu and Laqe. (1137) Although Ashurnasirpal eventually claimed to have subdued the whole of Laqe and Suhi as far as the city of Rapiqu (the northwestern boundary of Babylonia), there is no record of his armies penetrating even as far as Suru after 878. (1138)

Ashurnasirpal's later connections with the Suhi region cannot be dated with certainty. In the Banquet Stele erected to commemorate the solemn inaugural meal for the new capital city of Calah, Ashurnasirpal implied that Suhi was by that time subject to him. He referred to himself as "the king who ... had caused the land of Suhi as far as the city of Rapiqu to bow down at his feet." (1139) He mentioned that he had received from the governors of Suhi and Lubdu five live elephants as tribute. (1140) Envoys from Suhi were present at the banquet in an official capacity along with envoys from Syria (including Tyre and Sidon), Urartu, and Hindanu. (1141) Finally men of Suhi were listed among the "conquered" peoples who were settled in the new capital. (1142) The date for this claimed submission of Suhi cannot be established with certainty; but it should probably be placed somewhere between 874 and 867. (1143)

(1134) *AKA* 353 iii 26-27.

(1135) No eponym year is mentioned, so neither the revolt nor the subsequent campaign can be dated exactly. It occurred no earlier than 877 and no later than 870 or 869, according to the scheme of chronology accepted here. (See Appendix D below).

(1136) *AKA* 355 iii 32.

(1137) *AKA* 356-360 iii 37-48. The tribute of Hindanu is portrayed on a relief from Nineveh (*AAA* XVIII [1931] pl. 26 no. 1).

(1138) *AKA* 354-357 iii 31-38.

(1139) *Iraq* XIV (1952) 32-33:10-13 (the *šarru* preceding *ša* TA *ebertān* in line 10 has been inadvertently dropped from Wiseman's transliteration, though it is present in the cuneiform copy of the text). Cf. *AKA* 343-344 ii 127-128, etc.

(1140) *Iraq* XIV (1952) 34:95-96. Ashurnasirpal was so proud of these elephants that he took them along with him on his campaigns (*ibid.*, line 97).

(1141) *Iraq* XIV (1952) 35:143-147.

(1142) *Ibid.*, 33:33.

(1143) Wiseman in *Iraq* XIV (1952) 24-26 dated the banquet ceremonies described in the text to 879 B.C. and the erection of the stele itself "soon after 879 B.C." This is unlikely. In the titulary of the text, Ashurnasirpal mentions his journey to the mountains of Lebanon and to the Mediterranean; these events took place at the very earliest in 875 (though 874 is an even more probable *terminus a quo*—see Appendix D below), according to Ashurnasirpal's annals (*AKA* 372 iii 84-85). Secondly, though Ashurnasirpal himself had taken up residence in Calah by 878 (*AKA* 346 iii 1), there is no evidence that the capital was by then

The question arises: why did Suhi submit to Ashurnasirpal, if he fought no successful campaigns after 878 to subdue it? (1144) The most probable answer seems to be that Suhi did not actually submit to Ashurnasirpal at all. The fact that Suhi sent envoys (*šaprāte*) to the banquet festivities at Calah—in a manner similar to other independent cities and countries—indicates that Suhi was not an Assyrian subject in the strict sense. The claim that the governor (1145) of Suhi sent elephants as tribute is hardly proof of Suhian vassalage; for, when Ashurnasirpal was on his peaceful ceremonial and trade mission (largely to obtain building timber) to the Mediterranean, he claimed that all the kings of the great cities there offered him "tribute." (1146) It is more likely that there was a mutual exchange of gifts in that instance, and it is conceivable that some similar reality (trade or gifts) was involved in the Suhian "tribute." With regard to the "conquered" peoples settled in Calah, including people from Suhi and Syria (Hatti, Hattina), (1147) there is no evidence that any of them were ever conquered by Ashurnasirpal. If natives of these lands took up residence in Calah, they may have done so as free commercial agents, since Suhi, Hatti, and Hattina controlled important trade routes. Suhi not only remained substantially independent at this time but continued independent through the reign of Shalmaneser III. (1148)

Other than the brief encounter between the Assyrian army and the small body of Babylonian troops sent to help Kudurru at Suru in Suhi in 878, there are no recorded contacts between Assyria and Babylonia in the days of Ashurnasirpal II and Nabu-apla-iddina. Since both of these kings were monarchs who greatly enhanced the prestige of their respective countries, the silence of the sources is all

---

sufficiently completed for the formal royal inauguration. On the contrary, if we place any credit in Ashurnasirpal's statements about people attending the inaugural banquet, we could not date the ceremonies as early as 879: Suhi itself was then in revolt, and Syria (Hatti) was untouched by any of Ashurnasirpal's campaigns before 875 (earliest date). All indications are decidedly in favor of dating the stele itself sometime between 874 and 866 (before the recording of the campaign of Ashurnasirpal's eighteenth year) and of dating the banquet—if the Assyrian account is reasonably accurate—not long before the stele.

(1144) The 878 campaign was partially successful in that Suru was captured. But the success was short-lived, as the subsequent revolt testified. In Ashurnasirpal's first recorded campaign after 878 (earliest possible date: 877, latest possible date: 870 or 869), he succeeded in capturing only the cities on the northern bank of the Euphrates. After this campaign, no further military action of Ashurnasirpal against Suhi is recorded.

(1145) The title "governor" (*šaknu*, *Iraq* XIV [1952] 34:95) does not necessarily imply subordination. Compare the case of the clearly independent Shamash-resha-usur, the *šaknu* of Suhi who dated events by his own regnal years (*WVDOG* IV no. 4).

(1146) *AKA* 372-373 iii 85-88.

(1147) *nišē kišitti qātija ša mātāte ša apīlušināni* (*Iraq* XIV [1952] 33:33).

(1148) Marduk-apla-usur, governor (*šaknu*) of Suhi at the time of Shalmaneser III, is depicted as bringing "tribute" on the Black Obelisk. But Suhi was neither a province of the Assyrian empire at that time nor was it the object of any campaign of Shalmaneser III (see note 1127 above and notes 1231-1236 below). There is no question of Suhi enjoying diplomatic equality with Assyria in the ninth century or later, but the suzerainty claimed by Assyria seems to have been merely nominal.

the more regrettable. The only hint we get of other possible Babylonian-Assyrian contacts is in the standard titulary used by Ashurnasirpal in his longer inscriptions after his successful journeys to Carchemish and Syria. There Ashurnasirpal carefully delineated the lands east of the Tigris along the Assyro-Babylonian border which he claims to have restored to the territory of Assyria: (1149) "from the other side of the Lower Zab to Til-Bari, (1150) which is north of Zaban, (1151) from Til-sha-Abtani (1152) to Til-sha-Zabdani, (1153) and Hirimu and Harutu, fortresses of the land of Babylonia (Karduniash)." (1154) Thus, in the northeast, the Babylonian boundaries remained much the same as those fixed by the treaty between Nabu–

(1149) The pertinent portions of the standard titulary may be found in the following texts: (a) from Calah: *AKA* 163:12-16, 175 obv. 14-rev. 5, 180-181:25-28, 194:16-21, 216-217:9-11, 344-345:129-131, 383: 123-124, *Iraq* XIV (1952) 33:15-18; (b) from Assur: *KAH* I 25:4-5, *KAH* II 94:9-13; (c) from Nineveh: *AAA* XVIII (1931) 95 no. 8:25-27, *AAA* XIX (1932) 107-112 nos. 272, etc.:25-27; (d) from Balawat: *AKA* 169:13-18; (e) of unknown provenience: *Vivre et penser, IIe série* (1942), p. 316:⌈14-17⌉. Only the Assur recensions show real differences in phraseology from the standard edition translated here. Cf. Appendix D below.

(1150) The Assur texts read Til-Abari (DU_6*-a-ba-ri*, *KAH* I 25:4, II 94:10). This is the same place as Til-Bit-Bari in *CT* XXXIV 40 iii 20 (Synchronistic History). For the possible identification of this site with present-day Bargird, see Speiser, *AASOR* VIII (1926-27) 19 n. 36, with additional bibliography. It should be noted that both Speiser, *ibid.*, and Ebeling, *RLA* I 399, distinguish Til-(Bit)-Bari from Bara, also mentioned in the annals of Ashurnasirpal II.

(1151) Zaban is alternately written with the determinatives URU ("city") and KUR ("land"), e.g., *AKA* 163:13, 344:130. Much has been written on the location of Zaban. The treatments by Streck (*Asb.*, p. LXXXVIII) and by Olmstead (*AJSL* XXXVI [1919-20] 145 n. 3) contain abundant earlier bibliography; Poebel in *JNES* I (1942) 263 commented briefly on its occurrence in geographical lists. Weidner in his important article "Simurrum und Zaban" (*AfO* XV [1945-51] 75-80) has collected abundant references to Zaban in historical, geographical, religious, and economic texts, though he wished to place Zaban too far to the south (see Goetze, *JNES* XII [1953] 123). Zaban, also written at various times as Zabban, Zanban, and Zamban, was an important cult center of Adad (*AfO* XV [1945-51] 76); and Shalmaneser III offered sacrifices there on his way to Babylonia in 851 (*WO* IV/1 [1967] 30 iv 2-3). The Assyro-Babylonian border ran just north of Zaban at this time. See also note 1292 below.

(1152) Regularly written URU DU_6*-šá-ab-ta-(a)-ni* (*AKA* 217:10, etc.). The Assur recension, however, spells it as DU_6*-šá/ša-*m*A-ba-ta-(a)-ni* (*KAH* I 25:5, II 94:11). The Nineveh recensions sometimes write the name as URU DU_6-m*Ab-da-ni* (*AAA* XVIII [1931] 95:26, XIX [1932] 109:26). It is written in the Synchronistic History as DU_6 *šá* m*Ba-ta-a-ni* (*CT* XXXIV 40 iii 21). The order of this name and the following name, Til-sha-Zabdani, are sometimes reversed in Ashurnasirpal's titulary (*AKA* 194 n. 7, 217 n. 6; *AAA* XVIII [1931] 95:26, XIX [1932] 109:26, etc.).

(1153) Usually written URU DU_6*-šá-za-ab-da-(a)-ni* (*AKA* 217:10, etc.). A masculine personal determinative is sometimes inserted before *-zabdāni* (*AKA* 181:27, 217:10 [var.], *KAH* I 25:5, II 94:11, *AAA* XVIII [1931] 95:26, etc.); compare the name of Zabdanu, brother of Nabu-apla-iddina (*AKA* 351:20). This and the preceding name are written together as DU_6 *šá* m*Ba-ta-a-ni ù šá* URU *Zab-da-ni* in the Synchronistic History (*CT* XXXIV 40 iii 21). For a possible seventh-century reference, see note 1112 above.

(1154) The relevant portions of the titulary in the extant recensions from Assur are:

(a) "From the other side of the Lower Zab to Til-Abari (which is) north of the land of Zaban (and?) to Til-sha-Abatani, from Til-sha-Abatani to Til-sha-Zabdani, Hirimu and Harutu, fortresses of Babylonia (Karduniash)" (*KAH* I 25:4-5);

(b) *KAH* II 94:9-13, partially destroyed, runs roughly the same as the Calah and other recensions, with the exceptions noted in notes 1152-1153 above.

shuma–ukin I and Adad–nirari II a generation earlier, (1155) save that Ashurnasirpal claimed to have gained the Babylonian fortresses of Hirimu and Harutu. These fortresses are otherwise unknown in cuneiform literature and were presumably minor outposts, for there is no record of a campaign in which Ashurnasirpal captured them. (1156) All we know is that by the year 869 Ashurnasirpal was able to claim that his power extended into this area. (1157)

Besides preserving the Babylonian boundaries in the northwest and northeast substantially intact against an aggressive Assyrian ruler, Nabu–apla–iddina restored order within Babylonia. From the titulary which he claims on a stone tablet left at Sippar (*BBSt* no. 36), we learn of his program of achievements:

> Nabu–apla–iddina, king of Babylon, named by Marduk, beloved by Anu and Ea, who gladdens the heart of Sarpanitum, the courageous male, well suited for kingship, the wielder of an angry bow, who overthrew the wicked enemy, the Sutian (whose guilt was exceedingly great), into whose hand(s) the great lord Marduk entrusted the scepter of justice and the shepherding of the people: to avenge Akkad, to resettle the cult centers, to found shrines (lit.: daises), to draw (divine) symbols, to restore rites and rituals, to establish regular (food) offerings, to make more splendid the meals (for the gods) . . . (1158)

This passage is the only evidence we have for a military triumph of Nabu–apla–iddina over the Sutians. Otherwise, we know only that the king lent military assistance to the people of the middle Euphrates, which seems to have served as one of the avenues for the Sutian invasions of earlier centuries. But, with Sutian invaders no longer troubling the land, Nabu–apla–iddina was able to set about the work of reconstruction.

In Sippar, at the royal command, a new image of the god Shamash was fashioned and ritually consecrated to replace the old image which had disappeared during the Sutian disturbances two hundred years before. (1159) An old land grant was con-

(1155) *CT* XXXIV 40 iii 20-21 (Synchronistic History).

(1156) Millard (*Iraq* XXVI [1964] 25 and n. 52) connects Harutu with *Ḫi–rit*, the site of a battle between Assyria and Babylonia in the sixteenth year of Shamash–shuma–ukin (Chronicle of the Years 680-625 B.C., obv. 14), which is in the Diyala region.

(1157) I.e., sometime after his campaign to Carchemish. For the dating, see Appendix D.

(1158) *BBSt* no. 36 ii 18-iii 10.

(1159) *BBSt* no. 36 i 10-11, iii 19-iv 28. W. G. Lambert has plausibly suggested that the fortuitous finding of a clay model of the earlier statue (from which the new image could be made) might have been based on pious fraud (*AfO* XVIII [1957-58] 398). Gelb has gone much further and labelled the whole document (*BBSt* no. 36) a forgery, apparently because it fell into the category of texts "dealing with alleged acts of piety and large endowment established for the benefit of temples" (*JNES* VIII [1949] 348 n. 12).

firmed for the temple, which was also endowed with regular offerings, income, and festal vestments. (1160) In Uruk, record is preserved of the founding of regular food offerings; (1161) and we may assume that the king's largesse extended to other temples as well.

Also during this reign, after a lacuna of approximately a century, kudurrus make their appearance once again. And, in contrast to earlier documents of the same type, these texts all come from western Babylonia. (1162) The king granted lands along the Euphrates to two private individuals; one grant was made in his twentieth year (1163) and one in an unknown year. (1164) Unfortunately these fields cannot be located with more precision because the geographical names occurring are otherwise unknown. (1165) Also, a private legal text dealing with the disposition of an estate during this reign is preserved because it was incorporated into a document dated under the next king. (1166) In it we learn that Bel–iddina, the *šākin ṭēmi* of Dilbat, bestowed on Kidinnu, his second son, an inheritance consisting of income from the temple of Lagamal, a field and orchard outside the city, and a house and lot in the city itself; this section of the document is dated in the twenty-eighth year of Nabu–apla–iddina. (1167) The field in question was on the Euphrates and presumably near Dilbat, since the document was drawn up there. (1168)

This, then, was a king who could call himself *šar kiššati*, "king of the world," (1169) with more justification than his predecessors in the dynasty. Babylonia in its

---

This seems unlikely for the following reasons: (a) the food offerings established here (*BBSt* no. 36 v 10-38) are similar to the offerings established at the same time in Uruk (*OECT* I pls. 20-21); (b) the witness Marduk–shapik–zeri, son of Tuballat–Eshdar, the *šākin ṭēmi* (*BBSt* no. 36 vi 22-23) is also known from the slightly earlier document *BBSt* no. 28 rev. 23 (where the patronymic in line 22 should be read *Tú–ba–laṭ–Ešdar*); (c) prominent witnesses in the same two texts are *kartappu* officials from the Habban tribe (*BBSt* no. 36 vi 18-19, no. 28 rev. 21) and *bēl pīḫati* officials of the Arad–Ea family (*BBSt* no. 36 vi 24-26, no. 28 rev. 24—in each case the final witness); (d) similar legal phraseology is used in each text (*BBSt* no. 36 vi 17 = *BBSt* no. 28 rev. 18; cf. *BBSt* no. 36 vi 30-31 and *BBSt* no. 28 rev. 27); note also that both texts were drawn up in Babylon immediately after the New Year's festival on the same day, the twentieth of Nisan, though eleven years apart (*BBSt* no. 36 vi 27-28, no. 28 rev. 25-26) and that the king's titulary is the same in each case. Cf. also note 1237 below.

(1160) *BBSt* no. 36 iv 35-vi 16.

(1161) *OECT* I pls. 20-21 (obv. lines 6, 19 mention Nabu–apla–iddina by name). The faulty editing of this text is discussed in Appendix A under 24.3.2.

(1162) With the possible exception of an unpublished kudurru in the Louvre from Nabu–apla–iddina's thirty-third year. I have not been able to recognize any geographical names in the transliteration of this text provided me by Douglas Kennedy.

(1163) *BBSt* no. 28 rev. 26.

(1164) *BBSt* no. 29; for the dating of this text, see King, *BBSt*, p. 106 n. 2. It should be added that the date (according to King's speculations) is now a certainty because the name of the other monarch, "Marduk–shum–iddina," is now known to be "Marduk–zakir–shumi" and thereby ruled out as a possibility.

(1165) I.e., Abul–Ninurta, Bit–Atnaju, Balati, and the Mashe canal.

(1166) *VAS* I 35:1-31.

(1167) *Ibid.*, 30.

(1168) *Ibid.*, 29.

(1169) *BBSt* no. 29 ii 2.

entirety was under his sway, even according to the admission of Ashurnasirpal II. From Uruk in the south to Sippar and Rapiqu along the Euphrates in the northwest and to Til–Bari in the northeast, Nabu–apla–iddina controlled and protected the land. He was "king of Babylon" (1170) in its highest sense: protecting the people from outside enemies (both roving semi-nomads and Assyrians), preserving the old rites and endowing the temples of the gods, controlling the economy of the country, and, as we shall presently see, fostering the development of contemporary Babylonian letters.

Though this book is concerned chiefly with political history, it may not be amiss to mention briefly the evidence for the flourishing of literature during this reign. Editions of the *utukkī lemnūti* series (1171) and the s a . g i g medical texts (1172) were prepared. Moreover, as W. G. Lambert has plausibly argued, (1173) the Era Epic in its present form probably originated at this time: when the Sutian invasions of the recent past were no longer a threat and could be speculated on at leisure from a theological point of view. The invasions could then be used as a literary background against which was portrayed the prowess of the king destined by Marduk as the "vanquisher of the Sutians." (1174) Indeed, the halcyon days for Akkad predicted in a lyrical passage at the end of the Era Epic (1175) might be viewed as an apt portrayal of this reign.

The final years of Nabu–apla–iddina's reign saw a treaty concluded with Shalmaneser III, who had succeeded Ashurnasirpal II on the Assyrian throne. (1176) This treaty later proved of value when Shalmaneser came to the aid of Marduk–zakir–shumi I, Nabu–apla–iddina's son, and helped him to retain this throne. It

(1170) *BBSt* no. 28 rev. 26; *BBSt* no. 36 ii 19, iii 16, iv 37, v 4, vi 10, 29; *VAS* I 35:31. Cf. *AKA* 351 iii 19; *CT* XXXIV 40 iii 23, 26 (Synchronistic History); *CT* XVI 38 iv 20; *Iraq* XVIII (1956) pl. 24 rev. 10; *OECT* I pl. 20 obv. 6.

(1171) W. G. Lambert, *JCS* XI (1957) 5 n. 21.

(1172) *Ibid.*, 6 (reading of RN not entirely certain).

(1173) *AfO* XVIII (1957-58) 400.

(1174) *BBSt* no. 36 ii 26-27. *BBSt* no. 36 is a text with poetic passages reminiscent of *BBSt* no. 6, Nebuchadnezzar I's famous land grant.

(1175) Era Epic V 25-37, last edited by W. G. Lambert, *Iraq* XXIV (1962) 122.

(1176) *CT* XXXIV 40 iii 22-25 (Synchronistic History). The simple fact of the treaty is recorded in the usual formula, so we can make no definite statement as to the nature of the agreement. It is interesting to note the possibility that the Assyrian court may have profited from the loan of a Babylonian royal scribe about this time (see *JCS* XI [1957] 5 n. 21).

Olmstead, *AJSL* XXXVII (1920-21) 217 and *History of Assyria*, p. 121, suggested that this treaty marked the subjugation of Babylonia to Assyria and that this subordination was further evidenced during the reign of Nabu–apla–iddina (860) by Shalmaneser's exercising the prerogative of a sovereign by offering sacrifice in Babylon and Borsippa. This is unlikely for the following reasons. First, the treaty is reported in the Synchronistic History; and this document, well known for its boastfulness to the point of mendacity, would hardly be inclined to record a suzerainty treaty as a parity treaty. Secondly, Olmstead's date for Shalmaneser's visits to Babylon and Borsippa is ten years too early and is based on a faulty translation of the date of an inscription on a *sikkatu*-cone found at Assur. This translation, which renders the pertinent date as "Monat *Muḫur–ilâni*, 5. Tag, des 1. Jahres meiner Königsherrschaft," was published by

is probable that Nabu–apla–iddina lived to an old age (1177) to enjoy the achievements of his reign.

We may with justice look upon the reign of this monarch as a high point in the middle of the Post-Kassite period. Recovering rapidly from the semi-nomad depredations of the preceding two hundred years, preserving Babylonia's traditional borders against a powerful Assyrian opponent, fostering the economic, literary, and religious life of the land, Nabu–apla–iddina raised the realm to heights unequalled since the time of Nebuchadnezzar I. (1178) But, as with Hammurapi and Nebuchadnezzar I, the strength of Nabu–apla–iddina's kingdom did not long survive the king's own lifetime.

25. Marduk-zakir-shumi I (1179)

When the long reign of Nabu–apla–iddina had drawn to a close in the course of its fourth decade, Marduk–zakir–shumi I ascended his father's

---

Andrae in *MDOG* XXVIII (1905) 24-25. But, from the copy of the text published four years later by Andrae in *WVDOG* X 41 fig. 27, one can see that the date reads: ITI *mu–ḫur*–DINGIR.MEŠ UD *15* KAM MU *1* KAM *20* BALA.MEŠ–*ia*, which is to be translated "the fifteenth day of the month *Muḫḫur–ilāni*, the year of my twentieth *palû*" (MU *1* KAM=*šanat*). Furthermore, the extensive summary of conquests given at the beginning of the inscription, which mentions Lake Van (*tam–di ša* KUR *Na–i–ri*, i 2), the Persian Gulf ([Í]D? *Mar–ra–te*, i 3), and the Mediterranean Sea ([*tam–d*]*i ša* SILIM.SILIM.ME ᵈ*Šam–ši*, i 4), is hardly to be expected of a king writing in his first year. The references to sacrifices being offered (*niqê aqqi*, i 5-6) in Babylon and Borsippa may therefore be dated to Shalmaneser's ninth *palû*, as parallel texts show (e.g., *WO* I/4 [1949] 260 rev. 1-5, *WO* IV/1 [1967] 32 v 5-vi 2).

Another peculiar dating expression occurs in a text which also dates from the twentieth year of Shalmaneser III: *arḫu* MN UD *1* KAM *li–mu 20* BALA.MEŠ–*a* (*WO* II/1 [1954] 44 left edge 1-3). Was there some difficulty with the succession of eponym officials in that year?

(1177) He reigned at least thirty-three years. Is it possible that the Marduk–balassu–iqbi, "son" of Arad–Ea, who occurs as a witness in *BBSt* no. 36 vi 24 (dating in the king's thirty-first year) might be identical with this king's grandson, who came to the throne some thirty years later? Despite the difficulties in filiation, which should not be minimized, Marduk–balassu–iqbi may have been old enough to act as witness already at this time, since he was sufficiently mature to witness a kudurru drawn up in the second regnal year of Marduk–zakir–shumi I, Nabu–apla–iddina's successor.

(1178) There is some indication that the reign of Nabu–apla–iddina may have marked a high point also for ancient chronographers. Prof. D. Pingree has informed me of an Arab tradition concerning a Babylonian era which is calculated to have begun on Jan. 22, 863 B.C., a date which fell during the reign of Nabu–apla–iddina (Pingree, *The Thousands* of *Abū Maʿshar* [1968], p. 34 n. 1). This date is described as being connected with the "epoch (*ta'rīkh*) of the Babylonians *lī al–ʿArāmān* (?)" Since Nabu–apla–iddina's chief claim to fame was his vanquishing of the western semi-nomad invaders of Babylonia, the curious *al–ʿArāmān* might well allude to the Arameans who had for so long menaced western Babylonia before Nabu–apla–iddina's reign. (For the association of the Arameans and Sutians, see pp. 285-287 below).

(1179) *Marduk–zākir–šumi*: "Marduk has named an heir." (Literally, "Marduk is the namer of a name.") For remarks on the name type, see Stamm, *Namengebung*, p. 218. DN–zakir–shumi is attested at Dilbat in the Old Babylonian period (Ungnad, *BA* VI/5 [1909] 105) and was used during the Kassite (Clay, *CPN*, p. 172) and later periods (e.g., *Camb.* 276:5).

During the course of Babylonian history, the name Marduk–zakir–shumi was borne by several individuals other than Marduk–zakir–shumi I and II (the latter king ruled for one month early in the year

throne. (1180) The exact length of his reign is unknown, but it must have been at least twenty-seven years. (1181)

The king inherited from his father an alliance with Assyria which proved of benefit during his early years. At some point shortly after the beginning of his reign, (1182) his younger brother, (1183) Marduk–bel–usati, (1184) revolted against him

---

703 B.C.) The first man as yet known with the name held the office of *bēl pīḫati* under Merodach–Baladan I (*BBSt* no. 5 i 27). Men with the same name in later periods are mentioned in: *VAS* I 37 v 2 (probably the second king of that name before his accession, see *Studies Oppenheim*, pp. 24-25 n. 137), *YOS* III 43:1, *Camb*. 276:5. Because of the usual writing of the name, DN–MU–MU, names of the type DN–zakir–shumi cannot readily be distinguished from more common names like DN–shuma–iddina or DN–nadin–shumi, which are written with the same logograms. This is especially true in the Neo-Babylonian and Persian periods, when syllabic spelling of the name elements is comparatively rare.

Writing of RN: in contemporary Babylonian documents as ^{d}AMAR.UTU–MU–MU (*WVDOG* IV pl. 6 no. 2:4; *RA* XVI [1919] 126 iv 26; *VAS* I 35:53) and as ^{d}AMAR.UTU–*za–kir*–MU (*RA* XVI [1919] 125 ii 13); in the inscriptions of Shalmaneser III (here cited from cuneiform copies, where possible) as ^{md}AMAR.UTU–MU–MU (Layard, *ICC*, pls. 46:12, 76:14, 91:76; *TSBA* VII [1882] 98 iv 1, 103 v 3; *RT* XXV [1903] 83:24; *Sumer* VI [1949] photo opp. p. 26 and p. 13 ii 41; *Sumer* VII [1950] pl. I and p. 8 ii 31; *Iraq* XXI [1959] 149:44; *Iraq* XXV [1963] pl. X and p. 56:45, 46). The Synchronistic History writes the name as [^{md}Š]ID–MU–MU (*CT* XXXIV 40 iii 27) and ^{md}AMAR.UTU–MU–[MU] (iii 31); the synchronistic kinglists write it as ^{md}ŠID–M[U] (*KAV* 10 ii 9′) and as ^{md}PA–*za–kir*–MU (*KAV* 182 iii 12′), while Assur 14616c iii 20 has little more than the initial determinatives preserved. The New Babylonian Chronicle (rev. 4, 6) has ^{md}AMAR. UTU–*za–kir*–MU, and a later copy of a contemporary treaty has [AM]AR.UTU–MU–MU (*AfO* VIII [1932-33] 28:10).

Forrer in *MVAG* XX/3 (1915) 21 stated that there was another king named Marduk–zakir–shumi who ruled in the northern part of Babylonia during the reign of Marduk–balassu–iqbi, the son of Marduk–zakir–shumi I. This proposal by Forrer has not been generally accepted; and, in fact, the line on which it was based (New Babylonian Chronicle, rev. 6) is undoubtedly to be read: *ana tarṣi Marduk–balāssu–[iqbi mār] Marduk–zākir–šumi*, "in the time of Marduk–balassu–[iqbi, son of] Marduk–zakir–shumi."

(1180) *CT* XXXIV 40 iii 27 (Synchronistic History). For the reading of this passage, see note 1199 below.

(1181) The latest possible date for his accession year is 851, and the earliest possible date for his death is 824.

(1182) There is no decisive evidence to help in determining the exact year of Marduk–zakir–shumi's reign in which the rebellion began. A member of the Amukanu tribe was witness to a kudurru in Babylon in the king's second year (*RA* XVI [1919] 126 iv 20), so the southern tribes were apparently at peace with the central government in that year. But this kudurru could have been enacted either in 852 (or earlier), before the rebellion began, or as late as 849 (after Shalmaneser had quelled the rebellion). Though revolts more commonly broke out towards the beginning of a monarch's reign (i.e., before he had time to consolidate his position), this was not always the case, as is known from the later revolts of Ashur–dannin–apla against Shalmaneser III and of Shamash–shuma–ukin against Ashurbanipal.

(1183) Called *aḫu duppussû* (*WO* II/2 [1955] 150:74). In the *CAD* citation of this passage (*CAD* D 188b), quoted from the Layard edition, the RN should be corrected to read *Marduk–zākir–šumi* instead of *Marduk–nādin–šumi*. J. A. Craig in *Hebraica* II (1885-86) 140 suggested the restoration of *aḫu duppussû* in a parallel passage in the inscription on the statue of the enthroned Shalmaneser III, line 16; this restoration was accepted with minor reservations and changes by Delitzsch in *BA* VI/1 (1908) 152-153, though the bracket to denote the beginning of this restoration in the pertinent line was inadvertently omitted in Delitzsch's edition.

(1184) The name of Marduk–bel–usati is preserved in only one Babylonian source (New Babylonian Chronicle, rev. 5), and there it is written as ^{md}AMAR.UTU–EN–*ú–sat* (with apocope of the final vowel according to the principles established by Hyatt, *Final Vowels*, pp. 10-11; cf. a similar abbreviated writing of Nabu–bel–usat in *VAS* V 4:54). The name occurs chiefly in Assyrian sources, where it is written usually

and found support for his rebellion in large sections of Babylonia, especially the Diyala region and the tribal lands in the south near the Persian Gulf. ([1185]) Marduk–zakir–shumi was unable to cope with the uprising by himself and by the year 851 was obliged to send to his father's old ally, Shalmaneser III, for assistance. ([1186]) Shalmaneser replied immediately by personally leading an army down into rebel-held territory ([1187]) and claiming his first victory at Me–Turnat on the Diyala, where he despoiled the city. ([1188]) He then turned to face Marduk–bel–usati at the city of Gannanate and claimed a victory there. ([1189]) Shalmaneser shut Marduk–bel–usati up in the city, but was unable to take it and so had to content himself with destroying the harvest in the surrounding area, cutting down the orchards, and damming the river. ([1190])

In the next year, however, Shalmaneser renewed his efforts against the Babylonian rebels. He left Nineveh on the twentieth day of Nisan ([1191]) and plundered

---

as [md]AMAR.UTU–EN–*ú–sa–(a)–te* (*CT* XXXIV 40 iii ⌈28⌉, 33, Synchronistic History; *TSBA* VII [1882] 98 iv 1, 100 iv 4, 102 v 1, Balawat Gate inscription of Shalmaneser III). The Babylonian form of the name is to be normalized with a *–ti*, as may be seen from Babylonian writings of similar names (MB: *BE* XIV 2:27, 33; early NB: *BBSt* no. 27:2; later NB: *TCL* XII 14:22, *BIN* I 127:32, *YOS* VII 9:11). According to Delitzsch (*MDOG* XXXVI [1908] 16 n.), the name of Marduk–bel–usati is twice abbreviated as *Usatu* in an unpublished *sikkatu* inscription of Shalmaneser III from Assur.

([1185]) Both the Synchronistic History (*CT* XXXIV 40 iii 29-30) and the inscriptions of Shalmaneser III (*WO* IV/1 [1967] 30 iv 1, *WO* II/2 [1955] 150:75) say that Marduk–zakir–shumi and Marduk–bel–usati "divided the land (of Akkad) equally" (*malmališ izūzū*). The Synchronistic History adds that Marduk–bel–usati had captured Daban (location unknown: *RLA* II 96, but also mentioned in an omen, *CT* XXIX 48:5). Whether the Chaldeans were actively supporting Marduk–bel–usati is unknown.

The designation of Marduk–bel–usati as a "usurper" (*šar ḫammā'i*) by Assyrian sources and his omission from the Babylonian canon of kings are discussed above in notes 256-257.

([1186]) *WO* IV/1 (1967) 30 iv 1-2: *Marduk–zākir–šumi ana nīrārūtišu ana muḫḫi Šulmānu–ašarēd uma'era rakbašu.* Cf. the similar phraseology in the later inscription on the Nimrud throne base (*Iraq* XXV [1963] 56:45), where the shortened account gives the initiative to Shalmaneser.

([1187]) On the way to his first encounter with Marduk–bel–usati, Shalmaneser stopped briefly at the town of Zaban to offer sacrifice to Adad (*WO* IV/1 [1967] 30 iv 2-3); for Zaban, see note 1151 above and, for Adad of Zaban, see Weidner, *AfO* XV (1945-51) 76. M. Pancritius (*Assyrische Kriegführung*, pp. 117-118), basing her conclusions on the phrase *ana māt Akkadê alāka iqbi* (=*WO* IV/1 [1967] 30 iv 2), thought that Shalmaneser did not lead the army personally until the following campaign. This seems unlikely in view of the statement RN ... *iṣbat arḫu* (*ibid.*, iv 2) and the sacrifices personally offered by the king in Zaban. In the Balawat Gate inscription, the campaigns of both the eighth and the ninth *palû* are narrated for the most part in the first person singular.

([1188]) The fullest account of the taking of Me–Turnat is in the Balawat Gate inscription (*WO* IV/1 [1967] 30 iv 3). It is mentioned briefly also in *BA* VI/1 (1908) 147:79, *WO* I/6 (1952) 464:44, *WO* II/1 (1954) 32:34, *WO* II/2 (1955) 150:76. Weidner has suggested that Me–Turnat be located at the junction of the Narin–Su with the Diyala (*AfO* IX [1933-34] 96); for the equation Sirara=Me–Turnat in the geographical lists, see Poebel, *JNES* I (1942) 263.

([1189]) *WO* IV/1 (1967) 30 iv 3-4. For the location of Gannanate, northeast of the Jebel Hamrin on the Diyala, see Unger, *RLA* III 139-140 (with bibliography). Pancritius (*Assyrische Kriegführung*, pp. 119-121, 130-131) preferred to locate Gannanate in the lower reaches of the Jebel Hamrin itself.

([1190]) *WO* IV/1 (1967) 30 iv 4-5.

([1191]) *Ibid.*, iv 5.

the city of Lahiru (1192) before proceeding to Gannanate. (1193) Shalmaneser captured Gannanate, but not before Marduk-bel-usati had escaped and headed for the mountains of the land of Jasubi. (1194) Shalmaneser pursued him to Arman (Halman) (1195) and took the town; and here Marduk-bel-usati and his followers were finally de-

(1192) *Ibid.*, iv 6. The conquest of Lahiru is mistakenly placed in the preceding year by the later telescoped accounts in *BA* VI/1 (1908) 147:79, *WO* I/6 (1952) 464:44, *WO* II/1 (1954) 32:34. For the location of Lahiru, see note 1093 above.

(1193) Pancritius (*Assyrische Kriegführung*, p. 118) pointed out that Gannanate had probably been kept under siege since the preceding year.

(1194) *WO* IV/1 (1967) 30 v 1. The land of Jasubi, to be located somewhere northeast of Babylonia in the mountains from which the Diyala flows, is mentioned infrequently in the Neo-Assyrian period (e.g., in the geographical list II *R* 53 no. 1:16). In Nimrud Letter XII 44-45, probably to be dated about the time of Tiglath-Pileser III, tribes from Jasubi were ordered deported to the city of Kashpuna on the Mediterranean coast (for the location of this city, see Saggs, *Iraq* XVII [1955] 150). The GN also occurs in the gentilic PN: *Jasubaju* (Nimrud Letter II 9′, 16′, 18′). Almost certainly to be identified with the same GN are the (LÚ) *Jasubigal(l)aju*, a people linked with the Kassites as the object of Sennacherib's second campaign (*OIP* II 26:66 and *passim* in the accounts of this campaign). Is the land *Jasume*, mentioned together with Bit-Zamani in *ABL* 245 rev. 5, also to be viewed as a late variant of Jasubi?

(1195) Marduk-bel-usati's place of refuge is called Arman in the inscription on the Balawat Gates (*WO* IV/1 [1967] 30 v 1-2); other texts of Shalmaneser III call this place Halman (*KAH* II 110 rev. 1 [= *WO* I/2 (1947) 67]; *BA* VI/1 [1908] 147:80; *WO* I/6 [1952] 466:46). The city was in the mountains (*WO* II/1 [1954] 34:37-38, II/2 [1955] 150:79-80) in the land of Jasubi (*WO* IV/1 [1967] 30 v 1, see preceding note).

The "geographical treatise" of Sargon mentions a country *Ar-ma-ni-i*KI, whose borders were Ibla and Bit-Nanib (VAT 8006:13, previously published as *KAV* 92, latest copy by Weidner in *AfO* XVI [1952-53] pl. I; reading of Bit-Nanib uncertain [*ibid.*, 13 n. 97]). Weidner has connected this *Armanî* and Ibla with the Armanum and Ibla conquered by Naram-Sin (*UET* I 275 ii 4-6, iii 24-26, etc.) and located it in northwestern Mesopotamia or Syria (where Ibla is certainly to be placed: *AfO* XVI [1952-53] 12-13, with citation of earlier bibliography). The immediate context in VAT 8006:7-18, however, mentions only regions in Assyria or Babylonia or adjacent territories to the east; and one is led to suspect that the compiler of VAT 8006 may have thought that *Armanî* was identical with the Arman east of the Tigris. The city Arman of Ugarsallu, mentioned as being on the border between Assyria and Babylonia in the time of Adad-nirari I (*CT* XXXIV 38 i 30′), was east of the Tigris and between the Lower Zab and the Radanu (*AfO* XVIII [1957-58] 350-351:38); but whether it was identical with the Arman mentioned by Shalmaneser III can neither be proved nor disproved conclusively.

Halman is elsewhere connected with Babylonia: it was the center of a province under the Second Isin Dynasty (*BBSt* no. 6 ii 22), and in the Sargonid period the people of Halman were expected to provide annual offerings for Marduk (*ABL* 464:13-14). Its location in mountainous terrain is again proven by references to the pass of Halman in a text of Shilhak-Inshushinak (AŠ *Ḫal-ma-an-ni-r*[*i-pu-ni*]: König, *Die elamischen Königsinschriften*, no. 54b:3) and to the pass of Simesi at the head of the land of Halman (*WO* II/3 [1956] 232:190, Black Obelisk; contrary to E. Michel's remark *ibid.*, 233 n. 54, this Halman should not be connected with Syria, because Namri occurs in the same passage, line 187—though there is a homonymous Halman used elsewhere in the texts of Shalmaneser to indicate a city in Syria, e.g., III *R* 8 ii 86-87). KUR *Ḫal-man*KI also occurs in K. 5966:10 (published in Winckler, *Sammlung*, II 76 and now joined to K. 3703, etc., according to E. Leichty, *Bibliography of the Kuyunjik Collection*, p. 83). We do not know whether Arman and Halman represent dialectal variants for the same name, but this seems likely.

It is uncertain whether the Halman east of the Tigris is to be connected with the Alman in the titulary of Agum-kakrime (V *R* 33 i 38). Despite the similar sounding names, the city or district of Halman is not to be confused with the mountain Jalman, which is also east of the Tigris (see König, *Die elamischen Königsinschriften*, p. 129 n. 11 and note 1092 above). For the location of Halman and its possible identification with modern Holwan, see especially Albright, *JAOS* XLV (1925) 212-214, and Güterbock, *ZA* XLIV (1938) 73-74.

feated. ([1196]) With the collapse of the rebel leader, resistance in the Diyala region to the government of Marduk–zakir–shumi was at an end.

Although most editions of Shalmaneser's annals give the impression that the Assyrian king undertook the campaigns against Marduk–bel–usati single-handed, such was probably not the case. In the fullest and most nearly contemporary account of these events we learn that Shalmaneser went only to help Marduk–zakir–shumi ([1197]) and that Marduk–zakir–shumi shared in the victory. ([1198]) In a text written several years later, Shalmaneser was to claim that he had firmly established Marduk–zakir–shumi on his father's throne. ([1199])

([1196]) There is some question as to whether Marduk–bel–usati was killed in the suppression of the rebellion. The earliest surviving edition of Shalmaneser's annals dealing with this campaign (the Balawat Gate inscription, *WO* IV/1 [1967] 30 v 3) says that Shalmaneser smote Marduk–bel–usati and his fellow rebels with the sword (PN *ina kakkē ušamqit*); and the same phrase is frequently used in later editions of the annals: *Iraq* XXV (1963) 56:45-46, *BA* VI/1 (1908) 147:81, *WO* I/6 (1952) 466:49, *WO* II/1 (1954) 34: 38-40, *KAH* II 110 rev. 2 (= *WO* I/2 [1948] 67), *WO* II/2 (1955) 150:80-81. As far as can be judged from the traces of the inscription on the enthroned statue from Assur, however, only the defeat of Marduk–bel–usati is mentioned ([*abiktašu amḫ*]*aṣ*: *BA* VI/1 [1908] 152 ii 16-17); there appears to be no room for recording his death. The Synchronistic History (*CT* XXXIV 40 iii 34) uses the ambiguous *idūk*, which could mean either "defeated" or "killed." Marduk–bel–usati disappears from history at this point and was certainly not taken captive by the Assyrians; there is no unequivocal statement of his death, and it is possible that he escaped with his life.

([1197]) *ana nīrārūtišu* (*WO* IV/1 [1967] 30 iv 1), cf. *Iraq* XXV (1963) 56:45 and *CT* XXXIV 40 iii 31 (Synchronistic History).

([1198]) The Assyrian account of the campaign at one point states: "after Marduk–zakir–shumi had conquered his enemies . . ." (*issu* RN *ikšuda gārêšu*, *WO* IV/1 [1967] 30 v 3). This admission that an allied king substantially aided in an Assyrian campaign is practically unique. But Babylonia and Assyria were particularly close at this time because of intermarriage between the royal families (note 1111 above), recent treaties (notes 1111, 1176), and even loan(s) of court personnel (note 1176).

([1199]) RN *ina kussī abišu ukīn* (*Iraq* XXV [1963] 56:46). Whether this refers to restoring the king to his throne (P. Hulin, *ibid.*, p. 64) or simply to strengthening his previously precarious hold on the kingdom is uncertain. The only other similar textual reference is in the Synchronistic History, which mentions the accession of Marduk–zakir–shumi and is presumably to be restored [md*Ma*]*rduk–zākir–šumi ina kussī abišu ú–*[*šib*] (*CT* XXXIV 40 iii 27) because there is no room in the text to restore the subject expected for a verb like *ú–*[*kin*]; this passage, however, alludes to Marduk–zakir–shumi's acquiring of the throne prior to the outbreak of the revolt not to support received from Shalmaneser.

In 1962 the British excavations at Calah uncovered a limestone throne-base of Shalmaneser III, on which was pictured Shalmaneser grasping the hand of Marduk–zakir–shumi I (most recent photograph of this relief: M. E. L. Mallowan, *Nimrud and Its Remains*, II, 448-449d, close-up on p. 447). Weidner (*AfO* XXI [1966] 151) has claimed that this representation cannot be of Marduk–zakir–shumi, since he would have to be kneeling and kissing the ground before Shalmaneser; consequently, according to Weidner, this picture must be a double representation of Shalmaneser in his roles as king of Assyria and king of Babylonia. This is unlikely because: (a) Shalmaneser never claimed to be king of Babylon in his inscriptions, though he may have been *de facto* suzerain, and would hardly be likely then to claim the role in his reliefs; (b) this unique recognition of the equality of a foreign sovereign on an Assyrian relief is amply paralleled by the unique admission in the royal annals of Shalmaneser III that Marduk–zakir–shumi had a share in the victory (*WO* IV/1 [1967] 30 v 3), as cited above in this note); (c) a twofold representation of the same king would hardly show his hair shoulder-length on one side and extending down his back on the other side. For the close ties between the Assyrian and Babylonian courts at this time, see the preceding note.

Another pictorial representation of Marduk–zakir–shumi is on top of the obverse of the kudurru AO 6684 (photograph in *RA* XVI [1919] pl. I, opp. p. 132). The crown worn by the Babylonian king in

After the fall of Arman, the Assyrian king visited Cutha, Babylon, and Borsippa, the principal cult centers of northern Babylonia. (1200) He personally appeared at the chief shrines of the gods in the three cities, (1201) presented the shrines with lavish gifts and endowments, (1202) and feted the free citizens (1203) of Babylon and Borsippa at lavish banquets, presenting them with brightly-colored garments and other gifts. (1204)

When Shalmaneser had paid his respects to the gods of Babylonia, he turned his attention to the troublesome tribes in the south. He went down, he says, to the region of Chaldea (*Kaldu*) and approached Baqani, (1205) a fortified city of the Dakkuru tribe. Having surrounded the city, he captured it and took away much booty, including cattle. He burned Baqani (1206) and then set out for the capital city (1207)

---

this picture is roughly the same shape as the crown portrayed on the Assyrian relief, with minor differences in style (the shape of the band at the bottom, slight differences in height-width proportion, a long tassel hanging down the back). In Babylonia, this conical crown with the long tassel down the back is first known in the time of Nabu-apla-iddina, the father of Marduk-zakir-shumi (*BBSt*, pl. CIII), by which time it had replaced the earlier rectangular crown with feather-shaped top (and sometimes a knob as peak) which had prevailed during the Second Dynasty of Isin (*BBSt*, pl. LIV; *WVDOG* XV fig. 73) and down to the time of Nabu-mukin-apli (*BBSt*, pls. LXVII and LXXIV). The ceremonial garments worn by the Babylonian king on the two representations differ, as do the length of the hair and the beard style—but we are hardly dealing here with photographic likenesses.

(1200) Shalmaneser's tour through northern Babylonia is described in detail in *WO* IV/1 (1967) 30-32 v 4-vi 5; for briefer accounts in Shalmaneser's inscriptions, see Appendix A, 25.2.5. The campaign against Marduk-bel-usati and the subsequent tour of the cult centers are briefly summarized in the Synchronistic History (*CT* XXXIV 40 iii 28-35).

(1201) *WO* IV/1 (1967) 32 v 5-vi 3.

(1202) *Ibid.*, v 5-vi 4.

(1203) *ṣābē kidinni šubarê ša ilāni rabûti*: *WO* IV/1 (1967) 32 vi 4. For this terminology, see W. F. Leemans, "*Kidinnu*, un symbole de droit divin babylonien," *Symbolae van Oven*, pp. 36-61, and Seux, *Épithètes royales*, p. 103 n. 22. Further bibliography is given by Michel, *WO* IV/1 (1967) 33 n. 13.

(1204) *WO* IV/1 (1967) 32 vi 4-5. It is difficult to determine whether Shalmaneser's tour of northern Babylonia is to be interpreted as an exercise of suzerainty or as a concession by his grateful ally, Marduk-zakir-shumi. Olmstead (*AJSL* XXXVII [1920-21] 217 and *History of Assyria*, p. 122) was of the opinion that Marduk-zakir-shumi was a subordinate of Shalmaneser III even before the latter aided the former. For documentary and pictorial evidence in favor of Marduk-zakir-shumi's independence, see note 1199 above.

(1205) *WO* IV/1 (1967) 34 vi 6, written URU *Ba-qa-a-ni* (var.: *Ba-ni*). The city is otherwise unknown and is not mentioned among the cities of Bit-Dakkuri in 703 by Sennacherib (*OIP* II 52:36-39). In contrast to Unger's statements in *RLA* I 398, Baqani was inhabited by Chaldeans (rather than Arameans), whose leader was Adinu (not Ahuni). The siege of Baqani and Chaldean prisoners captured there are pictured on the Balawat Gate reliefs: Unger, *Mitteilungen des Deutschen Archäologischen Instituts, Athenische Abteilung* XLV (1920) 62-67 and pl. II, Platte 0 (partially reproduced in *RLA* I pl. 54 a-b); cf. also *RLV* IV (1926) 112. For a reconstruction of the original arrangement of the individual strips on the Balawat Gates, see H. G. Güterbock, *AJA* LXI (1957) 67-68 and pl. 22.

(1206) *WO* IV/1 (1967) 34 vi 6.

(1207) Michel in *WO* IV/1 (1967) 35 n. 15 states that the name of this city is probably written URU *Ḫu-da* (or *-zu*)*-di* and that, if the name is so interpreted, it would be different from the Hudadu in northern Babylonia (see note 1745 below). Pinches (*TSBA* VII [1882] 110 vi 6) and Delitzsch (*BA* VI/1 [1908] 137) read the city name as URU EN-ZU-DI, for which the reading *Sin-mušallim* was suggested by Leemans, *JEOL* X (1945-48) 433.

of Adinu, chief of the Dakkuru tribe. (1208) On his way, Shalmaneser had to cross the Euphrates; (1209) and shortly thereafter Adinu yielded without a struggle, (1210) paying an abundant tribute, including silver, gold, bronze, tin, iron, and ivory. (1211) Following the lead of Adinu, Mushallim-Marduk, chief of the (Am)-ukanu tribe, (1212) and Jakin, king of the Sealand, (1213) submitted voluntarily to Shalmaneser and paid similar tribute. (1214) Later editions of Shalmaneser's annals

(1208) *WO* IV/1 (1967) 34 vi 6-7. The personal name Adinu is similar to the name of the tribe Bit-Adini in upper Mesopotamia which had fought so bitterly against Ashurnasirpal II a few years before. A private inscription of a local official around this time probably refers to this same chieftain of the Dakkuru: *šá* ^{m}*Ab-di*-DINGIR LÚ GAR-*nu šá* ^{m}*A-di-ni* A ^{m}*Da-ku-ri* "belonging to Abdi-il, *šaknu* official of Adinu of the Dakkuru tribe." (*SPA* I 285 no. XIV) The expression *šakin* PN is quite rare, much less common than either *šakin* DN or *šakin* GN. A *šaknu* of Mushallim-Marduk, contemporary chief of the Amukanu tribe, bearing the name Zabdi-il (*RA* XVI [1919] 125 i 14) probably occurs in a kudurru drawn up in the second year of Marduk-zakir-shumi I (see note 1238 below); cf. also PN LÚ GAR *ša* PN_2 (Nimrud Letter XVIII 3-4), LÚ GAR *ša* ^{f}*ša-kin-te* (Nimrud Letter LXXXI 5), and *šá-kìn ša* PN (*HSS* IX 42:13).

The possibility (somewhat remote) that this Adinu might refer to a clan within the Dakkuru tribe rather than to a living person is raised by the mention of a Bit-Adini in southern Babylonia in the Assur Ostracon. See notes 1566-1567 below.

(1209) Written ÍD A.RAT (*TSBA* VII [1882] 110 vi 6). Delitzsch in *BA* VI/1 (1908) 137 reads ÍD *Pù*(A)-*rat*, following an older suggestion of Strassmaier (*Alphabetisches Verzeichniss*, no. 7126 and p. 1141 no. 483). *RLA* I 140 *sub voce* "Arat" gives only a cross-reference to "Euphrat"; and *RLA* II 483-484 *sub voce* "Eufrat" has nothing to say about the writing A.RAT. Gelb in *Hurrians and Subarians*, pp. 98-99, has collected evidence for reading A as bur_x; but, as he admits, the evidence is circumstantial.

Regardless of whether we read the name of the river as $Pu(r)_x$-*rat* or as A.RAT (=*Purattu*), the reference to the Euphrates is clear, as may be established from such passages as "the land/city of Sirqu (=earlier Terqa) on the other side of the Euphrates" (KUR/URU *Sirqu ša nēberti* ÍD A.RAT; *AKA* 185 rev. 10-11, Ashurnasirpal II). Thus Wiseman's suggestion that "*a-rat* is another form of the more common *arantu*" (=Orontes; *Iraq* XVIII [1956] 128, referring to ND 4301+4305 obv. 22') is to be disregarded, and that passage should also be translated "Euphrates."

A relief of Assyrians under Shalmaneser III crossing a stream in Chaldea over a bridge of boats appears on the Balawat Gates (King, *Bronze Reliefs*, pl. LXI, lower register).

(1210) Shalmaneser's inscription on the Balawat Gates says: "the fear and awesome splendor of the great Lord Marduk overwhelmed Adinu, 'son' of Dakkuru" (*WO* IV/1 [1967] 34 vi 7) and that he then brought valuable gifts to the Assyrian king.

(1211) *WO* IV/1 (1967) 34 vi 7. Reliefs of Adinu paying tribute are preserved on the Balawat Gates (King, *Bronze Reliefs*, pl. LXII, upper register) and on the Nimrud throne-base (see note 1214 below).

(1212) *WO* IV/1 (1967) 34 vi 8. The name of the tribe is written ^{m}*Ú-ka-ni* (with variants listed *ibid.*, 34 note cn) at this time, presumably for *Awukāni*.

(1213) ^{m}*Ia-ki-ni šar māt Tam-di* (*WO* IV/1 [1967] 34 vi 7). Note that Jakin is the only ruler accorded the title "king" in this account. Jakin, the eponymous ancestor of the tribe Bit-Jakin, is here spoken of as though he were a living person; but it is unlikely—considering the size of the tribe in the eighth century—that its reputed founder would have been living at such a late date. Since Jakin is mentioned only in the Balawat account, it is more likely that the Assyrians at this time had little to do with the most remote Chaldean tribe and that they mistook the name of the tribe for the name of its ruler. (Michel, *ibid.*, now restores the reference to this individual as [*mār*] *Jakīni*, i.e., with no personal name).

(1214) Silver, gold, tin, bronze, elephant hides, etc. (*WO* IV/1 [1967] 34 vi 8). The tribute of Mushallim-Marduk and Adinu is listed together in detail in the Nimrud throne-base inscription: silver, gold, tin, bronze, ivory, elephant hides, ebony, and sissoo-wood (*Iraq* XXV [1963] 56:49). Reliefs of the tribute procession led by Mushallim-Marduk and Adinu appear on the Nimrud throne-base (Mallowan, *Nimrud and Its Remains*, II, 448-449, sections e, f, g; commentary: *ibid.*, 446-447); superscriptions of reliefs: line 49 of the text as edited by Hulin, *Iraq* XXV (1963) 56. The reliefs on the throne-base also picture horses

sometimes shorten the account of these events and make the southern conquests of the Assyrian king more grandiose: he captured Chaldean cities, (1215) journeyed as far as the "Bitter Sea" (Persian Gulf), (1216) and received the tribute of all the Chaldean "kings" in Babylon. (1217)

This is the first appearance in history of the three tribes, the Amukanu, the Dakkuru, and the Jakin, (1218) which would loom so large in history in the days of the early Sargonids, when they would frequently rouse Babylonia to revolt against Assyrian domination. We known very little about them on the occasion of their first appearance. (1219) To judge from the articles of tribute which they paid to Shalmaneser, which included precious metals, ivory, and luxury woods, they were probably in control of the lucrative trade routes passing through southern Babylonia; and, taking tribal wealth as a criterion, we can see that foreign trade was thriving in the mid-ninth century as it had in past epochs. The tribes may have been nominally subject to the Babylonian crown; (1220) but they were practically autono-

---

brought as tribute, an item not mentioned in any of the inscriptions. For further reliefs depicting the tribute of Chaldea, see King, *Bronze Reliefs*, pls. LXII-LXV.

The tribute of Jakin and Mushallim-Marduk included *da i na* MEŠ, left untranslated by Pinches (*TSBA* VII [1882] 111 vi 8) and by Delitzsch (*BA* VI/1 [1908] 140). Michel (*WO* IV/1 [1967] 34) suggests emending to [GIŠ].MEŠ.MÁ!.GAN!.NA.MEŠ.

(1215) The capture of Baqani has now become the capture of "cities": *WO* I/6 (1952) 466:51; *WO* II/1 (1954) 34:43; restored in *KAH* II 110 rev. 3 (=*WO* I/2 [1947] 67); *WO* II/2 (1955) 150:83, etc.

(1216) *WO* I/6 (1952) 466:51; cf. *WO* I/4 (1949) 260:5-9. "The fear of my weapons extended to the Bitter (Sea)": *WO* II/2 (1955) 150:84; "I received the tribute of the kings of Chaldea as far as the sea and established my power and might over the Sealand": *Iraq* XXV (1963) 56:47. Inscriptions written late in Shalmaneser's reign which summarize his conquests in the titulary frequently mention the "Bitter Sea" or the sea of Chaldea as one of the areas reached by his arms: *WO* I/5 (1950) 387:4-6, *WO* I/4 (1949) 260: 7-9 (where the Bitter Sea of Chaldea is distinguished from the Upper Sea and the Lower Sea), *WO* III/1-2 (1964) 152:18-19 and 154:10, *WVDOG* X 41 i 3, *BA* VI/1 (1908) 145:38-39.

(1217) *BA* VI/1 (1908) 147:83-84; *WO* I/6 (1952) 466:52-54; *WO* II/1 (1954) 34:43-44. Since mention of Babylon is omitted in the two earliest accounts of this event which have survived (the Balawat Gate inscription and the Nimrud throne-base inscription [*Iraq* XXV (1963) 52-56]), as well as in the Black Obelisk, on the seated throne figure from Assur (*BA* VI/1 [1908] 151-155), and in shorter inscriptions (e.g., *WO* III/1-2 [1964] 152:20, 154:13), we should probably consider it as a later interpolation and devoid of any basis in fact. This conclusion is bolstered by information given in the earliest surviving redaction of the campaign, which says that Shalmaneser received the tribute of Jakin and Mushallim-Marduk while he was still in the Sealand: *kî ina aḫ tâmtimma usbākuni* (*WO* IV/1 [1967] 34 vi 7).

(1218) Despite my previous remarks on the spelling of the name *Dakkūru* in *Studies Oppenheim*, p. 7 n. 5, the spelling *Da-ak-ku-ri* in *WO* I/6 (1952) 466 ii 52 should probably be taken as indicative of the doubled *k* and the name interpreted as a *qattūl* formation. The observations on the spelling of *Amukānu* with a single *k* are still valid. The expected transcription of the third tribe as *Jakīn* is complicated by such *plene* spellings as É-m*Ja-a-ki-i-ni* and possibly *Jakīnā* (?) (M. Dietrich, *WO* IV/1 [1967] 73, 93).

(1219) Chaldea was mentioned in the inscriptions of Ashurnasirpal a generation earlier (*AKA* 352 iii 24), but nothing was said about individual tribes.

(1220) A member of the Amukanu tribe served as witness to a contemporary royal grant (*RA* XVI [1919] 126 iv 20), in which the chief of the Amukanu tribe is also mentioned (*ibid.*, 125 i 15).

mous, (1221) and Shalmaneser dealt with them as independent units. Though Shalmaneser claims that all three major tribes submitted to him, the submission was probably token; and his successor, Shamshi-Adad V, had to fight them once again. (1222)

Assyrian armies were also active during Shalmaneser's reign in a region which had previously belonged to northeastern Babylonia but had gained its independence around the middle of the ninth century. Namri, which had been under the Babylonian kings of the Second Isin Dynasty but seldom heard of in the meantime, had become politically independent, even though one of its contemporary rulers bore the Babylonian name Marduk-mudammiq. (1223) This prince was apparently creating trouble on the Assyrian frontier; and Shalmaneser defeated him in the year 843, (1224) setting Janzu, (1225) a member of the Hanban (Habban) tribe in his stead. (1226) This was part of an extensive campaign reaching from Zamua in the north and affecting the lands of Namri, Habban, and Tukliash (=Tupliash), all formerly within the Babylonian sphere of influence. (1227) Janzu, bearing the title "king of Namri," remained relatively docile in his nominal independence until 835, when Shalmaneser was forced to conduct an extensive campaign to subdue the area and brought back Janzu as a captive to Assyria. (1228) Finally, in the year 828, the

(1221) Both Adinu and Mushallim-Marduk had *šaknu*s subject to them, and the Chaldean chieftains were sometimes called "kings" in the Assyrian inscriptions (see note 1217 above for references). They paid tribute directly to the Assyrian kings and fought as allies of Babylonia against Shamshi-Adad V (see notes 1299 and 1322 below).

(1222) The Chaldeans are discussed in detail below, pp. 260-267.

(1223) *WO* I/1 (1947) 16 rev. 16, 21; *WO* I/6 (1952) 472 iv 7,13; *WO* II/2 (1955) 152:94.

(1224) Marduk-mudammiq commanded a large force of cavalry (*pitḫallūšu ma'dūte*), yet still lost the battle. Shalmaneser later despoiled the land of its goods, including horses (*WO* I/6 [1952] 472 iv 7-21). A macehead taken as booty from Marduk-mudammiq was provided with a suitable inscription and dedicated to Nergal by Shalmaneser III (*MAOG* III/1-2 [1927] 12-14 V.A.; photo: *ibid.*, p. 17 no. 1).

(1225) The details of the description also show the relative newness of the territory to the Assyrians. Janzu, while it might be an abbreviation of a proper name like Kashakti-Janzi or something similar, is the Kassite word for "king" and seems to have been turned into a proper name here. The name Janzu/i as a proper name is attested at this time only in Assyrian annals (Balkan, *Kassitenstudien*, I, 58) and may be regarded as an example of a generic designation taken as a proper name by the Assyrians. Cf. similar examples collected by Oppenheim, *RHA* V (1938-40) 111-112.

Kassite influence may also be detected in the land of Allabria, to the north of Namri. There the local ruler bore the Kassite name *Janzi-Buriaš* (*WO* I/6 [1952] 472 iii 63, only partially preserved in *WO* I/1 [1947] 16 rev. 10). For the interpretation of this name, see Balkan, *Kassitenstudien*, I, 58.

(1226) *WO* II/2 (1955) 152:95 (Black Obelisk). The omission of the installation of Janzu as king in the longest and most nearly contemporary accounts of this campaign (*WO* I/1 [1947] 16 and *WO* I/6 [1952] 470-472, both probably composed in 842) raises the suspicion that Janzu may not have assumed the throne in Namri immediately after the defeat of Marduk-mudammiq.

(1227) The campaign is described in *WO* I/1 (1947) 16 rev. 6-31; *WO* I/6 (1952) 470-472 iii 58-iv 25; *Iraq* XXIV (1962) 94:19-20; *WO* II/1 (1954) 36:33-37; *WO* II/2 (1955) 152:93-95; cf. also the mention of Namri in the short summary in *BA* VI/1 (1908) 145:38 and the mention of Tukliash in *AAA* XIX (1932) 113 no. 302:12. For the identification of Tukliash with Tupliash and its localization in the greater Diyala area (including Der), see the discussion of J. V. Kinnier Wilson in *Iraq* XXIV (1962) 113-115 with extensive earlier bibliography. Cf. also the general remarks on Tupliash by Jacobsen in *AS* VI 1 and *passim*.

(1228) *WO* II/2 (1955) 154-156:110-126 (Black Obelisk), with an almost verbally duplicate text on a statue from Nimrud (*Iraq* XXI [1959] 155-156, fragment F); cf. the shorter, but more nearly contemporary

year before the great Assyrian rebellion broke out, (1229) Shalmaneser had to send out a final campaign against Namri and the surrounding regions. (1230) This area had by now definitely passed into the Assyrian sphere of influence and was for some time to be a target for Assyrian attack whenever the local inhabitants asserted their independence too forcefully.

On the northwestern periphery of Babylonia, on the other hand, we have only the barest indication of contemporary conditions. Shalmaneser at some point during his reign (1231) collected tribute from Marduk–apla–usur of Suhi on the middle Euphrates. (1232) The Babylonian name of the ruler is expected, since most rulers of Suhi around this time bore good Akkadian names. (1233) The tribute consisted of "silver, gold, gold buckets, ivory, incense, byssos, bright-colored clothes, and linen" (1234) and shows the wealth of Suhi at this period, derived chiefly from trade passing along the middle Euphrates. On the Black Obelisk, a relief depicting the tribute of Marduk–apla–usur shows short-bearded attendants bearing tribute and a lion hunting a stag in a cluster of palm trees; (1235) there is no picture of Marduk–apla–usur submitting to Shalmaneser. (1236)

There are two kudurrus which date from the reign of Marduk–zakir–shumi I. The first, dated at Babylon in Nisan of his second year, (1237) is a royal grant of a

---

account from Assur (*WO* I/2 [1947] 58 iii 1-2). Despite the fact that Janzu fled to the mountains before the army of Shalmaneser III reached his area, the Assyrian king pursued and captured him. Janzu, his gods, his sons and daughters, many of his soldiers, and much of his property were carried away to Assyria (*WO* II/2 [1955] 156:125-126).

(1229) For the date, see *RLA* II 433 Cb4:15. Compare also note 1290 below.

(1230) *WO* II/3 (1956) 232:187-190. Upon the approach of Dajan–Ashur, the *turtānu*, who was conducting this campaign for the aged Shalmaneser, the population of Namri fled to the mountains; and the Assyrian army had to content itself with burning the local villages. The singular lack of success of Shalmaneser's chosen representatives in putting down the eastern rebellions in 829 and 828 may have been one of the factors in the revolt of the Assyrian cities in the following year.

(1231) Forrer in *MVAG* XX/3 (1915) 9-14 presented hypothetical arguments for dating a campaign against Suhi to the twenty-first year of Shalmaneser III (=838 B.C.). Then Ungnad in his edition of the eponym chronicles suggested the restoration of the entry for that year as *ana māt S*[*u*(?)–*ú*(?)]–*ḫi* (*RLA* II 433 Cb4:3). But the newly recovered eponym chronicle from Sultantepe now rules out that restoration because the end of the pertinent line reads [ ]–*is–ḫi* (*STT* 46:3′).

(1232) *WO* II/2 (1955) 142 D (Black Obelisk). An unpublished letter, found at Hama in Syria, was written by a Marduk–apla–usur, who O. E. Ravn thought could be identical with the ruler of Suhi: H. Ingholt, *Rapport préliminaire sur sept campagnes de fouilles à Hama en Syrie*, p. 115 n. 10.

(1233) See note 1127 for a brief history of Suhi and its rulers around this time.

(1234) *WO* II/2 (1955) 142 D. For the *bu–ú–ia* of the text (not just the copy, as *CAD* B implies), read *bu–ú–ṣi*! (*CAD* B 350a).

(1235) Black Obelisk, fourth tier of reliefs (see *ANEP*, nos. 351-354). For palm tress on this section of the middle Euphrates, see the inscription of Shamash–resha–usur (*WVDOG* IV no. 4 ii 37, iv 1-4) and *TuM* II-III 152:2.

(1236) Since there are no records of a campaign of Shalmaneser III against Suhi (note 1231 above) and no indication that Marduk–apla–usur brought tribute in person, it is probable that Marduk–apla–usur was at least a semi-independent vassal. See notes 1127 and 1128 for earlier and later rulers of Suhi who enjoyed a privileged independent status.

(1237) *RA* XVI (1919) 126 iv 25-26. One should note this is the third kudurru dated on the twentieth of Nisan within a space of about twenty years (cf. also *BBSt* no. 28 and 36 from the preceding reign, note

large amount of agricultural land, a house with eight rooms, two courtyards, (1238) an orchard, and a regular supply of food to a high temple official in Uruk—Ibni–Ishtar, who held the offices of *kalû* priest of Ishtar, *ērib bīti* of Nana, *šangû* of Usur–amassa, and scribe of Eanna. (1239) This text is interesting to us chiefly because it shows that, despite the relative independence of the Chaldean tribes, the king was still in sufficient control of land as far south as Uruk to bestow it in a direct royal grant. The text also reveals several features in the provincial officialdom which had not been present previously. The witnesses to the transaction included some of the highest government officials in the land in the following order of precedence:

Marduk–balassu–iqbi, crown prince,
Nabu–ahhe–iddina, *ša rēš šarri*,
Iddin–Marduk, (1240) "son" of Amukanu,
Nazi–Enlil, *šandabakku*, (1241)
Saggilu, *bēl pīḫati*,
Shuma–usur, (1242) *kalû* of Marduk and scribe. (1243)

Besides the lofty position assigned the *ša rēš šarri*, (1244) we observe that the office of *šandabakku* (governor of Nippur) is attested for the first time since the Kassite period. The *šaknu*, the official who served as provincial governor during the days of the Second Dynasty of Isin, (1245) is not mentioned in this text; and in most areas that title was losing its former political significance. (1246) Other noteworthy information in the kudurru includes the statements that the field given to Ibni–Ishtar

---

1159 above) and that Shalmaneser III also began his second campaign against the Babylonian rebels on the same day of the year (*WO* IV/1 [1967] 30 iv 5). The day was undoubtedly considered propitious for conducting business at the time.

(1238) The house was or had been inhabited by a man named Zabdi–il, who is described as LÚ GAR m*Mušallim–Marduk* (*RA* XVI [1919] 125 i 15). This is open to at least two possible interpretations: (a) that Zabdi-il (*amīlu ša* PN) and his family (*qinnišu*) of five persons were *glebae adscripti* and went with the house and garden made over to Ibni–Ishtar; (b) that Zabdi–il (*šakin* PN, cf. note 1208 above) had been the previous occupant of the house—and possibly the previous holder of the *kalû* office as well—and that he was now moving out, leaving the five slaves (*qinnišu* "his household") attached to the property behind; such a change in office might have been occasioned by the new reign (the text is dated in the king's second year) or even by the eclipse of the power of Mushallim–Marduk after Shalmaneser's visit to Chaldea (if 851 was Marduk–zakir–shumi's accession year).

(1239) *RA* XVI (1919) 126 iii 7-12. The goddess' name is written both dEŠ.DAR and d*Iš–tar* in the PN in this text (*RA* XVI [1919] 125 ii 15, 126 iii 7). For the family of Hunzu'u, to which Ibni–Ishtar belonged, see W. G. Lambert, *JCS* XI (1957) 4.

(1240) mSUM–dAMAR.UTU (iv 20), where the name of Mushallim–Marduk (i 15) might be expected. I know of no reading *mušallim* for SUM.

(1241) LÚ GÚ.EN.NA (*RA* XVI [1919] 126 iv 21), the governor of Nippur.

(1242) The signs mMU–ŠEŠ may also be read *Nādin–aḫi*.

(1243) *RA* XVI (1919) 126 iv 17-24.

(1244) Discussed on pp. 310-311 below.

(1245) *JESHO* VI (1963) 235-236.

(1246) The title does not die out completely, but is retained in some regions (see note 1957 below).

was in no provincial jurisdiction (NAM *la man–ma–an*) (1247) and that Babylonia outside of Uruk was considered as being divided currently into two principal sections: Akkad and the Sealand. (1248) This terminology—coupled with Shalmaneser's mention of Jakin as "king" of the Sealand (1249)—argues strongly that southern Babylonia outside older urban centers like Uruk was practically independent from the jurisdiction of the Babylonian king.

The second kudurru describes a private sale of land along the Euphrates near Dilbat. The only official witnessing the transfer was the local governor (*šākin ṭēmi*) of Dilbat, (1250) who was also the father of the buyer, though two other witnesses and the scribe were also present. (1251) The document holds little of interest for us save the information that business was going on as usual in Dilbat in the eleventh year of the king (1252) and that the local governor at that time had been in office for at least seventeen years. (1253)

Following in the footsteps of his father, Marduk–zakir–shumi made dedications to temples. Besides his grant of land, house, and food to the *kalû* official of Ishtar at Uruk, (1254) we know also of a lapis-lazuli seal which he presented to the god Marduk (to be worn around the neck of the divine statue in Esagila). (1255) In the dedicatory inscription on this seal, besides the expected reference to his role as "reverent prince," (1256) he calls himself "king of the world," (1257) a once grand, but rather shopworn title by this time. (1258)

(1247) *RA* XVI (1919) 125 i 8, possibly indicating the breakdown of the provincial system of administration in certain areas in the south.

(1248) KUR *Ak–ka–di–i*, KUR A.AB.BA (*RA* XVI [1919] 125 ii 31-32).

(1249) See note 1213 above.

(1250) *VAS* I 35:49. (1251) *Ibid.*, 50-52. (1252) *Ibid.*, 53.

(1253) I.e., from the twenty-eighth year of Nabu-apla-iddina (*VAS* I 35:1-2) to the eleventh year of Marduk–zakir–shumi I (*ibid.*, 49). This indicates that governors were no longer rotated in office from city to city, as they had been under the Second Dynasty of Isin, and bolsters the picture of stronger local governments at the expense of a weaker central administration.

(1254) *RA* XVI (1919) 125-126.

(1255) The seal was found in the mound Amran–ibn–Ali (earlier the site of Esagila) in Babylon in April 1900, in a basket filled with various kinds of stones to be used in making beads; the level at which it was found is dated to late Seleucid or Parthian times. The seal proper is made of lapis lazuli (NA_4.KIŠIB NA_4.ZA.GÌN *ebbi*) and was originally provided with golden handles (*ša ina ḫurāṣi ḫuššî kīniš kunnu*); it was designed to be worn around the statue's neck (*simat kišādišu*), probably to be attached by means of a cord. The seal bears a representation of the Marduk statue and an eight-line dedicatory inscription in the name of Marduk–zakir–shumi I.

Find-spot: *MDOG* V (1900) 3-5; *WVDOG* XV 46-48. Drawing of seal (or its representation): *MDOG* V (1900) 14 fig. 3; *WVDOG* IV 16 fig. 1; *WVDOG* LXII pl. 44b. Photos of seal: *WVDOG* XV fig. 74; *WVDOG* LXII pl. 43e-h. Copy of inscription: *WVDOG* IV pl. 6 no. 2. Editions of inscription: *MDOG* V (1900) 13-14 (translation); *WVDOG* IV 16-17. (transliteration, translation, notes).

(1256) *WVDOG* IV pl. 6 no. 2:4 (*rubû pāliḫšu*, lit.: " prince, revering him [i.e., Marduk]").

(1257) *Ibid.*, line 4 (LUGAL ŠÚ).

(1258) As we have noted several times before. If the seal was dedicated after his aid to Shamshi–Adad V, which we shall presently discuss, then there may have been some grounds for this grandiose claim. The same title was borne by this king's father (*BBSt* no. 29 ii 2) and by all the Assyrian kings of the ninth century (references collected by Seux, *RA* LIX [1965] 5).

The last event of major significance during the reign of Marduk–zakir–shumi was the widespread Assyrian revolt, which broke out in the year 827 and continued through 822. (1259) Beginning in the last years of the aged Shalmaneser III, who had helped Marduk–zakir–shumi solidify his own tenuous grasp of the Babylonian throne, the uprising spread to twenty-seven cities, some of which were the main cities of the realm, such as Nineveh, Assur, Arbail, and Arrapha. Though the account of Shamshi–Adad V does not mention Babylonian help in putting down the rebellion, (1260) a copy of a treaty has survived between him and Marduk–zakir–shumi I which puts the Assyrian on a lower footing than his Babylonian ally and can have resulted only from a quick change in the relative political positions of Babylonia and Assyria. (1261) It, therefore, seems likely that Shamshi–Adad V overcame his elder brother, Ashur–dannin–apla, (1262) and the widespread revolt throughout Assyria only with the aid of Marduk–zakir–shumi; and the treaty should be interpreted in the light of these circumstances.

Shalmaneser III had apparently been kind to Marduk–zakir–shumi I after rendering him similar help in the time of the Marduk–bel–usati rebellion. But Marduk–zakir–shumi does not seem to have been equally forbearing with Shamshi–Adad V. Only part of the text of the treaty between them survives; but one can see that Akkad precedes Assyria in the enumeration of the countries, (1263) that the Assyrian king is not given any royal title, (1264) that he is obliged to surrender fugitives from Babylonia, (1265) that he must promise to report a certain Marduk–rimanni if the latter plots against Babylonia, (1266) and that the treaty oath is sworn by Babylonian gods alone. (1267) Shamshi–Adad saved his throne, but probably lost face in the

(1259) *RLA* II 433 (eponym list). The extent of the revolt is described in the Monolith Inscription of Shamshi–Adad V (I *R* 29-31). Echoes of the rebellion may be seen in the unusual *arki* date in a text from Shibaniba, one of the rebellious cities, by which a year after the beginning of the revolt (i.e., after the second eponymate of Shalmaneser III) may be designated (date: *JCS* VII [1953] 137 no. 70:12-13).

(1260) I *R* 29 i 39-53.

(1261) The treaty (Rm. 2, 427), written in Babylonian script on a black stone tablet, was found by Hormuzd Rassam, at Kuyunjik. If, as suggested by Weidner (*AfO* VIII [1932-33] 27), it was the Babylonian copy of the treaty, it may have been removed later as booty to Nineveh from Babylonia. The text was originally published by Peiser, *MVAG* III/6 (1898) 14-17 (transliteration, translation); and later partial editions were done by Weidner, *AfO* VIII (1932-33) 27-29 (transliteration and translation of lines 16′-33′, copy of entire text, notes) and by Borger, *Orientalia N.S.* XXXIV (1965) 168-169 (transliteration of lines 22′-35′, largely restored on the basis of parallels from the Codex Hammurapi, and various notes on other lines). The acquaintance of ninth-century scribes with the text of the Codex Hammurapi offers an interesting insight into the traditional character of scribal education at this time. [See also the suggestion of Noth, *ZDPV* LXXVII (1961) 143 n. 73].

(1262) For the name Ashur–da'in/dannin–apla, see Stamm, *Namengebung*, p. 156.

(1263) Line 6′.

(1264) Line 8′.

(1265) Line ⌈13′⌉.

(1266) Lines 8′-9′.

(1267) Lines 16′-35′. S. Gevirtz, *Curse Motifs in the Old Testament and in the Ancient Near East* (unpublished Ph. D. dissertation, University of Chicago, 1959), p. 50 has rightly pointed out that the predom-

process. The treaty degrading to Assyria lasted during Marduk–zakir–shumi's lifetime; but his successors on the throne lived to rue the day that the treaty had been forced on the Assyrian king. (1268) The moment of weakness for the northern kingdom soon passed.

The circumstances of Marduk–zakir–shumi's death are unknown, but death from old age seems a plausible explanation. Over twenty-five years before the end of his reign, his son had been old enough to act as witness for a kudurru; (1269) and that son would now be at least forty-five years of age. As a consequence, it is probable that Marduk–zakir–shumi was a man advanced in years when his reign came to an end. His family, which had begun ruling over eighty years before, was to continue on the throne for one more reign before it lost control of the land.

26. Marduk-balassu-iqbi (1270)

As mentioned in the preceding paragraph, Marduk–balassu–iqbi had already passed the prime of life when he became king. (1271) The exact length of his reign

---

inance of Babylonian gods in the treaty does not necessarily prove the supremacy of Babylonia at this time (any more than the predominance of Phoenician gods in the treaty between Esarhaddon and Baal of Tyre [Borger, *Asarhaddon*, pp. 107-109] would argue for the supremacy of the latter). But the other factors mentioned above—Babylonia receiving preferential treatment to Assyria in several aspects of the wording of the treaty and the wholesale revolt of Assyrian cities at this time—do not support a theory which would hold that Assyria's hegemony remained undiminished early in the reign of Shamshi–Adad V. It is only later that Shamshi–Adad was able to recoup Assyria's former strength.

For various comments on the curse formulae in this treaty, see D. R. Hillers, *Treaty-Curses and the Old Testament Prophets*, p. 17 nn. 18-19 and p. 61.

(1268) Shamshi–Adad V personally overthrew the next two rulers in Babylonia, and their downfalls in quick succession paved the way for the years of anarchy which followed.

(1269) *RA* XVI (1919) 126 iv 17.

(1270) *Marduk–balāssu–iqbi*: "Marduk has promised his life." For this type of *Danknamen*, see Stamm, *Namengebung*, p. 206. The type DN-balassu-iqbi is not yet attested in either the Old Babylonian or the Kassite periods and seems to occur for the first time in the ninth century (*BBSt* no. 36 vi 24, possibly iden tical with this king, see note 1177 above and note 1271 below). It is quite popular in the Neo-Babylonian and Persian periods (Tallqvist, *NBN*, p. 329). Many private individuals with the same name as the king occur in later Babylonia (Tallqvist, *NBN*, p. 100).

Writing of RN: in a kudurru during his father's reign as ^{d}AMAR.UTU–TI–*su–iq–bi* (*RA* XVI [1919] 126 iv 17), on a stamped brick probably from his own reign as ^{d}⸢ŠID(?)⸣–DIN–*su–iq–bi* (*Tell Umar*, II, pl. XXV fig. 2, read from photograph and not collated), in a later copy of a text written during his reign as ^{md}AMAR.UTU–DIN–*su–iq–bi* (4 N-T 3:20′) and as ^{md}AMAR.UTU–TI–[ ] (4 N-T 3:4′), and in an inscription of Shamshi–Adad V as ^{md}AMAR.UTU–TI–*su–iq–bi* (*AfO* IX [1933-34] 93 iii 24, 95 iv ⸢2⸣). In the Assyrian synchronistic kinglist *KAV* 182 iii 13′, his name is written as ^{md}ŠID–TI–*su*–DUG$_4$(=KA). Traces of his name appear in the New Babylonian Chronicle, rev. 6 (^{md}AMAR.UTU–DIN–*su*–[ ]), in the Synchronistic History *CT* XXXIV 43 Sm. 2106 iv 6′ ([*i*]⸢*q–bi*⸣) and 8′ ([*s*]*u–iq–bi*), and probably in *KAV* 10 ii 11′ (undecipherable).

(1271) See above, especially note 1269. He might also be identical with the witness in *BBSt* no. 36 vi 24, late in the reign of his grandfather, who was a *bēl pīḫati* (see note 1177).

is unknown, but it probably did not occupy more than eleven years. (1272) At his death, the long reign of the family of Nabu–shuma–ukin I came to an end after four generations in power. (1273)

To date, we have only two documents from Babylonia coming from his reign. (1274) The first text is on a stamped brick found at the excavations at Tell Umar in 1931-32. Most of the brick is broken away; but the last line of the inscription, according to Prof. Waterman, reads: "Marduk–balatsu–iqbi king (or prince) of Karduniash." (1275) If the reading of this name is correct and if Marduk–balassu–iqbi was responsible for the brick inscription, then he presumably either built or repaired the large structure in which the brick was uncovered. (1276) This would fit well with his other activities in northern Babylonia described in Assyrian sources and which will be discussed below.

The second text is a legal document which survives only in a fragmentary Neo-Babylonian copy made—with several erasures—by a schoolboy and recently discovered at Nippur. (1277) Although the actual terms of the transaction are almost completely broken away, (1278) several interesting features may be detected in the list of witnesses that is partially preserved on the obverse of the document. This list shows that some high offices in Babylonia had become hereditary at this time. Considering the small number of officials known from the middle and late ninth century, there are a surprising number of families that recur in one official capacity

(1272) The earliest date for his first official year is 823; his reign probably ended in 813.

(1273) Baba–aha–iddina was not a descendant of the king, if we assume that he was identical with the witness to the 4 N-T 3 text whose father was Lidanu (17′) and who enjoyed a high office under Marduk–balassu–iqbi. Should this identification prove false, then there is no reason why the two kings could not be related.

(1274) The votive tablet published as *BBSt* no. 34 and elsewhere is not necessarily from this reign and cannot be dated precisely. King's explanation of the date in *BBSt*, p. 115 n. 2 still holds good.

(1275) The brick is published only in photo (*Tell Umar*, II, pl. XXV fig. 2) and in translation (*ibid.*, p. 78) by Waterman, who said that the pertinent line could be read "with a fair degree of certainty." Part of the line may be made out on the photo: ᵈ⌜ŠID(?)⌝–DIN–*su–iq–bi* NUN x (x). One should note that the rendering "prince of Karduniash" is unlikely, since *rubû* GN is unattested as a royal title in Babylonia (see Seux, *Épithètes royales*, pp. 251-256).

In the second-last line of the inscription seem to be traces of the name of the god Sin (⌜ᵈ30⌝). This reading, if correct, would prove to be interesting because of the known connection between Sin and Akshak–Opis, with which Umar has sometimes been identified (see Kraus, *ZA* LI [1955] 62-64 and note 608 above).

(1276) This burnt brick was found three feet below the loose debris on top of a large structure of unburnt bricks on the mound of Tell Umar (Waterman, *Tell Umar*, II, Fig. 12, section A-B).

(1277) 4 N-T 3, found Dec. 1, 1953 in fill. This unpublished document was brought to my attention by Prof. Jacobsen, who has graciously ceded publication rights to it.

(1278) The text mentions *x* MA.NA *kaspa kīmu isqi* (GIŠ.ŠUB.BA) *šuāti*, "x minas of silver in exchange for that prebend." Cf. the phrase *x* MA.NA KÙ.BABBAR *kūm isqi atûtu* PN *qīšta ana* PN_2 *iqtīš*, "x minas of silver PN gave as a gift to PN_2 for the prebend of the portership" (*VAS* V 37:15-17). Certain types of prebends were apparently not to be sold, hence the fiction of exchange of gifts (money for office). This document (4 N-T 3) was sealed by the king in the assembly of the "royal secretary and nobles" (UM.ME.A *u* LÚ.GAL.MEŠ).

or another. Nazi–Enlil, who was governor of Nippur (*šandabakku*) during the reign of Marduk–balassu–iqbi's father, (1279) had a son who held the same office during this reign. (1280) Tuballat–Eshdar (1281) had no fewer than three of his sons or descendants holding office over a period of about fifty years: two as *sukkallu*, (1282) one as *šākin ṭēmi*. (1283) Also, Saggilu and Esagil–shaduni, who held the office of *bēl pīḫati* during successive reigns, might be viewed as different versions of the same name. (1284) Thus, familial continuity in office at this time was not confined to kings. (1285) This document is dated on the twenty-second day of the eleventh month (Shabatu) in the second year of Marduk–balassu–iqbi. (1286) It gives the king the title "[king] of the lands of Sumer and Akkad." (1287) From the titles of witnesses listed in the text, it may be seen that Marduk–balassu–iqbi controlled both Nippur (1288) and Der. (1289)

Marduk–balassu–iqbi is much better known at present for his battles with Assyria. We have no idea of what provoked Shamshi–Adad V to turn so viciously against Babylonia after generations of friendly relations between the two countries, unless it was the humiliating terms imposed on him under the treaty with Marduk–zakir–shumi I. But the Assyrian king, after quelling the rebellion in his own land and then conducting three major campaigns against the Nairi to the west, north, and east of Assyria proper, undertook his next campaigns against Babylonia. (1290)

(1279) *RA* XVI (1919) 126 iv 21.

(1280) 4 N-T 3:11′. The son's name is Enlil–apla–usur.

(1281) The reading of the first element is uncertain. The name is always written *Tú–ba–laṭ–*dEŠ.DAR.

(1282) *BBSt* no. 28 rev. 22; 4 N-T 3:12′.

(1283) *BBSt* no. 28 rev. 23, no. 36 vi 22-23.

(1284) *RA* XVI (1919) 126 iv 22; 4 N-T 3:14′. In the first case no patronymic is given; in the second, Esagil–shaduni is called "son" of Arad–Ea. The identification of these two individuals is strictly hypothetical.

(1285) Indicative of some local autonomy in the provinces and a weakened central authority. See also note 1253 above.

(1286) 4 N-T 3:20′.

(1287) [LUGAL] KUR.KUR *šu–me–ri ù ak–kad–i*: 4 N-T 3:21′.

(1288) Known from the fact of a subject *šandabakku* in 4 N-T 3:11′. This text was probably written in Nippur.

(1289) The *šākin ṭēmi* of BÀD.AN.KI is a witness in 4 N-T 3:15′; only the theophoric element which ends his name is preserved: AN.GAL.

(1290) The chronology of the early campaigns of Shamshi–Adad's reign is uncertain. The eponym canon Cb4 (*RLA* II 433) apparently records campaigns for the years 821, 820, 819, 818, 817, 816 before breaking off. According to the newly recovered eponym chronicle *STT* 348, however, the revolt against Shamshi–Adad V terminated two years later than the date given in Cb4 (820 as opposed to 822); and the campaigns of Shamshi–Adad V began only in 819. Even then the traces of the regions fought against in 819 and 818 according to *STT* 348 do not match the traces in Cb4 (with the possible exception of the 819 campaign in *STT* 348, [*ana*] *māt Mannaja*, which might be equated with the 820 campaign in Cb4, of which only the trace [ ]–*a* remains). Thus the eponym chronicles record alternately seven or five campaigns of Shamshi–Adad before his campaign against Der, which is said to be his fifth (or fourth, see note 1291 below) campaign according to the annals. It is possible that some of these campaigns may have been combined in the annals or even that unsuccessful excursions were omitted altogether from the official ver-

The first of these campaigns probably took place in the year 814 and was noted in the eponym chronicle as "to the city of Der." (1291) After crossing the Lower Zab, he led his army through little-travelled mountain terrain, (1292) where he killed three lions. He crossed Mount Epih (the Jebel Hamrin) (1293) and besieged the city of Me-Turnat on the bank of the Diyala. The city surrendered apparently without struggle; some of its population together with their gods and movable goods were deported to Assyria. Shamshi-Adad then crossed the river, burnt the city of Qarne, (1294) one of the many Babylonian "royal cities" of the region, and surrounding hamlets. He went over Mt. Jalman and put the city of Di'bina under siege; when

---

sion of the royal exploits. The source mentioning three campaigns against Nairi before the first Babylonian campaign is the annals edition composed after the conclusion of Shamshi-Adad's official "fourth campaign" (I *R* 29-31).

(1291) *RLA* II 428 Cb1:3. Weidner in *AfO* IX (1933-34) 89, 94, 96 has discussed the dating of Shamshi-Adad's Babylonian campaigns; and his reconstruction is still the best, though his dates for the individual eponyms must now be placed one year later in each case. Weidner's position is based essentially on: (a) the return of AN.GAL to Der in the eponymy of Belu-balat (814, *RLA* II 428 Cb1:3), one year before the statue was removed in Shamshi-Adad's fifth campaign (813); (b) the equating of the city of Nimitti-sharri, attacked in Shamshi-Adad's fifth campaign, with the city Ahsanu mentioned as target for the campaign of 813 (see Weidner, *AfO* IX [1933-34] 94 for evidence for this equation in a geographical list).

The solution proposed by Weidner, however, has the obvious drawback of disassociating the campaign against Der recorded in the eponym chronicle for 814 from the capture of Der which is the culmination of the fifth campaign (813). Though it is still the most plausible solution, it may have to be revised slightly as further evidence becomes available. In that case, Shamshi-Adad's fourth campaign, in which he fought against Chaldeans, Arameans, Elamites, and people of Namri, may have to be dated to 815, which is characterized in the eponym canon Cb1 by the campaign *ana māt Zarat[e]*; if *zaratu* is interpreted as pertaining to "tents" (*CAD* Z 66), the *māt Zarate* could conceivably refer to the cityless encampment of the allied armies, some of whose forces were semi-nomads. This proposal, at present, has less to recommend it than Weidner's reconstruction. [Cf. perhaps URU *Zarāti* in an inscription of Sargon II (*Iraq* XVI [1954] 186 vi 53].

Throughout our present treatment, therefore, we date Shamshi-Adad's fourth through sixth campaigns to 814 through 812, even though we realize that these dates may eventually have to be adjusted slightly.

(1292) *ina birīt* (URU) *Zaddi* (URU) *Zaban abbalkit natbak šadê*: "I passed through the gorge (runoff?) of the mountain between Zaddi and Zaban" (I *R* 31 iv 2-3). The city of Zaddi was the northernmost town of Babylonia at this time (*miṣir māt Akkadî*); Shamshi-Adad in his first campaign had gone that far—but no farther—south (I *R* 30 ii 10-11). The same town is also mentioned in *ABL* 522 rev. 2.

The city of Zaban, on the other hand, is probably just within the border of Assyria at this time. Ashurnasirpal had stated that the border of Assyria was just upstream from there (*Iraq* XIV [1952] 33:16, etc.), as it had probably been also in the days of Adad-nirari II (Synchronistic History iii 20). Shalmaneser III had offered sacrifices to Adad there when on his campaign against Babylonia in 851 (*WO* IV/1 [1967] 30 iv 2); and the city had been involved in the widespread revolt among the cities of Assyria at the end of his reign (I *R* 29 i 48). In earlier times, in the days of Ashur-dan I, the city had been in Babylonian territory (*CT* XXXIV 42 K. 4401b ii 11, Synchronistic History); in later days, under the Sargonids, it seems to have been an Assyrian transportation center (*ABL* 311:10, 641:4, 1191:12). For further literature on Zaban, see note 1151 above.

(1293) T. C. Young, Jr. in *Iran* V (1967) 15 n. 35 has stated that the route of Shamshi-Adad V in his fourth campaign seems to have followed a line of march northeast of the Jebel Hamrin (in order to take the enemy in the rear and to separate the Elamites and the Babylonians). The general outline of the route may be correct; but it is unlikely that Shamshi-Adad V entirely skirted the Jebel Hamrin, since his annals explicitly state that he crossed Mt. Epih (I *R* 31 iv 4).

(1294) Attested only here (I *R* 31 iv 9) and in *ABL* 372:14.

it too surrendered, its people and their goods were deported. Finally, Datebir and Izduja, two suburbs of Gannanate, along with surrounding hamlets were captured and burnt; people, property, and gods were taken away and the fruit trees cut down. Gannanate itself was not taken at this time. (1295)

At this point in the campaign, after the spoliation and burning of the city Qiribti–alani, the Assyrian army attacked a large number of Babylonians who had fled to the city of Dur–Papsukkal, a royal residence situated on an island, possibly to be located further upstream from Gannanate. (1296) Marduk–balassu–iqbi, who had summoned large forces of Chaldeans, Elamites, Kassites (i.e., people of Namri), and Arameans (1297) to help oppose further encroachments of Shamshi–Adad east of the Tigris, did not arrive in time to save the beleaguered city. Shamshi–Adad took the town and massacred its defenders before putting it to the torch. The tardy Babylonian and allied forces drew up their battle lines near Dur–Papsukkal. Shamshi–Adad, despite his previous successes in the campaign and his unequivocal claim of victory here, may not have defeated the coalition of allies decisively et this juncture. This battle marked the limit of the Assyrian's advance for the year; (1298) and, though he boasted about capturing chariotry, cavalry, and some of the camp furniture, he did not manage to take the Babylonian king and had to return in the next year to finish the campaign. (1299)

Whatever the real outcome of the battle of Dur–Papsukkal, Shamshi–Adad definitely subdued Marduk–balassu–iqbi in the campaign of the next year, 813. (1300) The Assyrian king proceeded more quickly to his destination in this campaign, since in the previous year he had already brought under his control the territory towards the beginning of his line of march. After crossing the Lower Zab, Mount Epih, and the Diyala, he destroyed three small towns, (1301) after which he headed towards

(1295) It was captured only in the following year.

(1296) For the location of Dur–Papsukkal, see Unger in *RLA* II 248: it was on part of the river called Daban (*RLA* II 96), for which a tentative identification was suggested by Jacobsen and Adams, *Science* CXXVIII (1958) 1254 1256 (see also Adams, *Land behind Baghdad*, p. 48). Dur–Papsukkal was capital of a province in the late Kassite period (*MDP* II 87 i 37).

(1297) KUR *A–ru–mu* (I *R* 31 iv 39). Where these "Arameans" lived is uncertain. This is the first reference in the Neo-Assyrian period to Aramean activity in this area east of the Tigris.

(1298) In *CAH* II² xxxii 24, Labat erroneously dated this battle in 821. Hinz, *Das Reich Elam*, p. 115, followed that dating. In *Die altorientalischen Reiche* III (=*Fischer Weltgeschichte* IV) 39-40, Labat dates the fourth campaign to 816 and the fifth campaign to the following year; these dates are at least two years too early (see note 1291 above).

(1299) The fourth campaign of Shamshi–Adad V is narrated in I *R* 31 iii 70-iv 45 and in *AfO* IX (1933-34) 91-92 iii 1-16 (a badly broken account, probably dealing with Shamshi–Adad's return to Assyria).

(1300) For the dating of this campaign in the eponym year of Belu-balat, see Weidner in *AfO* IX (1933-34) 96. (The reading of the name of Belu–balat is uncertain; see note 1971 below).

(1301) Qai[ ]na, Padna, and Makurrite, none of which can be definitely located other than to say that they were probably southwest of Gannanate (deduced from Shamshi–Adad's line of march). Weidner (*AfO* IX [1933-34] 97) identifies Padna with Padan of the Kassite period.

Gannanate. (1302) Marduk–balassu–iqbi was evidently concerned with his own inability to defend the town; for he fled, probably in the direction of Der. (1303) Shamshi–Adad pursued him there, captured the city, and apparently took away images of several of the local gods to Assyria. (1304)

Here, unfortunately, there is a lacuna in the text which recounts the campaign. We cannot tell whether Marduk–balassu–iqbi received aid from his allies once again or where the final decisive battle of the campaign was fought. But it is clear that Shamshi–Adad eventually triumphed, captured the Babylonian king, and brought him back to Assyria. (1305)

We know nothing of Marduk–balassu–iqbi's fate after he was taken alive in exile to Assyria. (1306) His successor, as we have noted above, was probably not a member of the same family. (1307)

27. Baba-aha-iddina (1308)

After Marduk–balassu–iqbi had been removed to Assyria, Baba–aha–iddina succeeded him on the Babylonian throne. If identical with the *paqid mātāti* official

(1302) For the location of Gannanate, see Unger, *RLA* III 139-140. There is no evidence that Mount *Ḫa–ši–mur* (*AfO* IX [1933-34] 92 iii 24), mentioned here after Makkurite on Shamshi–Adad's line of march, is to be identified with the Hashmar pass of Ashurnasirpal (contra Weidner, *AfO* IX [1933-34] 97).

(1303) He went to the town of Nimitti–sharri, which Weidner (*AfO* IX [1933-34] 94) has shown to be identical with *Aḫišānu* or *Aḫsāna* (of the eponym chronicle—target of the campaign of 813). This was probably in the direction of Der, since Shamshi–Adad next fought against him at that city.

(1304) The fifth campaign of Shamshi–Adad is narrated in *AfO* IX (1933-34) 92 iii 17-iv 10 and also in the *Gottesbrief* (*ibid.*, 102). The deities whose statues were taken away at this time are discussed by Weidner, *AfO* IX (1933-34) 98-100. The Synchronistic History dates the removal of the patron god of Der (AN.GAL) to the next campaign, that against Baba–aha–iddina (*CT* XXXIV 41 iv 7-9).

Cameron (*History of Early Iran*, p. 146) mentions that at this time the inhabitants of Der fled to Elam. Though the name of Der is not preserved in the pertinent passage (*AfO* IX [1933-34] 102:21 ff.), it is probable that some of the inhabitants of eastern Babylonia are involved here.

(1305) *AfO* IX (1933-34) 92 iv 5, where this king's name is to be restored. Babylonia had a new king by the time of the next campaign. *CT* XXXIV 43 Sm. 2106 rev. 6′-9′ (Synchronistic History) also refers to a victory of Shamshi–Adad (rev. ⌈7′⌉) over Marduk–balassu–iqbi (rev. ⌈6′⌉).

(1306) Whether or not Marduk–balassu–iqbi was flayed alive like some of the other prisoners (*AfO* IX [1933-34] 92 iv 9-10) is uncertain.

(1307) See note 1273 above.

(1308) *Baba–aḫa–iddina*: "Baba has given me a brother." This is traditionally the name of a second son; see Stamm, *Namengebung*, p. 44. For the history of the type DN–ahhe/aha–iddina, see note 1078 above.

The reading of the god's name is not altogether certain, since the most common writing at this period is ^{d}*Ba–Ú*. The probability that it should be read in some such way as ^{d}*Ba–ba*$_6$ is increased by the writing of some Neo-Babylonian PN's as ^{md}KÁ– (e.g., *TCL* XIII 203:32). Shortened forms of names with the same theophorous element occur frequently written as ^{m}*Ba–ba–a* or ^{m}KÁ–*a*+*a* (e.g., *BRM* I 36:7; *VAS* V 116:13) in the same period. Akkadian names honoring this god occur in Babylonia as early as the Kassite period (Clay, *CPN*, p. 63). More evidence for reading the god's name as Baba might be adduced from Middle

of the previous reign, (1309) Baba–aha–iddina was not the son of his predecessor but rather of a certain Lidanu, who is unattested elsewhere. The first official regnal year of this king was probably 812, just after Marduk–balassu–iqbi had been captured by the Assyrians. (1310) How long Baba–aha–iddina remained on the throne is uncertain; but, as we shall presently see, it is likely that his first regnal year was also his last.

Events of this king's reign are known to date only from Assyrian sources, the annals of Shamshi–Adad V and the Synchronistic History. (1311) According to these, Baba–aha–iddina fared no better than his royal predecessor. In the year 812, Shamshi–Adad V conducted the third in his series of campaigns against Babylonia, proceeding by his usual route east of the Tigris. (1312) Shortly after crossing the Diyala, he shut up Baba–aha–iddina and his forces in a city whose name is only imperfectly preserved in the Assyrian account: NI–BU–[x–(x)]. (1313) Shamshi–Adad apparently besieged the Babylonian in the city and then captured it by breaching the wall. (1314) The king and his family were taken and brought back, along with Babylonian gods and rich booty, to Assyria. (1315)

Assyrian personal names, where a god [d]*Ba–bu* occurs (e.g., *KAJ* 178:15). This god's name (in a personal name) is also written [d]*Ba–ba* in a Hittite text referring to an Assyrian individual about the same time (*KUB* XXIII 103 rev. 8).

In Babylonia, other individuals with the name Baba–aha–iddina occur as early as the reign of Meli–Shipak in the early twelfth century (*BBSt* no. 4 i 16). There are three individuals of this name attested during the Second Dynasty of Isin (*AfK* II [1924-25] 61 rev. 2; *BBSt* no. 30 rev. 22, perhaps identical with the man in the preceding reference; *BBSt* no. 25 rev. 29). The name continues to be used through the Neo-Babylonian period (*Ev.-M.* 16:6, *Nbn.* 936:14). The name also occurs in the Middle- and Neo-Assyrian periods, e.g., *KUB* XXIII 103 rev. 8; *ADD* App. 1 xii 30.

Writing of RN: in an inscription of Shamshi–Adad V and in the Synchronistic History as [md]*Ba–ba*$_6$–PAB–AŠ (*AfO* IX [1933-34] 95 iv ⌈14⌉, 16; *CT* XXXIV 41 iv 1); in the Assyrian synchronistic kinglist *KAV* 182 iii 14′ only ⌈[md]*Ba*–⌉[ ] is preserved. An official bearing the same name and possibly to be identified with the king occurs in an economic text written during the reign of the preceding Babylonian monarch as [md]*Ba–ba*$_6$–ŠEŠ–SUM–*na* (4 N-T 3:17′).

(1309) 4 N-T 3:17′. See note 1273 above.

(1310) The chronology of this reign is discussed in note 1291 above.

(1311) Principal source for Shamshi–Adad's sixth campaign: *AfO* IX (1933-34) 100 iv 11-29; cf. *CT* XXXIV 41 iv 1-14, Synchronistic History. Though the Assyrian king is not mentioned explicitly in the preserved portion of the latter text, he is the only possible candidate between Shalmaneser III and Adad–nirari III, since the sections between lines in the latter part of the Synchronistic History are grouped according to Assyrian kings and Adad–nirari III should not be the subject of the section before iv 15.

(1312) I.e., across the Zab, Epih, and Diyala.

(1313) *AfO* IX (1933-34) 100 iv 15. No satisfactory reading of this geographical name has yet been suggested. One may speculate as to why both Marduk–balassu–iqbi and Baba–aha–iddina were using royal residences in the Diyala region at this time. Had the administrative capital been shifted from Babylon or did the monarchs deem it essential to defend this area in person?

(1314) *ina pilši u nāpi⌈li assibi ak⌉šud* (*AfO* IX [1933-34] 100 iv 15-16). Whether mining is involved in this technique is uncertain.

(1315) Included in the booty were the royal standard (*urigalli ālik pānišu*), precious stones, gold vessels, bronze, elephant hides, ivory, luxury woods, and some wooden objects overlaid with silver and gold (*AfO* IX [1933-34] 100 iv 17-27).

At this point, the name of Baba–aha–iddina vanishes from the page of history.(1316) Whether he regained the throne at a later date is doubtful; and there is no known connection between him and any of his successors. His kingdom, during his brief reign, had embraced at least the Diyala region(1317) and northern Babylonia.(1318) The southern part of the country, occupied by the Chaldean tribes, was possibly independent at this time, since Shamshi–Adad undertook a separate campaign against the south later in the same year.(1319)

The Synchronistic History adds some details about Shamshi–Adad's third Babylonian campaign. Besides his capture of Baba–aha–iddina, the Assyrian king despoiled many cities in eastern Babylonia—Der, Lahiru, Gannanate, Dur–Papsukkal, Bit–Riduti, and Me–Turnat—and took away more statues of the gods.(1320) Then Shamshi–Adad stopped to offer sacrifices in the northern cities of Cutha, Babylon, and Borsippa.(1321) Finally, he concluded his campaign by journeying south and receiving the tribute of the "kings of Chaldea."(1322) By this time, he had

(1316) Olmstead (*AJSL* XXXVII [1920-21] 222-223 and *History of Assyria*, p. 161) linked the final removal of Baba–aha–iddina to Assyria (*CT* XXXIV 41 iv 1-2, Synchronistic History), at which time the despoiling of Der also took place, with the entry preceding the return of AN.GAL to Der mentioned in the eponym chronicle (*RLA* II 429:32) and dated them both to 786. We now know, however, on the basis of the narrative of the sixth campaign of Shamshi–Adad V, published by Weidner in *AfO* IX (1933-34) 100, that this event should probably be identified with the eponym chronicle entry for 812 "to the land of Chaldea" (*RLA* II 428:5); see note 1319 below.

(1317) *AfO* IX (1933-34) 100 iv 11-29; cf. the cities captured by Shamshi–Adad V according to the Synchronistic History (*CT* XXXIV 41 iv 3-5).

(1318) This may be deduced from Shamshi–Adad's visits to Cutha, Borsippa, and Babylon immediately after his defeat of Baba–aha–iddina (*CT* XXXIV 41 iv 9-10, Synchronistic History).

(1319) *CT* XXXIV 41 iv 11-12, Synchronistic History. It is only the Chaldean phase of the campaign which is recorded in the eponym chronicle (*RLA* II 428:5). This is the most probable present interpretation of the data; because of the uncertainty of the chronology of Shamshi–Adad's reign, it is conceivable that this campaign may have to be dated to 811 or that the Synchronistic History described the campaigns of 812 and 811 together. See notes 1290-1291 above and note 1325 below.

Chaldea was probably at least *de facto* independent at this time, because it had joined the coalition of Elam, Namri, Babylon, and the Arameans on an apparently equal footing in 814.

(1320) The gods mentioned are AN.GAL, Humhummu, Belet Deri, Belet Akkadi, Shimalija, Palil (dIGI.DU), Annunitu, and Mar–biti of URU *Maliki* (*CT* XXXIV 41 iv 7-9, Synchronistic History). Some of these gods were supposed to have been removed following the previous campaign (*AfO* IX [1933-34] 92 iii 42-48). Mar–biti of Maliki (Malaki) is mentioned again in Streck, *Asb.*, 186:18; and Streck, *ibid.*, p. 187 n. 10, attempts to connect Maliki with earlier Malg(i)um. Bibliography for geographical names mentioned in the Synchronistic History iv 3-4: Der (=modern Badrah; Forrer, *Provinzeinteilung*, pp. 47, 97; Smith, *JEA* XVIII [1932] 28), Lahiru (note 1093 above), Gannanate (*RLA* III 139-140), Dur–Papsukkal (note 1296), Bit–Riduti (Streck, *Asb.*, p. CCCLXXIX n. 3 and note 473 above), Me–Turnat (note 1188).

(1321) *CT* XXXIV 41 iv 9-10, Synchronistic History. It is noteworthy that Shalmaneser III, Shamshi–Adad V, and Tiglath–Pileser III, when campaigning in Babylonia, stopped to pay homage to the principal gods of the northern cities; Adad–nirari III also received leftovers (*rīḫātu*) from the sacrifices to the principal gods of these cities and may himself have had sacrifices offered there (I *R* 35 no. 1:23-24). Throughout this period, whatever tensions there were between the two countries, the Assyrians retained their reverence for the Babylonian gods.

(1322) *CT* XXXIV 41 iv 11-12, Synchronistic History. The text (borrowed probably from an edition of Shamshi–Adad's annals that has not yet been recovered) switches from third to first person at this point. Further activities in Babylonia (lines 12-13) cannot be pieced together because of the poor preservation of the text.

assumed suzerainty over Babylonia and was claiming the title "king of Sumer and Akkad." (1323) The borders between Assyria and Babylonia were realigned, (1324) and Babylonia attempted to set up an independent government once again.

Years of Chaos: Kings 28-30

After the capture of Baba–aha–iddina, the campaigns of Shamshi–Adad V continued yet another year against Babylonia. For the year 811, the eponym chronicle records that the Assyrian army went "to Babylon"; (1325) but we have no other account of this campaign. Babylonia, exhausted by four successive Assyrian campaigns (two of which had culminated in the deportation of the reigning sovereign to Assyria), seems to have lapsed into a state of anarchy.

We have little information bearing on the political history of either Babylonia or Assyria during the years which elapsed between the deportation of Baba–aha–iddina and the accession of Eriba–Marduk. (1326) The New Babylonian Chronicle states that "for *x* years there was no king in the land"; (1327) and there is a text dated in "the fourth year in which there was no king in the land." (1328) The synchronistic kinglist *KAV* 13 and the Dynastic Chronicle reveal the names of three kings who followed this alleged kingless interval: Ninurta–apl?–[x], Marduk–bel–[zeri], and Marduk–apla–usur. (1329) Very little is known about any of these rulers; and only one known text is dated during their reigns, a small economic text from the reign of Marduk–bel–zeri.

(1323) *Archaeologia* LXXIX (1929) 123 no. 114:2, *AAA* XVIII (1931) pl. XX no. 44:2. Cf. also Scheil, *RT* XXII (1900) 37 c, which is probably also to be restored "king of [Sumer and Akkad]."

(1324) *CT* XXXIV 41 iv 14, Synchronistic History. Unfortunately, the text preserves for us none of the exact borders at this time.

(1325) *a–na* KÁ.DINGIR.RA.KI (*RLA* II 428:6). This was Shamshi–Adad's last campaign, and Olmstead (*AJSL* XXXVII [1920-21] 222 and *History of Assyria*, p. 157) has suggested that it was fatal to the Assyrian monarch.

(1326) We are not even certain how many years passed between these two events, but presumably no more than 42 (since the earliest probable date for Baba–aha–iddina's deportation is 812 and the latest possible date for Eriba–Marduk's accession year is 770).

(1327) New Babylonian Chronicle, rev. 7. The figure in the text is certainly at least *2*, probably at least *12* (traces of a preceding *Winkelhaken* may be seen in the copy), and possibly more; see also Weidner, *MVAG* XX/4 (1915) 101 n. 1. Depending on the validity of this reading, a "kingless" interval in Babylonia could have lasted down to at least 800.

(1328) *BRM* I 23: MU 4 KAM *šá* LUGAL *ina* KUR NU TUK–*ú*. Cf. *BRM* I 24: MU 8 KAM (no king mentioned); scribes in the Neo-Babylonian period rarely omitted the royal name deliberately from a date formula, though in the Kassite period this practice had not been at all uncommon.

(1329) *KAV* 13:1'-3'; *ADD* 888:3'.

Ninurta–apl?–[x], king no. 28, is named only in the synchronistic kinglist *KAV* 13; and the second element of his name cannot be read with certainty. (1330) Names attested in Akkadian with the same first two elements are:

(1) Ninurta–apil–Ekur: Assyrian king no. 82, who reigned 1192-1180;

(2) Ninurta–apla–ibni: attested only in a seventh-century Babylonian economic text (*TuM* II-III 36:11);

(3) Ninurta–apla–iddina: the name of several individuals, beginning in the last decades of the Kassite period (*BBSt* no. 5 ii 31); it occurs again in the middle of the tenth century (*BBSt* no. 9 i 13) and in the late seventh (*TuM* II-III 267:5) and fifth centuries (*TuM* II-III 7:21).

But the name could also be reconstructed in many other ways.

The second known monarch of this time is Marduk–bel–[zeri] (king no. 29). (1331) His name is restored from an economic text dated in the accession year of Marduk–bel–zeri (1332) and written in the city *Ú–da–ni*, which is to be located somewhere in the south. (1333) The text records simply that various parts of a wheeled vehicle had been entrusted to the temple of Palil in Udani by Belshunu, the *šangû* of Udani. (1334) Other than this minor text and a possible mention in the Dynastic Chronicle, (1335) we know nothing whatever concerning this king's reign.

(1330) *KAV* 13:1′ reads [^{m}]⌈^{d}MAŠ–A(?)⌉–[ ].

(1331) *Marduk–bēl–zēri*: "Marduk (is) lord of descendants (lit.: seed)," i.e., Marduk has it in his power to grant posterity. For the name type, see Stamm, *Namengebung*, p. 217, where we learn that this type starts in the Old Babylonian period. It continued to be used during the Kassite, Neo-Babylonian, and Persian periods (Clay, *CPN*, p. 163; Tallqvist, *NBN*, p. 308). This particular name seems to occur for the first time here, though later private persons also bear the same name, e.g., *Nbk.* 198:19, *VAS* III 134:12.

Writing of RN: ^{md}ŠID–⌈EN⌉–[ ] (*KAV* 13:2′, synchronistic kinglist), ^{d}AMAR.UTU–EN–NUMUN (*JAOS* XLI [1921] 313:10, contemporary economic text).

(1332) The text was published by Clay in *JAOS* XLI (1921) 313. This king was first identified with the *Marduk*-⌈*bēl*⌉–[x] of *KAV* 13:2′ by Sayce, *Babyloniaca* VII (1913-23) 242.

(1333) It might possibly be identified with the KUR *Ú*–⌈*da*⌉–*ni*–*i*^{KI} in *KAV* 92:47, despite the difference in writing. See also Weidner in *AfO* XVI (1952-53) 23. [See addendum, p. 395.]

(1334) Since the text has never been transliterated, I do so here. (1) *88* GIŠ.ŠÀ.KAL.MEŠ EN *1–en* ⌈BAR⌉ (2) *1* GIŠ *ma–šad–du* (3) *paq–du* É ^{d}IGI.DU (4) URU *Ú–da–ni* (5) ŠU^{III} EN–*šu–nu* É.⌈MAŠ⌉ (6) URU *Ú–da–ni* (rev., 7) URU *Ú–da–ni* (8) ITI AB UD *9* KAM (9) MU.SAG.NAM.LUGAL (10) ^{d}AMAR.UTU–EN–NUMUN LUGAL.E (11) LÚ.DUB ^{md}AG–*a–bi–lu–ú–da–ri* (12) LÚ.UŠ *ú–di–e*. "Eighty-eight *šakullu* together with one ... (and) one wagon-pole have been entrusted to the temple of Palil of Udani by Belshunu, the *šangû* of Udani. (Dated at) Udani, the ninth day of Tebetu, accession year of Marduk–bel–zeri, king. The scribe: Nabu–abi–lu–dari, custodian of the vessels." Commentary: (1) for GIŠ.ŠÀ.KAL (=*šak*(*k*)*ullu*) as part of a wheeled vehicle, see A. Salonen, *Landfahrzeuge*, pp. 135, 143; (2) *mašaddu*: *Landfahrzeuge*, pp. 122-123; (5) note the determinatives missing in front of the personal name and the occupation; (12) *rēdī udê*.

(1335) *ADD* 888:2′, which should refer to the predecessor of Marduk–apla–usur. Grayson reads the beginning of this line LÚ.MI[R], possibly to be restored LÚ.UK[U.UŠ] (cf. Dynastic Chronicle v 2′); if the reading is correct, it presumably refers to an office held by Marduk–bel–[zeri] before his accession to the throne.

The last of the three known monarchs is Marduk–apla–usur (king no. 30). [1336] He is mentioned only in the synchronistic kinglist *KAV* 13:3′ and in the Dynastic Chronicle. [1337] According to that chronicle, he came from Chaldea and was the lone king of his dynasty.

There are several texts which possibly pertain to the history of Babylonia in this period, but cannot be linked chronologically with any of the three monarchs just mentioned.

(a) Traces of the name of a Babylonian king occur in the Synchronistic History iv 15 (*CT* XXXIV 41). Since Baba–aha–iddina had already been deported to Assyria in the preceding episode (iv 1-2), these traces should refer to one of his successors on the Babylonian throne.

(b) There is a weight inscribed as belonging to the "palace (*ekal*) of Nabu–shumu–lishir," a member of the Dakkuru tribe. [1338] This formula "Palace of PN" is usually reserved for royal property, [1339] but there is no other indication that Nabu–shumu–lishir was ever king. He bears no royal title in the inscription; [1340] and his name is preceded by a masculine personal determinative, which hardly ever occurs in Babylonian inscriptions of this period before the names of reigning monarchs. [1341]

(c) A seal has survived which bears the name of Marduk–shakin–shumi, who may have been the father of Eriba–Marduk (king no. 31). [1342] This seal depicts "a royal or princely personage, with a long curved staff in his

[1336] *Marduk–apla–uṣur*: "O Marduk, protect the heir." For the history and a discussion of the name type, see Mar–biti–apla–usur, king no. 18 (note 1002 above). The earliest occurrence of this particular name may be in the mid-ninth century, when a prince of this name in Suhi paid tribute to Shalmaneser III (*WO* II/2 [1955] 142 D); the same person or another Marduk–apla–usur was the author of an unpublished letter found at Hama (according to Ingholt, *Rapport préliminaire sur sept campagnes de fouilles à Hama en Syrie*, p. 115; reference courtesy of Prof. Grayson). The name is fairly common in late Neo-Babylonian and Persian times, e.g., *YOS* VII 20:7, *TCL* XII 73:8, etc.

Writing of RN: ^{d}AMAR.UTU–A–ŠE[Š] (*ADD* 888:3′, Dynastic Chronicle), ^{md}ŠID–A–[x] (*KAV* 13:3′).

[1337] *ADD* 888:3′.

[1338] This small barrel-shaped weight made of green basalt was published by W. H. Ward in *JAOS* XIII (1889) lvi-lvii. The inscription reads: (1) $\frac{1}{3}$ GÍN GI.NA (2) É.GAL ^{md}PA–MU–SI.SÁ (3) A ^{m}*Da–kur* (4) LÚ x (x) x x ^{d}AMAR.UTU: "One-third true mina (lit.: one-third, true shekel). Palace of Nabu–shumu–lishir, member of the Dakkuru tribe (lit.: son of Dakkur), . . . Marduk." The signs in line four look like LÚ PA TE PA SI ^{d}AMAR.UTU, though the PA+TE after LÚ might be a single sign. For the idiom $\frac{1}{3}$ GÍN= "one-third mina," see Weissbach, *ZDMG* LXI (1907) 380. Last transliteration of the text: Weissbach, *ibid.*, p. 396, with bibliography of earlier treatments. A photograph of the weight has been published in J. L. Myres, *Handbook of the Cesnola Collection of Antiquities from Cyprus* (New York, 1914), p. 556 no. 4426. (The transliteration offered above has been compared with an impression made from the weight itself, which was kindly furnished to the author by Dr. Vaughn Crawford of the Metropolitan Museum).

[1339] *CAD* E 60.

[1340] In fact, the beginning of line 4 seems to record another title (prefixed by LÚ).

[1341] The convention for writing royal names in this period is discussed on pp. 289-290 below.

[1342] New Babylonian Chronicle, rev. 8. A reconstruction of the family tree of Eriba–Marduk has been given in *Studies Oppenheim*, pp. 28-31.

hand." (1343) On the seal, this Marduk–shakin–shumi states that he is the son of Marduk–zera–uballit (1344) and a member of the tribe of Jakin, (1345) the same tribe to which Eriba–Marduk belonged. (1346).

Both Nabu–shumu–lishir and Marduk–shakin–shumi may well have been minor Chaldean princes in the days of Babylonian weakness between 811 and 770 and may have been among the "kings" of Chaldea who paid tribute to Adad–nirari III. (1347)

Our lack of knowledge about internal affairs in Babylonia during these reigns is matched by a corresponding ignorance regarding the external affairs of the country. During the reign of Adad–nirari III (810-783), there were several contacts between Assyria and Babylonia. A broken passage in the Synchronistic History probably told of a battle between the two countries (1348) and the removal of the Babylonian army and of Babylonian gods to Assyria. (1349) After the account of the battle, the next lines read:

> He returned the deported people to their home (lit.: place). He established for them regular shares of food rations. The people of Assyria and Babylonia (Karduniash) intermingled, and they set up the borders and boundaries together. (1350)

The "he" mentioned in the first two lines is undoubtedly Adad–nirari III, and the "deported people" are presumably dispossessed Babylonians. (1351) The Assyrian king took an interest in the permanent welfare of the repatriates by granting them lasting revenues; and the people of Assyria and Babylonia enjoyed peaceful intercommunication. The propagandistic force of the document may be gathered from the final statement: both sides freely agreed on the stipulated boundaries (hence allowing no legitimate grounds for future border disputes). (1352)

(1343) Published by H. Carnegie (ed.), *Catalogue of the Collection of Antique Gems formed by James, Ninth Earl of Southesk*, II, 82-83 as Qβ39.

(1344) For the reading of the name of Marduk–shakin–shumi's father, see my remarks in *Studies Oppenheim*, p. 28 n. 159.

(1345) *liplippi* (ŠÀ.BAL.BAL) ᵐ*Ia–ki–na* (lines 3-4).

(1346) We know of Eriba–Marduk's membership in the Jakin tribe only indirectly, through the tribal affiliation of his direct descendant Merodach–Baladan II.

(1347) I *R* 35 no. 1:22-23.

(1348) *CT* XXXIV 41 iv 15-18.

(1349) Part of line 18 reads ⌜*um–ma–ni–šú* DINGIR.MEŠ⌝. Since Assyria inevitably wins the battles recorded in the Synchronistic History, there need be no guessing about the victor.

(1350) *CT* XXXIV 41 iv 19-22.

(1351) This can hardly be said with certainty; but, given the orientation of this document, it is unlikely that the text would admit that Assyrians needed repatriating.

(1352) Thus providing the reason for the writing of the document: "historical" propaganda to resolve an argument about boundaries. The anti-Babylonian bias of the document comes out clearly in the concluding phrases: "May (a future prince) extol the praises of Assyria forever. May he spread abroad the treachery of Sumer and Akkad to all the corners (of the earth)." (*CT* XXXIV 41 iv 28-30).

None of Adad–nirari's own inscriptions mentions a battle with Babylonia. But on a slab found at Nimrud he states that "all the kings of Chaldea" became his vassals ([1353]) and that he imposed tribute upon them. ([1354]) The temples in the northern cities of Babylon, Borsippa, and Cutha brought him leftovers from the sacral meals of the gods—a privilege usually accorded only to Babylonian monarchs—and he himself sent sacrifices to be offered there. ([1355]) He may have exercised at least suzerainty over Babylonia.

From the eponym chronicles we learn that Adad–nirari III campaigned for two years against Der, 795-794. ([1356]) The statue of the patron god of Der had been stolen twenty years earlier (813), and it was not returned to the city until 785. ([1357]) Also from the eponym chronicles we learn of Adad–nirari III's campaigns in 790 and 783 against the Itu' tribe, which lived just west of the Tigris, approximately opposite the mouth of the Adhaim river. ([1358])

Some of Adad–nirari's contacts with Babylonia—the submission of the Chaldeans, the presents given to and received from the temples in the cities of northern Babylonia, and the battle (probably) mentioned in the Synchronistic History—cannot be dated exactly. The submission of the Chaldean chieftains might be referred to in the eponym chronicle entry for the year 802: "to the Sea(land)"; ([1359]) but the interpretation of the phrase is uncertain.

In general, Adad–nirari III seems to have had relatively peaceful relations with Babylonia. He not only boasted of his reverence for the shrines of the ancient land, but considerably advanced the cult of the Babylonian god Nabu in his land. ([1360]) The Synchronistic History's account of Adad–nirari's restoration of the (Babylonian) deportees, his settling of food income on them, and the free communication between

([1353]) *ardūtī ēpušū* (I *R* 35 no. 1:22). The mention of kings (MAN.MEŠ–*ni*=*šarrāni*) attests to the plurality of independent tribes in southern Babylonia in these days, as in the days of Shalmaneser III.

([1354]) I *R* 35 no. 1:22-23.

([1355]) I *R* 35 no. 1:23-24. His own offering of sacrifices is based on a textual restoration (of some verb like *aqqi* after *niqê ellūti* in line 24).

([1356]) *RLA* II 429:22-23.

([1357]) AN.GAL *ana Dēri ittalak* (*RLA* II 430:33). The theft of 813 is recounted in the report of the fifth campaign of Shamshi Adad V, *AfO* IX (1933-34) 92 iii 42 ff.

([1358]) *RLA* II 429:27, 430:35. The campaign of 783 could fall in the accession year of Shalmaneser IV.

([1359]) *ana muḫḫi tam–tim* (*RLA* II 429:15). *Tâmtu*(*m*) usually means "sea" and could be interpreted as referring to either the Persian Gulf or the Mediterranean Sea (reached as a result of his campaigns in the west for the three preceding years, 805-803). But *tâmtu*(*m*) can also mean "Sealand" (see *Studies Oppenheim*, p. 12 n. 36); and, since the mention of a body of water as the destination of a campaign would be unique in an eponym chronicle, "Sealand" seems a more probable interpretation.

STT 46 rev. 2′ presents a slight variant: *ina ti–*[*amtim*] (see Gurney, *AnSt* III [1953] 19).

([1360]) Mallowan has summarized the evidence for the rise of the Nabu cult at Calah in *Nimrud and Its Remains*, I, 260-261. The building of a new temple for Nabu at Nineveh also took place during the reign of Adad–nirari III: the foundation was laid in 788 and the temple was dedicated in 787, according to the eponym chronicle C[b]2 (*RLA* II 431:24-25). It has sometimes been surmised, on the basis of the spectacular rise of the cult of Nabu under Adad–nirari III, that the Assyrian king's mother (Sammu–ramat) was a princess of Babylonian origin; but there is no cuneiform evidence for such an assertion.

the people of Babylonia and Assyria shows the Assyrian tradition concerning good relations between the two lands in his reign.

During the reign of Shalmaneser IV (782-773), contacts between Assyria and Babylonia are practically unattested. The eponym chronicle tells only of two campaigns of Shalmaneser against the Itu' tribe, in 782 and 777, just outside the Babylonian sphere of influence. (1361)

Relations between Babylonia and Assyria did not remain quiet during the reign of Ashur–dan III (772-755). Probably about the time of Eriba–Marduk's accession to the throne, (1362) Ashur–dan felt it necessary to launch several campaigns against the general area around northern Babylonia. The occasion for this may have been Eriba–Marduk's greater control over the north of his country; (1363) but Ashur–dan had to go against the city Gannanate on the Diyala in 771, against Marad in 770, against the Itu' in 769, and against Gannanate again in 767. (1364) Between 766 and 745, the year in which Ashur–nirari V died, there were no further Assyrian campaigns against Babylonia according to the eponym chronicles. (1365)

This was a period of local autonomy in Assyrian regions as well as in Babylonia. (1366) From this time dates the Saba'a stele written in the name of Adad–nirari III by Nergal–eresh, who was governor of a wide area along the middle Euphrates around the Habur. (1367) Slightly later is an inscription of Bel–harran–bel–usur, the *nāgir ekalli* official under both Shalmaneser IV and Tiglath–Pileser III, who founded a city and named it after himself: Dur–Bel–harran–bel–usur. (1368) From

(1361) *RLA* II 430:36, 41. As mentioned above, the campaign against them in 783 may have taken place in the accession year of Shalmaneser IV.

(1362) The latest possible date for Eriba–Marduk's accession year, according to the texts presently available, is 770. (See note 1384 below). If Eriba–Marduk ruled for more than nine years or if Nabu–shuma–ishkun ruled for more than thirteen (either or both for a total of two or more years), then the campaigns would easily fall after Eriba–Marduk's accession.

(1363) See pp. 222-223 below.

(1364) Eponym chronicle, *RLA* II 430:47-rev. 3. A new variant for the year 767 is provided by *STT* 46 rev. 41′: *ina* URU *Gán–na–a–na* (see also *AnSt* III [1953] 21).

We find it more convenient to treat Assyria between 810 and 745 as a unit here rather than attempt to split up the various portions of Assyrian-Babylonian relations among the several ill-dated Babylonian reigns of this era.

(1365) There were, however, campaigns against the land of Namri east of the Tigris in 749 and 748 (*RLA* II 430 rev. 22-23). [For possible Babylonian-Urartian contacts at this time, see p. 395].

(1366) Local autonomy in Babylonia in the early and middle eighth century is illustrated by such documents as *JAOS* XIII (1889) lvi-lvii (note the use of *ekal*), *JRAS* 1892 350-368, *BIN* II 31 (and duplicates). In the *JRAS* 1892 and *BIN* II texts, the local officials record that they were repairing temples in their own name and defending the land against marauding tribesmen; each text implies that the reigning king, mentioned only by name, was not performing this duty.

(1367) Unger, *Reliefstele Adadniraris III. aus Saba'a und Semiramis*. Note, however, that the installation of Nergal–eresh as governor over the various lands was accomplished under the at least nominal authority of Adad–nirari III (*AAA* XX [1933] 113-115 no. 105).

(1368) Unger, *Die Stele des Bel–Harran–beli–ussur, ein Denkmal der Zeit Salmanassars IV*. The original stele was inscribed with the name of Shalmaneser IV, over which was later engraved the name of Tiglath–Pileser III. The stele was found in 1894 at Tell Abta west of Mosul (*ibid.*, p. 5).

Til Barsip come the inscriptions of Shamshi–ilu, *turtānu* under Shalmaneser IV, Ashur–dan III, and Ashur–nirari V and eponym official in 780, 770, and 752, who recorded extensive conquests in his own name. (1369) Also probably from about this time dates the inscription of Shamash–resha–usur, who calls himself the "governor of the lands of Suhi and Mari." (1370) This individual, governing a territory on the middle Euphrates which had belonged chiefly to Assyria since the early ninth century, fought campaigns on his own behalf against the marauding Tumanu tribe, (1371) founded a city, (1372) dug canals, (1373) planted date palms, (1374) and boasted of introducing apiculture into his realm. (1375) To top off his assertion of authority, Shamash–resha–usur mentioned no king whatever in his inscription and dated the document in his own thirteenth official year. (1376) As in Babylonia proper under Nabu–shuma–ishkun and Nabonassar, (1377) the local officials in nominally Assyrian areas asserted considerable autonomy, yet did not claim a royal title.

The Synchronistic History, the Assyrian document retailing the history of Babylonian-Assyrian boundary disputes between the early fifteenth and the early eighth centuries, was probably composed at some time during these years. Since Adad–nirari III is the last monarch of Assyria mentioned in it, (1378) the text in its present form could have originated as early as the latter part of his reign. Since the purpose of the document is to bolster Assyrian boundary claims by a lavish appeal to tradition, one is led to suspect that it was written in a period when Assyrian arms were hard pressed to maintain the traditional borders. Thus the text might be dated in either those years when Assyrian campaigns in the southern border region were most frequent (i.e., from 797 to 766) or in the following years when the Assyrians were no longer able to mount campaigns in that area and yet wished to retain at least a verbal claim to the land (i.e., from 765 to 746). Beginning in the time of Tiglath–Pileser III, the Assyrian monarchs generally exerted sufficient

(1369) Thureau-Dangin, *Til–Barsib*, pp. 141-151. No Assyrian king is mentioned in the texts.

(1370) *šakin māt Su–ḫi u Ma–ri*: *WVDOG* IV 10 ii 27, etc. This inscription, published in *WVDOG* IV 9-15 and pls. 2-5, was one of the first two big finds of the German Babylonian expedition and was found in the "Schlossmuseum" of Nebuchadnezzar II on Sept. 14, 1899 (*MDOG* III [1899] 13-15; Unger, *Babylon*, p. 225). Schmidt (*Persepolis*, II 60) suggested a date in the late seventh century; but it seems unlikely that a relatively peaceful and independent thirteen-year reign could be fitted in at that time.

(1371) *WVDOG* IV 10 ii 17-26; the same tribe occurs also in *ABL* 1041 rev. 6. Probably not to be identified with the Tu'muna tribe which appeared in southeastern Babylonia at the time of Sargon II (Lie, *Sargon*, 20, etc.).

(1372) *WVDOG* IV 10 iii 1. The city was called *Gab–ba–ri–ni* (see Ebeling, *RLA* III 129).

(1373) *WVDOG* IV 10 ii 27 ff.

(1374) *Ibid.*, ii 37-39, etc.

(1375) *Ibid.*, iv 13-v 6.

(1376) *Ibid.*, iv 11. On the relief, Shamash–resha–usur wears headgear in the shape of a truncated cone, roughly similar to that worn by Assyrian kings (cf. the picture in Mallowan, *Nimrud and Its Remains*, II, 448-449d and note 1199 above)—as opposed to the Babylonian style.

(1377) See pp. 224-234 below.

(1378) *CT* XXXIV 41 iv 15.

authority to regulate the northern border of Babylonia east of the Tigris more or less as they saw fit.

Before concluding our brief discussion of this relatively unknown period of anarchy, we should mention that much of the governmental stability—however slight—which Babylonia enjoyed during the early eighth century seems to have been provided by Chaldeans. Marduk-apla-usur, king no. 29, according to the testimony of the Dynastic Chronicle, was connected with the "land of Chaldea." (1379) The two kings most responsible for the reviving of Babylonian fortunes at the close of these chaotic years, Eriba-Marduk and Nabu-shuma-ishkun, both hailed from southern tribes. (1380) After northern Babylonia had been decimated by Shamshi-Adad V, it seems that the Chaldean tribes, which had been relatively strong in the days of Marduk-zakir-shumi I in the middle of the ninth century, gained further political power. When the old checks from the northern part of Babylonia had largely disappeared, the Chaldeans were able to dominate all of the realm for the first time. In the future, the Assyrians would often regret that Shamshi-Adad V had so weakened northern Babylonia as to shift the balance of power to Chaldea; for, throughout the days of the mighty Sargonid empire, the Assyrians never succeeded completely in subduing the political aspirations of the south. Sargon, Sennacherib, Esarhaddon, Ashurbanipal—all were forced to carry on extensive military operations there; and none ever emerged complete master. Eventually the south was to win out over even the supposedly invincible Assyrians, when the new Chaldean Dynasty under Nabopolassar played a large part in vanquishing the once vast Assyrian empire.

(1379) *ADD* 888:5′. Note too that Adad-nirari III in his own inscription speaks of "kings" of Chaldea (I *R* 35 no. 1:22) and does not mention any king in northern Babylonia.

(1380) Eriba-Marduk: from the Sealand (*ADD* 888:6′) and probably from the Jakin tribe (note 1382 below); Nabu-shuma-ishkun: from the Dakkuru tribe (*JRAS* 1892 354 i 16′).

(1381) *Erība-Marduk*: "Marduk has provided me with a substitute." For this name type, normally given to a second or later son after an earlier one had died, see Stamm, *Namengebung*, p. 289. Erib(a)-DN begins in the late Old Akkadian period (*MAD* III 229) and continues down to Neo-Babylonian and Persian times (e.g., Ranke, *EBPN*, p. 227; Tallqvist, *NBN*, p. 59). The name Eriba-Marduk is first attested in the Old Babylonian period (I. M. Price, *Old Testament and Semitic Studies in Memory of William Rainey Harper*, I, 393:3), then in the Kassite era (*PBS* II/2 5:12, 130:15, etc.), in the early ninth century (*BBSt* no. 28 rev. 24), in the early eighth century (this king), and throughout Neo-Babylonian and Persian times (e.g., the forty-three individuals listed in Tallqvist, *NBN*, p. 59).

Writing of RN: in contemporary Babylonian inscriptions as *Eri-ba*-dAMAR.UTU (*JRAS* 1856 pl. opp. p. 222 no. 1:2; BM 40548, unpublished); in later Babylonian inscriptions as *Eri-ba*-dAMAR.UTU (*Iraq* XV [1953] 133:13, *VAS* I 37 ii 43, inscriptions of Merodach-Baladan II), m*Eri-ba*-dAMAR.UTU (*VAB* IV 274 iii 17, Nabonidus; New Babylonian Chronicle, rev. 14), SU-dAMAR.UTU (I *R* 5 no. XVII 6, *UVB* I pl. 27 no. 18:6, *VAS* I 37 iii 52, Merodach-Baladan II), m*Eri-ba*-dŠÚ (New Babylonian Chronicle, rev. 8, 15), and only partially preserved as m*Eri-ba*-[ ] (*ADD* 888:6′, Dynastic Chronicle; the masculine personal determinative is erroneously omitted in Johns' copy, but the text has been collated by Ungnad [*AfK* II (1924-25) 26] and by myself) and as [ ]x-dAMAR.UTU (*BBSt* no. 35:16, Merodach-Baladan II); in later Assyrian texts as m*Eri-ba-Mar-duk* (*YOS* I 40:13, Esarhaddon), mSU-*Mar*-[*duk*] (*KAV* 13:4′, synchronistic kinglist).

31. Eriba-Marduk (1381)

This king was the son of a certain Marduk–shakin–shumi (1382) and came from the Jakin tribe in the Sealand, as is explicitly stated by the Dynastic Chronicle (1383) and as is further confirmed by the similar origin of his direct descendant Merodach–Baladan II. The date and length of Eriba–Marduk's reign are unknown; but he ruled for at least nine years, (1384) and his reign presumably terminated shortly before 760 (the latest possible date for the first regnal year of his successor).

Any fame surrounding Eriba–Marduk has survived largely because of the high estimation in which later kings held him. Merodach–Baladan II, a forceful ruler in his own right, was wont proudly to trace his own lineage back to Eriba–Marduk in the following words: (1) "the legitimate (and) primary heir of Eriba–Marduk, king of Babylon, who re–established the foundation of the land"; (1385) (2) member of the "dynasty of Eriba–Marduk"; (1386) (3) "who makes the name of his father who begot him illustrious, offspring of Eriba–Marduk, king of Babylon, who re-established the foundation of the land"; (1387) (4) "[legitimate and] primary [heir], perduring royal seed, [offspring of Eriba]–Marduk, king of justice, who re[-established the foundation of the land]." (1388) From these passages one can infer that Mero-

---

(1382) New Babylonian Chronicle, rev. 8. This chronicle notes both royal and non-royal fathers of other kings, so we cannot tell anything about the paternal rank from the mere fact that a father is mentioned in the document. A seal of a Marduk–shakin–shumi is published in Carnegie (ed.), *Catalogue of the Collection of Antique Gems Formed by James, Ninth Earl of Southesk*, II, 82; in the seal, he gives himself no royal title, but indicates his affiliation with the Jakin tribe (the same tribe to which Merodach–Baladan II belonged and to which, therefore, Eriba–Marduk, the ancestor of Merodach–Baladan, probably belonged). It is likely that this man may have been the father of Eriba–Marduk.

In the Foroughi Collection at Teheran is a bronze situla inscribed with the name of Eriba–Marduk, son of m*Si–bu–ri* (Dossin, *Iranica Antiqua* II [1962] 164 no. 33). Though the remote possibility that the king Eriba–Marduk and Eriba–Marduk son of m*Si–bu–ri* were the same individual (cf. my earlier statement in *JCS* XVI [1962] 99 under 36.2.2) cannot be ruled out, it seems unlikely that the two men should be identified for the following reasons: (a) Eriba–Marduk was a relatively common personal name (see note 1381 above), (b) the two Eriba–Marduks are said to have different fathers, since the name of the king's father was Marduk–shakin–shumi, (c) the PN on the dagger is prefixed with the masculine personal determinative, which never precedes the names of Babylonian kings on Luristan bronze inscriptions and is almost never prefixed to the names of Babylonian kings of this period in contemporary inscriptions (see notes 1871-1872 below), (d) the person whose name is inscribed on the Luristan bronze situla bears no royal title, while other Babylonian kings with names inscribed on Luristan bronzes invariably bear at least one royal title.

(1383) *ADD* 888:6′.

(1384) The legal text, BM 40548, is dated in Babylon in the ninth year of his reign (information courtesy of Prof. Wiseman). Thus the latest possible date for his first regnal year is 769.

(1385) *Iraq* XV (1953) 133:13; the concluding titulary in the quotation belongs to Eriba–Marduk, since Merodach–Baladan was already called "king of Babylon" in the preceding line of the inscription. Such titularies appended to ancestors' names are known also from Assyrian royal inscriptions, e.g., Weidner, *Tn. I*, no. 52 a.

(1386) I *R* 5 no. XVII 6; *UVB* I pl. 27 no. 18:6.

(1387) *VAS* I 37 ii 41-44.

(1388) *BBSt* no. 35:15-16, restored according to Seux, *RA* LIV (1960) 206-208.

dach–Baladan attributed the reorganization of Babylonia after the period of anarchy in the early eighth century to his ancestor Eriba–Marduk. (1389) Whether Eriba–Marduk was his father or grandfather is uncertain from the language of the inscriptions, (1390) but the latter alternative seems chronologically more plausible. (1391)

Other later kings of Babylonia who mentioned Eriba–Marduk in their inscriptions were Esarhaddon and Nabonidus. Esarhaddon referred to Eriba–Marduk's expanding of the Ehilianna, the Nana shrine in the Eanna complex at Uruk, (1392) and Nabonidus to the fact that during the reign of Eriba–Marduk the people of Uruk removed an old statue of Ishtar from the temple and set up one less appropriate in its place. (1393)

Besides having Uruk under his control in the south, Eriba–Marduk was also in firm possession of Babylon and Borsippa in the north by his second year. The statement in the New Babylonian Chronicle that he took the hands of Marduk and Nabu in his second year (1394) would seem to imply that he was not in sufficient possession of these sites at the beginning of his first year to observe the usual installation rites there. But, despite the southern origin of Eriba–Marduk, he cared for the temples of Esagila and Ezida as well as for those in Uruk, though the extent of his repairs beyond the restoration of the throne of Marduk is not known. (1395)

One private legal text, still unpublished, survives from this reign. (1396) Drawn up in Babylon in Eriba–Marduk's ninth year, it is a land-sale document in which

(1389) It is interesting that the only other king of this period glorified with the title *mukīn išdī māti* was the great Nebuchadnezzar I (Hinke Kudurru ii 24), who resurrected Babylonia after the devastating Elamite incursions of the mid-twelfth century. For its use in the later eighth through sixth centuries, see Seux, *Épithètes royales*, pp. 131-132. Before the seventh century, it was used only as a "passive" epithet, in the sense that no king claimed it in his own inscriptions but it was assigned to him by someone else.

(1390) Merodach–Baladan II calls himself *mudammiq zikir abi ālidišu, ilitti Erība–Marduk, šar Bābili, mukīn išid māti* (*VAS* I 37 i 41-44), but it is impossible to tell whether *ilitti* modifies Merodach–Baladan or *abi* on grammatical considerations alone. In either case, it is not uncommon in Mesopotamia to refer to more remote ancestors as "father." See also my comments in *Studies Oppenheim*, p. 9 n. 18.

(1391) See my discussion, *ibid.*, p. 9 n. 15.

(1392) *ša ... Erība–Marduk šar Bābili ukeššû* (*YOS* I 40:12-14=Borger, *Asarhaddon*, 77 § 50). On the location of the Ehilianna, see Borger, *Asarhaddon*, 77 § 49:5; cf. also Ebeling, *RLA* II 302 and R. North, *Orientalia N.S.* XXVI (1957) 226.

(1393) *VAB* IV 274 iii 11-29. The statue of Ishtar in question was set up in a golden shrine and was connected with seven yoked lions (cf. the Neo-Babylonian letter, VAT 7, published by Meissner, in which a picture of the same statue is mentioned: *MVAG* XII [1907] 158:4-7). The people of Uruk changed her cult (*šuluḫḫīšu ušpellū*), removed her shrine (*atmānšu idkû*), and unyoked her team of lions (*ipṭurū ṣimittuš*). The old statue was then removed to a storage place: "she [Ishtar] departed from Eanna in anger and took up her dwelling in a house not her own" (*VAB* IV 274 iii 23-26). A new Ishtar statue, "unsuitable for Eanna" (*la simat Eanna*: *ibid.*, line 27, cf. line 34), was then installed in the Ishtar shrine (*ina simakkišu*, line 29).

Note that it was not Eriba–Marduk himself but local officials who altered the cult. This fits well with what we know of local autonomy in Babylonia during the middle of the eighth century (e.g., *JRAS* 1892 350-368, *YOS* IX 74, etc.).

(1394) New Babylonian Chronicle, rev. 9.

(1395) *Ibid.*, rev. 13.

(1396) BM 40548, to which Prof. Wiseman called my attention and of which he kindly furnished a copy.

members of a clan (*bīt errēši*, "House of the Cultivator") disposed of some of their land. (1397)

Although a tribesman himself, Eriba–Marduk was active in resisting the encroachments of Arameans from the west on the fields of citizens of Babylon and Borsippa. He defeated the Arameans who had gained possession of the land illegally, and he restored the fields and orchards to their rightful owners. (1398) His only extant royal inscription claims for him the simple title "king of Babylon," (1399) and he apparently did his best to live up to the epithet both by internal reconstruction and by defending the land against external aggressors. (1400) After years of anarchy, the land was still in a state of turmoil; (1401) and it seemed as though only a strong ruler of one of the powerful southern tribes would be able to restore a semblance of order to the country. (1402) The Aramean and Chaldean tribes were becoming more settled in Babylonia, adopting Babylonian names (1403) and to some extent observing Babylonian legal procedure. (1404)

(1397) The tablet concludes with the "finger-nail (marks) of the members (of the "House") of the Cultivator in place of their seals" *ṣupur mārē errēši kīma kunukkišunu*, rev. 16′). The land was bordered on its southern and eastern sides by roads (obv. 4, 6), on its western side by more land belonging to the "House of the Cultivator" (obv. 5), and on its northern side by land belonging to Iltihanu, the sheikh (*nasīku*).

(1398) New Babylonian Chronicle, rev. 10-12. Line 10, sometimes read as *ina Šigiltu u Subartu* (e.g., *CCEBK* II 67 "... the Aramaeans who were in Shigiltu and Subartu ..."; cf. Olmstead, *AJSL* XXXVII [1920-21] 223) should rather be interpreted as *ina ši–gil–tú u saḫ!–maš–tú*: "in (times of) lawlessness and destruction" (see already Winckler, *OLZ* X [1907] 590 n. 1). For the last word, compare the spelling of the plural *saḫ–ma–šá–a–ti* in *JRAS* 1892 354 i 16′ in an incident occurring in the time of Eriba–Marduk's successor.

King, *A History of Babylon*, p. 264, suggested that Eriba–Marduk may have owed his election to the throne to his success in driving the Aramean raiders from the fields of Borsippa and Babylon. The chronological arrangement of the chronicle, however, makes it probable that the expulsion of the Arameans took place in the second year of Eriba–Marduk's reign.

(1399) LUGAL DIN.TIR.KI: *JRAS* 1856 pl. opp. p. 222 no. 1:3. The inscription is on a syenite (or green basalt) duck weight, found by Layard in the Northwest Palace at Nimrud in his second series of excavations (Layard, *Discoveries among the Ruins of Nineveh and Babylon* [London: John Murray, 1853], p. 600). The weight is inscribed "30 true minas" and weighs slightly over 40 pounds 4 ounces (Weissbach, *ZDMG* LXI [1907] 395 no. 7). A photograph of this weight appears in *ANEP* as no. 120. It is now in the British Museum as BM 91433.

(1400) His titulary in later inscriptions includes "king of Babylon" (*Iraq* XV [1953] 133:13, *VAS* I 37 ii 44), "king of justice" (*BBSt* no. 35 rev. 16), "re-establisher of the foundation of the land" (*Iraq* XV [1953] 133:13, *VAS* I 37 ii 44, *BBSt* no. 35 rev. ⌜16⌝).

(1401) As exemplified by the tardy accession rites of the king, the local shift of cult at Uruk, the necessity for forcible ejection of the invading Arameans from around Babylon and Borsippa.

(1402) In the eighth century most of the rulers in Babylonia were either southern tribesmen (Marduk–apla–usur, Eriba–Marduk, Nabu–shuma–ishkun, [Nabu]–mukin–zeri, Merodach–Baladan II) or Assyrian-backed Babylonians (Nabonassar, Nabu–nadin–zeri, Bel–ibni).

(1403) E.g., the royal names mentioned in note 1402 (though some of these could be throne names) and such names as *Anu–imbuš*, *Amēl–Išum*, *Kabitu*, *Bēl–eṭir*, *Šaqi–ina–māti*, *Nabû–šarḫi–ilī*, *Eṭiru*, DN–*aḫḫē–erība*, *Sîn–erība* occurring alongside Aramaic names in BM 40548, the unpublished economic text from the ninth year of Eriba–Marduk's reign.

(1404) E.g., in the sale of land in BM 40548. It is interesting to observe in this document that not only the tribe owns land but also the sheikh as an individual (line 3: ᵐ*Il–ti–ḫa–ni* LÚ *na–si–ki*, probably in the genitive).

The Dynastic Chronicle indicates that Eriba–Marduk's successor, Nabu–shuma-ishkun, (1405) was not of the same family, since it refers to him as being from Chaldea rather than from the Sealand and also notes a change of dynasty at this juncture. (1406) No further evidence is available on this question at present. (1407)

32. Nabu-shuma-ishkun (1408)

Though we do not know the immediate antecedents of this ruler, the Dynastic Chronicle indicates that he came from southern Babylonia (Chaldea); (1409) and a private votive inscription informs us that he was originally from the Dakkuru tribe. (1410) He ruled over Babylonia for at least thirteen years, (1411) and his last regnal year was 748. (1412) Consequently, we know that he had begun to rule by at least 760.

The titulary of this monarch is quite ordinary. Contemporary economic texts refer to him variously as LUGAL or as LUGAL E. (1413) A private votive text also calls

(1405) The royal name is not preserved in the text, but the section follows immediately after that dealing with Eriba–Marduk.

(1406) *ADD* 888:6′-9′ (=Dynastic Chronicle vi). Eriba–Marduk is said to be from the Sealand (KUR A.AB.BA, *ADD* 888:6′, 8′); and he is the only king of his dynasty according to this tradition (*1* LUGAL.E BA[LA ...], *ADD* 888:7′). The next dynasty is from *māt Kaldi* (*ADD* 888:9′). It is interesting that both Eriba–Marduk and his (grand)son, Merodach–Baladan II, were considered as kings of the Sealand rather than of Chaldea in the strict sense (for the title of Merodach–Baladan, see *Studies Oppenheim*, p. 12 n. 36 and p. 36 n. 207).

(1407) Assyrian invasions into northern Babylonia which are to be dated about the time of Eriba-Marduk are discussed above on p. 218.

(1408) *Nabû–šuma–iškun*: "Nabu has established posterity." (Literally: "Nabu has set a name.") For the name type, see Stamm, *Namengebung*, pp. 41-42. The name class DN–shuma–ishkun is comparatively rare in Babylonia and begins only about this time; the theophorous element seldom refers to any god other than Nabu. (Contrast the slightly different form DN–shakin–shumi, which has approximately the same significance and yet enjoyed a much greater popularity, relatively speaking; for a discussion of the name type, see note 971 above).

Other individuals bearing this name in the Neo-Babylonian and Persian periods are listed in Tallqvist, *NBN*, pp. 145-146. Does the fact that a son of Merodach–Baladan II bore the same name (see the references collected in *Studies Oppenheim*, p. 47, 44.3.1a) perhaps indicate that Eriba–Marduk, Nabu–shuma–ishkun, and Merodach–Baladan may have belonged to the same family? Though Merodach–Baladan was himself a member of the Jakin tribe, he may have been related by marriage to the chief of the Dakkuru tribe (Nimrud Letter V 13′—it is uncertain which individual is the nephew of Balassu).

Writing of RN: in contemporary Babylonian texts as dPA–MU–GAR (*VAS* I 36 iv 12), dAG–MU–GAR–*un* (*BRM* I 2:7, 3:14), and dAG–MU–*iš–kun* (*JRAS* 1892 354 i 16′); in later texts as dAG–MU–GAR–*un* (Shamash–shuma–ukin Chronicle, 22) and as mdAG–MU–GAR–*u*[*n*(?)] (Kinglist A iv 2) and as mdPA–MU–[x] (*KAV* 13:5′).

(1409) *ADD* 888:9′.

(1410) *JRAS* 1892 354 i 16′.

(1411) *BRM* I 3:14.

(1412) Because the first official regnal year of Nabonassar, his successor, is known to have been 747.

(1413) *BRM* I 2:7, 3:14.

him simply LUGAL, (1414) while a more formal private stone inscription gives him a fuller title, LUGAL DIN.TIR.KI. (1415) These indicate little save that he was accepted as a legitimate ruler in the land.

No building or other activities of this king are yet attested, and the only original documents coming from his reign concern private individuals. There are two brief economic records, a grain receipt dated in the tenth year and a cattle account dated in his thirteenth year; (1416) one of them mentions a city Dur–sha–Ammeja–usur, (1417) which is otherwise unknown. From Borsippa there is a black kudurru-like stone carved with the symbols of various gods, which records the reception of one Nabu–mutakkil into the ranks of the *ērib bīti* officials of Nabu. (1418) The inscription on this stone describes how the gods Nana and Mar–biti chose Nabu–mutakkil, how they installed him as an *ērib bīti* of Nabu, assigned to him certain amounts of temple foodstuffs, and sealed the text with their own seals. (1419) Nabu–mutakkil belonged to the powerful family of Eda–etir, (1420) as did several important witnesses to the text: the governor of Borsippa (likewise an *ērib bīti* of Nabu), (1421) two other *ērib bīti* officials, (1422) and a scribe of Adad. (1423)

The most enlightening document, however, from the reign of Nabu–shuma–ishkun is a badly preserved clay cylinder, likewise from Borsippa, which was inscribed on the occasion of the repair of storerooms in the outer wall of Ezida by Nabu–shuma–imbi, governor of Borsippa and high priest of Nabu. (1424) This text gives the impression that Eriba–Marduk's adjudication of the land disputes around Borsippa had lost effect in his successor's reign. The rich fields near Borsippa were once again the object of bitter fighting; and the local citizens were attempting to stave off men of Babylon, Chaldeans, Arameans, and men of Dilbat from appropriating their land. The city of Borsippa was filled with "disorders, troubles, revolts, and disasters." (1425) The town was embroiled in fighting, even at night; and local

(1414) *JRAS* 1892 354 i 16′.

(1415) *VAS* I 36 iv 13.

(1416) *BRM* I 2-3.

(1417) *BRM* I 3:12.

(1418) *VAS* I 36. The text is dated at Borsippa (iv 11). Where it was found is unknown; it was presented to the Deutsche Orient-Gesellschaft by James Simon (*MDOG* IV [1900] 14-18).

(1419) *VAS* I 36 i 1-ii 15.

(1420) *VAS* I 36 ii 1. For the name *Ēda–eṭir* (always written mAŠ–ŠUR), see Landsberger, *Bischof*, p. 58 n. 110, and Stamm, *Namengebung*, p. 170. The misreading of this name as "Ashur" has led to an exaggerated estimate of the power of the Assyrians in Borsippa at this time (e.g., S. A. Strong, *JRAS* 1892 351; Olmstead, *History of Assyria*, p. 176; Millard, *Iraq* XXVI [1964] 30).

(1421) *VAS* I 36 iii 6-7.

(1422) *Ibid.*, iii 10, 17.

(1423) *Ibid.*, iii 12.

(1424) BM 33428, published by Strong in *JRAS* 1892 350-368. Nabu–shuma–imbi held the titles of *šākin ṭēmi* and *nišakku* (*JRAS* 1892 353 i 10′, etc.). For a similar combination of the chief religious and civil powers of a city in one person, compare Nusku–ibni at Nippur in the reign of Nebuchadnezzar I, who served as both *nišakku* of Enlil and *ḫazannu* of Nippur (Hinke Kudurru iii 10-12).

(1425) *JRAS* 1892 354 i 15′-20′.

officials were incapable of suppressing the trouble. On one nocturnal occasion, enemies battled around the city and temple and may have succeeded in capturing Ẹzida and part of the surrounding city; loyal citizens of Borsippa and their allies were put under siege. (1426) We do not learn how these particular difficulties were resolved since the text is broken here; but, according to the ancient writer, prayer to Nabu may have been one of the factors in arriving at a happy solution. (1427)

What impressions we gain of Babylonia at this time are necessarily confined to Borsippa because of the available documentation. In the fifth and sixth years of Nabu–shuma–ishkun, political affairs around Borsippa were so disrupted that the statue of Nabu could not go forth to take part in the New Year's festival at Babylon. (1428) This may have been the same occasion as the otherwise undated disturbances noted in Nabu–shuma–imbi's cylinder, when disorder was rampant and when the local governor (rather than the central government) felt it incumbent upon himself to quell the disturbances as well as to erect sections of the temple in his own name. (1429) Borsippa would continue to be a trouble spot even in the next reign, when it revolted against Babylon. (1430)

There is no family connection yet attested between Nabu–shuma–ishkun and his successor, Nabonassar.

33. Nabonassar (1431)

The accession of Nabonassar to the throne marked the beginning of a new era in Babylonia. (1432) From this point on, chronologically precise records of his-

(1426) *JRAS* 1892 354-355 ii 1-8. The enemies are probably described as fugitives (from the law); LÚ *ḫa*[*lqūti*] (ii 1). The hypothesis that some of these events may have represented civil war is proposed by Landsberger, *Bischof*, p. 58 n. 110, who interprets a broken passage as implying internal strife between Nabu–shuma–iddina, *šatammu* of Ẹzida, and Nabu–shuma–imbi.

(1427) *JRAS* 1892 355 ii 9-10.

(1428) See the chronicle published by Millard, *Iraq* XXVI (1964) 15:22.

(1429) *JRAS* 1892 350 ff., *passim*.

(1430) *CT* XXXIV 46 i 6-8 (Babylonian Chronicle).

(1431) *Nabû–nāṣir*: "Nabu (is) protector." For the name type, see Stamm, *Namengebung*, p. 219. DN–nasir names begin in the Old Akkadian period (*MAD* III 207) and continue in Babylonia down through Persian times (Ranke, *EBPN*, p. 242; Clay, *CPN*, p. 189; Tallqvist, *NBN*, p. 325); the type is also popular in Assyria from the Old Assyrian period on (Stephens, *PNC*, p. 91; Tallqvist, *APN*, pp. 297-298; *ADD* 203 rev. 1 and *passim*). The name Nabu-nasir itself is attested from the Old Babylonian period on (Ranke, *EBPN*, p. 127; Clay, *CPN*, p. 109; Tallqvist, *NBN*, pp. 140-142), in later Assyria (Tallqvist, *APN*, p. 156), and at Nuzi (Gelb *et al.*, *NPN*, p. 104).

Writing of RN: in contemporary economic texts and in the Babylonian Chronicle as dAG–PAB (*BRM* I 4:15, 5:14, 6:⌈12⌉, 7:5, 8:8, 9:10, 10:8, 11:5, 12:7, 13:4, 14:6, 15:9, 16:7, 17:15, 18:7, 19:⌈15⌉, 20:12, 21:6; *CT* XXXIV 46 i 6, 7, 9, 11, 12), in contemporary private votive texts as dAG–ŠEŠ–*ir* (*BIN* II 31:19, *YOS* IX 74:14′, BM 113205:19, all versions of the same text). In Kinglist A iv 3 the name is written mdAG–⌈PAB⌉, and it is partially preserved in the New Babylonian Chronicle, rev. 16 as [*n*]*a–ṣir*. In Greek the name is written Ναβονασσάρου (gen.) in the "Ptolemaic Canon" (var.: Ναβονασάρου) and Ναβονασάρου in Pseudo-Berossos of Cos (*FGrH* III C/1 p. 395 lines 31-35; var.: Βανασάρου [gen.]).

(1432) A new era from our point of view, not from that of the contemporary Babylonians. There is no evidence that a "Nabonassar Era" was in use in contemporary Babylonia (Kugler, *SSB* II 362-366),

torical events were kept systematically. The Babylonian Chronicle and the "Ptolemaic Canon" both commence their accounts with the beginning of this reign in 747. A Hellenistic tradition explained the dawn of the new historical epoch as follows:

> From the time of Nabonassar, the Chaldeans accurately recorded the times of the motion of the stars. The polymaths among the Greeks learned from the Chaldeans that—as Alexander (Polyhistor) and Berossus, men versed in Chaldean antiquities, say—Nabonassar gathered together (the accounts of) the deeds of the kings before him and did away with them so that the reckoning of the Chaldean kings would begin with him. (1433)

The commencing of more accurate astronomical observations and records in this reign fits in well with what we know of the period, (1434) though the story of the destruction of earlier documents seems contrived. (1435) From our point of view, a more likely explanation for the survival of historical documentation from this time on would be the greater stability of the country achieved under this king and the consequent likelihood of more systematic keeping of records and of their greater chance for survival. The Hellenistic tale presumably represents an attempt to explain why the ages before Nabonassar loomed so dark for later historians. (1436)

---

though later ages would often begin their reckoning with this time because of the abundant astronomical observations available. According to the later Ptolemaic reckoning, the era began at midday on February 26, 747 B.C. (Ptolemy, *Syntaxis Mathematica*, ed. Heiberg, I, 257:6-7, 325:20-22, 462:2-5, II, 293:25-294:1, 315:14-15, 357:19-20, 391:16-17, 425:5-6=K. Manitius, *Ptolemäus*: *Handbuch der Astronomie* [corrected edition by O. Neugebauer; Leipzig: Teubner, 1963], I, 185:2-3, 236:1-3, 338:21-22, II, 155:9-11, 171:2-3, 203:8-9, 227:13-14, 251:7-8).

(1433) *FGrH* III C/1 p. 395 no. 16 ([Pseudo]-Berossos of Cos).

(1434) The eighteen-year cycle texts (*ZA* VII [1892] 197-204, VIII [1893] 106-113) may be calculated to have begun their first eighteen-year cycle in 747, the first year of Nabonassar's reign. The astronomical observations available to Ptolemy also began at this time (*Syntaxis Mathematica*, ed. Heiberg, I, 254:8-13= Manitius, *Ptolemäus*: *Handbuch der Astronomie* [rev. ed., 1963], I, 183:3-8; see Neugebauer, *The Exact Sciences in Antiquity*, 2nd ed., p. 98). *LBAT* 1413 is a report of lunar eclipses which could be dated to about this time (748-746 B.C.). Kugler (*SSB* II 368-371) suggested that a possible reason why the Babylonians may have been motivated to begin keeping astronomical records now was the spectacular conjunction of the moon and the planets in the first regnal year of Nabonassar (747 B.C.).

We also note greater precision in synchronisms between Babylonia, Assyria, and Elam as listed in the Babylonian Chronicle. Kugler (*SSB* II 362-363) thought that the Babylonian Chronicle chose for its starting point the rise of Assyria to world power in 745 (rather than any native "Nabonassar Era"); but he failed to take into consideration that events before 745 are recorded in the variant A.H. 83-1-18, 1338 i 1' (*CT* XXXIV 44), before which several lines are damaged beyond restoration. But Kugler rightly stressed the beginning of more accurate astronomical observation in this period (*SSB* II 366-371).

(1435) It is difficult to hypothesize a reaction of Nabonassar against the records of his Chaldean predecessors, when we are uncertain of Nabonassar's own origin.

(1436) For the historical unlikelihood of the Hellenistic tradition, see already Weidner, *MVAG* XX/4 (1915) 105 and the literature cited there.

Weissbach, *Pauly-Wissowa*, XVI 1490 sub voce Ναβονάσσαρος, attempted to explain the tradition in a different way. He interpreted the verb ἠφάνισεν, usually translated as "destroyed" or "did away with," as meaning "concealed" and explained that Polyhistor meant that Nabonassar preserved only the names of his royal predecessors but not their deeds (which he did not consider worthy of mention). This interpretation is supported by the Armenian version of Eusebius' chronicle (*FGrH* III C/1 p. 374:13-18).

Nabonassar inherited from his predecessor, Nabu–shuma–ishkun, ([1437]) a kingdom torn by internal and external strife and little under the control of the central government. By virtue of a timely understanding with his Assyrian contemporary, Tiglath–Pileser III, who came to the throne in Assyria in Nabonassar's third year (745), Nabonassar was able to achieve relative stability in Babylonia for almost a decade and a half and to hand on his kingdom intact to his son. Though the central government in his time could hardly be considered strong, the land was more peaceful than it had been for many years.

The opening years of Nabonassar's reign were not auspicious. The Aramean and Chaldean tribes, which between them now hemmed in northern Babylonia on almost every side, were probably causing severe trouble to the more settled population of the region. ([1438]) Soon after his accession early in 745, Tiglath–Pileser, who had gained his throne as the result of a revolution in Assyria, ([1439]) undertook the restoration of order to his southern neighbor. ([1440]) For an Assyrian who nurtured grandiose ambitions in Syria and in Urartu, the first condition for tactically safe movement in those spheres was the securing of the frontiers to his south and east. Doubtless too, keeping the trade routes open was an important factor in Tiglath–Pileser's interest in the south, since the Arameans and Chaldeans controlled territory through which many of the key routes passed: through the Diyala from Iran, along the lower and middle Euphrates, and along the Tigris towards the head of the Persian Gulf. Accordingly, Tiglath–Pileser's first two campaigns, dating to his accession year (745) and to his first year (744), were directed against Babylonia and Namri. ([1441])

([1437]) No family relationship is attested between the two kings; Nabonassar's antecedents are as yet completely unknown.

([1438]) It is possible that political disorders within Babylonia had already disrupted the celebration of the New Year's festival in at least one of the first three years of Nabonassar's reign. Cf. the restoration of A.H. 83-1-18, 1338 i 1′ suggested by Landsberger and Bauer (*ZA* XXXVII [1927] 63 n. 2): [^{d}*Bēl*] *lā uṣ*[*â*], though *ul* is the more expected rendering of the negative here. The traces do indeed favor a reading [^{d}E]N NU ⌈È⌉.

It should be noted that there is no direct evidence for any Chaldean-Babylonian or Aramean-Babylonian conflict during this reign.

([1439]) Eponym list: *RLA* II 430 rev. 25-26.

([1440]) A. Anspacher, *Tiglath Pileser III*, p. 20, stated that Tiglath–Pileser legitimized his usurpation of the Assyrian throne by winning the acceptance of the principal priesthoods in Babylonia.

([1441]) *RLA* II 430 rev. 26-29. The campaign against Babylonia is described tersely as *ana birīt nāri ittalak*; the meaning of the phrase *birīt nāri* has been discussed at length by Finkelstein in *JNES* XXI (1962) 73-92.

The texts of Tiglath–Pileser III are here cited according to the edition of Rost, *Die Keilschrifttexte Tiglath–Pilesers III* (1893). Annals: Rost, *TP III*, pls. I-XXIII (=*ARAB* I 762-779). Nimrud Slab no. 1: Rost, *TP III*, pls. XXXII-XXXIII (=*ARAB* I 781-785). Nimrud Slab no. 2: Rost, *TP III*, pls. XXIX-XXXI (=*ARAB* I 808-814). Nimrud Tablet no. 1: Rost, *TP III*, pls. XXXV-XXXVIII (=*ARAB* I 787-804; cited here chiefly as II *R* 67). Nimrud Tablet no. 2: Rost, *TP III*, pl. XXXIV (=*ARAB* I 805-807; cited here chiefly as D.T. 3). Texts published since Rost's edition will be cited by their individual publications.

In his campaign which began in Tashrit 745, (1442) Tiglath–Pileser did not come to subjugate Babylonia to the Assyrian yoke; and there is no record of hostilities with the Babylonian administration. Rather, he came chiefly to aid the Babylonian king, who was unable to keep order in his own land, in repressing the Aramean and Chaldean tribesmen. (1443) The Assyrian campaign attacked many areas in northern, southern, and eastern Babylonia. Tiglath–Pileser claimed to have gained mastery over Aramean tribes over a wide area, ranging from the cities of Dur–Kurigalzu, Sippar (of Shamash), and Pazitu (of the Dunanu tribe) in the north to Nippur in central Babylonia and extending along the Tigris and Surappi rivers in the east as far as the place where the Uknu (Kerkha) reached the swamps at the head of the Persian Gulf. (1444) The Aramean tribes brought under control were the Itu', Rubu', Puqudu, Ru'a, and Li'tau (Litamu), (1445) plus the cities of Hamranu and

(1442) Attempting to isolate sources pertaining to the first campaign of Tiglath–Pileser is difficult, especially in the absence of any good edition of Tiglath–Pileser's annals. The arrangement of the annals fragments set forth by Rost is far from certain; and there is no guarantee that plate I (lines 1-7) in Rost's edition refers to the campaign of 745. (Prof. Tadmor has kindly informed me now by letter [July 1967] that plate I should be placed at the end of the annals rather than the beginning). Plate XII (lines 20-31) obviously alludes to some events in 745, because activities occurring in "my second year of reign" (i.e., 744) begin in line 26. It is possible that plate XI, because it alludes to the building and settling of Kar–Ashur (lines 8-11), which took place in or shortly after 745 (Nimrud Slab no. 1:6-7), refers to a time relatively early in the reign of Tiglath–Pileser.

The Assyrian source most pertinent to our reconstruction of the events of 745 is Nimrud Slab no. 1. This inscription, whose composition has often been dated in 734 or later (e.g., Rost, *TP III*, p. III; Luckenbill, *ARAB* I 780), should actually be dated in 743 or shortly thereafter (as seen already by Olmstead, *Assyrian Historiography*, p. 34). This slab tells only of the campaigns of 745 (lines 4-16), 744 (lines 17-20), and 743 (lines 20-36), as may be seen by comparing the destinations of these campaigns (Babylonia, the Namri–Habban area, and Urartu) with the entries for 745-743 in the eponym chronicle (*RLA* II 430 rev. 28-31). This is the only Assyrian source which can definitely be established as narrating the military campaign of 745 in Babylonia without also mixing in events from the 731-729 Babylonian campaigns (the Nimrud tablets and Nimrud Slab no. 2 describe Tiglath–Pileser's Babylonian campaigns geographically, without making chronological distinctions).

The Babylonian Chronicle i 1-5 (*CT* XXXIV 46) also tells of the events of 745.

Thus, our principal sources for Tiglath–Pileser's Babylonian campaign of 745 will be Nimrud Slab no. 1 and the Babylonian Chronicle. Parallels from the annals (Rost, *TP III*, pl. XI) will be shown in note 1457 below, but will not be used in the text because of the chronological uncertainty of their reference.

(1443) Anspacher, *Tiglath–Pileser III*, p. 19, suggested that Nabonassar invited the help of Tiglath–Pileser against the Arameans and Chaldeans. Though there is no direct proof for such a contention, it fits well with the later pattern of events.

The possibility has been raised that Arameans of southern Babylonia aligned themselves with Arameans of Syria against Assyria around this time. This is based on a proposed identification of KTK (mentioned in contemporary Aramaic treaties) with Kissik in southern Babylonia (Donner-Röllig, *Kanaanäische und aramäische Inschriften*, II, 273, with earlier bibliography). This possibility is strengthened by the fact that Babylonian gods such as Marduk, Sarpanitum, Nabu, and Nergal are invoked in a treaty between Barga'ja of KTK and Matiʿel (Donner-Röllig, *op. cit.*, no. 222 A 8-9). Difficulties with this position have been summarized by J. A. Fitzmyer, *The Aramaic Inscriptions of Sefîre* (1967), pp. 131-132.

(1444) Nimrud Slab Inscription no. 1:4-6. The last part of the phrase reads literally "all the Arameans of the bank(s) of the Tigris and Surappi as far as the Uknu of the shore of the lower sea." For the location and spelling of the Surappi, see notes 1731 and 1729 below.

(1445) Nimrud Slab Inscription no. 1:5, 12.

Rabbilu in Aramean territory. (1446) Some of these Arameans were deported and possibly resettled in the newly constructed city of Kar–Ashur. (1447) Tiglath–Pileser was able to boast: "I made the Arameans, as many as there were, submit at my feet; and I assumed kingship over their kings." (1448) The Chaldean tribe of Bit-Shilani was also vanquished: Sarrabanu, its capital, (1449) was destroyed and Nabu-ushabshi, its "king," was impaled. (1450) The rest of the ruling family of Bit-Shilani and much property was carried off. (1451) The tribe of Bit–Amukani was also attacked, and some of its people and goods was brought away to Assyria. (1452) Tribute was levied by Tiglath–Pileser upon the sheikhs of Chaldea. (1453) At this time, too, the gods of the city of Shapazzu were deported to Assyria; (1454) and in Hursagkalamma near Kish (1455) Tiglath–Pileser had sacrifices offered to the principal Babylonian

(1446) Babylonian Chronicle i 4. These names occur as Aramean tribes in II *R* 67:5 (Nimrud Tablet no. 1). The location of these cities is uncertain. On the basis of the occurrence of Hamranu among the cities taken on one of Sennacherib's Elamite campaigns (*AfO* XX [1963] 90:28, *OIP* II 40:69, etc.), Grayson has suggested that the city be located somewhere east of the Tigris on the Diyala along the route followed by Sennacherib to Elam. Elsewhere it is mentioned that the Hamranu tribe, noted plunderers of Babylonian caravans, fled to Sippar to escape the armies of Sargon (Lie, *Sargon*, 379-381, written LÚ *Ḫa–mar–a–na–a+a*); and it is possible that a branch of the tribe operated west of the Tigris as well.

M. Dietrich in *WO* IV/1 (1967) 77 attempts to connect the Hamuru (K. 1172:2, etc.) with the people of Hamranu; this is very unlikely since the *–ānu* ending in the latter name was an essential part of the form and Hamranu (*OIP* II 40:69, etc.) and Hamuru (*Camb.* 394:4) were different cities.

(1447) Nimrud Slab Inscription no. 1:13 (referring to the Puqudu, Ru'a, and Li'tau). Were some of the Itu' and Rubu' among the conquered peoples sent to Kar–Ashur (*ibid.*, 7)?

Olmstead (*AJSL* XXXVII [1920-21] 225-226 and *History of Assyria*, pp. 176-177) attempted to place Tiglath–Pileser's newly founded cities of Kar–Ashur and Dur–Tukulti–apil–Esharra near Babylonia, but there is little evidence for the location of these cities. Unger in *RLA* II 253-254 suggested that Dur–Tukulti–apil–Esharra might be identified with Arslan Tash; but see Thureau–Dangin *et al.*, *Arslan–Tash* (Texte), p. 7.

(1448) Nimrud Slab Inscription no. 1:13-14. The last part of the phrase should be read *šarrūt šarrīšunu aṣbat* (the LUGAL and MEŠ have become transposed in the text).

(1449) Note, however, that in Sennacherib's first campaign Sarrabanu is listed as belonging to Bit–Amukani (*OIP* II 53:42), while a similar-sounding Sarrabatu belongs to Bit–Sa'alli. Sarrabanu is also mentioned in the eponym chronicle Cb6 rev. for the year 704(?): *RLA* II 435.

(1450) Nimrud Slab Inscription no. 1:8-10. Since this text was written late in 743 or shortly thereafter (i.e., before Tiglath–Pileser's fourth campaign was completed), there can be no question of dating the defeat of Nabu–ushabshi and the capture of Sarrabanu to the period 731-729, as have Anspacher (*Tiglath Pileser III*, p. 66), Olmstead (*AJSL* XXXVII [1920-21] 227), and Labat (*Die altorientalischen Reiche* III [=*Fischer Weltgeschichte* IV] 55).

(1451) Nimrud Slab Inscription no. 1:10-11.

(1452) *Ibid.*, 11-12.

(1453) *Ibid.*, 14-15. *Ra'sāni* ("headmen") has sometimes been translated as the proper name of a tribe; its meaning is discussed in note 1705 below.

(1454) Babylonian Chronicle i 5, where the name of the city is written as URU *Šá–pa–az–za* (var.: *–zu*). The gods of Shapazzu are also mentioned in Wiseman, *Chronicles*, 52 rev. 19 (referring to the year 625). It occurs also in the later Babylonian family name (*mār*) LÚ *šangû* URU *Šá–pa–za* (*UET* IV 56:14; *VAS* VI 248:15, the following line in the same text may contain a gentilic referring to the same GN: URU *Šá–pa–zu–ú–a*).

(1455) Hursagkalamma was the name of the eastern section of Kish (perhaps reckoned as a separate city in this period); see the tablets and bricks found there which are discussed by Langdon, *Excavations at Kish*, III, 17-20.

and Assyrian gods. (1456) According to this account of Tiglath–Pileser's deeds, he must have affected a wide area of Babylonia at this time. (1457)

We have no explicit statement from either the Babylonian or the Assyrian side concerning Tiglath–Pileser's relations with Nabonassar. It seems that the Assyrian king did not visit Babylon itself at this time, (1458) nor did he attempt to depose the Babylonian king. Yet, if we can believe the official Assyrian accounts of his campaign of 745, Tiglath–Pileser must have travelled through much territory that nominally belonged to Nabonassar. Furthermore, the Assyrian king claimed to have become master of the land of Karduniash and of all the Arameans who lived along the Tigris and Surappi rivers as far south as the Uknu and the Persian Gulf; (1459) and, shortly after his first campaign, he adopted the title "King of Sumer and Akkad," (1460) implying some claim to suzerainty over Babylonia. What such suzerainty actually involved is uncertain, since it is clear that Nippur, mentioned as

(1456) Labat's statement in *Die altorientalischen Reiche* III (=*Fischer Weltgeschichte* IV) 51 that Tiglath–Pileser at this time visited all the great shrines from Sippar to Uruk is based on II *R* 67:11-12, a narrative which combines the events of 745 and 731-729 in topical rather than chronological order; it is more likely that Tiglath–Pileser's homage to these shrines should be dated to the later time, since it is mentioned only in the later text.

(1457) Later editions of Tiglath–Pileser's inscriptions, i.e., K. 3751 (=II *R* 67; Rost, *TP III*, pls. XXXV-XXXVIII) and D.T. 3 (=Rost, *TP III*, pl. XXXIV), which combine the king's earlier (745) and later (731-729) campaigns against southern Babylonia, offer additional details which may pertain to the earlier campaign. Nabu–ushabshi was defeated outside his city (K. 3751:15), Sarrabanu fell only after an earthen ramp was built up to its walls (K. 3751:16), fifty-five thousand people and various gods were deported from the region (K. 3751:16-17). The cities of Tarbasu and Jaballu may also have been captured at this time and their people, property, and gods carried off (K. 3751:18, D.T. 3:13-14); and some cities east of the Tigris—Lahiru, Hilimmu, Pillutu—may likewise have been taken in 745 rather than later (K. 3751: 13-14). If the text in pl. XI of Rost's edition of the annals were eventually to be assigned here as referring to 745 [the correctness of this attribution has been kindly confirmed for me now (July 1967) by Prof. Tadmor in a letter], further details of the campaign would become known (contact with the Nakri, Tane, Adile[?] tribes and with the land of Budu and the city of Pahhaz). The section of the annals (pl. I), which Rost interpreted as its earliest preserved portion, does not agree well with what we know of the 745 campaign (since no religious contact with Babylon, Borsippa, or Cutha is mentioned in Nimrud Slab no. 1, but only relations with Hursagkalamma [see now also note 1442 above]).

Barnett in *The Sculptures of TP III*, pp. xvi-xvii, identifies and interprets Assyrian reliefs which he believes portray some of the events of this first campaign of Tiglath–Pileser III. (The reliefs themselves appear *ibid.*, pls. I-XII). The reliefs depict Assyrian officials and soldiers (pls. I-XII), siege engines (pls. III-IV), the siege of Babylonian cities (pls. X-XII), prisoners and cattle being tallied and led away (pls. III-VI), and statues of gods being carried away into captivity (pl. VII); plates III-VI are published as a composite in *ANEP* no. 367. Barnett's suggestion (pp. xvi-xvii) that the gods being led off include Marduk and Nabu from Babylon is unlikely, since there is no mention of Assyrian dealings with Babylon or Borsippa at this time. In fact, the only gods mentioned in the texts as being carried off now are the gods of the city of Shapazzu (note 1454); and it is probable, if the relief does refer to events of 745, that the gods pictured are from Shapazzu or from some other minor city—not the famous statue of Marduk from Babylon.

(1458) Anspacher in *Tiglath Pileser III*, p. 23, is wrong in claiming that the Assyrians took cities like Babylon, Borsippa, and Uruk in this campaign. Nimrud Tablet no. 1 (K. 3751=II *R* 67) draws a composite picture of the campaigns of 745 and 731 and cannot be used to pinpoint incidents confined to the campaign of 745.

(1459) Nimrud Slab Inscription no. 1:5-6, 13-14.

(1460) Nimrud Slab Inscription no. 1:1 (written in or shortly after 743).

terminus of one of his thrusts into Babylonia, continued under at least nominal Babylonian administration. ([1461])

Before his next long campaign in Babylonia, which began in 731, Tiglath-Pileser seems to have fought several times in outlying regions which had been nominally Babylonian early in the preceding century. In 744, in his campaign against Namri, he subdued the old Kassite tribal area of Bit-Hamban. ([1462]) Sometime around 738 ([1463]) the Assyrians deported 600 captives from the city Amlatu of the Aramean tribe of Damunu and 5400 captives from Der ([1464]) and settled them in cities in Syria (*Unqi*). ([1465]) In an undated encounter, which Rost also placed around this time, Assyrian armies crossed the Lower Zab and fought against Ahlamu and Arameans. ([1466]) In 737, Tiglath-Pileser once more marched against areas east of the Tigris, including the land of the Medes and also the land of Tupliash. ([1467]) In another undated section of the annals, assigned by Rost to approximately this time, the towns of Silhazi and Niqqu, ([1468]) formerly part of northeastern Babylonia, were taken by the Assyrians. ([1469])

([1461]) A transaction referring to Nippur in late 745 is dated early in 744 under Nabonassar (*BRM* I 6:3, 11-12). Nippur, however, was to prove clearly on the Assyrian side in the subsequent Mukin-zeri troubles (see note 1517 below).

([1462]) Nimrud Slab Inscription no. 1:17, *RLA* II 430 rev. 29; cf. Annals, 49. Bit-Hamban is the Bit-Habban of earlier periods, e.g., *BBSt* no. 6 ii 50. In the description of an occurrence dated by Rost to the same campaign, *mār Bābili* (DUMU KÁ.DINGIR.R[A.(KI)]) is mentioned in broken context (Annals, 57 = Rost, *TP III*, pl. XXIVB); but the placing of this fragment of the annals is still open to question.

([1463]) These events, according to the most likely arrangement of the annals, would occur in the campaign immediately preceding the ninth *palû* (=737). That plate XV (lines 142-152) in Rost should go just before plate XVI (lines 153-164) seems reasonably certain because plates IV (lines 148-154) and V (lines 149-155) overlap the juncture between those two plates (lines 152-153) and show the overall continuity of the section. Since line 157 on plate XVI begins the narrative of the ninth *palû*, the events in lines 142-156 should presumably be dated to the eighth *palû* (=738).

([1464]) Written URU BÀD (Rost, *TP III*, pl. XV 3) and [URU/LÚ] *Di-ra-a+a* (*ibid.*, pl. III 2).

([1465]) Annals, 143-145.

([1466]) Annals, 134-140 (pl. XXI). This poorly preserved section of the annals cannot definitely be dated, nor can one say with certainty that the deportations to Syria (*Ḫatti*) and the imposing of Assyrian provincial administration refer to the Ahlamu and Arameans.

([1467]) Annals, 157-158.

([1468]) The spelling of this town as Niqqu is assured by the writing URU *Ni-iq-qu* in *BOR* I (1886-87) 76:6 and elsewhere. The location of Niqqu has been discussed by Albright, *JAOS* XLV (1925) 215-217, S. I. Feigin, *JAOS* LIX (1939) 107-108, and Weidner, *AfO* XVI (1952-53) 14-15.

([1469]) Annals, 175-176 (pl. XVII). The town of Til-Ashuri (line 176, here called a country), which had a temple of Marduk, was either taken at this time or earlier; it too is called a "fortress of the Babylonians" (Nimrud Slab no. 2:24), as was Silhazi. The city of Niqqu of Tupliash had been brought under Assyrian control already in 744 (Nimrud Slab no. 1:17-18) and had presumably become free in the meantime. The date to be assigned to the conquests of Til-Ashuri and Niqqu is not yet certain. Annals, 178-179, may also refer to Niqqu (the context is broken so the reference is dubious); if so, Tiglath-Pileser resettled part of the Diyala region at this time (see Adams, *Land behind Baghdad*, p. 175 n. 2).

Barnett in his *The Sculptures of TP III*, p. xviii, suggests that some reliefs of Tiglath-Pileser III from Nimrud (pls. XXXI-XXXIV) refer to a second Babylonian campaign (after 745); if so, it is more likely that they deal with events taking place in 731 or later, since this is the earliest certain evidence for an attack on Babylonia proper (i.e., the date-palm country of the reliefs) after 745.

We know little about the activities of Nabonassar himself. (1470) The Babylonian Chronicle informs us that he waged a fight against Borsippa after that city had revolted; but no account of the battle was preserved for the later chronicler. (1471) Although we hear of no Aramean disturbances during Nabonassar's reign after Tiglath–Pileser III's campaign in 745, we know that Uruk in the south was not very firmly under his control. There two local officials, after castigating the king and other administrators for neglecting the repair of an *akītu* temple, restored the edifice in their own name. They acknowledged the nominal sovereignty of the king by dating the document in his fifth year, but showed little respect for or allegiance to the central government. (1472)

More economic texts have survived from Nabonassar's reign than from any other reign in the period between Kashtiliash IV and Shamash–shuma–ukin. A collection of eighteen documents explicitly dated to Nabonassar's tenure in office, ranging from the twenty-third of Siman in his first year to the seventeenth of Tebet in his fourteenth (and last) year, has been published by A. T. Clay. (1473) Clay stated that these texts were supposed to have been found at a single site; (1474) but their exact provenience is unknown and their contents are such that it cannot definitely be settled whether or not they come from the same site. The majority of the texts are short: eighty percent are less than fifteen lines long. They are administrative in character, chiefly records of supplies coming in or out. (1475) The geographical names occurring in the texts are few (1476) and do not shed much light on the extent of the realm governed by Nabonassar. Some Aramean names are mentioned in the documents, e.g., ^{m}*Ba–ru–qa–a'*; (1477) but this is only to be expected when we consider the number of tribesmen supposedly residing in and around Babylonia who were objects of Tiglath–Pileser's campaigns. (1478) A fragmen-

(1470) No royal inscriptions of his have survived.

(1471) "In the time of Nabonassar, Borsippa fought with Babylon. The battle which Nabonassar waged against Borsippa is not recorded": Babylonian Chronicle i 6-8. Borsippa had also during the preceding reign been the scene of civil disturbances.

King, *A History of Babylon*, p. 268, refers to a revolt of Sippar in the time of Nabonassar. Since no revolt of Sippar is mentioned in the texts currently available, "Sippar" is presumably a slip of the pen for "Borsippa."

(1472) *YOS* IX 74; duplicates: *BIN* II 31 and BM 113205 (unpublished). Traces of this building have not yet been unearthed at Warka, though a *bīt akītu* probably to be dated to the Seleucid period has been excavated there (*UVB* XIII 35-42 and pl. 7; see also the remarks by North, *Orientalia N.S.* XXVI [1957] 245).

(1473) *BRM* I 4-21.

(1474) *BRM* I, p. 9.

(1475) The texts deal with sheep ("sheep of the king" [*BRM* I 6], sheep shearing [4], wool of several kinds [5, 7], including wool belonging to the goddess Nana [21]), other cattle (19), dates (11, 14), millet (13), barley (8, 9, 15, 20), oil (16), and are records of various types (goods dispensed, goods received, sales, etc.).

(1476) Babylon (*BRM* I 15:7), Uruk (19:4, 9), Nippur (6:3).

(1477) *BRM* I 12:4. These names are discussed on p. 272 below.

(1478) The percentage of Aramean names in the texts may run as high as forty percent, though many of the names are imperfectly preserved or difficult to classify. This might indicate that the tablets came from a peripheral area, possibly somewhere in the south or east.

tary legal text dated in Babylon in the second year of Nabonassar also survives. (1479)

Nabonassar was a contemporary of Ashur–nirari V and Tiglath–Pileser III in Assyria and of Ummanigash and his predecessor in Elam. The Babylonian Chronicle records the simple fact that in the fifth year of Nabonassar (743) Ummanigash came to the throne in Elam, (1480) where he was to reign until 717. (1481)

In summary, Nabonassar's reign in Babylonia was overshadowed by the more powerful figure of Tiglath–Pileser III. The Assyrian king campaigned extensively in regions under nominal Babylonian control and, with his assumption of the title of "King of Sumer and Akkad," claimed some form of suzerainty over Babylonia. Borsippa, long a center of disturbances under Nabonassar's predecessor, revolted from Babylon in the time of Nabonassar. Officials in Uruk, though acknowledging nominal allegiance to the Babylonian king, complained that he neglected his royal functions there; and so they repaired the *akītu* temple in their own names. Nabonassar's weak reign, under the partial peace ensured by Assyria, lasted until its fourteenth year, when Nabonassar died in his palace following an illness. (1482) He was succeeded by his son, Nabu–nadin–zeri. (1483)

34. Nabu-nadin-zeri (1484)

This little-known king, whose name is abbreviated as Nadinu or Nadin in the Babylonian Chronicle, (1485) succeeded his father, Nabonassar. In the second year of his reign, he was deposed in the midst of a revolt led by Nabu–shuma–ukin, one

(1479) BM 38114, kindly called to my attention by Prof. Wiseman. Too much is missing from the text for one to make any statement about its contents other than it is a legal document (with witnesses and with finger-nail marks in lieu of seals) and that the item which changed hands was worth 24 shekels of silver.

(1480) Babylonian Chronicle i 9-10.

(1481) *Ibid.*, i 38.

(1482) *Ibid.*, i 11.

(1483) Saggs, *Iraq* XVII (1955) 44, says that upon the death of Nabonassar in 734 a revolt broke out in Babylonia. The revolt in question actually began two years later at the time of the death of Nabu–nadin–zeri, the son of Nabonassar.

(1484) *Nabû–nādin–zēri*: "Nabu (is) the giver of offspring." For the name type, see Stamm, *Namengebung*, p. 217. The class DN–nadin–zeri is comparatively rare and apparently begins only in the Neo-Babylonian period (Tallqvist, *NBN*, p. 324). Other than the king, references to persons with the same name are few: *YOS* VII 198:8; *YOS* III 3:3, 57:2; *ADD* 892:6.

Writing of RN: m[dA]G–MU–NUMUN (Kinglist A iv 4), (m)*Na–di–nu* (*CT* XXXIV 46 i 13, 14, Babylonian Chronicle), *Na–din* (*ibid.*, i 15), Ναδίου (gen.; "Ptolemaic Canon"; var.: Νάβιος [nom.]).

(1485) Babylonian Chronicle i 13, 14, 15. Nadinu is a common abbreviation for longer proper names in the Neo-Babylonian period (Tallqvist, *NBN*, pp. 156-157). The variant Νάβιος (for *Νάδιος) in Synkellos is discussed in note 301 above.

of his provincial officials, who succeeded him on the throne. (1486) We have as yet no contemporary documents from his reign.

35. Nabu-shuma-ukin II (1487)

Nabu–shuma–ukin, whose complete name is known only from Kinglist A, (1488) was a provincial official (*bēl pīḫati*) under Nabu–nadin–zeri and led the successful rebellion which killed the king. (1489) His victory was short-lived, however; for, after slightly over one month on the throne, (1490) he was replaced by Mukin–zeri, chief of the southern Amukanu tribe. (1491)

36. (Nabu)-mukin-zeri (1492)

Chief of the Amukanu tribe in southern Babylonia, Mukin–zeri took advantage of the instability in Babylonia which attended the revolt against Nabu–nadin–zeri. He deposed the leader of the rebellion, Nabu–shuma–ukin II, and assumed the throne

(1486) Babylonian Chronicle i 14. MU 2 *Nādinu ina sīḫi dīk*(GAZ). Since *dīk* (from *dâku*) can be translated either "was killed" or "was defeated" (*CAD* D 35-43), the precise fate of Nabu–nadin–zeri is uncertain. In the context, since no military encounter is being described, "killed" would be the more probable translation; but this is too slight a premise on which to base any conclusions.

(1487) For a discussion of the royal name, see note 1105 above. Writing of RN: m[dA]G–MU–DU (Kinglist A iv 5), mMU–GI.NA (*CT* XXXIV 46 i 16, Babylonian Chronicle), [m]⌈MU⌉–DU (*ibid.*, i 17).

(1488) Kinglist A iv 5.

(1489) Kinglist A refers to Nabu–shuma–ukin II as the son of his predecessor. This is doubtful since it would certainly have likewise been recorded by the Babylonian Chronicle, which is usually careful to note the family relationships between the various kings (*CT* XXXIV 46-50 i 13, 40; ii 29, 32; iii 38; iv 13, 33). Kinglist A is not always accurate in its dynastic designations, especially towards the end of the list (see note 120 above).

(1490) Babylonian Chronicle i 16-18. The exact length of the king's reign—given variously as 1 month and 2 days or 1 month and 13 days—is discussed in note 304 above.

(1491) Babylonian Chronicle i 18. It is interesting to note that Mukin–zeri had a son whose name was likewise abbreviated as Shuma–ukin (Nimrud Letter LXV 10).

(1492) *Nabû–mukīn–zēri*: "Nabu gives legitimate offspring" (literally: "Nabu [is] the establisher of seed"). For the name type, see Stamm, *Namengebung*, p. 219. I have been unable to find any trace of the type DN–mukin–zeri before the Neo-Babylonian period, but it becomes fairly common then (Tallqvist, *NBN*, p. 319). With the exception of the person noted in note 1497 below, the king here seems to be the first person attested bearing the name Nabu–mukin–zeri; but there are numerous later private individuals with the same name (Tallqvist, *NBN*, p. 136).

Writing of RN: mDU–NUMUN (Kinglist A iv 7; *CT* XXXIV 46 i 18, Babylonian Chronicle; D.T. 3:16 [=Rost, *TP III*, pl. XXXIV]; II *R* 67:23; Nimrud Letters I 33, II obv. 6′, 13′, rev. 5′, 6′, 8′, 11′, III A 7′, 12′, IV B ⌈4′⌉, V 3′, ⌈15′⌉, VI A 12′, VII A 8′, LXV 9; the determinative is omitted in *CT* XXXIV 47 i 19, 21, 22, Babylonian Chronicle, where the name occurs in the middle of a line), dAG–DU–NUMUN (*BRM* I 22: 13), Χινζῆρος (genitive, "Ptolemaic Canon," sometimes wrongly emended to Χίνζιρος; var.: Χϊήρεος in Cod. Paris., see E. Schrader in *Sitzungsberichte der Königlich Preussischen Akademie der Wissenschaften zu Berlin*, Jahrgang 1887, p. 606).

himself a little more than a month after the assassination of Nabu–nadin–zeri. According to later Babylonian tradition, his reign in Babylonia lasted for three years. (1493)

We know little about Mukin–zeri before his accession to royal power. Kinglist A designates him as a member of the dynasty of Shapi, (1494) a variant spelling for the name of his capital city, Shapija. (1495) Tiglath–Pileser's royal inscriptions call him a member of the Amukanu tribe, (1496) but we otherwise know nothing of his descent. (1497)

Tiglath–Pileser was besieging Damascus in 732 when the revolts against Nabu–nadin–zeri and Nabu–shuma–ukin broke out; and the Assyrian king was unable to march into Babylonia until the next year, 731, the first full year of the reign of Mukin–zeri. (1498) A detailed chronology of Tiglath–Pileser's campaign against Mukin–zeri cannot be reconstructed with any degree of certainty, since the Assyrian royal inscriptions dealing with events in Babylonia during the years 731-729 narrate them in geographical rather than chronological order. The only chronologically arranged texts with pertinent information are the Babylonian Chronicle and the eponym chronicle C^b1. The eponym chronicle says that Tiglath–Pileser went against Shapija in 731, but then stayed in the land of Assyria during 730. (1499) The Babylonian Chronicle records another campaign to Babylonia in 729, in which Mukin–zeri was defeated and his tribal area of Bit–Amukani devastated. (1500) As a result, Tiglath–Pileser was able to become king of Babylonia formally at the end of that year. (1501)

(1493) Kinglist A iv 7; Babylonian Chronicle i 19-22. For a Babylonian report on lunar eclipses pertinent to the year 731/0 B.C., see *LBAT* 1414.

(1494) BALA *Šá–pi–i* (Kinglist A iv 7). All credit is due to Prof. Grayson for reviving the correct reading of the dynasty *Šapî* in Kinglist A. In a letter of June 19, 1962, Grayson proposed to me a reading of *Šá–pi–ja* (based on a photograph of the text), but said that this reading should be regarded as tentative pending a collation by W. G. Lambert (it was this tentative reading that I cited in *JCS* XVI [1962] 101). Lambert's collation subsequently proved that the reading should be *Šá–pi–i*, as Grayson informed me in a letter of April 13, 1963; and I noted the correction in *Studies Oppenheim*, p. 11 n. 28. This reading had been totally lost sight of since its proposal by Rost in *MVAG* II/2 (1897) 27 and n. 3 and its acceptance by Streck in *MVAG* XI/3 (1906) 19.

(1495) For the spellings of this name (*Šapīja, Šapî, Sapīja, Sapê*) and its possible identification as a hypocoristic for *Šapî–Bēl*, see my remarks in *Studies Oppenheim*, p. 11 n. 28, and also Streck, *MVAG* XI/3 (1906) 19-20. Shapi–Bel seems to have been on an island according to *AS* V 70 vi 24 (*ša qereb nārē nadât šubassu*).

(1496) E.g., II *R* 67:23.

(1497) It is not impossible that he might be identified with the high official who was chief witness to a private votive inscription dated in Uruk in 743 in the reign of Nabonassar: *BIN* II 31:20 (= *YOS* IX 74:15 and BM 113205:20). This man, who bears the title GÌR.NITÁ UG.UD.KI (the GN is not as yet interpreted), is described as the son of Nabu–apkal–ili. This official occupied an important position in the south only twelve years before Mukin–zeri seized the throne and could eventually prove to be the same man.

(1498) *RLA* II 431 rev. 42-43.

(1499) *Ibid.*, rev. 43-44.

(1500) Babylonian Chronicle i 19-21.

(1501) *RLA* II 431 rev. 45. For the chronology of Tiglath–Pileser's accession, see note 1547 below.

Some of our uncertainty about political affairs in Babylonia at this juncture may be attributed to our almost total ignorance of Babylonian politics even before the revolt of Nabu–shuma–ukin II. Judged in the light of Tiglath–Pileser's vaunted control over the Arameans and Chaldeans won in **745** (1502) and his subsequent assumption of the title "king of Sumer and Akkad," (1503) one would surmise that some of the tribal areas in Babylonia owed at least nominal allegiance to him. This conclusion is bolstered by an accusation made by Tiglath–Pileser against Zakiru, chief of the Sha'allu tribe, namely that he had violated his oaths of fealty to Assyria, (1504) and by the assurance given by the Litamu tribe to Tiglath–Pileser before his later campaigns into Babylonia that they were remaining loyal subjects of the king. (1505)

Actually there seem to have been conflicting loyalties throughout Babylonia at this time. Representatives of the citizens of Babylon were willing to listen in public to oral arguments presented in behalf of the Assyrian king, while an official of Mukin–zeri stood by. (1506) The upshot of this conversation was that the Babylonians would submit to the Assyrian king if he came in person, but they did not believe he would come. (1507) An Assyrian camp had been set up at Kar–Nergal near Cutha, (1508) and reports on conditions in Babylonia were being sent from this camp to the Assyrian king. (1509) There is some evidence that Aramean tribes like the Itu' (1510) and Ru'a (1511) may have been working for Assyria. Even in the south the Chaldean chiefs did not present a solid front, and letters of intrigue passed back and forth. (1512) After considerable disillusionment, (1513) Balassu, chief of the Dakkuru tribe, (1514) gave aid to the Assyrians; (1515) and, after the defeat of Mukin–zeri, Balassu also paid tribute. (1516) Cities like Nippur (1517) and Dilbat (1518) were on the Assyrian side; and Mukin–zeri attempted to persuade the people of Babylon to wreak reprisals on the people of Dilbat by cutting down their date palms. (1519) Mukin–

(1502) Nimrud Slab Inscription no. 1:5-6, 13-15 (excluding mention of Arameans along the Euphrates).
(1503) *Ibid.*, no. 1:1.
(1504) II *R* 67:19.
(1505) Nimrud Letter I 39-40.
(1506) Nimrud Letter I 5-38.
(1507) Nimrud Letter I 26-30.
(1508) For the location of Kar–Nergal, see Saggs, *Iraq* XVIII (1956) 51.
(1509) E.g., Nimrud Letters I, VIII, LXXVI.
(1510) Nimrud Letters II ⌈7'⌉, III A ⌈9'⌉, VIII ⌈6⌉. None of these references is certain; but there are other clear allusions to the Itu' in the Nimrud Letters (XII 19, XX 30, etc.).
(1511) Nimrud Letter VIII ⌜12⌝ in broken context.
(1512) Nimrud Letter V.
(1513) *Ibid.*
(1514) II *R* 67:26.
(1515) Nimrud Letter XI rev. 4'-5'.
(1516) II *R* 67:26.
(1517) Nimrud Letters II rev. 16', X 6.
(1518) Nimrud Letters II and LXXXIII (probably to be dated to this time).
(1519) Nimrud Letter II rev. 11'-13'.

zeri himself sallied forth to destroy fortifications in southern Babylonia (1520) and to steal cattle. (1521) Moreover, fear of Mukin–zeri sometimes kept areas sympathetic to Assyria from giving active aid to the Assyrians (1522) and prevented more Babylonians and tribesmen from taking advantage of the liberal amnesty terms offered by Tiglath–Pileser. (1523)

While it is impossible to establish the chronology of the gradual triumph of Assyria between 731 and 729, the results of the campaigns are clear. Tiglath–Pileser emerged as king of northern Babylonia (1524) and as nominal sovereign over most of the south. (1525) He had broken the power of Mukin–zeri, (1526) confined him to his capital city of Shapija, (1527) burnt the surrounding villages, and cut down the date palms around the city. (1528) Though Mukin–zeri remained at large and Shapija may have remained independent, (1529) the Chaldean's jurisdiction was decided-

(1520) *Ibid.*, rev. 6′-7′ (interpretation not altogether certain).

(1521) *Ibid.*, rev. 9′-10′. The phrase *ša Mukīn–zēri iḫtabtuni* ("which Mukin–zeri plundered") is a syntactic unit, with the verb in the subjunctive. The interpretation of the end of line 9′ is uncertain; one would not expect objects stolen to be *followed* by a number.

(1522) *Ibid.*, obv. 4′-28′.

(1523) Nimrud Letters II rev. 3′-5′ (interpretation not entirely certain because of broken context), LXVI.

(1524) *RLA* II 431 rev. 45; Babylonian Chronicle i 23. It is noteworthy that in the date formulae of economic texts coming from Babylonia during his reign his name is either followed by no title (*TCL* XII 1:19, 2:8, 3:18) or by the grandiose but noncommittal "king of the four quarters" (BM 78156:1 [Akk.], 35 [Sum.]; BM 40717:1 [Akk.] and possibly to be restored in rev. 4′). He calls himself "king of Babylonia" only in his Assyrian inscriptions (Nimrud Slab Inscription no. 2:2, D.T. 3:1).

(1525) In the sense that the Aramean tribes there were supposedly subject to him and that chieftains of the Dakkuru and Jakin tribes and of Larak paid him tribute. In Nimrud Tablet no. 1 (II *R* 67:3), one of the boundaries of Tiglath–Pileser's domains is said to be "the Bitter Sea of Bit–Jakin."

(1526) "He conquered Mukin–zeri" (Babylonian Chronicle i 21). "I (Tiglath–Pileser) inflicted a great defeat on him in front of his city gate" (II *R* 67:23). That this defeat was not inflicted by Tiglath–Pileser in person is now shown by Nimrud Letter LXV, in which Ashur–shallimanni reports the defeat of Mukin–zeri *ina libbi abullāte* (obv. 7) to the king.

(1527) II *R* 67:23.

(1528) II *R* 67:24-25.

(1529) Some historians, e.g., Anspacher (*Tiglath Pileser III*, p. 68), King (*A History of Babylon*, p. 268), and Labat (*Die altorientalischen Reiche* III [=*Fischer Weltgeschichte* IV] 55), have assumed that Tiglath–Pileser captured Mukin–zeri. But Tiglath–Pileser nowhere makes such a claim, which he surely would have done had the wily Chaldean fallen into his hands. Furthermore, there is a text dated under Mukin–zeri in the year 728, the year after Tiglath–Pileser's forces had supposedly vanquished him (see note 1530 below).

There is no direct textual evidence for the fall of Shapija. In fact, since the capture of Shapija is mentioned neither in the inscriptions of Tiglath–Pileser III nor in the Babylonian Chronicle, it may be assumed that it did not fall at this time. A tantalizing reference to the (imminent) fall of an unnamed, but probably important Babylonian city is contained in Nimrud Letter LXV, a battle report to the Assyrian king from Ashur–shallimanni, the governor of Arrapha, who was in command of some of the Assyrian forces fighting in Babylonia:

> "We have engaged within the city gates. We are winning a victory. Mukin–zeri is defeated; Shuma–ukin, his son, is defeated. The city is taken."

Saggs (*Iraq* XXV [1963] 70) suggests that the city involved was Babylon, but there is no evidence that the Chaldeans or their supporters offered active military resistance there. One suspects that the city in-

ly restricted: one economic text survives from the third month of his fourth year, (1530) and this is his last notice in history. The tribe of Bit–Sha'alli suffered more severely from the campaigning of Tiglath–Pileser. Its capital, Dur–Illataju, (1531) was taken after a siege and levelled to the earth; (1532) Zakiru, its chieftain, was treated as a rebel and taken in chains to Assyria. (1533) His family, his people, his gods, and considerable property were also taken away. (1534) The city of Amlilatu was likewise captured and its people and property carried off. (1535) Balassu, (1536) chief of the Dakkuru, and Nadinu of Larak, which was a vassal city of Mukin–zeri, (1537) submitted without a struggle to the Assyrians and paid a tribute of gold, silver, and precious stones. (1538) Merodach–Baladan, chief of the Jakin tribe and king of the Sealand, was overcome by "the reverential fear of (the god) Ashur" and brought "tribute" to Tiglath Pileser while the latter was besieging Shapija. (1539) The "tribute" was splendid—gold ore as well as jewelry made of gold, precious stones, beams of wood, plants with medicinal properties, (1540) aromatics, and cattle—and shows the wealth of the southern chieftains at this time. It is difficult to tell from the Assyrian account alone whether these lavish gifts were really tribute, i.e., a token of Merodach–Baladan's submission to Assyrian might, or whether they were part of an exchange of presents between the Assyrian king and the king of the Sealand. (1541)

---

volved in Nimrud Letter LXV may be Shapija, especially since Tiglath–Pileser elsewhere mentions the decisive action in the war as taking place "in front of his (Mukin–zeri's) city gate" (II *R* 67:23).

Tiglath–Pileser, however, did gain sufficient control of Bit–Amukani to deport people from there (Assur Ostracon: Donner-Röllig, *Kanaanäische und aramäische Inschriften*, no. 233 i 15).

(1530) *BRM* I 22. No geographical name is mentioned in the text, but the document has the earliest known cuneiform inscription with Aramaic notation added; for the approximate dating, see R. A. Bowman, *JNES* VII (1948) 73-74. But it is an isolated phenomenon—the only Aramaic writing in Babylonia before the sixth century—and possibly subject to doubt (see p. 284 below).

BRM I 23, dated in the ninth month of "the fourth year, in which there was no king in the land" may date from 728 and reflect the uncertainty of the south concerning who was king; for another possibility for the date of this text, see note 1328 above. A similar confusion regarding this time is reflected in the "Ptolemaic Canon," which assigned a combined reign of five years to Χινζῆρος καὶ Πώρου.

(1531) Written URU.BÀD–dKASKAL.KUR–*a*+*a* (Nimrud Slab Inscription no. 2:14).

(1532) II *R* 67:21. For possible reliefs of siege(s) undertaken at this time, see note 1469 above.

(1533) II *R* 67:19-20.

(1534) II *R* 67:21.

(1535) II *R* 67:22. The same city is written URU *Ma–li–la–tu* in D.T. 3:13 (Rost, *TP III*, pl. XXXIV).

(1536) Olmstead (*AJSL* XXXVII [1920-21] 228) has suggested that Balassu became famous in Hellenistic tradition as Belesys, the Chaldean priest who aided the Median Arbaces in overthrowing the first Assyrian empire (Ctesias apud Diodorus Siculus, ii 24, cited in *FGrH* III C/1 pp. 443-445).

(1537) Larak was part of Bit–Amukani (*OIP* II 53:42); for a possible identification of the site as Tell al–Wilaya, see *Sumer* XV (1959) 51. Though Nadinu held only a minor position in southern Babylonia, he is presumably mentioned here to show that at least one of Mukin–zeri's subordinates had defected.

(1538) II *R* 67:26.

(1539) II *R* 67:27-28; cf. D.T. 3:19.

(1540) The *amīlānu* and *ašqulālu* plants. Merodach–Baladan's traditional interest in plants is also reflected in the text published in *CT* XIV 50 (see *Studies Oppenheim*, p. 37).

(1541) Olmstead (*AJSL* XXXVII [1920-21] 228) made a similar suggestion. Certainly, throughout the later career of Merodach–Baladan (*Studies Oppenheim*, pp. 12-27), there is no evidence that the Chaldean

Merodach–Baladan was to replace Mukin–zeri as the principal political figure in Chaldea.

In eastern Babylonia, Tiglath–Pileser between 731 and 729 subdued the Aramean tribe of the Puqudu and put it together with the cities of Lahiru, Hilimmu, and Pillutu under the jurisdiction of the Assyrian governor of Arrapha. [1542] The Assyrian king also had people from Labdudu, likewise an Aramean center, deported to Assyria. [1543].

37. Tiglath-Pileser III (Pulu) [1544]

Tiglath–Pileser III climaxed his career as empire-builder by becoming the first Assyrian king in almost five centuries to assume the crown of Babylo-

---

prince ever submitted to Assyrian rule. On the other hand, Sargon II claimed that Merodach–Baladan had been a vassal of Assyria, had violated his oath of fealty, and withheld his tribute (*adê māmīt ilāni rabûti ēbukma ikla tāmartuš*: Lie, *Sargon*, 264-265). For the conflict between the Babylonian and Assyrian traditions regarding Merodach–Baladan, see *Studies Oppenheim*, pp. 13-18.

(1542) II *R* 67:13-14.

(1543) II *R* 67:14-15. For the connection of the Arameans with Labdudu, see note 1726 below.

(1544) *Tukultī–apil–Ešarra*: "My trust is (in) the son of Esharra" (i.e., in the god Ashur). This name is attested to date only for Assyrian kings, beginning with Tiglath–Pileser I (1115-1077) and ending with Tiglath–Pileser III (744-727). Tiglath–Pileser was this king's official name both in Assyria and Babylonia. Pulu was a shorter, less formal name which was later used in non-Assyrian texts to designate Tiglath–Pileser; it was not the king's throne name in Babylonia (see pp. 61-62 above).

Pūlu: meaning and origin of the name are unknown. We read the first sign as *pu* rather than *bu* because the Hebrew and Greek translations of the name employ the unvoiced consonant. Because the same name is attested in Assyria for private citizens (*ABL* 951:5, 975:2; *ADD* 281 rev. 8, 642 rev. 17, and possibly 350 rev. 13), it has sometimes been supposed that Tiglath–Pileser was a commoner and bore this name before his spectacular rise to power. Since his royal pedigree is attested in only one of his royal inscriptions (*KAH* I 21:2), one may with some justification have doubts about its veracity; but, contrary to *Studies Oppenheim*, p. 12 n. 39, this need not necessarily be taken as an indication that the king was a usurper: Sennacherib, whose legitimacy was unquestioned, never cited his ancestry (probably because of Sargon's ill-fated demise). The name is transcribed with the first syllable long because the names of the Assyrian private citizens are usually written *Pu–ú–lu*, etc. The identification of Tiglath–Pileser and Pulu was discussed on pp. 61-62 above.

Writing of RN:

(a) as Tukulti–apil–Esharra (cuneiform): in his own Assyrian inscriptions regularly as ^{m}(GIŠ).TUKUL–*ti*–A–É.ŠÁR.RA (*passim*, with minor variants); in the inscription of Bel–harran–bel–usur, as ^{m}TUKUL–*ti*–A–É.ŠÁR (line ⸢9⸣); in the SDAS kinglist as [^{m}GI]Š.TUKUL–*ti*–A–É.ŠÁR.RA (iv 24); in the eponym lists as TUKUL–*ti*–IBILA–É.ŠÁR.RA (C^{b}1, *RLA* II 430), GIŠKIM–A–É.ŠÁR.RA (C^{a}5, C^{c}, *RLA* II 424-425); in the Babylonian Chronicle as TUKUL–*ti*–IBILA–É.ŠÁR.RA (*CT* XXXIV 47 i 19, 24, 25; in i 23 with masculine personal determinative prefixed, because RN begins the line of text, and with *ina* mistakenly inserted in the name before É.ŠÁR.RA; –A– for –IBILA– in *CT* XXXIV 44 i 9′); in contemporary Babylonian economic texts as TUKUL–*ti*–IBILA–É.ŠÁR.RA (*TCL* XII 2:8, 3:18), TUKUL–*ti*–A–É.ŠÁR.RA (BM 78156:1, 38; BM 40717:⸢1⸣, rev. 3′), TUKUL–*tu*–A–É.ŠÁR!(IM).RA (*TCL* XII 1:19); in the New Babylonian Chronicle, rev. 18, traces of [É.ŠÁR].⸢RA⸣;

(b) as Pulu (cuneiform): ^{m}*Pu–lu* (Kinglist A iv 8);

(c) as Tiglath–Pileser (Aramaic, Hebrew, Greek): Aramaic תכלתפלסר (Assur Ostracon [=Donner-Röllig, *Kanaanäische und aramäische Inschriften*, no. 233], line 15; תגלתפלסר (Donner-Röllig, *op. cit.*, no. 215:13, 15,

nia; (1545) and this assumption of the dual monarchy was to set a precedent for many of his successors over the next century.

Tiglath–Pileser had made himself master of Western Asia by his own ability. Claiming to be a member of a cadet branch of the royal house, he had succeeded to the throne in Assyria after a revolution which capped half a century of political atrophy in that land. Having made himself king by means outside the ordinary channels for succession, he proceeded to devise extraordinary plans to make Assyria great. By extensive campaigning and by thorough reorganization of the provincial structure of Assyria to include the conquered territories, he laid the foundations for the vast Neo-Assyrian empire which would reach its apogee only in the course of the seventh century. The ancient cultural center of Babylon, of course, could not be humbled to the status of a province; so Tiglath–Pileser made the decision to rule as king of Babylonia as well as king of Assyria, thus allowing the older civilization a nominal independence under the rule of his person. (1546)

When the Chaldean tribal chieftains failed to support Mukin–zeri in his bid to retain the kingship of Babylonia, the royal power had passed easily to Tiglath–Pileser. The Assyrian took the hands of Marduk in the annual New Year's festival (1547) and was solemnly inaugurated as king in Babylon. He claimed sovereignty

---

16), and תגלתפליסר (Donner-Röllig, *op. cit.*, no. 216:3, 6; no. 217:[1]-2); Hebrew תגלת פל(א)סר (II Kings 15:29, 16:7, 16:10), תלגת פלנ(א)סר (I Chronicles 5:6, 5:26; II Chronicles 28:20, some variants have the same form as in II Kings); Θαγλαθφελλασαρ (IV Kings 15:29, 16:7, 16:10; with many variants Θαλγαθφελλασαρ, αλγαθφ–, Θαλγαλφασαρ, αγλαθφαλλ–, Θεγλαθφαλσαρ); Θαγλαθφαλνασαρ (I Paralipomenon 5:6, 5:26, variants include Θαλγαβανασαρ and Θαγναφαμασαρ); Θαγλαθφελλασαρ (II Paralipomenon 28:20; variants include Θαλγαφελλαδαρ and Θαγλαθφαλνασαρ); Θαγλαθφαλλάσαρ (Josephus, *Antiquities of the Jews*, IX xi and xii [-ασάρην, acc.]; vars.: Θελλαφαλασσάρ, Θαγλαφαλασάρ, Θαιγλαφαλασάρ, Θεγλαφαράσσαρ, Θαιγλαφαρασαρ, Lat.: Theglaphaassar); (d) as Pul, etc. (Hebrew, Greek); פול (I Chronicles 5:26; II Kings 15:19); Φουλ (IV Kings 15:19); Φαλωχ (I Paralipomenon 5:26, var.: Φαλως); Πώρου (gen.: "Ptolemaic Canon"; var.: Πόρου); Phulos (Berossos in *FGrH* III C/1 p. 385:2-3); Φούλου (gen.; Josephus, *Antiquities of the Jews*, IX xi; vars.: Φούλλου, Φίλου, Lat.: Phoiulus).

(1545) Tukulti–Ninurta I had earlier claimed the titles of "king of Babylon(ia)" and "king of Sumer and Akkad," but had not been recognized as king in the native Babylonian tradition; for references, see my note in *JNES* XXIV (1965) 161 n. 1. Shamshi–Adad V had claimed suzerainty under the title "king of Sumer and Akkad" (note 1323 above). Tiglath–Pileser III, however, was accepted as king in the full native tradition and was listed in Kinglist A, the Babylonian Chronicle, and the later "Ptolemaic Canon."

(1546) Olmstead has speculated on the reasons underlying Tiglath–Pileser's assumption of the Babylonian throne in *The American Political Science Review* XII (1918) 73-75.

(1547) *RLA* II 431 rev. 45. The eponym chronicles (C^b1 and C^b3) date the two years in which Tiglath–Pileser took the hands of Bel to the years 729 and 728. Tiglath–Pileser, however, according to the Babylonian chronological tradition, ruled over Babylonia during the years 728 and 727. This apparent contradiction is resolved when we remember that the New Year's festival in Babylon, which took place in early Nisan, was regarded as the culminating event of the old year. This is certainly true in Sargon's narrative regarding the New Year's festival in 709 (Lie, *Sargon*, 56:384-58:15), which is included in the account at the end of the *palû* of 710; the explanation in *Studies Oppenheim*, p. 20 n. 104, on the basis of the *limmu* office changing hands only in Ajaru is now obviated. Compare too the account in the later Babylonian chronicle concerning the New Year's festival in 604 (Wiseman, *Chronicles*, p. 68:14), which is included in events at the end of Nebuchadnezzar's accession year (see also *ibid.*, p. 27).

over the whole of Babylonia (1548) and had sacrifices offered in the major religious centers of the realm: Sippar, Nippur, Babylon, Borsippa, Cutha, Kish, Dilbat, and Uruk. (1549) He likewise claimed to have conquered all the Aramean tribes settled along the Euphrates, Tigris, and Surappi (1550) rivers as far as the region where the Uknu river (modern Kerkha) flows into the southern swamps; (1551) and in his inscriptions he enumerated thirty-six of these Aramean tribes by name. (1552) How fleeting the Assyrian power over these tribes was is shown by the fact that both Sargon and Sennacherib had to reconquer many of them at a later date. (1553)

We know practically nothing about Tiglath–Pileser's activities as king of Babylonia. That he was duly accepted as monarch there by at least part of the population is shown by three Babylonian economic texts of unknown provenience dated in his first year (1554) and by two texts pertaining to a case of property exchange dated at Babylon in his second year. (1555) The three documents from his first year, though mentioning no geographical names, stem from the same archive and record amounts of beer given or received by various persons. (1556) The two legal texts from his second year record briefly the settling of a lawsuit involving inheritance (as historical background) and the trade of real estate in Babylon and the city of *Šamanê*. (1557) In the texts of his first year, Tiglath–Pileser's name is followed by no title; in those of his second year, he is called simply "king of the four quarters." (1558)

Tiglath–Pileser did not enjoy the dual monarchy long; for, in Tebet of his second year of reign in Akkad, he died and left his empire in the hands of his son, Shalmaneser V. It is noteworthy, however, that up to the end of his reign he was still intent on expanding his empire, since, even after the reducing of Babylonia, an offi-

(1548) Adding "king of Babylonia" to his titulary (Nimrud Slab Inscription no. 2:2, D.T. 3:1).

(1549) II *R* 67:11-12, cf. Nimrud Slab Inscription no. 2:15-16 (only Marduk and Babylon mentioned).

(1550) The location of the Surappi in southeastern Babylonia is discussed in note 1731 below.

(1551) Nimrud Slab Inscription no. 2:7-8; II *R* 67:9. The Nimrud Slab Inscription no. 2 says "all the Arameans of the banks of the Tigris, Euphrates, and Surappi, (and) Uknu up to the Lower Sea (=Persian Gulf) in the east", while Nimrud Tablet no. 1 (=II *R* 67) says "all the Arameans of the banks of the Tigris, Euphrates, and Surappi up to the Uknu of the shore of the Lower Sea." This would seem to indicate that the swamps at the mouth of the Uknu were sometimes considered as an extension of the Lower Sea. That the region was swampy even in those days is confirmed by Lie, *Sargon*, 281.

(1552) See pp. 269-272 below. The cities of Dur–Kurigalzu and Adidu(?) are also mentioned, along with the fortresses of Sarragiti, Labbanat, and Kar-Bel–matati.

(1553) See note 1797 below.

(1554) *TCL* XII 1-3.

(1555) BM 78156, BM 40717; the texts appear to be duplicates.

(1556) Because of the phrase *ana šatê ša* SAL ŠÀ É.GAL (*TCL* XII 2:3, 3:13-14), these texts probably concern the provisioning of palace personnel at Babylon.

(1557) Written URU *šá–ma–ni–e*.

(1558) For references see note 1524 above. Bar–rakib of Sam'al in an Aramaic inscription on an orthostat likewise refers to Tiglath–Pileser, his suzerain, as "king of the four quarters" (Donner-Röllig, *Kanaanäische und aramäische Inschriften*, no. 217:2).

cial campaign was organized in the very last year of his reign against a region whose name has not been preserved in the eponym chronicles. (1559)

38. Shalmaneser V (Ululaju) (1560)

Shalmaneser V inherited the dual monarchy of Assyria and Babylonia from his illustrious father, Tiglath–Pileser III, and held it for five years. (1561) The Babylonian Kinglist A adds the designation "dynasty of BAL.TIL" after his name, referring to his connection with the city of Assur. (1562)

We have no cuneiform record of Shalmaneser's activity in Babylonia save for a lawsuit initiated in Der in his third year. (1563) In fact, because of the almost complete lack of royal inscriptions of this ruler in Assyria, (1564) we know very little

(1559) *RLA* II 432: eponym canon Cb3 under 727: *a–na* [ ]. It need not be assumed that the king led the campaign in person, and it is also possible that it took place after Shalmaneser's accession.

(1560) *Šulmānu–ašarēd*: "Shulmanu is pre-eminent." For the name type DN–ashared, see Stamm, *Namengebung*, pp. 225-226. The name Shalmaneser was borne by five Assyrian kings, beginning with Shalmaneser I (1274-1245) and ending with Shalmaneser V (726-722). The god Shulmanu has been discussed by Albright in *AfO* VII (1931-32) 164-169 and by J. Lewy in *RHR* CX (1934) 62-63 and in *JBL* LIX (1940) 519-522. Ululaju is not the Babylonian throne name of this ruler but rather a popular variant name attested chiefly in later texts (see p. 62 above).

Ululaju: "(One born in the month) of Ululu." For the Mesopotamian practice of naming children after their birth dates (whether month or day), see Stamm, *Namengebung*, p. 272. I have been unable thus far to unearth any Ululaju earlier than the Neo-Babylonian or Neo-Assyrian periods, when the adjectival name was used for private persons (Tallqvist, *NBN*, p. 215; Tallqvist, *APN*, pp. 239-240); but the noun from which the adjective was derived (the festival and month Elulu = Ululu, see *CAD* E 136a) was used as a personal name as early as the third millennium (e.g., *MAD* II^2 8). The name Ululaju seems to have been more common in Assyria than in Babylonia. The feminine form of the adjective was used in personal names of the Kassite period: f*Ululitum* (*BE* XV 184:9, 200 ii 18) and *mār* m*Ú–lu–lí–ti* (*PBS* II/2 72:15).

Writing of RN:

(a) as Shalmaneser: md*Šùl–man*–BAR (*CIS* II/1 p. 4 no. 2:1, p. 7 no. 6:1; the RN is only partially preserved but presumably to be restored in the same way *ibid.*, p. 6 nos. 4-5:1, p. 8 no. 7:1); m*Šùl–ma–nu*–BAR (*VAS* I 70 i 1); d*Šùl–ma–nu*–BAR (eponym list Ca1, *RLA* II 424); md*Šùl–ma–nu*–BAR (SDAS Kinglist iv 26; *CIS* II/1 p. 5 no. 3:⌈1⌉; traces [*–n*]*u*–BAR are preserved also in Cb3:7, *RLA* II 432); *Šul–man–a–šá–red* (*CT* XXXIV 47 i 27, 29, 30, Babylonian Chronicle); שלמנאצר (II Kings 17:3, 18:9); Σαλμανασ(σ)αρ (IV Kings 17:3, 18:9; vars.: Σαλαμανασ(σ)αρ, Σαμενναсαρ); Σαλμανάσσης (Josephus, *Antiquities of the Jews*, IX xiv);

(b) as Ululaju: m*Ú–lu–la–a+a* (Kinglist A iv 9); אללי (Assur Ostracon, line 15); ʼΙλουλαίου (gen.; "Ptolemaic Canon").

(1561) Babylonian Chronicle i 27-30.

(1562) Kinglist A iv 9. The meaning of BAL.TIL is discussed on p. 168 and in note 1031 above.

(1563) *VAS* I 70 i 1 ff. Der, however, had been incorporated as part of Assyria by this time and had an Assyrian provincial governor (*šaknu*) in residence (for references see *Studies Oppenheim*, p. 13 n. 42).

(1564) The only royal inscription attributed to Shalmaneser V by Luckenbill in *ARAB* I 828-830 is now known to belong to Esarhaddon; see Meissner, *AfO* III (1926) 13-14 and Borger, *Asarhaddon*, no. 20. The only published cuneiform inscriptions presently assignable to Shalmaneser V, which have been almost universally overlooked by bibliographers, are on six bronze lion weights found at Nimrud by Layard. The inscriptions on the lions—in Aramaic and in cuneiform—were partially published by Layard, *Discoveries in the Ruins of Nineveh and Babylon* (London: Murray, 1853), pl. opp. p. 601 and fully published in 1889 in

about his activities anywhere except for occasional glimpses afforded us by later writers:

(1) the Babylonian Chronicle tells us that Shalmaneser destroyed the city of Samaria: URU *Šá–ma–ra–'i–in iḫ–te–pi*; (1565)

(2) an ostracon found at Assur (1566) refers to the deportation by Ululaju (אללי) of captives from Bit–Adini (בית עדן); (1567)

(3) the Bible tells of his siege of Samaria and of the subsequent deportation of the conquered Israelites; (1568)

(4) Josephus relates old stories concerning the siege of Samaria (an echo of the older biblical account) and of a five-year siege of Tyre, which Shalmaneser conducted against an "Eloulaios" (Ἐλούλαιος), king of Tyre. (1569)

CIS II/1 pp. 3-8 nos. 2-7 (with bibliography of earlier treatments on p. 2). The six lions are now in the British Museum and bear the following numbers: BM 91221 (=*CIS* II/1 no. 2), BM 91226 (=no. 3), BM 91222 (=no. 4), BM 91223 (=no. 5), BM 91224 (=no. 6), BM 91230 (=no. 7). Recently D. Oates in *Sumer* XIX (1963) 73 called attention to a fragmentary unpublished brick inscription from Tell Abu Marya, which in the opinion of Prof. Laessøe must be assigned to the reign of Shalmaneser V.

A few Nimrud Letters (nos. XXXI, L, LI, LIII) are written by a man named Ululaju. Since these letters are reports to an unidentified king and contain reports on the well-being and security of Assyria (presumably while the king is on campaign), it is quite possible that these were letters written by Shalmaneser when he was crown prince to his father, Tiglath–Pileser III. This possibility is strengthened when we observe the similarity of the beginning of these letters with the beginning of letters written by Sennacherib when crown prince to his father, Sargon (e.g., *ABL* 197). Dietrich has recently called attention to a passage in an unpublished Neo-Babylonian letter (K. 4740+) which may mention Shalmaneser V (*WO* IV/1 [1967] 68).

(1565) Babylonian Chronicle i 28. For the interpretation of this passage, see Tadmor, *JCS* XII (1958) 33-40.

(1566) Primary publication: Mark Lidzbarski, *Altaramäische Urkunden aus Assur* (*WVDOG* XXXVIII), pp. 5-15, pl. I. Most recent edition (with bibliography): Donner-Röllig, *Kanaanäische und aramäische Inschriften*, no. 233. Found in the excavations at Assur (Assur no. 10229) by the expedition of the Deutsche Orient-Gesellschaft, the text was joined together from six sherds; but there are still several pieces missing. The ostracon is now VA 8384 in the Staatliche Museen, Berlin.

(1567) Assur Ostracon, line 15. Bit–Adini as a locality in southern Babylonia—not to be confused with its homonym on the upper Euphrates, which flourished in the ninth century—occurs only here and in Sennacherib's inscriptions (*OIP* II 43:47, cf. *AfO* XX [1963] 90:51). That it is to be identified as a part of Bit–Dakkuri (thus E. Honigmann, *RLA* II 34; Donner-Röllig, *Kanaanäische und aramäische Inschriften*, II, 285-286) seems possible on the basis of two ninth-century references to individuals: (a) Adinu of the tribe of Dakkuru, and (b) Abdi–il, *šaknu* of Adinu, belonging to the tribe of Dakkuru; one wonders whether Adinu might not have been a clan name rather than the name of an individual. In both of these instances, Adinu is clearly linked with the Dakkuru tribe. (For references to the ninth-century texts, see note 1208 above).

(1568) II Kings 17:5-6, 18:9-12. Note, however, that in the biblical narrative the "king of Assyria" who took Samaria and deported its population is only by implication Shalmaneser, the king who initiated the siege. The (same?) "king of Assyria" repopulated Samaria partly with people from Babylon and Cutha (II Kings 17:24).

It is interesting that these documents refer mainly to military activity in the west. Thanks to the Assur Ostracon, we know also of his deportation of locals from Bit–Adini in Babylonia; but this was not considered significant enough to be mentioned in the Babylonian Chronicle.

Shalmaneser V reigned for a few days less than five calendar years, (1570) dying in Tebet of his fifth official year. (1571) At the time of his death, Babylon was apparently still under his control; but his successor in Assyria, Sargon II, was unable to retain sovereignty over Babylonia. (1572) In the confusion that ensued in Assyria upon the death of the old king and the coming of Sargon to the throne, Merodach–Baladan II, head of the Jakin tribe in Chaldea, managed to gain sufficient support throughout Babylonia to proclaim himself king of the land and to be installed formally in Babylon at the next New Year's festival. (1573) Welding together the normally discordant Chaldean tribes through his great personal diplomacy and securing an Elamite military alliance to strengthen his position, (1574) he headed a powerful movement for Babylonian independence from Assyria. This movement, eminently successful for the first twelve years, later degenerated into a series of petty combats between the two lands, with each side installing its own ruler in the land every few years. This state of affairs continued until 689 when Sennacherib, whose forbearance had at last been overtaxed by the murder of Ashur–nadin–shumi, his eldest son, whom he had made king of Babylonia, utterly annihilated the capital city. Thereafter, the native drive for independence slumbered or sputtered rather ineffectively until the rise of the Chaldean Dynasty under Nabopolassar.

(1569) *Antiquities of the Jews*, IX xiv, including the mention of people deported from Cutha to Samaria. Josephus claims to have derived the extra-biblical account of the siege from Menander's translation of the Tyrian archives. For a discussion of this account, see Lehmann, "Menander und Josephos über Salmanassar IV," *Klio* II (1902) 125-140, 466-472.

(1570) He ascended the throne on 25 Tebet 727; his successor succeeded on 12 Tebet 722.

(1571) Babylonian Chronicle i 30.

(1572) Sargon may have belonged to a junior branch of the royal house, according to his claim of descent from Tiglath–Pileser III in an isolated inscription (evidence in *Studies Oppenheim*, p. 12 n. 39, with a correction in note 1544 above).

The official line of propaganda adopted by Sargon, as revealed in the Assur Charter (K. 1349, published most recently in Winckler, *Sammlung*, II, no. 1), apparently condemns his royal predecessor—Shalmaneser, whose name is not preserved in the text—for imposing tax on the exempt city of Assur. Sargon conceived of himself as supplanting Shalmaneser rather than continuing his policies, and from this might be inferred a political unrest in Assyria at the time of Sargon's accession which occupied his attention and prevented him from preserving the Assyrian hold on Babylon.

(1573) Babylonian Chronicle i 32.

(1574) See my remarks in *Studies Oppenheim*, pp. 30-31 and "Elamite Military Aid to Merodach–Baladan," *JNES* XXIV (1965) 161-166.

CHAPTER IV

FOREIGN POPULATION GROUPS IN BABYLONIA

Between 1158* and 722 B.C., several large groups of foreigners residing in or on the outskirts of Babylonia left their imprint on Babylonian political history. The best known groups are: (a) the Kassites, one-time rulers of Babylonia, whose fortunes remained linked for a time with the land which they had formerly governed; (b) the Chaldeans, comprising several large tribes unmentioned in history before 878, who gained sufficient power to dominate southern Babylonia for approximately three centuries, commencing about 850; (c) the Arameans, the eastern branch of a large family of West Semitic peoples, who first appeared as raiders in northwestern Babylonia in the closing centuries of the second millennium and many of whom had settled on the fringes of Babylonia by the late eighth century. Less known are: (d) the Sutians, also raiders of Babylonia around the turn of the millennium; and (e) the "Ahlamu" or "Ahlamu Arameans," people closely related to the Arameans, who harassed the western frontiers of Babylonia and Assyria in the late second and early first millennia. (1575) There is very little evidence concerning the Sutians and the Ahlamu (Arameans) in this period, perhaps because the nomenclature as applied in this time was slightly anachronistic. (1576)

The Kassites, Chaldeans, and Arameans living in and around Babylonia during this period are somewhat better known. These peoples often appear as groups foreign to Babylonian society. Though the individual members of each of these groups rapidly assimilated Babylonian culture and many of them bore Babylonian names, they frequently preserved a distinctive tribal or clan structure which is reflected chiefly by the way in which their ancestry was cited. Individual native

(1575) There were also two men described as *Ḫapiraju* in the time of the Second Dynasty of Isin, but by that time the epithet plainly had no ethnic connotations. The two individuals were named Harbi-Shipak (*AfO* X [1935-36] 2:5, 5:11) and Kudurra (*BE* I/2 149 i 21-22).

Another person of foreign extraction was Mar-biti-apla-usur (king no. 18), who was of Elamite descent (Dynastic Chronicle v 13′). Also two men attested in kudurrus from the twelfth and ninth centuries respectively bore Hurrian names: ᵐ*Ṭu-bi-ia-en-na* (*BBSt* no. 6 ii 15) and ᵐ*Am-me-en-na* (*BBSt* no. 9 top 6); both of these men were *ša rēši* officials; cf. also Napsamenni, ***nišakku*** of Enlil at Nippur in the early eleventh century (H.S. 157 iv 14, 9 N 99:2, both unpublished). For the supposed Assyrian colony at Borsippa in the time of Nabu-shuma-ishkun, see note 1420 above.

(1576) These groups are hardly distinguishable from the Arameans in this period, as we shall see below, note 1799 and pp. 285-287.

Babylonians of this period were usually referred to as "PN, son of PN_2" (i.e., "So-and-so, son of So-and-so"), with PN_2 representing the name of the individual's father. (1577) An apparently similar type of nomenclature was used for individual Kassites and Chaldeans, i.e., "PN, son of PN_2," but with this fundamental difference: the PN_2 stands for the eponymous ancestor of the House (i.e., tribe or clan), not the real father of the individual. (1578) Thus PN *mār Karziabku* or PN *mār Dakkūri* means "PN, member of the House of Karziabku" or "PN, member of the Ḍakkuru tribe." By contrast, the ancestry of Arameans in and around Babylonia is hardly ever cited; and their tribal affiliation, if mentioned at all, is usually indicated in a way different from the Kassites or Chaldeans: "PN, the Puqudian" (LÚ *Puqudaju*, member of the Puqudu tribe). (1579) These diverse methods of describing tribal or clan affiliation not only serve to differentiate members of these population groups from native Babylonians occurring in the same texts but point up the survival of non-Babylonian institutions in foreign groups otherwise heavily influenced by Babylonian civilization.

In the following pages, we will deal with each of these foreign population groups separately: Kassites, Chaldeans, Arameans, and Sutians. (1580) The chapter will conclude with a few general observations on the impact of these groups on Babylonia in this period.

The Kassites

In sketching the history of the Kassites in and around Babylonia after the fall of the Kassite Dynasty, we divide our treatment into three major sections, dealing with the onomastic, cultic, and politico-military evidence respectively. (1581) The onomastic evidence concerns people in Babylonia bearing Kassite names or with

(1577) The system of "family names" for Babylonians, in vogue in the later Neo-Babylonian period (see, e.g., Ungnad, "Babylonische Familiennamen," *AnOr* XII 319-326), was just beginning at this time. The only provable examples thus far which antedate the middle ninth century are chiefly scribes and provincial officials (*bēlē pīḫati*) belonging to the family of Arad-Ea (W. G. Lambert, *JCS* XI [1957] 9-10, 112).

(1578) This seems to be almost universally true for the early Chaldeans and generally so for the later Kassites. Some of the later Kassite patronymics, however, may have designated actual fathers rather than clan ancestors, though a single instance of this has yet to be conclusively demonstrated. In such texts as *BBSt* no. 9, reference to people of Kassite descent as *mār* PN denotes clan ancestry, while *māršu ša* PN is used to denote real fatherhood.

(1579) For a single exception, see note 1821 below. This observation does not hold true for the western Arameans nor for the MB Ahlamu.

(1580) The term Ahlamu will be discussed in note 1799 below.

(1581) We are concerned here with the history of the Kassites between 1158* and about 700, principally in so far as it affects Babylonia. I shall deal in a separate article with the entire history of the Kassites after the fall of the Kassite Dynasty (as outlined in my paper delivered before the American Oriental Society at Yale University, New Haven, Conn., on March 22, 1967).

some indication of Kassite ancestry. [1582] The cultic evidence relates to the survival of the worship of Kassite gods. The political and military evidence deals with the political allegiance of the Kassites, especially those in the regions of Namri and Bit–Habban: their early allegiance to Babylonia and their later struggles for independence against Assyria.

We begin then with the onomastic evidence. This evidence will be discussed in four separate though not necessarily mutually exclusive categories: (a) living persons bearing Kassite names, [1583] (b) living persons bearing hybrid names (Kassite–Akkadian), (c) persons with Kassite ancestral names, (d) persons bearing Akkadian names with Kassite gods serving as theophoric elements. These are the only persons for whom we can trace Kassite descent; others may have been living in Babylonia at this time, but cannot now be detected.

There were relatively few living individuals [1584] in this period within the political boundaries of Babylonia [1585] who bore Kassite names. Including the king Simbar–Shipak of the Second Sealand Dynasty, purely Kassite names were borne by only eight persons (six of whom lived during the Second Dynasty of Isin): [1586]

(a) [m]*Burramasaḫ*, witness to a kudurru in the early eleventh century (*YOS* I 37 iv 33); [1587]

(b) [m]*Ḫarbi–Šipak*, courtier serving the Assyrian king, middle twelfth century, described as *Ḫapiraju* (*AfO* X [1935-36] 2:5, etc.);

(c) [m]*Kadašman–Buriaš*, governor of the province of Dur–Kurigalzu around the middle of the eleventh century, "son" of Itti–Marduk–balatu (*AKA* 133 iii 7, Broken Obelisk); [1588]

[1582] This is not to say that each individual bearing a Kassite name was necessarily Kassite, any more than each person bearing a Babylonian name was Babylonian. This is manifestly untrue when brothers in the same family bear Kassite and Akkadian names (e.g., the sons of Arad–Sibitti in *BBSt* no. 9). As stressed by Gelb in "Ethnic Reconstruction and Onomastic Evidence," *Names* X (1962) 45-52, personal names help to give a proportional picture of ethnic backgrounds represented in an area, not life histories of individuals. What is of more significance in establishing a person as Kassite, for example, is his clan affiliation.

[1583] As a working criterion for distinguishing Kassite elements in personal names, we accept with minor modifications Balkan's glossaries in *Kassitenstudien*, I, which includes analysis of personal names occurring after the Kassite period. To this must be added the names of such Kassite groups as (Bit-) Habban, Hanbi, and Hunna.

[1584] As opposed to persons occurring only in patronymics or in names of tribal or clan organizations.

[1585] Therefore excluding ninth- and eighth-century individuals such as Janzu (*TCL* III 306-307, etc.) and Janzi-Buriash (*WO* I/6 [1952] 472 iii 63, etc.), who headed areas politically independent from Babylonia. Such persons would presumably have gained local support by acknowledging their Kassite heritage.

[1586] In this and the following lists of this section, the gender determinatives will be prefixed to the transcribed name forms; other determinatives (e.g., URU and DINGIR) will be omitted, save where readings of following signs are uncertain.

[1587] This name should be added to Balkan, *Kassitenstudien*, I, 51.

[1588] For the reading of the name of Kadashman–Buriash's father, see note 861 above. Its interpretation as Kassite rather than Akkadian is not entirely certain (see note 1631 below).

(d) ᵐ*Kara–Šuqamuna,* witness to a kudurru in the early eleventh century, "son" of ᵐ*A–a–ri* (*YOS* I 37 iv 27); (1589)

(e) ᵐ*Muktarissaḫ, ša bāb ekalli* official in the late twelfth century, "son" of ᵐ*Ṣapru* (*BBSt* no. 6 ii 16); (1590)

(f) ᵐ*Nibi–Šipak,* witness to a kudurru in the early eleventh century, son of ᵐ*Ka–re–e–a* (*YOS* I 37 iv 26);

(g) ᵐ*Simbar–Šipak,* first king of the Second Dynasty of the Sealand (1026*-1009*), son of Eriba–Sin (Dynastic Chronicle v 2′-4′, etc.);

(h) ᵐ*Uzibia* (hypocoristic), member of the clan of Bit–Abirattash, participant in legal action dated in 975* (*BBSt* no. 9 i 14).

It is noteworthy that at least five of these individuals had fathers—or more remote ancestors—who bore Babylonian names. (1591) Several of these men with Kassite names held high office: Simbar–Shipak as a king, Muktarissah and Harbi–Shipak as court or palace officials, and Kadashman–Buriash as provincial governor.

The hybrid names Nazi–Marduk and Nazi–Enlil were also borne by living individuals; but such hybrid formations were generally unproductive in the later Babylonian onomasticon. (1592) Nazi–Marduk was *kartappu* of Akkad in the time of Nebuchadnezzar I (1126*-1105*), (1593) and Nazi–Enlil was *šandabakku,* i.e., governor of Nippur, in the reign of Marduk–zakir–shumi I (c. 854-c. 819). (1594)

Kassite names were more commonly used as patronymics or as clan designations during this period; but, because of the scanty documentation pertaining to the Kassite clans or "Houses," it is often difficult to determine whether a designation such as "son of Abirattash" should be interpreted literally as "son of Abirattash" or as "member of the House of Abirattash" or even occasionally as "descendant of Abirattash." (1595) Consequently, we prefer to treat such ambiguous designations together under the general heading "of (acknowledged) Kassite descent," no matter how remote the descent may be. There are more than fifty known individuals of Kassite descent in this period; and with the exception of Nazi–Marduk, "son" of Shad-

(1589) For the reading of *Kar/Kara,* see Balkan, *Kassitenstudien,* I, 191 nn. 1-2.

(1590) For *Ṣapru,* see note 1617 below.

(1591) This shows that adoption of Babylonian names in one generation does not mean that all successive generations would eschew Kassite names.

(1592) Nazi–Enlil occurs rarely in later patronymics (*VAS* I 37 v 1; *BE* VIII 149:10, 17), while Nazi–Marduk occurs chiefly as a clan name (*BBSt* no. 5 i 10, ii 35; *BBSt* no. 9 top 18, ivb 1).

(1593) *BBSt* no. 6 ii 12.

(1594) *RA* XVI (1919) 126 iv 21. Nazi–Enlil had a son with an Akkadian name (*Enlil–apla–uṣur*) who succeeded him as *šandabakku* (4 N-T 3:11′).

(1595) We should note, however, that the majority of these references can be proven to mean "member of the tribe/clan of PN" and that none of them has as yet been demonstrated to mean "son of PN" or "descendant of PN."

dagme, and Uzibia, "son" of Abirattash, none of them bears a Kassite name. In fact, practically all of them have good Babylonian names—indicating the increasing Babylonization of Kassite stock with the passing of time. These men of Kassite descent may be grouped alphabetically by "ancestor" as follows:

descendants of *Abirattaš* (1596)

1. ᵐ*Aḫḫē-šullim,* early tenth century (*BBSt* no. 9 i 23, iva 20);
2. ᵐ*Arad-Sibitti, bēl bīt Maḫila* in the early tenth century (*BBSt* no. 9 top 2, etc., face A:1-2);
3. ᵐ*Ekallaju,* early tenth century (*BBSt* no. 9 i 14);
4. ᵐ*Illataju,* early tenth century (*BBSt* no. 9 i 23);
5. ᶠ*In*[*a-x*]*-šērī,* early tenth century (*BBSt* no. 9 face A:4-5);
6. ᵐ*Išnukû,* early tenth century (*BBSt* no. 9 i 23);
7. ᵐ*Kaššaju,* early tenth century (*BBSt* no. 9 i 12, iii 8, iva 19);
8. ᵐ*Kaššû-nādin-aḫḫē,* early tenth century (*BBSt* no. 9 i 13);
9. ᵐ*Larak-zēra-ibni,* early tenth century (*BBSt* no. 9 i 12);
10. ᵐ*Mār-bīti-šuma-ibni,* early tenth century (*BBSt* no. 9 i 19, etc., iva 3-4, 20);
11. ᵐ*Nabûti,* early tenth century (*BBSt* no. 9 i 22);
12. ᵐ*Ninurta-apla-iddina,* early tenth century (*BBSt* no. 9 i 13);
13. ᶠᵈSAG*-mudammiq-šarbe,* early tenth century (*BBSt* no. 9 i 16-17, etc.);
14. ᵐ*Šá-pi-x,* early tenth century (*BBSt* no. 9 i 22);
15. ᵐ*Uzibia,* early tenth century (*BBSt* no. 9 i 14);
16. ᵐ*Zēra-ibni,* early tenth century (*BBSt* no. 9 i 14);

descendants of *Aḫu-bānī* (1597)

17. ᵐ*Kaššû-bēl-zēri, šakin māt Tâmti*(*m*), uncertain date (1598) (*RA* XIX [1922] 86:8);
18. ᵐ*Kaššû-nādin-aḫḫē, ša rēši,* early tenth century (*BBSt* no. 9 iva 34-35);

(1596) These members of the group *Bīt-Abirattaš* belong to two successive generations of one family: Arad-Sibitti, his brothers, and his sons and daughter(s). They occur in the text *BBSt* no. 9, which tells of events occurring between the second year of Ninurta-kudurri-usur I (987*) and the twenty-fifth year of Nabu-mukin-apli (955*).

(1597) Despite its Babylonian form, this name, beginning in late Kassite times, is used only as a patronymic (*MDP* II 88 ii 31, 91 first subscript 2; *MDP* VI 34 ii 25, iii 2; *MDP* XIV 34:3), though it is amply attested as a personal name for living individuals earlier in the Kassite period (*BE* XIV 6:2, 23:9, etc.; *PBS* II/2 100:15, etc.). That it is probably to be interpreted as a Kassite group may be inferred from the personal name *Kašakti-Šugab* (*MDP* II 88 ii 31, etc.), who is said to be a "son" of Ahu-bani in the late Kassite period and from the names with the theophorous element *Kaššû* listed here (such names are other-

descendants of *Bāzi*

19. ᵐ*Eulmaš–šākin–šumi, sakrumaš ša mātāti*, early eleventh century (*BBSt* no. 8 i 29-30; *PSBA* XIX [1897] 71 ii 12);
20. ᵐ*Eulmaš–šākin–šumi*, first king of the Bazi Dynasty (1005*-989*) (Dynastic Chronicle v 9′);
21. ᵐ*Kaššû–mukīn–apli, sakrumaš*, early tenth century (*BBSt* no. 9 top 17);
22. ᵐ*Ninurta–kudurrī–uṣur* I, second king of the Bazi Dynasty (988*-986*) (Dynastic Chronicle v 10′);
23. ᵐ*Širikti–Šuqamuna*, third king of the Bazi Dynasty (986*) (Dynastic Chronicle v 11′);

descendant of *Gandu* (1599)

24. ᵐ*Sîn–bēl–ilī, šakin Bīt–Piri'–Amurru*, middle eleventh century (*BE* I/2 149 i 3-4); (1600)

descendants of *Ḫabban* (1601)

25. ᵐ*Aḫa–erība, kartappu*, middle ninth century (*BBSt* no. 28:21);
26. ᵐ*Amurru–ušallim, sakrumaš*, middle ninth century (*BBSt* no. 29 ii 11-12);
27. ᶠ*Dūr–Šarru–kīn–ajiti* (gen.), daughter of ᵐᵈMUŠ–*nāṣir, mār Ḫabban*, early eleventh century (I *R* 70 i 14-15);
28. ᵐ*Enlil–nādin–šumi, šakin māt Namar*, late twelfth century (*BBSt* no. 6 ii 23);

---

wise attested only of individuals of Kassite descent, as will be seen below). The reading of the name is assured from writings like ᵐ*A–ḫu–ba–ni* (*BE* XIV 6:2) and ᵐŠEŠ–*ba–ni–i* (*MDP* VI 34 iii 2) alongside ᵐŠEŠ–DÙ–*i* (*MDP* II 88 ii 31); and the writing of the final vowel as long seems to imply that the second element of the name should be interpreted as a participial form plus pronominal suffix and the first element of the name as at least latently theophoric. (But cf. writings like ᵐŠEŠ–*ba–nu–ú* [*MDP* VI 34 ii 25], probably to be interpreted as nominative back formations).

The name of this Kassite group may well have derived from a time early in the Kassite period when the name was commonly borne by individuals. In the later Neo-Babylonian period, beginning in the reign of Neriglissar (*TCL* XII 63:5, 17), Ahu–bani was a well-known family name.

(1598) But see p. 257 below.

(1599) This could be interpreted as a reference to an individual. The same name is written as ᵐ*Ka–an–du* (*WZJ* VIII [1958-59] 573:⌈19⌉, 23, Kassite period letter).

(1600) This reference to a son of Gandu and the references in note 1599 may be added to Balkan, *Kassitenstudien*, I, 53.

(1601) Bit–Habban is attested in I *R* 70 i 3, etc. Shalmaneser appointed "Janzu, son of Hanban" as king of Namri after his campaign of 843 (*WO* II/2 [1955] 152:95). *Janzi*, the Kassite word for "king" (Balkan, *Kassitenstudien*, I, 155), need not necessarily be viewed here as a personal name, though it could have been a hypocoristic for a name like Janzi–Buriaṣh or Kashakti–Janzi. But, even if interpreted as a title which was misunderstood by the Assyrians as being a personal name, it would nonetheless indicate the Kassite affiliation of the individual.

29. ᵐ*Marduk–šuma–ukīn, kartappu,* middle ninth century (*BBSt* no. 36 vi 18-19);

30. ᵐᵈMUŠ–*nāṣir,* (1602) early eleventh century (I *R* 70 i 13); (1603)

descendant of *Ḫanbu* (1604)

31. ᵐ*Amēl–Enlil,* probably early eleventh century (*BBSt* no. 7 i 10-11);

descendant of *Ḫašmar* (1605)

32. ᵐ*Ea–mukīn–zēri,* second king of the Second Sealand Dynasty (1009*) (Dynastic Chronicle v 5′);

descendants of *Ḫunna* (1606)

33. ᵐ*Amēl–Išin,* late twelfth century (Hinke Kudurru v 21);
34. ᵐ*Baba–šuma–iddina, šakin Bābili* and *šakin Bīt–Sîn–šeme,* late twelfth century (*BBSt* no. 6 ii 18; Hinke Kudurru ii 17, etc.);
35. ᵐ*Gula–zēra–iqīša,* late twelfth century (Hinke Kudurru v 23);
36. ᵐ*Kaššû,* late twelfth century (Hinke Kudurru v 22);

descendants of *Ina–Esagila–zēru* (1607)

37. ᵐ*Marduk–ṣulūlī, sukkallu, bēl bīti ša Bīt–Ada,* early eleventh century (*BBSt* no. 8 i 8-9, A 4-6);
38. ᵐ*Ṭāb–ašāb–Marduk, sukkallu, šakin māt Ḫalman,* late twelfth and early eleventh centuries (*BBSt* no. 6 ii 22; I *R* 70 i 15-17, etc.; *BBSt* no. 25:31-32 and dupl.);

(1602) ᵈMUŠ is possibly to be read ᵈ*Niraḫ*. Compare *MSL* IV 5:19 (Emesal I) and *MSL* VIII/2 7:9 (Ḫḫ XIV).

(1603) Another descendant of Habban who may date from this period is *Nergal–apla–uṣur,* a *sakrumaš* and probably a witness in the broken and undated kudurru *VAS* I 57 ii 5-6.

(1604) Bit–Hanbi occurs in *BBSt* no. 7 i 2, 3, etc. (cf. the [AŠ *Pi*]*–it Ḫa–ni–pi* mentioned by Shilhak–Inshushinak: König, *Die elamischen Königsinschriften,* no. 54 iii 38). The name Hanbu is uncommon, and serves chiefly as a patronymic in the Kassite and Neo-Babylonian periods (e.g., *PBS* II/2 6:17, *BIN* I 107:7, etc.).

(1605) Bit–Hashmar is attested in the Dynastic Chronicle v 6′.

(1606) The name occurs in this period only as a patronymic and only during the reign of Nebuchadnezzar I (1126*-1105*); so it could designate a single individual (real father). To the best of my knowledge, it occurs elsewhere as a PN only in *PBS* I/2 21:1, ⌜5⌝ (MB letter).

(1607) Probably a clan name, but could prove to be the name of a real father (because all the texts in which it occurs are within the span of one generation). Note that *Marduk–ṣulūlī* is a semi-independent *bēl bīti* in northeastern Babylonia.

descendants of *Karziabku*

39. ᵐLAK–*ti–Marduk, bēl bīti ša Bīt–Karziabku,* late twelfth century (*BBSt* no. 6 i 25, etc.);
40. ᵐ*Šuqamuna–apla–iddina, šākin ṭēme māti,* early tenth century (*BBSt* no. 9 ivb 2-3);
41. ᵐ*Zēra–ukīn,* early tenth century (*BBSt* no. 9 iva 3, etc.);

descendant of *Kašakti–Janzi* (1608)

42. ᵐ*Uballissu* (*Uballiṭsu*), early eleventh century (*BBSt* no. 8 ii 9-10);

descendant of *Kurigalzu* (1609)

43. ᵐ*Bēl–erība,* middle ninth century (*VAS* I 35:27);

descendant of *Meli–Ḫala* (1610)

44. ᵐ*Mār–bīti–šākin–līti, šakin Išin,* early tenth century (*BBSt* no. 9 iva 33-34);

descendants of *Mili–Ḫarbe* (1611)

45. ᵐ*Anu–bēl–aḫḫēšu,* early eleventh century (*BBSt* no. 8 ii 17-18);
46. ᵐ*Šuqamuna–aḫa–iddina,* early eleventh century (*BBSt* no. 8 ii 13-14);

descendants of *Namri* (1612)

47. ᵐ*Ea–zēra–iqīša, ērib bīti* ᵈ*Ea,* late eleventh century (*BBSt* no. 27:7-8); (1613)
48. ᵐ*Nabû–nādin–aḫḫē, šatam bīt unâti,* early eleventh century (*PSBA* XIX [1897] 71 ii 16-17; *BBSt* no. 25:35-36; cf. Walters Art Gallery 21.10 rev. ii 4-5 [*RA* LXI (1967) 71]);

descendants of *Nazi–Marduk* (1614)

49. ᵐ*Kaššû–šuma–iddina, sukkallu,* early tenth century (*BBSt* no. 9 top 18-19);
50. ᵐ*Zērija, sukkallu,* early tenth century (*BBSt* no. 9 ivb 1-2);

(1608) Could prove to be the name of a real father.

(1609) Probably the name of a real father, since the name Kurigalzu is not uncommon for living individuals in the later Neo-Babylonian period (references in note 1635 below).

(1610) Could prove to be the name of a real father.

(1611) Since both "descendants" occur in the same text, Mili–Harbe may have been their real father.

(1612) Connected with Bit–Habban in the time of Nebuchadnezzar I (*BBSt* no. 6 ii 23, 27-28) and also later (e.g., *WO* II/2 [1955] 152:95).

(1613) Patronymic preserved only partially: ᵐ*Nam–[ri]*.

(1614) Bit–Nazi–Marduk is known from *BBSt* no. 5 i 10 (reign of Merodach–Baladan I, early twelfth century). Most known descendants of Nazi–Marduk held the office of *sukkallu*: besides the two named

descendant of *Piri'-Amurru* (1615)

51. m*Nergal-šá-li-*[*x*], (1616) middle ninth century (*BBSt* no. 29 ii 13-14);

descendant of *Ṣapru* (1617)

52. m*Muktarissaḫ, ša bāb ekalli*, late twelfth century (*BBSt* no. 6 ii 16);

descendant of *Šaddagme* (1618)

53. m*Nazi-Marduk, kartappu* of Akkad, late twelfth century (*BBSt* no. 6 ii 12);

descendant of *Tunamissaḫ* (1619)

54. m*Eulmaš-nāṣir, šākin ṭēme māti*, early tenth century (*BBSt* no. 9 top 19-20);

descendant of *Uzib-Ḫala* (1620)

55. m*Amēl-Eulmaš*, early eleventh century (*BBSt* no. 8 ii 19-20);

descendant of *Uzib-Šipak* (1621)

56. m*Nabû-mudammiq, sakrumaš Tâmti*, late eleventh century (*BBSt* no. 27 rev. 15). (1622)

---

here, there was also a *sukkallu* named *Nabû-nāṣir* in the late Kassite period (*BBSt* no. 5 ii 34-35). There is also an undated votive inscription of a *Šat-indar*, "son" of Nazi-Marduk (not "Vater" as claimed by Balkan, *op. cit.*, p. 78), published by Dhorme in *RB* XX (1911) 277-278; but this may belong to the Kassite period.

The name Nazi-Marduk also occurs as the name of a living individual in the late twelfth century (*BBSt* no. 6 ii 12).

(1615) Bit-Piri'-Amurru had the status of a province under the Kassite and Second Isin dynasties (*BBSt* no. 4 i 3, cf. *MDP* VI 40 ii 4; *BE* I/2 149, *passim*).

(1616) Possibly to be interpreted as *Nergal-šākin*(GAR)*-lī*[*ti*].

(1617) *Bīt-Ṣapri* is attested in *BBSt* no. 30:6. *Ṣapru* as a personal name occurs in the OB and Kassite periods (e.g., *VAS* XIII 98:3; *MDP* XXII 77:11; *MDP* XXIII 170:33; Clay, *CPN*, pp. 134-135), but, to my knowledge, is attested only as a patronymic after Kassite times. For the reading and meaning of the name, see Stamm, *Namengebung*, p. 265.

(1618) Possibly the name of a real father.

(1619) For Bit-Tunamissah, see *MDP* II 100 i 45, *BBSt* no. 5 i 14, I *R* 70 i 8.

(1620) Read *Ueš*(?)*-Ḫala* in Balkan, *op. cit.*, p. 87; cf. the ZIB sign in *BBSt* no. 14:7. This may be the name of a real father.

(1621) Bit-Uzib-Shipak is attested in *BBSt* no. 14:7.

(1622) The following patronymics, though unrecognized in Balkan, *op. cit.*, may eventually have to be interpreted as Kassite:

(a) m*Ḫab-bur-ri*: "ancestor" of m*Ilu-bāni*, early eleventh century (*YOS* I 37 iv 25);
(b) m*Ki-*⌈*ri*⌉*-ik-me*: "ancestor" of m*I-da-a-a*, early eleventh century (*YOS* I 37 iv 28);
(c) m*Ni-ga-zi*: "ancestor" of m*Baba-aḫa-iddina, sakrumaš*, early eleventh century (*BBSt* no. 25: 29-30);
(d) m*Šá-zu-ú-ti*: "ancestor" of m*Enlil-nādin-šumi*, early eleventh century (*BBSt* no. 8 ii 11-12);

Of these fifty-six persons of Kassite "descent," the overwhelming majority (fifty) have Akkadian names. Two (nos. 15, 52) bear Kassite names, and one (no. 53) bears a hybrid (Kassite–Akkadian) name. Three (nos. 13, 14, 39) have names of uncertain derivation, which, however, are presumably to be interpreted as Akkadian because of the occurrence within them of Akkadian elements. That some supposedly Kassite "Houses" have men with Akkadian names as their eponymous ancestors probably implies that these "Houses" were established only after the Kassites were partially Babylonized.

Many of these people held office within Babylonia, often high office. Four (nos. 20, 21, 23, 32) were kings. Six (nos. 17, 24, 28, 34, 38, 44) were governors (*šaknu*), including governors of Babylon (no. 34), Isin (no. 44), and the Sealand (no. 17). Three were tribal chieftains of gubernatorial rank (*bēl bīti*), i.e., nos. 2, 37, 39. Two held the post of *šākin ṭēme māti* (nos. 40, 54). Four (nos. 19, 21, 26, 56) served as *sakrumaš*, including *sakrumaš ša mātāti* and *sakrumaš* (*māt*) *Tâmti* (nos. 19, 56). Four held office as *sukkallu* (nos. 37, 38, 49, 50), three as *kartappu* (1623) (nos. 25, 29, 53), and one each as *ērib bīti* ᵈ*Ea* (no. 47), *šatam bīt unâti* (no. 48), and *ša bāb ekalli* (no. 52).

Though assessment of the institutions of these Kassite groups should await a further study which would also include material of the Kassite period, we may perhaps make brief preliminary remarks here. Noteworthy is the institution of the *bēl bīti* (lit.: "Lord of the House"), the head of the clan, the equivalent of a governor for one of the Kassite groups. Since individual *bēlū bīti* did not always bear in their patronymic the name of the group which they headed, (1624) it may be supposed that there was an interlocking hierarchical structure of *bītātu* (smaller within larger), that *bēlū bīti* could be selected from outside the group which they headed, or that the *bītātu* sometimes retained older names for the group than were commonly in vogue.

(e) ᵐ*Ú-za-an-nu-uḫ-li-ia*: "ancestor" of ᵐ*Ninurta-nādin-aḫḫē*, middle eleventh century (VA 5937: 1-2, unpublished);

besides the following possible "clans" with "ancestors" bearing Semitic names:

(f) *Atta-ilumma*: "ancestor" of *Šamaš-šumu-līšir*, *šakkanak Agade* in the early twelfth century (*BBSt* no. 4 ii 9-10, late Kassite period) and of *Šamaš-nādin-šumi*, *šakin Išin* in the late twelfth century (*BBSt* no. 6 ii 17);

(g) *Nūr-Marduk*: "ancestor" of *Gula-balāssu-ibni*, *šatam bīt unâti*, early tenth century (*BBSt* no. 9 ivb 5-6), of *Ibni-Marduk*, *ša rēši*, middle ninth century (*BBSt* no. 29 ii 10), and of *Šamaš-mudammiq*, *zazakku*, early tenth century (*BBSt* no. 9 top 22);

(h) *Tuballaṭ-Ešdar*: "ancestor" of *Marduk-šāpik-zēri*, *šākin ṭēmi māti*, middle ninth century (*BBSt* no. 28 rev. 23, no. 36 vi 22-23), of *Nergal-ušebši*, *sukkallu*, middle ninth century (*BBSt* no. 28 rev. 22); and of [DN]-*nāṣir*, *sukkallu*, late ninth century (4 N-T 3:12′).

The "House of Atnaju" in *BBSt* no. 28 is at best a remote possibility, since it is in western Babylonia. Obviously, with the little evidence available, one can hardly assert that (a-e) were Kassite or that (f-h) were not real fathers or even precursors of "family names."

(1623) For the reading of this title (written KA.DIB) see p. 305 below.

(1624) See nos. 2 and 37 in the list of persons of Kassite descent above.

Also noteworthy is the fratriarchal structure of such Kassite groups as Bit–Abirattash, in which the alienation of property in favor of a daughter had to be approved by her uncles as well as by her oldest brother [1625] and then confirmed by her other brothers after the death of the eldest brother; [1626] these formal acts were performed in the ancestral town of residence, "in the city of his brothers." [1627]

We should make clear at this point that each of these groups which defined its ancestry in a specifically non-Babylonian fashion need not be viewed as an ethno-linguistic purity, i.e., as people of impeccable Kassite descent who were affected in greater or lesser degree by Babylonian language and customs. While it is conceivable that some of these groups or "Houses" originated late enough to have as eponymous ancestors Kassites who had become partially assimilated to Babylonian ways and bore Akkadian names (e.g., Ahu–bani) or that some of them derived fictitious eponymous ancestors from the regions where they were dwelling (e.g., Bazi), it is likewise possible that outsiders may occasionally have become assimilated into the institutions of surrounding Kassites. Note too that the gods of Bit–Habban, one of the most prominent of the Kassite "Houses," were Sin and Belet Akkadi, [1628] possibly Kassite deities who had received Babylonian names, but also perhaps older gods of the region who had been taken over by the Kassites. Many aspects of the Kassite–Babylonian symbiosis remain to be investigated, but one of the few clear legacies which later Babylonized Kassites retained from earlier days was their clan or "House" structure.

We come now to the use of the names of Kassite deities as the theophoric element in some personal names (chiefly Akkadian) during this period. The divine names so used are Shuqamuna and Kashshu. [1629] Shuqamuna is used in the names of four individuals of this period: [1630]

(a) ᵐ*Kara*(KAR)–*Šuqamuna*, "son" of ᵐ*A–a–ri*, early eleventh century (*YOS* I 37 iv 27); [1631]

(b) ᵐ*Širikti–Šuqamuna*, "son" of Bazi, third king of the Bazi Dynasty (986*);

(c) ᵐ*Šuqamuna–aḫa–iddina*, "son" of Mili–Harbe, early eleventh century (*BBSt* no. 8 ii 13-14);

(1625) *BBSt* no. 9 i 12-15. That these men were uncles of Kashshaju and his sister may be seen by comparison with the list of the latter's brothers, *ibid.*, i 22-23 (after the death of Kashshaju).

(1626) *BBSt* no. 9 i 18-29.

(1627) *BBSt* no. 9 i 11, 22.

(1628) *BBSt* no. 6 ii 50.

(1629) For the possibility that these might be two names for the same god, see Balkan, *Kassitenstudien*, I, 109.

(1630) Shuqamuna is also used in personal names in the Kassite period (references *ibid.*, I, 122).

(1631) It is uncertain whether KAR is to be read as Kassite *Kara* or as Akkadian *Eṭir*, *Mušēzib*, *vel al.* Since the other names in this category (with Kassite theophoric elements) during this period are Akkadian, this name should perhaps also be interpreted as Akkadian.

(d) ^{m}*Šuqamuna–apla–iddina,* "son" of Karziabku, *šākin ṭēme māti,* early tenth century (*BBSt* no. 9 ivb 2).

After the time of Nabu–mukin–apli (979*-944*), the theophoric element Shuqamuna does not occur in Babylonian personal names. ^{d}*Kaššû,* "the Kassite god," is used in the names of six individuals:

(e) ^{m}*Kaššû–bēl–zēri,* "son" of Ahu–bani, (1632) *šakin* (*māt*) *Tâmti,* date unspecified (*RA* XIX [1922] 86:8);

(f) ^{m}*Kaššû–mukīn–apli,* "son" of Bazi, *sakrumaš,* early tenth century (*BBSt* no. 9 top 17);

(g-h) ^{m}*Kaššû–nādin–aḫḫē*

(g) "son" of Abirattash, early tenth century (*BBSt* no. 9 i 13);

(h) "son" of Ahu–bani, (1633) early tenth century (*BBSt* no. 9 iva 34);

(i) ^{m}*Kaššû–nādin–aḫi,* "son" of Bazi, third king of the Second Sealand Dynasty (1008*-1006*);

(j) ^{m}*Kaššû–šuma–iddina,* "son" of Nazi–Marduk, *sukkallu,* early tenth century (*BBSt* no. 9 top 18).

Five of these individuals (f-j) can be dated between 1008* and 955*. Only Kashshu–bel–zeri (a) occurs in an undated text; but, since Kashshu as a theophoric element in personal names is attested only in the late eleventh and early tenth century, the text may presumably be dated around the same time. (1634) Except for the king, Kashshu–nadin–ahi, and the undated Kashshu–bel–zeri, the other individuals whose names are formed with ^{d}*Kaššû* are attested only in the text *BBSt* no. 9 and seem to be restricted to one region. Almost all these individuals whose names have either ^{d}*Šuqamuna* or ^{d}*Kaššû* as the theophoric element were members of Kassite tribal or clan groups: Bit–Abirattash (g), *(Bit)–Ahu–bani (e, h), Bit–Bazi (b, f, i), Bit–Karziabku (d), Bit–Nazi–Marduk (j).

Thus, with the exception of Kurigalzu, a name also used in later Neo-Babylonian times, (1635) most Kassite names or Akkadian names formed with a Kassite theophoric element die out after the middle of the ninth century. Even before that time they comprise a very small minority of the names of living individuals, and

(1632) The text has ^{m}ŠEŠ–DÙ not ^{m}ŠEŠ–NUMUN (wrongly given by Balkan, *ibid.*, I, 110).

(1633) Balkan (*ibid.*, I, 110) reads ^{m}ŠEŠ–DÙ^{i}. The name is written with DÙ (*BBSt*, pl. LXXV). For the reading of the PN see note 1597 above.

(1634) Thureau–Dangin (*RA* XIX [1922] 86-87) attempted to date this document to the Kassite period on the basis of this personal name; but ^{d}*Kaššû* does not occur as a theophoric element in personal names of the Kassite period.

(1635) E.g., *BIN* I 159:34, *BRM* I 32:1, cf. *ABL* 1185:13, etc.

most of these persons seem to have lived around the Sealand or in northeastern Babylonia. (1636)

Another trace of surviving Kassite influence in Babylonia may be found in religious references in the texts. The goddess Shimalija (Shumalija) was invoked in a kudurru in the time of Nebuchadnezzar I (1126*-1105*) (1637) and was still worshipped in Babylonia in the time of Baba-aha-iddina (c. 812). (1638) Shuqamuna and Shimalija were named in texts as late as the reign of Esarhaddon, when their statues were returned to Sippar-Aruru. (1639) Though there is no reference to a cult of ᵈ*Kaššû*, "the Kassite god," mention is made of cults of ᵈ*Kaššītu*, "the Kassite goddess," at Uruk and at Babylon. (1640)

The political history of the Kassites after the collapse of the Kassite Dynasty may now be sketched briefly. After the fall of the last Kassite king in Babylonia, the Elamite Shilhak-Inshushinak campaigned against Kassite regions east of the Tigris. (1641) A short time later, some of the Kassites in the eastern mountains may have been smitten by Nebuchadnezzar I (1126*-1105*), to judge from his vaunted title "despoiler of the Kassites"; (1642) but Kassites continued to hold office in Babylonia in his time. (1643) The eastern mountain region remained linked with the central government in Babylonia during the eleventh and tenth centuries; (1644) and, between the years 1026* and 986*, no fewer than six kings of Kassite descent or bearing Kassite or Kassite-related names sat on the throne of Babylonia. (1645) Also from these times, i.e., from the late Kassite period through the middle of the tenth century, date the great numbers of Luristan bronze weapons inscribed with the names of Babylonian kings—presumably another indication of the close links

(1636) Personal names like *Kaššû/ê/î* (later also *Kaššâ* and *Kaššât*) occur in Mesopotamia beginning in the MA and MB periods. *Kaššâ* remains popular, especially as a feminine personal name, into Persian times (e.g., *Camb.* 15:1, 244:3).

(1637) *BBSt* no. 6 ii 46. Balkan does not believe that the name Shumalija itself was Kassite, but Shuqamuna and Shumalija were the gods of the Kassite royal family (*Kassitenstudien*, I, 118).

(1638) *CT* XXXIV 41 iv 8 (Synchronistic History).

(1639) References in Landsberger, *Bischof*, p. 55 n. 106.

(1640) Balkan, *Kassitenstudien*, I, 108. But there seem to be no personal names formed with ᵈ*Kaššītu* as the theophoric element.

(1641) König, *Die elamischen Königsinschriften*, no. 54, *passim*; e.g., Bit-Kadashman (ii 77), Sha Kattarsah (iii 39), [M]urrattash (iii 37).

(1642) *BBSt* no. 6 i 10. Seux translates the epithet "qui a déporté les N.," (*Épithètes royales*, p. 281); but one wonders whether any widespread forcible movement of Kassites was involved, either into or out of Babylonia proper. See note 656 above.

(1643) *BBSt* no. 6 ii 12, 16.

(1644) Shown by the names of men of Kassite descent occurring in the texts of this time (see the list on pp. 250-254 above).

(1645) Eulmash-shakin-shumi, Ninurta-kudurri-usur I, and Shirikti-Shuqamuna were "sons" of Bazi; Ea-mukin-zeri was a "son" of Hashmar. Simbar-Shipak had a Kassite name (though his father bore an Akkadian one), and the name of Kashshu-nadin-ahi has ᵈ*Kaššû* as its theophoric element. Are we then to view the Second Sealand and Bazi dynasties as a renaissance of the Kassites after the native Babylonian Second Dynasty of Isin?

of the inhabitants of the eastern mountains with Babylonia. As late as the thirty-first year of Nabu–apla–iddina (probably c. 856), a member of the "House" of Habban was serving as a *kartappu* official in Babylonia. [1646] During this time and continuing through the days of Ashurbanipal, Assyrian texts repeatedly alluded to Babylonia as "Karduniash"; [1647] and a document of Ashurnasirpal II (883-859) referred to a Babylonian military force as "the widespread troops of (the land of) the Kassite(s)." [1648] It is possible that these allusions to the southern land by names connected with its former alien rulers may have been intended as derogatory.

By the year 850, the land of the Kassites at the northeastern edge of Babylonia seems to have passed from the Babylonian to the Assyrian sphere of influence. [1649] In 843 or shortly thereafter, Janzu, a member of the "House" of Hanban (=Habban) was appointed king of Namri (earlier Namar) by Shalmaneser III. [1650] Namri, however, remained a trouble spot for the Assyrians, and the armies of Shalmaneser had to campaign there again in 835 and 828. [1651] Namri was clearly once more independent by the time of the fourth campaign of Shamshi–Adad V (c. 814) and fought as an ally on the Babylonian side at the battle near Dur–Papsukkal. [1652] The Assyrian eponym chronicles record further campaigns against Namri in 797, 749, 748, and 744. [1653] Both Namri and Bit–Hamban (older Bit–Habban) were subdued by Tiglath–Pileser III[1654] and later by Sargon;[1655] but Sennacherib had to march against the Kassites again on his second campaign. [1656] In later days, the Kassites were able to maintain their independence even in the face of the Persians and Greeks. [1657]

[1646] *BBSt* no. 36 vi 18-19.

[1647] *Passim* in the Assyrian royal inscriptions (see Luckenbill, *ARAB*, II, p. 467 *sub voce*). After the Kassite period, Babylonians only rarely referred to their land as Karduniash (e.g., *BBSt* no. 24:5).

[1648] *AKA* 351 iii 17.

[1649] Just when the regions of Namri and Habban gained their independence from Babylonia is uncertain. Men from those areas were still serving in Babylonian officialdom late in the reign of Nabu–apla–iddina (c. 887-855), according to *BBSt* no. 28 rev. 21, no. 29 ii 11, no. 36 vi 19. But a half century earlier, Adad–nirari II had marched "as far as the passes of the land of Namri" (*KAH* II 84:24).

[1650] *WO* II/2 (1955) 152:95. An interpretation of the name Janzu is given above in note 1225. The previous king of Namri had had the Babylonian name Marduk–mudammiq (see note 1223 above). For the location of Namri, see the recent remarks of T. C. Young in *Iran* V (1967) 15 n. 39 and the map, *ibid.*, 18.

Kings with Kassite names are also attested in more northerly regions outside the Babylonian area of interest: Janzi–Buriash in Allabria in the time of Shalmaneser III (*WO* I/6 [1952] 472 iii 63, cf. *WO* I/1 [1947] 16 rev. 10) and Janzu of Nairi in the time of Sargon II (*TCL* III 306-307, etc.). Cf. also R. M. Boehmer's remarks connecting some aspects of the Manneans with the Kassites, *Bagh. Mitt.* III (1964) 18-19.

[1651] References in notes 1228 and 1230 above.

[1652] I *R* 31 iv 38.

[1653] *RLA* II 431-432, *passim*. Note also that Shamshi–ilu, Assyrian *turtānu* in the early eighth century, claimed to have ruled over "Syria (*māt Ḫatti*), the land of the Guti, and all the land of Namri" (Thureau-Dangin, *Til–Barsib*, p. 146:9).

[1654] Annals, 49; Nimrud Slab Inscription no. 1:17; II *R* 67:29, 34.

[1655] Lyon, *Sargon*, 3:14-15, etc.; *TCL* III 39-41.

[1656] *OIP* II 58:20-26, etc.

[1657] I shall treat Kassite relations with the Assyrians, Greeks, and Persians in a separate article, as mentioned in note 1581 above.

The Chaldeans [1658]

The first documentary hint concerning the presence of Chaldeans in southern Babylonia comes in the annals of Ashurnasirpal II, when the annalist refers to that area as "Chaldea" (*māt Kaldu*) after the account of the Assyrian campaign of 878. [1659] Ashurnasirpal himself had no direct contact with the region; but, according to his official annals, the king's reputed prowess in war caused fear even in the distant land of Chaldea.

A generation later, in 850, Shalmaneser III conducted a campaign in southern Babylonia, again referred to as *māt Kaldi*, [1660] where he encountered for the first time the three principal Chaldean tribes: Bit–Dakkuri, Bit–Amukani, and Bit–Jakin. [1661] Shalmaneser came into extended contact with only the northernmost of these groups, Bit–Dakkuri. He successfully besieged and burnt one of their fortified cities and was then marching to attack another city when he received the submission of their chief. It is understandable that the author of the redaction of Shalmaneser's annals inscribed on the Balawat Gates was less acquainted with the other two groups, Bit–Amukani and Bit–Jakin, with whom the Assyrians did not fight. He referred to the first of these as (Bit)–Ukani [1662] (perhaps reproducing a spoken Awukani or Awkani) and interpreted Jakin, the name of the other tribe, as the personal name of its chief, whom he termed "king of the Sealand." [1663]

Several interesting features emerge from Shalmaneser's account. Bit–Jakin, as often on later occasions, appeared as the strongest of the tribes; and its chief was the only sheikh accorded the title "king" by the Assyrian annalist. [1664] Already

[1658] For a general history of the Chaldeans and for a bibliography of earlier treatments of the subject, see Leemans, "Marduk–apal–iddina II, zijn Tijd en zijn Geslacht," *JEOL* X (1945-48) 432-455.

[1659] *AKA* 352 iii 24.

[1660] The principal written account of this campaign is in the Balawat Gate inscription, edited most recently by Michel in *WO* IV/1 (1967) 32-34 vi 5-8. This is supplemented by information given in the inscription on Shalmaneser's throne base, published by Hulin in *Iraq* XXV (1963) 48-69 and plate X. Further brief summaries mentioning Shalmaneser's conquests in Chaldea are listed in notes 1215-1217 above. Pictorial representations of the campaign or the tribute received from the Chaldeans appear on the Balawat Gates (King, *Bronze Reliefs*, pls. LX-LXV and Unger, *Mitteilungen des Deutschen Archäologischen Instituts, Athenische Abteilung* XLV [1920] pl. II, Platte 0) and on the Nimrud throne base (Mallowan, *Nimrud and Its Remains*, II, 448-449, e-g).

[1661] On the spelling of Dakkuru, Amukanu, and Jakin, see note 1218 above. The two lesser Chaldean tribes, Bit–Shilani and Bit–S(h)a'alli, are not attested in the ninth century, but only under Tiglath–Pileser (e.g., Nimrud Slab Inscription no. 1:8, II *R* 67:20), Sargon (e.g., Winckler, *Sargon*, pl. 30 no. 64:21), and Sennacherib (e.g., *OIP* II 43:47—read KUR É m*Šil–la–na*—, 53:41).

[1662] Written m*Ú–ka–ni* (but see *WO* IV/1 [1967] 34 vi 8, note). Cf. בית אוכן in the Assur Ostracon (line 15) and the partial list of writings cited by Unger, *RLA* II 35.

[1663] *šar māt Tam–di* (*WO* IV/1 [1967] 34 vi 7). For the name of Jakin, see note 1213 above.

[1664] Over a century later the official accounts of Tiglath–Pileser III's campaigns against the Chaldeans likewise bestowed the title of "king" only on Merodach–Baladan, head of the Jakin tribe (see Brink-

at this date, many of the Chaldeans could hardly be regarded as even semi-nomads. Some of them were living in walled towns, which belonged to the tribes; (1665) and, according to a contemporary royal grant, others dwelt in older cities of the south, such as Uruk. (1666) The Assyrian reliefs portray the regions of southern Babylonia in which the Chaldeans lived as filled with flourishing date palm plantations; (1667) and the Chaldeans also raised horses and cattle, some of which were presented to Shalmaneser. (1668) To judge from the articles of "tribute" paid to the Assyrians—ebony, sissoo, ivory, elephant hides, gold, and silver (1669)—the Chaldeans were benefitting from their location on the trade routes which passed through southern Babylonia.

Though the Chaldean tribes seem to have been nominal subjects of the Babylonian king, they enjoyed *de facto* independence. (1670) Shalmaneser III launched a campaign directly against them in 850 and claimed to have received tribute from them. (1671) There is no record of any further Assyrian–Chaldean relations before 814, when Chaldea sent soldiers to aid the Babylonian army of Marduk–balassu–iqbi, which was fighting against the troops of Shamshi–Adad V near Dur–Papsukkal in the Diyala region. (1672) Chaldea in this context appears as an independent ally of Babylonia, joining other allies—Elam, Namri (i.e., the Kassites), and the Arameans—in resisting Assyrian encroachments east of the Tigris.

In the years 813 and 812 Shamshi–Adad V effectively weakened the political power of northern Babylonia by removing two successive Babylonian kings, Marduk–

---

man, *Studies Oppenheim*, p. 12). One should note, however, that in the more compressed versions of Shalmaneser III's Chaldean conquests the chieftains were collectively referred to as "kings" (*WO* II/1 [1954] 34:43-44).

(1665) *WO* IV/1 (1967) 34 vi 6. The fortified cities of Chaldea in the time of Shalmaneser III are pictured in King, *Bronze Reliefs*, pls. LXIII-LXV and in Unger, *Mitteilungen des Deutschen Archäologischen Instituts, Athenische Abteilung*, pl. II, Platte 0. Models of walled cities presented by Chaldeans to Shalmaneser III in token of submission are portrayed on the reliefs of the Nimrud throne base (Mallowan, *Nimrud and Its Remains*, II, 448-449, f-g). Fortified cities in Chaldea are also depicted on later Assyrian reliefs, e.g., those of Tiglath–Pileser III (Barnett and Falkner, *The Sculptures of TP III*, pls. III-IV, X, XXXIII-XXXIV). At a later date Sennacherib claimed that Chaldeans were settled in some of the older cities in Babylonia (*OIP* II 25:39-41, etc.).

(1666) *RA* XVI (1919) 125 i 14-16.

(1667) King, *Bronze Reliefs*, pls. LX-LXV. Cf. also the date palms pictured as background scenery in the reliefs of the campaigns of Tiglath–Pileser III in Chaldea (Barnett and Falkner, *The Sculptures of TP III*, pls. III-VII, X-XII, XXXI-XXXIV).

(1668) *WO* IV/1 (1967) 34 vi 6. King, *Bronze Reliefs*, pl. LXIII; Mallowan, *Nimrud and Its Remains*, II, 448-449, g. Cattle as tribute from Chaldea are also shown in reliefs from the time of Tiglath–Pileser III (Barnett and Falkner, *op. cit.*, pls. V-VI).

(1669) *WO* IV/1 (1967) 34 vi 7-8, *Iraq* XXV (1963) 56:49.

(1670) See notes 1220-1221 above.

(1671) *WO* IV/1 (1967) 34 vi 6-8, etc. This may have included hostages, according to one interpretation of the young Chaldean princelings pictured on the Nimrud throne base (Mallowan, *Nimrud and Its Remains*, II, 447).

(1672) I *R* 31 iii 70-iv 45; *AfO* IX (1933-34) 91-92 iii 1-16. For the date, see note 1291 above.

balassu–iqbi and Baba–aha–iddina, from the throne. [1673] In 812 the Assyrian concluded his Babylonian campaign by journeying south to collect the tribute of the "kings of Chaldea." [1674] There is no record of Assyrian military action in the south at that time.

Adad–nirari III (810-783), like his father and grandfather before him, claimed to have exacted tribute from Chaldea. On an undated slab found at Nimrud, he states: "all of the kings of Chaldea became my vassals; I imposed on them tribute and dues for all future time." [1675] There is no record of a campaign by Adad–nirari against Chaldea. [1676]

After Adad–nirari III, a period of weakness set in in Assyria. This military nadir, combined with the continuing debility of northern Babylonia, which had been reduced to chaos by Assyrian raids, produced a favorable climate for the political rise of the Chaldeans. The earliest known Chaldean to sit on the throne of Babylonia was Marduk–apla–usur, [1677] but the date of his reign is unknown. He was succeeded by Eriba–Marduk, a member of the Jakin tribe, [1678] whose first regnal year cannot be dated later than 769. [1679] We do not as yet have enough information to determine whether any of the immediate royal predecessors of these two kings were also Chaldean. But about this time, probably between 820 and 770, may be dated the inscriptions of Nabu–shumu–lishir, a member of the Dakkuru tribe, [1680] and Marduk–shakin–shumi, a member of the Jakin tribe, [1681] both of whom might have been among the "kings of Chaldea" spoken of in the Assyrian sources pertaining to the time of Shamshi–Adad V and Adad–nirari III; whether these chieftains ever ruled over northern Babylonia is uncertain.

Despite his tribal origin, Eriba–Marduk was credited with stabilizing the whole of Babylonia once again. He inflicted a military defeat on Arameans who had appropriated fields belonging to the inhabitants of Babylon and Borsippa and returned those fields to their rightful owners. [1682] For his success in restoring political

[1673] *AfO* IX (1933-34) 92-100 iii 17-iv 29, cf. *ibid.*, 102; *CT* XXXIV 41 iv 1-14, Synchronistic History.

[1674] *CT* XXXIV 41 iv 11-12, Synchronistic History; cf. the eponym chronicle entry, *RLA* II 428:5.

[1675] I *R* 35 no. 1:22-23.

[1676] With the possible exception of his campaign for 802, which is recorded as *ana muḫḫi tâmti(m)* in the eponym chronicle (*RLA* II 429). For the interpretation of this entry, see note 1359 above.

[1677] *ADD* 888:5′, Dynastic Chronicle.

[1678] Evidence for Eriba–Marduk being a member of the Jakin tribe has been given by the present writer in *Studies Oppenheim*, p. 9 n. 13. The Dynastic Chronicle describes Eriba–Marduk's dynastic affiliation as the Sealand (*ADD* 888:6′-8′). The connection between Bit–Jakin and the Sealand has also been noted in the case of "Jakin" (note 1663 above) and in the case of Merodach–Baladan II (*Studies Oppenheim*, p. 12 n. 36).

[1679] See note 1384 above.

[1680] *JAOS* XIII (1889) lvi-lvii. See note 1338 above.

[1681] Carnegie (ed.), *Catalogue of the Collection of Antique Gems Formed by James, Ninth Earl of Southesk*, II, 82-83, Qβ39. For the reading of the name Marduk–zera–uballit, see *Studies Oppenheim*, p. 28 n. 159.

[1682] New Babylonian Chronicle, rev. 10-12.

stability, he was later accorded the comparatively rare honorific "establisher of the foundation of the land," reserved in this time for preeminent rulers in Babylonia. (1683) He was succeeded by Nabu–shuma–ishkun, a member of the Dakkuru tribe, (1684) during whose reign the governor (*šākin ṭēmi*) of Borsippa voiced strenuous complaints about chaotic political conditions. (1685)

The Dynastic Chronicle refers to the reigns of Marduk–apla–usur, Eriba–Marduk, and Nabu–shuma–ishkun as each comprising a separate dynasty; (1686) and it is possible that the hegemony over all of Babylonia may have rotated among the various powerful tribes.

With the accession of Nabonassar, the hegemony perhaps revived in northern Babylonia again. At any rate, Nabonassar's ascendancy was apparently maintained only by the arduous campaigning of Tiglath–Pileser III against Aramean and Chaldean tribesmen in 745 (1687) and by the Assyrian's assumption of protective suzerainty over Babylonia. (1688) Later, when Tiglath–Pileser was occupied with the conquest of Syria, a revolt broke out against the son of Nabonassar; (1689) and, following a second upheaval a month later, the Babylonian throne passed into the hands of Mukin–zeri of the Amukanu tribe. (1690)

Thus Tiglath–Pileser fought against the Chaldeans on at least two separate occasions: in 745 to assist Nabonassar and from 731 to 729 to depose Mukin–zeri. In 745 he devastated the regions occupied by the Shilanu and Amukanu tribes; and it was presumably on this occasion that Zakiru, chief of the Sha'allu tribe, swore oaths of fealty to Assyria. (1691) In the campaign(s) of 731-729, Tiglath–Pileser had to fight against the Sha'allu and Amukanu again. (1692) The forsworn Zakiru was removed in chains to Assyria, and many of his people were deported. (1693) Bit–Amukani was again brought low. Though Mukin–zeri remained unharmed, he was confined to his citadel of Shapija; and the surrounding countryside was plundered. (1694) Other Chaldean chieftains, who had been intriguing among themselves even before Mukin–zeri was defeated, hastened to pay tribute to Tiglath–Pileser. Nadinu of Larak, a city belonging to the Amukanu tribe, and Balassu of the Dakkuru brought

(1683) *Iraq* XV (1953) 133:13, *VAS* I 37 ii 44, *BBSt* no. 35:⌈16⌉ (texts of Merodach–Baladan II).

(1684) *JRAS* 1892 354 i 16′.

(1685) *JRAS* 1892 351-357.

(1686) *ADD* 888:5′-9′.

(1687) Sources listed in note 1442 above.

(1688) Shown by his claiming the title "King of Sumer and Akkad" by the year 743 (Nimrud Slab Inscription no. 1:1).

(1689) Babylonian Chronicle i 14.

(1690) Babylonian Chronicle i 16-18.

(1691) Inferred from the later Assyrian claim that Zakiru had violated his oaths (II *R* 67:19).

(1692) Babylonian Chronicle i 19-24, II *R* 67:19-25, etc.

(1693) II *R* 67:19-20.

(1694) II *R* 67:23-25.

gold, silver, and precious stones; (1695) and Merodach–Baladan of the Jakin tribe, whom the annals call "king of the Sea(land)," gave expensive gifts of gold, precious stones, exotic woods and plants, brightly colored garments, frankincense, cattle, and sheep. (1696)

In the course of the next seven years, according to a tradition from the middle of the seventh century, Shalmaneser V deported captives from Bit–Adini, probably a clan within the Dakkuru tribe. (1697)

The early history of the Chaldeans down to 729 B.C. is a curious mixture of economic prosperity and political impotence in the face of the Assyrians. Their walled cities, their agriculture and animal husbandry, their income from international trade availed them little because they were not united among themselves and because they were militarily weak. Leadership passed from one to another of the great tribes, but the nominal leader was seldom supported by the other tribes: once the principal protagonist had been subdued by the Assyrians, the rest of the tribes were prone to give in without a struggle. (1698) The Assyrian records allude to tribal chieftains as "kings" or "headmen," (1699) presumably indicating their mutual independence and supposed self-sufficiency. This state of affairs, as far as one can see, did not change for the better until the gifted Merodach–Baladan, who seized the Babylonian throne after the death of Shalmaneser V in 722, welded the Chaldean tribes into an anti-Assyrian alliance and utilized the wealth of his land to secure the assistance of the powerful Elamite army. (1700) With Merodach–Baladan a new era dawned for the Chaldeans.

We know little about the internal organization of the Chaldean tribes. As with the Kassite clan groups, the individual tribes are called *Bīt*–PN, "House of So–and–so," and members of the tribe are referred to as *mār* PN, "son of So–and–so." (1701) Chieftains of the tribes often bear no title other than *mār* PN, i.e., their tribal affiliation, in the Assyrian sources, (1702) though leaders of the Jakin tribe sometimes have the additional title "king of the Sealand." (1703) The Chaldean chieftains are referred to collectively as "kings of Chaldea" (1704) several times in late-

(1695) II *R* 67:26; cf. D.T. 3:18.

(1696) II *R* 67:27-28; cf. D.T. 3:19.

(1697) Assur Ostracon, line 15 (see note 1567 above).

(1698) This is true both in 850 and in 731-729, the only two times (before 722) for which we have detailed accounts of the Assyrians' fighting against the Chaldeans.

(1699) See notes 1704 and 1705 below.

(1700) See my remarks in *Studies Oppenheim*, p. 40 n. 236 and in *JNES* XXIV (1965) 161-166. Merodach-Baladan also was able to muster some troops of his own (e.g., Lie, *Sargon*, 276; *OIP* II 50:17, 51:27).

(1701) "So-and-so" being the personal name of the supposed eponymous ancestor of the tribe.

(1702) E.g., *WO* IV/1 (1967) 34 vi 6, II *R* 67:26.

(1703) E.g., II *R* 67:26.

(1704) *šarrāni* (*ša*) *māt Kaldi*: *Iraq* XXV (1963) 56:47, *WO* II/1 (1954) 34:43-44, *WO* II/2 (1955) 150: 84; *CT* XXXIV 41 iv 11-12 (Synchronistic History); I *R* 35 no. 1:22.

ninth- and early-eighth-century Assyrian sources and as "headmen" (1705) in the time of Tiglath–Pileser III. (1706) Despite their squabbles, the leading families of the tribes are known to have intermarried. (1707) Subordinate officials within the tribes are seldom attested: two individuals are referred to as *šakin* PN in the mid-ninth century, (1708) and one man is called a *ṣīru* (MAḪ) in the second half of the eighth century. (1709) In each case, these subordinate officials are described as attached to the chieftain of the tribe, i.e., *šaknu* (*ša*) PN, *ṣīru ša* RN, rather than to the tribe itself; they were presumably appointed by and responsible to the chieftain himself.

Where did the Chaldeans come from and what were their ethno-linguistic affiliations? There is no sure trace of the Chaldeans before they are found settled in southern Babylonia in the early ninth century. (1710) There is no extensive corpus of Chaldean personal names available. For the period between 878 and 722, we have the names of only eighteen individuals who are known to have been Chaldean; and fourteen of these names are Akkadian, showing that the Chaldean tribes—or at least their leaders—had rapidly become assimilated to Babylonian ways. (1711)

(1705) The earliest known references to the sheikhs or "headmen" of the Chaldeans occur in the time of Tiglath–Pileser III. The word is perhaps one that the Chaldeans themselves used. It occurs in Assyrian sources only in the stereotyped phrase "the headmen of Chaldea" (LÚ *r. ša māt Kaldi*[var.: *Kaldu*]). It is written variously as LÚ *ra–a'–sa–a–ni* (Rost, *TP III*, pl. XXXII 14, Nimrud Slab no. 1; cf. Rost, *TP III*, pl. I:⌜3'⌝, Annals, and pl. XXIX ⌜17⌝, Nimrud Slab no. 2, in which places only the beginnings are preserved—LÚ *ra*–⌜*a'*⌝–[ ] and LÚ *ra*–[ ]), LÚ *ra–šá–a!–nu* (Nimrud Letter VI A:18'), LÚ *ra–šá–ni* (*ABL* 418 rev. 6), and LÚ *re–e'–sa–ni* (Nimrud Letter V 5). The determinative before Kaldu in Nimrud Letter VI A:18' is apparently written as LÚ rather than KUR; but the removal of the bottom horizontal wedge in the LÚ would leave a perfect KUR, and its occurrence before *Kaldu* (rather than *Kaldaju*) points to a scribal oversight here.

(1706) In Tiglath–Pileser's description of the building of his palace at Calah, he alludes to building materials that were part of the tribute "of the princes of the Arameans and of Chaldea" (*malkī ša māt Areme u māt Kaldi*: II *R* 67:74).

(1707) Balassu of the Dakkuru tribe refers to one of the other tribal leaders (either Merodach–Baladan or Mukin–zeri, the contextual reference is not entirely clear) as his nephew (DUMU NIN–*ia*, Nimrud Letter V 13').

(1708) References and discussion of the reading in note 1208 above.

(1709) LÚ.MAḪ *ša Mukīn–zēri* (Nimrud Letter III A:7').

(1710) Arguments drawn from the etymology of *Kaldu* and (supposed) relationships with *Kešed/Kašdîm* and *Kardu*(*niaš*) are indecisive on this question of the origin of the Chaldeans. See Leemans, *JEOL* X (1945-48) 437 and R. P. Dougherty, *The Sealand of Ancient Arabia*, pp. 133 141 (both with bibliography of earlier discussions).

(1711) The fourteen Akkadian names are: *Balāssu* (chief of the Dakkuru tribe c. 730, II *R* 67:26, D.T. 3:18), *Erība–Marduk* (king), *Marduk–apla–iddina* (king of the Sealand in 729 and later king of Babylonia), *Marduk–apla–uṣur* (king), *Marduk–šākin–šumi* (father of Eriba–Marduk; prince of Jakin tribe, see p. 215 above), *Marduk–zēra–uballiṭ* (father of Marduk–shakin–shumi, see p. 216 above), *Mušallim–Marduk* (chief of the Amukanu tribe in 850, *WO* IV/1 (1967) 34 vi 8, etc.), (*Nabû*)–*mukīn–zēri* (king), *Nabû–šuma–iškun* (king), *Nabû–šumu–līšir* (member of the Dakkuru tribe in late-ninth or early-eighth century, see note 1338 above), *Nabû–ušabši* (chief of the Shilanu tribe in 745, Nimrud Slab no. 1:9, II *R* 67:15, D.T. 3:12), *Nādinu* (member of the Dakkuru tribe and head of Larak c. 730, II *R* 67:26, D.T. 3:18), *Šuma–ukīn* (son of Mukin–zeri, Nimrud Letter LXV 10), and *Zākiru* (presumably a hypocoristic for some name like DN–*zākir–šumi*; chief of the Sha'allu tribe c. 730, II *R* 67:19, D.T. 3:12).

The interpretation of the name *Zākiru* is probable, but not certain. The name is written only in Assyrian sources, and there it occurs twice as [m]*Za–qi–ru*. Since (a) the root ZQR is not productive of

Four names (Zabdi–il, Abdi–il, Jadi'–ilu, and Adinu) (1712) seem to be West Semitic, as is the tribal name Jakin. (1713) The name Adinu, attested both for a ninth-century individual and for a clan Bit–Adini in southern Babylonia in the time of Shalmaneser V, (1714) invites comparison with the well-known Aramean tribe of Bit–Adini in upper Mesopotamia in the ninth century. But whether or whence the Chaldeans are likely to have come from the West Semitic area cannot as yet be established. (1715)

Thus, what slim evidence is presently available suggests a West Semitic relationship for the Chaldeans and possibly some kinship with the Arameans. The Chaldeans, however, apparently preceded the Arameans as inhabitants of southern Babylonia by a century or more. But from the late eighth century on, the two groups occupied adjacent territory, especially in southeastern Babylonia. Though they worked together as allies, particularly in the days of Sargon and Sennacherib, the Chaldeans and Arameans were always regarded as distinct entities by the As-

---

personal names in Akkadian or nearby Semitic languages, while (b) the root ZKR (*ḎKR) is used in Akkadian, Amorite, Canaanite, and Aramaic personal names, and (c) the names of the other four contemporary Chaldean chieftains are all clearly Akkadian, it seems preferable to interpret the name as the common Akkadian PN *Zākiru* comparable to the other abbreviated names *Nādinu* and *Balāssu*, despite the Assyrian spelling with *q* (which may represent a partial adaptation of a Babylonian form to Assyrian). Even should the interpretation of this name some day prove to be different, it would not affect the basic conclusions reached here on the personal names of the Chaldeans.

(1712) Zabdi–il: *šaknu* of Mushallim–Marduk c. 850 (*RA* XVI [1919] 125 i 14); another man of the same name, not called a Chaldean, occurs in BM 40548:12, dated at Babylon in the ninth year of Eriba–Marduk. Abdi–il: *šaknu* of Adinu c. 850 (*SPA* I 285 no. XIV); a Bit–Abdi–il occurs in a fragmentary legal text drawn up in the second year of Nabonassar (BM 38114:7, unpublished). Jadi'–ilu: *ṣīru* of Mukin–zeri, according to Nimrud Letter III; for the writing of this PN, see Saggs, *Iraq* XVII (1955) 31. Adinu: chief of the Dakkuru tribe in 850 (*WO* IV/1 [1967] 34 vi 6, etc.).

(1713) We have not considered the mention of "Jakin" by the Assyrians in 850 as an occurrence of a Chaldean personal name for reasons given in note 1213 above.

The place names of Chaldea do not seem to offer much hope of linguistic analysis, save that some begin with the prefix *Ia*–. But place names are notoriously hard to date (see Gelb, "Ethnic Reconstruction and Onomastic Evidence," *Names* X [1962] 45-52) and may have nothing to do with the Chaldeans at all.

(1714) Assur Ostracon, line 15. See note 1567 above.

(1715) In *BASOR* CXXVIII (1952) 44-45, Albright presented arguments for Chaldean infiltration into southern Babylonia from eastern Arabia along the shores of the Persian Gulf in the tenth and ninth centuries B.C. These arguments were based on occurrences of an early South Arabic ("Chaldean") script in southern Babylonia, beginning in the seventh century B.C., and apparent instances of Babylonian names written in this script (see now also Biggs, *BASOR* CLXXIX [1965] 36-38 with additional editorial remarks by Albright in note 2 of that article). Is the script to be regarded as a form of writing used by native inhabitants of Babylonia (i.e., Chaldeans with Babylonian names) or as an import by traders or travellers from Arabia (cf. the Phoenician inscriptions found in roughly contemporary levels at Ur: Brinkman, *Orientalia N.S.* XXXIV [1965] 258 n. 1)? The fact that the script is found on bricks, tablets, and crude pots suggests that the inscribed objects themselves were probably not imports.

B. Moritz in the *Haupt Anniversary Volume*, pp. 205-206 also speculated on the relationship between the Chaldeans and the Arabs on the basis of Old Testament genealogies and the occurrence of the root *ksd/kld* in later Arabic geographical names.

syrians and the Babylonians; and any tribe or individual was considered as belonging to one group or the other—not both. (1716)

The Arameans

The Arameans play an important role in the history of the ancient Near East between 1150 and 700. At the time of their first clear appearance under the name Aramean, (1717) during the reign of Tiglath-Pileser I, they are already found spread out over a large area along the upper and middle Euphrates; (1718) and, before the death of Tiglath-Pileser, they had occupied a substantial portion of Syria (1719) and had invaded Assyria itself. (1720) By the middle of the tenth century, most of Syria and upper Mesopotamia was in Aramean hands; (1721) and northwestern Babylonia was subject to periodic Aramean raids. (1722) By the middle of the eighth century the Arameans were dispersed over an area roughly equivalent to that occupied by the Amorites at their height. (1723) From the late tenth century through the late

(1716) Though the Chaldeans and Arameans were both West Semitic, the two groups were never confused by the Babylonians. Also, despite the meager evidence we have at hand, we see that the Chaldeans had relatively larger and more unified tribes than the Arameans, that the Chaldeans were more Babylonized (to judge from the personal names occurring in both groups), that the Chaldeans described their tribal affiliation by calling themselves "son" of the eponymous ancestor, e.g., "son of Amukanu" (while the Arameans were called by a gentilic, e.g., "Puqudian"), and that Chaldean chieftains were called *ra'sāni* and Aramean leaders *nasīkāni* or *nasīkāte*. See also p. 273 and n. 1762 below.

The later tradition associating the Chaldeans and the Chaldean language with Aramaic (even to the point of calling Aramaic "Chaldee") presumably goes back to Daniel ii 4, in which the Chaldeans (כשדים, Septuagint Χαλδαῖοι) speak to Nebuchadnezzar in Aramaic (ארמית, Septuagint Συριστί). This statement undoubtedly reflects the state of affairs in later Neo-Babylonian and Persian times, when all the inhabitants of Babylonia used Aramaic as the vernacular.

A further interesting parallel is provided by Ibn Waḥshiyyah, a writer from southern Iraq in the ninth or tenth century A.D. who purportedly translated some ancient texts of his people into Arabic and who was given the gentilic epithet *al-Kasdānī* (also *al-Kaldānī*: Gustav Flügel, *Kitâb al-Fihrist*, I, 311). He translated these compositions from *lisān al-Kasdānī* (D. Chwolson, *Über die Überreste der altbabylonischen Literatur in arabischen Übersetzungen*, p. 18), which was a later form of Aramaic. It should be noted that the "Chaldeans" (*al-Kasdāniyyūn*) are also sometimes called "Kardians" (*al-Kardāniyyūn*; see *ibid.*, p. 101). See further Chwolson, *Die Ssabier und der Ssabismus*, I, 703-713. This interchange of forms in *Kald-*, *Kasd-*, and *Kard-* in Arabic is reminiscent of the older *Kaldu*, *Kaśdîm*, *Kardu* in the older Semitic languages.

(1717) Strictly speaking, "Ahlamu Aramean," i.e., (KUR) *Aḫlamê* (KUR) *Armaja* (*AfO* XVIII [1957-58] 350:34, etc.), in the time of Tiglath-Pileser I. For earlier, more dubious references to the Arameans see S. Moscati, "Sulle origini degli Aramei," *RSO* XXVI (1951) 16-22; A. Dupont-Sommer, "Sur les débuts de l'histoire araméenne," *Vetus Testamentum*, Supplement I (1953) 40-49; Kupper, *Nomades*, pp. 112-114. Whether the third- and second-millennium references to *Aram*, *Aramu*, *Army*, etc., should be related to the later Arameans is open to debate.

(1718) *AKA* 73 v 49-50.

(1719) *AfO* XVIII (1957-58) 344:29-35, etc.

(1720) *AfO* XVII (1954-56) 384:3′-5′, 12′.

(1721) The sources are analyzed by Kupper, *Nomades*, pp. 116-120.

(1722) *JCS* XIX (1965) 123-124; Religious Chronicle iii.

(1723) There is also a KUR *A-ri-ma-a+a* among the Nairi regions conquered by Shamshi-Adad V on his third campaign (I *R* 30 iii 51); but this is probably not to be connected with "Aramean" for which the usual Assyrian gentilic is *Armaju* (see note 1724 below).

eighth century, the Assyrians conducted campaigns against the Arameans in many sections of Mesopotamia and Syria, at first with varying success, but eventually subduing them effectively almost everywhere except in eastern Babylonia.

The Arameans in the vicinity of Babylonia, especially along the lower Tigris and on the middle Euphrates just northwest of Sippar, represent a substantial chapter in the overall story of Aramean political power. Situated as they were, they were in a position to menace several important trade routes passing along the Euphrates, Diyala, and Tigris. Though called "Arameans" by both Babylonians and Assyrians, (1724) who did not distinguish them by name from their western counterparts, the origin of these peoples is obscure; and the relationship between them and the western Arameans is largely undetermined. The Arameans around Babylonia are found settled there in large numbers in the time of Tiglath–Pileser III; and it is generally assumed that they had originally come from the west, migrating along the middle Euphrates and filtering gradually into Babylonia, beginning in the eleventh century. But evidence regarding this supposed migration is frustratingly sparse; and, in many instances, one may question whether the prevailing historical reconstructions are entirely satisfactory.

Because of the paucity of evidence, I propose to present an analysis of the subject in reverse chronological order, dealing first with the better-known Aramean tribes established around Babylonia in the time of Tiglath–Pileser III and then sifting the available evidence to determine their antecedents. This treatment, then, will have three principal parts: (a) the Arameans from 745 to 722, (b) the Arameans from 1150 to 746, (c) the origins of the Arameans in eastern Babylonia.

The Arameans 745-722 B.C. (1725)

The inscriptions of Tiglath–Pileser III mention by name thirty-six Aramean tribes settled in Babylonia whom the contemporary Assyrian armies conquered. (1726)

(1724) The land of the Arameans is referred to in Babylonian as *Aramu*, gentilic *Aramû* (New Babylonian Chronicle, obv. 8′). In Assyrian, the short second syllable is affected by vowel harmony: *Arumu*, *Areme*, *Arama*, gentilic *Armaju*; beginning in the time of Sargon II, the Babylonian forms also appear occasionally in Assyrian (e.g., as listed in Lie, *Sargon*, p. 87).

(1725) The most detailed and systematic studies of the Arameans in and around Babylonia in the eighth century are still: Streck, "Keilschriftliche Beiträge zur Geographie Vorderasiens, I.," *MVAG* XI/3 (1906); the pertinent sections in Schiffer, *Die Aramäer* (1911), especially pp. 115-135; and Moritz, "Die Nationalität der Arumu-Stämme in Südost-Babylonien," *Haupt Anniversary Volume*, pp. 184-211. These studies are still valuable, especially in so far as they touch upon the period under consideration here.

Though our treatment here is concerned only with the Arameans in Babylonia down through the reign of Shalmaneser V, we will occasionally call attention to relevant information in slightly later sources, e.g., the inscriptions of Sargon or Sennacherib or the Harper letters. Such information will be explicitly labelled as later.

(1726) II *R* 67:5-8 contains a list of thirty-five names, with the Puqudu listed *ibid.*, 13 (the Puqudu are called Aramean in Nimrud Slab Inscription no. 2:6). Similar lists in inscriptions of Tiglath–Pileser III are shorter but contain no different names. Two tribes, the *Nakri* and *Tanê*, occur only in Annals 13

According to the texts of Tiglath–Pileser written in 729 or shortly thereafter, (1727) these Aramean tribes were settled along the Tigris, Euphrates, (1728) Surappi, (1729) and Uknu rivers as far as the shore of the Persian Gulf. (1730) The Uknu is traditionally identified with the Kerkha, and the Surappi may perhaps be identified with the Tib or one of the other streams flowing from the mountains east of the Tigris. (1731) Attempts to localize the Aramean habitats along these large rivers with greater precision are as yet principally speculative, (1732) but there is evidence that the Arameans may have occupied areas along the Tigris north of present-day Baghdad (1733) and on the Euphrates around Sippar. (1734) The greatest concentration of Arameans,

---

(probably campaign of 745); but they are not specifically called Aramean. The people of the land of Labdudu (II *R* 67:14), who were deported by Tiglath–Pileser but not specifically called Aramean in his inscriptions, are classified as Arameans by Sargon (Winckler, *Sargon*, pl. 30 no. 64:18, pl. 39:72). The inscriptions of Sargon and Sennacherib mention still more Aramean tribes.

(1727) I.e., after the events of his seventeenth *palû* (presumably to be dated in 729 because his accession year, 745, was reckoned as his first *palû*).

(1728) Written ÍD A.RAT. For the interpretation of this writing, see note 1209 above.

(1729) The name of this waterway occurs to date only in the inscriptions of Tiglath–Pileser III and Sargon II. The earliest attested writing is ÍD *Su–ra–pi* (Nimrud Slab Inscription no. 1:5), and the usual writing is ÍD *Su–rap–pi* (II *R* 67:9 and *passim*). The writing ÍD *Su–ra–ap–pi* (Lie, *Sargon*, 278) establishes that the name should be spelled with a doubled *p*.

(1730) With allowance for minor variations in wording, both D.T. 3:7-8 and Nimrud Slab Inscription no. 2:7-9 refer to "all the Arameans of the bank(s) of the Tigris, Euphrates, and Surappi, (and) Uknu as far as the Lower Sea of the rising sun." II *R* 67:9 describes the tribes as "all the Arameans of the bank(s) of the Tigris, Euphrates, and Surappi as far as the Uknu of the shore of the Lower Sea" (*adi libbi Uknê ša kišād tâmti(m) šaplīti*). The earliest inscription, Nimrud Slab Inscription no. 1:5-6, omits the Euphrates in its enumeration—"all the Arameans of the bank(s) of the Tigris (and) Surappi as far as the Uknu of the shore of the Lower Sea" (*adi Uknê ša aḫ tâmti(m) šaplīti*)—presumably because Tiglath–Pileser's campaign of 745 did not affect the Arameans on the Euphrates.

(1731) The only passage that might give some indication of the location of the Surappi is in Sargon's annals (Lie, *Sargon*, 274-282), where a channel was cut from the Surappi to flood the environs of Dur–Athara (site unknown). When that town was taken, fugitives went to the marshes of the Uknu river—presumably nearby—to hide from the Assyrians. Streck (*MVAG* XI/3 [1906] 3) identified the Surappi with the modern eastern branch of the Tigris (as opposed to the Shatt el–Hai). Schiffer (*Die Aramäer*, p. 119) presented plausible arguments for the Surappi being a canal connecting the Uknu with the Tigris.

(1732) One tantalizingly broken passage in the cylinder BM 113203, relating the first campaign of Sennacherib, originally divided the names of the Arameans into three groups, the first two of which were distinguished by the fact that they dwelt near a specific river (lines 12-14). Despite the ingenious restorations of Smith (*The First Campaign of Sennacherib*, pp. 58-59, 79), later followed by Luckenbill (*OIP* II 49), there is no real clue as to which rivers should be restored here; and, actually, Smith's restoration of the *Uknû* in line 14 as the habitat of the Hindaru, Puqudu, etc., is probably wrong, since Sargon specifically states that in the year 710 the Puqudu and Hindaru fled at his approach from their own locale to the Uknu—which would lead us to conclude that the two regions were distinct. But the grouping of the tribes in the text of Sennacherib is an item of information which may be utilized at some future date.

(1733) The traditional homeland of the Itu' (Utu') was on the west bank of the Tigris north of Dur–Kurigalzu (Scheil, *Annales de Tn. II*, obv. 49). A broken section of the annals of Tiglath–Pileser III (lines 134-136) may indicate that there were also Arameans up towards the Lower Zab.

(1734) In the time of Sargon II, the Ham(a)ranu tribe was raiding Babylonian caravans, probably near Sippar (Lie, *Sargon*, 379-382). For the location of the Hamranu, see note 1446 above.

however, was probably in southeastern Babylonia in the neighborhood of ʿAmara between the Tigris and Elam. ([1735])

The names of the thirty-six tribes specifically called Aramean in the inscriptions of Tiglath-Pileser III are:

1. Itu'	19. Gurumu
2. Rubu'	20. Hudadu
3. Hamaranu	21. Hinderu
4. Luhuatu	22. Damunu
5. Hatal(l)u	23. Dunanu
6. Rubbu	24. Nilqu
7. Rapiqu	25. Rade
8. Hiranu	26. Da-[ ]
9. Rabilu	27. Ubulu
10. Nasiru	28. Karma'
11. Gulusu	29. Amlatu
12. Nabatu	30. Ru'a
13. Rahiqu	31. Qabi'
14 Ka-[ ]	32. Li'tau
15. Rummulutu	33. Marusu
16. Adile	34. Amatu
17. Kipre	35. Hagaranu
18. Ubudu	36. Puqudu. ([1736])

Some of these tribes, e.g., the Itu', ([1737]) Rubu', Hamaranu, Li'tau, ([1738]) Ru'a, and Puqudu, are quite well known. Others of lesser renown are nonetheless also attes-

([1735]) It was in this region that the principal encounters between the Assyrians and the Arameans took place in the days of Sargon and Sennacherib, as well as in the time of the later Harper Letters.

([1736]) The principal source for this list is the summary of the Aramean tribes conquered by Tiglath-Pileser III between 745 and 729 as given in II *R* 67:5-8 (names 1-35) supplemented by *ibid.*, 13 (name 36). Shorter summaries are given in D.T. 3:5-6 (=Rost, *TP III*, pl. XXXIV; names 1-7, 12, 19, 23, 27, 30, 32-33), in Nimrud Slab no. 2:4-6 (=Rost, *TP III*, pl. XXIX; names 1-4, 12, 21, 30, 32-33, 36), and in ND 5419:5-6 (=*Iraq* XXVI [1964] pl. XXVI, fragmentary list including names 3-6 and 32-33). Tiglath-Pileser's annals allude to the Dunanu (line 13), the Adile (line 14), and the city Amlatu of the Damunu tribe (line 143). Nimrud Slab no. 1 refers to the Dunanu, Itu', Rubu' (lines 4-5) and the Puqudu, Ru'a, and Li'tau (line 12) in the campaign of 745. See also note 1726 above.

([1737]) Sometimes called Utu': see Streck, *MVAG* XI/3 (1906) 27, Thureau-Dangin, *Til-Barsib*, p. 146: 10, and *ABL* 349 rev. 3; cf. Scheil, *Annales de Tn. II*, obv. 49. For their location, see note 1733 above.

([1738]) In the inscriptions of Tiglath-Pileser III and Sennacherib, the name of the tribe is written regularly as LÚ *Li-i'-ta-(a)-ú* (Nimrud Slab no. 1:12; Nimrud Slab no. 2:6; II R 67:7; *Iraq* XXVI [1964] 120:6; *OIP* II 25:49, 49:14, 54:56, 57:15) and once as LÚ *Li-ta-a-ú* (D.T. 3:6, Tiglath-Pileser III). In the inscriptions of Sargon II the name appears variously as LÚ *Li-i'-(it)-ta-a+a* (Winckler, *Sargon*, pl. 30 no. 64:19) and LÚ *Li-ta-a+a* (*ibid.*, pl. 39:74). Outside of the Assyrian annals, however, the name invariably occurs as Litamu or Li'tamu (presumably for a spoken Li'tawu). In an unpublished economic

ted in either the annals of Sargon or Sennacherib or in the Harper Letters: Luhuatu, (1739) Hatal(l)u, (1740) Rubbu, Nabatu, Rahiqu, Kipre (*Kiprê*), Ubudu, Gurumu, Hinderu, (1741) Damunu, Ubulu, Hagaranu. Some "tribes" appear elsewhere only as cities, and their tribalization may have been an Assyrian fabrication or simplification: Rapiqu, (1742) Hiranu, (1743) Rabilu, (1744) Hudadu, (1745) Rade (*Radê*), (1746) Karma', (1747)

---

text from the reign of Eriba–Marduk in the early eighth century, a man is called the "son" of ᵐ*Li–ta–me* (BM 40548:10). In the Nimrud Letters, the name is written as LÚ *Li–iʾ–ta–mu–*[(*ú*?)] (IV A 9′; IX 8′, ⌈12′⌉) and as ⌈LÚ *Li*⌉*–ta–ma–a+a* (I 39); in a Harper Letter written in the time of Sargon, the name appears as LÚ *Li–ta–mu* (ABL 436:9). In an economic text from the reign of Shamash–shuma–ukin, a *tāmirtu Li–ta–mu* is connected with the Euphrates (*TCL* XII 11:1-2); and in economic texts from the reign of Darius a city (URU) or *tāmirtu Li–ta–mu/–me/–mi* is frequently linked with the province of Babylon (*Dar.* 152:3, 172:2, 290:1, 202:3, 227:4, 273:1, 26:⌈3⌉; *BRM* I 73:2; cf. *Bīt Li–ta–mu* in *Dar.* 329:3); whether the Litamu tribe was also in western Babylonia in earlier days is unknown.

(1739) Occurs only in the inscriptions of Tiglath–Pileser III and in Neo-Assyrian letters (*ABL* 1175:8 and 468 rev. 8, where it is written Lihuataju; see also Dietrich, *WO* IV/1 [1967] 79). This is not related to the Syrian land of *Luḫuti* (*AKA* 372 iii 83).

(1740) Sometimes previously normalized as Harilu. The name is usually written LÚ *Ḫa–*RI*–lu* (e.g., *Iraq* XXVI [1964] 120:5) or LÚ *Ḫa–*RI*–la–a+a* (e.g., *ABL* 721:8, rev. 4). Streck in *MVAG* XI/3 (1906) 23-24 proposed reading the name *Ḫatallu* on the basis of a supposed connection with the city Hatallua, which occurs in the Persian period texts from Nippur; this connection is unproven. The reading *Ḫatal(l)u* (possibly with a single *l*), however, may be deduced from the writing LÚ *Ḫa–*RI*–a+a* which occurs in *ABL* 1175:9, 12 in the same context as the Luhuatu tribe (which immediately precedes Hatal(l)u in the lists of Tiglath–Pileser III).

(1741) Also occurs as Hindaru in the inscriptions of Sargon II (e.g., Lie, *Sargon*, 48:2) and Sennacherib (e.g., *OIP* II 49:13).

(1742) This is the only name in the list not prefixed with a LÚ determinative. Rapiqu was the well-known border city at the northwestern edge of Babylonia, e.g., *AfO* XVIII (1957-58) 350:35. See note 748 above.

(1743) The city Hiranu was a place along the middle Euphrates, possibly near Sippar (Scheil, *Une saison*, p. 27). The second syllable of the name is long according to the writing URU *Ḫi–ra–a–nu* in *AKA* 376:97. A supposed first-millennium reference to a Hiranu tribe in *ABL* 1468 rev. 7 (LÚ *Ḫi–i–ra–*[*a–nu*]) is based on a doubtful restoration, since Hiranu elsewhere is never written with a long first syllable (*AKA* 376:97; *Nbn.* 505:3; *ADD* 210 rev. 7; cf. also the MB references cited in the next paragraph).

In the Kassite period, however, Hiranu, is apparently used of a tribe or group of Ahlamu, which appear occasionally as troops or guards in contemporary Babylonian texts. In *PBS* II/2 114, six men on guard duty (*manzalti* PN) are described as ᵐ*Ḫi–ra–a–nu* (presumably for *mār Ḫirānu*, cf. *ibid.*, lines 1-2) after their own personal names; all the individuals in this text are explicitly labelled *Aḫlamû* (line 16). In a ration text, *BE* XV 198, two individuals are described as *mār* ᵐ*Ḫirāni* (lines 50 and 105). In a letter found at Dur–Kurigalzu (*Iraq* XI [1949] 139 no. 10:4, ⌈21⌉), *ḫurād Ḫirāna*, "troops of (the) Hiranu," are described as stationed in territory normally belonging to Assyria and in the regions of Suhi and Mari on the middle Euphrates.

(1744) URU *Rab–bi–lu* (Babylonian Chronicle i 4), URU *Rab–bi–i–li* (*BOR* I [1886-87] 76:7).

(1745) The city Hudadu, well known in the MB and NB periods, was the seat of a province under the Kassite Dynasty and the Second Dynasty of Isin (Brinkman, *JESHO* VI [1963] 234-235). Besides the references to the city assembled by Forrer in *RLA* I 391 (under Bagdadu, a reading long ago suggested, e.g., by Delitzsch, *Wo lag das Paradies?*, p. 206), we should also note I *R* 70 i 6, *BIN* I 159:20, *YOS* III 142:8, and possibly *AfO* X (1935-36) 41 no. 92:⌈7⌉ (MA) and *TCL* I 196:1 (OB). The city was probably located in northern Babylonia somewhere between Sippar and the Tigris (see already Thureau-Dangin, *RA* IX [1912] 3) and perhaps not too far from later Baghdad (hence some justification for Delitzsch's reading). For the possibility of another Hudadu in southern Babylonia, see Michel, *WO* IV/1 (1967) 35 n. 15.

(1746) URU *Ra–di–e*: *ABL* 281 rev. 16, 1464:6.

(1747) Perhaps identical with URU *Kar–me–e* in *ABL* 574:6, *ADD* 778:7.

Amlatu, (1748) Amatu. (1749) Other tribal names are apparently unattested as yet outside the inscriptions of Tiglath–Pileser III: Nasiru (LÚ *Na–ṣi–ru*), (1750) Gulusu, Rummulutu, Adilu, (1751) Dunanu, Nilqu, Qabi', Marusu.

There is also a small corpus of Aramean personal names from about this time in Babylonia which may be culled from economic texts dated in the reigns of Nabonassar and Tiglath–Pileser III and from the slightly later inscriptions of Sargon. Though the names in documents from the time of Nabonassar and Tiglath–Pileser III are not specifically designated as Aramean, they may be identified as such by comparison with similar names explicitly labelled as Aramean in the inscriptions of Sargon II. In the texts of Sargon we can detect some patterns in the names of Aramean individuals, principally the occurrence of the *ia*– prefix, the –*ān*(*u*) suffix, and final aleph. Names of Arameans mentioned by Sargon which fall into these categories include:

(a) *ia*– prefix: [m]*Ia–a–di*, [m]*Ia*–[ ], [m]*Ia*–⌈*x*⌉–*ia–nu*, [m]*Ú–si–ia–da–a'*, [m]*Ia–nu–qu*;
(b) –*ān*(*u*) suffix: [m]*A–si–an*, [m]*Ḫa–ma–da–a–ni*, [m]*Ia*–⌈*x*⌉–*ia–nu*, [m]*Sa–a'–da–ni*, [m]*Ḫa–u–ka–nu*; (1752)
(c) final aleph: [m]*Ú–si–ia–da–a'*, [m]*Ra–a–pi–i'*, [m]*Sa–me–e'*. (1753)

We then find non-Babylonian names of similar formation occurring in Babylonian texts from the reigns of Nabonassar and Tiglath–Pileser III: [m]*Ba–ruq–qa–a'* (*TCL* XII 3:5, cf. 1:7) and [m]*Ba–ru–qa–a'* (*BRM* I 12:4), [f]*I–me–ta–a'* (*TCL* XII 3:3, 8), [f]*Ma–a'–ia–nu* (*BRM* I 5:13), [m]*Ia–qa–a–a–ta* (*BRM* I 12:3, 14:4), [[m]]*Ba–aḫ–ia–nu* (*BRM* I 17:3), [ ]*x–ia–pa–a'* (*BRM* I 17:4), [m]*Ia–ti–ri* (*BRM* I 19:1, 14). Such names as [md]*A–ra–mu* (*BRM* I 18:2), [m]*Na–si–ku* (i.e., "sheikh," *TCL* XII 1:6), and [m]*Ab–di*!–*il* (BM 38114:7, unpublished) are also presumably Aramean. (1754)

(1748) A city of the Damunu tribe according to Tiglath–Pileser's annals, line 143.

(1749) Listed as a city along the Uknu according to Lie, *Sargon* 50:12 (restoration from parallel text). This phenomenon of tribalized city names may be compared with a slightly later usage of the determinative URU in the Harper letters where URU *Pu–qu–du* (*ABL* 268:9, etc.), URU *Ru–u'–ú–a* (*ABL* 268:10), URU *Gam–bu–lu* (*ABL* 269:9, rev. 5), and even URU *Bīt–Dakkūru* (*ABL* 336:5, 16) show that the city determinative is being prefixed to larger units. [See also addendum, p. 396].

(1750) Schiffer, *Die Aramäer*, p. 122, suggested connecting the tribe with the city (URU) *Na–ṣir* in *Dar.* 110:2.

(1751) Connected by Streck, *MVAG* XI/3 (1906) 13, with the city whose name is written URU *A–di–* DINGIR (*ADD* 443:6, 396 rev. 4; II *R* 53 no. 1:29).

(1752) Some of the names ending in *–an* could be interpreted as –AN (=*il*).

(1753) Sheikhs or (eponymous) masters of villages listed in Lie, *Sargon*, 288-326.

(1754) Abdi–il could, of course, be another type of West Semitic. Moritz in his article, "Die Nationalität der Arumu-Stämme in Südost-Babylonien," *Haupt Anniversary Volume*, pp. 184-211, concluded from a study of the tribal and personal names that these groups must have been Arabic. It seems doubtful, however, that his evidence need be interpreted so literally; and the ties of the Arameans (and most other Semitic groups) with the Arabian peninsula could be explained in a more remote and generic fashion.

Little is known about the Arameans and their tribes except what is recorded in the Assyrian royal inscriptions and official correspondence. In general, the Aramean tribes were smaller units than their Chaldean counterparts ([1755]) and were less given to relying on fortified cities for protection against the Assyrians. ([1756]) They were much less Babylonized than the Chaldeans, to judge from the names of their sheikhs, who seldom bore Babylonian names. Yet the Arameans in Babylonia possessed a number of cities and towns, ([1757]) although they may also have lived in small villages ([1758]) or in travelling bands (like the later raiders near Sippar). ([1759]) The inscriptions of Sennacherib record that there were also Arameans living in major cities of Babylonia—Uruk, Nippur, Kish, Cutha, and Sippar—who supported the anti-Assyrian cause in 703; ([1760]) and administrative texts from the time of Nabonassar and Tiglath-Pileser III show that persons with Aramean names had settled down and were drawing rations as part of the Babylonian economy. ([1761])

The Aramean tribes in Babylonia do not seem to have been as unified as the Chaldeans, i.e., with each tribe subject to a single powerful leader. ([1762]) Some tribes have more than one sheikh (*nasīku*), and as many as six are attested for one group. ([1763]) We do not know whether each sheikh governed a part of the tribe or whether the tribe as a whole was subject to several leaders; the former alternative seems more

([1755]) To judge from the more than thirty-five of them occupying smaller areas than the five large Chaldean tribes. But a tribe like the Gambulu, first mentioned in the time of Sargon, must have been quite large, to judge from the extent of its holdings cited in the Assyrian annals (Lie, *Sargon*, 286-p. 48:1).

([1756]) The only city in Aramean territory in Babylonia which attempted to hold out against the Assyrians was Dur-Athara in 710 (Lie, *Sargon*, 274-280); and its defense was organized by Merodach-Baladan, a Chaldean.

([1757]) See the references in notes 1741 to 1749 above and the city Pazitu mentioned in Nimrud Slab Inscription no. 1:4. Sargon mentions 44 fortified cities (*ālāni dannūti*) of the Gambulu (Lie, *Sargon*, 48:1).

([1758]) E.g., an eighth-century sheikh (*nasīku*) owned agricultural land in a small community (BM 40548:3, unpublished inscription from the reign of Eriba-Marduk).

([1759]) Lie, *Sargon*, 379-382. Cf. *Iraq* XVI (1954) 192 vii 45-74.

([1760]) *OIP* II 25 i 39-41 mentions Arabs, Arameans, and Chaldeans in these cities.

([1761]) *TCL* XII 3:3, 5, 8; *BRM* I 5:13, etc.

([1762]) We have noted above that, in contrast to the Chaldeans, the Aramean tribal organizations were not referred to in terms of "houses" of eponymous ancestors (*bīt* PN) and that individuals were not referred to as "sons" of the eponymous ancestor. Rather, the tribes were given simple names such as the Puqudu or the Damunu; and individual tribal members, seldom referred to by name before the time of Sargon II and not too commonly even then, were usually distinguished by some gentilic such as the "Puqudian" (*Puqudaju*), if their tribal affiliation was indicated at all. The only instance I have been able to find of an Aramean tribesman in Babylonia who is called a "son" of his tribe is in an unpublished economic text of the early eighth century (ninth year of Eriba-Marduk), in which a man named *Kābitu* is called DUMU ^{m}*Li-ta-me* (BM 40548:10). Since this is the earliest known reference to one of these Aramean tribesmen in Babylonia, this may explain why his patronymic is given in the same form as a Chaldean; the Babylonians may have been unacquainted with the correct form of genealogical citation or perhaps the convention was fixed only later. (But compare the Bit-Litamu attested in *Dar.* 329:3).

([1763]) This is known from texts from the reign of Sargon (e.g., Lie, *Sargon*, 48:5-6, 52:2, etc.); but note that Lie restores a reference to "8 sheikhs" in the annals, line 281. Cf. *ABL* 906:1-2, 1112:3-4. Plurals of *nasīku*, "sheikh," are *nasīkāti/u* (*ABL* 280:19, etc.) and less commonly *nasīkāni* (*ABL* 1065:5, 12; *ADD* 955:2; etc.).

plausible, as we shall see below. On what basis sheikhs were chosen is unknown; (1764) but they could be deposed by their followers, as may be seen in the time of Sargon II when the Tu'muna tribe ousted their chief, (1765) presumably a pro-Assyrian, and handed him over to Merodach-Baladan. (1766)

The history of the word *nasīku*, "sheikh," reveals some aspects of the history of this important institution. Before the time of Sargon II there are only isolated occurrences of the term *nasīku*. The first clear references (1767) to the Aramean *nasīku* occur in the texts of Ashurnasirpal II: two rulers of Aramean lands west of Assyria proper (the land of Nairi and the land of Laqe) are referred to as *nasīku*, (1768) as is the ruler of the eastern land of Dagara, part of Zamua. (1769) Next in time is an unpublished Babylonian economic text from the ninth year of Eriba-Marduk, in which an individual is called LÚ *nasīku* (no tribe or region mentioned). (1770) There is also possibly a reference in Nimrud Letter no. XXXIII (line 14), but the reading of the signs is uncertain.

From the time of the Sargonids, however, there are abundant references to the *nasīku*, who, as far as we can tell at present, was then restricted chiefly to Aramean tribes dwelling in southeastern Babylonia. *Nasīku* was used to refer to the sheikh of a people (or tribe), a land, a city, or even a river. (1771) A sheikh or sheikhs are thus far attested from:

PEOPLES *Babilaju* (*ADD* 478 rev. 3), (1772) *Ḫalat* (*ABL* 520:14), *Iašiān* or *Iaši-il* (*ABL* 280:14), *Naqiraju* (ND 259, *Iraq* XII [1950] 194), *Nugû'*, (*ABL* 280:20), *Pillat* (*ABL* 520 rev. 17), *Puqudu* (Lie, *Sargon*, 48:5-6), *Tu'muna* (Lyon, *Sargon*, 3:18);

LANDS *Ḫindaru* (Lie, *Sargon*, 327), *Iadburu* (Lie, *Sargon*, 52:2), *Iakimānu* (*ABL* 1109 rev. 7-9 = *RMA* 90), *Kaldu* (*OIP* II 47 vi 25), *Manānu* (*ABL* 520:4);

(1764) In the early ninth century, Ashurnasirpal II appointed an individual to sheikhdom (*ana nasīkūte*) among the Arameans living in the Nairi lands (*AKA* 239 rev. 42).

(1765) Not "chiefs," as translated by Lyon (*Sargon*, p. 33, "Fürsten") and Luckenbill (*ARAB* II 118). The word is plainly singular: LÚ *na-sik-šú-nu* (Lyon, *Sargon*, 3:18).

(1766) Lyon, *Sargon*, 3:18. Sargon describes himself as "the despoiler of the Tu'muna, who had arrested (*ipīdu*) their sheikh and sent him to the king of Chaldea." For *pâdu*, "to take prisoner," "to bind with fetters," see Landsberger, *ZDMG* LXIX (1915) 508.

(1767) Earlier apparent, but dubious references occur: (a) in an economic text from the time of Rim-Sin of Larsa, in which an individual is called LÚ *na-zi-ku* (*TCL* X 80:11); (b) in an epithet of Nebuchadnezzar I, *nasīk/q šarrī* (*BBSt* no. 6 i 11). Seux, *Épithètes royales*, p. 201, reads the latter reference as *nasīq šarrī* and translates "d'élite parmi les rois." These two early references are isolated and may bear no relation to the later, typically Aramean institution of the *nasīku*. (N.B.: There is only one certain instance in which the later term *nasīku* is known to have been used of a group not Aramean—when a group of Chaldean chieftains are once referred to as *nasīkāni* [*OIP* II 47 vi 25, Sennacherib]).

(1768) *AKA* 239 rev. 42 (abstract *nasīkūte*, genitive), 359 iii 45.

(1769) *AKA* 303 ii 24.

(1770) BM 40548:3 (genitive).

(1771) Presumably the region around the river.

(1772) KÁ.DINGIR-*a*+*a*. Probably not referring to the city of Babylon, but possibly to a sheikh as "Babylonian" or to a homonymous town such as (URU) *ša Babilê* (Lie, *Sargon*, 298).

CITIES *Laḫīru* (*ABL* 280:20), *Murmašu* (*ABL* 831 rev. 5-6), *Upî* (*ABL* 608 rev. 7), *Zāmê* (Lie, *Sargon*, 48:4);

RIVER *Tupuli'aš* (*ABL* 906:1-2, 1112:3-4). (1773)

Since there is usually more than one official of *nasīku* rank attested for the larger Aramean tribes (e.g., Puqudu) and lands (Hindaru, Jadburu, Jakimanu) and for the river area (Tup(u)liash) and only one for cities and peoples that do not occur elsewhere in the lists of the principal Aramean tribes, we might conclude that sheikhs in the larger groups generally ruled over sub-tribal units and that only smaller groups like the Tu'muna had a single sheikh. (1774)

The economy of the Arameans, to judge from textual evidence from the time of Sargon, was based at least partially on animal husbandry and on agriculture. Horses, mules, oxen, sheep, and goats were captured from the Aramean tribes by the Assyrians. (1775) A percentage of the annual increase of the Aramean flocks was designated for tribute to Assyria (1776) and for the maintenance of the cults of Marduk and Nabu. (1777) Date palms belonging to the Arameans were cut down by Assyrian troops, (1778) and part of the annual tribute was to be paid in grain. (1779) Since another portion of the yearly tribute was levied in money (silver), (1780) the Arameans do not seem to have lived wholly on a barter economy.

What must have been fairly extensive military activities by Tiglath–Pileser III against the Arameans are only slightly illuminated by his surviving royal inscriptions from Calah. Despite Tiglath–Pileser's claims to have subdued 36 Aramean tribes between 745 and 729, there is no detailed record of his defeat of any of them. Though probably seven tribes are mentioned by name as having been brought into submission in 745 (1781) and two more are mentioned in a campaign about 738, (1782)

(1773) To be connected with the ÍD *Tup-li-áš* near the Uknu in southeastern Babylonia (Lie, *Sargon*, 48:3), as distinguished from the region Tupliash near the Diyala.

(1774) Poebel comments on the etymology and origin of *nasīku* in *AS* XIV 62-63; see also earlier remarks by Peiser, *OLZ* XX (1917) 367, and Meissner, *MAOG* III/3 (1929) 31-32. There is no evidence for a form *nasīkatu* as a feminine counterpart of *nasīku*; in *ABL* 1109 rev. 8-9 read "and all the sheikhs of Jakimanu" (*u nasīkātu ša māt Iakimānu gabbi*). m*Nasīku* is also used as a personal name (e.g., *TCL* XII 1:6). Cf. Hebrew and later Aramaic נסיך.

(1775) Lie, *Sargon*, 280 and p. 52:2 ("sheep and goats" = *ṣēnu*). Note also the quantities of animals captured from the Arameans around Babylonia by Sennacherib (*OIP* II 57:16, 25 i 51-52, etc.).

(1776) Lie, *Sargon*, 284-285.

(1777) *Ibid.*, 331-332.

(1778) *Ibid.*, 335-336.

(1779) *Ibid.*, 284.

(1780) *Ibid.*, 284.

(1781) The Itu' and Rubu' (Nimrud Slab Inscription no. 1:5); the Puqudu, Ru'a, and Litamu (*ibid.*, 12). The conquest of the Dunanu and Adile is mentioned in a section of the annals (lines 13-⌈14⌉) which is probably to be assigned to 745; see also the possible addenda in note 1726 above.

(1782) Gurumu (Annals, 134) and Damunu (*ibid.*, 143).

the conquest of the other 25 or 26 tribes [1783] was not related in detail in the annals of Tiglath–Pileser; and their names occur chiefly in the summary of his conquests through the year 729. [1784] Though it is likely that the Assyrian king achieved most of his victories against the Arameans in the years 745, c. 738, or in 731-729, we cannot as yet date many of these conquests with certainty. But, by the year 729, Tiglath–Pileser could claim to have subdued 36 Aramean tribal groups along the Tigris, Euphrates, Surappi, and Uknu rivers.

Tiglath–Pileser frequently mentioned that he had defeated or conquered the Arameans; [1785] and, in one broken passage, he speaks of a battle line drawn up, probably by Arameans. [1786] These statements imply that the Arameans did on occasion engage the Assyrians in battle and that flight, though their usual tactic, was not their sole strategy. [1787] As the result of his military successes, Tiglath–Pileser claimed to rule over the Arameans and even said that he "assumed the kingship of their kings." [1788] After his campaign of 745 he apparently settled some of the Arameans (the Itu' and the Rubu') in the newly built city of Kar–Ashur, [1789] perhaps to be located slightly east of the Tigris and north of the Diyala; [1790] some of these Arameans, principally the Itu', later furnished special contingents for Assyrian military service. [1791] Groups of the Puqudu, Ru'a, and Litamu were also uprooted and settled elsewhere in 745. [1792] All of these Arameans who were conquered in 745 were jurisdictionally incorporated into Assyria and put under the control of Assyrian provincial officials. [1793] Further trouble, which came from Arameans living near the Lower Zab (i.e., from the Gurumu [1794] and from part of the Damunu tribe living in the city of Amlatu) [1795], resulted in sizable numbers of

(1783) The city of Amlatu, also mentioned in the Annals, 143, is counted as a separate tribe in Nimrud Tablet no. 1 (=II *R* 67); hence the question as to the exact total.

(1784) Fullest example: II *R* 67:5-8, 13.

(1785) II *R* 67:9, 13; Nimrud Slab Inscription no. 2:9.

(1786) Annals, 136 (*iškuna sidirtu*). LÚ *Arumu* seems to be the only likely subject, but the passage is slightly damaged.

(1787) The Arameans also opposed the Assyrians in the battle near Dur–Papsukkal about 814 (I *R* 31 iv 39).

(1788) *šarrūt šarrī*(LUGAL.MEŠ)*–šunu aṣbat* (Nimrud Slab Inscription no. 1:14). The LUGAL and MEŠ are transposed in the text.

(1789) Nimrud Slab Inscription no. 1:5-6; cf. Annals, 10. Also during his reign some of the Labdudu were uprooted and deported to Assyria (II *R* 67:14-15).

(1790) This may be judged from its being mentioned in a context with Urzuhina, Mazamua, Arrapha, and Lahiru in *ADD* 950 rev. 4-8.

(1791) E.g., Nimrud Letters XII, LX, LXXXVI, and *passim* in the Nimrud and Harper letters.

(1792) Nimrud Slab Inscription no. 1:13. Nimrud Letters XXV and XXVI deal with the resettlement of Arameans at some time in the late eighth century.

(1793) Nimrud Slab Inscription no. 1:7, 14; cf. Annals, 15, etc. The chieftains of the Arameans and Chaldeans also paid tribute (*biltu*) to help build Tiglath–Pileser's palace at Calah (II *R* 67 rev. 24).

(1794) Annals, 134. Is *Kiši* (determinatives missing; Annals, 135-136) to be interpreted as a personal name?

(1795) Annals, 143.

these groups being deported to Syria. (1796) But Tiglath–Pileser's general policies of conquest, deportation, and incorporation into the Assyrian provincial structure did not have lasting effects on these Aramean tribes. In succeeding decades, during the reigns of Sargon II and Sennacherib, practically every major Aramean tribe in Babylonia which had been conquered by Tiglath–Pileser III was again in revolt. (1797)

The Arameans 1150-746 B.C.

Material for reconstructing the history of the Arameans in Babylonia for the four centuries preceding the time of Tiglath–Pileser III is quite scanty. In the days of Tiglath–Pileser I (1115-1077), the Arameans along the Euphrates to the west of Assyria and Babylonia proper became a source of grave concern to the two older civilizations of Mesopotamia; (1798) they appear in the royal inscriptions of Tiglath–Pileser I under the name KUR *Aḫlamê* KUR *Armaja*, which could be translated as "Ahlamu Arameans" or as "Aramean Ahlamu." (1799) Beginning in the fourth year

(1796) Annals, 139(?) and 143-145.

(1797) If we exclude city names from our consideration (notes 1742-1749 above), then 16 of the remaining 28 tribes mentioned in Nimrud Tablet no. 1 (=II *R* 67) rebelled against Sargon or Sennacherib—this includes all the principal tribes. In shorter summaries, where only the names of important tribes are given, the percentage of future rebels is much higher: 10 out of 13 in D.T. 3 and 8 out of 10 in Nimrud Slab Inscription no. 2 (two of the tribes in these texts who are not mentioned as rebels later are the Luhuatu and the Marusu, both groups of little consequence).

(1798) Ashur–resha–ishi I, the father of Tiglath–Pileser I, had already had to fight against "the widespread forces of the Ahlamu" (*ummānāt Aḫlamî rapšāti*; Weidner, *Tn. I*, no. 60:6).

(1799) *Aḫlamû* has also been interpreted as a common noun meaning "companions, confederates." This etymology, based on a comparison with the Arabic *ḫilm* (plural *aḫlām*), has been demonstrated as unlikely by Moscati, *JSS* IV (1959) 303-307. (Albright in *CAH* II² xxxiii 47 translates the phrase as "Aramean bedawin.")

Moscati, however, goes on to state that there is no connection between the Arameans and the Ahlamu in the fourteenth through twelfth centuries (*JSS* IV [1959] 304) and ends by concluding "that Aḫlamū is to be regarded as the proper name of a population-group, and not a common name applied to a group of populations forming a 'confederacy'; and that the Aḫlamū are independent, in origin and in nature, of the Aramaeans, who can neither be identified with them nor regarded as forming part of them" (*ibid.*, 307). Few people would dispute Moscati's observations on the unlikelihood of interpreting Ahlamu as "confederacy." But Moscati has presented no evidence to prove that Ahlamu should be regarded as the proper name of a specific population group; indeed, one could raise the question whether the name might not rather refer to a certain type of semi-nomad, whatever his ethno-linguistic affiliation, somewhat as *Sutû* and *Ḫapiru* were used at various times. A further and much more serious question bypassed by Moscati is the usage of *Aḫlamû* and its derivatives as an appellative for "Aramaic" or "Aramean" in later times. Though this later usage can hardly be taken as proof that the *Aḫlamû* and the *Aramu/Arumu* are to be identified in all instances in earlier times, it does suggest strong historical ties between the two (a supposition supported by the recurring doublet *Aḫlamê Armaja*).

It should be remarked that *Aḫlamê Armaja* occurs only in Assyrian royal inscriptions of Tiglath–Pileser I, Adad–nirari II, and Ashurnasirpal II. The KUR determinative is sometimes omitted before *Aḫlamê* (e.g., *AfO* XVIII [1957-58] 350:34, var.; *AKA* 240 rev. 47) and a single MEŠ after *Armaja* usually suffices for the two names, thus indicating that the phrase is to be regarded as a unit rather than as naming two distinct groups. In the time of Tiglath–Pileser I, the phrase is used for semi-nomads on the middle

of his reign, [1800] Tiglath–Pileser I conducted a series of police actions against the *Aḫlamê Armaja* principally on the upper and middle Euphrates, but eventually reaching into Syria as well. [1801] Tiglath–Pileser burned some of their villages near Jebel Bishri [1802] but, despite numerous campaigns, was unsuccessful in containing their raids. In his early encounters with them, Tiglath–Pileser ranged only between Carchemish and Suhi on the Euphrates. [1803] Later he was forced to fight with them as far as Rapiqu, the northwestern border of Babylonia. [1804] In the west, Tiglath–Pileser in his later campaigns had to leave the Euphrates and protect the caravan routes in Syria all the way to the Lebanon; [1805] but subsequently he was able to protect the area only as far as Palmyra (*Tadmar*). [1806] Eventually Arameans [1807] penetrated Assyria itself, including the district around Nineveh, and forced Tiglath–Pileser to withdraw to the mountains. [1808]

---

and upper Euphrates and in Syria. In the inscriptions of Adad–nirari II, it designates a group on the middle Euphrates (*KAH* II 84:33); and, in the Kurkh monolith of Ashurnasirpal II, it refers to men in the service of Bit–Zamani in the Nairi lands (*AKA* 240 rev. 47).

If we consider the use of *Aḫlamû* as distinct from *Aḫlamê Armaja,* we find the term used during the Middle Babylonian period down to the time of Ashur–resha–ishi I to denote raiders and soldiers hostile to Babylonia and Assyria (*JCS* VI [1952] 144:14, 145:12-16; *AOB* I 62:23, 118 ii 39; *KBo* I 10:36-54; Weidner, *Tn. I*, no. 16:70), mercenaries in the Babylonian army (*Iraq* XI [1949] 139 no. 10), merchants (*PBS* I/2 51:22), gate guards at Nippur (*PBS* II/2 56:3), and other people settled within Babylonia (*BE* XVII 31:25; *PBS* II/2 114, probably also a type of guard). While it is difficult to affirm without qualification that the Ahlamu were forerunners of the later Arameans, it is noteworthy that they inhabited much of the same territory along the middle and upper Euphrates and that the Hiranu tribe, classified as Ahlamu in the Kassite period (*PBS* II/2 114), was later classified as Aramean (II *R* 67:4); and the two groups were at least very closely related. By the later Neo-Assyrian period, the designation *Aḫlamû* used of people seems to have become largely an anachronism, chiefly confined to omina and prayers (Kupper, *Nomades*, pp. 133-134), where it almost certainly refers to Arameans; it is used rarely in Neo-Assyrian royal inscriptions to describe groups principally east of the Tigris who are identical with or at least geographically close to the Arameans (Tiglath–Pileser III, Annals, 134; Sennacherib, *OIP* II 77:13; cf. also the GN *Bīt Aḫlamê* near the Elamite frontier which was conquered by Sennacherib, *OIP* II 39:62, *AfO* XX [1963] 90:24). In the early Persian period, a slave had the name of his owner written on his hand in Akkadian (*akkadattu*) and Aramaic (*aḫ!-la-ma-at-ti*, *CAD* A/1 192-193); and Aramaic words are described as *ina aḫlamê* in bilingual lists (*ibid.*, 193). In the Seleucid-period sage list published by van Dijk, it is stated that Esarhaddon's *ummânu* was called Ahiqar (m*A-hu-u'-qa-a-ri*) by the Arameans ([LÚ] *Aḫ-la-*MI*-mu-ú*, UVB XVIII 45:20).

(1800) *AKA* 73-74 v 46-63.

(1801) E.g., *AfO* XVIII (1957-58) 344:31-32.

(1802) *AKA* 74 v 59-63. On Jebel Bishri, see most recently G. Buccellati, *The Amorites of the Ur III Period*, pp. 236-237 (with citation of earlier literature).

(1803) *AKA* 73 v 48-50.

(1804) *AfO* XVIII (1957-58) 344:33, 350:35-38, cf. 351:41-43 (where gods and property of the land of Suhi are carried off by the Assyrians). Ahlamu infiltration as far as Rapiqu, however, need not have been new in the time of Tiglath–Pileser I. Tukulti–Ninurta I had also fought against "the land of Mari, the land of Hana, the land of Rapiqu, and the 'mountains' (*šadân*) of the *Aḫlamî*" (Weidner, *Tn. I*, no. 16: 69-70), implying that these areas were hostile territory even then.

(1805) *AfO* XVIII (1957-58) 344:31-32.

(1806) *AfO* XVIII (1957-58) 350:35.

(1807) Described as *bītāt māt Armaja* (*AfO* XVII [1954-56] 384:3′, ⌈11′⌉) rather than *Aḫlamê Armaja*.

(1808) *AfO* XVII (1954-56) 384:11′-13′. Some of the Assyrians had fled to the land of Kirriuri at a slightly earlier date to escape the Arameans (*ibid.*, line 6′); for the location of the land of Kirriuri (probably

What was happening in Babylonia at the same time is unclear. The only sources which mention the Arameans in the time of Marduk–nadin–ahhe and Tiglath–Pileser I are Assyrian and are concerned chiefly with Assyria proper and with Assyrian military actions. They tell us only that the Arameans had reached the northwest border of Babylonia (Rapiqu) in the reign of Tiglath–Pileser I (1809) and then, at the very time when the Arameans were advancing into Assyria, the Babylonian throne changed hands (1810)—possibly as the result of a simultaneous wave of Arameans invading Babylonia. (1811)

From the time of Adad–apla–iddina (1069*-1048*) on, there are isolated references to Aramean contacts with Babylonia. Adad–apla–iddina himself, according to a Babylonian chronicle, was an Aramean usurper. (1812) During his reign, Arameans and Sutians were said to have ransacked the venerable Babylonian shrines at Sippar and Nippur. (1813) Tukulti–Mer, contemporary king of Hana in Aramean territory on the middle Euphrates, dedicated a votive object to Shamash at Sippar, (1814) showing that he had access to the shrine and that the intentions of westerners towards the Babylonian religious centers were not always spoliative. During these years, Assyria continued to conduct campaigns against the Arameans (1815) and recaptured some of the temple property stolen from Babylonia at the time of Adad–apla–iddina, which they returned to its rightful owners. (1816)

In the next century during the reign of Nabu–mukin–apli (979*-944*), hostile Arameans were active on the Euphrates around Babylon and Borsippa. They seized the river crossing at Kar–Bel–matati and prevented the journeys of the divine statues of Nabu and Marduk for the New Year's festival. (1817)

By the ninth century, we find in Babylonia that a change of attitude had taken place towards the Arameans. In 878 Nabu–apla–iddina sent a contingent of Babylonian troops under the command of his brother to aid the traditionally Aramean state of Suhi in resisting the advance of Ashurnasirpal II along the middle Euphra-

---

Herir), see the discussions of Michel in *WO* I/2 (1947) 65 n. 2 and R. Boehmer, *BJV* V (1965) 192-193 (both citing earlier bibliography, to which now may be added *AfO* XVII [1954-56] 384:6′, Kinnier Wilson in *Iraq* XXIV [1962] 105, and Hulin in *Iraq* XXV [1963] 59).

(1809) *AfO* XVIII (1957-58) 344:33, 350:35-36.

(1810) *AfO* XVII (1954-56) 384:8′-9′.

(1811) For a possible reference to Ahlamu around Babylonia in the time of Marduk–shapik–zeri, see p. 133 above.

(1812) New Babylonian Chronicle, obv. 8′ (see note 840 above).

(1813) *JCS* XIX (1965) 123:10-13 (inscription of Simbar–Shipak). This inaugurated the era of Aramean and Sutian disturbances reflected in the Era Epic, *BBSt* no. 36, etc.

(1814) *AnOr* XII 336-338.

(1815) *AKA* 132-137 (Broken Obelisk).

(1816) *JCS* XIX (1965) 123:14-19.

(1817) Religious Chronicle iii 4′-15′. The abbreviated references in the New Babylonian Chronicle, obv. 14′-17′ may refer to similar disturbances.

tes. [1818] Two generations later, about **814**, Aramean forces allied with Babylonians, Chaldeans, Elamites, and Kassites (i.e., men of Namri) to fight against the armies of Shamshi-Adad V near Dur-Papsukkal east of the Tigris. [1819]

In the eighth century we find Arameans affecting Babylonia in still a different way. By the time of Eriba-Marduk, Arameans had taken over fields near Babylon and Borsippa and had to be ousted forcibly from them. [1820] From the same reign, an economic document from Babylon records the name of a member of the Litamu tribe [1821] and the names of four other people which are presumably Aramean: *ᵐḪa-di-ia-a-ni*, *ᵐḪa-as-sa-a-nu*, *ᵐGa-ú-ma-nu*, *ᵐIl-ti-ḫa-ni* (a sheikh). [1822] In the following reign, that of Nabu-shuma-ishkun, Arameans were involved in fighting for possession of fields near Borsippa. [1823] These are the earliest instances of substantial Aramean settlement in Babylonian territory, and they occur just before the widespread attestation of Aramean tribes all around Babylonia in the time of Tiglath-Pileser III.

In surveying the evidence available on the Arameans who affected Babylonia between **1150** and **746**, we find that we are not in a position to answer even such essential questions as: who were these Arameans and where did they come from, why did they come into Babylonia, and what effects did they have there? First, our presently available evidence is almost entirely restricted to Arameans active along the northern section of the western border of Babylonia and says nothing about that segment of the Arameans which was most important in the days of Tiglath-Pileser III, i.e., the tribes east of the Tigris. Secondly, the group or groups called *Aramu* in this period by the Babylonians and *Arumu* by the Assyrians are not well defined; and one frequently wonders whether at least some of the same peoples were also described as *Sutû*. [1824] We have little evidence as to the language spoken by these people, and few personal names are mentioned for the Aramean groups in contact with Babylonia.

In summary, we may say that the known history of the Arameans around Babylonia during this period falls roughly into three phases. The first phase, which lasted until about the second half of the tenth century, shows the Arameans as raiders, active chiefly along the Euphrates from Sippar to Borsippa but sometimes penetrating into the interior of the land. These raiders were most likely to attack the settled areas of Babylonia in times of famine, when they were unable to procure

(1818) *AKA* 351 iii 19-20.
(1819) I *R* 31 iv 39.
(1820) New Babylonian Chronicle, rev. 10-12.
(1821) ᵐ*Ka-bi-tu* DUMU ᵐ*Li-ta-me* (BM 40548:10, unpublished) is one of the parties involved in a land sale. For an explanation of this writing, see note 1762 above.
(1822) BM 40548:8-11, 3, ᵐ*Zab-di-ìl* (*ibid.*, 12) may also be an Aramean name.
(1823) *JRAS* 1892 354 i 18′.
(1824) See pp. 285-287 below.

food by peaceful means and when the inhabitants of Babylonia were apt to be weaker than usual. (1825) Though these Arameans were known to plunder cities and to seize key transportation points, they were not known to settle down in Babylonia itself in this period. That they were not mere uncouth barbarians is hinted by the dedication inscription of Tukulti-Mer, king of Hana, to the god Shamash; (1826) and the fact that a king is attested suggests that the invasions may not have been haphazard razzias by roving marauder groups but planned sorties by politically organized and settled units. The Babylonians were probably not very successful in withstanding the Arameans, especially if the latter could plunder as far south as Nippur. Furthermore, the Babylonians were slow to recoup their losses: they rebuilt at Nippur only after the Assyrians had recovered some of the stolen property for them; (1827) and, at Sippar, the attempts made under the Second Sealand and Bazi Dynasties to restore the cult and regular food offerings in the temple of Shamash were largely ineffectual. (1828)

The second and third phases of the history of the Arameans around Babylonia between 1150 and 746 may be described more succinctly. In the second phase, covering most of the ninth century, we find Babylonians and Arameans allied against the Assyrians and lending each other military aid. The third phase, commencing about the year 800, shows the Arameans beginning to settle down in Babylonia, usurping fields near the large western cities of Borsippa and Babylon and making isolated appearances in the economic documents.

But, as mentioned above, this evidence regarding the Arameans between 1150 and 746 is confined almost entirely to western Babylonia. In the following section, we will consider what indications there are for the origin of the more important Aramean groups east of the Tigris.

The Origins of the Arameans in Eastern Babylonia

The proximate origin of the Arameans who are found settled east of the Tigris in or near Babylonia in the time of Tiglath-Pileser III is obscure. The often accepted theory, namely that these Arameans migrated into Babylonia in large numbers beginning in the eleventh century, is only one of several possible—but not provable—hypotheses on the subject. I wish here to present rough sketches of three

(1825) The earliest recorded instances of the Arameans overrunning Assyria, in the time of Tiglath-Pileser I, came in times of severe famine and crop failure; and Ahlamean and Sutian disturbances in settled areas were frequently connected with food shortages. This topic is discussed at length in Appendix C below.

(1826) *AnOr* XII 336-338.

(1827) *JCS* XIX (1965) 123:13-124:24.

(1828) *BBSt* no. 36 i 13-ii 17.

different theories on the origins of these eastern Arameans, not necessarily the only theories which might validly be projected, but those which seem to be more plausible at present.

The first of the three theories regards the relationship of the Arameans with the earlier Amorites. Even a superficial glance at the geographical distribution of the Amorites in the early part of the second millennium and a comparison with the areas occupied by the Arameans in the second half of the eighth century will show that they inhabited many of the same regions in Syria, along the middle Euphrates, and in southeastern Babylonia. Furthermore, we have practically no information about the population of southeastern Babylonia between the end of the First Dynasty of Babylon and the middle of the eighth century, when the Arameans are found settled there en masse. Since there is no substantial evidence for the Arameans coming into this area in the intervening period and since there is no trace of an older Babylonian or Amorite population being displaced, one is led to wonder whether the southeastern Arameans might not be either remote descendants of earlier Amorites or at least a group speaking a related West Semitic language. This speculation is enhanced when one reflects on the frequent occurrence of the *ia–* prefix and *–ān(um)* suffix in the personal names of southeastern Aramean sheikhs—exactly the same elements that have been cited as characterizing many names of the old Amorite invaders of Babylonia. [1829] Though this evidence is hardly more than circumstantial, it raises the interesting—if somewhat remote—possibility that the Arameans may have been living in eastern Babylonia earlier than is usually assumed.

The second of the three theories would argue for an invasion and settlement of Arameans in Babylonia beginning in the eleventh century. [1830] Towards the end of the reign of Tiglath–Pileser I, the first waves of Aramean invaders hit Assyria. At the same time or shortly thereafter, Babylonia was also affected. The first obvious sign of Aramean influence there was during the reign of Adad–apla–

(1829) M. Noth's thesis, presented at length in 1928 in *Die israelitischen Personennamen im Rahmen der gemeinsemitischen Namengebung* and updated recently in his *Die Ursprünge des alten Israel im Lichte neuer Quellen* (1961), that the Amorite language is to be interpreted as "Proto-Aramean," seems to go too far in attempting to explain the similarities between the two tongues. See the justified criticism of this position by Edzard, "Mari und Aramäer?" *ZA* LVI (1964) 142-149.

(1830) Cameron, *History of Early Iran*, p. 116, suggested that the GN Reshu mentioned in the account of the twelfth-century Babylonian campaigns of Shilhak–Inshushinak (König, *Die elamischen Königsinschriften*, no. 54 iii 19) "is probably the Rashi tribe of Arameans, well known to the Assyrians from Sargon onward and located in the mountains east of Der"; and this tentative interpretation was again mentioned by Labat, *CAH* II² xxxii 11. While Reshu and Rashi could conceivably be identical, Rashi is not an Aramean tribe, but a land located near the Elamite–Babylonian border and much involved in Elamite affairs (e.g., *ABL* 295:1, 1022:6, 1260:2). Though sometimes mentioned by Neo-Assyrian kings campaigning in eastern Babylonia (Sargon: Lie, *Sargon*, 52:5, etc.; Sennacherib: *AfO* XX [1963] 90:⌈33⌉, cf. Babylonian Chronicle iii 10) and therefore connected with campaigns that also went against the Arameans in nearby regions, Rashi and its inhabitants are never referred to as Aramean in the texts. For a possible location of Rashi south of modern Ilām, see T. C. Young, Jr., *Iran* V (1967) 13 n. 21.

iddina, the so-called "Aramean usurper," [1831] when Arameans and Sutians invaded the land and sacked the sanctuaries of Nippur and Sippar. [1832] Over the next centuries, western raiders, called variously Arameans or Sutians by different sources, continued to harass western Babylonia, seizing small transportation centers and generally obstructing traffic and commerce. [1833] This time of weakness for the Babylonian central government would have afforded ample opportunity for Arameans to settle in Babylonian territory.

The third of the three theories would see the southeastern Arameans settling on the fringes of Babylonia around or not too long after 800. Neither Assyrian nor Babylonian sources mention them as being present in the area before that. The Assyrian kings, who campaigned extensively east of the Tigris in the ninth and eighth centuries, did not encounter Arameans settled there before the time of Tiglath–Pileser III. [1834] The earliest mention of Arameans settled down in Babylonia comes in the first half of the eighth century, when the Arameans are reported to have taken over fields near Babylon and Borsippa and Arameans participated in a legal transaction at Babylon. [1835]

It is especially striking that before 745 there is practically no mention of the more than thirty-five Aramean tribes found around Babylonia in the days of Tiglath–Pileser III. The full-scale concentration of named Aramean tribal groups in eastern Babylonia is preceded by almost total silence, since very few of these tribes are known by name before the time of Tiglath–Pileser. The sole notable exception is the Utu' or Itu' tribe, which lived along the western banks of the Tigris north of Babylonia and which had been fought against by Tukulti–Ninurta II in the early ninth century. [1836] In addition, Shamshi–ilu, Assyrian *turtānu* in the early eighth century, claimed that he had overcome the Utu', Rubu', Hatallu, and Labdudu tribes. [1837] Though Shamshi–ilu did not state where these tribes were situated, the locations of the Utu' and of the Labdudu (along the Elamite border near Der) are known; and it is possible that the Rubu' and Hatallu were also living somewhere in the general region which had been northeastern Babylonia and which was the

[1831] New Babylonian Chronicle, obv. 8′. This, however, is an isolated instance of an Aramean settling in Babylonia at this time. His Babylonian name and his building of Babylonian temples and fortifications lead us to suspect that he was or at least aimed to be culturally assimilated. (See note 840 above).

[1832] *JCS* XIX (1965) 123:10-13: New Babylonian Chronicle, obv. 10′-11′; probably also *BBSt* no. 36 i 4-8.

[1833] See note 1817 above.

[1834] Except perhaps in the Nairi region (see note 1723 above). The location of the land of *Arumu* which furnished troops to aid Babylonia at the battle near Dur–Papsukkal about 814 (note 1819 above) is unknown; it could, but need not, represent an Aramean population living east of the Tigris at this time.

[1835] See p. 280 above.

[1836] Scheil, *Annales de Tn. II*, obv. 49.

[1837] Thureau-Dangin, *Til–Barsib*, p. 146:10-11.

frequent object of Assyrian campaigns in the early eighth century. [1838] These are the only sure references in Assyrian sources to Aramean tribes in eastern Babylonia before the time of Tiglath–Pileser III.

Another factor which might argue for heavy Aramean settlement in Babylonia only in the eighth century is the relative lateness of the use of Aramaic writing in Babylonia as compared to Assyria. In Assyria, where Arameans were deported in number already in the first half of the ninth century, the use of Aramaic writing is attested in the eighth century [1839] and quite common in the seventh century. [1840] In Babylonia on the other hand, with the exception of a fragmentary document which is possibly to be dated to the year 728, [1841] there is no Aramaic writing dating before the sixth century. In fact, the peak period of Aramaic writing in Assyria in the seventh century is matched in Babylonia by a contemporary dearth of Aramaic script and paralleled only by the rise of Aramaic writing in the next century under Nebuchadnezzar II. [1842] This slender evidence might suggest that the settlement of Arameans in Babylonia also took place a century later than their settlement in Assyria.

It should be noted that the time of chaos between the deposing of Baba–aha–iddina and the accession of Eriba–Marduk, a period during which there were years when "there was no king in the land," [1843] would have provided a suitable opportunity for the Arameans to consolidate their position in Babylonia without interference from an organized central government. Even under Chaldean monarchs like Eriba–Marduk and his successor Nabu–shuma–ishkun, the central government was unable to assert much power; and, only with the advent of Assyrian aid to Nabonassar, were the outlying regions of Babylonia put under any sort of political control.

These three theories regarding the origins of the eastern Arameans all revolve around a single point, the silence of the documents, and how that silence is to be interpreted. Depending on whether the silence is seen as indicating the presence, absence, or movement of the Arameans, one may opt for any of the three theories or some modification of them. My purpose here has been simply to emphasize that we do not have sufficient evidence now to do more than speculate vaguely on the

(1838) See the eponym chronicle entries for the years 795, 794, 790, 783, 782, 777, 771, 769, 767 (*RLA* II 429-430).

(1839) *CIS* II/1 pp. 3-13 nos. 2-13. A scribe writing on parchment, presumably in Aramaic, is pictured on a relief from the time of Tiglath–Pileser III (Barnett and Falkner, *The Sculptures of TP III*, pls. V-VI).

(1840) E.g., *CIS* II/1 pp. 13 ff.

(1841) *BRM* I 22, docket. For the dating of the cuneiform text, see note 1530 above.

(1842) Pinches, *An Outline of Assyrian Grammar*, p. 62 n. 2 (=Louis Delaporte, *Épigraphes araméens*, p. 54, no. 44); *TuM* II-III 19; *TCL* XII 58; *BE* VIII/1 17, 27, 28; *CIS* II/1 nos. 54-57.

(1843) New Babylonian Chronicle, rev. 7.

origins of the Arameans in eastern Babylonia. With further discoveries, we may some day have better materials with which to work and be able to reach more definite conclusions.

The Sutians

The Sutians are seldom mentioned in this period and almost exclusively in Babylonian texts. (1844) Their distribution in time and place roughly matches the distribution of the contemporary Arameans, (1845) and one is led to suspect that in Babylonian parlance the terms "Sutian" and "Aramean" may not always have designated distinguishable groups.

The Sutians are mentioned in connection with the semi-nomad disturbances in Babylonia in the eleventh and tenth centuries. In the reign of Adad–apla–iddina (1069*-1048*), the Sutians despoiled Sumer and Akkad, attacking the cult centers of Nippur and Sippar in conjunction with the Arameans (1846) and perhaps also ravaging Der and Dur–Kurigalzu. (1847) The Era Epic, which probably alludes to the disruption of the land beginning at this time, refers to Sutians howling in the city of Uruk (1848) and also mentions the cities of Babylon, Sippar, Dur–Kurigalzu, and Der as being afflicted at this time. (1849) With the resurgence of Babylonia in the ninth century, Nabu–apla–iddina (c. 887-c. 855) claims to have overthrown the Sutians, his principal enemy, (1850) and then to have restored Akkad; (1851) he mentions no Aramean role at all in the earlier disturbances. In a similar passage in the Era Epic, Era gives orders to Ishum for crippled Akkad to throw down the mighty Sutians and to restore the land. (1852)

With the exception of the allusion to the attack on Der in the middle of the eleventh century and the poetic mention of Uruk, the other references to Sutian

(1844) The term "Sutian" is not attested in Assyrian royal inscriptions between the time of Adad–nirari I and Sargon II.

(1845) In the sense that, wherever Sutians are mentioned, Arameans may generally be linked with them—not vice versa.

(1846) *JCS* XIX (1965) 123:10-13; cf. New Babylonian Chronicle, obv. 9′-10′, and *BBSt* no. 36 i 1-12.

(1847) New Babylonian Chronicle, obv. 9′-10′. Among the geographical names occur [(x?)]*di–ri* and [*Pàr*(?)]*–sa–a*.

(1848) Era Epic IV 54.

(1849) *Ibid.*, IV 5-51, 63-71.

(1850) *BBSt* no. 36 ii 26-28.

(1851) *BBSt* no. 36 ii 29-iii 10.

(1852) Era Epic V 25-39, last edited by W. G. Lambert, *Iraq* XXIV (1962) 122. Line 38 and the beginning of line 39 should be translated: "Cause the provisioner of Esagil and Babylon to rule over the regents of all inhabited areas for years without number!" This is the first attestation of the Š-stem of *bêlu*, and it should be added to *CAD* and *AHw*. Some of the variants ("may they rule," i.e., *libīlū* for *šubēl*; "regent" for "regents") may indicate that later copyists no longer understood the meaning of the line. Compare V 51: *šarru ša šumī ušarbû libēl kibrāti*, "may the king who magnifies my fame rule the world."

raids indicate an area of penetration in northwestern Babylonia ranging from Dur–Kurigalzu to Nippur—approximately the same area as (though slightly larger than) that subject to Aramean incursions at the same time. The only known military activity of Nabu–apla–iddina, the vaunted vanquisher of the Sutians, was on the middle Euphrates, assisting the state of Suhi in resisting the Assyrians; (1853) this was just outside the western border of Babylonia proper, in traditionally Aramean territory. With the exception of the inscription of Simbar–Shipak, the Babylonian texts describing the semi-nomad raids on western Babylonia in the eleventh through ninth centuries blame either the Sutians or the Arameans, not both. But the two groups were clearly carrying on the same type of activity in the same area.

Another trace of Sutian influence in Babylonia is the cult of the goddess ᵈ*Sutītu*, "the Sutian goddess," in Borsippa in the middle of the eighth century and later. (1854)

Shortly after the period under consideration here, the Assyrian sources begin to mention the Sutians again. Just after the earliest appearance of the Arameans in southeastern Babylonia near Elam, the "Sutians" were first found there too—in the time of Sargon II, whose inscriptions call them "country folk," *ṣāb(ē) ṣēri.* (1855) At the same time we find that the Sutians were being blamed for the age-old crime of the Arameans, (1856) i.e., seizing fields near Babylon and Borsippa. (1857) These two references strongly suggest that a Sutian–Aramean distinction was not carefully made by Assyrians of this time. The only roughly contemporary Sutian individual whose name is known bears the Babylonian name *Nergal–nāṣir* and served in the armies fighting for Babylonia in the time of Merodach–Baladan II. (1858) In the days of Esarhaddon, the Sutians were called tent-dwellers (*āšibūte kultārē*). (1859)

It is a striking coincidence that in the late second and early first millennia, wherever Sutians are mentioned, Arameans are usually in some way connected with the same time and place. It is not inconceivable that references to Sutians in this

(1853) *AKA* 350-353 iii 16-26.

(1854) An *ērib bīti* ᵈ*Sutīti* and a *šangû* ᵈ*Sutīti* are attested at Borsippa in the eighth year of Nabu–shuma–ishkun (*VAS* I 36 iv 2, 9). Though Sutitu is said to be the "child of Ishtar" (*bu–kur* ᵈ*Ištar, BRM* IV 25:44; note *bukur* rather than *bukrat* in this late text), she is more often associated with Nana (*VAS* VI 113:2, from Borsippa; S. Pallis, *Akitu*, pl. xi rev. 21). Sutitu is rarely used in personal names in the Persian period: Amat–Sutiti (*BE* VIII 115:36, from Borsippa) and Arad–Sutiti (*Dar.* 388:4, 8, probably from the vicinity of Borsippa). The name of the goddess also occurs on a stone votive fragment A. 829, published in Delaporte, *Catalogue des cylindres orientaux*, II, p. 180 and pl. 93, and on inscribed Mesopotamian votive eye-stones found at Persepolis (Schmidt, *Persepolis*, II, 58 PT4 455 [with inscription of Ashurbanipal] and probably to be restored *ibid.*, II, 59 PT4 1180).

(1855) As opposed to city dwellers. Lie, *Sargon*, 266, etc.

(1856) New Babylonian Chronicle, rev. 10-12; see note 1398 above.

(1857) Lie, *Sargon*, 64:9-11, etc.

(1858) *OIP* II 49:8.

(1859) Borger, *Asarhaddon*, 58:15.

period may designate a more mobile type of semi-nomad (1860) (especially among Aramean-related groups) rather than a specific ethno-linguistic entity (tribe or tribes).

Conclusion

The Kassites, Chaldeans, and Arameans were important and influential foreign population groups settled in or on the fringes of Babylonia during this period. The Kassites and Chaldeans especially became Babylonized in many ways, adopting Babylonian names, entering national office, and sometimes even coming to live in the old cities of the realm. Yet a significant portion of these groups, despite the Babylonizing tendencies, retained their distinctive tribal or clan structure as opposed to the smaller Babylonian family structure. Furthermore, though these groups possessed towns and cities of their own, they were less likely to rely on fortified sites for protection in war and, because of their relative mobility, enjoyed greater advantage than native Babylonians against the Assyrian military machine. (1861) The Arameans showed much less inclination to Babylonize; and, even though some of them settled in the old cities, they tended to retain Aramean names and to remain aloof from the government of Babylonia. (1862)

Kassites and Chaldeans, however, were very apt to take part in Babylonian government, and at the highest levels. There is some reason for believing that the Second Sealand and Bazi Dynasties may be viewed as Kassite attempts to restore stability in Babylonia after the collapse of the Second Dynasty of Isin. (1863) In addition, between the twelfth and ninth centuries, many officials in Babylonia were of Kassite descent. (1864) After the collapse of northern Babylonia under the repeated attacks of Shamshi–Adad V between 814 and 811, the Chaldeans benefited from the ensuing power vacuum to set the first of a long line of their princes on the Babylonian throne: Marduk–apla–usur, Eriba–Marduk, and Nabu–shuma–ishkun. This tradition would continue in the famous rulers of Babylonia and the Sealand

(1860) Especially since they appear almost always on the move, not settled in cities (cf. notes 1855 and 1859). The word "Sutian" seems to have become almost a synonym for "highwayman" or "brigand" (cf. the remarks of Kupper, *Nomades*, pp. 100-105, on the Sutians in the late second millennium).

(1861) The relative mobility of such groups at this time may be reflected in the coeval sparse pattern of permanent settlements found in the Diyala region, as noted by Adams, *Land behind Baghdad*, p. 56.

(1862) Arameans did not become kings of Babylonia, with the notable exception of the eleventh-century Babylonizer Adad–apla–iddina (for the possibility that "Aramean" as applied to Adad–apla–iddina, whose father also bore a Babylonian name, may have been intended as an opprobrious epithet rather than as an ethnic designation see note 840 above).

(1863) See note 1645 above. Note too that the next dynasty, the Elamite Dynasty, was also supposed to be of foreign extraction.

(1864) See pp. 250-254 above.

in the late eighth and the seventh centuries: Mukin–zeri, Merodach–Baladan II, Mushezib–Marduk, Nabu–zer–kitti–lishir, Nabu–bel–shumati, and Nabopolassar. With the notable exceptions of Nebuchadnezzar I and Nabu–apla–iddina, some of the strongest rulers in Babylonia between 1158* and 605 were of Kassite or especially Chaldean descent.

How were the Kassites, Chaldeans, Arameans, and Sutians accepted by the Babylonians, principally the native stock of northern Babylonia? By the time of the Second Dynasty of Isin, the Kassites had long been in Babylonia and were accepted almost without question. (1865) The Aramean and Sutian invaders who attacked northwestern Babylonia were obviously feared and disliked, though Babylonian hostility towards the Arameans must have dulled by the eighth century when Arameans began to settle in the villages and towns. (1866) The Babylonian attitude towards the Chaldeans is somewhat harder to fathom. Kings like Eriba–Marduk who drove out the Aramean squatters near Babylon and Borsippa and who "established the foundation(s) of the land" should have been well received in northern Babylonia. Several Chaldeans were accepted as king over the whole land, and there is no instance of a northern Babylonian revolt against the Chaldeans. On the contrary, in the late eighth century, many of the older cities of Babylonia actively supported Merodach–Baladan II against Sennacherib. (1867) There was no Babylonian tradition of hostility against the Chaldeans, (1868) at least expressed in writing, though there do seem to have been certain elements in Babylon in the late eighth century that welcomed Assyrian liberation from Chaldean rule (according to the official Assyrian account). (1869)

(1865) The sole hostile reference to the Kassites in this period is explained on p. 258 above.

(1866) Obviously the Arameans who were attempting to take over the fields of the citizens of Borsippa and Babylon would not have been regarded so kindly.

(1867) See Brinkman, *Studies Oppenheim*, pp. 15-18.

(1868) In contradistinction to Assyrian anti-Chaldean feeling, e.g., against Merodach–Baladan (*Studies Oppenheim*, p. 13).

(1869) Lie, *Sargon*, 371-373.

CHAPTER V

GOVERNMENT AND ARMY

In this chapter we shall deal with the political administration and military organization of Post-Kassite Babylonia. We shall first discuss the institution of the monarchy, then the provincial administration, and finally the army.

The Monarchy

The supreme political and military power of the Babylonian state was vested in the king. Though the few reticent sources relating to this period hardly permit a comprehensive treatise on the contemporary monarchy, we wish to make a few remarks on the king and his functions as seen in the light of the available materials.

As in preceding periods in Babylonia, the king was the dominant individual in the land. Documents were dated in terms of his regnal years, and his royal name and the principal events of his reign were carefully recorded for posterity. Though the king was not deified, [1870] as sometimes happened in other lands, he was a man set apart; and even in such a simple matter as the writing of his name, the king was carefully distinguished from other persons. In contemporary Babylonian documents, the king's name was not preceded by the masculine personal determinative, as were the names of other men. [1871] This distinction was not usually accorded any other living individual, [1872] not even the heir to the throne; [1873] and, though merely a

(1870) In this period, the divine determinative begins the royal name only in cases where there is an initial theophoric element. Where there is no initial theophoric element (as in the name of Itti-Marduk-balatu, Eulmash-shakin-shumi, and Tiglath-Pileser III), the name begins without any determinative in contemporary Babylonian documents (see notes 490, 971, and 1544 above).

(1871) Exceptions to this statement are few and perhaps only apparent. Two occur in late copies of royal inscriptions of kings from this period and could have been added by the later copyists (*JCS* XIX [1965] 123:7 and 4 N-T 3:20′, 40′; cf. also *Studia Orientalia* I [1925] 32:6, where there is room to restore the masculine personal determinative). One occurs in an undated kudurru which refers to the action of a king who is usually but need not be regarded as contemporary (*BE* I/2 149 i 15).

(1872) The supposed exception in *Iranica Antiqua* II (1962) 161 no. 20 does not seem to be borne out by the published photograph (*ibid.*, pl. XXVIII). But, to judge from the photo of *BBSt* 30 rev. 22, early in the Second Isin Dynasty, the scribe seems to have omitted the masculine personal determinative before his own name; also in an eighth-century economic text, the personal determinative is omitted before the name of the *šangû* of Udani (note 1334 above).

(1873) *BBSt* no. 9 iva 30; Amandry, *Antike Kunst* IX/2 (1966) 59 fig. 3. The sole exception seems to be Marduk-balassu-iqbi, heir of Marduk-zakir-shumi (*RA* XVI [1919] 126 iv 17).

scribal convention, it implies a respectful appreciation for the unique character of the monarch. ([1874])

The king was responsible for the internal stability and prosperity of the land. Through a specially appointed bureaucracy, he oversaw the efficient operation of the extensive irrigation system on which the predominantly agricultural economy of Babylonia depended. Local officials were designated to keep the canals functioning and to see that the irrigation water was distributed equitably. ([1875]) Other public utilities such as roads and bridges ([1876]) had special officials to supervise their upkeep. ([1877]) In the interests of national security, the king saw to the building and repair of fortifications, including city walls. ([1878]) He showed great devotion to the gods, deferring to their pleasure in matters of national and international policy ([1879]) and aiding their cults in various ways: by setting aside land and food revenues for their temples and temple personnel, ([1880]) by presenting sacred vestments and sundry precious votive offerings, ([1881]) and by repairing temple buildings. ([1882])

The king was also a key figure in the administration of the Babylonian legal system. For the validity of certain legal actions such as land grants and tax exemptions, the king's physical presence was required; and this was attested by the affixing of the distinctive royal seal to the document. ([1883]) The king was also the ultimate court of appeal in legal cases, especially those dealing with land ownership ([1884]) or damages. ([1885]) Though we might suspect some bias would be present in judg-

([1874]) In earlier periods, the masculine personal determinative was sometimes omitted before personal names of men, especially when these names occurred in medial or final position in a line.

([1875]) Hinke Kudurru iii 25 (see also note 1900 below).

([1876]) The word *titurru* can probably be translated as either "bridge" or "causeway." As a means of traversing water, the *titurru* was more commonly connected with canals (*palgu*, e.g., Reiner, *Šurpu*, III 49; *VAB* IV 88 no. 8 ii 9; cf. *Nbn.* 753:15-16), though a *titurru* could also provide access across swampland (Lie, *Sargon*, 407) or across rivers (e.g., *AKA* 65 iv 69; III *R* 8 ii 101, simile). A *titurru* could be built of wood (*AKA* 65 iv 69), of brick (*MDP* IV 10), or of brick and limestone (*OIP* II 102:90). Note too that in the synonym list *LTBA* II 2:301 *titurru* is connected with *arammu*, which means wharf, ramp, or causeway. See also the remarks of Meissner in *OLZ* XXII (1919) 112-14 and Thureau-Dangin in *RA* XX (1923) 109 n. 7.

([1877]) *BBSt* no. 6 ii 2. Cf. the Kassite text *MDP* II 103 iii 22-27.

([1878]) *BE* I/2 148; *MDOG* LIII (1914) 28; Place, *Ninive et l'Assyrie*, II, 308.

([1879]) E.g., *BiOr* VII (1950) pl. III 16b (see note 575 above); cf. *CT* XIII 48:5-10.

([1880]) E.g., *BBSt* nos. 24 and 36; *RA* XVI (1919) 125-126; *OECT* I pl. 20:6, 19.

([1881]) See especially *BBSt* no. 36 v 39-vi 8.

([1882]) *BiOr* VII (1950) 42-46; 2 N-T 483; *UET* I 306; *UET* VIII 101; *LIH* I 70; I *R* 5 no. XXII; *UET* I 166-167; *JCS* XIX (1965) 123-124.

([1883]) The king's seal of administration (*kunuk šarri ša šiprēti*) was a unique object and not to be copied (*ša la tam*[*šīli*]: *BBSt* no. 10 rev. 8, etc.; cf. *VAS* I 37 v 48-49). The only such seal that has been recovered (H. Frankfort, *Cylinder Seals*, pl. XXXVI k) is a distinctive eight-sided prism. I have discussed these seals at more length in *RA* LXI (1967) 70-74.

The impressing of the royal seal on the document was important, since its omission could lead to future litigation (see note 1896 below).

([1884]) *BE* I/1 83; *BBSt* no. 12 ii 1-12; *BBSt* no. 28 obv. 1-rev. 17.

([1885]) E.g., *BBSt* no. 9 top 8-10.

ments respecting supposed crown lands, we find that the king was capable of handing down equitable decisions even against province or crown interests, [1886] basing his judgment—as far as we can gauge—on oral historical tradition. [1887] Though historical possession was ideally the criterion for judgment, sometimes it seems that troublesome litigants had to be bought off before relinquishing their claims, since, unless their claims were somehow compensated for and the fact duly recorded, they could continue to bring suit under each successive king to the perpetual harass ment of the landholder. [1888] In dubious cases, the king could settle disputes by sending a man to the water ordeal, if he deemed it necessary. [1889]

The king possessed vast government lands from which he drew revenue and which he used from time to time for making land grants. Thus he might reward outstanding service on the battlefield with grants of royal land, [1890] or he might provide handsome endowments for temples or temple officials with similar grants. [1891] The king could make such grants either by direct royal charter [1892] or by authorizing local officials to draw up documents of their own. [1893] In the latter case, the customary procedure probably consisted of several steps:

(1) the royal authorization for the land grant, communicated to the ranking province official, the governor (*šaknu*);

(2) the deputizing by the governor of certain officials to supervise the surveying of the land (frequently the mayor of the local village and a scribe were included in this committee); [1894]

(3) the certification by the governor and the deputized officials that the plot of land had been deeded over to the individual; [1895]

(4) the affixing of the royal seal to the document. [1896]

(1886) *BE* I/1 83.

(1887) *BBSt* no. 6 i 50; *BE* I/1 83 rev. 9; cf. *MDP* VI 34 ii 27 (late Kassite). By contrast, if the historical tradition concerning property were written, the case would presumably be capable of solution before it reached the king.

(1888) E.g., *BBSt* no. 9 ii 32-38; cf. *BBSt* no. 3 (Kassite).

(1889) *BBSt* no. 9 iva 2-6; cf. BBSt no. 3 v 14-18 (Kassite).

(1890) *BBSt* no. 8; cf. *MDP* II 93-94 (Kassite).

(1891) *BBSt* nos. 24, 36.

(1892) E.g., *MDP* II 101 ii 1-5 (Kassite).

(1893) E.g., *BBSt* nos. 8 and 24; Hinke Kudurru. This was the more common procedure after the Kassite Dynasty.

(1894) The king, of course, may authorize the surveying directly, e.g., *BBSt* no. 24:27-28. In such cases, the governor might serve on the measuring committee (e.g., *MDP* VI 44:5-8, Kassite).

(1895) Akkadian: *ana* PN *kunnu* (*BBSt* no. 4 i 19).

(1896) *BBSt* no. 8 B 5. Cf. *BBSt* no. 12 ii 11; *BBSt* no. 24:16; *PSBA* XIX (1897) 71 ii 5. This step is sometimes omitted, e.g., *MDP* VI 33 ii 13, which may prove a cause for future litigation.

These grants were usually made in perpetuity, but there are indications that private land could once again become crown or province property. (1897)

The right of private ownership of land, however, was strictly respected; and, according to a late Kassite kudurru, if the king wished a tract of land which was privately owned, he had to make arrangements to purchase it. (1898) But private individuals and local officials owed the crown certain taxes and services, which could include:

(a) a fixed percentage of crop yields and of increase in flocks; (1899)

(b) conscription of men and animals for work on public projects, such as dredging canals, improving roads, building causeways, erecting fortifications; (1900)

(c) impressing of men, animals, and materials (e.g., a chariot) into the royal service for an extended period of time; (1901)

(d) forced provision for royal officials, troops, and animals: supplying wood, straw, fodder for royal cattle, quartering royal soldiers, etc. (1902)

Villages disliked having roads, causeways, or fortifications built in their vicinity lest they be forced to provide burdensome maintenance for these public facilities. (1903) The king occasionally granted exemptions (*zakûtu*) from performing these onerous public duties, usually as a reward for meritorious military service or because the lands involved were owned by temple personnel. (1904) It seems that royal tax officials were extremely zealous in the performance of their duties, since decrees of tax exemption contain numerous clauses to guard against various ingenious means of indirect pressure by tax collectors. Tax-exemption grants frequently forbade tax officials even to enter a town. (1905) Likewise such timely devices as shutting off the irrigation water supply for tax-exempt areas were frowned upon. (1906)

(1897) *BE* I/1 83:15; cf. *CT* XXXVI 7 ii 25 (Kassite).

(1898) *MDP* X 93 viii 6-19 (Kassite).

(1899) *BBSt* no. 6 i 55-57; *BBSt* no. 8 top 21-22. Cf. the Kassite text *MDP* X 88 i 20, 91 iii 32-33. Animals were also accepted in payment for land taxes (*BBSt* no. 9 iii 1-15).

(1900) *BBSt* no. 6 ii 1-2; Hinke Kudurru iii 25. Cf. the Kassite kudurrus *MDP* II 101-102 ii 18-33 (including a detailed description of types of corvée work done on canals) and *MDP* X 88-89 i 21-25.

(1901) *BBSt* no. 6 i 58-59, ii 5; *BBSt* no. 24:35-37; *BBSt* no. 25:7-9. Cf. the Kassite texts *MDP* II 102 ii 34-42, 51-53 and *MDP* X 89 i 24.

(1902) *BBSt* no. 6 i 53-54, 60, ii 3-4, 9; Hinke Kudurru iii 26. Cf. the Kassite documents *MDP* II 102 ii 43-50, 103 iii 13-21 (where cattle of the king and cattle of the provincial governor are not to be let loose on the individual's pasture lands) and *MDP* X 89 i 26.

(1903) *BBSt* no. 6 ii 1-2; cf. the Kassite text *MDP* II 103 iii 22-27.

(1904) Military service: *BBSt* no. 6, *BBSt* no. 8 (freedom from local tax jurisdiction). Temple personnel: *BBSt* no. 24.

(1905) *BBSt* no. 6 i 51-54, 58; *BBSt* no. 8 top 16-17, 23-24; *BBSt* no. 24:33-35; cf. *MDP* X 89 ii 1-2 (Kassite period).

(1906) *BBSt* no. 8 top 20; cf. the Kassite *MDP* II 102-103 ii 54-iii 12 and *MDP* X 89 ii 3-7.

The king was also the commander-in-chief of the army and led important military expeditions in person. (1907) Royal stables, presumably chiefly for military purposes, were kept at Dur–Sumulael not far from Babylon. (1908) In semi-independent lands, e.g., in the Kassite–populated regions east of the Tigris, powerful local leaders were induced to help the king in his military campaigns, principally by liberal rewards of land or by tax exemptions given to warriors who distinguished themselves in battle. (1909) In border districts, where trouble with foreign raiding parties was an ever present possibility, the king stationed garrisons of troops against such a contingency. (1910) The organization of the army is treated more fully in a separate section below.

The king was also responsible for diplomatic relations, including the making of treaties (1911) and the adjustment of territorial boundaries. (1912) On more than one occasion during this period, political alliances between Babylonia and Assyria were cemented by marriages between the royal families of the two countries. (1913)

There is practically no direct evidence concerning the location of the seat of the Babylonian government during this period; but it seems generally to have been in Babylon, with the following possible exceptions. Just after the end of the Kassite Dynasty, the kings may have governed from Isin. (1914) During the three short-lived dynasties—Sealand, Bazi, and Elamite—which followed the Second Dynasty of Isin, the king may have resided in the southern or eastern portions of the land. (1915) There is also some evidence that Nabu–mukin–apli, the first king after the Elamite Dynasty, may have lived outside Babylon, since he was prevented from reaching the city by Aramean advances. (1916) Later, Eriba–Marduk, early in his reign, does not seem to have been in possession of Babylon or at least could not perform the New Year's festival there during his first year. (1917) Finally, Mukin–zeri was in-

(1907) *BBSt* no. 6 i 23, 28-29; I *R* 31 iv 37-42; cf. K. 2660 rev. (*JNES* XVII [1958] 138).

(1908) *AfK* II (1924-25) 56:61 Gron. 847-849.

(1909) *BBSt* nos. 6 and 8.

(1910) *BBSt* no. 6 ii 3-4.

(1911) *AfO* VIII (1932-33) 27-29; *CT* XXXIV 39 ii 27′-28′, 40 iii 24-25 (Synchronistic History).

(1912) *CT* XXXIV 40 iii 20-21, 41 iv 14, 22 (Synchronistic History).

(1913) The Synchronistic History tells of the marriage of the daughter of Adad–apla–iddina to Ashur–bel–kala (*CT* XXXIV 39 ii 33′-35′) and of the exchange of daughters in marriage between Adad–nirari II and Nabu–shuma–ukin(!) I (*CT* XXXIV 40 iii 17; Babylonian and Assyrian kings are certainly involved in this broken passage, and their identity as specified here is highly probable).

(1914) Because of the temporary Elamite occupation of Babylon (see pages 80-82 above) and because of the name of the "Isin" Dynasty.

(1915) The Bazi Dynasty was connected with the city of Kar–Marduk, where there was a palace (Dynastic Chronicle v 9′; cf. *BBSt* no. 9 top 23). There is no evidence of activity at Babylon during this time.

(1916) Religious Chronicle iii 5′.

(1917) Inferred from the mention only of the festival celebrated in his second year in the New Babylonian Chronicle, rev. 8-9.

stalled in the southern stronghold of Shapija, when the Assyrians put an end to his effective rule as king over Babylonia. (1918)

The monarchy experienced many periods of political debility during this era in Babylonia. No fewer than four dynasties came and went during the years between 1158* and 980*; and the E Dynasty, which ruled during the decades immediately preceding 732, seems to have been an artificial historiographical creation which did not win unanimous acceptance even among the Babylonian scribes. (1919) Besides the decisive changes in hegemony represented by changes in dynasty, there were also revolts (1920) and usurpations (1921) within dynasties—perhaps more than we are presently aware of. (1922) At some periods the strongest leader in Babylonia did not control the northern part of the country or could not reside in Babylon; this later gave rise to the question whether these individuals could be considered legitimate kings, (1923) especially if they had not gained control of the capital during the course of their short reigns. (1924) And, even when the king did rule over Babylon, there were times—especially in the tenth century—when he did not have sufficient control in the outskirts of the capital to permit the full ceremonies of the New Year's festival (by which the monarch's claim to the kingship was annually renewed) (1925) to take place. (1926) Further evidences of the weakness of the central administration were apparent in the ninth century, when some of the high provin-

(1918) II *R* 67:23, D.T. 3:16. Note too that Mukin–zeri does not seem to have been in Babylon when an emissary of Tiglath–Pileser III attempted to negotiate the city's surrender early in the struggle against Assyria between 732 and 729 (Nimrud Letter I).

(1919) See note 163 above.

(1920) Marduk–bel–usati against Marduk–zakir–shumi I (*CT* XXXIV 40 iii 28, Synchronistic History, etc.), Borsippa against Nabonassar (*CT* XXXIV 46 i 6-7, Babylonian Chronicle), Nabu–shuma–ukin II against Nabu–nadin–zeri (*CT* XXXIV 46 i 14-17, Babylonian Chronicle).

(1921) Adad–apla–iddina (New Babylonian Chronicle, obv. 8′) and Ea–mukin–zeri (Dynastic Chronicle v 5′) were usurpers.

(1922) In addition, Shamshi–Adad V (*Archaeologia* LXXIX [1929] 123 no. 119:2; *AAA* XVIII [1931] pl. XX no. 44:2) and Tiglath–Pileser III before 729 (Nimrud Slab no. 1:1) claimed hegemony over Babylonia without actually occupying the throne. At such times they assumed the title "king of Sumer and Akkad" but not the title "king of Babylonia" (which implied actual possession of the Babylonian throne).

(1923) This may be what is behind the "kingless" years recorded in the New Babylonian Chronicle, rev. 7.

(1924) Kings like Eriba–Marduk who did gain control of the capital during their reign (New Babylonian Chronicle, rev. 8-9) were counted as legitimate.

(1925) The importance of the king's annual participation in the New Year's festival cannot be overlooked. Though it took place in early Ṇisan, it was usually recorded with the last events of the old year (*RLA* II 431 rev. 45-46; Lie, *Sargon*, 384-386; Wiseman, *Chronicles*, 68:14); and the new year for official purposes, e.g., royal campaigns, was considered as beginning after the festival (Lie, *Sargon*, 58:15; Wiseman, *Chronicles*, 68:15). The crucial importance of the festival may be gauged from its frequent mention in the Neo-Babylonian chronicles (e.g., Religious Chronicle ii-iii, *passim*; New Babylonian Chronicle, rev. 9 and possibly obv. 14′-17′; *Iraq* XXVI [1964] 15:22; *BHT* 13 rev. 8-14, 23:1-24:8, 24 rev. 1-3, 111-112 ii *passim*) and from the apparent psychological impact on Babylonia when it was not celebrated.

(1926) Religious Chronicle ii 1-5, 16-18, iii 5′, 8′, 9′, 13′-15′; possibly also the New Babylonian Chronicle, obv. 14′-edge.

cial offices had become *de facto* hereditary, (1927) and in the eighth century, when local officials repaired temple buildings in their own name rather than in that of the king. (1928)

The throne was as a rule passed down within the same family, from father to son if possible. (1929) But revolts, usurpations, and changes of hegemony within the land were of sufficiently frequent occurrence that no single family was able to retain the royal power for so long as a century. (1930) During the eighth century, when Chaldean dynasts often held the kingship, the throne was occupied at different times by members of all three major tribes. (1931)

Royal princes and other members of the royal family are seldom attested during this period. Only from the extraordinarily long reign of Nabu–mukin–apli (thirty-six years) do any of the king's sons leave contemporary inscriptions. (1932) Royal princes, however, on several occasions served as witnesses to legal documents, (1933) principally to those in which a special action by the king was recorded; presumably they added to the solemnity of these occasions and stood as an additional guarantee for the royal presence at, or the royal favor towards, the recorded transaction or deed. Once in this period the brother of a king made an appearance, leading a contingent of three thousand Babylonian troops to support the land of Suhi in its stand against Ashurnasirpal II. (1934) Daughters of the king are not attested by name from this period and are known only from references to diplomatic marriages in the Synchronistic History. (1935)

(1927) See pages 206-207 above. This situation should be contrasted with conditions prevailing under the Second Isin Dynasty, when the governors could be transferred from province to province at the king's will.

(1928) Nabu–shuma–imbi at Borsippa (*JRAS* 1892 350-368) and Bel–ibni and Nabu–zera–ushabshi at Uruk (*YOS* IX 74, *BIN* II 31, BM 113205).

(1929) Note, however, that Enlil–nadin–apli, who probably died as a minor, was succeeded by his father's brother, Marduk–nadin–ahhe. Also Ninurta–kudurri–usur II, who died after a reign of a few months, was succeeded by his younger brother, Mar–biti–ahhe–iddina; the second brother, Rimut–ili, was a temple official and may have been ineligible to succeed (or he may have been dead by this time).

(1930) The only possible exception during this period might be the family of Nabu–shuma–ukin I, which held the throne for about eighty years in the ninth century. If Nabu–shuma–ukin's immediate predecessors should prove to have been his ancestors (a fact not yet established), then the family may have held the throne for more than a century.

(1931) Mukin–zeri was a member of the Amukanu tribe. Nabu–shuma–ishkun was a member of the Dakkuru tribe. Eriba–Marduk and later Merodach–Baladan II were members of the Jakin tribe. Marduk–apla–usur was also a Chaldean, but his tribal affiliation is unknown.

(1932) Both inscriptions are on Luristan bronze situlae (Pope, *SPA* I 284 no. XIII and Amandry, *Antike Kunst* IX/2 [1966] 59 fig. 3).

(1933) *mAbullu–te–ta–par–a–a–ú*, son of Marduk–nadin–ahhe, was a witness in *BBSt* no. 8 ii 26. Ninurta–kudurri–usur, Rimut–ili, and Mar–biti–ahhe–iddina, sons of Nabu–mukin–apli, were witnesses in *BBSt* no. 9 iva 30-32. Marduk–balassu–iqbi, son of Marduk–zakir–shumi I, was a witness in *RA* XVI (1919) 126 iv 17.

(1934) *AKA* 351 iii 20.

(1935) References in note 1913 above.

That there was a special burial place or mausoleum for kings of Babylonia during at least part of this epoch is suggested by remarks in the Dynastic Chronicle, which mentions that certain kings were interred in the "palace (of Sargon)" in contradistinction to a usurper, who was said to have been buried in his native swampland. (1936) E. Unger proposed a possible location for a royal mausoleum in the south corner of the "New City" (*ālu eššu*) in Babylon; (1937) but this is very uncertain. (1938)

Provincial Administration (1939)

Babylonia at this time was divided into administrative districts called *pīḫatu*, (1940) a word which we translate as "province." These provinces were small, mutually independent units with governments functioning directly or indirectly under the king. They took their names either from a previously existing country (e.g., the Sealand), from a local tribe (e.g., Bit–Sin–magir), or from the principal

(1936) Dynastic Chronicle, v 3′-11′. Simbar–Shipak was buried in the "palace of Sargon" (see note 934 above) and Ea–mukin–zeri in the "swamp of Bit–Hashmar." Kashshu–nadin–ahi was buried in the "palace" (not further specified), as was Shirikti–Shuqamuna. Eulmash–shakin–shumi was buried in the "palace of Kar–Marduk" (see note 1915 above).

(1937) *Babylon*, pp. 51-52 and pl. 2, relying on a slight textual basis in the "Stadtbeschreibung," section I, lines 4-5 (*Babylon*, p. 237 and *WVDOG* XLVIII 89).

(1938) See Landsberger, *ZA* XLI (1933) 297. Note that *CAD*'s translation of the name of this section of the city as "In–It–Is–Created..." (*CAD* B 90b) is based on a misunderstanding of the text; the verb *banû* here is part of the preceding relative clause introduced by *ša* and should be translated "the É.NAM.BAD(?), inside which was built the É.EŠ.MAḪ" and so should be classified under *CAD*'s meaning 7a rather than 7c.

(1939) I have dealt with the more restricted subject of "Provincial Administration in Babylonia under the Second Dynasty of Isin" in a paper delivered before the American Oriental Society at Harvard University in April, 1962. This paper was subsequently published in *JESHO* VI (1963) 233-242. Pertinent sections of this previous presentation are incorporated here.

(1940) Usually written NAM. The Babylonian word is *pīḫatu*; the Assyrian forms are *pāḫatu* and possibly *paḫātu*. The transcription of vowel length in these words is uncertain. In Babylonian and in Middle Assyrian, the second syllable is short; and Middle Assyrian forms show vowel harmony (nominative singular unattested, genitive singular written as *pa–ḫi–ti* [*KAJ* 121:4, 187:5, etc.] or *pa–ḫe–te* [*KAJ* 133:6, 182:10; *KAH* II 56:3; *AfO* XVII (1954-56) 268:7, etc.], construct *pa–ḫa–at* [*KAJ* 224:13, etc.]). In an Akkadian text from Boghazkoy, the second syllable drops out completely: *bēl pa–aḫ–ti–šu* (*KUB* III 48:7). In two letters from Kibri–Dagan found at Mari, the forms *bēl pa–ḫa–tim* (*ARM* II 91 rev. ⌈2′⌉, 7′) and LÚ.MEŠ *be–el pa–ḫa–tim* (*ARM* III 59:17) are attested, probably indicating *pă̄ḫatum* in current use in some places along the Euphrates in the OB period. In Neo-Assyrian, a form *pă̄ḫātu* is used (genitive singular *pa–ḫa–ti* in *AAA* XX [1933] 113 no. 105:19, *pa–ḫa–ṭu*! in *ABL* 307:10; from this late form are borrowed the Hebrew and Aramaic words פחה, which suggest that the late Assyrian form should probably be interpreted as *paḫātu* (regardless of etymology). A form *paḫātu* is also occasionally used in Babylonian in the Persian period (e.g., *Darius* 338:4, 14) and is presumably influenced by official Aramaic usage.

The first vowel is transcribed long because of presumed derivation from a root P'Ḫ and because the Babylonian forms do not exhibit contraction. One should, however, note Landsberger's well-founded reservations on the subject in *MSL* I 126-127.

city of the region (e.g., Isin). There are at least fourteen provinces known from the period under consideration, [1941] and there were probably more. [1942] These provinces ranged all the way from the southern coastland of Babylonia (Sealand) [1943] to the lands between the Diyala and the Lower Zab (e.g., Namar). The heavy concentration of provinces north of the parallel of Nippur suggests that at this time much of southern Babylonia was already thinly populated swamp—a geographical condition well attested in later Assyrian annals. [1944]

Till about the middle of the ninth century, the chief official of the province was normally the *šaknu* [1945] or "governor," who held office by royal appointment and could be shifted from province to province at the king's will. [1946] This official was the channel through whom business regarding crown or province lands in the area was transacted; for example, the king gave the basic order but the governor made the actual grant of land to the private individual. [1947] Similarly, when land was considered to have lapsed from private ownership, the governor was the one who reclaimed it as a province possession. [1948]

In some areas, however, governors bore other titles. For instance, in Nippur the governor was called the *šandabakku*. [1949] And in provinces east of the Tigris, where Kassite tribal or clan organization was still strong, powerful native governors called *bēl bīti* held office. [1950] The *bēl bīti* could preside over an independent province

(1941) Babylon, Bit-Ada, Bit-Piri'-Amurru, Bit-Sin-magir, Bit-Sin-sheme, Borsippa, Der, Dur-Kurigalzu, Halman, Hudadu, Isin, Namar, Nippur, and the Sealand. The somewhat complex documentation on the provinces other than Borsippa and Der has been discussed in detail in *JESHO* VI (1963) 234 n. 1. The provinces of Borsippa and Der are attested through *šākin ṭēmi* officials (*JRAS* 1892 350 ff., *VAS* I 36 iii 7; 4 N-T 3:15'). A fifteenth province, namely that of Bit-Riduti, may be attested, if Streck's interpretation (*Asb.*, CCCLXXIX n. 3) of the office of *šakin rīdûti* is correct (see note 473 above).

(1942) E.g., Ur.

(1943) The Sealand may have been at least *de facto* independent at certain times during this period. *BBSt* no. 11 mentions no king by name, but alludes only to a *rubû* (i 3), who may have been a governor. Note too that the private dedication made to Usur-amassu of Uruk by Kashshu-bel-zeri, a governor of the Sealand, probably in the late eleventh or early tenth century (for the date, see p. 257 above).

(1944) It cannot be argued that the institution of the kudurru was restricted to the northern and eastern sections of Babylonia, since *BE* I/1 83 and *BBSt* no. 27 originate in the south and *BBSt* nos. 28 and 29 in the western areas near the Euphrates.

(1945) The original title was probably *šakin māti* (*MDP* II 89 iii 5); but it had become *šaknu* by this time, as is shown by the abstract *šá-ak-nu-ti* (*BBSt* no. 8 i 15). Compare the pseudo-logogram ŠÁ.KÌN-*ú-ti* in *BBSt* no. 6 ii 28, which adds the abstract ending directly to the frozen writing of the construct *šá-kìn*.

(1946) Baba-shuma-iddina served as *šaknu* at Bit-Sin-sheme and then held the same office at Babylon during the reign of Nebuchadnezzar I (Hinke Kudurru iii 9; *BBSt* no. 6 ii 18). Ekarra-iqisha appeared as *šaknu* at Bit-Sin-magir and at Isin during successive reigns (and probably in successive years: *BE* I/1 83 rev. 3-4, *BBSt* no. 25:26-27.

(1947) E.g., Hinke Kudurru iii 9-13.

(1948) See note 1897 above.

(1949) Written (LÚ) GÚ.EN.NA. For the reading of the title, see most recently Landsberger, *Bischof*, pp. 75-76. It is not yet attested, however, during the time of the Second Dynasty of Isin. During the ninth century, Nazi-Enlil and his son Enlil-apla-usur held the office during the reigns of Marduk-zakir-shumi I (*RA* XVI [1919] 126 iv 21) and Marduk-balassu-iqbi (4 N-T 3:11') respectively.

(1950) *BBSt* no. 6 i 25, etc.; *BBSt* no. 8 A 6, etc.; *BBSt* no. 9 A 2.

such as Bit–Ada, ([1951]) which then had no *šaknu*; ([1952]) in this case, the *bēl bīti* transmitted royal land grants just as the *šaknu* did in other provinces. ([1953]) Or the *bēl bīti* could be the head of a subordinate area within a province, powerful enough to have his friendship cultivated by the king in time of war, but nonetheless technically subordinate to a *šaknu*. ([1954]) In *BBSt* no. 6, such a subordinate tribal chieftain was granted *de jure* independence from the provincial administration. ([1955]) The institution of the *bēl bīti* should not be regarded as a usual feature of the contemporary hierarchy of Babylonian officialdom but rather as an untamed element of the tribal regime in the nominally Babylonian outlying areas.

From about the middle of the ninth century, the title of the chief official of the province varies. The official most commonly found exercising the office of governor is the *šākin ṭēmi*, previously a minor provincial official. ([1956]) Later examples of the *šaknu* as provincial governor occur, chiefly in the seventh century. ([1957]) At Nippur, the office of *šandabakku* is attested once again, beginning in the middle of the ninth century. ([1958]).

Numerous subordinate officials served within the province, though their precise function in many instances is yet to be determined. This incomplete state of knowledge is due to the reticence of our principal sources, the kudurrus, which refer to many officials, but seldom in any more revealing guise than as witnesses to legal transactions. ([1959]) Thus our treatment of these officials will be largely skeletal, expanded only in the case of the half dozen officials who occur most frequently in the texts of this period.

In many instances, it is difficult to determine even whether certain officials served on a local or a province-wide level. The *šākin ṭēmi* and the *bēl pīḫati* were officials on the province level; ([1960]) and it is possible that the *ša rēši* and the *sakrumaš* were on the same level. ([1961]) The *ḫazannu* served in the local village administration,

([1951]) *BBSt* no. 8 top 12.

([1952]) Note that *šakin māti* alternates with *bēl bīti* in the sequences in *BBSt* no. 8 top 7-11, 12-14.

([1953]) *BBSt* no. 8 i 10-13, save that it was sometimes necessary to bribe the *bēl bīti* in order to secure title to land, while in other areas the royal behest was sufficient (see column A of *BBSt* no. 8).

([1954]) *BBSt* no. 6 i 45-48.

([1955]) *BBSt* no. 6 i 50-ii 11.

([1956]) By the time of the Chaldean Dynasty, the chief officials of the different sections of the land bore a variety of titles, including *bēl pīḫati* (as attested in the *Hofkalender* of Nebuchadnezzar II; see Unger, *Babylon*, p. 285).

The office of *šākin ṭēmi* is treated separately below, pp. 307-309.

([1957]) E.g., the case I have discussed in *Orientalia N.S.* XXXIV (1965) 246 n. 3 and the late-eighth-century governor of Kish (Langdon, *Excavations at Kish*, III, pl. XI, W. 1929, 136:4).

([1958]) References in note 1949 above.

([1959]) These sources produce an inevitable distortion in our portrayal of the provincial administration, since we learn chiefly of officials concerned with land ownership and taxes.

([1960]) See notes 1990-1994 and 2049 below.

([1961]) See notes 2035-2038 and 2073-2075 below.

as did the *massû*. (1962) Tax collectors such as the *mākisu*, the *kallû*, (1963) and the *rē'ī sīsê* (1964) may have served on both levels; but there is no clear evidence for this. (1965)

(1962) In twelfth-century kudurrus, the *massû* are individuals consulted by the kings (Merodach-Baladan I, Nebuchadnezzar I, and Enlil–nadin–apli) to ascertain information about the past: where the boundaries of a field had been located, what tax exemptions a town had had, who had owned a field (*MDP* VI 34 ii 27-30, *BBSt* no. 6 i 50, *BE* I/1 83 rev. 9). The term is used in a generic sense to refer to local "experts" who would be acquainted with the tradition of their neighborhood. The title of *massû* does not refer to an office either in this time or in later Neo-Babylonian times. (Von Soden's reference in *AHw* 619b to NB *massû* officials is based on Steinmetzer's misreading [*ArOr* VII (1935) 315:10] of a text he had copied in *AnOr* XII 303-306; the passage in question should be read LÚ GAR *ṭ*[*è*]*–me lu–ú* LÚ.SAG.LUGAL. For the writing *šākin ṭēme*, cf. Hinke Kudurru v 16-17. The correct form of the sign SU in the Steinmetzer kudurru occurs in rev. 2).

In Old Assyrian texts (*CCT* 1 26b:1, 27a:6, 12 [=*CCT* V 48d]), and in Old Babylonian texts from Mari (*ARM* II 78:35), the *massûm* is a city official (usually occurring in a phrase like *massûm ša* GN). Whether or not the similar *massu* (?) officials in the Alalakh and Amarna texts (references in *AHw* 619a) refer to the same title is uncertain.

The epithet *massû* in the meaning "prince" or "sage" is occasionally used of kings and gods; see Seux, *Épithètes royales*, p. 161. Apparent byforms of this epithet are *mansû* and *maššû* (references in *AHw* 619a-b).

(1963) The word **kallû*, as used in the late Kassite period and under the Second Dynasty of Isin, is a generic term attested thus far only in the plural form *kallê*. It is written variously as *kal–li–e* (*MDP* X 89 i 23; *BBSt* no. 6 i 51; Hinke Kudurru iii 26; *BBSt* no. 25:6, 7), *ka–al–li–e* (*BBSt* no. 8 top 3-4) and *kal–li* (*BBSt* no. 24:33, twice). Since no individual ever bears the title *kallû* in this period and since the office never occurs in the many curse formulae in kudurrus, it is to be regarded as a generic term at this time. It is possible that the LÚ *pānû*, the LÚ *lāsimu* (=*mu'irru*?, written KAŠ$_4$, see note 1967 below), and the LÚ *ṣu–ḫi–li*, mentioned in *BBSt* no. 24:34, were specific types of *kallû* officials.

The *kallû* are mentioned only in tax-exemption (*zakûtu*) clauses in kudurrus and were known for requisitioning men, animals, and materials (e.g., chariots) for public works projects (such as digging canals or cutting fodder) or for public defense (Hinke Kudurru iii 25-26; *BBSt* no. 24:36-37; *BBSt* no. 25:8-9; *BBSt* no. 8 top 5; cf. the Kassite text *MDP* X 89 i 23). Such public works projects are described variously as *ina ilki tupšikki* (*BBSt* no. 24:38), *ina ilki dikûti* (Hinke Kudurru iii 25), *ina all*[*u*] *tupšikki* (*BBSt* no. 8 top 2). The interpretation of the last-mentioned passage in *CAD* A/1 357b as "the *kallû*-officials... shall not take (away persons for their own use) from the hoe and corvée basket assigned to GN" is erroneous, since the whole purpose of the writing of this kudurru was to exempt certain lands from obligations towards the civil administration of GN; the passage should rather be translated: "the *kallû* officials shall not take away (persons) for hoe- or corvée-duty for GN." Note too that in *MDP* X 89 i 23 the LÚ is to be interpreted as part of the phrase *ṣabāt amēli* rather than as a determinative for the following *kallê*.

Two principal types of *kallû* officials are mentioned, the *kallû nāri* and the *kallû tābali*, in charge of projects on the waterways and on the land respectively (*BBSt* no. 24:33; Hinke Kudurru iii 26; *BBSt* 25:6-7; *BBSt* no. 8 top 3-4; cf. the Kassite *MDP* X 89 i 23). *Kallû šarri*, mentioned only once (*BBSt* no. 6 i 51), is probably to be regarded as a more general term embracing all types of *kallû* in the royal service.

For the Neo-Assyrian and late Neo-Babylonian *kallû* (*kalliu*), who seem to serve as couriers and soldiers, see Saggs, *Iraq* XXI (1959) 173 n. and Wiseman, *Chronicles*, p. 87.

(1964) The *rē'ī sīsê* (called the *rē'ī sīsê ša isqi* in *BBSt* no. 9) collected regular payments of animals from Bit–Abirattash over a period of thirty-two years (*ibid.*, iii 1-15). Compare *YOS* I 37 ii 9-10, where a *rē'ī sīsê* of the province of Bit–Sin–magir receives a payment.

(1965) In a kudurru from northeastern Babylonia drawn up in the reign of Marduk–nadin–ahhe occur four witnesses in succession with unique titles: the *sakrumaš ša mātāti*, the *ša rēši ša mātāti*, the *bēl pīḫati ša mātāti*, and the *šākin ṭēmi ša mātāti* (*BBSt* no. 8 i 30-ii 6). These are the only titles with the qualification *ša mātāti* attested in this period, and it is conceivable that the "lands" (*mātāti*) spoken of in these titles may refer to the tribal lands for which the kudurru was drawn up, i.e., in the area of Irrea (NI*–ri–e–a*), under the jurisdiction of the *bēl bīti* of Bit–Ada. It is hardly necessary to view these officials as possessing

The *ša rēš šarri* and the *kartappu* officials were probably court personnel, (1966) as were the *sukkallu,* (1967) the *sukkalmaḫḫu,* (1968) and perhaps even the *šatam bīt unâti.* (1969) Certain temple or divinatory officials such as the *nišakku,* (1970) the *šatam ekurrāti,* (1971) and the *bārû* (1972) may also have had political influence, since some

---

plenipotentiary power over all of Babylonia. A LÚ *pa–qid mātāti* (KUR.MEŠ) is attested two and one-half centuries later in an unpublished document from the reign of Marduk–balassu–iqbi (4 N-T 3:17′).

Officials are also attested in this period with the designation *māti* appended to their titles, e.g., *šākin ṭēmi māti* (*BBSt* no. 6 ii 13; *BBSt* no. 9 top 20; *BBSt* no. 9 ivb 3; *BBSt* no. 28 rev. 23; 4 N-T 3:13′) and *sukkalmaḫ māti* (VA 5937:3, unpublished kudurru from the reign of Adad–apla–iddina). Since the same officials are called alternately *šākin ṭēmi* and *šākin ṭēmi māti* (see note 2059 below), it is conceivable that the forms with *māti* represent fuller and perhaps the original forms of the titles (cf. *šakin* GN derived from an earlier *šakin māti*).

(1966) See pp. 305 and 310-311 below.

(1967) *BBSt* no. 6 ii 24; I *R* 70 i 17, 19; *BBSt* no. 25:32; *BBSt* no. 8 i 9, A 5, B 4 (note that this *sukkallu* is also *bēl bīti* of Bit–Ada); *BBSt* no. 9 top 19, ivb 2; *BBSt* no. 28 rev. 22; *BBSt* no. 36 vi 21; 4 N-T 3:12′. These officials were frequently members of the clans of Ina–Esagila–zeru, Nazi–Marduk (cf. also the late Kassite text *BBSt* no. 5 ii 35), or Tuballat–Eshdar.

In kudurrus from the reign of Meli–Shipak, a witness Hashardu bore a title written alternately as LÚ SUKKAL LÚ KAŠ$_4$ (*MDP* VI 35 iii 18) and LÚ SUKKAL *mu–ir–ri* (*BBSt* no. 4 i 11) [there is no question of there being two different individuals named Hashardu here, since there are two other witnesses in common between these texts]. This suggests that KAŠ$_4$ here should be read as *mu'irru;* and one wonders whether other instances of (LÚ) KAŠ$_4$ in the late second millennium in Babylonia (see *AHw* 539 under *lāsimu*[*m*]) might rather be interpreted as *mu'irru,* since the title *lāsimu* is not attested in a syllabic spelling at this time while the title *mu'irru*—spelled syllabically—is attested in kudurru curse formulae in the late Kassite period (*MDP* VI 35 iv 4, 40 ii 3; *MDP* X 89 ii 18).

(1968) In the context of Babylonian kudurrus, *sukkalmaḫḫu* officials are attested once in late Kassite times (*BBSt* no. 4 ii 7) and once under the Second Dynasty of Isin (LÚ SUKKAL.MAḪ KUR, i.e., *sukkalmaḫ māti,* in VA 5937:3, unpublished).

(1969) *BBSt* no. 6 ii 20; *BBSt* no. 25:36 (cf. Walters Art Gallery 21.10 rev. ii ⌜5⌝), *PSBA* XIX (1897) 71 ii 17; VA 5937 rev. ⌜4′⌝, unpublished kudurru from the reign of Adad–apla–iddina; *BBSt* no. 9 ivb 6. The office occurs rarely outside this period; in late Kassite times in *BBSt* no. 4 ii 4 (written logographically as *šà–tam* É.NÍG.GÚ.NA, reign of Meli–Shipak) and in Neo-Babylonian times in *Nbn.* 43:2 (LÚ *šà–tam* É *ú–na–*[*a–ti*]). It is uncertain whether this office was on the court, provincial, or local level or even whether it was a strictly political office at all.

(1970) At Nippur, the *nišakku* of Enlil in the time of Nebuchadnezzar I was also mayor (*ḫazannu*) of the city (Hinke Kudurru iii 10-12, etc.). A few years later, the *nišakku* of Enlil there held the office of "chief of the seers" (*akil bārê*: 9 N 99:3, unpublished; in the slightly earlier H.S. 157 iv 14, unpublished, the same individual was called simply *bārû*). At Borsippa in the middle of the eighth century the *nišakku* also served as governor (*šākin ṭēmi*: *JRAS* 1892 353 i 10′). In late Kassite times, a *nišakku* of Enlil had also served as *šandabakku* (*BBSt* no. 3 i 46-47). J. Renger in a forthcoming *ZA* (probably LIX) will discuss the derivation of *nišakku* (*nêšakku*) from Sumerian n u . è š and the Old Babylonian occurrences of the office.

(1971) *BBSt* no. 9 iva 31; *SPA* I 284 no. XIII; *VAS* I 36 iii 9. The title *šatam ekurrāti* is also one of the titles borne by the *turtānu* in Assyria in the late ninth and early eighth centuries, as attested on the Assur stele of Belu–balat (*WVDOG* XXIV 52 no. 44:4; reading of PN questionable: written mEN–*lu*–TI.LA *ibid.*, line 1 and mEN–*ba–laṭ* in *RLA* II 420 Ca1 iii 2) and on the lion inscriptions of Shamshi–ilu from Til–Barsip (Thureau-Dangin, *Til–Barsib,* p. 143:⌜8⌝, ⌜14⌝). Cf. the *šatam ekurri* mentioned in the *Fürstenspiegel* (*BWL* 114:55, 56).

(1972) Seers appear in high religious, military, and political positions. The high priest (*nišakku*) of Enlil at Nippur in the time of Marduk–nadin–ahhe and Marduk–shapik–zeri was a seer (eventually called chief seer, i.e., *akil bārê,* in the time of Marduk–shapik–zeri: 9 N 99:3, unpublished). Two officials who

of them commonly occur as witnesses in kudurrus. It should be noted that titles such as *aklu*, (1973) *šāpiru*, (1974) and *šakkanakku* (1975) also occur in kudurrus, but only in the traditional curse formulae; the offices had become obsolete in government. (1976)

It is impossible in our present limited state of knowledge to establish a hierarchy among these subordinate officials. But several brief observations may be made concerning the sequence in which certain officials occur when serving as witnesses to the same document. The table presented on page 302 lists the sequences of officials serving as witnesses to five legal transactions concluded between the beginning of the eleventh century and the middle of the ninth century. (1977) The striking similarity of the sequences is apparent and leads to several tentative conclusions.

It is noteworthy that in each of the texts the total number of witnesses is seven, save in *BBSt* no. 9 iva, where three royal princes precede the other witnesses (making a total of ten there). Other witness lists occasionally reflect certain parts of this sequence, e.g., *BBSt* nos. 28 and 36 list offices 4-6 in the same order (preceded in each case by the *kartappu*). (1978) In other witness lists, officials 2-3 and 5-6 occur next to each other or only slightly separated, but sometimes in reverse order (i.e., 3-2, 6-5). (1979) It seems likely that, for some legal purposes, seven witnesses may have been required; and it is conceivable that the seven officials who recur may have

---

served as *šangû* of Sippar were seers (*BBSt* no. 36 i 21-23, 30-31, ii 15-16, iii 28-29, iv 51-52; *ibid.*, iii 26-27, iv 40-41, vi 11-12). A seer led the Babylonian troops assisting the people of Suhi in the early ninth century (*AKA* 351 iii 20). A seer held the position of scribe to the governor of Bit–Piri'–Amurru in the latter part of the eleventh century (*BE* I/2 149 i 16-17); another seer was the scribe who wrote *BBSt* no. 30 (rev. 22-23). A witness in a kudurru from the time of Nebuchadnezzar I was called "the seer of Bit–Sin–sheme" (Hinke Kudurru v 14).

(1973) Hinke Kudurru iii 19; *BE* I/1 83 rev. 12; *BBSt* no. 7 i 31; *BBSt* no. 8 iii 14; *BBSt* no. 12 iii 2; *RA* XVI (1919) 125 ii 25; *VAS* I 36 ii 17. Cf. *BBSt* no. 14:18 (uncertain date). Note, however, that the *aklu* continued to occur as overseers of certain professions, e.g., seers and cooks (9 N 99:3, unpublished; *VAS* I 36 iv 3).

(1974) Hinke Kudurru iii 19; *VAS* I 36 ii 18. Cf. the Kassite *MDP* II 97:11.

(1975) Hinke Kudurru iii 19. In a late Kassite text, an individual is referred to as the "*šakkanakku* of Agade" (*BBSt* no. 4 ii 10); it is possible that this is a laudatory allusion to the governor of Babylon (note that the city of *Ak–ka–di* is designated as the residence city of the late Kassite kings in *BBSt* no. 3 v 19).

(1976) *Šakkanakku* occurs in royal titulary at this time (*VAS* I 112:7; *BBSt* no. 6 i 3; Hinke Kudurru ii 20). It was also used as an honorific title for governor (*šaknu*) in late Neo-Babylonian times (references presented in *Orientalia N.S.* XXXIV [1965] 246 n. 3) and perhaps in Kassite times (see note 1975 above).

(1977) In the table, the titles of the witnesses in the kudurru in the second column (*PSBA* XIX [1897] 71) may be restored by comparison with *BBSt* no. 8 i 29-ii 6, where most of the titles of these same men are preserved. Note that the titles borne in *BBSt* no. 8 are each followed by the designation *ša mātāti*.

(1978) *BBSt* no. 28 rev. 21-24; *BBSt* no. 36 vi 18-26. 4 N-T 12′-14′ lists offices 4-6 in the same order, preceded by the *kar*[*tappu*] (10′) and *šan*[*dabakku*] (11′). Cf. also the sequence *kartappu, šākin ṭēmi, sukkallu* in *BBSt* no. 6 ii 12-14. *BBSt* no. 6 ii 19-20 lists the *bēl pīḫati* and *šatam bīt unâti* in order towards the end of the list of witnesses. In the very fragmentary kudurru VA 5937, the *šatam bīt u*[*nâti*] occurs at the end of the witnesses (rev. 4′); but the titulary of the earlier witnesses is entirely broken away.

(1979) Hinke Kudurru v 9-11, 15-17; *BBSt* no. 8 i 29-ii 6.

BBSt no. 25 dated 1100*	*PSBA* XIX (1897) 71 dated 1088*	*BBSt* no. 9 top dated 987*	*BBSt* no. 9 iva-b dated c. 955*	*BBSt* no. 29 c. 887-855
			royal princes	
1 governor of Isin	1 [ ]	1 governor of Isin	1 governor of Isin	1 governor of Isin
2 *ša rēši*	2 [*ša rēši*]	2 *ša rēši*	2 *ša rēši*	2 *ša rē*[*ši*]
3 *sakrumaš*	3 [*sakrumaš*]	3 *sakrumaš*	3 *sakrumaš*	3 *sakru*[*maš*]
4 *sukkallu*	4 [ ]	4 *sukkallu*	4 *sukkallu*	4 [ ]
5 *šākin ṭēme*	5 [*šākin ṭēme*]	5 *šākin ṭēme* (*māti*)	5 *šākin ṭēme* (*māti*)	5 [ ]
6 *bēl pīḫati*	6 [*bēl pīḫati*]	6 *bēl pīḫati*	6 *bēl pīḫati*	6 *bēl* [*pīḫati*]
7 *šatam bīt unâti*	7 *šatam bīt unâti*	*zazakku*	7 *šatam bīt unâti*	7 [ ]

served as some sort of judicial committee under the presidency of the governor of Isin to attest to the validity of royal actions. (1980)

In the following sections, I shall discuss briefly the evidence available on several of the more significant provincial officials: the *bēl pīḫati*, the *kartappu*, the *sakrumaš*, the *šākin ṭēmi*, the *ša rēši* and *ša rēš šarri*.

bēl pīḫati (1981)

The term *bēl pīḫati* is first used in the Old Babylonian and early Kassite periods with the meaning "person responsible." (1982) Officials named *bēl pāḫatim* are rarely attested at Mari in the Old Babylonian period, (1983) but begin to be attested more frequently in Babylonia commencing in the late fourteenth century. (1984) Despite the fact that *pīḫatu* by this time meant "province" (i.e., the governmental administrative unit), the *bēl pīḫati* was until at least the middle of the eighth century a lowly administrative official. With the notable exceptions of Marduk–zakir–shumi (the voluble recipient of a munificent royal land grant in the early twelfth century who recounted his lineage back three generations and then concluded with the claim of being a "descendant of Arad–Ea") (1985) and of Nabu–shuma–ukin II (the *bēl pīḫati* who led the revolt against Nabu–nadin–zeri in 732), (1986) most of the *bēl pīḫati* officials were singularly undistinguished. In the texts they appear usually as minor witnesses to kudurrus, (1987) and the title occurs in a relatively low position among the officials cited in kudurru curse formulae. (1988) Most of them were called simply *bēl pīḫati* without a following geographical name; (1989) but *bēlū pīḫati* of Bit–Sin–sheme, (1990) Bit–Ada, (1991) Irrea (NI–*ri–e–a*), (1992) Bit–Piri'–

(1980) When there are more than or less than seven witnesses, the order in which the witnesses are listed varies.

(1981) For the writing *pīḫatu*, see note 1940 above.

(1982) E.g., *TCL* VII 51:30, *PBS* I/2 73:27.

(1983) *ARM* II 91 rev. ⌜2'⌝, 7'; *ARM* III 59:17.

(1984) *MDP* II 89 iii 6; *Iraq*, Supplement 1944, pl. XVIII right column 7.

(1985) *BBSt* no. 5 i 27-ii 3.

(1986) *CT* XXXIV 46 i 16 (Babylonian Chronicle).

(1987) This is especially true after the Kassite period, when only one *bēl pīḫati* is attested as a witness (*MDP* VI 35 iii 23). *Bēl pīḫati* officials as witnesses in kudurrus drawn up from the time of the Second Dynasty of Isin through the late ninth century occur in: *BBSt* no. 6 ii 19; Hinke Kudurru v 15; *BBSt* no. 8 ii 4; *BBSt* no. 8 ii 23; *BBSt* no. 25:34 (cf. Walters Art Gallery 21.10 rev. ii ⌜3⌝); *BBSt* no. 9 top 21, ivb 5; *BBSt* no. 28 rev. 24; *BBSt* no. 29 ii ⌜18⌝; *BBSt* no. 36 vi 26; *RA* XVI (1919) 126 iv 22; 4 N-T 3:14'. See also my remarks in *JESHO* VI (1963) 237 n. 2.

(1988) I.e., after the governor of the province or his equivalent. *MDP* II 89 iii 6; *MDP* VI 35 iv 1; *CT* XXXVI 13:12' (preceding references are from the Kassite period); *BBSt* no. 8 iii 9, top 7, top 12; *BBSt* no. 11 ii 3; *RA* XVI (1919) 125 ii 24; cf. *BE* I/2 149, ii 2.

(1989) E.g., *BBSt* no. 5 i 28, *BBSt* no. 6 ii 19, and *passim*.

(1990) Hinke Kudurru v 15.

(1991) *BBSt* no. 8 ii 23, cf. *ibid.*, iii 9, top 12.

(1992) *BBSt* no. 8 top 7; cf. *MDP* VI 44 i 9-10 (Kassite).

Amurru, [1993] and "of the lands," [1994] are attested under the Second Dynasty of Isin. [1995]

The exact function of the *bēl pīḫati* in the Kassite and Post-Kassite periods is unknown, since he does not often appear outside of witness lists and curse formulae. Marduk–zakir–shumi, already mentioned above, received a royal land grant. [1996] Bel–ana–kala–bani acted as purchasing agent for the king in a real estate transaction. [1997] Kidin–Marduk together with four other officials supervised the measuring of a field. [1998] Marduk–shumu–lishir served as scribe in the recording of a kudurru. [1999] These four men all lived in the Kassite period. A probable Post-Kassite reference to a *bēl pīḫati* before the middle of the eighth century occurs on a Luristan bronze dagger, though the personal name has not as yet been read. [2000] A late-ninth-century treaty between Babylonia and Assyria also mentions *bēl pīḫati*, but in a broken context. [2001] It is noteworthy that, of the ten *bēl pīḫati* officials during the Kassite and Post-Kassite periods whose ancestry is legibly recorded, eight are descendants of the famous scribal family of Arad–Ea; [2002] and, considering that the earliest accurately dated *bēl pīḫati* official also served as a scribe, [2003] it is possible that one of the functions of the *bēl pīḫati* may have been to keep certain province records.

After the middle of the eighth century, the *bēl pīḫati* in certain areas was a province governor. [2004].

In the Persian period, the word (LÚ) *pīḫatu* [2005] (rarely *paḫātu*) [2006] sometimes served as the Babylonian equivalent of satrap (i.e., governor).

[1993] *BE* I/2 149 ii 2 (curse).

[1994] *BBSt* no. 8 ii 4. For the interpretation of "of the lands," see note 1965 above.

[1995] In the Kassite period a *bēl pīḫati* may also be attested for Bit–Belani (*Iraq*, Supplement 1944, pl. XVIII, right column; but the GN could also be interpreted as the place where the document was written), and for *Bit–[x]* (*BBSt* no. 3 ii 3).

[1996] *BBSt* no. 5. Whether the grandiose epithets (*ibid.* i 29-30) claimed by Marduk–zakir–shumi describe his *ex officio* functions as *bēl pīḫati* is uncertain.

[1997] *MDP* X 93 viii.

[1998] *MDP* VI 44 i 9-10 (cf. *BBSt* no. 3 ii 1-3, where the context is uncertain).

[1999] *Iraq*, Supplement 1944, pl. XVIII right column 6-7.

[2000] Dossin, *Iranica Antiqua* II (1962) 162 no. 25.

[2001] *AfO* VIII (1932-33) 28:3′.

[2002] Not of the family of Arad–Ea: *BBSt* no. 3 ii 1-3; *BBSt* no. 8 ii 21-23. Of the family of Arad–Ea: *MDP* VI 35 iii 22-23; *BBSt* no. 5 ii 3; *BBSt* no. 6 ii 19; *BBSt* no. 8 ii 4; *BBSt* no. 25:34 (and dupl.); *BBSt* no. 9 top 21; *BBSt* no. 28 rev. 24; 4 N-T 3:14′. The reading of the patronymic in *BBSt* no. 9 ivb 5 is uncertain; but, in the light of the overwhelming predominance of "Arad–Ea" names, it is possible that the scribe did not have sufficient space to complete the writing of the theophoric element of the PN in this instance.

[2003] *Iraq*, Supplement 1944, pl. XVIII right column 6.

[2004] E.g., *ABL* 989:3; Unger, *Babylon*, p. 285 no. 26 iv 28-29.

[2005] E.g., *BRM* I 101:5.

[2006] *Darius* 338:4, 14.

(LÚ) *kartappu* (2007)

This official, whose title in this period is always written KA.DIB and usually with a preceding LÚ determinative, (2008) is attested in texts from the early twelfth century through the late ninth century. (2009) His official function is unknown, since he occurs only as a witness to kudurrus (two in the late Kassite period, (2010) one from the Second Dynasty of Isin, (2011) two from the middle ninth century, (2012) and one from the late ninth century) (2013) and once in a curse formula in a mid-ninth-century kudurru. (2014) The title is usually LÚ *kartappu* without further specification, the sole exception being the "*kartappu* of Akkad" (KA.DIB KUR.URI.KI), chief witness to the famous LAK–ti–Marduk kudurru drawn up in the reign of Nebuchadnezzar I. (2015) That the *kartappu* was an important official is suggested by his invariable occurrence towards the top of a list of witnesses—never lower than third in order and once preceding even the governors of Isin and Babylon (2016)—and from the sequence *šarru, mār šarri, ša rēš šarri, kartappu, bēl pīḫati,* etc. in a curse formula. (2017) It is noteworthy that, wherever the patronymic of a *kartappu* is legibly preserved, the official is of Kassite descent. (2018)

sakrumaš (2019)

The *sakrumaš*, first attested in the Kassite period, (2020) held a military position often connected with chariotry or horses. (2021) According to one Middle Babylonian letter, a *sakrumaš* was to command two chariots on a campaign; (2022) in another

(2007) For the reading of this title, see von Soden, *AHw* 451.

(2008) In *BBSt* no. 6 ii 12, KA.DIB is written without a determinative.

(2009) But the KA.DIB is also attested in the Old Babylonian (e.g., *VAS* XIII 104 iii 32, v 12, 15, etc.) and earlier periods. In the Kassite period, a KA.DIB of Nazimaruttash is attested in *UVB* XIII 43:5.

(2010) *BBSt* no. 4 ii 5; *MDP* VI 35 iii 19.

(2011) *BBSt* no. 6 ii 12.

(2012) *BBSt* nos. 28 rev. 21 and 36 vi 19.

(2013) 4 N-T 3:⌜10′⌝.

(2014) *RA* XVI (1919) 125 ii 23.

(2015) *BBSt* no. 6 ii 12. For KA.DIB RN, see note 2009 above.

(2016) Arranged in chronological order: *BBSt* no. 4 ii 5 (second of seven witnesses), *MDP* VI 35 iii 19 (third of four witnesses, but the preceding two are *ša rēši* and *sukkallu*), *BBSt* no. 6 ii 12 (first of thirteen witnesses, not including the scribe), *BBSt* no. 28 rev. 21 (second of five witnesses, preceded only by the governor of Isin), *BBSt* no. 36 vi 19 (first of four witnesses), 4 N-T 3:⌜10′⌝ (second of eight witnesses, not including the scribe; title of first witness not preserved).

(2017) *RA* XVI (1919) 125 ii 20-24.

(2018) "Sons" of Shaddagme (*BBSt* no. 6 ii 12) and of Habban (*BBSt* nos. 28 rev. 21 and 36 vi 19).

(2019) For the reading of this title, see Balkan, *Kassitenstudien*, I, 137.

(2020) Prof. Gelb has kindly pointed out to me a possible OB precursor of *sakrumaš* in a date formula from Tell Dhiba'i: mu 1 kam sa-ak-ru-aš ba-úš (var.: aḫ(?)-sa-ak-ru-aš, *Sumer* V [1949] 143 no. 4). A form *sakru'aš* or *sakruwaš* could be written later as *sakrumaš*, though the identity of the *sakru'aš* and the *sakrumaš* must at present be regarded as hypothetical.

(2021) To speak of "cavalry" is perhaps an anachronism in the Kassite period.

(2022) *BE* XVII 33a:28 ff. Or, if the commander did not wish to order the *sakrumaš* into the field, then the *sakrumaš* could be made to stay behind with two chariots to guard the fortress (*birtu*).

document, a *sakrumaš* received material to be used for constructing or repairing chariot equipment. (2023) Thirty-two *sakrumašātu* served among the guards of a gate (*ṣāb bābi*) at Nippur in Kassite times. (2024) *Sakrumašātu* appear on ration lists, including those lists dealing with the royal stables early in the Second Isin Dynasty. (2025) Later under the same dynasty, Marduk–nadin–ahhe presented land to a *sakrumaš* who had favorably acquitted himself in a battle against Assyria; (2026) and the *sakrumaš* had the land grant confirmed by bestowing a generous "gift" of thirty horses on the local tribal governor (*bēl bīti*). (2027) Lastly, probably dating from the early tenth century, there is a Luristan bronze arrowhead inscribed with the name of Mar–biti–shuma–ibni, a *sakrumaš*, (2028) again supporting the connection of this title with the military.

In dealing with the title of *sakrumaš*, we should probably distinguish between an original meaning, designating a member of a profession or class, and a later meaning, designating an official. Since such an interpretation of the *sakrumaš* differs from the conclusions reached by Balkan, (2029) I summarize my evidence regarding the earlier meaning of this word as follows. Three occurrences of *sakrumaš* in the plural (2030) (the highest number attested being thirty-two *sakrumašātu*) (2031) show that a number of persons could hold this title in one place (especially since two of these instances are in ration texts). The fact that a *sakrumaš* belonged to or was employed by a private individual (2032) speaks against the title's designating some sort of government office. Also, revealingly, the *sakrumaš* never occurs in the Kassite kudurrus either as the title of a witness or in the long lists of officials cited in curse formulae. Lastly, a person in the early eleventh century is called "son of LÚ *sakrumaš*"; (2033) and such family names are usually derived from the names of professions not from titles of governmental officials.

After the Kassite Dynasty, there is some evidence that *sakrumaš* should be regarded as the title of an official. Beginning in the time of Nebuchadnezzar I, *sakrumaš* occurs frequently as the title of witnesses in kudurrus. (2034) There are

(2023) *BE* XV 13.

(2024) *PBS* II/2 56:2.

(2025) *BE* XV 154:41; *PBS* II/2 56:2, 133:26; *AfK* II (1924-25) 61, Gron. 849:7.

(2026) *BBSt* no. 8 i 1-23; the recipient of the land is elsewhere called a *sakrumaš* (*ibid.*, A 4).

(2027) *BBSt* no. 8 A-B.

(2028) *Iranica Antiqua* II (1962) 161 no. 20. For the dating of this inscription, see note 46 above.

(2029) *Kassitenstudien*, I, 137-138.

(2030) *PBS* II/2 56:2; *AfK* II (1924-25) 61, Gron. 849:7; *BBSt* no. 11 i 5.

(2031) *PBS* II/2 56:2.

(2032) Kassite ration lists speak of a *sakr*[*umaš*] *ša* PN (*PBS* II/2 133: 26-27) and also of a *sakrumaš* of the king (*BE* XV 154:41).

(2033) *BBSt* no. 8 ii 6.

(2034) References in the following notes. The exceptions are on the bronze arrowhead mentioned above (note 2028) and in a kudurru's description of the borders of a field, where one side is said to be ad-

four passages which show individual *sakrumašātu* officials connected with specific geographical areas: Bit–Sin–sheme, [2035] the Sealand, [2036] Bit–Ada, [2037] and "the lands." [2038] In most other instances, however, a person bearing this title is described simply as (LÚ) *sakrumaš*, which could technically be interpreted as the name of either an official or a profession. [2039] But, since most titles borne by witnesses in kudurrus of the time of the Second Dynasty of Isin and later are officials rather than members of professions, it seems more likely that these individuals should also be regarded as officials. [2040]

It is noteworthy that, from the beginning of the Second Dynasty of Isin on, in the seven cases in which the ancestry of a *sakrumaš* is indicated he is invariably of non-Babylonian descent. Five of the patronymics clearly indicate Kassite parentage, [2041] while two of the patronyms are not Babylonian and could be Kassite. [2042] This suggests that the Kassites, who were much concerned with horse-training and similar matters [2043] and who had first introduced the title of *sakrumaš*, may have retained exclusive right to the title even after the end of the Kassite Dynasty.

šākin ṭēmi [2044]

The office of *šākin ṭēmi* originates in the Kassite period. [2045] Up until the middle of the ninth century, the *šākin ṭēmi* seems to have been a rather minor provincial

---

jacent to (the field of) ᵐ*Amēl–Marduk sak–ru–maš*.MEŠ (*BBSt* no. 11 i 5). The use of the plural here is surprising, unless another PN was omitted next to Amel–Marduk; it is also conceivable that *u*, "and," could be understood after Amel–Marduk. But these are only conjectures.

[2035] Hinke Kudurru v 9 (*maš* written over erased É).

[2036] *BBSt* no. 27 rev. 15.

[2037] *BBSt* no. 8 A 4.

[2038] *BBSt* no. 8 i 30. For the interpretation of this title, see note 1965 above.

[2039] *BBSt* no. 25:30; *BBSt* no. 9 top 17; *BBSt* no. 9 iva 36; *BBSt* no. 29 ii 12. Also probably dating from about this time are *VAS* I 57 ii 7, *Iranica Antiqua* II (1962) 161 no. 20.

[2040] This is strengthened by the consideration that the *sakrumaš* is not attested in the plural after the close of the twelfth century. But it should be noted that the *sakrumaš* is still unattested among the officials listed in the kudurru curse formulae from any period.

[2041] "Sons" of Bazi (*BBSt* no. 8 i 30; *BBSt* no. 9 top 17), of Habban (*BBSt* no. 29 ii 11-12; *VAS* I 57 ii 6-7, precise date unknown), and of Uzib–Shipak (*BBSt* no. 27 rev. 15). To these might be added "son" of Abirattash, if Mar–biti–shuma–ibni the *sakrumaš* (*Iranica Antiqua* II [1962] 161 no. 20) is to be identified with Mar–biti–shuma–ibni of *BBSt* no. 9 i 19, etc. (see note 46 above).

[2042] "Sons" of Nigazi (*BBSt* no. 25:30) and of ᵐ*Še–rik* (*BBSt* no. 9 iva 36).

[2043] Balkan, *Kassitenstudien*, I, 11-33.

[2044] Written both syllabically (e.g., *MDP* VI 44 i 12, late Kassite period), and logographically (LÚ GAR KU, e.g., *BBSt* no. 36 vi 23). Towards the end of the Kassite Dynasty and under the Second Dynasty of Isin, the most common writing is with the first element expressed logographically and the second syllabically; GAR(*–in*) *ṭè–mi*/*–me* (e.g., *MDP* VI 35 iii 30, *BBSt* no. 11 i 10, *BBSt* no. 25:33). The LÚ determinative is frequently omitted (e.g., *BBSt* no. 11 ii 2, *BBSt* no. 8 ii 6). Purely logographic writing is the rule after the early tenth century, especially in titulary, though there are exceptions (e.g., *YOS* III 57:7).

[2045] The earliest reference seems to be in *BE* XVII 9:16. Other Kassite references are *MDP* II 108 vi 9, *MDP* VI 35 iii 30, *MDP* VI 44 i 12. A *ša–ki–in ṭe–mu* is also mentioned in the (MB?) Susan recension of the Anzu myth (*RA* XXXV [1938] 20:11).

official since, except for occasional appearances as witness to kudurrus (2046) or general references to the office in the kudurru curse formulae, (2047) he appears only as a surveyor of local land. (2048) During this period, *šākin ṭēmi* officials are attested principally in the provinces of northeastern or southern Babylonia, (2049) probably because almost all contemporary kudurrus come from that region.

About the middle of the ninth century, the *šākin ṭēmi* seems to have gained new stature and began to serve as chief public magistrate or "governor" in several important provincial cities. (2050) Between 860 and 722, there are gubernatorial *šākin ṭēmi* attested at Dilbat, Der, and Borsippa. (2051) Other major Babylonian cities which have *šākin ṭēmi* officials as governors in a slightly later period include Babylon, (2052) Cutha, (2053) Kish, (2054) Ur, (2055) and Uruk. (2056) The office of *šākin ṭēmi* continued as late as the reign of Darius I. (2057).

A possible variant of this office, *šākin ṭēm(i) māti*, occurs several times in Babylonia between the late twelfth and the late ninth centuries. (2058) Since the same

(2046) *BBSt* no. 6 ii 13; *BBSt* no. 25:33 (cf. Walters Art Gallery no. 21.10 rev. ii 2); Hinke Kudurru v 16-17; *BBSt* no. 8 ii 6; *BBSt* no. 9 top 20; *BBSt* no. 9 ivb 3; *BBSt* no. 28 rev. 23; *BBSt* no. 36 vi 23; *VAS* I 35:49; 4 N-T 3:13′, 15′.

(2047) *BBSt* no. 11 ii 2; *BBSt* no. 8 iii 11, top 9-10; *BE* I/2 149 ii 3; *RA* XVI (1919) 125 ii 28; *VAS* I 36 ii 19; 4 N-T 3:23′. Late Kassite: *MDP* II 108 vi 9; *MDP* VI 35 ii 30. Cf. *BBSt* no. 14:14, undated.

(2048) Hinke Kudurru iii 15-16; *BBSt* no. 11 i 10; *BE* I/2 149 i 18. Late Kassite: *MDP* VI 44 i 12. This need not imply that the *šākin ṭēmi* was a surveyor by profession, but simply that he was one of the local officials called upon to supervise field measurements.

(2049) Down through the early ninth century, *šākin ṭēmi* officials are attested from Bit-Ada (*BBSt* no. 8 iii 11, Second Isin Dynasty, curse formula), Bit-Piri'-Amurru (*MDP* II 108 vi 9, Kassite, curse formula; *BE* I/2 149 i 18, Second Isin Dynasty, cf. *ibid.* ii 3, curse formula), Bit-Sin-magir (*BE* XVII 9:16, Kassite, letter), Bit-Sin-sheme (Hinke Kudurru iii 15-16, cf. *ibid.* v 16-17, Second Isin Dynasty; and probably also *UET* I 165 ii 4, date unknown, curse formula), Hudadu (*MDP* VI 35 iii 30, Kassite, curse formula), Irrea (*MDP* VI 44 i 12, Kassite; *BBSt* no. 8 top 9-10, Second Isin Dynasty, curse formula), Sealand (*BBSt* no. 11 i 10, Second Isin Dynasty, cf. *ibid.* ii 2, curse formula), and in a kudurru found at Za'aleh near Babylon (*BBSt* no. 25:33, Second Isin Dynasty). The only *šākin ṭēmi* said to be from an area lower than province rank is one from Dur-Rim-Sin of Bit-Sin-sheme (Hinke Kudurru v 16-17), but the same official is elsewhere in the same text said to be the *šākin ṭēmi* of Bit-Sin-sheme itself (iii 15-16). There is no evidence that there was more than one *šākin ṭēmi* per province.

For the offices of *šākin ṭēmi māti* and *šākin ṭēmi ša mātāti*, see below.

(2050) The earliest reference is in *VAS* I 35:2, dated in the twenty-eighth year of Nabu-apla-iddina.

(2051) Dilbat: *VAS* I 35:2, 49. Der: 4 N-T 3:15′. Borsippa: *VAS* I 36 iii 7; *JRAS* 1892 353 i 10′ (and *passim* in this text). The governor of Dilbat is known to have retained his office for at least seventeen years about the middle of the ninth century (see note 1253 above).

(2052) E.g., *VAS* V 5:28.

(2053) E.g., *VAS* I 37 v 13.

(2054) E.g., W. 1929,145:6 (Langdon, *Kish*, III, pl. 13).

(2055) *UET* IV 8:28-29, cf. *UET* IV 206 rev. 3.

(2056) E.g., *BIN* II 134:17, 19.

(2057) *VAS* VI 128, edge. The office of *šākin ṭēmi* is usually Babylonian, though a text of Sargon II refers to LÚ *šākin ṭēm mātišu* (of the land of the Manneans, *TCL* III 58).

(2058) *BBSt* no. 6 ii 13; *BBSt* no. 9 top 20; *BBSt* no. 9 ivb 3; *BBSt* no. 28 rev. 23; 4 N-T 3:13′. *MDP* VI 44 i 12 (late Kassite period) refers to a *šākin ṭēmi māt* URU GN; but the double determinative *māt* URU goes with the GN (cf. *BBSt* no. 8 i 2), so the *māt* does not belong to the preceding title.

individuals are called alternately *šākin ṭēmi* and *šākin ṭēmi māti* in different documents, the former may have been a shorter form of the latter. ([2059]) A person called *šākin ṭēmi ša mātāti* occurs as a witness to a kudurru under the Second Dynasty of Isin ([2060]) and is probably to be connected with the tribal "lands" in northeastern Babylonia, for which the kudurru was drawn up. ([2061])

ša rēši and *ša rēš šarri* ([2062])

The meaning of the term *ša rēši* is known from abundant evidence in the Neo-Assyrian period. Here *ša rēši* was used of officials not wearing beards in distinction to the *ša ziqni*, who were bearded officials. ([2063]) In addition, it is generally assumed that the unbearded officials were eunuchs; and "eunuch" often serves as the translation of *ša rēši*. In the Neo-Assyrian period, *ša rēši* attendants are attested for some of the high court personnel:

(a) king: *ša rēši* (*ša*) *šarri* (e.g., *ADD* 249:6′, 1104:8);
(b) prince: *ša rēši* (*ša*) *mār šarri* (e.g., *ADD* 334:1, 854:18);
(c) queen mother: *ša rēš ummi šarri* (*ADD* 857:21);
(d) "palace woman": *ša rēš*(*i*) (*ša*) SAL.É.GAL (e.g., *ADD* 316:6′, 287:7);
(e) *turtānu*: *ša rēši ša* PN *turtānu* (Delaporte, *Catalogue des cylindres orientaux*, II, 165-166, no. A.678:1-3)

and also for a *šakintu* (*ADD* 356:6), *bēl bīti* (*ADD* 344:2), and for temples (*ADD* 805:5, etc.). Furthermore, the Neo-Assyrian royal annals frequently use the plural *šūt rēši* as a generic term for Assyrian officials engaged in provincial administration. ([2064])

Justification for the translation of Assyrian *ša rēši* as "eunuch" may be found in texts of the Middle Assyrian period. The Middle Assyrian Law Code imposes gelding (*ana ša-ri-še-en turru*) ([2065]) as a penalty in certain cases involving adultery

([2059]) Arad-Nana, son of Mudammiq-Adad, is called *šākin ṭēmi māti* in *BBSt* no. 6 ii 13 and *šākin ṭēme* in *BBSt* no. 25:33. Marduk-shapik-zeri, son of Tuballat-Eshdar, is called *šākin ṭēmi māti* in *BBSt* no. 28 rev. 23 and *šākin ṭēmi* in *BBSt* no. 36 vi 23.

([2060]) *BBSt* no. 8 ii 6.

([2061]) See note 1965 above.

([2062]) Usually written (LÚ) SAG and (LÚ) SAG LUGAL respectively. The *ša* is only occasionally expressed in writing, e.g., *CT* XLIII 44:9, *BBSt* no. 8 ii 2. That (LÚ) SAG is to be interpreted as (LÚ) *ša rēši* during this period in Babylonia may be seen from the writing of the titles of Babilaju, son of Sin-lishir; in *BBSt* no. 25:28 he bears the title LÚ SAG and in *BBSt* no. 8 ii 2 the title of (LÚ) *šá* SAG (*ša mātāti*).

([2063]) *CAD* Z 126-127, where earlier literature is cited.

([2064]) E.g., Lie, *Sargon*, 215 and *passim* in the Neo-Assyrian royal annals. This hardly implies that all officials embraced by the term *šūt rēši* were eunuchs.

([2065]) (*ša*)*rēšēn* is formally a dual in these earliest Assyrian references.

or homosexuality. (2066) The *ša rēši* is also an official involved with the administration of the royal women's quarters, as abundantly attested in the Middle Assyrian Harem Edicts. (2067)

There is no evidence for a meaning "eunuch" for *ša rēši* in Babylonia. (2068) The term is attested rarely in the Old Babylonian period, (2069) and is used about four times in the Kassite period. (2070) There is no indication of the *ša rēši*'s function at that time, though there is a *ša rēši* who occurs twice as a witness in kudurrus in late Kassite times. (2071) Also, in a ration list from the Kassite period, an individual is designated as PN LÚ SAG *ša* PN_2, (2072) presumably indicating that the *ša rēši* could serve in some sort of household capacity for a private person.

Under the Second Isin and Second Sealand dynasties, the *ša rēši* was apparently sometimes an official title, since there was a *ša rēši* of Bit–Sin–sheme, (2073) a *ša rēši* of the Sealand, (2074) and a *ša rēši* "of the lands." (2075) Between the late twelfth and middle ninth centuries there are seven known instances of *ša rēši*s who served as witnesses in kudurrus; (2076) with the exception of the three officials mentioned in the preceding sentence, the rest of these men were designated simply as LÚ SAG (with no geographical name following). One individual, Babilaju, son of Sin–lishir, was described as *ša rēši* in one text and as *ša rēši ša mātāti* in another text written nine years later; (2077) the latter title is presumably to be regarded as a more specific rendering of an abridged form. (2078) The *ša rēši* does not occur in curse formulae in kudurrus; and it is possible that at least some of the *ša rēši*s should be regarded as members of a class rather than as officials. (2079)

The *ša rēš šarri* occurs as a royal official as early as the Kassite period and is more commonly attested at that time than the *ša rēši*. (2080) A *ša rēš šarri* was given

(2066) *KAV* 1 ii 54, 97.

(2067) References listed by Weidner, *AfO* XVII (1954-56) 264.

(2068) The literal meaning of the term is "of the head," presumably referring to the position of an attendant standing at the head of or near an individual.

(2069) *CT* XLIII 44:9.

(2070) *PBS* II/2 20:27, 136:15; *MDP* VI 35 iii 17; *BBSt* no. 4 ii 6.

(2071) *MDP* VI 35 iii 17; *BBSt* no. 4 ii 6.

(2072) *PBS* II/2 20:27.

(2073) Hinke Kudurru v 11.

(2074) *BBSt* no. 27 rev. 15.

(2075) LÚ *šá* SAG *šá* KUR.MEŠ (*BBSt* no. 8 ii 2).

(2076) *BBSt* no. 6 ii 15; Hinke Kudurru v 11; *BBSt* no. 8 ii 2; *BBSt* no. 27 rev. 15; *BBSt* no. 9 top 16, iva 35; *BBSt* no. 29 ii 10. Of unknown date, but probably around this time: *VAS* I 57 ii 4. Three of these individuals have foreign names, two of which are Hurrian (m*Ṭu–bi–ia–en–na* [*BBSt* no. 6 ii 15] and m*Am–me–en–na* [*BBSt* no. 9 top 16]) and one of which cannot be readily analyzed (m*Ši–ta–ri–ba* [Hinke Kudurru v 11]).

(2077) *BBSt* no. 25:28; *BBSt* no. 8 ii 2.

(2078) See also note 1965 above.

(2079) Especially those bearing no geographical name or other specification in their title.

(2080) Both offices occur once in the same text: *BBSt* no. 4 i 17, ii 6 (late Kassite).

a royal land grant by Adad–shuma–usur, (2081) and another *ša rēš šarri* was described as a land owner. (2082) The *ša rēš šarri* was sometimes in charge of work projects, (2083) and twice officials bearing that title were delegated by the king to assist in surveying land. (2084) Other men described as *ša rēš šarri* are likewise mentioned in the Kassite period, (2085) and *ša rēš šarri* occurs among the officials in a kudurru curse formula. (2086) Furthermore, we have two seals inscribed with the name and title of an individual who describes himself as *ša rēš* RN: Kidin–Marduk, the *ša rēš Burnaburiaš* (II); one of these seals was found at recent excavations at Thebes in Greece. (2087)

After the Kassite dynasty, the *ša rēš šarri* is less commonly attested. Marduk–nasir, a *ša rēš šarri*, purchased land from a member of the "House" of Hanbu; (2088) and from the extensive amounts of goods, including a chariot, horses (mares), asses, grain, oil, silver, and garments paid out for the land, it may be concluded that Marduk–nasir was a wealthy individual and that he possessed military equipment. (2089) That the *ša rēš šarri* may have had some military function in the Post-Kassite period is also suggested by the fact that some of the Luristan bronze weapons are inscribed with the names of *ša rēš šarri* officials. (2090) According to a kudurru from the middle of the ninth century, the *ša rēš šarri* enjoyed a high position in the governmental hierarchy and was mentioned just after the king's son and before the governor of Nippur in a witness list. (2091)

Both *ša rēši* and *ša rēš šarri* officials continue to occur in economic documents in Babylonia down into the Persian period, chiefly in connection with the temple administration at Uruk. (2092)

(2081) *MDP* VI 42 i 20.

(2082) *MDP* II 99 i 14.

(2083) *BE* XVII 13:5, rev. 6′.

(2084) *MDP* II 100 i 32; *BBSt* no. 4 i 17.

(2085) *BE* XVII 1:5 (to be restored in line 19?); *MDP* II 113 i 2. Cf. *MDP* VI 43 ii ⌈13⌉.

(2086) *MDP* II 108 vi 3.

(2087) Moortgat, *Vorderasiatische Rollsiegel*, no. 554. A photograph of the Theban seal was published in *Kathimerini* for April 19, 1964; translations, transliterations, and brief commentaries were published on the seal by M. T. Larsen in *Nestor* no. 79 (July 1, 1964) 335-336 and by Falkenstein in *Kadmos* III/1 (1964) 108-109. See also the *Illustrated London News* for November 28, 1964, p. 860, figs. 2-3, and *Bulletin de Correspondance Hellénique* LXXXVIII (1964) 777-779.

(2088) *BBSt* no. 7.

(2089) A Marduk–nasir, possibly the same man, dedicated a Luristan bronze dagger to the god Erija (Dossin, *Iranica Antiqua* II [1962] 153 no. 7).

(2090) *SPA* I 284 no. XI; Dossin, *Iranica Antiqua* II (1962) 162 no. 26 (is this rather to be interpreted as a type of macehead?).

(2091) *RA* XVI (1919) 126 iv 19, mentioned also in the curse formula *ibid.* 125 ii 22. The *ša rēš šarri* is also mentioned in a curse formula in a seventh-century kudurru (*AnOr* XII 305 rev. 10) and in an undated and fragmentary kudurru (*BBSt* no. 18 A 6).

(2092) *YOS* VII 190:18, *VAS* III 71:14, etc. There the *ša rēš šarri* title developed more complex sub-species such as the (*ša*) *rēš šarri bēl piqitti Eanna* (*TCL* XIII 163:5, etc.) and the (*ša*) *rēš šarri ša muḫḫi quppi* (*ša*) *Eanna* (*AnOr* VIII 41:1, etc.).

The Army

The Babylonian army during this period was probably a small force, used primarily for defense purposes. Its occasional aggressive actions were quick raids into enemy lands; (2093) attempts to capture and hold enemy territory were restricted to frontier fortifications which could be taken by siege and readily retained. (2094) The Babylonian army did not attempt permanent territorial conquests, and most large-scale battles in which it participated were defensive actions against invaders.

The Babylonian armed forces were composed of chariotry, (2095) infantry, (2096) and cavalry. (2097) During the Second Dynasty of Isin, chariotry still played a significant part in Babylonian warfare; and the victories of Nebuchadnezzar I over Hulteludish–Inshushinak (2098) and of Marduk–nadin–ahhe over Tiglath–Pileser I attest to the skill of the Babylonian chariotry. (2099) Some ration lists from the royal stables have survived from the time of Itti–Marduk–balatu. (2100) Chariots could be owned and maintained by individual officers, as may be seen from the fact that Marduk–nasir, a *ša rēš šarri*, handed over a fully equipped chariot to another person in part payment for a parcel of land. (2101) Chariotry officials bore special titles, e.g., "(Commander) of the Chariotry of the Right Wing" (*ša magarrašu bīt imitti*), (2102) which suggest a highly organized chariotry corps. After the Second Dynasty of Isin, chariots are less commonly heard of, though Shamash–mudammiq had chariots and (horse) teams captured by Adad–nirari II (2103) and the combined Babylonian–Suhian forces against Ashurnasirpal II in 878 included chariotry. (2104) One hundred Babylonian chariots were captured at the battle of Dur–Papsukkal c. 814. (2105)

Infantry is seldom mentioned explicitly in the texts. The Synchronistic History tells of infantry (*zūku*) in the army of Nebuchadnezzar I which attacked Assyrian border fortresses. (2106) Otherwise this element in the composition of the army

(2093) *AfO* IV (1927) 215; *BBSt* no. 6 i 14-43; *BBSt* no. 24:7-8; *OIP* II 83:48-50. The kudurrus *BBSt* nos. 6 and 24 describe the raids into Elam by the word *šiḫṭu*, "razzia" (*BBSt* no. 6 i 15; no. 24:7).

(2094) *CT* XXXIV 39 ii 2′-13′, Synchronistic History.

(2095) *BBSt* no. 6 i 34, etc.; *CT* XXXIV 39 ii 8′, 12′, 15′ and 40 iii 6, Synchronistic History; I *R* 31 iv 44.

(2096) *CT* XXXIV 39 ii 8′, Synchronistic History.

(2097) See notes 2108 and 2109 below. The triple division of Babylonian troops is described in the annals of Shamshi–Adad V (I *R* 31 iv 43-44).

(2098) *BBSt* no. 6 i 14-43.

(2099) See p. 128. The first encounter blocked the Assyrian advance east of the Tigris for that year.

(2100) *AfK* II (1924-25) 56-61: Gron. 847, Gron. 848, Gron. 849. The first and third of these texts mention *sīsê ša ekalli*, the second only *sīsê*.

(2101) *BBSt* no. 7 i 15.

(2102) *BBSt* no. 6 i 26, etc.

(2103) *CT* XXXIV 40 iii 6-7, Synchronistic History (the verb "captured" is restored).

(2104) *AKA* 352 iii 22.

(2105) I *R* 31 iv 44.

(2106) *CT* XXXIV 39 ii 8′, Synchronistic History.

was regularly taken for granted and rarely mentioned in the texts. The army on foot also included bowmen and siege troops such as miners and the men who operated the wooden siege engines. (2107)

Cavalry seems to have been a minor factor in the Babylonian army. During the Second Dynasty of Isin, riding animals were subject to confiscation by the master of the cavalry (LÚ *ša pitḫalli*), (2108) though the connection of this official with the military can only be surmised. According to an Assyrian account, two hundred Babylonian cavalry were captured near Dur–Papsukkal c. 814. (2109)

The manner in which troops were recruited and mustered in this period is unknown. Probably tenancy of certain land within Babylonia still carried with it an obligation to military service; but the conscription which furnished manpower for public works projects may also have provided fighting personnel. (2110) Rewards for distinction in battle, including land grants (2111) and tax exemptions, (2112) may have been an inducement to potential recruits from nominally Babylonian outlying regions. The big cities such as Babylon and Nippur also apparently maintained troops for the cause of national defense. (2113) There is little evidence for a standing army, though some contingents of soldiers were regularly quartered in the eastern frontier regions under Nebuchadnezzar I. (2114)

On major campaigns, the army in the field was commanded by the king, (2115) assisted by subordinate commanders. Minor expeditions were commanded by leaders called *ālik pān ummān(āt)i*, (2116) who were sometimes supervised by a member of the royal family such as the king's brother. (2117) It is conceivable that strong local leaders in outlying areas, such as LAK–ti–Marduk in the time of Nebuchadnezzar I, may have possessed armed forces of their own.

We know little about battle techniques in this period. Apparently, however, during the days of the Second Dynasty of Isin, the most remarkable results of Babylonian military forces were achieved by striking deep into enemy territory at unexpected times. Nebuchadnezzar I picked the hot summer months to advance

(2107) The army of Nebuchadnezzar I employed siege engines (*nēpišū*) to attack Assyrian forts and was forced to burn them on retiring from the scene (*CT* XXXIV 39 ii 3′-6′, Synchronistic History).

(2108) *BBSt* no. 6 i 58-59.

(2109) I *R* 31 iv 44.

(2110) E.g., Hinke Kudurru iii 25.

(2111) E.g., *BBSt* no. 8.

(2112) E.g., *BBSt* no. 6.

(2113) *BBSt* no. 6 ii 3.

(2114) *BBSt* no. 6 ii 4, 9.

(2115) *BBSt* no. 6 i 23, 28-29, 42; I *R* 31 iv 37-42; cf. K. 2660 rev. (*JNES* XVII [1958] 138).

(2116) *CT* XXXIV 39 ii 13′, Synchronistic History; *AKA* 351 iii 20. This term is recorded only in Assyrian sources and may probably be regarded as a generic term rather than a military rank. In the time of Nabu-apla-iddina, the "leader" of the troops was a seer (*bārû*).

(2117) *AKA* 351 iii 20.

unperceived deep into Elam and vanquish Hulteludish–Inshushinak on his home ground. (2118) Nebuchadnezzar's father, Ninurta–nadin–shumi, had achieved military fame by penetrating near Arbail in the Assyrian homeland. (2119) Nebuchadnezzar's younger brother, Marduk–nadin–ahhe, won lasting renown by raiding north on the Tigris and carrying off the gods of Ekallate. (2120)

Most of the recorded battles of this time were fought between Babylonia and Elam or between Babylonia and Assyria. But on occasion Babylonia joined with foreign allies to fight battles. Nabu–apla–iddina sent a contingent of 3000 men to help the Suhians against Assyria. (2121) Shalmaneser III came with Assyrian troops to assist Marduk–zakir–shumi I in putting down the rebellion of his brother. (2122) Elamite, Chaldean, Kassite, and Aramean troops assisted Marduk–balassu–iqbi in his fight against the Assyrians. (2123) But during the eighth and seventh centuries, until the rise of the Chaldean Dynasty under Nabopolassar, Babylonian armies were increasingly reluctant to take the field. Nabonassar allowed Assyrian armies to fight against the Arameans and Chaldeans. (2124) Mukin–zeri let himself be sieged by the Assyrians rather than risk a major conflict in the field. (2125) Even the later Merodach–Baladan II, who profited by military victory over the Assyrians, preferred to let the Elamites do the active fighting for him. (2126)

Except under the Second Dynasty of Isin, the Babylonian army at this time does not seem to have been an effective fighting force. (2127) The slight strength of the Babylonian military, especially the chariotry, which may have been built up under the Kassites, suffered heavily during the last century of Kassite rule and, after a brief revival under the family of Nebuchadnezzar I, went into eclipse until the late seventh century.

(2118) The difficulty of the season is described in *BBSt* no. 6 i 16-21.
(2119) *AfO* IV (1927) 215 rev. ii.
(2120) *OIP* II 83:48-50.
(2121) *AKA* 351 iii 20.
(2122) *WO* IV/1 (1967) 30 iv 1-v 3, etc.
(2123) I *R* 31 iv 38-39.
(2124) See pp. 229-231 above.
(2125) II *R* 67:23-25, etc.
(2126) Brinkman, *JNES* XXIV (1965) 161-166.
(2127) This conclusion may be prejudiced because of the dearth of Babylonian documents dealing with military activities. Our views of Babylonian military organization are seen principally through Assyrian eyes.

Conclusion

The political history of independent Babylonia, which extended from the time of Sumu-abum (1894-1881) down to Nabonidus (555-539), was dominated largely by monarchs and dynasties who were not of Babylonian descent. Babylon as an independent political power was born under the aegis of an Amorite dynasty; and the first three dynasties of Babylon, which ruled for a total of over seven hundred years, were comprised of foreign families—Amorites, Sealanders, and Kassites. The three most powerful and most renowned dynasties in Babylonian history, those which reigned during the heydays of the Old, Middle, and Neo-Babylonian periods, were of foreign extraction: Amorites, Kassites, and Chaldeans. These groups were able to provide a military basis for Babylonian political power that was stronger than that which native Babylonians managed to furnish.

The years treated in the present volume, from 1158* to 722, represented a period of transition in Babylonia: from the hegemony of the Kassites to the hegemony of the Chaldeans. The main power of the Kassites had been broken by the Elamites when they destroyed the Kassite Dynasty around the year 1158*. Into the power vacuum created by the demise of this dynasty stepped native Babylonian rulers associated with the city of Isin. During the centuries that followed, a period which in many ways seemed a political nadir for Babylon in the international sphere, emerged some of the strongest rulers of Babylonian descent—and, indeed, some of the only rulers of Babylonian descent—who ever sat on the throne in Babylon: men of the caliber of Nebuchadnezzar I, (2128) Marduk-nadin-ahhe, Nabu-apla-iddina, and Marduk-zakir-shumi I. (2129) Yet the ambitions and achievements of these monarchs were modest: they neither essayed to hold permanently extensive territory outside Babylonia, nor did they succeed in handing down their power long within their own families. In general, these rulers had no noteworthy impact on the international scene, though they did manage to compete successfully—at least for a time—against Assyrian monarchs like Tiglath-Pileser I, Ashurnasirpal II, Shalmaneser III, and Shamshi-Adad V.

This period, however, cannot be characterized as uninterrupted political hegemony for native Babylonians. One of the rulers of the Second Isin Dynasty, Adad-apla-iddina, may have been an Aramean. The Kassites seem to have regained a temporary ascendancy in the Second Sealand and Bazi dynasties; and a ruler of Elamite descent occupied the Babylonian throne in the early tenth century. We cannot speak with certainty of the dynastic affiliation of most Babylonian rulers

(2128) Explicitly termed a native of Babylon (*ṣīt Bābili*) in *BBSt* no. 6 i 2.

(2129) There is no indication that the latter two rulers were of foreign extraction, though we do not know the name of their dynasty.

during the tenth and ninth centuries. And in the eighth century, following the brutal blows of Shamshi–Adad V against northern Babylonia, the Chaldeans gradually emerged as the power to be reckoned with in the land.

Two threads run throughout the Babylonian history of this period. The first is the impact of foreign invasions on the vulnerable northern part of Babylonia, which profoundly altered the political situation within the land itself. The second is the part played by foreign or provincial individuals and families, who profited from the weakness of the area around Babylon. The Elamite invasions in the middle of the twelfth century effectively removed the hegemony of the Kassites. The Assyrian invasions towards the end of the ninth century removed any native obstacles to Chaldean rule. We have seen how rulers connected with the provincial city of Isin took advantage of the Elamite victories and how, when the Isin Dynasty had departed from the scene, the small dynasties from the Sealand and from Bit–Bazi and a lone ruler of Elamite extraction came and went in quick succession. Later the Chaldean ruler Eriba–Marduk was hailed as the king who reestablished the stability of the land and put an end to the anarchy left in the wake of Shamshi–Adad V. Then, following such leaders as Mukin–zeri and Merodach–Baladan II, the Chaldeans continued to harass Assyrian attempts to rule Babylonia until eventually in the latter part of the seventh century a Chaldean dynasty was to assist in the final dismembering of the once great Assyrian empire. But these political movements were largely engendered by forces outside Babylonia and carried on by provincial and foreign elements within Babylonia.

In this period, before the eighth century, Babylonian official records—such as royal inscriptions and chronicles—exhibit a profound disinterest in most military or political events. (2130) Instead, their orientation is largely religious; and, when Babylonian military exploits are recorded in detail, as in the case of Nebuchadnezzar's feats against Elam, it is principally because of the religious significance of these events (i.e., the recovery of the Marduk statue). Only with the advent of Nabonassar were precise and full native records kept of Babylonian military matters; (2131) and this helps to explain not only why there is so little documentation available for Babylonian political history of the Post-Kassite period but also why much of what is known is seen through foreign—chiefly Assyrian—eyes.

Babylonian-Assyrian relations are undoubtedly the best known facet of Babylonian political life during this period, but only because the Assyrians took the trouble to set them down in writing. Thus we learn of Assyrian invasions of Babylonia, Babylonian raids into Assyria, frontier skirmishes and squabbles, treaties,

(2130) It is difficult to say whether this attitude reflected in the documents should be regarded as resulting from or effecting the frequent debility of the native Babylonian military. Perhaps there is some truth to each view.

(2131) Providing some justification for the later Hellenistic legend recorded by (Pseudo-Berossos), as explained on p. 227 above. Yet the Babylonians before Nabonassar kept a very careful record of their individual kings and dynasties (and some religious events), even if they did note few royal military achievements.

diplomatic marriages between the royal families, weaknesses of kings, insolence of courtiers, and the sharing of a scribe between the royal courts. We learn of indirect Babylonian opposition to Assyria through support given anti-Assyrian forces on the middle Euphrates. We see the peripheral areas of Babylonia—Namri, Bit-Habban, Chaldea, and the Aramean settlements east of the Tigris—slipping away from the jurisdiction of the Babylonian central government; and we can watch growing Assyrian interest in these regions with resultant campaigns designed either to incorporate these areas into Assyria or to insure at least a token submission to the Assyrian monarch. In general, Babylonia and Assyria preserved a precarious political balance between the end of the Kassite Dynasty and the time of Shamshi-Adad V, with neither side managing to gain anything more than a temporary advantage over the other. But, with the reign of Shamshi-Adad V, the balance was permanently altered (perhaps because of humiliating terms of a treaty imposed by Babylonia): the power of northern Babylonia was destroyed, and henceforth Assyrian rulers like Shamshi-Adad V, Tiglath-Pileser III, and Shalmaneser V would claim either suzerainty or direct rule over Babylonia. This would lead to long and bitter Babylonian revolts and eventually to the downfall of Assyria.

Babylonian-Elamite contacts in this period are less well known. Elamite raids on Babylonia in the thirteenth and twelfth centuries under kings from Kidin-Hutrutash to Shilhak-Inshushinak must have created chaos, especially in northern and eastern Babylonia. The crowning blow was the removal of the Marduk statue to Elam by Kudur-Nahhunte. Later, when Nebuchadnezzar I succeeded in his daring effort to restore the statue to Babylon, his defeat of the Elamite ruler Hulteludish-Inshushinak apparently ushered in a "Dark Age" for Elamite power. With the exception of Mar-biti-apla-usur, a Babylonian king of Elamite descent in the early tenth century, nothing more is heard of Elam until it sent troops to assist against the Assyrians at the battle near Dur-Papsukkal around the year 814. Then, though the Babylonian Chronicle notes a royal synchronism between Elam and Babylonia, the next attested contact between the two countries is on the occasion of the battle of Der in 720, when Ummanigash fought against Assyria on behalf of Merodach-Baladan II. Thus Babylonia and Elam were enemies in the late second millennium, but later united in opposition to Assyria in the early first millennium. With the weakening of the Babylonian monarchy, the Babylonian army also declined as an effective force: whereas Babylonian kings under the Second Isin Dynasty and occasionally in the ninth century could muster Babylonian military forces, by the late eighth century there is little trace of a Babylonian army and eventually—under Merodach-Baladan II—the Elamites bore the brunt of campaigning on behalf of Babylonia.

At the same time, we witness a decline in the urban and village settlements of Babylonia: the Merkes quarter of Babylon shows fewer and poorer habitations than in preceding centuries, and in the Diyala region the number of villages and the amount of land under cultivation reaches a low point for the Babylonian period.

The political power base within Babylonia gradually shifts from the old cities to the outlying regions and to the less sedentary foreign populations, which increase in number and importance as time goes on. The Kassites and later the Chaldeans represent the real strength in the land. There are probably several reasons for the decline of the urban centers during this period: as targets for raids and looting by Elamites, Arameans (Sutians), and Assyrians, they were undoubtedly weakened by spoliation; but famine and plague in the eleventh and tenth centuries may also have hastened their wane.

Yet urban life and culture continued in Babylonia during this period. Babylon itself retained its reputation as a cultural and religious center. Literature flourished with the composition of poetry and of bilingual (Sumerian-Akkadian) royal inscriptions. Among Babylonian literary works, the Theodicy was composed during the latter part of the Second Dynasty of Isin and the Era Epic probably in the first half of the ninth century. Editions of scientific texts—medical series, documents with formulae for making artificial gems, and astrological treatises—continued to be made. Scribal education throve on bygone classics such as the Codex Hammurapi. The royal scribes of Babylonia were not only in demand at the Assyrian court but also achieved a lasting fame reflected in later literary catalogues as well as in synchronistic kinglists and the Seleucid-period *apkallu* list (all of which recorded the names of illustrious Babylonian *ummânu*s of this time). Even texts such as those in the Nebuchadnezzar I epic cycle were well represented in the later library assembled by Ashurbanipal at Nineveh. This Babylonian literary virtuosity, as noted above, was largely exercised on religious themes: the chronicles and royal inscriptions recorded events of religious importance (the recovery of Marduk, the celebration of the New Year's festival), which sometimes had military overtones (the defeat of the Elamites, the raids of the Arameans and Sutians). Babylonian religion in this time also underwent change and development with the final triumph of Marduk in the pantheon and the subsequent rise of Nabu.

All in all, the history of Babylonia during this period—in so far as it is presently known—may be characterized as a time of military decline (with a few exceptional bright spots under kings like Nebuchadnezzar I) and international insignificance (at least beyond its near neighbors, Assyria and Elam). Within Babylonia, this was an era of political transition from the hegemony of the Kassites to the hegemony of the Chaldeans and the attendant decline of both the old urban centers and the Babylonian army. Despite continued cultural excellence and the respect paid on all sides to the religious eminence of the old cities of northern Babylonia, the real political power in the country shifted to peoples residing in the outlying areas; and it would be these peoples, principally the Chaldeans, who would wage the Babylonian fight for independence in the late eighth and seventh centuries and usher in the final period of Babylonian political greatness, the Neo-Babylonian Empire.

APPENDIX A

CATALOGUE OF WRITTEN SOURCES [2132]

In the following catalogue, the written sources have been arranged in chronological order according to the kings mentioned. Documents which have been tentatively assigned to certain monarchs (pending further evidence) are prefixed with an asterisk; unpublished texts are enclosed in brackets. Texts which cannot be linked to an individual ruler with any degree of probability are listed in the supplement at the end of the catalogue. All texts are written in Akkadian, unless noted to the contrary.

Under each king in the catalogue, the sources have been grouped as follows:

(a) chronological material: kinglists and chronicles which mention the monarch and help to place him in the sequence of Babylonian rulers during this epoch;

(b) contemporary material: documents from Babylonia and Assyria which mention the king and date from his lifetime;

(c) later material: texts (excluding kinglists and chronicles) referring to the king which were written after his death.

Since new major editions of the kinglists and chronicles are being prepared by Röllig and Grayson, we list here only the principal publications referring to these chronological sources; the interested reader may obtain fuller bibliography from the projected comprehensive editions. In the case of contemporary texts, we have attempted to give a complete list of pertinent publications (excluding minor or insignificant corrections or commentaries). For later sources, additional bibliography is cited only when it directly concerns the interpretation of the passage involved.

(2132) A preliminary version of this catalogue appeared in *JCS* XVI (1962) 83-109. The numbers in the preceding catalogue which differ from the numbers in the present catalogue are indicated in section V of this appendix.

The succeeding portions of this appendix will be divided into five sections:

I. Bibliography of Chronological Sources
II. Chronological Catalogue of Sources
III. Index of Publications
IV. Index of Museum and Excavation Numbers
V. Concordance between Preliminary and Final Catalogues

I. BIBLIOGRAPHY OF CHRONOLOGICAL SOURCES

A. Simple Kinglists

1. Kinglist A (BM 33332, formerly Rm. 3, 5)

Principal publications:

1884 Pinches, *PSBA* VI 193-198 (description; printed copy on two unnumbered plates; tables, notes)
1889 Winckler, *Untersuchungen*, pp. 146-147 (copy by L. Abel)
1893 Knudtzon, *Assyrische Gebete an den Sonnengott*, I, 60 (copy); II, 277 (notes)
1897 Rost, *MVAG* II 241-242 (copy)
1898 Lehmann, *Zwei Hauptprobleme*, pls. 1-2 (photo, copy, discussion of collation), pp. 13-29 (notes)
1921 Gadd, *CT* XXXVI 24-25 (copy; reproduced in Schmidtke, *Der Aufbau der babylonischen Chronologie*, pls. 2-3)
Important collations were also published by Delitzsch in *Berichte über die Verhandlungen der Königlich Sächsischen Gesellschaft der Wissenschaften zu Leipzig, philologisch-historische Classe*, XLV (1893), 183-189.

2. Kinglist C (tablet presently [July 1967] in private collection)

Principal publication: Poebel, *AS* XV (copy, transliteration, translation, commentary). Reviews: Falkenstein, *OLZ* LI (1956) 417-419; M. Lambert, *RA* L (1956) 104-105; Matouš, *ArOr* XXIV (1956) 640-642; Pohl, *Orientalia N.S.* XXV (1956) 426-427; Weidner, *AfO* XVII (1954-56) 383-385; Edzard, *ZA* LIII (1959) 308-309; Schmidtke, *ZDMG* CIX (1959) 204-205; von Soden, *WZKM* LV (1959) 156.

B. Synchronistic Kinglists

1. Assur 14616c (=excavation number; tablet presently in the Istanbul museum)

   Principal publications:

   1920 Schroeder, *KAV* 216 (copy of reverse made from excavation photo)
   1921 Weidner, *MVAG* XXVI/2 pls. 1-4 (unnumbered; copy made from excavation photo), pp. 13-16 (transliteration)
   1926 Weidner, *AfO* III 70-71 (copy made from new photo)
   Important discussions of the tablet and its present condition: Weidner in *AfO* III (1926) 66-77, XVII (1954-56) 383-384 n. 1, XIX (1959-60) 138.

2. Assur 13956 d h (=excavation number)

   Principal publications:

   1920 Schroeder, *KAV* 182 (copy of reverse made from excavation photo)
   1921 Weidner, *MVAG* XXVI/2 11 (transliteration)

3. VAT 11261+VAT 11345

   Principal publications:

   1915 Weidner, *MVAG* XX/4 4-5 (Frags. E-F; transliteration)
   1920 Schroeder, *KAV* 10 and 13 (copy)
   Weidner noted in *MVAG* XX/4 (1915) 5 and XXVI/2 (1921) 23 that these two texts belong to the same tablet.

4. VAT 11338

   Principal publications:

   1915 Weidner, *MVAG* XX/4 3-4 (Frag. D; transliteration)
   1920 Schroeder, *KAV* 12 (copy)
   Weidner commented further on this text in *MVAG* XXVI/2 (1921) 9-10.

C. Babylonian Chronicles

1. Chronicle P (BM 92701, formerly 82-7-4, 38)

   Principal publications:

   1894 Pinches, *JRAS* 1894 807-833 (printed copy, transliteration, translation, notes)
   1895 Winckler, *AOF* I 297-303 (copy); cf. *ibid.*, 115-130 (notes, published 1894)

1904 King, *Records of the Reign of Tukulti–Ninib I*, pp. 51 (photo), 96-101 (transliteration, translation), 157 (copy); this edition pertains to col. iv 1-13 only;

1906 Delitzsch, *Die babylonische Chronik*, pp. 43-46 (transliteration, including collations)

1959 Weidner, *Tn. I*, no. 37 (transliteration, translation, notes pertaining to iv 1-13)

2. New Babylonian Chronicle (BM 27859)

Published by King, *CCEBK*, II, 57-69 (transliteration, translation) and 147-155 (copy). Important commentary by Winckler, *OLZ* X (1907) 589-593.

3. Religious Chronicle (BM 35968)

Published by King, *CCEBK*, II, 70-86 (transliteration, translation) and 157-179 (copy).

4. Dynastic Chronicle (K. 11261+K. 11624, K. 8532+K. 8533+K. 8534, 81-7-27, 117; all three of these pieces probably come from the same tablet, but do not join)

K. 11624 was published by Jacobsen in *AS* XI, plate at end (copy) and p. 60 n. 113 (transliteration, translation); W. G. Lambert has published K. 11261+K. 11624 as *CT* XLVI 5 (copy) and has later suggested that the fragment belongs to this chronicle. Fragments K. 8532+K. 8533+K. 8534 were published principally by King, *CCEBK*, II, 46-56 (transliteration, translation) and 143-145 (copy); see *ibid.*, p. 46 n. 1 for bibliography of earlier editions. 81-7-27, 117 was published originally by Johns as *ADD* 888 (copy); see the additional remarks made by Johns in *PSBA* XL (1918) 125-130, by Gadd in *JRAS* 1922 394-396, and by Ungnad in *AfK* II (1924-25) 25-27 (including collations). [Information courtesy of Prof. Grayson.]

5. Babylonian Chronicle (BM 92502, formerly 84-2-11, 356; duplicates: BM 75976-75977, formerly A.H. 83-1-18, 1338 and 1339)

The most recent complete copies of this text were published by King in *CT* XXXIV 43-50 in 1914. For full bibliography on this chronicle, see Grayson's forthcoming edition of the Assyrian and Babylonian chronicles.

6. Shamash–shuma–ukin Chronicle (BM 96273)

Published by Millard, *Iraq* XXVI (1964) 14-35 and pls. VI-VII (photo, copy, transliteration, translation, commentary).

7. [BM 48498: to be published by Grayson in his forthcoming edition of the Assyrian and Babylonian chronicles]

D. Assyrian Chronicles

1. Ashur–resha–ishi I Chronicle (VAT 10281)

Published by Weidner in *AfO* IV (1927) 213-217 (copy, transliteration, translation, commentary). See also Weidner, *Tn. I*, no. 70 and Borger, *EAK* I 105-106 (who believes the obverse and reverse of this test should be interchanged).

2. Tiglath–Pileser I Chronicle (VAT 10453+VAT 10465)

Published by Weidner in *AfO* XVII (1954-56) 384 (copy). Transliteration, translation, and notes by Tadmor, *JNES* XVII (1958) 133-134.

3. Synchronistic History (K. 4401a+Rm. 854; duplicates: K. 4401b, Sm. 2106)

The most recent complete copies of this text were published by King in *CT* XXXIV 38-43 in 1914. For a full bibliography on this chronicle, see Grayson's forthcoming edition of the Assyrian and Babylonian chronicles.

E. "Ptolemaic Canon"

For remarks on the nomenclature and origin of this kinglist (written in Greek), see Neugebauer in *A Locust's Leg*, p. 209, and page 22 above. Recent editions of this list include Wachsmuth, *Einleitung in das Studium der alten Geschichte* (Leipzig, 1895), pp. 304-306 and Schmidtke, *Der Aufbau der babylonischen Chronologie,* pp. 98-99. See also Joh. Bainbridge, *Procli Sphaera; Ptolemaei de Hypothesibus Planetarum ... cui accessit ejusdem Ptolemaei Canon Regnorum* (London, 1620), pp. 47-51.

II. CHRONOLOGICAL CATALOGUE OF WRITTEN SOURCES

1. Marduk-kabit-ahheshu

1.1 Chronological material

1.1.1 Kinglist C, 1—18 (years) and complete RN.

1.1.2 *Kinglist A ii 17′—17 (years) and broken beginning of RN. See p. 40 above.

1.1.3 *Assur 14616c ii 12′—beginning of RN, opposite Ninurti–tukulti–Ashur of Assyria.

1.1.4 *[BM 48498:12—possible (but doubtful) reference to the thirteenth year of RN; see note 485 above. Text to be published in Grayson's edition of the Assyrian and Babylonian chronicles.]

1.2 Contemporary material: none.

1.3 Later material

1.3.1 *VAS* I 112:4—mentioned in filiation in royal inscription of his son and successor. (For the complete document, see 2.2.1 below).

2. Itti-Marduk-balatu

2.1 Chronological material

2.1.1 Kinglist C, 2—8 (years) and complete RN.

2.1.2 *Kinglist A ii 18′—6 (years) and very fragmentary beginning o RN. See p. 41 above.

2.1.3 *Assur 14616c ii 13′—name of RN expected here or rather in the following line; but traces are quite uncertain. See p. 41 above.

2.2 Contemporary material

2.2.1 VA 2577—stone bearing a fragmentary fifteen-line inscription (chiefly RN and titulary). Pre-publication study including transliteration and translation by Winckler, *Untersuchungen*, pp. 139-140. Principal publication by Ungnad as *VAS* I 112.

2.2.2 BM 91015—diorite tablet recording private sale of land dated during the king's reign, exact year broken away; RN occurs in rev. ⌜10, 24⌝. Principal publication by King as *BBSt* no. 30 (photo, transliteration, translation, notes). Catalogued by Steinmetzer, *Kudurru*, pp. 40-41, no. 30 (=L 30).

2.2.3 Gron. 846-850—five economic (administrative) tablets, one dated in the accession year of RN, three dated in his first year, and one not dated but presumably from the same archive. Published by Böhl in *AfK* II (1924-25) 49-64 (copy, transliteration, translation, notes).

2.3 Later material: none.

3. Ninurta-nadin-shumi

3.1 Chronological material

3.1.1 Kinglist C, 3—6 (years) and complete RN (see note 529 above).

3.1.2 *Assur 14616c ii 14′—RN expected here (or in following line), opposite Ashur–resha–ishi I of Assyria.

3.1.3 VAT 10281—fragmentary Assyrian chronicle, part of which (rev. ii 7 ff.) narrates military maneuvers of Ninurta–nadin–shumati(sic) and Ashur–resha–ishi I in the vicinity of Arbail. Bibliography for this text above in section I under D.1.

3.2 Contemporary material

3.2.1 Two Luristan bronze daggers inscribed with RN and brief titulary; presently in the Foroughi Collection, Teheran. Published by G. Dossin, *Iranica Antiqua* II (1962) 151-152 no. 3 (transliteration, translation) and pls. XV-XVI (photos). Presumably identical with the dagger(s) first mentioned by Contenau in *RA* XXIX (1932) 29 and catalogued by Langdon in Pope, *SPA* I 283 no. VI and by Nagel, "Königsdolche," no. 5.

3.3 Later material

3.3.1 *SPA* I 284 no. X—RN mentioned in filiation on Luristan bronze dagger of Marduk–nadin–ahhe. (Bibliography for this dagger under 6.2.3 below).

3.3.2 *YOS* I 45 i 30—mentioned by Nabonidus as father of Nebuchadnezzar I. (Bibliography for the full text under 4.3.4 below).

3.3.3 *CT* XLVI no. 48 ii 6′—same context as preceding reference. (Bibliography under 4.3.5 below).

4. Nebuchadnezzar I

4.1 Chronological material

4.1.1 Kinglist C, 4—22 (years) and complete RN.

4.1.2 *Assur 14616c ii 15′—possible traces of RN here (or in following line), opposite Ashur–resha–ishi I of Assyria.

4.1.3 *KAV* 12:1-3—[ ]-NÍG.DU–PAB, opposite Ninurta–tu[kulti–Ashur] of Assyria, in line 1. Lines 2-3 presumably contained MIN ("ditto"), opposite Mutakkil–[Nusku] and Ashur–resha–[ishi] I.

4.1.4 Synchronistic History ii 1′-13′ (*CT* XXXIV 39)—military encounters between RN and Ashur–resha–ishi I.

4.1.5 *[BM 48498:13—reference to the ninth year of a Nebuchadnezzar, possibly this king; see note 600 above. Text to be published in Grayson's forthcoming edition of the Assyrian and Babylonian chronicles.]

4.2 Contemporary material

4.2.1 Böhl Collection, no. 1530—broken limestone tablet with an interlinear Sumerian–Akkadian royal inscription of Nebuchadnezzar I recording repairs on the Ekidurhegaltila temple of Adad in Babylon in gratitude for the god's help in battle. Acquisition for the Böhl collection noted in *JEOL* VI (1939) 263 no. 3; published by Böhl in *BiOr* VII (1950) 42-46 and plates I-III (photo, copy, transliteration, translation, notes). An additional fragment (Photo Babylon 715), probably from the same stone tablet, was partially published by E. Weidner in *AfO* XVI (1952-53) 72 (copy of reverse made from photo); this fragment is now A. 3647 in the tablet collection of the Oriental Institute, Chicago. If both these pieces belong to the same tablet, it may originally have consisted of two columns on each side (see Weidner, *AfO* XVI [1952-53] 72).

4.2.2 Luristan bronze dagger inscribed with RN and brief titulary, presently in the National Museum, Teheran. Published in transliteration by G. Contenau, *RA* XXVIII (1931) 107 and in copy, transliteration, and translation by S. Langdon in Pope, *SPA* I 283 no. VII. (=Nagel, "Königsdolche," no. 2).

4.2.3 [Several bricks, still unpublished, stamped with Sumerian inscriptions of Nebuchadnezzar I, were found in the recent American excavations of the Enlil temple at Nippur. One of these bricks has been numbered 2 N-T 483. The bricks are approximately 29×29×6 cm. For their findspots, see McCown and Haines, *OIP* LXXVIII 13-14, 17. Transliteration and translation of 2 N-T 483 in note 624 above].

4.2.4 Luristan bronze hatchet inscribed with a prayer to Marduk and with the name of Nebuchadnezzar, presently in the Foroughi Collection, Teheran. Published by Dossin in *Iranica Antiqua* II (1962) 158 no. 14 (transliteration, translation, notes) and pl. XXIV (photo). Partially revised transliteration and translation in note 575 above.

4.2.5 Three Luristan bronze daggers inscribed with RN and brief titulary, presently in the Foroughi Collection, Teheran. Published by Dossin in *Iranica Antiqua* II (1962) 152 no. 4 (transliteration, translation) and pl. XVII! (wrongly numbered as XVIII; photo). The text on these daggers is practically identical with that on 4.2.2.

4.2.6 Photograph Bab. K. 713 (preserved in the Staatliche Museen, Berlin): picture of a tablet copied in the reign of Nebuchadnezzar I which contained chemical recipes for making artificial gems. The present whereabouts of the tablet are unknown; but the photograph of it has been reproduced in *RA* LX (1966) 30 fig. 1 and the text has been edited (with transliteration, translation, and commentary) by Oppenheim, *ibid.*, 30-35. See also note 642 above.

4.2.7 MLC 383 (published as *BRM* I 1) and *BRM* I 1a (unnumbered): administrative texts dated in the eighth and eleventh years respectively of Nebuchadnezzar I.

4.2.8 Hinke Kudurru—stone stele recording a royal grant of land to the high priest (*nišakku*) of Enlil at Nippur in RN's sixteenth year; formerly in the possession of Frau Prof. Hilprecht and presumably in the Hilprecht Sammlung, Jena. Published in transliteration and translation by Hinke, *Boundary Stone*, pp. 142-155 (with commentary, *ibid.*, pp. 156-187). Copy published by Hinke in *Selected Babylonian Kudurru Inscriptions* (*Semitic Study Series*, XIV), no. 5, pp. 21-27. Catalogued by Steinmetzer, *Kudurru*, pp. 89-90, no. 79 (=Neb. Nipp.).

4.2.9 BM 90858—stone stele recording a royal grant of freedom from taxes and from the jurisdiction of the province of Namar to the villages of Bit–Karziabku after military services rendered by its chief on RN's campaign to Elam. Chief publication by King as *BBSt* no. 6 (photos, transliteration, translation, notes). Further bibliography in *BBSt*, p. 29, n. 4 and in the catalogue of Steinmetzer, *Kudurru*, pp. 12-14, no. 6 (=L 6).

4.2.10 BM 92987—stone tablet engraved with a royal grant of lands to a god and his two priests, whose previous residence had become dangerous because of the military situation on the Babylonian–Elamite border. Chief publication by King as *BBSt* no. 24 (photos, transliteration, translation, notes). Further bibliography may be found in *BBSt*, p. 96 n. 1 and in Steinmetzer, *Kudurru*, pp. 34-35, no. 24 (=L 24).

4.3 Later material

4.3.1 *BE* I/1 83:7—Nebuchadnezzar mentioned in a kudurru dated in the fourth year of Enlil–nadin–apli, his son and successor, as part of a chronological calculation: "696 years from Gulkishar, king of the Sealand, to Nebuchadnezzar, king of Babylon." (Bibliography for this kudurru in 5.2.2 below).

4.3.2 *JCS* XIX (1965) 123:9—mention in a royal inscription of Simbar–Shipak that Nebuchadnezzar had made the throne of Enlil in the Ekurigigal at Nippur. (Bibliography for this document in 12.2.1 below).

4.3.3 *UET* IV 143: 11, 13—RN listed as one of the royal donors in an inventory of temple objects at Ur.

4.3.4 YBC 2182 i 26-35—mention in a royal inscription of Nabonidus that Nebuchadnezzar (I) had erected at Ur a stele which depicted an *entu* priestess with all her insignia. The inscription was published by Clay as *YOS* I 45 (copy; transliteration and translation *ibid.*, pp. 69-75).

4.3.5 BM 34375+34896+34995 ii 5′-8′—approximately the same context as 4.3.4 above, but more fragmentary. BM 34896 (= Sp. II, 407) was first published in copy by Strassmaier in *Hebraica* IX (1892-93) 4-5, where it was incorrectly identified as an inscription of Nebuchadnezzar I; Weidner in *JSOR* VI (1922) 117-121 correctly identified this fragment as belonging to Nabonidus and offered a partial transliteration and translation. The joined fragments were published by W. G. Lambert as *CT* XLVI no. 48 (cf. *ibid.*, no. 47).

4.3.6 K. 710 rev. 4-5—mention in an astrologer's report from Nineveh of an omen series based on Nebuchadnezzar's devastation of Elam: *kî Nabû-kudurrī-uṣur Elamta iḫpûni*. Published by Thompson, *RMA* 200. Weidner in *MAOG* IV (1928-29) 238-239 transliterates, translates, and comments on this passage; for a possible restoration of the end of line 4, see Weidner, *AfO* XIV (1941-44) 176.

4.3.7 W 20030, 7:18—Seleucid tablet listing *apkallu*s and *ummânu*s in earlier Mesopotamia mentions Esagil-kini-ubba as *ummânu* in the time of Nebuchadnezzar (I). The text has been published by van Dijk in *UVB* XVIII 44-52 (transliteration, translation, notes) and plates 20 (photo) and 27 (copy).

4.3.8 K. 3426—poetic document dealing with Nebuchadnezzar's recovery of the statue of Marduk from the Elamites. Principal publications: Winckler, *Sammlung*, II, 72 (copy); Boissier, *Revue Sémitique* II (1894) 76-78 (partial transcription, translation, comments); Winckler, *AOF* I/6 (1897) 542-543 (transliteration, translation, notes); King, *CT* XIII 48 (copy).

4.3.9 *K. 2660—poetic text relating military encounters between Elam and Babylonia during the closing years of the Kassite Dynasty and the early years of the Second Dynasty of Isin. (The name of the king who supposedly recorded the ultimate triumph of Babylonia is not preserved in the text, but Nebuchadnezzar seems at present to be the most likely candidate). Principal publications: III *R* 38 no. 2 (copy); Winckler, *AOF* I/6 (1897) 534-538 (transliteration, translation, notes); Tadmor, *JNES* XVII (1958) 137-139 (transliteration based on photographs of the tablet, translation, notes). Hallo in *IEJ* XVI (1966) 238 suggests a date later in the Second Isin Dynasty as the historical background for this text.

4.3.10 *K. 3444+BM 99067 (formerly Ki. 1904-10-9, 96): interlinear Sumerian-Akkadian text describing events preceding the return of the Marduk statue from Elam and the joyous installation of the statue in Babylon. Duplicates: K. 3317+3319, K. 5191, BM 35000 (formerly Sp. II, 524), all still unpublished. Principal publications: Pinches, IV R^2 20 no. 1 (copy of K. 3444, partially restored from K. 3317+3319); Meek, *AJSL* XXXV (1918-19) 139 (copy of BM 99067); Winckler, *AOF* I/6 (1897) 538-540 (transliteration and translation of Akkadian lines of K. 3444); F. Martin, *RT* XXIV (1902) 96-99 (transliteration, translation, notes on IV R^2 20 no. 1); J. Hehn, *BA* V (1906) 339-344 (transliteration, translation, and notes on IV R^2 20 no. 1); R. Jestin, *RA* LII (1958) 193-202 (transliteration, translation, and notes for Sumerian version only). Further bibliography: Bezold, *Catalogue*, II, 534; Borger, *Handbuch der Keilschriftliteratur*, I, 402; Lambert, *The Seed of Wisdom*, p. 9 no. 19 [2133].

4.3.11 *K. 3766:21-22—statement in an astrological omen that Bel will go into exile in Elam but that vengeance will be taken after thirty years. Principal publications: III *R* 61 no. 2 and Virolleaud, *Sin*, IV. Duplicate: BM 34031 rev. 1-3 (formerly Sp. 127, published as *LBAT* 1526).

5. Enlil-nadin-apli

5.1 Chronological material

5.1.1 Kinglist C, 5—4 (years) and complete RN, plus designation of the king as the son of his predecessor.

5.1.2 *Assur 14616c ii 16′—RN expected here (illegible traces) opposite Ashur–resha–ishi I of Assyria.

5.1.3 *KAV* 12 i 4—[ ]-A, opposite Ashur–resha–ishi I (implied in [MIN] from the preceding line).

5.2 Contemporary material

5.2.1 Luristan bronze dagger with RN and brief titulary, presently in the Foroughi Collection, Teheran. Published by Dossin, *Iranica Antiqua* II (1962) 153 no. 6 (partial transliteration and translation, notes) and pl. XIX (photo). For the identification of this dagger as belonging to Enlil–nadin–apli, see p. 117 above.

(2133) Cf. D.T. 71, a badly broken text dealing with inimical Elamite(s), which might be referring to approximately this time (*AOF* I [1893-97] 540-542; *BA* V [1906] 386-388, etc.).

5.2.2 CBM 13—stone tablet recording royal adjudication of a dispute concerning land ownership in the fourth year of the king. Principal publication by Hilprecht, *BE* I/1 83 (copy). See also Hilprecht, *Assyriaca* I (1894) 1-58 (transliteration, translation, notes); Hinke, *Boundary Stone,* p. 12 fig. 3 (photo of obverse); Hinke, *Selected Babylonian Kudurru Inscriptions,* no. 6, pp. 28-29 (copy); Ungnad, *Orientalia N.S.* XIII (1944) 96-97 (translation). Further bibliography in Steinmetzer, *Kudurru,* pp. 90-91, no. 80 (Ph 1).

5.2.3 *BM 102485—stele inscribed with land grant, dated to about the time of this reign on the basis of personal names occurring in the text. Principal publication by King, *BBSt* no. 11 (photos, transliteration, translation, notes). Catalogued by Steinmetzer, *Kudurru,* pp. 23-24, no. 11 (L 11).

5.3 Later material: none.

6. Marduk-nadin-ahhe

6.1 Chronological material

6.1.1 Kinglist C, 6—18 (years) and complete RN. The name is written mdAMAR.UTU–SUM–MU on the tablet (see note 187 above).

6.1.2 *Assur 14616c ii 17′—name expected here or in following line (traces uncertain) opposite Tiglath–Pileser I of Assyria.

6.1.3 *KAV* 12 i 5—[ ].MEŠ, opposite Tiglath–Pileser I.

6.1.4 Synchronistic History ii 14′-24′ (*CT* XXXIV 39)—battles of Tiglath–Pileser I with Babylonia in the time of Marduk–nadin–ahhe.

6.1.5 VAT 10453+10465:8′-9′—demise of the king and the accession of his successor. Bibliography for this text above in section I under D.2.

6.1.6 *New Babylonian Chronicle, obv. 1′-3′—possible reference to Tiglath–Pileser's devastation of Babylonia.

6.2 Contemporary material

6.2.1 U. 7818—four limestone gate sockets containing identical fifteen-line royal inscriptions in Sumerian commemorating the rebuilding of the Eganunmah temple at Ur. Principal publication by Gadd, *UET* I 306 (copy, transliteration, translation, notes). For further bibliography (including information on find spot), see note 694 above. At least one of these sockets is now CBS 17244 in Philadelphia.

6.2.2 Two Luristan bronze daggers inscribed with RN and brief titulary.

(a) The first, in the collection of Mrs. Christian R. Holmes, was originally published by Arthur Upham Pope in the *Illustrated London News,*

Oct. 29, 1932, p. 666 and figs. 4-5 (photo and translation; note, however, that—contrary to Pope's statements—fig. 4 shows the reverse of the dagger, fig. 5 the obverse, and that the translation given fits the Louvre dagger [6.2.3 below] but not the Holmes dagger). The inscription was also published by Weidner in *AfO* VIII (1932-33) 258-259 (copy, transliteration, translation) and by Langdon in *SPA* I 283 no. VIII (copy, transliteration, translation, notes) and IV pl. 55 D,E (photos) and catalogued by Nagel, "Königsdolche," as no. 6.

(b) BM 123061, bearing an inscription identical to the preceding dagger. First published by C. J. Gadd in *BMQ* VII (1932) 44-45 (photo, description, translation). Subsequently catalogued by Langdon in *SPA* I 283 no. IX (with photo in *ibid.*, IV pl. 55 A) and by Nagel, "Königsdolche," no. 3. Another photo of the dagger appeared in an article by K. R. Maxwell-Hyslop and H. W. M. Hodges in *Iraq* XXVI (1964) pl. XII no. 5, with a discussion of the typology of the dagger, *ibid.*, p. 52.

6.2.3 Luristan bronze dagger in the Louvre inscribed with RN, short titulary, and filiation. First published by Contenau in *RA* XXVIII (1931) 105-106 (photo, copy, transliteration, translation, notes). A translation of the inscription on this dagger was given by Langdon in the *Illustrated London News*, Oct. 29, 1932, p. 667 (where he wrongly assumed that the inscription on the Holmes dagger [6.2.2 (a) above] was identical with that on the Louvre dagger); a photo of the dagger appeared *ibid.*, p. 666, fig. 3. Republished by Langdon in *SPA* I 284 no. X (copy, transliteration, translation) and IV pl. 55 B (photo). Nagel, "Königsdolche," no. 1.

6.2.4 Luristan bronze dagger inscribed with RN and brief titulary, presently in the Foroughi Collection, Teheran. Published by Dossin in *Iranica Antiqua* II (1962) 152-153 no. 5 (transliteration, translation, notes) and pl. XVIII (photo).

6.2.5 BM 123124 (accession number: 1932-10-8,8; excavation number: U. 17627a)—copper cylinder with 62-line Sumerian inscription of RN. Published by Sollberger, *UET* VIII 101. For further bibliography and information on the find-spot of the cylinder, see note 695 above.

6.2.6 BM 90938—stone tablet recording tax exemption granted in the first year of RN. Principal publications: I *R* 66 and *BBSt* no. 25. For further bibliography, see *BBSt*, p. 98 n. 1 and Steinmetzer, *Kudurru*, pp. 35-36, no. 25 (L 25). For a possible duplicate, see 6.2.7 below.

6.2.7 Walters Art Gallery 21.10—broken black limestone stele, originally found by the German excavators at Babylon in 1900 in a Parthian building in the mound Amran–ibn–Ali. The text has never been fully published. Drawings of the stone were published with commentary by Koldewey in *MDOG* VII (1901) 25-29; the same drawings were reproduced in Hinke, *Boundary Stone,* p. 45 fig. 19 and p. 136 fig. 50. A photo of the obverse was published in *WVDOG* XV fig. 73; and photos of the obverse and reverse appeared in D. Hill, *The Fertile Crescent,* p. 12. A transliteration of the more legible portion of the inscription has been published by Brinkman, *RA* LXI (1967) 71. For the dating of this text, see Delitzsch in *MDOG* VII (1901) 29 n., King in *BBSt* p. 38 n. 1, and Brinkman, *RA* LXI (1967) 70-74; and it may be a duplicate to 6.2.6 above. [2133a] This document is listed in Steinmetzer, *Kudurru,* p. 84, no. 74 (B 7), though it never seems to have been in the Berlin Museum.

6.2.8 [H.S. 157—unpublished economic tablet from Nippur in which the latest activity is dated *ina* MU 5 KAM ᵈAMAR.UTU–*na–din–aḫ–ḫe* (no title, H.S. 157 iv 31, transliteration courtesy of J. Aro). According to Hilprecht, *Excavations in Assyria and Babylonia,* p. 519, a tablet found in the early Pennsylvania excavations at Nippur was dated "in the fifth year of Marduk–na–di–in–akh–khi, king of the world (*shar kishshati*)"; this may be a different tablet. But since H.S. 157 iv 15-17 reads "*ina* ITI BÁR *ša* MU 2 KAM ᵈAMAR.UTU–*na–di–in–aḫ–ḫe* LUGAL ŠÁR" (Aro), it is possible that Hilprecht may have confused the wording of the two dates in his semi-popular account. But it is equally possible that two different tablets may be involved].

6.2.9 YBC 2154—fragmentary stone stele, preserving in rev. ii a list of witnesses and a date in the eighth year of RN. Principal publication by Clay in *YOS* I 37 (copy); catalogued in Steinmetzer, *Kudurru,* p. 92, no. 82 (Y 1). [2134]

6.2.10 BM 90840—stele inscribed with royal land grant bestowed on an individual for military services rendered during a battle with Assyria; dated in RN's tenth year. Principal publications: III *R* 43 (copy) and *BBSt* no. 8 (photos, transliteration, translation, notes).

(2133a) As I have stated in *RA* LXI (1967) 71 n. 7, one cannot state categorically that texts 6.2.6 and 6.2.7 were duplicates. I have in the meantime uncovered another instance in which four witnesses are probably cited in the same order in different texts: *MDP* VI 43 ii 11-17, to be restored by comparison with *MDP* VI 35 iii 18-22, both texts (not duplicates) drawn up in the reign of Merodach–Baladan I. This makes the theory that texts 6.2.6 and 6.2.7 were duplicates less likely than formerly.

(2134) I am classifying *YOS* I 37 iv and *YOS* I 37 ii as though these were separate documents. For the second column of the text and a more complete bibliography, see 7.2.5 below.

Further pertinent bibliography in Steinmetzer, *Kudurru*, pp. 17-18, no. 8 (L 8) and in Borger, *Handbuch der Keilschriftliteratur*, I, 220.

6.2.11 Fragmentary black stone kudurru recording a royal grant of land to a leather worker in the king's thirteenth year; in the Museum of Warwick (1897). Published by A. H. Sayce in *PSBA* XIX (1897) 70-73 (printed facsimile, transliteration, translation, notes). Listed in Steinmetzer, *Kudurru*, p. 91, no. 81 (W 1). Further notes are given in note 707 above.

6.2.12 *BM 90841—stele recording private sale of land. King, *BBSt*, p. 37 n. 4, has given reasons for dating the text to approximately this time; see also note 688 above. Principal publications: III *R* 41 (copy) and *BBSt* no. 7 (photos, transliteration, translation, notes). Additional bibliography in *BBSt*, p. 37 n. 2, and in Steinmetzer, *Kudurru*, pp. 14-16, no. 7 (L 7).

6.2.13 *"Caillou Michaux"—stele concerning private disposition of land. Dated to approximately this time because of personal names occurring (see note 688 above). Principal publication: I *R* 70 (copy); further bibliography in Steinmetzer, *Kudurru*, pp. 86-87, no. 76 (CMich).

6.2.14 Inscriptions of Tiglath–Pileser I describing his two campaigns against Babylonia during the reign of Marduk–nadin–ahhe. Principal publication by Weidner, *AfO* XVIII (1957-58) 350:37-351:51 (bibliography of text numbers *ibid.*, 347-348).

6.3 Later material

6.3.1 BM 118898 i 17 (*AKA* 129)—mention of Marduk–nadin–ahhe in fragmentary context in the "Broken Obelisk." For the reading of the RN, see note 729 above.

6.3.2 *OIP* II 83:48-50—note in Sennacherib's Bavian inscription that Marduk–nadin–ahhe had stolen the statues of the gods Adad and Shala from Ekallate 418 years earlier. For a discussion of this date, see p. 84 above.

6.3.3 BM 99030 (=Ki. 1904-10-9,59)—astrological report written in 657 B.C., alluding to an earlier report (lines 28-29) sent by Ea–mushallim to his lord, Marduk–nadin–ahhe, presumably this king. Published in copy in 1914 independently by R. F. Harper, *ABL* 1391, and by King, *CT* XXXIV 10-11. In 1930 Waterman published a transliteration and translation of the text in *RCAE* II 472-473 and in 1931 a commentary in *RCAE* III 358-359. L. F. Hartman has recently made a study of the document in its historical context, including a transliteration, translation, and commentary, in *JNES* XXI (1962) 25-37.

7. Marduk-shapik-zeri

7.1 Chronological material

7.1.1 Kinglist C, 7—13 (years) and complete RN; also mentioned in line 9 of the same text in obscure context.

7.1.2 *Assur 14616c ii 20′—uncertain traces of RN, opposite Ashur–bel–kala.

7.1.3 New Babylonian Chronicle, obv. 4′-7′—contents of the first two lines are uncertain, but lines 6′-7′ tell of peaceful relations between the king and Ashur–bel–kala of Assyria and of RN's journey to Sippar.

7.1.4 Synchronistic History ii 25′-30′ (*CT* XXXIV 39)—alluding to peace between Babylonia and Assyria in the days of Marduk–shapik–zeri and Ashur–bel–kala and to the death of Marduk–shapik–zeri while the other king was still reigning.

7.1.5 VAT 10453+10465:8′-9′—accession of RN after the demise of his predecessor. Bibliography for this text above in section I under D.2.

7.2 Contemporary material

7.2.1 BM 26295: clay tablet containing a copy (made in the fifteenth year of Kandalanu) of a royal inscription of RN written in Sumerian recording repairs made on Ezida during his reign. Published by King as *LIH* I 70 (copy; transliteration and translation in *LIH* III 254-255).

7.2.2 Fragmentary baked clay cylinder, once in the possession of Dr. Talcott Williams, Philadelphia. The inscription contains extensive titulary and mentions repairs on the walls and gates of Babylon, where it was probably used originally as a building deposit. Principal publications by M. Jastrow, Jr., *ZA* IV (1889) 301-323 (printed copy, transliteration, translation, notes), and by Hilprecht, *BE* I/2 148 (copy). See also further remarks by Knudtzon, *ZA* VI (1891) 163-165, by Hilprecht, *ZA* VIII (1893) 116-120, by Jastrow, *ibid.*, 214-219, and by Poebel, *AS* XV 16.

7.2.3 (Royal Ontario Museum) 938.35—Luristan bronze dagger inscribed with RN and brief titulary. Published by Meek in *BASOR* LXXIV (1939) 8 (transliteration, translation; photo: *ibid.*, 1 fig. 1). Catalogued in Nagel, "Königsdolche," no. 7. Transliteration in note 773 above.

7.2.4 [*UET* VII 6—fragmentary unpublished economic text dated at Ur on the last day of Ajar in the third year of the reign of RN.]

7.2.5 YBC 2154—fragmentary stone stele, partially preserving in obv. ii an account of a transaction listing prices current in RN's twelfth year. (For the rest of the text, see 6.2.9 above). Principal edition of the text: Clay, *YOS* I 37 (copy); see also Ungnad, *Orientalia N.S.* XIII (1944) 86-96 (transliteration, translation, notes) and Poebel's comments in *AS* XV 16-20. Catalogued in Steinmetzer, *Kudurru*, p. 92, no. 82 (=Y 1).

7.2.6 BM 104404—fragmentary stele recording RN's restoration of land to its rightful owner. Published as *BBSt* no. 12 (copy, transliteration, translation, notes). Catalogued in Steinmetzer, *Kudurru*, pp. 24-26, no. 12 (L 12).

7.2.7 [Stone duck weight, originally weighing 10 minas, with five-line Sumerian inscription in the name of Napsamenni, high priest (*nišakku*) of Enlil and chief of the seers at Nippur under RN. Found at Nippur in the 1964-65 excavation season (excavation number 9 N 99)].

7.3 Later material.

7.3.1 *UET* IV 143:15—RN occurs in temple inventory among royal donors of ex-voto objects.

7.3.2 83-1-18, 1 (published as *ABL* 1237), rev. 24—a report from Babylon to Esarhaddon mentions an oracular utterance of Marduk in which Esarhaddon is compared to Marduk–shapik–zeri. Transliteration and translation by Waterman, *RCAE* II 358-361; commentary: *ibid.*, III 325-326. [2135]

8. Adad-apla-iddina

8.1 Chronological material

8.1.1 *Kinglist A iii 1′—22 (years) plus traces of the initial determinatives.

8.1.2 *Assur 14616c ii 21′—traces of RN (dubious) opposite Ashur–bel–kala of Assyria.

8.1.3 New Babylonian Chronicle, obv. 8′-11′—describes RN as son of Itti–Marduk–balatu, an Aramean, a usurper, during whose reign the Sutians raided Sumer and Akkad.

8.1.4 Synchronistic History ii 31′-37′ (*CT* XXXIV 39)—describes RN as son of Esagil–shaduni and tells of his marrying his daughter to Ashur–bel–kala; peace flourished between Babylonia and Assyria at this time.

[2135] For colophons in Seleucid astronomical texts which mention the name of Marduk–shapik–zeri, see note 769 above.

8.2 Contemporary material

8.2.1 Fragment of brick stamped with a four-line inscription (partially illegible) of Adad–apla–iddina, found at Babylon in the 1913-14 season of excavations. Excavation number: Bab. 59431; present whereabouts unknown. Published in transcription with brief commentary by Fr. Wetzel in *MDOG* LIII (1914) 28. For the find spot of the brick, see *WVDOG* XLVIII 64, 79, and pl. 37 (for further bibliography see note 843 above).

8.2.2 BM 79503—clay tablet containing copy of an earlier Sumerian-Akkadian interlinear votive inscription of Adad–apla–iddina which had been engraved on a belt of gold presented to the statue of Nabu at Borsippa. This copy was made during the reign of Esarhaddon from an already damaged version of the text by the scribe Arad–Gula, who added a brief colophon. Published by Gadd in *Studia Orientalia* I (1925) 29-33 (copy, transliteration, translation, notes).

8.2.3 Bricks stamped with a nine-line Sumerian inscription of Adad–apla–iddina, commemorating his repair of the Emeteursag temple at Kish. Fifteen of these bricks were noted in 1818 by Sir Robert Ker Porter, and a copy of their identical inscriptions was published by him in *Travels,* II (London, 1822), pl. 77 (a). In 1861, Rawlinson and Norris published another copy of the inscription in I *R* 5 no. XXII. Bricks bearing the same inscription were also found by the Oxford-Field Museum expedition to Kish in 1923-1924, and a transliteration and translation of the text was offered by Langdon, *Excavations at Kish,* I, 16-17 (the site where these bricks were found is noted *ibid.,* I, 16, 65). One of these bricks is on exhibit in the Field Museum, Chicago, as no. 156011.

8.2.4 Small truncated cone of clay with a ten-line inscription recording Adad–apla–iddina's repairs of Nemed–Marduk, the outer wall of Nippur. The cone was found at Khorsabad and published in 1870 by Oppert in Place, *Ninive et l'Assyrie,* II, 308 (printed copy, transliteration, translation, notes; a heliograph facsimile of the cone, with part of the inscription visible, is given *ibid.,* III, pl. 78, no. 4). Winckler published a transliteration and translation of the text in *Untersuchungen,* p. 28 n. 2.

8.2.5 BM 116989 (excavation number: U. 3130)—brick from Ur inscribed with Sumerian text of RN. Published by Gadd in *Studia Orientalia* I (1925) 27-28 (transliteration, translation, notes) and in *UET* I 166 (photo, copy, transliteration, translation, notes). See also note 847 above. [According to *UE* VIII, p. 103, this brick fragment is IM 1038 in Baghdad; but we are probably dealing with duplicate copies of the same brick, cf. *UE* VIII, p. 69.]

8.2.6 CBS 16482 (excavation number: U. 2877)—brick from Ur inscribed with Akkadian text of RN (=translation of 8.2.5). Published by Gadd as *UET* I 167 (copy, transliteration, translation, notes). See also note 847 above.

8.2.7 Luristan bronze dagger in the J. Ternbach Collection, on loan to the Queens College Art Collection, Flushing, New York. Published by Herzfeld, *Iran in the Ancient East,* p. 134 (transcription) and pl. XXVIII, 3 (photo). Catalogued in Porada (ed.,), *Man in the Ancient World* (Flushing, N.Y., 1958), p. 15, no. 45. The inscription contains the RN and the title *šar kiššati*. Nagel, "Königsdolche," no. 8.

8.2.8 [Unpublished economic text from his tenth year, found at Nippur and mentioned by Hilprecht in *Excavations in Assyria and Babylonia,* p. 519.]

8.2.9 BM 103215—fragmentary stone tablet recording a land grant made by RN. Published by King as *BBSt* no. 26 (copy, transliteration, translation, notes) and listed by Steinmetzer, *Kudurru*, p. 36, no. 26 (L 26).

8.2.10 [VA 5937—unpublished fragmentary stone tablet recording legal transaction (with witnesses) dated in the first year of RN. Kindly called to my attention by Prof. Weidner.]

8.2.11 *BM 90940—fragmentary boundary stele, in which RN is mentioned in the first line; date uncertain. Published by King as *BBSt* no. 13 (copy, transliteration, translation, notes) and catalogued by Steinmetzer, *Kudurru*, p. 26, no. 13 (L 13).

8.2.12 *BM 118898—the "Broken Obelisk," in which an Assyrian ruler recounts a campaign through the Babylonian province of Dur–Kurigalzu (iii 4-8) and claims to have conquered as far as Babylon itself (iv 38). Principal publication of the text: King, *AKA* 128-149 (for further bibliography and commentary, see Borger, *EAK* I 135, 138-142). If this inscription is to be dated to Ashur–bel–kala (as seems most likely: Weidner, *AfO* VI [1930-31] 75-94; Jaritz, *JSS* IV [1959] 204-215; Borger, *EAK* I 135), then the Babylonian campaign probably took place either during the reign of Adad–apla–iddina or late in the reign of his predecessor.

8.3 Later material

8.3.1 *JCS* XIX (1965) 123:10-13—mention in a royal inscription of Simbar–Shipak that during the reign of Adad–apla–iddina Arameans and Sutians had raided Babylonia and despoiled its temples. (Bibliography for this document in 12.2.1 below).

8.3.2 *JNES* XIII (1954) 220 iv 1-4 and 221 iii 33-36 (Khorsabad and SDAS kinglists)—Shamshi-Adad IV came up from Babylonia and deposed Eriba-Adad II of Assyria. From chronological considerations, we know that this event can have taken place only towards the end of the reign of Adad-apla-iddina.

8.3.3 [K. 6156, an unpublished astrological fragment has a colophon which states that the tablet was copied from an original made in the eleventh year of Adad-apla-iddin[a]. See Bezold, *Catalogue*, II, 767. K. 6156 is now joined to K. 6141, 6148, 9108.] (2136)

8.3.4 W 20030, 7:17—Seleucid tablet listing *apkallu*s and *ummânu*s in earlier Mesopotamia mentions Esagil-kini-ubba as *ummânu* in the time of Adad-apla-iddina. For bibliography of the whole text, see 4.3.7 above.

8.3.5 K. 10802 rev. 2—mention of [Adad-apl]a-iddina in literary catalogue (the *Theodicy* was composed during his reign). See W. G. Lambert, *JCS* XVI (1962) 62, 67, 76 and van Dijk, *UVB* XVIII 46.

9. Marduk-ahhe-[eriba]

9.1 Chronological material

9.1.1 Kinglist A iii 2′—1 year 6 months plus beginning of RN: [md]ŠÚ-ŠEŠ(?)-[ ].

9.1.2 *Assur 14616c ii 22′—practically illegible traces of an RN opposite Ashur-bel-kala of Assyria.

9.2 Contemporary material

9.2.1 Stele recording grant of land in Bit-Piri'-Amurru by Marduk-ahhe-eriba (2137) to one of his subordinates. The present whereabouts of the text are unknown; but it is presumably still in private possession in Istanbul. Principal publications: *BE* I/2 149 (copy); Hinke, *Boundary Stone*, pp. 188-199 (transliteration, translation, notes); see

(2136) Royal names ending in -apla-iddina occur in other colophons, but it is uncertain whether they refer to Adad-apla-iddina, Nabu-apla-iddina, or Marduk-apla-iddina (II): see my remarks in *JCS* XVI (1962) 96 and n. 19 and in *Studies Oppenheim*, p. 37.

(2137) Borger (*Handbuch der Keilschriftliteratur*, I, 191) mistakenly attributes this text to "Marduk-nādin-aḫḫī."

also the comments by Steinmetzer, *OLZ* XXIII (1920) 199 and the bibliography by Steinmetzer, *Kudurru*, p. 88, no. 78 (C 2).

9.3 Later material: none.

10. Marduk-zer-[x]

10.1 Chronological material

10.1.1 Kinglist A iii 3′—12 (years) plus mdŠÚ–NUMUN(?)–[x].

10.1.2 *Assur 14616c ii 23′—traces of the masculine personal determinative opposite Ashur–bel–kala.

10.2 Contemporary material: none.

10.3 Later material: none.

11. Nabu-shumu-libur

11.1 Chronological material

11.1.1 Kinglist A iii 4′—8 (years) and mdAG–MU–[x].

11.1.2 *Assur 14616c ii 24′—traces of a masculine personal determinative opposite Ashur–bel–kala.

11.1.3 Religious Chronicle i 16′—[mdA]G–MU–*li–bur* LUGAL in broken context in a list of portents. (The first element of the RN might be written [P]A here.)

11.2 Contemporary material

11.2.1 BM 91432: thirty-mina duck weight made of fine-grained white marble, found in the rubble covering the Northwest Palace at Nimrud by Layard (*Nineveh and Its Remains*, 3rd ed. [London, 1849], II, 316; see also R. D. Barnett, *A Catalogue of the Nimrud Ivories*, p. 4). The stone contains a two-line inscription including the RN and the title *šar kiššati* and weighs 39 pounds 1 ounce 1 dt. 6 grains, about a pound short of the expected weight (because of the damaged condition of the head). A sketch of the weight was published by Layard in *The Monuments of Nineveh*, First Series (London, 1853), pl. 95a no. 11 and the inscription in *ICC*, pl. 83F. The text was also copied by Norris, *JRAS* 1856 pl. opp. p. 222 no. 2, mentioned by J. Brandis, *Das Münz- Mass- und Gewichtswesen in Vorderasien*, pp. 46-47, and transcribed by Winckler, *Untersuchungen*, p. 46. Further bibliography: Weissbach, *ZDMG* LXI (1907) 394-395 no. 6, and Nachtrag p. 948. A printed cuneiform text with transliteration and translation was published by King in *PSBA* XXIX (1907) 221. Recently, Poebel transliterated the text in *AS* XV 23.

11.3 Later material: none.

12. Simbar-Shipak

12.1 Chronological material

12.1.1 Kinglist A iii 6′—18 (years) plus RN (abbreviated as ^{m}*Sim–bar–ši*).

12.1.2 *Assur 14616c iii 1-2—no traces of RN identifiable in the section here, but the king belongs in these lines opposite Eriba–Adad II.

12.1.3 Dynastic Chronicle v 2′-4′—RN, son of Eriba-Sin, starting as a minor official in the Sealand, rises to the throne and rules 17 years until he is assassinated. Burial place also indicated (see note 934 above).

12.1.4 New Babylonian Chronicle, obv. 12′-13′—origins of the king and note on his construction in the Ekurigigal.

12.2 Contemporary material

12.2.1 UIOM 2499—copy of a royal inscription of Simbar–Shipak probably made sometime between the late seventh and early fifth century B.C., describes RN's restorations in the Enlil temple at Nippur after the Aramean depredations some years earlier. Published by Goetze in *JCS* XIX (1965) 121-135 (copy, transliteration, translation, notes). For further comments on the text, see Hallo, *IEJ* XVI (1966) 239, and p. 170 and notes 922-924 above.

12.2.2 BM 90937—stone tablet recording a private sale of land and other business transactions; dated in the twelfth year of RN. Published first by Layard, *ICC*, pl. 53 (copy) and later by King, *BBSt* no. 27 (copy, transliteration, translation, notes). Catalogued by Steinmetzer, *Kudurru*, p. 37, no. 27 (=L 27).

12.3 Later material

12.3.1 *BBSt* no. 36 i 13-23—attempts by RN to restore the cult of Shamash at Sippar. For the complete document, see 24.2.3 below.

12.3.2 *AKA 325:84—mention of ^{m}*Si–bir*, a previous Babylonian king, in the annals of Ashurnasirpal II. For a discussion of this passage, see p. 154 above.

13. Ea-mukin-zeri

13.1 Chronological material

13.1.1 Kinglist A iii 7′—5 months plus RN (abbreviated as [md]BE–*mu–kin*).

13.1.2 *Assur 14616c iii 3—possible beginning of RN (but the traces do not seem to fit this king); opposite Sham⟨shi⟩–Adad IV.

13.1.3 Dynastic Chronicle v 5′-6′—RN, a usurper from Bit–Hashmar, reigned for three months and was buried in swampland of his native region.

13.2 Contemporary material

13.2.1 **BBSt* no. 27, bottom edge 1—possibly the same individual, occurring as a witness to a private document drawn up in the reign of the previous monarch (see note 939 above). For the whole document, see 12.2.2.

13.3 Later material: none.

14. Kashshu-nadin-ahi (now to be read Kashshu–nadin–ahhe; see p. 395 below)

14.1 Chronological material

14.1.1 Kinglist A iii 8′—3 (years) plus RN.

14.1.2 Assur 14616c iii 4—[md]*Kaš–šu*–[ ], opposite Ashurnasirpal I.

14.1.3 **KAV* 182 iii 1′—RN expected here, if the list were complete; all that is visible is part of the masculine personal determinative.

14.1.4 Dynastic Chronicle v 7′—RN, son of [m]SAP–*pa–a+a*, ruled for three years and ⟨was buried⟩ in the palace (see p. 157 above).

14.2 Contemporary material: see addendum, p. 395.

14.3 Later material

14.3.1 *BBSt* no. 36 i 24-28—mention in a later temple endowment that food offerings in Ebabbar in Sippar were discontinued during the hard times in RN's reign. For the whole document, see 24.2.3 below.

15. Eulmash-shakin-shumi

15.1 Chronological material

15.1.1 Kinglist A iii 10′—17 (years) plus RN.

15.1.2 Assur 14616c iii 5—^{md}*Ul–maš*–[ ], opposite Shalmaneser II.

15.1.3 *KAV 182 iii 2′—masculine personal determinative and horizontal wedge of the beginning of the next sign are preserved.

15.1.4 Dynastic Chronicle v 9′—RN, member of Bit–Bazi, ruled for 15(?) years and (was buried) in the palace at Kar–Marduk.

15.1.5 New Babylonian Chronicle, obv. 14′-15′—cryptic references "in Nisan of the fifth year of RN" and "the fourteenth year" (of RN). See note 978 above.

15.2 Contemporary material

15.2.1 Fourteen Luristan bronze arrowheads inscribed with the name of Eulmash–shakin–shumi and the title *šar kiššati*. One, in the M.-J. Chappée collection, was published by Contenau in *RA* XXIX (1932) 29 (copy, transliteration, translation) and by Langdon in *SPA* I 284 no. XII (transliteration, translation). Thirteen duplicates are in the Foroughi Collection, Teheran, and the text on them has been published by Dossin in *Iranica Antiqua* II (1962) 160 no. 17 (transliteration, translation) and pl. XXVI (photo).

15.3 Later material

15.3.1 *BBSt* no. 36 i 29-ii 17, iv 49-53—mention in a later temple endowment that this king provided for the resumption of the Shamash cult in Sippar. For the whole document, see 24.2.3 below.

16. Ninurta-kudurri-usur I

16.1 Chronological material

16.1.1 Kinglist A iii 11′—3 (years) plus abbreviated RN (^{md}MAŠ–⌈NÍG.DU⌉).

16.1.2 Assur 14616c iii 6—^{md}MAŠ–*ku*–[ ], opposite Ashur–nirari IV.

16.1.3 **KAV* 182 iii 3′—^{md}[ ] in broken context.

16.1.4 Dynastic Chronicle v 10′—RN, member of Bit–Bazi, ruled for two years.

16.1.5 Shamash–shuma–ukin Chronicle, 21—RN (erroneously written as Nabu–kudurri–usur, i.e., ^{d}AG–NÍG.DU–ŠEŠ) mentioned as a brother of Shirikti–Shuqamuna. See note 995 above.

16.2 Contemporary material

16.2.1 Two Luristan bronze arrowheads inscribed with RN and the title *šar kiššati*; presently in the Foroughi Collection, Teheran. Published by Dossin in *Iranica Antiqua* II (1962) 160 no. 18 (transliteration, translation) and pl. XXVII (photo.) ([2138])

16.3 Later material

16.3.1 *BBSt* no. 9 top 1, 24; ii 36; iii 13—mention in a later kudurru of business which took place during the second year of his reign. For the whole document, see 19.2.2 below.

17. Shirikti-Shuqamuna

17.1 Chronological material

17.1.1 Kinglist A iii 12′—3 months plus abbreviated RN ([m]*Ši*–⌈*x*–(*x*)–*šu*–*qa*⌉–*mu*).
17.1.2 Assur 14616c iii 7—[m]*Ši–rík–tú*–[d][ ], opposite Ashur-rabi II.
17.1.3 *KAV* 182 iii 4′—[m]*Š*[*i*–].
17.1.4 *KAV* 10 ii 1′—[m]*Š*[*i*–].
17.1.5 Dynastic Chronicle v 11′—[Shirikti]-Shuqamuna, member of Bit-Bazi, reigned for three months and [was buried] in the pa[lace of x].
17.1.6 Shamash-shuma-ukin Chronicle, 20-21—Shirikti-Shuqam[u]nu, brother of Ninurta!(text: Nabu)-kudurri-usur (I), reigned for three months.

17.2 Contemporary material: none.

17.3 Later material: none.

18. Mar-biti-apla-usur

18.1 Chronological material

18.1.1 Kinglist A iii 14′—6 (years) and [m]DUMU.⌈É⌉–[ ]
18.1.2 Assur 14616c iii 8—[md]DUMU.É–[ ], opposite Ashur-resha-ishi II.
18.1.3 *KAV* 182 iii 5′—[m][ ]–⌈A⌉–PAB.
18.1.4 *KAV* 10 ii 2′—[md]DU[MU(?).É–].
18.1.5 Dynastic Chronicle v 13′-15′—[RN], descended from an Elamite family, ruled six years and was buried in a manner befitting a legitimate king (see note 934 above).

([2138]) For the dating of this text and another possible text from this reign, see note 993 above.

18.1.6 New Babylonian Chronicle, obv. 16′—allusion to "the fourth year of RN."

18.2 Contemporary material

18.2.1 Four Luristan bronze arrowheads inscribed with RN and the title *šar kiššati*; presently in the Foroughi Collection, Teheran. Published by Dossin in *Iranica Antiqua* II (1962) 160 no. 19 (transliteration, translation) and pl. XXVII (photo).

18.3 Later material: none.

19. Nabu-mukin-apli

19.1 Chronological material

19.1.1 *Kinglist A iii 15′—⌜36⌝ years, RN broken away.
19.1.2 Assur 14616c iii 9—[ ]⌜x⌝[ ]-A, opposite Tiglath-Pileser II.
19.1.3 *KAV* 182 iii 6′—^{m}[ ]-DU-A.
19.1.4 *KAV* 10 ii 3′—^{md}PA-D[U-].
19.1.5 New Babylonian Chronicle, obv. 17′—abbreviated reference to "the first year of RN, king."
19.1.6 Religious Chronicle iii 1′-iv 7′—list of animal portents and other prodigies occurring during the reign of RN, from his seventh through twenty-sixth years; Aramean advances into Babylonia are also noted.

19.2 Contemporary material

19.2.1 Four Luristan bronze arrowheads inscribed with RN and the title *šar kiššati*; presently in the Foroughi Collection, Teheran. Published by Dossin in *Iranica Antiqua* II (1962) 161 no. 21 (transliteration, translation, notes) and pl. XXVIII (photo).
19.2.2 BM 90835—stone stele recording the settlement of a land title and the payment of back taxes, etc. Principal publication by King, *BBSt* no. 9 (photos, transliteration, translation, notes). Further bibliography by Weidner in *MVAG* XX/4 (1915) 92 n. 5 and by Steinmetzer, *Kudurru*, pp. 18-21, no. 9 (=L 9).
19.2.3 *[Unpublished economic text in the Geneva Museum mentioned by Sollberger in *JCS* V (1951) 19 no. 2.9 as possibly belonging to this reign.]
19.2.4 *Luristan bronze situla inscribed with the name of Ninurta-kudurri-usur (son of RN) and the title A LUGAL; presently in private

collection. Published by Amandry in *Antike Kunst* IX/2 (1966) 59 no. 3 and fig. 3 (copy), pl. 13 nos. 3a-3b (photo), p. 66 (translation); transliterated by P. Calmeyer, *BJV* VI (1966) 69. (2139)

19.2.5 *Luristan bronze situla bearing the name of Rimut–ili, *šatam ekurrāti*, probably identical with the prince of the same name (and occupation) who occurs as a witness in *BBSt* no. 9 iva 31. The situla, in the Mrs. William H. Moore collection, was published by Langdon in Pope, *SPA* I 284 no. XIII (copy, transliteration, translation, notes) and *SPA* IV pl. 70A (photo); further bibliography: *SPA* I 280 n. 1. For the reading of Rimut–ili, see note 1067 above.

19.2.6 *Luristan bronze arrowhead inscribed with the name of Mar–biti–shuma–ibni, *sakrumaš*; presently in the Foroughi Collection, Teheran. Published by Dossin in *Iranica Antiqua* II (1962) 161 no. 20 (transliteration, translation) and pl. XXVIII (photo). For the probable dating of this individual, see p. 12 above.

19.3 Later material: none.

20. Ninurta-kudurri-usur II

20.1 Chronological material

20.1.1 *Kinglist A iii 16′—8 months 12 [days]; RN missing.
20.1.2 Assur 14616c iii 10—[ ]–PAB, opposite Tiglath–Pileser II.
20.1.3 *KAV* 182 iii 7′—mdMAŠ–[NÍG.D]U–PAB.
20.1.4 *KAV* 10 ii 4′—complete RN.

20.2 Contemporary material

20.2.1 *Situla of RN as prince. See 19.2.4 above.
20.2.2 *BBSt* no. 9 iva 30—mentioned as witness to a legal transaction during his father's reign, where he was listed first among the three royal princes who acted as witnesses to the document. For the whole text, see 19.2.2 above. (2140)

20.3 Later material: none.

(2139) For the dating of this text, see note 993 above.
(2140) For another possible text from this reign, see note 993 above.

21. Mar-biti-ahhe-iddina

21.1 Chronological material

21.1.1 *Kinglist A iii 17′—possible traces of a number referring to the length of reign of this king. See p. 49 above.
21.1.2 Assur 14616c iii 11—[ ]–PAB–AŠ, opposite Tiglath–Pileser II.
21.1.3 *KAV* 182 iii 8′—complete RN (but with *–aḫa–* in place of *–aḫḫē–*).
21.1.4 *KAV* 10 ii 5′—complete RN (but with *–aḫa–* for *–aḫḫē–*).
21.1.5 New Babylonian Chronicle, edge—end of RN ([ ].ME–MU).

21.2 Contemporary material

21.2.1 *BBSt* no. 9 iva 32—mentioned as third of three royal princes among the witnesses to a kudurru dated in his father's reign. For the whole document, see 19.2.2 above.

21.3 Later material: none.

22. Shamash-mudammiq

22.1 Chronological material

22.1.1 Assur 14616c iii 13-14—complete RN and MIN, opposite Ashur–dan II and Adad–nirari II.
22.1.2 *KAV* 182 iii 9′—complete RN.
22.1.3 *KAV* 10 ii 6′—^{md}UTU–S[IG$_5$].
22.1.4 New Babylonian Chronicle, rev. 1—faint traces of RN, occurring with the almost completely obliterated name of Adad–nirari II of Assyria.
22.1.5 Synchronistic History iii 1-8 (*CT* XXXIV 40)—RN's battle with Adad–nirari II at the foot of Mt. Jalman, his "defeat," and subsequent death.

22.2 Contemporary material

22.2.1 VAT 8288: 26-29, 33-34—undated sections of the annals of Adad–nirari II relating his defeat of Shamash–mudammiq, the extension of the Assyrian border east of the Tigris, the defeat of the Ahlamu Arameans, the receiving of tribute from Suhi, and the return of Hit and Zaqqu on the Euphrates to the jurisdiction of Assyria. Principal publication: *KAH* II 84 (copy), subsequently re-edited by J. Seidmann in *MAOG* IX/3 (1935), with transliteration, translation, collations, and notes. The pertinent sections are translated in Luckenbill, *ARAB* I 360, 362.

22.3 Later material: none.

23. Nabu-shuma-ukin I

23.1 Chronological material

23.1.1 Assur 14616c iii 16—mdPA–MU–⌈x⌉[x], opposite Tukulti–Ninurta II.
23.1.2 *KAV* 182 iii 10′—complete RN.
23.1.3 *KAV* 10 ii 7′—mdPA–MU–[x].
23.1.4 New Babylonian Chronicle, rev. 2-3—[M]U–*ú–kin*, occurring in the same line with Tukul[ti–Ninurta] II of Assyria; and mdAG–MU–⌈*ú*⌉–[*kin*] occurs as the father of Nabu–apla–iddina.
23.1.5 Synchronistic History iii 9-21 (*CT* XXXIV 40)—tells of Adad–nirari II's victory over Nabu–shuma–ukin!(text: –ishkun), followed by accounts of booty taken; the two kings exchanged daughters in marriage, concluded a peace, and realigned the boundaries between the two lands.

23.2 Contemporary material: none.

23.3 Later material: none.

24. Nabu-apla-iddina

24.1 Chronological material

24.1.1 Assur 14616c iii 18—mdPA–A–SUM–[*na*], opposite Ashurnasirpal II.
24.1.2 *KAV* 182 iii 11′—complete RN.
24.1.3 *KAV* 10 ii 8′—mdPA–A–[x].
24.1.4 New Babylonian Chronicle, rev. 3—[DUMU].UŠ–MU, son of Nabu–shuma–u[kin].
24.1.5 Synchronistic History iii 22-26 (*CT* XXXIV 40)—peaceful relations between RN and Shalmaneser III; death of RN during Shalmaneser's reign.

24.2 Contemporary material

24.2.1 BM 90922—stone tablet recording the royal restoration of land after adjudication of a title dispute; written in the king's twentieth year. Principal publications: King in *CT* X 3 (copy) and in *BBSt* no. 28 (photo, copy, transliteration, translation, notes); further bibliography in Steinmetzer, *Kudurru*, pp. 38-39, no. 28 (L 28).

24.2.2 BM 90936—stone tablet recording a royal land grant made by RN. Published by King as *BBSt* no. 29 (photos, transliteration, translation, notes; see also Steinmetzer, *Kudurru*, pp. 39-40, no. 29, L 29). For the dating of this text, see King, *BBSt*, p. 106 n. 2 and note 1164 above.

24.2.3 BM 91000—stone tablet recording the endowment by RN of the Ebabbar temple at Sippar and including a brief history of the Sutian attacks and famines which had disrupted the cult over the preceding two centuries; dated in the thirty-first year of the king. Found at Abu Habba (Sippar) by H. Rassam in 1881 (see Rassam, *Asshur and the Land of Nimrod* [Cincinnati and New York, 1897], p. 402); for the possibility of a second, duplicate tablet of Nabu–apla–iddina having been found at the same time, see Jastrow, *AJSL* XV (1898-99) 68-69, 86. Principal publications: V *R* 60-61 (copy) and *BBSt* no. 36 (photos, transliteration, translation, notes); further bibliography in *BBSt*, p. 120 n. 2 and in Steinmetzer, *Kudurru*, pp. 45-48, no. 35 (=L 36). Numerous photos of the tablet have been published, including recently Parrot, *The Arts of Assyria*, pp. 166 and 168 nos. 213, 215, and *ANEP* no. 529.

24.2.4 [Unnumbered kudurru in the Louvre, preserving an account of a transaction dated in the thirty-third year of Nabu–[apla–id]dina. To be published by Douglas Kennedy.]

24.2.5 *AKA* 350-353 iii 16-26—passage in the annals of Ashurnasirpal II recounting the capture of the Babylonian troops of Nabu–apla–iddina at the city of Suru in the land of Suhi. Translation of this passage in Luckenbill, *ARAB* I 470.

24.3 Later material

24.3.1 VA 208:1-31—copy of a legal document drawn up at Dilbat in RN's twenty-eighth year, cited in the introduction to a contract written in the reign of RN's successor. Published as *VAS* I 35; see 25.2.3 below for the whole document.

24.3.2 W.-B. 10 obv. 6, 19—mention of gifts of RN (*rīmūt* RN) in a list of offerings (*ginê*) for the goddesses Ishtar of Uruk and Nana. The principal edition of the text by Langdon (copy: *OECT* I pls. 20-21; partial translation: *ibid.* pp. 25-27), even with additional notes and collations by A. Salonen apud H. Holma, *Orientalia N.S.* XIII

(1944) 223-233, leaves much to be desired. The copy is inaccurate, omitting at least four lines completely, (2141) interpreting an independent line as a runover, (2142) and reproducing many signs inaccurately (e.g., AN.LU for SIBA in rev. 17) or omitting them altogether (e.g., LÚ ÌR É.GAL in rev. 31). A new edition of this text is badly needed.

24.3.3 *JCS* XI (1957) 5-6 and n. 21—various occurrences of Nabu–apla–iddina in colophons (see also notes 1119 and 2136 above).

25. Marduk-zakir-shumi I

25.1 Chronological material

25.1.1 *Assur 14616c iii 20—initial determinatives of RN, opposite Shalmaneser III.

25.1.2 *KAV* 182 iii 12′—Marduk!(text: Nabu)–zakir–shumi and the name of his *ummânu*.

25.1.3 *KAV* 10 ii 9′—mdŠID–M[U–], followed by the name of his *ummânu* (see note 257 above).

25.1.4 New Babylonian Chronicle, rev. 4-6—RN, filiation (broken), brief notice of revolt of RN's brother, and mention of RN as father of his successor.

25.1.5 Synchronistic History iii 27-36 (*CT* XXXIV 40)—RN's accession to the throne after his father's death, the revolt of his brother, Shalmaneser's success in quelling the rebellion and subsequent visit to the principal cult centers of northern Babylonia.

25.2 Contemporary material

25.2.1 VA Bab. 646—lapis-lazuli seal with eight-line inscription, presented to Marduk by RN. Principal publication: Weissbach, *WVDOG* IV pl. 6 no. 2 (copy) and pp. 16-17 (transliteration, translation, notes). Photos of seal: *WVDOG* XV fig. 74; *WVDOG* LXII pl. 43e-h. Drawings of seal or its representation: *MDOG* V (1900)

(2141) (a) On the obverse, between lines 35 and 38, there are three rather than two lines as copied. (b) On the obverse, there is an additional line between lines 39 and 40 of the copy. (c) On the reverse, there is a line omitted between the fourth and fifth lines of the copy (probably ending in LUGAL, as does obv. 30). (d) On the reverse, there is one line omitted between lines 30 and 31 of the copy. Furthermore, practically all horizontal lines drawn across the tablet are omitted on the copy. The reverse also has a clear guide-line on which the second half of most lines begins; this is completely neglected on all lines after line 22 on the copy.

(2142) As may be seen from a photo, the second half of rev. 14, according to Langdon's numbering, is a separate line, not a runover (cf. obv. 30).

14 fig. 3; *WVDOG* IV 16 fig. 1; *WVDOG* LXII pl. 44b. For further bibliography and information on the find spot of the seal, see note 1255 above.

25.2.2 AO 6684—royal grant of property and income to a *kalû* priest of Ishtar of Uruk, dated in the second year of RN. Published by Thureau-Dangin in *RA* XVI (1919) 117-141 (copy, photos of part of stele, transliteration, translation) and catalogued by Steinmetzer, *Kudurru*, pp. 74-75, no. 65 (P 30). A photo of the obverse is published in Parrot, *The Arts of Assyria*, p. 170, no. 217.

25.2.3 VA 208—stone stele recording private disposal of land in RN's eleventh year. Principal publication: *VAS* I 35; see also Steinmetzer, *Kudurru*, pp. 76-77, no. 68 (=B 1). Cf. 24.3.1 above.

25.2.4 Rm. 2, 427—broken black stone tablet containing part of a treaty between Marduk–zakir–shumi I and Shamshi–Adad V; originally found by H. Rassam at Kuyunjik. Published by Peiser in *MVAG* III (1898) 240-243 (transliteration, translation) and by Weidner in *AfO* VIII (1932-33) 27-29 (reproduction of a copy made by Peiser, partial transliteration and translation). Lines 22-35 of the text are transliterated (with restorations) and discussed by Borger, *Orientalia N.S.* XXXIV (1965) 168-169.

25.2.5 Royal inscriptions of Shalmaneser III dealing with his campaigns against the Babylonian rebels in his eighth and ninth years:

(a) Balawat Gate inscription, iv 1-vi 8 (published in *TSBA* VII [1882] 98-111, re-edited in *BA* VI/1 [1908] 135-137 and in *WO* IV/1 (1967) 30-35; *ARAB* I 622-625);

(b) ND 11000, inscription on throne base from Nimrud, lines 45-47 and 49 (published by Hulin in *Iraq* XXV [1963] 55-56 and pl. X);

(c) IM. 54669 ii 41-54 (published by Cameron in *Sumer* VI [1950] 13-14, re-edited by Michel, *WO* I/6 [1952] 464-467, 31. Text);

(d) Layard, *ICC*, pl. 46:12-17 (re-edited in *BA* VI/1 [1908] 147:78-84; *ARAB* I 649-650);

(e) IM. 55644 ii 31-44 (published by F. Safar in *Sumer* VII [1951] 8, re-edited by Michel, *WO* II/1 [1954] 32-35, 32. Text);

(f) VAT 9536 rev. 1-5 (published as *KAH* II 110, edited by Michel, *WO* I/2 [1947] 67, 7. Text; *ARAB* I 666);

(g) IM. 60496:43 (published by Laessøe, *Iraq* XXI [1959] 149-151)—beginning of campaign of eighth year;

(h) Black Obelisk, lines 73-84 (published by Layard, *ICC*, pl. 91; edited most recently by Michel, *WO* II/2 [1955] 150-151; *ARAB* I 565-566);

(i) A. 2529 rev. 1-5 (edited by Michel, *WO* I/4 [1949] 259-261; *ARAB* I 706)—brief mention of Shalmaneser's trip to Babylon, Borsippa, and Cutha in his ninth year;

(j) Assur 5999 i 5-6 (*sikkatu*-cone found at Assur, published by Andrae in *MDOG* XXVIII [1905] 24-25 and in *WVDOG* X 41 fig. 27; see also note 1176 above)—mention of sacrifices offered in Babylon and Borsippa;

(k) Layard, *ICC*, pl. 76:14-20 (edited in *BA* VI/1 [1908] 152; *ARAB* I 674);

(l) *AAA* XIX (1932) 113 no. 302:14-15—mention of sacrifices in Borsippa;

(m) [unpublished fragmentary inscription on a *sikkatu* from Assur, mentioned in *MDOG* XXXVI (1908) 16 and note—recounts campaign of Shalmaneser's ninth year];

(n) Tigris Tunnel inscriptions also briefly mention Shalmaneser's visits to cult centers of northern Babylonia and his conquest of Chaldea (most recently edited by Michel, *WO* III/1-2 [1964] 152:19-20, 154:11-13, with earlier bibliography).

25.3 Later material: none.

26. Marduk-balassu-iqbi

26.1 Chronological material

26.1.1 *KAV* 182 iii 13′—complete RN.

26.1.2 **KAV* 10 ii 11′—very slight traces of RN (indistinguishable).

26.1.3 New Babylonian Chronicle, rev. 6—reference to "at the time of Marduk-balassu-iqbi, ⌈son⌉ of Marduk-zakir-shumi."

26.1.4 Synchronistic History, Sm. 2106 rev. 6′-9′ (*CT* XXXIV 43)—brief reference to [Marduk-balass]u-iqbi, presumably being defeated by [Shamshi]-Adad V.

26.2 Contemporary material

26.2.1 *[Brick from Tell Umar, supposedly inscribed with the name of RN. Photo published by Waterman, *Tell Umar*, II, pl. XXV fig. 2 (with translation, *ibid.*, p. 78). For further information see notes 1275-1276 above.]

26.2.2 [4 N-T 3—unpublished late copy of a legal document originally drawn up in the second year of RN. Only the end of the transaction is preserved, chiefly the names of witnesses and curses. The text was called to my attention by Prof. Jacobsen].

26.2.3 *RA* XVI (1919) 126 iv 17—witness to a royal grant drawn up in the second year of his father's reign. For the whole document, see 25.2.2 above.

26.2.4 (a) I *R* 31 iii 70-iv 45—annals recounting the fourth campaign of Shamshi–Adad V (against Babylonia); translated in *ARAB* I 723-726;
(b) Assur 6596 iii 1-iv 10—annals of Shamshi–Adad V recounting his defeat of Marduk–balassu–iqbi during his fourth and fifth campaigns. Principal publication of the whole text by Weidner, *AfO* IX (1933-34) 90-101.

26.2.5 VAT 9628—*Gottesbrief* from Shamshi–Adad V describing the victories of his fifth campaign. Principal publications: *KAH* II 142 (copy) and *AfO* IX (1933-34) 101-104 (transliteration, translation, and notes by Weidner).

26.3 Later material: none.

27. Baba-aha-iddina

27.1 Chronological material

27.1.1 *KAV* 182 iii 14′—⌈^{md}*Ba*⌉–[ ].

27.1.2 Synchronistic History iv 1-14 (*CT* XXXIV 41)—victory of Shamshi–Adad V over Baba–aha–iddina and the deportation of the Babylonian king to Assyria; the text also lists the spoils of the Assyrian king, cult offerings made in Babylonia, a campaign against Chaldea, and the realigning of the Assyro-Babylonian border.

27.2 Contemporary material

27.2.1 *[4 N-T 3:17′—possible occurrence of this Baba–aha–iddina as a witness to a private document dated in the second year of the preceding reign. For the whole document, see 26.2.2 above.]

27.2.2 Assur 6596 iv 11-29—account in the annals of Shamshi–Adad V of the defeat of RN in the Assyrian's sixth campaign; RN and his family are then deported to Assyria. Principal publication: Weidner, *AfO* IX (1933-34) 90-101.

27.3 Later material: none.

Lacuna

King no. 28 apparently did not succeed king no. 27 immediately, as is indicated by the New Babylonian Chronicle, rev. 7: "For 12(+x) years, there was no king in the land." Further documentation pertaining to this time is discussed on pp. 213-220 above. ([2143])

28. Ninurta-apl?-[x]

28.1 Chronological material

28.1.1 *KAV* 13:1′—[m]⌈dMAŠ–A(?)⌉–[ ].

28.2 Contemporary material: none.

28.3 Later material: none.

29. Marduk-bel-[zeri]

29.1 Chronological material

29.1.1 *KAV* 13:2′—mdŠID–⌈EN⌉–[x]. The identification of this king with the ruler in 29.2.1 is possible, but by no means certain.

29.2 Contemporary material

29.2.1 Economic text once in the possession of Mr. C. C. Garbett, London. Published by Clay in *JAOS* XLI (1921) 313 (copy, partial translation). A fuller transliteration and translation are given in note 1334 above.

29.3 Later material: none.

30. Marduk-apla-usur

30.1 Chronological material

30.1.1 *KAV* 13:3′—mdŠID–A–[x].

30.1.2 *ADD* 888:3′—dAMAR.UTU–A–ŠE[Š] in broken context. Apparently mentioned as a king of *māt Kaldi* (line 5′) and as ruling before Eriba–[Marduk] (line 6′).

([2143]) Traces of a royal name occur in the Synchronistic History iv 15 (CT XXXIV 41). This should refer to a Babylonian successor of Baba–aha–iddina (who occurred in the preceding section of the chronicle).

30.2 Contemporary material: none.

30.3 Later material: none.

31. Eriba-Marduk

31.1 Chronological material

31.1.1 *Kinglist A iv 1—illegible traces, where the name of Eriba–Marduk is expected.

31.1.2 *KAV* 13:4′—ᵐSU–*Mar*–[*duk*].

31.1.3 New Babylonian Chronicle, rev. 8-14—RN, son of Marduk–shakin–shumi, "took the hand" of Marduk and Nabu in his second year, drove out Arameans from western Babylonia, and made cultic restorations. (Line 15 may refer to Eriba–Marduk or to his successor).

31.1.4 *ADD* 888:6′—broken reference to ᵐ*Eri–ba*–[ ].

31.2 Contemporary material

31.2.1 BM 91433—30-mina duck weight made of green stone (syenite or basalt), found in the Northwest Palace at Nimrud by Layard during his second expedition to Mesopotamia (1849-1851); see Layard, *Discoveries among the Ruins of Nineveh and Babylon* (1853), p. 600, where the three-line text of the inscription appears in printed cuneiform. The weight of the stone is 40 lbs. 4 oz. 4 dts. 4 grains. The text was also published in copy by Norris, *JRAS* 1856 pl. opp. p. 222 no. 1, with a translation on p. 217; it was also published in translation by Brandis, *Das Münz- Mass- und Gewichtswesen in Vorderasien* (1866), p. 46 and in transliteration and translation by Winckler, *Untersuchungen*, p. 32. Further bibliography and description by Weissbach, *ZDMG* LXI (1907) 395 no. 7 and *RLA* II 463-464. Photo: *ANEP* no. 120.

31.2.2 [BM 40548: unpublished legal document dealing with a sale of land, dated in Babylon on the fifteenth day of Siman, ninth year of RN. This text was kindly called to my attention by Professor Wiseman.]

31.3 Later material

31.3.1 ND 2090:13—mention of RN as ancestor of Merodach–Baladan II in a royal inscription of the latter. Text published by Gadd, *Iraq* XV (1953) 123-134.

31.3.2 VA 2663 ii 43, iii 52—mention of RN as ancestor of Merodach–Baladan II in a royal land grant of the latter. Text published as *VAS* I 37.

31.3.3 Bricks of Merodach–Baladan II mentioning RN in brief account of ancestry: I *R* 5 no. XVII 6, *UVB* I pl. 27 no. 18:6, etc. (see also *Studies Oppenheim*, p. 42, no. 44.2.2).

31.3.4 BM 40006:16—temple endowment of Merodach–Baladan II in which [R]N is mentioned as an ancestor of the king. Principal publication: *BBSt* no. 35. See Seux, *RA* LIV (1960) 206-208 for the dating and pertinent restoration.

31.3.5 YBC 2146:13—RN noted as restorer of a shrine at Uruk, according to an inscription of Esarhaddon. Principal editions of the text: Clay, *YOS* I 40; Borger, *Asarhaddon*, p. 77 no. 50.

31.3.6 *VAB* IV 274 iii 17—reference in a building inscription of Nabonidus that alterations in a cult at Uruk took place during the reign of RN.

32. Nabu-shuma-ishkun

32.1 Chronological material

32.1.1 Kinglist A iv 2—mdAG–MU–GAR–*u*[*n*(?)]; regnal years not preserved.

32.1.2 *KAV* 13:5′—mdPA–MU–[ ]. (2144)

32.1.3 Shamash–shuma–ukin Chronicle, 22—the statue of Nabu did not participate in the procession of Marduk in the fifth and sixth years of RN.

32.2 Contemporary material

32.2.1 VA 3031—stone stele recording "divine" grant of income to an official upon his induction into temple service; dated in RN's eighth year. Principal publications: *VAS* I 36 (copy of text; copy of symbols in *VAS* I, Beiheft I, pl. I) and *MDOG* IV (1900) 14-18 (photos); transliteration and translation by Thureau-Dangin in *RA* XVI (1919) 141-144. See also Steinmetzer, *Kudurru*, pp. 82-84, no. 73 (=B 6).

32.2.2 MLC 1812-1813—two economic texts dated in the tenth and thirteenth years of RN, respectively. Principal publication: Clay,

(2144) *ADD* 888:9′ ff. might be expected to refer to Nabu–shuma–ishkun. The New Babylonian Chronicle rev. 15 may refer either to Eriba–Marduk or to Nabu–shuma–ishkun.

BRM I 2-3 (copy). Commentary and translations of individual sections: San Nicolò, *Orientalia N.S.* XVIII (1949) 302-303; Landsberger, *MSL* VIII/1 70, 77.

32.2.3 *BM 33428 (previously Rm. 3, 105)—private votive inscription of Nabu-shuma-imbi, governor of Borsippa, inscribed at the time of the repair of outer storehouses in Ezida. The text notes disturbances occurring in the city during the reign of Nabu-shuma-ishkun and is probably contemporary or only slightly later. Principal publication by S. A. Strong in *JRAS* 1892 350-368 (printed copy, transliteration, translation, notes); Winckler also published a transliteration, translation, and commentary in *AOF* I (1893-97) 254-263.

32.3 Later material: none.

33. Nabonassar

33.1 Chronological material

33.1.1 Kinglist A iv 3—ᵐᵈAG–⌈PAB(?)⌉; regnal years not preserved.

33.1.2 *New Babylonian Chronicle, rev. 16—[*n*]*a-ṣir*, in broken context.

33.1.3 Babylonian Chronicle i 1-12 (*CT* XXXIV 46)—record of RN's fourteen-year reign, containing synchronisms with the current Assyrian and Elamite monarchs, brief mention of Tiglath-Pileser III's campaign of 745 and of the revolt quelled by RN in Borsippa. Variant version: *CT* XXXIV 44 i 2′-8′.

33.1.4 "Ptolemaic Canon"—RN and 14 (year) reign.

33.2 Contemporary material

33.2.1 MLC 1814-1815, 1789-1804—eighteen economic texts, probably from the same archive (more texts from the same group are listed in 32.2.2 above and in 36.2.1 and supplement [w] below). The dates on the tablets range from 23 Siman 1 (747 B.C.) to 17 Tebet 14 (734 B.C.). Principal publication: *BRM* I 4-21 (copy).

33.2.2 [BM 38114—fragmentary legal text dated in Babylon in the second year of RN. Called to my attention by Prof. Wiseman.]

33.2.3 Three small clay cylinders containing duplicate versions of a private votive inscription recording the rebuilding of an *akītu* temple for the goddess Usuramassu by Bel-ibni and Nabu-zera-ushabshi at Uruk in the fifth year of Nabonassar. The texts are: (a) NBC 2502, published as *BIN* II 31; (b) YBC 2170, published as *YOS*

IX 74; (c) BM 113205, unpublished. The text of (a), with variants from (b), was published in transliteration and translation by Keiser in *BIN* II, pp. 48-50.

33.3 Later material

33.3.1 (a) Berossos, *FGrH* III C/1 p. 374:11-20—compiling of ancient Babylonian history in the time of Nabonassar (Armenian version of Eusebius' chronicle);
(b) Pseudo-Berossos, *FGrH* III C/1, p. 395:32-p. 396:1—Nabonassar's suppressing of the deeds of earlier Babylonian rulers (Synkellos).

33.3.2 (a) Ptolemy: *Syntaxis Mathematica* (ed. Heiberg), I, 254:8-13—astronomical observations available to Ptolemy begin in the time of Nabonassar. German translation of this passage available in Manitius, *Ptolemäus*: *Handbuch der Astronomie* (rev. ed. by O. Neugebauer, 1963), I, 183:3-8;
(b) Ptolemy, *Syntaxis Mathematica* (ed. Heiberg), I, 257:6-7, 325:20-22, 462:2-5, II, 293:25-294:1, 315:14-15, 357:19-20, 391:16-17, 425:5-6—the date of the beginning of the Nabonassar Era. German translation of these passages available in Manitius, *op. cit.*, I, 185:2-3, 236:1-3, 338:21-22, II, 155:9-11, 171:2-3, 203:8-9, 227:13-14, 251:7-8.

34. Nabu-nadin-zeri

34.1 Chronological material

34.1.1 Kinglist A iv 4—⌜2⌝ (years) assigned to ^{m}[^{d}A]G–MU–NUMUN, son of predecessor.

34.1.2 Babylonian Chronicle i 13-15 (*CT* XXXIV 46)—Nadinu, son of predecessor, succeeded to the throne after Nabonassar's death. He was deposed in a rebellion during his second regnal year.

34.1.3 "Ptolemaic Canon"—RN appears in an abbreviated form (Ναδίου [gen.], var.: Νάβιος [nom.]) and is assigned a reign of 2 (years).

34.2 Contemporary material: none.

34.3 Later material: none.

35. Nabu-shuma-ukin II

35.1 Chronological material

35.1.1 Kinglist A iv 5—ITI 1 13 UD ^{m}[^{d}A]G–MU–DU, son of predecessor.

35.1.2 Babylonian Chronicle i 16-17 (*CT* XXXIV 46)—ᵐMU–DU/GI.NA, provincial administrator, led the rebellion which killed his predecessor. He ruled for ITI 2 UD (see note 304 above).

35.2 Contemporary material: none.

35.3 Later material: none.

36. (Nabu)-mukin-zeri

36.1 Chronological material

36.1.1 Kinglist A iv 7—3 (years), abbreviated RN (ᵐDU–NUMUN), of the dynasty of *Šá–pi–i* (see note 1494 above for a history of this reading).

36.1.2 Babylonian Chronicle i 18-22 (*CT* XXXIV 46-47)—ᵐDU–NUMUN deposed his predecessor and took over the throne. In his third year, RN's reign was terminated by Tiglath–Pileser III. Possible variant version: *CT* XXXIV 44 i 9′-10′.

36.1.3 "Ptolemaic Canon"—RN linked with his successor, Πώρου; and the two are given a combined reign of 5 (years).

36.2 Contemporary material

36.2.1 MLC 1805—economic text dated in RN's fourth year (this is the only text which gives the full name of the king). Publication: *BRM* I 22 (copy).

36.2.2 Royal inscriptions of Tiglath–Pileser III narrating in detail his contacts with Babylonia in the time of RN:

(a) K. 3751:3-28 (published as II *R* 67 and in Rost, *TP III*, pl. XXXV; *ARAB* I 787–794);

(b) D.T. 3:3-19 (published in Rost, *TP III*, pl. XXXIV; *ARAB* I 805-806).

36.2.3 Nimrud Letters dealing with various aspects of the military and diplomatic strategy of the Assyrians in winning Babylonia from Mukin–zeri. Letters especially pertinent are nos. I-XI, LXV-LXVI (published by H. W. F. Saggs in *Iraq* XVII [1955] 21-50, pls. IV-X; *Iraq* XXV [1963] 71-73, pl. XI). RN is mentioned by name in nos.:

I (ND 2632) 33;
II (ND 2717) obv. 6′, 13′; rev. 5′, 6′, 8′, 11′;
III (ND 2700) face A 7′, 12′;
IV (ND 2360) face B 4′(?);

V (ND 2603) obv. 3′, 15′;
VI (ND 2674) face A 12′;
VII (ND 2636) face A 8′;
LXV (ND 2385) 9.

One may also compare the unpublished ND 2435 (referred to by Saggs in *Iraq* XXV [1963] 150) and even possibly the later *ABL* 1365:6.

37. Tiglath-Pileser III (Pulu)

37.1 Chronological material

37.1.1 Kinglist A iv 8—2 (years) ᵐ*Pu–lu*.

37.1.2 Babylonian Chronicle i 19-26 (*CT* XXXIV 47)—his devastation of southern Babylonia in the third year of Mukin–zeri, his accession to the Babylonian throne, his reign of two years. (Cf. also *ibid.*, i 2-5, where his accession to the Assyrian throne and his campaign of 745 are mentioned).

37.1.3 *New Babylonian Chronicle, rev. 18—possible traces of final sign of RN: [É.ŠÁR].⌜RA⌝ LUGAL KUR *Aš+šur ina* AŠ.TE DÚR–*ab*.

37.1.4 "Ptolemaic Canon"—RN and his predecessor ruled for a combined total of 5 (years).

37.2 Contemporary material

37.2.1 AO 4422-4424—three administrative tablets recording amounts of beer given or received, dated in the first year of RN (as king of Babylonia). AO 4423-4424 were first published by Thureau-Dangin in *RA* VI/4 (1907) 134-137 (copy, transliteration, translation). Principal publication: Contenau, *TCL* XII 1-3; transliterated and translated by E. W. Moore, *Neo-Babylonian Business and Administrative Documents*, pp. 2-5.

37.2.2 [BM 78156 (formerly 88-4-19, 9)—unpublished legal text dealing with an inheritance dispute, dated at Babylon on the twenty-fifth day of Dumuz, second year of RN. Fragmentary duplicate: BM 40717 (formerly 81-4-28, 262, noted by Thureau-Dangin in *RA* VI/4 [1907] 137), also unpublished. These texts were called to my attention by Prof. Wiseman.]

37.3 Later material

37.3.1 VA 8384:15 (Assur Ostracon)—mention of deportations from Bit–Amukani under Tiglath–Pileser. Most recent edition of the text (with full bibliography): Donner-Röllig, *Kanaanäische und aramäische Inschriften*, no. 233.

37.3.2 Berossos, *FGrH* III C/1 p. 385:1-3—Phulos, king of the Chaldeans, led a campaign against Judea (Armenian version of Eusebius' chronicle).

38. Shalmaneser V (Ululaju)

38.1 Chronological material

38.1.1 Kinglist A iv 9—5 (years) assigned to Ululaju of the dynasty BAL.TIL.

38.1.2 Babylonian Chronicle i 27-30 (*CT* XXXIV 47)—Shalmaneser succeeded his father on both the Assyrian and Babylonian thrones and held the dual monarchy for five years. During his reign he devastated the city URU *Šá–ma–ra–'i–in*.

38.1.3 "Ptolemaic Canon"—RN assigned a reign of 5 (years).

38.2 Contemporary material

38.2.1 BM 91221-91224, 91226, 91230—six bronze lion weights inscribed with the name of Shalmaneser. Principal publication: *CIS* II/1 pp. 3-8 nos. 2-7 (with bibliography). For find spots and correlation between BM numbers and *CIS* numbers, see note 1564 above. (2145)

38.3 Later material

38.3.1 VA 209 i 1ff.—reference in a text from the reign of Sargon II to a business transaction which took place at Der in the third year of Shalmaneser V. Principal publication: *VAS* I 70.

38.3.2 VA 8384:15 (Assur Ostracon)—mention of deportations from Bit–Adini under Ululaju. Most recent edition of the text (with full bibliography): Donner-Röllig, *Kanaanäische und aramäische Inschriften*, no. 233.

38.3.3 II Kings 17:3-6 and 18:9-12—Shalmaneser's campaign against Samaria.

38.3.4 Josephus, *Antiquities of the Jews*, IX xiv— Shalmaneser's sieges of Samaria and Tyre.

(2145) For some letters possibly written by Shalmaneser V when he was crown prince, see note 1564 above.

Supplement

(a) *Chronicle P iv 12-13—at the time of Tukulti-Ashur, the statue of Marduk was returned to Babylon, whence it had been taken by Tukulti-Ninurta I. If Tukulti-Ashur is to be identified with Ninurta-tukulti-Ashur (which is uncertain), then this may have taken place during the early years of the Second Isin Dynasty.

(b) *BM 35496 (formerly Sp. III, 2), BM 34062 (formerly Sp. 158+ Sp. II, 962), BM 35404 (Sp. II, 987)—the so-called Kedor-laomer texts, poetic documents which deal in part with the fall of Babylon at the end of the Kassite Dynasty. Principal publications: Pinches in *JTVI* XXIX (1897) 43-90 and A. Jeremias in *MVAG* XXI (1916) 69-97. [See also addendum, p. 396.]

(c) Elamite royal inscriptions of Shilhak-Inshushinak telling of places in Babylonia which submitted to him in the course of his campaigning. Most recent publication (with earlier bibliography): König, *Die elamischen Königsinschriften*, nos. 54-55. These campaigns took place early in the Second Isin Dynasty.

(d) Khorsabad Kinglist iii 34-35 and SDAS Kinglist iii 20-21—Mutakkil-Nusku, Assyrian king no. 85, deported his brother Ninurta-tukulti-Ashur to Babylonia sometime during the early years of the Second Isin Dynasty. Text publication of this passage by Gelb, *JNES* XIII (1954) 218-219.

(e) K. 212+K. 4448 and BM 104727 (formerly 1912-5-13, 2)—fragmentary letter(s) written by a Babylonian king early in the Second Isin Dynasty to his weaker Assyrian counterpart. Principal publications: Pinches, IV R^2 34 no. 2 (copy of K. 212+K. 4448); Pinches, *JRAS* 1904 407-417 (copy of 1912-5-13, 2; transliteration, translation, commentary on both fragments); Weidner, *AfO* X (1935-36) 2-9 (transliteration, translation, commentary, and extensive bibliography on both fragments). For further commentary and bibliography, see Borger, *EAK* I 100 and *Handbuch der Keilschriftliteratur*, I, 395 (repeated *ibid.*, 404), to which may be added Böhl's discussion in *MAOG* XI/3 (1937) 33-34 and Wiseman's observations in *CAH* II^2 xxxi 9.

(f) *Luristan bronze dagger with a four-line inscription of Eriba-Nusku, a scribe who presumably lived around the time of the Second Isin Dynasty; now in the Museum für Vor- und Frühgeschichte, Berlin. Published in copy, transliteration, and translation by Nagel, *AfO* XIX (1959-60) 96. Nagel, "Königsdolche," no. 10.

(g) *Luristan bronze dagger bearing a short votive inscription of Marduk–nasir to the god Erija; now in the Foroughi Collection, Teheran. Published by Dossin in *Iranica Antiqua* II (1962) 153 no. 7 (transliteration, translation) and pl. XIV (photo).

(h) *Luristan bronze dagger inscribed *na–pu* (PN?); now in the Joseph Ternbach collection. Published in 1941 by Herzfeld, *Iran in the Ancient East,* p. 134 (partial transcription) and pl. XXVIII (photo); catalogued in Porada (ed.), *Man in the Ancient World* (1958), pp. 15-16, no. 46. Nagel, "Königsdolche," no. 9.

(i) *BM 123060—Luristan bronze dagger with brief inscription of Shamash–killani, a *ša rēš šarri* official. Published by Contenau in *RA* XXVIII (1931) 107 (translation only), by Gadd in *BMQ* VII (1932) 44 and pl. XVIII (description, translation, photo), and by Langdon in *SPA* I 284 no. XI (transliteration, translation) and *SPA* IV pl. 55C (photo). Date uncertain, but presumably sometime between twelfth and ninth centuries. This dagger was said to have been found in the same cave as a dagger inscribed with the name of Marduk–nadin–ahhe (no. 6.2.2(b) above), according to Meek in *BASOR* LXXIV (1939) 9-10. Nagel, "Königsdolche," no. 4.

(j) *Two Luristan bronze daggers in the Foroughi Collection, Teheran, with brief private inscriptions. Published by Dossin, *Iranica Antiqua* II (1962) 154 nos. 8-9 (transliteration, translation) and pl. XX (photo). Exact dates uncertain.

(k) Religious Chronicle, col. ii—portents dating from the reign of some king(s), presumably either Simbar–Shipak and/or Eulmash–shakin–shumi. See note 926 above.

(l) Era Epic—a theological myth describing the divine machinery behind the Sutian invasions in Babylonia from the eleventh through ninth centuries. Principal recent edition: Gössmann, *Das Era–Epos.* Recent commentaries, additions, reviews, re-editions: N. M. Bailkey, *Osiris* IX (1950) 106-130; Borger, *Orientalia N.S.* XXVI (1957) 143; Borger and W. G. Lambert, *Orientalia N.S.* XXVII (1958) 137-149; Bottéro, *RHR* CLIV (1958) 231; M. Civil, *JCS* XVII (1963) 58; van Dijk, *OLZ* LIV (1959) 379-385; Falkenstein, *DLZ* LXXIX (1958) 13-16 and ZA LIII (1959) 200-208; R. Frankena, *BiOr* XIV (1957) 2-10 and pls. I-II, *JEOL* XV (1957-58) 160-176, *BiOr* XV (1958) 12-15 and pl. I; Garelli, *RA* LIV (1960) 104-106; Kienast, *ZA* LIV (1961) 244-249; W. G. Lambert, *JCS* X (1956) 99-100, *AfO* XVIII (1957-58) 395-401, *Iraq* XXIV (1962) 119-125 and pl. XXXVI (re-edition of tablet V); Reiner, *JNES* XVII (1958) 41-48 and XIX (1960) 148-155.

(m) *Luristan bronze arrowhead inscribed with the name of Ninurta–ushallim, *šangû*; in the Foroughi Collection, Teheran. Published by Dossin, *Iranica Antiqua* II (1962) 161 no. 24 (transliteration, translation) and pl. XXIX (photo).

(n) *Luristan bronze arrowheads inscribed with the names of private individuals; in the Foroughi Collection, Teheran. Published by Dossin, *Iranica Antiqua* II (1962) 161-162 nos. 22, 23, 25 (transliterations, translations, and copy of no. 25) and pl. XXIX (photos of nos. 22-23).

(o) Scheil, *Annales de Tn. II*, obv. 41-73—account of the campaign of Tukulti–Ninurta II in 885 which passed through northern Babylonia. At that time, either Nabu–shuma–ukin I (king no. 23) or Nabu–apla–iddina (no. 24) was on the throne.

(p) Bronze bowl in the possession of Mrs. Christian R. Holmes, bearing inscription of Abdi–il, an official of Adinu, chief of the Dakkuru tribe (c. 850). Published by Langdon, *SPA* I 285 no. XIV (copy, transliteration, translation, commentary) and *SPA* IV pl. 68 A (photo); transliteration also in note 1208 above.

(q) *Bronze macehead(?) inscribed with the name of a *ša rēš šarri* official. Published by Dossin, *Iranica Antiqua* II (1962) 162 no. 26 (transliteration, translation) and pl. XXX (photo).

(r) I *R* 35 no. 1:22-24—Adad–nirari III recounts that the kings of Chaldea became his vassals and that he imposed tribute on them; he also offered homage in the cult centers of northern Babylonia. Cf. also *CT* XXXIV 41 iv 15-22 (Synchronistic History), where Adad–nirari is involved with a Babylonian king whose name has not been preserved.

(s) MMA 74.51.4426—barrel-shaped weight made of green basalt, containing a four-line Akkadian inscription of Nabu–shumu–lishir of the Dakkuru tribe; weight 164.3 grams, provenience unknown. Inscription published by Ward in *JAOS* XIII (1889) lvi-lvii (copy, transliteration, translation, notes). [2146] Transliteration, translation, notes, and additional bibliography by Weissbach, *ZDMG* LXI

(2146) Ward stated that the weight had been brought to the United States by the Wolfe Expedition to Babylonia; but, according to the records of the Metropolitan Museum, New York, it was obtained by them during the preceding decade (1874). Presumably Ward was in error regarding the source of the weight (the probability of there being two identical such weights obtained around the same time is minimal).

(1907) 395-396, no. 8. Photo: John L. Myres, *Handbook of the Cesnola Collection of Antiquities from Cyprus* (New York, 1914), p. 556, no. 4426. A new transliteration and translation of this inscription (made from an impression of the original kindly furnished by Dr. Vaughn E. Crawford) are given above in note 1338.

(t) BM 129532—a seal bearing the inscription of Marduk–shakin–shumi, who is probably to be identified with Eriba–Marduk's father (see *JCS* XVI [1962] 98 and n. 24; *Studies Oppenheim*, pp. 28-29). Published in copy with transliteration, translation, and notes in H. Carnegie (ed.), *Catalogue of the Collection of Antique Gems Formed by James, Ninth Earl of Southesk*, II, 82-83 as Qβ39; the text has also been transliterated and translated by Leemans, *JEOL* X (1945-48) 438, and further collation is noted in *Studies Oppenheim*, p. 28 n. 159. The seal depicts "a royal or princely personage, with a long curved staff in his hand."

(u) *Luristan bronze situla inscribed with the name of Eriba–Marduk son of ᵐ*Si–bu–ri*; now in the Foroughi Collection, Teheran. Published by Dossin, *Iranica Antiqua* II (1962) 164 no. 33 (transliteration, translation, notes) and pl. XXXIV (photo). See note 1382 above for further discussion and bibliography.

(v) *BM 90834—votive stele erected by a Marduk–balassu–iqbi containing a twenty-line inscription and an image of the donor's father. Published by Strong, *JRAS* 1892 345-349 (copy, transliteration, translation, notes), and by King, *BBSt* no. 34 (photo, transliteration, translation, notes). Date uncertain (erroneously connected with the king Marduk–balassu–iqbi by Pinches in *PSBA* VI [1884] 181).

(w) MLC 1806-1811—six economic texts presumably dating from Babylonia in the eighth century; they apparently belong to an archive whose dated tablets come from about 750-728 B.C. (see 32.2.2, 33.2.1, 36.2.1 above). Published in *BRM* I 23-28 (copy). Three of these texts bear no date, three have incomplete or cryptic dates:

(i) *BRM* I 23: MU 4 KAM *šá* LUGAL *ina* KUR NU TUK–*ú*, "the fourth year in which there was no king in the land"; for the interpretation of this date, see note 1328 above;

(ii) *BRM* I 24: MU 8 KAM (no king mentioned; date uncertain, but see note 1328 above);

(iii) *BRM* I 28: ITI KIN UD 23 KAM, year omitted.

III. INDEX OF PUBLICATIONS [2147]

[2147] Books not having a well-known, short abbreviation will be found listed under the author's last name, as will the catalogues of Nagel (for Luristan daggers) and Steinmetzer (for kudurrus).

ARAB I 666	= 25.2.5 (f)
674	= 25.2.5 (k)
706	= 25.2.5 (i)
723-726	= 26.2.4 (a)
787-794	= 36.2.2 (a)
805-806	= 36.2.2 (b)
AS XI 60 n. 113 and plate at end	= I.C.4
AS XV 3	= 1.1.1 and *passim*; bibliography in I.A.2
Assur Ostracon	= 37.3.1, 38.3.2
BA V 339-344	= 4.3.10
BA V 386-388	= note 2133
BA VI/1 135-137	= 25.2.5 (a)
BA VI/1 147	= 25.2.5 (d)
BA VI/1 152	= 25.2.5 (k)
Babylonian Chronicle i 1-12	= 33.1.3
13-15	= 34.1.2
16-17	= 35.1.2
18-22	= 36.1.2
19-26	= 37.1.2
27-30	= 38.1.2
BASOR LXXIV 7-11	= 7.2.3
BBSt no. 6	= 4.2.9
BBSt no. 7	= 6.2.12
BBSt no. 8	= 6.2.10
BBSt no. 9	= 19.2.2 (see also 16.3.1, 20.2.2, 21.2.1)
BBSt no. 11	= 5.2.3
BBSt no. 12	= 7.2.6
BBSt no. 13	= 8.2.11
BBSt no. 24	= 4.2.10
BBSt no. 25	= 6.2.6
BBSt no. 26	= 8.2.9
BBSt no. 27	= 12.2.2 (see also 13.2.1)
BBSt no. 28	= 24.2.1
BBSt no. 29	= 24.2.2
BBSt no. 30	= 2.2.2
BBSt no. 34	= supplement (v)
BBSt no. 35	= 31.3.4
BBSt no. 36	= 24.2.3 (see also 12.3.1, 14.3.1, 15.3.1)
BE I/1 83	= 5.2.2 (see also 4.3.1)
BE I/2 148	= 7.2.2

Dynastic Chronicle v 5′-6′	= 13.1.3
7′	= 14.1.4
9′	= 15.1.4
10′	= 16.1.4
11′	= 17.1.5
13′-15′	= 18.1.5
Dynastic Chronicle vi	= (see *ADD* 888)
Era Epic	= supplement (l)
FGrH III C/1	
p. 374	= 33.3.1 (a)
p. 385	= 37.3.2
pp. 395-396	= 33.3.1 (b)
Hebraica IX 4-5	= 3.3.3, 4.3.5
Herzfeld, *Iran in the Ancient East*, p. 134	= 8.2.7, supplement (h)
Hill, *The Fertile Crescent*, p. 12	= 6.2.7
Hilprecht, *Excavations in Assyria and Babylonia*, p. 519	= 6.2.8, 8.2.8
Hinke, *Boundary Stone*, pp. 142-155	= 4.2.8
pp. 188-199	= 9.2.1
Hinke, *Selected Babylonian Kudurru Inscriptions*, no. 5	= 4.2.8
ICC, pl. 46	= 25.2.5 (d)
ICC, pl. 53	= 12.2.2
ICC, pl. 76	= 25.2.5 (k)
ICC, pl. 83F	= 11.2.1
ICC, pl. 91	= 25.2.5 (h)
ILN, Oct. 29, 1932, pp. 666-667	= 6.2.2 (a), 6.2.3
Iranica Antiqua II	
pp. 151-152 no. 3	= 3.2.1
p. 152 no. 4	= 4.2.5
pp. 152-153 no. 5	= 6.2.4
p. 153 no. 6	= 5.2.1
p. 153 no. 7	= supplement (g)
p. 154 nos. 8-9	= supplement (j)
p. 158 no. 14	= 4.2.4
p. 160 no. 17	= 15.2.1
p. 160 no. 18	= 16.2.1
p. 160 no. 19	= 18.2.1
p. 161 no. 20	= 19.2.6

KAH II 110	= 25.2.5 (f)
KAH II 142	= 26.2.5
KAV 10	= 17.1.4 and *passim*; bibliography in I.B.3
KAV 12	= 4.1.3, 5.1.3, 6.1.3; bibliography in I.B.4
KAV 13	= 28.1.1 and *passim*; bibliography in I.B.3
KAV 182	= 14.1.3 and *passim*; bibliography in I.B.2
KAV 216	= 12.1.2 and *passim*; bibliography in I.B.1
Ker Porter, *Travels*, II, pl. 77 (a)	= 8.2.3
Kinglist A	= 1.1.2 and *passim*; bibliography in I.A.1
Kinglist C	= 1.1.1 and *passim*; bibliography in I.A.2
King, *Records of the Reign of Tukulti-Ninib I*, pp. 116-119	= 6.3.2
pp. 51, 96-101, 157	= bibliography in I.C.1
II Kings 17-18	= 38.3.3
König, *Die elamischen Königsinschriften*, nos. 54-55	= supplement (c)
Langdon, *Excavations at Kish*, I, 16-17	= 8.2.3
Layard, *Discoveries among the Ruins of Nineveh and Babylon*, p. 600	= 31.2.1
Layard, *The Monuments of Nineveh*, First Series, pl. 95a no. 11	= 11.2.1
LBAT 1413	= (see note 1434)
LBAT 1414	= (see note 1493)
LBAT 1526	= 4.3.11
LIH I 70	= 7.2.1
LIH III 254-255	= 7.2.1
MAOG IX/3 8-35	= 22.2.1
MDOG IV 14-18	= 32.2.1
MDOG V 14 fig. 3	= 25.2.1
MDOG VII 25-29	= 6.2.7
MDOG XXVIII 24-25	= 25.2.5 (j)
MDOG XXXVI 16	= 25.2.5 (m)
MDOG LIII 28	= 8.2.1
MDP XI no. 92	= supplement (c)
MVAG III 240-243	= 25.2.4
MVAG XX/4 3-5	
Fragment D	= *KAV* 12: bibliography in I.B.4
Fragment E	= *KAV* 10; bibliography in I.B.3
Fragment F	= *KAV* 13; bibliography in I.B.3
MVAG XXI 69-97	= supplement (b)

Porada (ed.), *Man in the Ancient World* p. 15, no. 45	= 8.2.7
pp. 15-16, no. 46	= supplement (h)
PSBA VI 193-198	= I.A.1
PSBA XIX 70-73	= 6.2.11
PSBA XXIX 221	= 11.2.1
"Ptolemaic Canon"	= 33.1.4 and *passim*; bibliography in I.E
I *R* 5 no. XVII	= 31.3.3
I *R* 5 no. XXII	= 8.2.3
I *R* 31	= 26.2.4 (a)
I *R* 35 no. 1	= supplement (r)
I *R* 66	= 6.2.6
I *R* 70	= 6.2.13
II *R* 67	= 36.2.2 (a)
III *R* 14:48-50	= 6.3.2
III *R* 38 no. 2	= 4.3.9
III *R* 41	= 6.2.12
III *R* 43	= 6.2.10
III *R* 61 no. 2	= 4.3.11
IV *R*[2] 20 no. 1	= 4.3.10
IV *R*[2] 34 no. 2	= supplement (e)
V *R* 60-61	= 24.2.3
RA VI 134-137	= 37.2.1
RA XVI 117-141	= 25.2.2 (see also 26.2.3)
RA XVI 141-144	= 32.2.1
RA XIX 86-87	= (see p. 257)
RA XXVIII 105-106	= 6.2.3
RA XXVIII 107	= 4.2.2, supplement (i)
RA XXIX 29	= 15.2.1, 3.2.1
RA LII 193-202	= 4.3.10
RA LX 30-35	= 4.2.6
RA LXI 71	= 6.2.7
Religious Chronicle i 16′	= 11.1.3
ii	= supplement (k)
iii-iv	= 19.1.6
Revue Sémitique II 76-78	= 4.3.8
RMA 200	= 4.3.6
Rost, *TP III*, vol. II	
pl. XXXIV	= 36.2.2 (b)
pl. XXXV	= 36.2.2 (a)

IV. INDEX OF MUSEUM AND EXCAVATION NUMBERS

83-1-18,1338-1339	= I.C.5
84-2-11,356	= I.C.5
88-4-19,9	= 37.2.2
1904-10-9,59	= 6.3.3
1904-10-9,96	= 4.3.10
1912-5-13,2	= supplement (e)
1932-10-8,8	= 6.2.5
A. 2529	= 25.2.5 (i)
A. 3442	= 24.3.3
A. 3647	= 4.2.1
AO 4422-4424	= 37.2.1
AO 6684	= 25.2.2 (see also 26.2.3)
Assur 5999	= 25.2.5 (j)
Assur 6596	= 26.2.4 (b), 27.2.2
Assur 13956 d h	= I.B.2
Assur 14616c	= I.B.1
Assur 18438	= 6.2.14
Assur 18641	= 6.2.14
Bab. 59431	= 8.2.1
Bab. K. 713 (Photo)	= 4.2.6
Bab. 715 (Photo)	= 4.2.1
BM 26295	= 7.2.1
BM 27859	= I.C.2
BM 33332	= I.A.1
BM 33428	= 32.2.3
BM 34031	= 4.3.11
BM 34062	= supplement (b)
BM 34375	= 4.3.5 (see also 3.3.3)
BM 34896	= 4.3.5 (see also 3.3.3)
BM 34995	= 4.3.5 (see also 3.3.3)
BM 35000	= 4.3.10
BM 35404	= supplement (b)
BM 35496	= supplement (b)
BM 35968	= I.C.3
BM 38114	= 33.2.2
BM 40006	= 31.3.4
BM 40548	= 31.2.2
BM 40717	= 37.2.2
BM 48498	= I.C.7
BM 75976-75977	= I.C.5

D.T. 3	= 36.2.2 (b)
D.T. 71	= (see note 2133)
Field Museum (Chicago), no. 156011	= 8.2.3
Gron. 846-850	= 2.2.3
H.S. 157	= 6.2.8
IM 1038	= 8.2.5
IM 54669	= 25.2.5 (c)
IM 55644	= 25.2.5 (e)
IM 60496	= 25.2.5 (g)
K. 212	= supplement (e)
K. 710	= 4.3.6
K. 2660	= 4.3.9
K. 3317+3319	= 4.3.10
K. 3426	= 4.3.8
K. 3444	= 4.3.10
K. 3751	= 36.2.2 (a)
K. 3766	= 4.3.11
K. 4401a	= I.D.3
K. 4401b	= I.D.3
K. 4448	= supplement (e)
K. 5191	= 4.3.10
K. 6156	= 8.3.3
K. 8532-8534	= I.C.4
K. 10802	= 8.3.5
K. 11261	= I.C.4
K. 11624	= I.C.4
MLC 383	= 4.2.7
MLC 1789-1804	= 33.2.1
MLC 1805	= 36.2.1
MLC 1806-1811	= supplement (w)
MLC 1812-1813	= 32.2.2
MLC 1814-1815	= 33.2.1
MMA 74.51.4426	= supplement (s)
9 N 99	= 7.2.7
NBC 2502	= 33.2.3
ND 2090	= 31.3.1
ND 2360	= 36.2.3
ND 2385	= 36.2.3
ND 2435	= 36.2.3
ND 2494	= 36.2.3

VAT 10281	= I.D.1, 3.1.3
VAT 10453+10465	= I.D.2
VAT 11261	= I.B.3
VAT 11338	= I.B.4
VAT 11345	= I.B.3
W 20030,7	= 4.3.7, 8.3.4
W.-B. 10	= 24.3.2
Walters Art Gallery 21.10	= 6.2.7
YBC 2146	= 31.3.5
YBC 2154	= 6.2.9, 7.2.5
YBC 2170	= 33.2.3
YBC 2182	= 4.3.4 (see also 3.3.2)

V. CONCORDANCE BETWEEN PRELIMINARY AND FINAL CATALOGUES

The following section presents a list of texts appearing in the preliminary catalogue (*JCS* XVI [1962] 83-109) which do not bear the same numbers in the catalogue given above.

old	*new*
I.B.5	= I.B.3
4.2.6	= 4.2.7
4.2.7	= 4.2.8
4.2.8	= 4.2.9
4.2.9	= 4.2.10
4.3.2	= 4.3.3
4.3.3	= 4.3.4
4.3.4	= 4.3.5
4.3.5	= 4.3.6
4.3.6	= 4.3.8
4.3.7	= 4.3.9
4.3.8	= 4.3.10
5.2.1	= 5.2.2
5.2.2	= 5.2.3
6.2.4	= 6.2.6
6.2.5	= 6.2.8
6.2.6	= 6.2.9
6.2.7	= 6.2.10

old		*new*
6.2.8	=	6.2.11
6.2.9	=	6.2.12
6.2.10	=	6.2.7
6.2.11	=	6.2.13
6.2.12	=	6.2.14
6.3.1	=	6.3.2
6.3.2	=	6.3.3
7.2.4	=	7.2.6
7.2.6	=	7.2.4
8.2.8	=	8.2.9
8.2.9	=	8.2.11
8.2.10	=	8.2.8
8.2.11	=	8.2.12
8.3.1	=	8.3.3
12.2.1	=	12.2.2
19.2.1	=	19.2.2
19.2.2	=	19.2.3
20.2.1	=	20.2.2
24.2.4	=	24.2.5
25.2.5 (a)	=	25.2.5 (h)
25.2.5 (b)	=	25.2.5 (a)
25.2.5 (c)	=	25.2.5 (d)
25.2.5 (d)	=	25.2.5 (k)
25.2.5 (e)	=	25.2.5 (f)
25.2.5 (f)	=	25.2.5 (i)
25.2.5 (g)	=	25.2.5 (c)
25.2.5 (h)	=	25.2.5 (e)
25.2.5 (i)	=	25.2.5 (g)
26.2.1	=	26.2.2
26.2.2	=	26.2.3
26.2.3	=	26.2.4
26.2.4	=	26.2.5
28-32 (a)	=	supplement (s)
28-32 (b)	=	supplement (t)
28-32 (c)	=	supplement (r)
33.1.1	=	28.1.1
34.1.1-34.2.1	=	29.1.1-29.2.1
35.1.1-35.1.2	=	30.1.1-30.1.2

old		*new*
36.1.1-36.2.1	=	31.1.1-31.2.1
36.2.2	=	supplement (u)
36.3.1-36.3.3	=	31.3.1-31.3.3
36.3.4-36.3.5	=	31.3.5-31.3.6
37.1.1-37.1.2	=	32.1.1-32.1.2
37.2.1	=	32.2.3
37.2.2	=	32.2.1
37.2.3	=	32.2.2
38.1.1-38.1.4	=	33.1.1-33.1.4
38.2.1	=	33.2.3
38.2.2	=	33.2.1
38.3.1	=	33.3.1
39.1.1-39.1.3	=	34.1.1-34.1.3
40.1.1-40.1.2	=	35.1.1-35.1.2
41.1.1-41.2.3	=	36.1.1-36.2.3
42.1.1-42.2.1	=	37.1.1-37.2.1
42.3.1	=	37.3.2
43.1.1-43.3.1	=	38.1.1-38.3.1
43.3.2	=	38.3.3
43.3.3	=	38.3.4
appendix (g) [2148]	=	supplement (k)
appendix (h)	=	supplement (l)
appendix (i)	=	19.2.5
appendix (j)	=	supplement (o)
appendix (k)	=	supplement (p)
appendix (l)	=	supplement (i)
appendix (m)	=	supplement (v)
appendix (n)	=	supplement (w)

[2148] The "appendix" in the *JCS* XVI catalogue is equivalent to the "supplement" here.

Appendix B

THE INTERNAL CHRONOLOGY OF THE BROKEN OBELISK

To historians concerned with the later years of the Second Dynasty of Isin, the Broken Obelisk has been and will remain a problematic and tantalizing document. Over the years much ink has been spilled in efforts to date this important text, which does not preserve the name of its royal author. The various monarchs proposed have ranged from Shalmaneser I to Adad–nirari II. [2149] In recent years, the most generally accepted view has been that the inscription was the work of Ashur–bel–kala. Some of the reasons advanced for this position are:

(a) the limmu of Ashur–ra'im–nisheshu occurs both in the annals of Ashur–bel–kala and in the Broken Obelisk; [2150]

(b) the Broken Obelisk was found in conjunction with another inscription of Ashur–bel–kala; [2151]

(c) the Arameans in the Broken Obelisk are referred to as living in (KUR) *A–re–me*; in the time of Tiglath–Pileser I, they were called KUR *Aḫlamê* KUR *Armaja*; [2152]

(d) the many phrases borrowed from the annals of Tiglath–Pileser I may reflect a desire of Ashur–bel–kala to imitate the exploits of his renowned father and also show that the inscriptions of Tiglath–Pileser I—and perhaps even his scribes—were still ready to hand; [2153]

(e) the month names employed in the text are Babylonian, in contrast to the texts of Tiglath–Pileser I, in which the changeover from Assyrian to Babylonian month names was still going on. [2154]

Weidner, Jaritz, and Borger have been the chief spokesmen for dating the Broken Obelisk to the time of Ashur–bel–kala.

[2149] A brief bibliography of the more notable opinions has been assembled by Jaritz, *JSS* IV (1959) 206 n. 1 and by Borger, *EAK* I 135.

[2150] *AfO* VI (1930-31) 86, Teil IV; *AKA* 133 iii 3. See also Jaritz, *JSS* IV (1959) 213. Stamm (*Namengebung*, p. 228) and Borger (*EAK* I 5 n. 2) present arguments for reading the *limmu* name as Ashur–rim–nisheshu.

[2151] Jaritz, *JSS* IV (1959) 204.

[2152] *AfO* XVIII (1957-58) 350:34, etc.

[2153] The resemblances between the inscriptions of the two have been summarized by Jaritz, *JSS* IV (1959) 210-211; see also Borger, *EAK* I 140.

[2154] E.g., *AfO* XVIII (1957-58) 353.

While there is little disagreement today about the date of the Broken Obelisk, there is still considerable confusion about the dating of the campaigns within the text itself. In general, modern attempts to deal with the internal chronology of the Broken Obelisk are characterized by their propensity to assume disorder within the text itself. The most recent extensive treatment by Jaritz, (2155) for instance, erects an elaborate chronology on two assumptions:

(a) *ina šattimma šiāti,* an often-repeated formula in the text, does not here have its usual idiomatic meaning "in the same year," but rather means "in that year" with an indefinite point of reference; (2156)

(b) the eponym officials at this time in Assyria were assuming office in the month of Ajar. (2157)

With these two assumptions, Jaritz wonders why he finds inconsistency in the text, "why the name of the contemporary eponym is given in some instances only," (2158) especially at his hypothetical beginning of the eponym year. Yet, with these foundations, Jaritz proceeds to erect a chronology of events described in columns ii-iii of the Obelisk which spreads out over at least eight years. (2159) Borger, while rejecting Jaritz's interpretations, fails to give any positive proposals of his own, commenting merely that "merkwürdigerweise sind die Monate nur zum Teil chronologisch richtig geordnet." (2160)

But a different analysis of the Broken Obelisk is possible, one which is not based on presumptions of disorder in the text. This analysis is based on the following principles:

(a) the military events described in columns ii-iii are described in chronological order;

(b) each event is introduced with a stereotyped date formula;

(c) the formulae are of three kinds:

(i) *ina* ITI MN *li–me* PN "in the month MN, in the limmu of PN,"

(ii) *ina šattimma šiāti ina* ITI MN "in the same year, (2161) in the month MN,"

(iii) *ina šattimma šiāti ina* ITI KIMIN–*ma* "in the same year, the same month"

(2155) *JSS* IV (1959) 205-208.

(2156) *Ibid.*, 206 n. 2.

(2157) *Ibid.*, 207. The Broken Obelisk ii 13 can be used to prove only that the eponym official took office sometime between the fifth and the third month not, as Jaritz assumes, that it had to take place during the preceding month. By the same logic he should have said that the eponymate of Ilu–iddina (iii 20) began in the eighth month.

(2158) *JSS* IV (1959) 208.

(2159) Three in col. ii, five in col. iii.

(2160) *EAK* I 139.

(2161) I.e., in the last-mentioned eponymate.

(d) these formulae should be interpreted as follows:
(i) this is the first recorded event in the eponymy under discussion; ([2162])
(ii) the eponym official was installed in a month preceding this in the year under discussion, i.e., this is not the first month in the eponym cycle;
(iii) this is not the first event described in the month and year under discussion.

In the succeeding paragraphs we will assemble all preserved dates and then apply the above principles in an attempt to understand the dating within the text.

Chart of Chronological Data in the Broken Obelisk

			(*ina*)		
ii	8	[ ]	ITI GAN	[	IX]
	11	*ina šattimma* [*ši*]*āti*	ITI ŠU		IV
	13		ITI SIG$_4$	*li–me Aššur*–[ ]	III
	16	*ina šattimma šiāti*	ITI KIMIN–*ma*		III
	19	*ina šattimma šiāti*	ITI GAN		IX
			. . . . .		
iii	1	*ina šattimma šiāti*	ITI KIMIN–*ma*		
	2	*ina šattimma šiāti*	ITI ŠU		IV
	3		ITI [ ]	*li–me Aššur–rā'im–nišēšu*	
	4	*ina šattimma šiāti*	ITI ZÍZ		XI
	8	*ina šattimma šiāti*	ITI GU$_4$		II
	9	*ina šattimma šiāti*	ITI KIMIN–*ma*		II
	10-11	*ina šattimma šiāti*	ITI SIG$_4$		III
	11-12	*ina šattimma šiāti*	ITI KIMIN–*ma*		III
	13	*ina šattimma šiāti*	ITI NE		V
	15	*ina šattimma šiāti*	ITI KIMIN–*ma*		V
	17-18	*ina šattimma šiāti*	ITI KIN		VI
	19	*ina šattimma šiāti*	ITI ⌈APIN⌉		VIII
	20		ITI GAN	*li–me Ilu–iddina*	IX
	21-22	*ina šattimma šiāti*	ITI KIMIN–*ma*		IX
	23	*ina šattimma šiāti*	ITI KIMIN–*ma*		IX
	24	[*ina šattimma ši*]*āti*	ITI KIMIN–*ma*		IX
	28	[*ina*] *šattimma šiāti*	ITI APIN		VIII
	30	[*ina šattimma šiāti*	ITI]KIMIN–*ma*		VIII

([2162]) So the eponym official was installed either in this month or in a month elapsing since the last explicitly mentioned month date.

Now let us see what can be deduced from the chart. In line 11 of column two, we can see that the eponym official was installed before the fourth month of the year. In line 13 of the same column, we can see that the eponym official was installed in or before the third month of the year; but the third month was the first occasion during the eponymate in which noteworthy military activity took place. From line 4 of column three, we can see that Ashur–ra'im–nisheshu was installed as eponym sometime before the eleventh month. Since the last recorded event in the same eponymate took place in the eighth month (line 19), the installation presumably took place in the ninth or tenth month (unless a full year without military activity intervened). From line 20, we see that the eponymate of Ilu–iddina probably began in the ninth month and from lines 28-30 that it ended in the eighth month. There is some likelihood then that the eponymates described in column three began in the ninth month and ended in the eighth.

Note, however, that this conclusion cannot be followed for the whole document. In line 19 of column two, the ninth month clearly cannot have been the first of the eponymate (formula ii). It seems logical, therefore, to conclude that the beginning month of the eponymate was subject to variation at this time, in short that the earlier Assyrian lunar calendar ([2163]) had not yet been adjusted to the Babylonian system of intercalary months, despite the recent introduction of Babylonian month names into Assyria.

This solution, though hardly incontrovertible, has the following obvious advantages. In contrast to Borger's opinion, it asserts that the events whose dates are preserved in the document with such elaborate care were listed in chronological order. In contrast to Jaritz's theory, *ina šattimma šiāti* can be translated idiomatically as "in the same year" rather than a meaningless indefinite "in that year." It also removes the apparent inconsistency in the citing of eponym names which Jaritz must postulate in the inscription (because of his belief that a new eponymate began in each Ajar, whether a new official was named or not [e.g., iii 8]). The solution would also fit with the early Assyrian lunar calendar, which lacked intercalary months and which would therefore begin at different times of the solar year. But, because of the fragmentary condition of the text and our uncertain knowledge of the contemporary Assyrian calendar, we can present the above opinion only tentatively at this time.

([2163]) On the lunar calendar, see Rowton, *CAH* I² vi 58-59; Weidner, *AfO* V (1928-29) 184-185; *idem*, *AfO* X (1935-36) 27-29.

Appendix C

THE ROLE OF FAMINE IN THE SEMI-NOMAD DISTURBANCES IN POST-KASSITE BABYLONIA

In the late second and early first millennia, Babylonia was often troubled by raids from semi-nomad groups living around its periphery, especially Arameans and Sutians. The circumstances surrounding these raids are difficult to elucidate, primarily because of the lack of documentation. But the few texts which are pertinent reveal an interesting pattern of food shortage, which may help to explain some of the underlying motivation for these common and frequently disastrous invasions. The following paragraphs will sketch briefly the evidence for the connection of famine conditions with semi-nomad disturbances.

In the eighteenth and final year (1083*) of the reign of Marduk–nadin–ahhe, according to an Assyrian chronicle, Assyria was afflicted with a severe famine. (2164) This famine also affected the semi-nomad Arameans living on the fringes of Assyria, and they poured into the weakened settled areas in quest of food and spoil. (2165) They blocked the roads to prevent the relief of the famished Assyrians, forced the people to flee for their lives to the Kirriuri mountains north of Assyria, and then proceeded to despoil the abandoned property of the inhabitants. (2166) Although the Assyrian chronicle is less concerned with parallel events in Babylonia, it mentions that in this same ill-fated year the throne in Babylonia changed hands. (2167) We are left to infer whether or not similar conditions prevailed in the southern country at this time.

In a succeeding year, (2168) the Assyrian harvest was again woefully inadequate. (2169) The hungry Aramean tribes once again surged into the country and oc-

(2164) *AfO* XVII (1954-56) 384:2′. The interpretation adopted here follows in many points the translation proposed by Tadmor in *JNES* XVII (1958) 133-134. It should be mentioned that the texts used for the historical reconstruction of this section are often damaged and somewhat ambiguous; therefore, the interpretations proposed here should be treated as hypothetical.

(2165) *AfO* XVII (1954-56) 384:3′-4′.

(2166) *Ibid.*, 4′-7′.

(2167) *Ibid.*, 8′-9′.

(2168) Possibly the immediately succeeding year, i.e., 1082*.

(2169) Perhaps because of crop damage due to storms (*AfO* XVII [1954-56] 384:10′; see Tadmor, *JNES* XVII [1958] 134).

cupied the area around Nineveh. (2170) On this occasion, Tiglath–Pileser I beat a strategic retreat to Katmuhi and left the Arameans in temporary possession of the land. (2171) These events occurred during the early years of the reign of Marduk–shapik–zeri (1082*-1070*) of Babylonia.

Referring to other events which took place during the reign of Marduk–shapik–zeri, a broken passage in the New Babylonian Chronicle states: "*105* kings of the lands of the *A*[*ḫlamû* came into the land (Babylonia)] and enjoyed abundance and [prosperity]." (2172) Mention of so many "kings" (or kinglets) suggests the leaders of the many tribes (*bītāti*) of the Arameans, (2173) since there can be little question of so many settled areas around Babylonia to speak of "kings" in any literal sense. The reference to "abundance" or "plenty" (*ḫegallu*) calls to mind the lack of food which drove the Arameans into Assyria in the time of Tiglath–Pileser I. Though one does not wish to overinterpret a broken passage, there would seem to be little point in a Babylonian chronicle referring to many "kings of the lands [of GN]" and their "experiencing of plenty" unless this event—presumably referring to the relief of famine—took place in or around Babylonia, peacefully or not.

In the time of the next king, Adad–apla–iddina (1069*-1048*), Arameans and Sutians plundered Babylonian cities, notably Sippar and Nippur. (2174) In the wake of this destruction, food became scarce; and, according to a later record from Sippar, attempts over the next two centuries to restore food offerings for the cult of Shamash there proved generally ineffective. Simbar–Shipak (1026*-1009*) re-established the offerings, (2175) but they were broken off again during a famine in the reign of Kashshu–nadin–ahi (1008*-1006*). (2176) In the reign of Eulmash–shakin–shumi (1005*-989*), some temple revenues were diverted from Esagila in Babylon to help the Shamash cult; and land was given to the high priest of Sippar in Babylon. (2177) But it was not until the reign of Nabu–apla–iddina (c. 887-c. 855), the self-styled "vanquisher of the Sutians," (2178) that the cult of Shamash was adequately restored in Sippar. (2179)

Conditions in Babylonia between the close of the Second Dynasty of Isin (1027*) and the reign of Nabu–apla–iddina (c. 887-c. 855) are poorly documented, perhaps

(2170) *AfO* XVII (1954-56) 384:11′-12′.
(2171) *Ibid.*, 13′. See Tadmor's note (c) in *JNES* XVII (1958) 134.
(2172) Obv. 4′-7′. For the restorations, see also pp. 132-133 above.
(2173) *AfO* XVII (1954-56) 384:3′, 11′. Rulers of small areas in Aramean territory at this time could call themselves "king," e.g., Tukulti–Mer of Hana (*AnOr* XII 336).
(2174) New Babylonian Chronicle, obv. 10′-11′; *JCS* XIX (1965) 123:10-13; cf. *BBSt* no. 36 i 1-12.
(2175) *BBSt* no. 36 i 20.
(2176) *Ibid.*, i 24-27.
(2177) *Ibid.*, i 29-ii 17.
(2178) Paraphrase of *BBSt* no. 36 ii 26-27.
(2179) *BBSt* no. 36 iii 19-vi 16.

because of repeated Aramean and Sutian irruptions into the land. (2180) There is, however, one text dealing with tax payments and other business affairs of the clan of Abirattash dated about 955* B.C. (2181), which describes the exorbitantly high price of grain in Babylonia at that time. (2182) This provides supporting evidence for the general scarcity of food-stuffs in this period. It is also noteworthy that the archeological survey of the Diyala region conducted by Jacobsen and Adams revealed "large-scale abandonment of settled irrigation agriculture" about this period. (2183)

This evidence for famine as a factor in semi-nomad disturbances in settled territories is not unparalleled in Babylonian history. The semi-nomads, whether their livelihood was derived at various times from the raising of cattle or from trade, needed to obtain at least some food supplies from the more settled areas. In times of famine, when there was not enough food to go around even in the settled areas themselves, the semi-nomads were quite likely to cause trouble and steal food. Even in more prosperous years, the semi-nomads were interested in food as well as other plunder. Thus, for example, in the Kassite period, the Ahlamu, who are often considered as forerunners of the Arameans, were accused of stealing part of the date crop near Dilmun (2184) and of agitating for food (in a context that also mentions the king of Babylonia). (2185) (Some of these groups even settled down in the cities: in Kassite Nippur some of the Ahlamu held jobs as guards and drew regular wage rations). (2186) Thus this pattern of hungry semi-nomads stealing food and other goods from settled areas is not an isolated phenomenon in Babylonian history.

(2180) These invasions form the background for the Era Epic. The fact that the plague god plays such a prominent role in the literary portrayal of these dark days in Babylonia suggests that plague and famine may have stalked the land hand-in-hand during this time, just as they have often done in other periods of history.

(2181) Literally 958* B.C. (*BBSt* no. 9 ivb 8-9), but see note 1048 above.

(2182) *BBSt* no. 9 iva 15, 13. Cf. *BBSt* no. 7 i 21 for the price of grain in more normal times.

(2183) Adams, *Land Behind Baghdad*, p. 56.

(2184) *JCS* VI (1952) 144:13-14.

(2185) *EA* 200:8-11. The passage is badly broken and difficult to interpret; but it mentions the Ahlamu, the king of Karduniash, and food within a single section.

(2186) *PBS* II/2 56:3, cf. *ibid.* 114:16 (summary).

Appendix D

THE STANDARD TITULARY OF ASHURNASIRPAL II IN INSCRIPTIONS FROM CALAH

At Calah, the longer stone inscriptions of Ashurnasirpal which were written after his journey to Carchemish often include a standard summary of his conquests. Because this titulary is so repetitious, it has received little attention. Available publications of the pertinent texts often combine the variant copies of the titulary together in such a way that the different recensions are indistinguishable; (2187) and the current inaccessibility of some of the texts prevents the present author from attempting a critical edition at this point. But the different recensions of this titulary are significant, perhaps more significant than can be established here. It is hoped that the following preliminary survey will point out directions for future study when a critical edition of these texts will become feasible.

Sources:

1. *AKA* 179:17-181:32, limestone tablets from city wall; contain sections A, B, C-1, D, E-1, F, G-1, H;
2. *AKA* 215:6-218:12, slabs from Northwest Palace; contain sections A, B, C-1/C-2, D, E-1/E-2, F, G-1, H;
3. *AKA* 174:6-176:8, limestone tablets recording palace building; contain B, C-2, D, E-1, F, G-2;
4. *AKA* 162:6-164:18, limestone tablet recording the restoration of the temple of Ishtar, queen of Kitmuri; contains sections B, C-2, D, E-1, F, G-2;
5. *AKA* 343:127-345:131, section of the final edition of the annals immediately after campaign of 879; contains sections B, C-2, D, E-1, F, G-2;
6. *AKA* 382:119-384:126, concluding section of the final edition of the annals; contains sections A, B, C-2, D, E-1, F, G-1, H;

(2187) E.g., *AKA* 212-221.

7. *AKA* 192:7-195:5, inscriptions on colossal bulls and lions; contain sections A, B, C-2, D, Ẹ-2, F, G-1, H;

8. *Iraq* XIV (1952) pl. VII 10-20, stele recording the inauguration of the new capital; contains sections B, C-2, D, Ẹ-2, F, G-1. (2188)

Similar titulary with variations in phraseology occurs also in inscriptions from Assur (*KAH* I 25:1-6, II 94:1-14), Balawat (*AKA* 168:6-170:21), Nineveh (*AAA* XIX [1932] 109:19-27, cf. *AAA* XVIII [1931] 94:19-95:27), and an unknown site (Tournay, *Vivre et penser* II [1942] 316:6-19); but these were different editions prepared for these places and—because of the paucity of surviving recensions from any one of these sites—do not yet lend themselves to an analysis such as that attempted here for the Calah inscriptions.

Transcription: (2189)

A. *ummānāt* (*māt*) *Lullumê rapšāti ina qereb tamḫāri ina kakkē lu ušamqit ina rēṣūte ša* ^{d}*Šamaš u* ^{d}*Adad ilāni tiklīja ummānāt mātāt Nairi māt Ḫabḫi māt Šubarê u māt* ^{a}*Nirbe*^{a} *kīma* ^{d}*Adad rāḫiṣi elišunu ašgum*

B. *šarru ša ištu ebertān* ÍD *Idiglat*

C-1. *adi* URU *Kargamiš ša māt Ḫatte*

C-2. *adi* KUR *Labnāna u tâmte rabīte*

D. *māt Laqê ana siḫirtiša māt Sūḫi adi* URU/*māt Rapiqi ana šēpēšu ušekniša ištu rēš*^{b} *ēni* ÍD *Subnat*

Ẹ-1. *adi māt* ^{c}*Nirbi*^{c} *ša bītāni qāssu* ^{d}*ikšud*^{d}

Ẹ-2. *adi māt Urarṭi qāssu* ^{d}*ikšud*^{d}

(2188) The edition of this section of the stele (lines 10-20) in *Iraq* XIV (1952) 24-44 has a number of errors, which may be corrected by comparison with the photograph of the stele published *ibid.*, pl. II:

(10) transliteration: insert *šarru*(MAN) before *ša ištu ēbirtan*
(12) transliteration: for *si–ḫir–ti–šu* read *si–ḫir–ti–šá*
(12) transliteration: the second *a–di* does not occur on the stele (despite the editor's "sic")
(14) for *Ú–ra–ar–tu* (copy) and *Ú–ra–ar–ṭi* (transliteration) read *Ú–ra–ar–ṭi* (photo)
(14) copy: insert ŠU before *–su*
(17) transliteration: for *ša* read *šá*
(17) transliteration: for *Ḫar–* read *Ḫa–*
(18) transliteration: for *ša* read *šá*

(2189) This is not a critical edition, which must one day be done from the original documents. Thus there is some inconsistency in the transcriptions, as there is in the texts themselves, between Babylonian and Assyrian forms and orthography. (Minor orthographic variants such as *–te* for *–ti*, etc., are not noted, save in the case of geographical names). The logogram TA is transcribed here as *ištu* because of the syllabic writings attested in *AKA* 180:21 var., 216:8 var., 343:127, 344:128.

F. *ištu* (*māt*) [e]*nīribē*[e] *ša māt Kirruri adi māt Gilzāni*
ištu ebertān ÍD *Zaba šupalî adi* URU *Til–Bāri ša ellān māt*/URU *Zaban*
[f]*ištu* URU *Til–ša–Abtāni adi* URU *Til–ša–Zabdāni*[f]
URU[g] *Ḫirimu* URU *Ḫarutu* (*māt*/URU) *birāte ša māt* [h]*Karduniaš*[h] *ana miṣri*/*miṣir mātija* [i]*utēr*[i]

G-1. *ištu* (*māt*) [j]*nīribē*[j] *ša māt*/URU *Babite*[k] *adi māt Ḫašmar ana nišē mātija amnu*

G-2. *u rapšāti mātāt Nairi ana pāṭ gimriša apīl*

H. *ina mātāte ša apīlušināni* LÚ *šaknūteja altakan*
[l]*urdūtī uppušu kudurru ēmessunūti*[l]

[a-a]*Nirbi*: *AKA* 179:20 var., 193:10 var., 215:7 var.; *Nirib*: *AKA* 193:10, 215:7

[b]*AKA* 344:128 inserts an ÍD before *ēni*

[c-c]*Nirib*: *AKA* 216:9 var., 344:129, 383:122; *Niribe*: *AKA* 163:10; *Niribi*: *AKA* 175:12 var.

[d-d]*ik–šú–du*: *AKA* 175:13; *ik–šu–du*: *AKA* 180:24 var., 216:9 var.

[e-e]*nīribī*: *AKA* 175:13, 180:24 var., 216:9 var., 383:122; *nīrbē*: *AKA* 216:9 var. (also *nirbi*?); *nirbī*: *AKA* 194:15 var.; *nīrib*: *AKA* 163:11, 194:15; *ni–⟨ri⟩–be*: *AKA* 180:24 var.

[f-f]*adi* URU *Til–ša–Zabdāni u* URU *Til–ša–Abtāni*: *AKA* 181:27, 383:123-124; *ištu* URU *Til–ša–Abtāni u* URU *Til–ša–Zabdāni AKA* 217:10; *ištu* URU *Til–ša–Zabdāni u* (var.: *adi*) URU *Til–ša–Abtāni*: *AKA* 194:18-19; cf. also the transposition sometimes in *AKA* 217:10; the names *Abtāni* and *Zabdāni* are sometimes prefixed with the masculine personal determinative

[g]*māt*: *AKA* 194:20 var.

[h-h]*Kar–du–ni–šá*: *AKA* 181:28;

[i-i][*ú*]*–te–ri*: *AKA* 194:21

[j-j]*nīribī*: *AKA* 181:29 var.; *nīrbī*: *AKA* 195:1, 217:11 var.; *nīrib*: *AKA* 195:1 var., 217:11

[k]*Babete*: *AKA* 217:11 var.

[l-l]*urdūtī uppušū*: *AKA* 195:5 var., 218:12; *urdūtī uppuš*: *AKA* 195:5, 218:12 var. (i.e., these versions omit *kudurru ēmessunūti*, presumably interpreting *uppušū* as a stative)

Translation:

A. In battle I felled with weapons the widespread troops of the land of Lullume. With the help of Shamash and Adad, my divine supporters, I thundered like Adad, the destroyer, over the armies of the Nairi lands, the land of Habhi, the land of the Subarian(s), and the land of Nirib.

B. (I am) the king who has caused to bow at his feet (the lands) from the far side of the Tigris

C-1. to the city Carchemish of the land of Hatte,

C-2. to the mountain of Lebanon and the Great Sea,

D. the entire land of Laqe, the land of Suhi as far as Rapiqu. His (i.e., Ashurnasirpal's) hand has conquered from the source of the Subnat River

E-1. as far as the interior of the land of Nirbi.

E-2. as far as the land of Urartu.

F. I have restored to the borders of my land (the territory) from the mountain passes of the land of Kirruri to the land of Gilzanu, from the other side of the Lower Zab to the city of Til–Bari, which is north of the land/city of Zaban, from Til–sha–Abtani to Til–sha–Zabdani, and Hirimu and Harutu, fortresses of the land of Babylonia.

G-1. From the mountain passes of the land/city of Babite to the land of Hashmar, I have reckoned (the inhabitants) as people of my land.

G-2. I have become master of all the Nairi lands.

H. Over all lands of which I have become master, I have appointed governors. I have imposed obeisance and (the carrying of) the corvée-basket upon them.

Remarks:

1. Sections B-G are contained in all versions of the titulary, though sections C, E, and G each have two variant forms. Sections A and H are omitted in shorter versions.

2. Versions having C-1 ("to the city Carchemish of the land of Hatte") are chronologically prior to versions with C-2 ("to the mountain of Lebanon and the Great Sea"). Though the final edition of the annals has been interpreted as including the expedition to Carchemish and the Mediterranean in a single year, (2190) this interpretation is probably incorrect. It is clear from the variations (C-1, C-2) in the Calah standard titulary as well as from an Assur recension (2191) that sufficient time elapsed between the trip to Carchemish and the trip to the Mediterranean for a number of inscriptions to be written. New official editions of royal inscriptions would hardly have been prepared for the short space of time it would have taken Ashurnasirpal to go directly from Carchemish to the Mediterranean, so it may be presumed that these destinations were not reached in one and the same year. It is likewise

(2190) *AKA* 363:56-374:92 (see *ARAB* I 475-479).

(2191) *KAH* I 25:3 mentions reaching *māt Ḫatti* but not the Mediterranean.

noteworthy that the march to the Lebanon and the Mediterranean commences in the annals with the phrase *ina ūmešūma,* (2192) which marks a transition from the preceding narrative (the expedition to Carchemish). Thus it is probable that at least four campaigns were recorded in Ashurnasirpal's annals for the years 877-867. (2193)

3. There is no presently detectable chronological significance in the other variants noted. The omission or retention of A and H as well as the G-1/G-2 variation are not likely to have chronological bearing, since these variants occur in different portions of the same text, the final annals edition. (2194) The E-1/E-2 variation may have some chronological significance, but it cannot be traced until all the pertinent texts are re-edited; and its probability at present is rather slight. (2195)

4. Sections A and H always occur together. They are always accompanied by section G-1. On the other hand, section G-1 occurs only once in a shorter version (i.e., without A and H) and this is in the inaugural stele for the new capital.

5. Section E-2 is less common than E-1 and always occurs with section G-1, never G-2. Section G-2 always occurs with C-2 and E-1 and never in the longer versions of the titulary (i.e., those with A and H); it never occurs in the earliest versions of the titulary (i.e., those with C-1).

(2192) *AKA* 372:84.

(2193) Much work remains to be done on elucidating the campaigns of Ashurnasirpal between 877 and 867 (*AKA* 353:26-374:92). The traditional division into three campaigns (i.e., lines 26-50, 50-56, 56-92, e.g., by Luckenbill, *ARAB* I 471-479) is not entirely satisfactory for the reasons noted above. Whether other transitional phrases (e.g., lines 55, 63, 77) might also mark passage of time is yet to be determined.

(2194) *AKA* 343:127-345:131, 382:119-384:126.

(2195) Principally because E-1 is shared both by the earliest inscriptions (the tablets from the city wall) and by one of the latest known inscriptions (the most complete edition of the annals).

Addenda

P. 94 n. 490. The personal name Itti–Marduk–balatu also occurs on a tablet dated in the year 185 of the Seleucid era: *BOR* IV (1889-90) 132:9, etc.

P. 114 n. 630. *gigursallû* (*UET* IV 143:12): this reference should be added to *AHw* 287-288. It here designates a gold object made in the shape of a reed basket. The *kursālum* (*ARM* VII 237:3′, cited in *AHw* 511) should also be interpreted as a basket-shaped object made of gold.

P. 136 n. 807. One advantage to reading the DN as Nin–Isinna would be that the dedication would honor the tutelary deity of the old dynasty, which was native to Isin. But, since the reading of the DN and the origin of Adad–apla–iddina are both obscure, this possibility can be raised only quite tentatively.

P. 154 n. 930. For the recent Iraqi excavations at Bakrawa and the texts found there, see *Sumer* XVII (1961) 1-2 and 17-66, XVIII (1962) 141-164 (Arabic), and XXI (1965) 75-88 (Arabic).

Pp. 156-157 and note 942. In letters of January 23, 1968 and March 8, 1968, Dr. Peter Calmeyer has been kind enough first to call to my attention and then to send photographs of a Luristan bronze spear point inscribed with the name of ᵈ*Kaš–šú–ú*–SUM–ŠEŠ.MEŠ, who bears the title *šar kiššati*. This is the first known inscription of this king. It is somewhat surprising to find that we should read the name of this king as Kashshu–nadin–ahhe, since all three of the later Babylonian texts which have preserved this king's name (*BBSt* no. 36, the Dynastic Chronicle, and Kinglist A) uniformly write its final element in the singular. But a contemporary writing of the RN should undoubtedly be given preference, and note 942 above should be altered accordingly. (For the name type, DN–nadin–ahhe, see the discussion in note 679). The spear point in question is in the collection of Dr. Bach, Aachen; and Dr. Calmeyer is planning to publish it in the near future.

P. 214 n. 1333. The city *Ú–da–ni* is probably to be identified with the city *Ú–dan–nu* (*Ú–da–an–num*), which is attested in later Neo-Babylonian and Persian times (Unger, *Babylon*, p. 286 v 9, Hofkalender; *YOS* III 91:18, 95:17; *BIN* I 167:9, without determinative; *YOS* VII 74 15.17.21, 137:8, 174:9) down till the late fourth century (*TCL* XIII 249:3, time of Philip). It was probably in southern Babylonia, since in the Hofkalender it is grouped with Kullab, Larsa, and Kissik (v 8-11); and, if *TCL* XIII 249:3 is to be restored [*ḫarrān*] *šarri ša ana Ú–dan–nu tallak*, then Uruk and Udannu may have been only a short distance apart and connected by a road. (Cf. also Landsberger, *MSL* II 97). The *šangû* of this city (Belshunu in the early eighth century: see above p. 214 and n. 1334) may well have been its chief executive, since the same official is mentioned among the high-ranking dignitaries in the Hofkalender (v 9).

Pp. 216-220. In Urartian inscriptions of the early eighth century, a land Babilu is mentioned as affected by the campaigns of Argishti I and Sardur II. The land, once prefixed with the determinative for city (URU) rather than that for country (KUR), is written variously—with and without suffixes—as KUR *Ba–bi–lu–ú*, KUR *Ba–bi–lu–ni–e*, and URU *Ba–bi–lu–i–ni–e* (König, *Handbuch der chaldischen Inschriften*, no. 103 § 16 III 5, 4 and no. 80 § 5 V 11 = Melikišvili, *Urartskie Klinoobraznye Nadpisi*, no. 155 A 5,4 and no. 127 III 11). According to the context of the Urartian inscriptions, Babilu is to be located somewhere in the Zagros area, probably around the region inhabited by the Manneans (König, *op. cit.*, p. 129 n. 2 and p. 177; Melikišvili, *op. cit.*, p. 422), and is unlikely to be directly connected with Babylonia. Diakonov (cited apud Melikišvili, *ibid.*) has proposed that the area called Babilu by the Urartians may have been Namri, northeast of Babylonia proper, which was certainly heavily Babylonized in the ninth century.

P. 240. Pillutu: see under p. 274 below.

Pp. 271-272. Dr. Michael Rowton has kindly pointed out to me that these tribes bearing city names may have been groups who had taken over or were centered around a city (cf. his forthcoming article currently scheduled to appear in *JESHO* XI [1968]).

P. 274. Pillat: referring to a spot near the Elamite border (cf. *ABL* 1007 rev. 21, 1315:14; see Streck, *Asb.* p. 803). The same place is referred to as Pillutu (vowel harmony) in the inscriptions of Tiglath–Pileser III (II *R* 67:14) and Sargon II (Lie, *Sargon*, p. 52:4) where it is said to be "of the border of Elam". It is often linked with the city/tribe of Hilim(mu): *ABL* 1000:6, 13, rev. 8; *ABL* 1007 rev. 21; II *R* 67:13-14; Lie, *Sargon*, p. 52:4; *OIP* II 38 iv 38, etc., where it is mentioned among the provinces (*nagê*) of Elam; Streck, *Asb.*, 42:116. Cf. also Forrer, *Provinzeinteilung*, p. 96.

Pp. 274-275. Sheikhs (*nasīku* or *nasīkāni*) are also attested for the city of Laban, to the west of Mesopotamia, in the time of Sargon II (*AfO* XIV [1941-44] 43 B 7) and in Nimrud Letters LXXXIII 13, LXXXVII rev. 7′, etc. Cf. now also *AHw* 754a.

Pp. 309-311. On the *ša rēši* and the *ša rēš šarri*, see also the remarks of Borger, *Babylonisch-assyrische Lesestücke*, LXXVI.

P. 361 (b). For further bibliography and discussion of the Kedor-laomer texts, see Michael C. Astour, "Political and Cosmic Symbolism in Genesis 14 and in Its Babylonian Sources" in Alexander Altmann (ed.), *Biblical Motifs: Origins and Transformations* (Cambridge, Mass.: Harvard University Press, 1966), pp. 65-112. The passages dealing with Kudur–Naḫhunte are discussed by Astour especially on pp. 90-94.

General Index

In this study the following rules have been observed for transcribing Akkadian proper names into English: (1) names which have a well-known English form, such as names occurring in the Bible (e.g., Nebuchadnezzar), retain that form here; (2) names which are generally transcribed into English in a certain form, such as Enlil, Adad-nirari, Ashurnasirpal, Kassites, retain this customary form, even though the transcription may be slightly inaccurate; (3) names not commonly occurring in English are rendered phonetically in English script without length marks or diacritical signs (i.e., *s* serves for *s* and *ṣ*, *t* for *t* and *ṭ*, *sh* for *š*, *h* for *ḫ*, etc.). Nouns in personal names are uniformly written with proper case endings, even though many of these terminations were presumably dropped in the speech of the period.

Index of Akkadian

This list includes Akkadian words other than personal names and month names which are cited in the text. It embraces most geographical names and divine names, where quoted in Akkadian, and also individual common nouns discussed in the analysis of royal names.

Index of Sumerian and Logograms

The following list includes Sumerian words quoted in the text as well as some of the logograms mentioned, especially those whose reading is unknown or not readily determinable.